INTELLECTUAL PROP.

THE INITIATIVE FOR POLICY DIALOGUE SERIES

The Initiative for Policy Dialogue (IPD) brings together the top voices in development to address some of the most pressing and controversial debates in economic policy today. The IPD book series approaches topics such as capital market liberalization, macroeconomics, environmental economics, and trade policy from a balanced perspective, presenting alternatives, and analyzing their consequences on the basis of the best available research. Written in a language accessible to policymakers and civil society, this series will rekindle the debate on economic policy and facilitate a more democratic discussion of development around the world.

Intellectual Property Rights

Legal and Economic Challenges for Development

Edited by
MARIO CIMOLI, GIOVANNI DOSI,
KEITH E. MASKUS, RUTH L. OKEDIJI,
JEROME H. REICHMAN,
and
JOSEPH E. STIGLITZ

OXFORD
UNIVERSITY PRESS

OXFORD

UNIVERSITY PRESS

Great Clarendon Street, Oxford, OX2 6DP,
United Kingdom

Oxford University Press is a department of the University of Oxford.
It furthers the University's objective of excellence in research, scholarship,
and education by publishing worldwide. Oxford is a registered trade mark of
Oxford University Press in the UK and in certain other countries

Published in the United States of America by Oxford University Press
198 Madison Avenue, New York, NY 10016, United States of America

British Library Cataloguing in Publication Data

Data available

Library of Congress Cataloging in Publication Data

Data available

ISBN 978-0-19-966075-9 (Hbk)
978-0-19-966076-6 (Pbk)

Printed in Great Britain by
CPI Group (UK) Ltd, Croydon, CR0 4YY

Contents

List of Figures and Graphs

List of Tables

List of Contributors

Minna Allarakhia, University of Waterloo

Leonardo Burlamaqui, The Ford Foundation, New York

Sarah Chan, Institute for Science Ethics and Innovation, University of Manchester

Mario Cimoli, ECLAC, United Nations, Santiago and University of Venice Ca' Foscari

Robert Cook-Deegan, Duke University

Benjamin Coriat, Université Paris 13

Carlos M. Correa, Centre of Interdisciplinary Studies on Industrial Property and Economics, Law Faculty, University of Buenos Aires

Giovanni Dosi, Sant'Anna School of Advanced Studies, Pisa

Timo Goeschl, University of Heidelberg

Michael Halewood, Policy Research Unit, Bioversity International

John Harris, Institute for Science Ethics and Innovation, University of Manchester

Albert G.Z. Hu, National University of Singapore

Adam B. Jaffe, Motu Economic and Public Policy Research, New Zealand

Amy Kapczynski, Yale Law School

Keith E. Maskus, University of Colorado Boulder

Roberto Mazzoleni, Hofstra University

Richard G. Newell, Duke University

Alessandro Nuvolari, Institute of Economics, Sant' Anna School of Advanced Studies, Pisa

Ruth L. Okediji, University of Minnesota Law School

Luigi Orsenigo, University Institute for Advanced Studies, Pavia

Arti K. Rai, Duke University School of Law

Jerome H. Reichman, Duke University School of Law

Pedro Roffe, International Centre for Trade and Sustainable Development (ICTSD)

Bhaven N. Sampat, Mailman School of Public Health, Columbia University

Anthony D. So, Sanford School of Public Policy, Duke University

Christoph Spennemann, United Nations Conference on Trade and Development (UNCTAD)

Joseph E. Stiglitz, Columbia University

John Sulston, Institute for Science Ethics and Innovation, Manchester University

Timothy Swanson, The Graduate Institute, Geneva

Valentina Tartari, Department of Innovation and Organizational Economics, Copenhagen Business School

Robert Weissman, Public Citizen, Washington, D.C.

Jonathan B. Wiener, Duke University School of Law

1

The Role of Intellectual Property Rights in the Development Process, with Some Lessons from Developed Countries: An Introduction[1]

Giovanni Dosi and Joseph E. Stiglitz

This book analyzes the impact of diverse intellectual property rights (IPR) regimes upon the development process.

The relationship between IPR and development has become a source of increasing concern over the past fifteen years, for two related reasons: (a) it has become increasingly recognized that what separates developed from developing countries is a gap in knowledge, and that inappropriately designed IPR regimes can present an important impediment to closing the knowledge gap, and therefore to development; and (b) at the same time, the Agreement on Trade-Related Intellectual Property Agreements (TRIPS)[2] of the Uruguay Round imposed a Western-style IPR regime on developing countries, one which many developing countries rightly worried might impede their access to knowledge, and thus their development.

So concerned have many of those in the developing countries become about the adverse effects of this intellectual property regime that they have called for a "development-oriented intellectual property regime," just as they had, at Doha, called for a development-oriented trade regime. On 4 October 2004 the General Assembly of the World Intellectual Property Organization (WIPO), decided to advance an IPR agenda that was, for the first time, explicitly developmentally oriented. The adoption of the Brazilian and Argentinean proposal for a development agenda was a major step forward for several reasons. First, it recognized that intellectual property "is not an end in itself."[3] Second, it reiterated WIPO's mission to "promote creative intellectual activity" and "the transfer of technology to developing countries." The new development agenda calls for ascertaining how different intellectual property regimes affect developing countries. This volume can be seen, in part, as providing some of the intellectual foundations for that analysis.

Developing countries have claimed that the IPR regime that the West advocates impairs their development not only by failing to give them access to knowledge, but also by failing to protect *their* intellectual property—both traditional knowledge and the knowledge embedded in biodiversity. This asymmetry too has adverse effects on development, for it necessitates developing countries paying large rents to Western firms for their intellectual property, but not receiving in return rents from what the developing countries view as *their* intellectual property. Indeed, in some cases, developing countries would have to pay Western firms rents for what developing countries view as their own property.

The United States has, for instance, granted patents for traditional knowledge (such as traditional medicinal uses of certain plants), which developing countries argue should not be patentable. Traditionally, this type of knowledge was held by communities and made freely available. Developing countries have widely criticized the patents on neem oil, basmati rice, and the medicinal uses of turmeric.[4] But the United States has not even ratified the Convention on Biological Diversity, under pressure from the pharmaceutical companies that fear it would provide (what they consider to be) "excessive" protection for the intellectual property associated with the use in their products of genetic material derived from plants or animals in, say, developing countries—even if the countries from which they had taken the plant or animal had devoted considerable resources to preserving their biodiversity. Evidently, in this line of argument, while incentives are important for the pharmaceutical companies, they are not for countries; and while companies should be rewarded for "discovery," countries should not be rewarded for protecting their biodiversity—without which the discovery would not have been possible. The one point of intellectual consistency in the position of the United States is that it seeks an IPR regime that maximizes the rents for its companies and minimizes the rents that its companies might pay to others.

Developed countries have tried to argue that "strong" IPR (in which traditional medicine can be patented, but genetic material that developing countries believe is theirs is left unprotected[5]) is in the best interests of developing countries. The papers in this book, and the discussion below, suggest such contentions are incorrect.

Indeed, the IPR regime that the United States has pushed on the world was not the one its scientists and innovators advocated. It was the IPR regime that the drug and entertainment industries advocated. One of us (Stiglitz) had the opportunity to see this first hand:[6]

> When I served on President Clinton's Council of Economic Advisers, we provided our assessment of the TRIPS agreement, the intellectual property provisions of the 1994 WTO Uruguay Round agreement, which sought to impose an American style intellectual property regime on developing countries. Both we and

the Office of Science and Technology Policy within the White House basically opposed TRIPS, believing that it was bad for American science, global science, and the economies of the U.S. and developing countries alike. Many of America's own innovative firms are trying to change its IPR regime, which is designed not to maximize innovation but rents from those who have had the good luck receiving a patent (and the two are not the same).

Along with many of the authors of the papers in this volume, we believe that there is a need for reform in the U.S. IPR regime and that it would be wrong to impose such a flawed regime on others. (Indeed, the United States has been reforming its regime;[7] there is a worry that others will be left with an IPR regime that even the United States has rejected.) As badly designed as the American IPR regime is for the United States, it is even worse suited for developing countries. But even if the American IPR regime *were* ideal for the United States, that does not mean that it would be ideal for others.

Among the central theses of this introduction, and the papers in this book, are the following:

(i) Intellectual property is man-made; it is a social contrivance purportedly designed to increase welfare, by supposedly enhancing innovation (though, as we shall see, it may actually have exactly the opposite effect). Moreover, the focus on intellectual property *rights* ignores the fact that all property rights come with restrictions; they are never unfettered (Kennedy and Stiglitz, 2013). In the case of intellectual property rights, there are restrictions associated both with abuses— they cannot (or should not) be used to unduly restrict competition— and also with public uses—compulsory licenses can and have played an important role in ensuring access to knowledge when it is deemed central for the public interest. Part of the granting of a patent is full disclosure of relevant information, so that others can build upon the knowledge. Different countries may come to different judgments about which abuses are unacceptable or which public interests are essential.

(ii) In general, the private returns to innovation with intellectual property are not well-aligned with social returns.[8]

(iii) Most broadly, the link between stronger IPR and innovation is ambiguous at best.[9]

(iv) The impact of IPR on welfare and innovation depends on details of the IPR regime and the nature of the sector—institutional details matter. Advocates of IPR in advanced industrial countries have not only focused excessively on IPR. They have also typically argued that the better and stronger intellectual property rights are, the more innovative the economy will be.[10] We show, to the contrary, that there is considerable subtlety in the design of a good IPR regime. In the discussion below, we will explain that there are many details in the design of an intellectual property regime that affect the extent to which it promotes or impedes innovation. It is not just a question of "strong" or "weak" intellectual property rights. Rather, the design of the whole intellectual property regime, with its myriad of provisions, is what matters.[11]

(v) Poorly designed IPR systems may not enhance welfare, both in the short run and in the long; and such systems may well impede innovation. We will explain that the IPR regime in the United States, and which the United States has attempted to foist on developing countries, may actually be welfare reducing. Both the levels and patterns of innovation may be adversely affected. Interestingly, as we have noted, even many in the United States high-tech sectors have come to recognize this, and there have been marked changes in the IPR regime in recent years. Not all have been positive, but even the positive ones have not yet been incorporated into other countries' IPR regimes.

(vi) Intellectual property is only one way of incentivizing innovative research; it is only one part of what might be thought of as a country's *innovation system*, the collection of institutions that promote innovation; there has been too much emphasis on IPR, to the exclusion of other ways of stimulating innovation and learning.

(vii) An intellectual property regime that might be appropriate for one country or one sector might be inappropriate for another.

(viii) In particular, the IPR regimes of the advanced developed countries are likely to be inappropriate for many developing countries, and this is likely to be especially so in areas like health and agriculture. One reason that an IPR regime designed for advanced developed countries may be inappropriate for developing countries is that *institutional transplants generally don't work*. Indeed, one-size-fits-all policy prescriptions are rarely a good idea in any field,[12] but this is one area where they may work particularly badly. Institutional structures have to be sensitive to differences in objectives and circumstances—including the broader set of institutional arrangements, which inevitably differ from country to country, shaped by circumstances and history. There are, for instance, large distributional consequences of different IPR regimes, and developing countries may not have the resources to easily offset those effects. Moreover, much innovation occurs within and is supported by non-market institutions. The excessive focus on IPR—a market-based approach to promoting innovation—ignores the effects on and interactions with these other parts of countries' innovation systems.

The implications of this analysis can be summarized briefly: Intellectual property rights—like other institutions—are social constructions whose objective is to promote the well-being of society. In the case of intellectual property rights, well-designed intellectual property regimes attempt to do this through the expansion and deepening of its knowledge base. But all institutions (including intellectual property rights) need to be adapted to the circumstances, history, and objectives of each country. In many circumstances, intellectual property rights may not be the best way of promoting innovation. Developing countries need to design their own IPR regimes, appropriate to their economies and circumstances.

As we noted, a country's IPR system does not exist in isolation; it is part of the country's innovation system. And the innovation system does not exist in isolation. It can, for instance, affect the competitiveness and efficiency of the entire economy, the extent of inequality in society, and the health of its citizens. It can even have large budgetary consequences, as in the United States, where the government pays pharmaceutical companies large amounts for drugs, the production costs of which are but a fraction of what the government pays—in some cases, even for drugs largely based on government-financed research. The United States may be able to afford such largesse (though that is increasingly being questioned). For developing countries, the opportunity cost of these expenditures is enormous—the money could have been better spent promoting education or innovation—and there are even better ways to spend the government's health budget.

The discussions in this book will hopefully point the way to a developmentally oriented intellectual property regime.

The discussion of this chapter is divided into six parts. The first presents the general theory of innovation, in the context of which we can evaluate the consequences of stronger IPR. The second employs this general theory to make some critical observations of the role of IPR in promoting innovation. The third discusses some of the evidence on the role of IPR in promoting innovation, looking particularly at the empirical evidence on the relationship between patents, appropriability, and innovation. The fourth presents the central elements of what we may call the "portfolio approach to an effective innovation system." The fifth focuses on the special problems of developing countries engaged in late industrialization and catching-up. We conclude with a brief discussion of some recent developments in intellectual property regimes that shed light on the issues raised here.

I. THE GENERAL THEORY OF INNOVATION AND THE ROLE OF IPR

That profit-motivated innovators are fundamental drivers of the "unbound Prometheus" of modern capitalism (Landes, 1969) has been well appreciated since Smith, Marx, and later, Schumpeter. And the last half a century has also seen in-depth analyses of determinants of the pace of technological progress and entrepreneurs' and business firms' propensity to innovate (for a thorough survey, see Dosi and Nelson, 2010).

There are many sources of innovation. Some come from outside the industry such as the advances in applied science, generally stemming from public laboratories and universities. However, at least equally important in a modern economy are the activities of search, including of course research and development expenditures, undertaken by business firms—explicit investments in developing new products that consumers and firms value, or new processes that reduce the costs of production. But if firms are to make these investments, they have to reap a return. If they appropriate for themselves less than the full social return to their innovation (and if firms were able *ex ante* to make accurate predictions on actual costs and returns), then there might be private underinvestment in innovation. The intent of the patent (IPR) system is to enable individuals and firms to garner for themselves a larger fraction of the social returns resulting from their innovative activity.[13]

But there are circumstances in which, especially under a strong patent system, the returns they reap can actually be in excess of the marginal social product. The marginal social product is related to the fact that the innovation is available earlier than it otherwise would have been. A firm's contribution can be negligible, and yet its rewards large. Moreover, an innovation may garner for a firm high profits in an imperfectly competitive industry, by seizing a fraction of its rivals' profits with a me-too innovation. These are not just theoretical niceties: me-too innovations abound in the pharmaceutical industry. So do attempts to appropriate advances in scientific knowledge: a good example is the medical diagnostic company Myriad, which rushed to beat the human genome project in identifying the BRCA genes related to breast cancer, so that it could get patents from which it could extract large rents from any woman wanting to find out whether she had a high risk of getting cancer. In that case, the net social return was negative, for the patents allowed the company to charge a high fee, well beyond the ability of anyone who is poor without insurance to pay. After years of legal wrangling, the Supreme Court finally struck down Myriad's patents on human genes in June 2013. However, this did not happen before many women were forced to make agonizing life-or-death decisions about treatment and preventative measures, with incomplete information, either because they could not afford the tests or because the patents prevented second opinions.[14]

Sometimes knowledge is produced as a by-product of production and investment. In that case, there may be little need to provide incentives;[15] but a patent can reduce access by others to the benefits of the knowledge so produced. Again, in that case, patents can have a negative social impact.

Later in this introduction, we will explain other ways in which the patent system may impede innovation.

Knowledge as a (quasi-) public good

Any analysis of innovation and the patent system begins with the question, how is the production of knowledge different from that of ordinary goods? In the case of ordinary goods, there is a presumption that markets are efficient, and there is little controversy about the definition of "property rights." In the case of the production of knowledge, there is, as we have just seen, no presumption that private production, with or without "intellectual property rights," is efficient.

The fundamental problem with knowledge, it has come to be recognized, is that it is a quasi-public good (it is often hard to exclude others from the knowledge a person or corporation acquired,[16] and even if it were possible, it is inefficient to do so, since one person's access to knowledge does not detract from the knowledge of others).[17] But unlike other public goods where we rely on government provision, we turn to the private sector for both production and financing of much innovation. The challenge has been how to get private markets to provide the desirable level and form of such a public good. Efficient competitive markets might be unable to generate a stream of quasi-rents sufficient to motivate profit-seeking firms to invest resources in the production of such goods (Arrow 1962a). A long line of economists (from Smith to Marx to Schumpeter (1943)) argued that in order to provide such incentives, it was necessary to depart from pure competition.[18]

Granted that, however, what is empirically the extent of such a departure, and what are the consequences? Clearly, if there is to be private provision of research, those engaging in research have to be able to appropriate *some* returns. But any such appropriation necessitates an impediment to the efficient utilization of knowledge. Heller (1998) and Heller and Eisenberg (1998) have referred to the underutilization of knowledge as a result of patents as the "tragedy of the anti-commons." The tragedy of the commons was the (alleged) inability, without property rights, to exclude individuals from the use of the commons, leading to over-utilization, e.g. overgrazing. The tragedy of the anti-commons is that knowledge, for which utilization is non-rivalrous, is restricted. Those that argued that property rights were essential for preventing the tragedy of the commons were wrong; regulatory mechanisms can be just as effective, without the adverse distributive consequences (see e.g. Ostrom, Gardner, and Walker, 1994.) So too we argue here that property rights are not always the best solution to the appropriability problem.

This raises the question, what is the "desirable" degree of appropriability? And through which mechanisms?

Appropriability occurs through patent and copyright protection, but there are alternative, perhaps more important, mechanisms. Because of lead times and the costs and time required for duplication and learning, and because of the availability of specific manufacturing facilities and sales networks, the first innovator can typically appropriate some returns to his innovation, even without IPR; secrecy and the fact that much relevant knowledge is "tacit" can enhance the ability of firms to appropriate returns on their investments in knowledge (these mechanisms of appropriation are discussed at length in Dosi and Nelson, 2010).

The choice of the appropriability mechanism may be largely dictated by the nature of technology, with some industries relying on trade secrets, lead times, and the sheer complexity of products, rather than IPR.[19] The diversity mechanisms through which firms benefit from innovation, however, has been lost in a good deal of contemporary literature on innovation, in which it seems to be assumed that the *only* way by which appropriability occurs is through IPR.

In fact, there seems to be no compelling evidence of a positive relation, above some threshold, between appropriability in general—and even more so, the tightening of IPR regimes—on the one hand, and the rates of innovation, on the other. The discussion below will explain why this empirical result should not come as a surprise.

While the evidence that IPR *in general* promotes innovation is far from convincing, there is good evidence that there may be adverse effects, especially with poorly designed "tight" IPR regimes: access to life-saving medicines may be restricted and so too access to knowledge that is necessary for successful development, and even for follow-on innovation. As governments have to spend more money to purchase the drugs they need, because of reduced availability of low-cost generic medicines, other expenditures—from those necessary to promote growth to those devoted to alleviating poverty—are reduced. Conversely, there may be perverse links between IPR protection and income distribution. Moreover, even if an IPR regime promoted growth in, say, some sector in some industrial country, it does not mean it will do so in other sectors and/or in other countries.

Some failures of the "market failure" arguments

We begin by considering the main arguments supporting IPR, then turn to why the traditional analyses fail to provide an adequate description of the innovation process—and thereby why they fail to provide a persuasive analysis of the role of IPR in supporting the innovation process.

The economic foundations of the theory supporting IPR rest upon a standard market failure argument: Markets perfectly fulfil their allocative role only in the absence of externalities. Without full appropriability, there will be, as we have noted, positive externalities to research, and this in turn leads to underinvestment and underproduction of knowledge. There is a (partial) market-based solution: even though knowledge is "non-rivalrous" one can attempt to make it partially excludable, e.g. through patents. This will mean that more of the benefits of the knowledge will be appropriated by those who invest in knowledge.

But it also means that, because of the artificial scarcity, the knowledge that has been produced is not being used efficiently. This tension between purported incentives for the creation of knowledge and its efficient utilization is a theme that plays out throughout most analyses of the appropriate design of IPR.

As this volume illustrates, matters are even worse: granting exclusivity to the use of knowledge is tantamount to granting a (limited) monopoly; but sometimes the monopoly power thus granted is leveraged further to create market power in segments of the economy. Sometimes, at great expense, governments have acted to curb some of the abuses of this market power (as in the case of Microsoft), but even after taking actions to limit anticompetitive practices, monopoly power persists. Not only does this result in a distorted, less efficient economy, but, as we shall comment later, even innovation may be hurt—ironic, since the putative purpose of IPR is to promote innovation.

The core of the design of a good IPR regime then becomes (a) balancing out the detrimental effect of the deadweight loss implied by a legally enforced monopoly, on the one hand, and the beneficial effect of investments in R&D and more generally in knowledge generation, on the other; and (b) detailed provisions which limit the adverse static costs and maximize the dynamic benefits. Of course, if IPR actually impedes innovation, then there is no trade-off: the economy loses in the short run and the long. Unfortunately, it appears that too often the dynamic consequences are at best mixed—some forms of innovation are helped, others are hurt. Well-designed IPR regimes are those that minimize both the short-run allocative costs, the long-run dynamic impediments to innovation, and the incentives for rent-seeking innovations which have minimal positive, or even negative, effects on welfare, while enhancing the positive incentives for welfare-enhancing innovations.

But IPR regimes can only go so far: IPR more broadly needs to be seen as part of a country's innovation system (Stiglitz, 2012; Freeman, 1987; Lundvall, 2010; Nelson, 1993, 2004a, 2004b, 2006); and the design of a good innovation system consists of looking for ways of enhancing simultaneously dynamic and static efficiency—a high level of knowledge generation combined with a system of efficient utilization of knowledge.

Patents and monopolization

Advocates of strong IPR discount the adverse effects of monopolization, thinking that monopolies would be short-lived, since the force of "Schumpeterian competition" would lead one monopolist to be replaced by another. Schumpeter and quite a few after him thought there would be competition for the market, rather than competition in the market, and that competition for the market would be sufficiently keen that consumers would reap large benefits. Schumpeter and many of his followers touted the advantages that arise from the greater level of innovation, arguing that they more than outweighed the distortions associated with monopoly.

But research over the past three decades has shown that all of these contentions are questionable. Monopolists have the ability and incentives to deter others from entering, so that monopolies can persist (see, e.g. Dasgupta and Stiglitz, 1980 and Gilbert and Newbery, 1982).

While Arrow (1962a) suggested that monopolies have far weaker incentives to innovate (compared to the social optimum), Dasgupta and Stiglitz (1980), Stiglitz (1988), and Fudenberg et al. (1983) have shown that matters are far worse than Arrow thought: a monopolist can maintain his position simply by getting a little bit ahead of his rivals, enough ahead that the rivals know that should they enter the fray, he will outcompete them. Worse still, recent years have seen monopolists using their monopoly power to squelch innovators who represent a threat to their dominant position; and the knowledge that they have the incentive, resources, and tools to do so provides a disincentive to innovation. Microsoft has provided the example par excellence of this behaviour. Integrating Internet Explorer into its operating system meant providing the browser at an essentially zero price, making it impossible for the market innovator in browsers, Netscape, to compete. Even though Microsoft was charged with anticompetitive practices in Europe, America, and Asia, and agreed to discontinue these practices, Netscape never recovered.

Patents, access to knowledge, and innovation

There are other reasons that IPR may be bad for innovation: one of the most important inputs into research is knowledge, and IPR reduces access to knowledge.[20]

Matters might not be so bad in a world with perfect information, in which the owner of the patent could act as a perfectly discriminating monopolist, charging each potential user a price which extracts the maximum rents without adversely affecting innovation. But this is not the world we live in, and restrictions in access to knowledge do impede follow-on innovation. More rents to earlier innovators result in less to follow-on innovators, thus reducing their incentives to innovate.

Who has access to information and knowledge today may affect who can engage in research. Reduced access to knowledge can, as we noted, lead to reduced possibilities to invest in research and to reduced innovation. The U.S. patent system recognized this, requiring wide disclosure as a quid pro quo for granting a patent. But the disclosure requirements may not suffice to offset the adverse effects from the "enclosure of the commons." And worse, some who are the most ardent defenders of patent rights are fighting against such disclosures, and in practice, disclosure has been far from complete.[21]

Patent thicket

Matters have become even worse with the development of what is called the patent thicket, an overlay of intellectual property claims that makes progress difficult, at best.[22] With thousands of patents being issued every year, in some areas (including many high-tech ones) it is hard to avoid trespassing on someone else's patent, and expensive and time consuming to engage in the research (reviewing patents that have been granted) that might avoid this. Modern complex products involve a myriad of components, many of which may be essential to the success of the product; and even if not essential, it may be very expensive to innovate around the patent.[23]

Such a patent thicket slowed the development of the airplane in the years before World War I, and it was only strong government action to override these claims by the creation of a patent pool that allowed the development of the airplane that was so central to that war (see Stiglitz, 2008; Bradshaw, 1992).

More recently, a whole industry has developed—firms that buy up patents, waiting until someone successfully produces a product that *might* have infringed on their patent, to sue, "holding them up", in effect, for ransom.[24] To the extent that they can get more for themselves, there is less left over for the "real innovators."

The consequences of such holdups are particularly important in those industries where successful innovation requires putting together various pieces of distributed knowledge. But even without holdups, the IP system may impede innovation. The IP regime gives too many subjects the right to exclude others from using fragmented and overlapping pieces of knowledge, with the result that no one can make effective use of them (Heller and Eisenberg, 1998 and Heller, 1998). One by-product of the recent surge in patenting is that, in several domains, knowledge has been so finely subdivided into separate but complementary property claims that the cost of reassembling constituent parts/properties in order to engage in further research imposes a heavy burden on technological advance. This means that a large number of costly negotiations might be needed in order to secure critical licenses, discouraging the pursuit of certain classes of research projects. Not surprisingly, at the beginning of this century, Barton (2000) noted that "the number of intellectual property lawyers is growing faster than the amount of research." Since then, matters have become worse. In these circumstances, the proliferation of patents may well turn out to have the effect of discouraging innovation.

Other distortions in the allocation of R&D

Holdup patents are but one example of socially unproductive "innovation" or innovations where social returns are markedly lower than private returns. The Myriad patent race, described earlier, provides another. But there are still others, including me-too patents—in which an innovator tries to grab part of the rents of existing patent holders; and innovation designed to extend the life of the patent, or more generally, to enhance the patent holder's monopoly returns. Some of the research (in some fields, perhaps much) is directed at getting around an existing patent, i.e. to avoid unreasonable charges for the use of a patent.[25] Much of the patenting is defensive—to protect oneself against a claim of someone else. Huge amounts are spent on patent lawyers.[26]

Thus, while the advocates of a strong patent system champion its ability to increase the allocation of resources into innovation, critics (rightly, in our view) point out the distortionary effects, both in the short run and the long, with the result that not only may patents interfere with the efficient use of information today, but a poorly designed patent system may not even lead to a faster pace of innovation. Thus, even the classic distinction between "static" and "dynamic" efficiency may be misplaced.

More generally, rules affecting access to knowledge affect the patterns of technological evolution in directions which are, in general, far from optimal. Later in this introduction, we shall discuss how reforms in the patent system can mitigate some of the adverse effects of currently dominant IPR regimes.

The multiple drivers of the innovation process

Much of the early theoretical literature on the design of IPR was overly simplistic. It failed to take into account key aspects of the production of knowledge, the variety of ways by which the returns to innovation are appropriated, and the many problematic aspects of the IPR regimes. As we have previously commented, for instance, the most important input into the production of knowledge is knowledge itself, and any product in today's complex economy is based on a large number of separate and complementary innovations.[27] This means that innovation cannot be viewed from the perspective of a one-off event. Each innovation builds on prior innovations, and works in conjunction with other innovations. It is difficult, if not impossible, to identify the productivity of one innovation in isolation from others (they are "joint" inputs).[28]

Part of the deficiencies in the standard theory arise from treating knowledge much like any other form of capital and property, ignoring the many subtleties and complexities. For instance, while the boundaries of real estate property are easy to establish, those of intellectual property are not. Each idea builds on others. Intellectual property was intended to encourage *new* ideas, but how do we define "novelty"? What ideas are the obvious consequence of previous ideas, and therefore should not be patentable?

Moreover, as we already mentioned, while many aspects of knowledge can be viewed as a "public good," for which exclusion exists only as a result of government actions through the enforcement of intellectual property rights, in fact there are many non-public aspects of knowledge—tacit knowledge that may in fact be hard to transfer, and the returns to which are easy to appropriate without IPR. In some sectors, trade secrets play a far more important role than IPR, and in most sectors, they and other returns associated with being the first entrant into a market play a major role.

Indeed, there are marked differences in the nature of "knowledge" and its production in different industries. In some cases, it is primarily tacit knowledge, which arises as a by-product of production and investment.[29] In the chemical industry, identifying compounds and their effects is critical, but so are the processes by which the chemicals are synthesized. In some countries, in some periods, naturally existing compounds could not be patented—after all, they are a fact of nature, not a creation of man. Only the production processes could be patented. Analogous debates are now playing out in biotechnology: some jurisdictions have ruled that genes can be patented, others that they cannot.[30]

More generally, to transform information into "useful knowledge" requires a lot of search and development activities, partially based on pre-existing knowledge, processes which are to a large extent tacit and embedded in organizations. Such processes through which new knowledge is generated are strongly dependent on the specificities of each technological paradigm (More in Dosi, 1982, and Dosi and Nelson, 2010).

The standard theory suffers from another deficiency. It focuses on the private production of knowledge, not taking into account the important interactions between the production of knowledge by profit-seeking firms and that of other actors in the economy (governments, not-for-profit research institutes, universities). But private production of applied knowledge typically rests on a foundation of basic research provided by these other institutions. Moreover, the level and direction of research is affected by a whole variety of motivations and instruments, besides that of property rights stressed in the IPR literature. Viewing markets as embedded in and depending upon a whole ensemble of non-market institutions allows us to appreciate the fact that technological innovation is highly dependent on a variety of complementary institutions (e.g. public agencies, public policies, universities, professional communities and, of course, corporate organizations with their rich inner structure) which can hardly be called "markets" and, at best, are governed and regulated by pure market incentives only to a limited extent.[31] This institutional embeddedness of innovative activities makes it very unlikely that a "market failure" approach such as the one we sketched above could provide a fully satisfactory account of the relationship between appropriability and propensity to innovate.

In short, one needs to see IPR as part of a country's *innovation system*, in which there are many institutions involved in the innovation process and in which there are a variety of mechanisms by which research is financed and funded and by which those engaging in research can be motivated and appropriate returns. Indeed, in some of these institutional settings (universities, for example) motivations are unrelated to standard concerns about appropriability, and enhanced appropriability has almost surely unambiguously adverse effects on innovation.[32] This reinforces the earlier conclusion that there may not only be adverse static consequences from stronger IPR but adverse dynamic effects.

Both static and dynamic efficiency are affected by this broader range of instruments; and it is accordingly wrong to focus simply on market-based "tools," and among the potential market based instruments, to focus just on intellectual property rights. (See section III on alternative ways to promote innovation.)

While IPR is part—but only a part—of a country's innovation system, data presented below shows that intellectual property rights play a different role in different industries. In some industries, where follow-on (sequential) innovations are important and/or where successful projects require large numbers of complementary "ideas" and components IPR (and especially poorly designed IPR regimes) can have an especially adverse effect on innovation.

II. SOME THEORETICAL AND INSTITUTIONAL ASPECTS OF IPR AND INNOVATION

What we have said so far should have made clear that the conventional wisdom, that the stronger the intellectual property regime, the better—the higher the level of innovation—is wrong. In fact, there has long been doubt about the role of IPR in promoting innovation. To some extent, the effect of IPR on innovation depends on the design of the IPR regime. And some of the "reforms" in the IPR regime in recent years may have made matters worse.

Historical scepticism about the role of patents

Scepticism about the role of intellectual property rights is not new. A half century ago, as Fritz Machlup, whose research focused on knowledge, put it: "If we did not have a patent system, it would be irresponsible, on the basis of our present knowledge of its economic consequences, to recommend instituting one. But since we have had a patent system for a long time, it would be irresponsible, on the basis of our present knowledge, to recommend abolishing it" (1958: 80). Similar doubts are expressed in David (1993, 2002) who argues that IPR is not necessary for new technologies and suggests that different institutional mechanisms more similar to open science might work more efficiently.

It is worth noting that as different countries have debated the benefits and costs of IPR, over time, there have been marked changes—largely influenced by special interests, but also sometimes influenced by public policy. We remarked earlier that at some times, in some countries, chemical entities could not be patented, and patents were only granted for the processes through which the entities could be synthesized. Through all of these changes, though, much of basic research—such as mathematical concepts—were not patentable. There is a broad consensus that the costs of extending patents would exceed the benefits. The worry, however, is that, under the influence of corporate interests, the boundaries of what is patentable have been extended, especially in the United States, in ways that are adverse to the advances of science and innovation.

Details matter: the challenge of designing a pro-innovation IPR system

The same criticism can be levelled against many other provisions of the current IPR regime. While some of the observed problems with current patent systems could be obviated with a better designed system, some of them may have indeed been made worse with changes in the patent system in the United States in recent years. *Details matter.* For instance, while there has been much discussion of the length of the patent, equally important are questions of the breadth of the patent, the standards of novelty under which a patent can be granted, and the processes by which patents can be granted (or opposed). (Not all of the changes have been bad. Later, we will note at least one instance where a Court decision has reduced the scope for enforcement actions for holdup patents, which can be adverse for innovation.)

Because the boundaries of knowledge and thus also of intellectual property are fuzzy, excessively broad patent protection can be especially adverse to innovation.[33] Ford had to challenge a broad patent that had been granted on self-propelled vehicles to produce his low cost "people's" car. A broad patent in genetically modified organisms (the "OncoMouse") has suppressed research and innovation in the field of cancer (see Murray et al., 2011). Patents can easily embrace existing knowledge, rewarding the patent holder well beyond his contribution. But in "fencing in the commons" access of others to incumbent knowledge and the returns that others will reap from their true contributions are reduced, again diminishing future innovation (see Boyle, 2003).

The asymmetries in getting and challenging patents worsen the problem: getting a patent privatizes what might have been public knowledge. Successfully challenging a patent converts what would have been a private good into the public domain. It is providing a public good, and, as in the case of other public goods, there will be an underprovision. That is why it is important to lower the costs of challenging the issuance of patents. European intellectual property framework is, in this respect, somewhat better than that of the United States (see Henry and Stiglitz, 2010).

These problems become more severe the lower the standard of "novelty" that is imposed in granting a patent. Several U.S. patents have been rightly criticized: Amazon's "one click" for buying online, or Apple's claim on rectangular smartphones and tablets with rounded corners are good cases to the point.

Making things worse: the expansion of the IPR domain to scientific exploration and public-funded search[34]

The last thirty years not only witnessed a tightening of the IPR regime in most developed countries, but brought about also (a) a significant *shrinkage of the legal domains of the commons of open source*; (b) a related (but not fully overlapping) *extension of* the domain of *matters considered patentable*; and (c) a significant *extension of the depth and breadth* of patents themselves.

The first regime change, in shorthand, goes under the heading of the Bayh-Dole (BD) Act, encouraging American universities to patent results obtained with public funding and sell them under exclusive terms to private profit-making actors. The issue is discussed at much greater detail by So et al. in Chapter 6 of this volume.

Bayh-Dole was a fundamental change in the premises underlying research universities, which were based on an ethos of free disclosure, and in which curiosity and the quest for knowledge drove research. Peer recognition, not monetary rewards, provided any additional incentives if required.[35]

Of course, the *commodification* of scientific inquiry stemming from Bayh-Dole has little to do with the incentives for research provided to the scientists actually doing the research. Their research is financed *ex ante* by taxpayers, universities, and research institutions.[36] The purported aim is an easier *commercialization* of its results. As we discuss below and in Chapter 6, there is little evidence of the latter, but a growing evidence on the distortion in the *directions* of scientific search linked with deep transformations in the institutional mission of research universities.

Of particular concern, as David (2004a and 2004b) convincingly argues, *"open science"* is a relatively fragile institutional arrangement. The Bayh-Dole "philosophy" may turn out to be a serious blow to open science. And because of "path dependence," once open science is undermined, it may be hard to restore. Indeed, as Chan, Sulston, and Harris argue (Chapter 5 in this volume) the domain of open science is consistent with ethical motivations supporting the value of knowledge and discovery per se, which commodification excludes. They argue that if there are rights to intellectual property, they have to compete with other (*higher*) rights of an ethical and moral kind. (These issues become especially relevant when IPR encroaches on access to medicines and to knowledge relevant to global warming—where overzealous enforcement of IPR can adversely affect the right to life, or even the survival of the planet.)

There have been other extensions of the domain of patentability that may have adversely affected innovation: the patentability of research tools and with that also the downstream restriction on research and on the ability of multiple researchers to draw upon each other's knowledge, building on common platforms and investments (Maskus, 1997).

This is particularly the case with patents on inventions concerning fundamental pieces of knowledge. Good examples are patents on genes or the Leder and Stewart patent on a genetically engineered mouse that develops cancer. To the extent that such techniques and knowledge are critical for further research that proceeds cumulatively on the basis of the original invention, the attribution of broad property rights might severely hamper further developments. Even more so if the patent protects not only the product the inventors have achieved (the "OncoMouse") but all the class of products that could be produced through that principle ("all transgenic non-human mammals") or all the possible uses of a patented invention (say, a gene sequence), even though they are not named in the application. In this respect, Murray et al. (2011) offers a striking illustration of how "opening up upstream" research paths can yield more search and more diverse explorations of "downstream" research paths.

Historical examples, such as those discussed by Merges and Nelson (1994) of the Selden patent of a four-wheel self-propelled vehicle (the automobile) and the Wright brothers' patent on an efficient stabilizing and steering system for flying machines illustrate how the IPR regime probably considerably retarded the subsequent development of automobiles and aircrafts. Earlier, at the beginning of the Industrial Revolution, the breadth of Watt's patent hindered innovation in high pressure steam engines (Nuvolari, 2004). The current debate on property rights in biotechnology suggests similar problems, where granting very broad claims on patents may have a detrimental effect on the rate of innovation, insofar as they preclude the exploration of alternative applications of the patented invention.

III. EMPIRICAL EVIDENCE

The ambiguous relation between appropriability (and even more so, IPR forms of appropriability) and rates of innovation puts the burden of proof upon the actual empirical record.

Indeed, the past two decades have witnessed the broadening of the patenting domain, including into areas that previously could not be so protected. This has been associated with an unprecedented increase in patenting rates. Between 1988 and 2000, patent applications from U.S. corporations more than doubled—a rate of increase of 6 per cent—well beyond the pace of innovation itself.

The relation between patenting and innovation—especially significant improvements, innovations that significantly lower, say, costs of production or providing valued services at a higher cost—has been subject to extensive controversy (for discussion, see Hu and Jaffe in Chapter 3 of this volume; Kortum and Lerner (1998); Hall (2005); Lerner (2002); Jaffe and Lerner (2004); and Jaffe (2000)).

Causal links

Even if there is a relationship between innovation and the explosion of patents, the direction of causality is not clear. One hypothesis claims that the increase of patents has been largely the consequence of the acceleration of the rates of innovation, which would have taken place even with weaker protection. This acceleration in innovation may, for instance, reflect a general increase in "technological opportunities" related, in particular, to the emergence of new technological paradigms such as those concerning information technologies and biotechnologies. (The latter is a field in which patents are a more important way to appropriability than in others. As search in the future shifts to other areas, this may no longer be true.)

The contrary hypothesis, suggested by tight IPR supporters, in our view without much evidence to back it, is that the changes in IPR regime are a primary "cause" of increased innovation rates. Conversely, those that doubt that the increase in patenting has caused an increase in innovation sometimes go further, suggesting that changes both in the legal and institutional framework, and in firms' strategies may have led to more patenting, with little relation to the underlying innovative activities.

While it is difficult to come to sharp conclusions in the absence of counterfactual experiments, some circumstantial evidence does lend some support to the latter hypothesis.

Explaining the growth of patents

Certainly part of the growth in the number of patents is simply due to the expansion of the patentability domain to new types of objects such as software, research tools, business methods, genes and artificially engineered organisms (see also Tirole, 2002, on the European case). Moreover, new actors have entered the patenting game, most notably universities and public agencies (see for example Mowery, Nelson, Sampat, and Ziedonis, 2001).

Finally, corporate strategies vis-à-vis the legal claims of IPR also appear to have significantly changed. Patents have acquired importance among the non-physical assets of firms as a means to signal the enterprise's value to potential investors, even well before the patented knowledge has been embodied in any marketable good. In this respect, the most relevant institutional change is to be found in the so called "Alternative 2" under the Nasdaq regulation (1984). This allowed "market entry and listing of firms operating at a deficit on the condition that they had considerable 'intangible' capital . . . composed of IPR" (Coriat and Orsi 2006: 170).[37]

At the same time, patents seems to have acquired a strategic value, quite independently from any embodiment in profitable goods. Even in those industries in which they were not considered as an important mechanism for appropriating the benefits from innovation: extensive portfolios of legal rights are considered means for entry deterrence (Hall and Ziedonis, 2001), and for infringement and counter-infringement suits against rivals. Texas Instruments, for instance, is estimated to have gained almost $1 billion a year from patent licenses and settlements resulting from its aggressive enforcement policy (Lerner 2010: 35). It is interesting to note that this practice has generated a new commercial strategy called "defensive publishing." According to this practice, firms who find it too expensive to build an extensive portfolio of patents tend to openly describe an invention in order to place it in the "prior art" domain, thus preserving the option to employ that invention free from the interference of anyone who might eventually patent the same idea.

The increased role that patent litigation is playing has, in turn, lead to increased patenting: patenting is designed both to build fences (not just to extend the effective life of the patent, but to deter others from entering into the fray, lest they encroach on one of the myriad of patents), and to increase one's arsenal in response to a patent infringement suit, enhancing the likelihood of a counter-suit. While such patent fences may possibly raise the private rate of return to patenting itself (Jaffe 2000), they may do so without increasing the underlying rate of innovation—and they could even have an adverse effect.

Kortum and Lerner (1998) present a careful account of different explanations of recent massive increases in patenting rates, comparing different interpretations. They look carefully at two changes in the institutional structure that may account for increased patenting. First, according to the "friendly court hypothesis," the balance between costs related to the patenting process (in terms e.g. of loss of secrecy) and the value of the protection that a patent affords to the innovator had been altered by an increase in the probability of successful application granted by the establishment in the United States of the Court of Appeals for the Federal Circuit (CAFC) specialized in patent cases—regarded by most observers as a strongly pro-patent institution (cf. Merges, 1996).

Second, the "capture" hypothesis (that the patent system has been captured by large corporate interests) tries to explain the surge of U.S. patent applications tracking it back to changes in the patent regime. Business firms in general and in particular larger corporations (whose propensity to patent has traditionally been higher than average) succeeded in inducing the U.S. government to change patent policy in their favor by adopting a stronger patent regime.

Patents and innovation

What we really care about, of course, is not whether there are few or more patents, but whether the patents are associated with more innovations, and in particular, whether there are more welfare-enhancing innovations—not me-too innovations, and not innovations that serve to block others from engaging in innovation.

Lerner (2002) presents evidence that if rates of innovation have increased in recent years, the increases were not the result of the change in the IPR regime and the associated increase in patents that it caused. Rather the growth in (real) R&D spending predates the strengthening of the IP regime.

The apparent lack of effects of different IPR regimes upon the rates of innovation appears also from broad historical comparisons. For example, based on the analysis of data from the catalogues of two nineteenth-century world fairs—the Crystal Palace Exhibition in London in 1851 and the

Centennial Exhibition in Philadelphia in 1876—Moser (2005) finds no evidence that countries with stronger IP protection produced more innovations than those with weaker IP protection, though there is significant evidence of the influence of IP laws on the sectoral distribution of innovations. In weak IP countries, firms did innovate in sectors in which other forms of appropriation (e.g. secrecy and lead time) were more effective, whereas in countries with strong IP protection significantly more innovative effort went to the sectors in which these other forms were less effective. Hence, one can draw from Moser's study the interesting conclusion that patents' main effect could well be on the direction rather than on the rates of innovative activity. (And we have to remember that we are concerned not with just innovation per se, but welfare-enhancing innovation. If the patent system shifts resources into research designed to innovate around a patent, the net welfare benefit may be negative.)

More generally, the evidence suggests that the relationship between patents and innovation depends on the very nature of industry-specific knowledge bases, on industry stages in their life cycles, and on the industrial structure. Various surveys highlight both the differences among sectors and the limited role that patents play in many sectors. Levin, Klevorick, Nelson, and Winter (1987), for instance, report that patents are by and large viewed as less important than learning curve advantages and lead time in protecting product innovation, and are the least effective among the means of appropriating returns from innovative investments for process innovations (see Table 1.1). Cohen, Nelson, and Walsh (2000) present a follow-up to Levin et al. (1987), also addressing the impact of patenting on the incentive to undertake R&D. Again, they report on the relative importance of the variety of mechanisms used by firms to protect their innovations—including secrecy, lead time, complementary capabilities and patents: see again Table 1.1. The table suggests that the most effective instruments for product innovations are secrecy and lead time while patents are the least effective, with the partial exception of drugs and medical equipment. Interestingly, the most important reasons given for not patenting an innovation were (i) the difficulty of demonstrating novelty (that is, satisfying the conditions required to get a patent) (32 per cent), (ii) information disclosure (24 per cent), and (iii) ease of inventing around the patent (25 per cent).

The uses of patents also differ for "complex" and "discrete" product industries. Complex products industries are those in which a product is protected by a large number of patents while discrete product industries are those in which a product is relatively simple and therefore associated with a small number of patents. In complex product industries, patents are used to block rival use of components and acquire bargaining strength in cross-licensing negotiations. In discrete product industries, patents are used to block substitutes by creating patent "fences" (cf. Gallini, 2002; Ziedonis, 2004).

Table 1.1 Effectiveness of appropriability mechanism in product and process innovations, 1983 and 1994 surveys, United States, 33 manufacturing industries

1.1(a). Product innovation

Mechanism	Rank of importance of mechanisms, and number of industries in which a mechanism achieved that rank							
	1st		2nd		3rd		4th	
	1983	1994	1983	1994	1983	1994	1983	1994
Patents	4	7	3	5	17	7	9	4
Secrecy	0	13	0	11	11	2	22	5
Lead time	14	10	14	8	5	7	0	7
Sales & service	16	4	16	4	1	7	0	10
Manufacturing*	n.a.	3	n.a.	3	n.a.	14	n.a.	7

1.1(b). Process innovation

Mechanism	Rank of importance of mechanisms, and number of industries in which a mechanism achieved that rank							
	1st		2nd		3rd		4th	
	1983	1994	1983	1994	1983	1994	1983	1994
Patents	2	1	4	5	3	3	24	16
Secrecy	2	21	10	10	19	1	2	0
Lead time	26	3	5	7	2	16	0	3
Sales & service	4	0	16	0	7	3	6	11
Manufacturing*	n.a.	10	n.a.	12	n.a.	10	n.a.	0

The table shows the relative importance of each mechanism (e.g. patents) to appropriability in 33 different sectors. The column on the left lists the various mechanisms. The other columns list the possible ranking of their importance to appropriability (1st, 2nd, 3rd, or 4th), and the number of sectors in which a mechanism held that rank of importance for appropriability, in 1983 and 1994 respectively. *Manufacturing capabilities. *Source*: Levin et al. (1987) and Cohen, Nelson and Welsh (2000) as presented in Winter (2002) (n.a. for observations not available).

It is interesting also to compare Cohen, Nelson and Walsh (2000) with the older Levin et al. (1987), which came before the changes in the IPR regime and before the massive increase in patenting rates. Even with this increased use of patents, Cohen, Nelson and Walsh (2000) report that patents are not the key means to appropriate returns from innovations in most industries. Secrecy, lead time and complementary capabilities are often perceived as being more important appropriability mechanisms.

The example of the semiconductor and other ICT industries

Given that patents clearly play different roles in different industries, further insights can be gleaned by in-depth studies of particular industries. A number of scholars (Bessen and Maskin, 2000; Hall and Ziedonis, 2001) have focused on the role of patents in the semiconductor industry, one of the most dynamic sectors of the economy in recent decades. Bessen and Maskin (2000) observe that computers and semiconductors, while having been among the most innovative industries in the last forty years, have historically had weak patent protection and rapid imitation of their products. The short product life cycles and fast-paced innovation also may have played a role in this historical pattern. But then the software industry in the United States experienced a rapid strengthening of patent protection in the 1980s. Bessen and Maskin suggest that "far from unleashing a flurry of new innovative activity, these stronger property rights ushered in a period of stagnant, if not declining, R&D among those industries and firms that patented most" (2000: 2). Bessen and Maskin (2000) argue that this phenomenon is likely to occur in those industries characterized by a high degree of sequentiality (each innovation builds on a previous one) and complementarity (the simultaneous existence of different research lines enhances the probability that a goal might be eventually reached). A patent, in this perspective, actually prevents non-holders from the use of the idea (or of similar ideas) protected by the patent itself and in a sequential world full of complementarities this turns out to slowdown innovation rates. Conversely, it might well happen that firms would be better off in an environment characterized by easy imitation, whereby it would be true that imitation would reduce current profits but it would also be the case that easy imitation would raise the probability of further innovation taking place and of further profitable innovations being realized later on.[38]

In these sectors, the growth in patents might have been associated with the use of patents as "bargaining chips" in the exchanges of technology among different firms and in the attempts of rent extraction from each other.

Again, the social value of research directed at obtaining such patents is likely to be limited, with the private value of such patents most likely exceeding the social value.

Drugs: a second example

In several respects, pharmaceuticals are an archetypical case for examining the role of IPR. It is one of the sectors for which IPR represents one of the more important mechanisms for appropriability. It is also the sector in which research is most affected by the Bayh-Dole Act and more generally by the exclusive appropriation of the results of research itself and the retreat of the boundaries of Open Science. It represents a sort of crucial institutional experiment (more on it in Angell, 2004; Mazzucato and Dosi, 2006; and Avorn, 2004).

But the tightening of the patenting regime was followed by a fall in the rate of innovation—as proxied e.g. by the number of FDA-approved New Chemical Entities (NCE) per year.[39] While a good deal of the new discoveries were and are based on research funded by or conducted by government agencies (Angell, 2004), a big share of early discoveries appropriated by biotech firms and "big pharma" companies have remained unfulfilled promises of new drugs, that is they never went all the way to clinical trials. Part of the explanation of the seeming lack of innovation is that meaningful innovations are only part of the drug companies' concern: currently, marketing, enforcement of IPR-related rent extraction and search of *me-too drugs* (that is, marginal variations on incumbent, typically mass-market drugs for high income patients), all have a big share of major pharmaceutical companies' activities, while the uncertain experimentation of NCE, possibly effective only for subsets of patients with a certain disease, is far from a priority. All this is a powerful test—and indeed a very expensive one for the taxpayer and purchaser of health care services—of the ineffectiveness, at best, of tightening and widening IPR as an incentive to greater efforts of innovative search, even *in the presence of seemingly increasing science-driven notional opportunities.*

Part of the explanation of the failure of tighter IPR to enhance innovation may be the impediments that are posed for follow-on research and the adverse effects of the "institutional innovations" on the research process itself, by encouraging more secrecy. Part may rest in the effect that it had on the directions of search in favor of high-end, not-too-difficult to find "blockbusters" and subsidized me-too drugs, addressing rich and aging populations.[40]

As we shall discuss below, the picture is bleaker for developing countries.

The role of appropriability more generally

So far we have primarily discussed the relations between the regimes of IPR protection and rates of innovations, basically concluding that either the relation is not there, or if it is there that it might be a perverse one, with strong IPR enforcement actually deterring innovative efforts.

However, we also know that IPR protection is only one of the mechanisms for appropriating returns from innovation, and certainly not the most important one. We should, then, also consider the impact of appropriability more generally. The question is not whether an increase in the extent of appropriability increases investments in innovation in some sort of *partial equilibrium model*, given the inflow of knowledge. The question is what the broader impacts of stronger conditions for appropriability are, taking into account how they affect both incentives for investments and the dissemination of knowledge. In particular, stronger appropriability implies that the pool of "ideas" that are publicly available for researchers to draw upon may be smaller, and since technological opportunities are a (perhaps *the*) major driver of innovation, a reduced set of opportunities may actually lead to reduced innovation.

Considering together the evidence on appropriability from survey data (cf. Cohen, Nelson and Walsh, 2000; and Levin, Klevorick, Nelson and

Winter, 1987), the cross-sectoral evidence on technological opportunities (cf. Klevorick, Levin, Nelson and Winter, 1995) and the evidence from multiple sources on the modes, rates and directions of innovation (for two surveys, cf. Dosi, 1988; and Dosi and Nelson, 2010), the broad conclusion is that appropriability conditions above a minimum threshold generally have at most a limited effect on the level and pattern of innovation. Obviously, with zero appropriability, the incentive to innovate for private actors would vanish—everybody would want to be a free rider—but, as our previous discussion emphasized, with few exceptions innovators are always able to appropriate some returns from their innovations; flows of information are never perfect; and technological knowledge is often quite sticky indeed. Open source software shows that the threshold level of appropriability might indeed be very low.

Opportunities, capabilities and greed: some general properties of the drivers of innovation and its private appropriation

There are some basic messages from the foregoing discussion of the theory and empirical evidence on the relationship between the extent of IPR protection and rates of innovation. For corporate investments in research, it is obvious that there must be some private *expectation* (whether fulfilled or not) of "profiting from innovation." Nevertheless, there are neither strong theoretical reasons nor strong empirical evidence suggesting that modifying appropriability mechanisms for innovations in general—and appropriability by means of IPR in particular—has any clear, strong effect on the amount of resources that private, self-seeking agents devote to innovative search, nor on the rates at which they discover new products and new production processes. As Jaffe concluded after surveying the available literature, "there is little empirical evidence that what is widely perceived to be a significant strengthening of intellectual property protection had significant impact on the innovation process" (2000: 540).

Indeed, we have explained why "stronger" IPR may actually have an adverse effect on innovation. Again, as Jaffe concluded:

> to the extent that firms' attention and resources are, at the margin, diverted from innovation itself toward the acquisition, defence and assertion against others of property rights, the social return to the endeavour as a whole is likely to fall. While the evidence on all sides is scant, it is fair to say that there is at least much evidence of these effects of patent policy changes as there is evidence of stimulation of research.
> (2000: 555; see also Hu and Jaffe, Chapter 3 in this volume)

But if IPR regimes have, at best, second-order effects on the rates of innovation, the question remains of what the main determinants of the rates and directions of innovation are. Our basic answer, as argued in more detail elsewhere (cf. Cimoli, Dosi, and Stiglitz, 2009; and Dosi and Nelson, 2010) is the following. The fundamental determinants of observed rates of innovation in individual industries/technologies appear to arise from the extent of the *opportunities* that each industry faces. To understand this, it may be useful to think of an "opportunity sea" in which incumbents and entrants go fishing for innovation. A broader, deeper, richer sea contains more opportunities for innovation, stemming from a variety of sources. In part, they are generated by research institutions outside the business sector. Others spring from the search efforts incumbent firms have undertaken in the past. Moreover, yet others are generated and flow through the economic system via the relationships between suppliers and users[41] (see the detailed inter-sectoral comparisons and taxonomy in Pavitt, 1984, and Klevorick, et al., 1995). But patents restrict the flow of knowledge into the "opportunity sea," and in doing so, have an adverse effect on the most important determinant of progress. Conversely, in most industries, the possibilities for appropriating returns—even with a weak IPR regime—are sufficient to induce firms to go out to "fish in the sea of opportunities."

In short, a full analysis has to take into account not just the effect of an IPR regime in inducing more innovation *given the set of technological opportunities*, but how a tighter IPR regime enables successful innovators to "enclose the commons," which reduces the amount of knowledge in the knowledge pool that could be the basis for further patentable research; as well as reducing the extent to which the induced innovations contribute to the pool of knowledge from which others may eventually draw. Tighter IPR regimes enable innovators to take more out of the pool and to contribute less to the pool, so that the size of the pool is diminished, so much so that the actual level of innovation may be diminished (Stiglitz, 2013c).

Indeed, one observes large differences in the innovative activity of different firms having little to do with any legal regime governing the access to the use of supposedly publicly disclosed but legally restricted knowledge, such as that associated with patent-related information. While the "rates of fishing" depend essentially on the size and richness of the sea, idiosyncratic differences in the rates of success in the fishing activity itself depend to a large extent on firm-specific capabilities.[42] Increasing appropriability has little effect—given a particular level of capabilities and opportunities—upon the rates of investment and R&D spending. And if that is so, then the adverse effects of stronger IPR on the technological opportunity set may dominate any positive effect of a change in how much society decides to compensate the fishermen for their catch. (Tighter IPR may itself impede the diffusion of learning capabilities among firms, thereby further diminishing the overall pace of innovation.)

While the effects of a stronger IPR regime on innovation are ambiguous, its effects on distribution are not. It gives rise to monopoly power. This leads to higher prices and lower consumer welfare (at any given level of innovation).[43] But in some sectors, like pharmaceuticals, the adverse effects of patents can be even worse: how are we to evaluate the unnecessary deaths associated with higher drug prices?[44] As a result, the overall benefits of stronger IPR are even more questionable.

We should, of course, bear in mind our earlier important message: details matter. It is not only a matter of the "strength" of the IPR regime, but also its design. We have described some of the effects of the IPR regimes that the United States and other countries have had, and how some of the changes in the IPR regime have affected innovation. There are some changes in the IPR regime (and other associated legal regimes) that would reduce the adverse effects. For instance, more extensive use of compulsory licensing would reduce some of the adverse welfare effects from unnecessary deaths and from the adverse budgetary consequences; more effective enforcement of competition laws would reduce some of the adverse welfare effects from anticompetitive practices of those who attempt to leverage the monopoly of the patent into more general market power. Later, we will describe a recent change in the U.S. IPR regime that may reduce the adverse effects of the patent thicket, by reducing the scope for holdups.

IV. PATENTS AND A COUNTRY'S INNOVATION SYSTEM[45]

A country's innovation system is the collection of institutions that promote innovation; it fosters the accumulation of technological capabilities in individuals and corporations; it provides incentives and finance, and allocates resources among researchers and research projects. The innovation system is concerned with the production and dissemination of knowledge throughout the economy, including the creation of new products and the improvement of production processes.

There are many components of an innovation system besides intellectual property rights (see e.g. Freeman (1987), Lundvall (2010) and Nelson (2004b).) Much research—and especially basic research, the most foundational—goes on within universities, not-for-profit research institutions, and government laboratories, typically financed by government, sometimes in partnership with the private sector, sometimes supported by foundations.[46]

In evaluating alternative innovation systems, there are several criteria. The ultimate objective is the well-being of society and its dynamics (that is, not just well-being now, but in the future). That, in turn, is affected by the pace and direction of innovation and the efficiency with which resources devoted to research are used. But the innovation system does not exist in isolation. It can, for instance, affect the competitiveness and efficiency of the entire economy, the extent of inequality in society and the health of its citizens. It can even have large budgetary consequences, as in the United States, as government pays pharmaceutical companies large amounts for drugs, the production costs of which are but a fraction of what the government pays—in some cases, even for drugs based largely on government-financed research.

In recent years, two other institutional arrangements (besides IPR and government supported research) have grown (and regrown) in importance as part of a modern innovation system: prizes and open source.

The prize system represents one alternative to the patent system for providing incentives for research. This entails giving a prize to whomever comes up with an innovation, or at least those innovations that meet announced objectives. For instance, the person who finds a cure or a vaccine for AIDS or malaria would get a big prize. Someone who comes up with a drug with slightly different side effects than existing drugs (but which is otherwise no more effective) might get a small prize. The size of the prize is calibrated by the magnitude of the contribution.

The idea is an old one. The UK's Royal Society for the Encouragement of Arts, Manufactures and Commerce has been advocating and using prizes to incentivize the development of needed technologies for more than a century. For instance, an alternative was needed for chimney sweeps, those small, underfed boys who used to be sent down chimneys. It was not good for their health, but not cleaning chimneys meant increasing the risk of fire, with serious consequences. So the Royal Society offered a prize to anybody who invented a mechanical way of cleaning chimneys. The prize provided an incentive—and it worked. A patent system might also have motivated the development of a mechanical device (though it did not), but if it had, there would have been a problem: the owner of the patent would have wanted to maximize the return on his innovation by charging a high fee for its use. That would have meant that only rich families could have afforded to use the mechanical device, and young boys' lives would have continued to be put at risk. With the prize system, everyone ended up benefitting from this socially important innovation.

The current patent system is, of course, similar to a prize system, but it is an inefficient one, because the "prize" is a grant of monopoly power, and with monopoly power there are incentives to restrict the use of the knowledge. One of the characteristics of a desirable innovation system is that the ideas and innovations, once developed, are widely used and disseminated; to the contrary, the patent system is designed to restrict the use of knowledge. With the prize system, a competitive market ensures a reasonably efficient dissemination: giving licenses to a large number of actors enables competition to drive down the price and to increase the use of the knowledge. With both patents and prizes, market forces are used: one is the incentive of a monopoly to restrict knowledge and raise prices, the other is the force of competitive markets to drive down prices and extend the benefit of knowledge widely.

Moreover, the prize system has the advantage of creating fewer incentives to waste money on advertising and to engage in anticompetitive behaviors designed to enhance monopoly profits. Drug companies spend more on advertising and marketing than they do on research.[47] Much of these marketing expenditures are designed to reduce the elasticity of demand, which allows the owner of the patent to raise prices and increase monopoly profits. From a social point of view, these expenditures are dissipative.

The patent system also distorts the pattern of research: drug companies have insufficient incentives to develop medicines for the diseases that tend to afflict poor people, simply because there is no money in those drugs.[48]And as we have already noted, there are other distortions: incentives for research to get a share of the rents through me-too patents, to extend the life of the patent, through evergreening, to get "blocking" patents that can extract rents in holdups.

The fourth alternative way of promoting innovation, open source, has become especially important in IT, but has spread from there to other sectors (see Henry and Stiglitz, 2010; Hertel, Krishnan and Slaughter, 2003; Lerner and Tirole, 2002; Weber, 2005). It highlights and strengthens the collaborative nature of research that is the hallmark of academia, and the open architecture facilitates follow-on research, in contrast to the patent system which closes it down. As in academia, in some instances non-pecuniary returns play a crucial role in motivating research; in other cases, firms have found a variety of ways of appropriating returns, e.g. through the sale of services or tailoring software based on open source to the needs of particular clients.

There is still a fifth alternative, already described: let firms appropriate returns through natural markets using the non-IPR mechanisms (the advantage of being first, etc.) described earlier.

Table 1.2 provides a chart of some of the attributes of the five alternatives we have described.

Any innovation system has to solve the problems of finance, selection (who gets research money) and incentives. There are, in addition, problems of coordination of research efforts. How these tasks are solved will affect the efficiency of the system—including the uncertainty and transaction costs facing market participants. Every country should have a portfolio of instruments, but in our view, too much weight has been assigned to patents in the current U.S. portfolio.

The first attribute listed is *selection*. One problem facing any innovation system is how to select those to engage in research activities. A possible advantage (but also a possible bias) of both the patent and prize system is that they are decentralized and based on self-selection. Those who think that they are able to successfully undertake the research in a particular

Table 1.2 Comparing alternative systems

Attribute	Innovation system				
	Patent	Prize	Government-funded research	Open source	Non-IPR market appropriation
Selection	Decentralized, self-selection. Lacks coordination.	Decentralized, self-selection. Lacks coordination.	Bureaucratic. More coordination possible.	Decentralized, self-selection. Sometimes "self" coordination.	Decentralized, self-selection. Lacks coordination.
Finance (tax)	Highly distortionary and inequitable.	Can be less distortionary and more equitable.	Most efficient.	May be underfinanced. Foundations, government, by-product of other activities.	Likely to be less distortionary than patent.
Risk	Litigation risk.	Less risk.	Least risk.	Limited.	Limited.
Innovation incentives	Strong but distorted.	Strong, less distorted. Requires well-defined objectives.	Strong non-monetary incentives.	Strong—often non-pecuniary.	Strong, less distorted.
Dissemination incentive	Limited—monopoly.	Strong—competitive markets.	Strong.	Strong.	Limited—returns depend on secrecy.
Transaction costs	High.	Lower.	Lower.	Low.	Low.

technological field make the investment, risking their own money, in the belief that they have a good chance of winning the prize (the formal prize or the prize of the patent). This would seem to be a significant advantage of the prize and patent systems over government-funded research, in which there is a group of peers (or bureaucrats) deciding on the best searchers.[49,50] In some countries, there is obviously also a concern about "capture" of the research-awarding process, e.g., by political or economic interests whose agendas may be separate from or counter to the advancement of science and technology. At the same time, self-selection does not necessarily result in the best researchers undertaking research, but rather the most confident, or those with the deepest pockets. Thus, patent races and prizes put smaller firms at a disadvantage. To the extent that those that enter the fray are those that are the most overconfident, though innovation might proceed more slowly than it would in an alternative system, at least the costs of the mistakes are not borne by the public.

With respect to *finance*, the patent system is the worst of the systems. It is highly distortionary and inequitable in the way in which funds to support research are raised—by charging monopoly prices, e.g., in the case of pharmaceuticals, on the sick.

By the same token, the transaction costs (especially those associated with litigation) and the distortions in the economic system are much higher with a patent system than with the other two. (And there is some evidence that those costs are increasing, together with the firms' propensity to litigate.)[51]

Regarding the *dissemination* of knowledge and its efficient use, government-funded research, the prize system and open source are best (because knowledge is generally made freely available), and the patent system is the worst, given that it relies on monopolization, which entails high prices and restricted usage. In short, under the prize and the government-funded research systems, knowledge, once acquired, is more efficiently used. These are among the key advantages of these alternatives.

There is a big difference in the nature of the *risk* faced by researchers (which in modern economies often happen to be firms) operating in the different systems. With respect to risk, the patent system is the worst and the government-funded system is the best, because it has the advantages of paying for the input rather than the output. That is to say, a researcher gets money for his time and other resources spent doing the research, whereas in the prize and the patent systems researchers are rewarded only if their research is successful—and successful before their rivals.

Risk is increased too within the prize and patent system by problems of coordination. One of the disadvantages of both the patent and the prize systems is the lack of *coordination*. The lack of coordination reduces the efficiency of the innovation process and increases risk. The difficulties of coordination are increased by secrecy which is encouraged by the IPR regime. Relatedly, one of the *risks* that each researcher faces is that of costly litigation.

One of the reasons that risk (in fact, most often in the case of innovation, "Knightian" uncertainty which cannot be reduced to objective probabilities) is important is that users and consumers ultimately have to pay for the risk borne by researchers. People and firms[52] tend to be risk averse, and if they must bear risk, they demand to be compensated for doing so (through higher prices and mark-ups). The patent system makes society bear the cost of that risk in an inefficient way. Under the government-financed research system, not only is risk lower, but it is shared by society in a more efficient way.

Innovation incentives are strong in the patent system, but they are distorted. The prize system can provide strong incentives, but the incentives are designed to foster socially desirable innovation, in contrast to the distorted incentives of the patent system, discussed earlier in this introduction.[53]

On most accounts, the prize system dominates the patent system; but the prize system has one limitation: it does not work when the objective is not well-defined. There are, however, many areas, such as health, energy conservation and carbon emissions reductions, in which there are well-defined objectives. The prize system will never fully replace the patent system. At the same time, in basic research—the foundation on which everything else is built—government-funded research will continue to remain at the core of the innovation system. It would be a disaster otherwise: the costs of restricting the usage of more basic knowledge associated with the patent system far outweigh any purported benefits.

V. IPR IN THE DEVELOPMENT PROCESS

What we have said so far applies to countries more or less on the "technological frontier." The drawbacks of IPR, especially poorly designed IPR regimes, are significantly amplified when tight IPR regimes are applied in countries attempting to catch up with the more advanced industrial countries. As we note in the preface, what separates developed from developing countries today is as much a gap in knowledge as a gap in resources. Access to knowledge is essential. But the intellectual property regime denies them access to knowledge and/or requires that they pay large rents to firms in the developed countries.

This is a core topic of this book analyzed from different angles, especially in the Chapters 2, 3, 4 and 7 of this volume and also in Odagiri, Goto, Sunami and Nelson (2010), which is in many respects complementary to this one, as it takes a historical perspective of inter-country comparisons.

"Tight" intellectual property rights regimes tend to hinder the development of local technological capabilities in general and *absorptive capabilities* in particular, since they hinder the activities of reverse engineering and imitative experimentation which are typically at the core of the development process.

As discussed in the introduction to Odagiri et al. (2010), and also in Chapters 2 and 16, learning in catching-up countries takes place mainly via the following (partly complementary) mechanisms:

(i) *Mobility of people* either in the form of the "peaceful conquest" (Pollard, 1981), i.e. the emigration of technicians from frontier countries to catching-up ones—as it occurred in the nineteenth century in Continental Europe and the United States, with many coming from the U.K.; or in the form of students and technicians coming for periods of training in Europe and the United States from Japan and later South Korea, China, etc. and then returning back home.

(ii) *Open source* forms of knowledge dissemination, including exhibitions—quite important in the nineteenth century—conferences, papers, more recently internet and even patent documents.

(iii) *Investment goods*—especially machine tools and instruments—that "embody" advances in knowledge. Knowledge is also transmitted and developed as those in the catching-up countries learn how to effectively use these advanced investment goods.

(iv) *Imitation, reverse engineering*, or sheer *copying* of foreign products and capital inputs by *domestic* firms.

(v) *Formal licensing* of patented technologies and know-how by domestic firms.

(vi) *Inter-firm technology transfer by MNCs* to their subsidiaries in emerging economics.

(vii) *Technological spillovers* from MNCs themselves to other firms in catching-up countries, especially as a result of the training of workers.

In addition, several emerging markets (particularly China and Brazil) have become a source of innovations in their own right. In some areas, they have moved to the frontier: China, for instance, in solar technology; Brazil in deep-water drilling for oil and sugar-based ethanol. Patent grants to residents of China have soared in recent years, from 5,395 in 2001 to 112,347 in 2011.[54]

The reason we have provided this long list of channels through which the knowledge gap is reduced is that Western advocates of IPR emphasize only a few channels that might be enhanced by stronger IPR—including MNC-mediated and license-mediated transfer of technology. But IPR may have adverse effects on other channels (e.g. those associated with the transfer of knowledge/products/processes via imitation and learning from developed to developing countries). Indeed, the historical record shows that these other mechanisms have typically been paramount in successful episodes of industrialization (more in Cimoli, Dosi and Stiglitz, 2009).[55] And if the latter are more important (as they probably are in most developing countries), then negative effects outweigh the positive. In fact, the evidence that stronger IPR regimes are effective in fostering technology transfer is far from conclusive (more in Fink and Maskus, 2005; Odagiri et al., 2010; Hu and Jaffe, Chapter 3 in this volume).

VI. THE IMPACT OF TRIPS

TRIPS has brought increased international harmonization. But is it likely to bring increased innovation to developing countries? Was there excessive harmonization? And was the harmonization around the right standards?

We suggest that this new IPR regime tends to be, other things being equal, a *hindrance* to the process of development and catching-up, precisely because it impedes many of the ways by which knowledge is transferred to developing countries: it tends to hinder, for instance, imitation by domestic firms and accumulation of local technological capabilities. These were indeed the instruments which developed countries—from the United States, to Germany, to Japan—used abundantly during the course of their catching up. Interestingly, later, those same countries "kicked away the ladder" (Chang, 2002), re-writing history as they sought to depict their earlier success as a result of *free-trade with strong IPR* (more in Odagiri et al., 2010; and in Chapter 2 in this volume).[56]

For developing countries, there is a further concern: the "new" IPR regime may result in massive transfers of money from developing to developed countries (that, of course, was the intent when setting it up!). To reduce the gap in knowledge, developing countries are being asked to increase the gap in resources. Under the new TRIPS regime the flow of international licenses from developed to developing countries in *monetary terms* significantly increased (Maskus, 2005; Arora, Fosfuri and Gambardella, 2001). However it is less clear-cut whether this is due to an actual increase in the flow of technology transfers (the flow of knowledge) or in the costs of such transfers—that is, ultimately in the rents extracted out of the licensing of each piece of technological knowledge.

In some circumstances, such as in the pharmaceutical industry, the evidence is particularly striking. Before TRIPS, generics obtained under loose IPR regimes were able to dramatically reduce the cost of drugs available to

Table 1.3 Costs of first and second line HIV treatments in Western and developing countries

	Lamivudine/stavudine/ nevirapine (1st line)	Tenofovir/didanosine/ opinavi (2ndline)	2nd line vs. 1st line
Western countries[a]	U.S. $8,773/yr	U.S. $13,551/yr	1.5 times more expensive
Developing countries	U.S. $154/yr CiplaTriomune[b]	U.S. $3,950/yr Originator product	26 times more expensive
Reduction	−98%	−70%	

[a] Australian EXW prices: Schedule of Pharmaceutical Benefits for Approved Pharmacists and Medical Practioners, May 2004. Exchange rate used for conversion 1 AUD = 0.72213 USD, 1 May 2004.
[b] Clinton Foundation price (FOB) + 10% due to transportation and importation taxes.
Source: E. t'Hoen (2005) and elaborations by Coriat, Orsi, and d'Almeida (2006).

developing countries. A vivid illustration concerns anti-retroviral drugs against the HIV virus where generics were able to reduce the cost by between 98 per cent and 70 per cent (cf. Table 1.3, from Coriat et al, 2006; and Chapter 7 in this volume).

More generally, the evidence discussed in Coriat and Orsenigo in this volume suggests that large increases in the prices of drugs in developing countries, ranging between 50 per cent and 400 per cent, resulted from the implementations of TRIPS. And all that, of course, without evidence that these higher prices have led either to more drug innovation in general, let alone more innovation attempting to address the needs of those in developing countries.

There are no major pharmaceutical companies in the developing world and a good deal of learning and catching-up—in India, Israel, Thailand, China and Brazil—occurred precisely with the production of generics, under loose IPR protection most often covering *only processes* of production but *not products*. And all this is now banned, or at least, significant barriers have been imposed to the introduction of generics, and so innovation in developing countries is impeded. (Note that the benefits of establishing a generics industry may go well beyond the lower prices; on the basis of the learning associated with generics, a broader industry can be established.)

Yet another archetypal case is agriculture. If one takes the long-term view as the chapters by Nuvolari and Tartari, and by Halewood do—this is a sector where technological improvements have taken place over decades and centuries, in the absence of any IPR protection, though at a slower pace until the nineteenth century, when—still without any IPR protection—dramatic agricultural advances occurred (allowing a small proportion of the labor force to produce all of the food demanded even as incomes rose), significantly helped by public institutions such as Land Grant Colleges in the United States and similar ones in Europe.

The scenario changed a good deal with the introduction of high-productivity, (quasi-) sterile seeds. The originators of innovation began to successfully demand a powerful "technical protection" on the flow of outputs from their innovations. Chapter 9 in this volume explores the difference between "if you want a seed as productive as last year, you are bound to come back to me, and at my prices" as compared to "if you buy the seeds which I originated, without paying some royalty to me I will bring you to court in Burkina Faso." The outcome, as Swanson and Goeschl highlight, is much lower rates of innovation diffusion and a greater *divergence* vis-à-vis the moving international productivity boundaries—no matter how measured.

An intellectual property regime for developing countries

This book offers a detailed diagnostics of the impact of IPR on developing countries at multiple levels—including the rates and direction of scientific search and technological innovation, the rates and patterns of international diffusion of technological knowledge, and more generally its effects on the developing countries' catching-up process.

At the same time, this book is equally rich in the exploration of policy measures fostering the international diffusion of knowledge, the accumulation of capabilities in catching-up countries and the access by the populations in emerging economies of the fruits of technological innovation. Chapter 6 draws upon U.S. experiences in formulating policy lessons for governance of publicly financed research by developing countries. Chapter 7 discusss the policy agenda in the area of pharmaceuticals in the post-2005 international TRIPS regime. Chapter 10 analyzes the possibilities of securing a global common in plant genetic resources, while Chapter 11 deals with the ways of nurturing open source modes of governance of biotech knowledge in emerging economies. Chapter 12 examines the role of IPR with respect to innovations curbing greenhouse gases in general, and in developing countries in particular, while Chapter 13 considers different arrangements aimed at the diffusion to the developing countries of environmentally sound technologies.

Finally, the last three chapters look at IPR and their consequences from the point of view of the international governance institutions and the role of IPR policies in the broader context of industrial policies. Chapter 14 discusses in depth the "opportunities" (i.e. the "flexibilities") still available to developing countries under the TRIPS regime, opportunities which bilateral and multilateral trade agreements attempt to restrict, as Spenneman and Roffe show in Chapter 15. Burlamaqui and Cimoli in Chapter 16 continue in this vein, exploring links between IPR, industrial policy, and the reach and limits of the "governance of knowledge."

We have suggested that excessive attention has been given to IPR-related policies, and that more progress would have been made if IPR had been viewed within the broader context of an innovation system, of which IPR is only one component. Equally or more important from the perspective of "catching up" are industrial policies focusing on the development of domestic technological and organizational capabilities. This is the thrust of Chapter 16. Unfortunately, the 1995 Uruguay Round not only created an intellectual property regime that was not pro-development, but also imposed restrictions on the ability of developing countries to effectively use industrial policies.

We shall come back to several of these policy themes in the conclusion to this book.

VII. RECENT DEVELOPMENTS IN IPR AND INNOVATION SYSTEMS

Everywhere, intellectual property rights are in flux, as changes in technology and the economy pose challenges to existing perspectives. The battle is not just one between civil society and consumer groups, on the one hand, and large corporations on the other. There is also a battle among different business interests, battles that illustrate the central themes of this book—intellectual property is man-made, designed to enhance societal well-being, and there can be large distributive effects. But if we don't design the IPR system well, it may impede innovation. It may help large established firms, with their army of patent lawyers, at the expense of small firms.

It is not just the laws themselves that matter, but how they are interpreted by the courts and the agencies that administer them. In the concluding section of this introduction, we discuss two recent developments that illustrate how courts and administrative agencies are trying to come to terms with the dangers of unbalanced IPR regimes.

The first is a path-breaking decision of the Supreme Court in a case called *eBay Inc. v. MercExchange, L.L.C.*[57] In the past, patents have typically been enforced through "injunctions"—others cannot trespass on a patent without the permission of the patent holder, who can extract as much "rent" as he wishes. This is in contrast with many other areas, where there is compensation for violating someone's rights or property. The Supreme Court itself has raised questions about the consequences of what might be termed excessive enforcement though actions by patent holders that in effect "exclude" those who might infringe upon the patent. In *eBay*, the Court ruled that a permanent injunction (against infringement) would only be granted if a four-part test was satisfied:

A [patent] plaintiff must demonstrate: (1) that it has suffered an irreparable injury; (2) that remedies at law, such as monetary damages, are inadequate to compensate for that injury; (3) that, considering the balance of hardships between the plaintiff and defendant, a remedy in equity is warranted; and (4) that the public interest would not be disserved by a permanent injunction.

An extreme version of exclusion is still part of America's trade laws, where a firm that the International Trade Commission finds has violated an American's intellectual property rights can have the infringing products excluded from importation into the United States. In 2012, a small company, X2Y, sued Intel, Apple and HP to exclude all of Intel's advanced microprocessors, all of Apple's computers (which employ these microprocessors), and those HP computers that do so. The claim was that these microprocessors infringed, in their "packaging," on a X2Y patent. X2Y had offered to sell this and a bundle of other patents for a few million dollars. Intel viewed it as a holdup and refused. The cost to Intel, Apple and HP—let alone to the U.S. economy—of the exclusion would have been in the order of billions of dollars.[58]

The law providing for the exclusion had a narrow exception—the exclusion order was not to be issued if it was against the public interest. But the ITC had so narrowly defined the exception that it had been used only four times in forty years. The irony, of course, was that a law designed to protect American firms against foreign firms who violated the intellectual property rights of Americans was being used by a small American firm that had spent a miniscule amount on research—and far more on lawyers—to hold up some of America's leading IT companies who were spending billions on research. Those who argued against the exclusion order contended that exclusion would not only have a large negative effect on the economy in the short run, but also that it would actually be counterproductive, inhibiting innovation.

The second example is from a developing country—India—and shows once again how the interpretation of laws can be critical. Before TRIPS, India had had a thriving generic drug industry. The patent laws that India passed as part of its implementation of the obligations it undertook as part of TRIPS had put this important industry in jeopardy. A recent Court decision refusing to grant a patent to a Western drug company provided new life, and not only for the generic drug industry. The lower price of drugs of the generics provided lifesaving medicines for those in the developing countries that otherwise would never have been able to afford them.

Earlier in this paper, we noted the influence of special interest groups in shaping the intellectual property regime. It is not designed to maximize innovation or societal well-being, even in the developed countries, but even less so in developing countries; rather, it is more concerned with maximizing rents to certain types of innovation activities. Even within TRIPS, developing countries have much more discretion than they have taken advantage of.

They should shape the intellectual property regime to advance the well-being of their citizens. For instance, drug companies regularly try to extend the life of their patents through "ever-greening." But most such attempts fail a reasonable standard of "obviousness." It is, for example, obvious how to move from the standard version of a drug to the time release version. Hence, developing countries should not grant patents for the time release version, even if the drug companies succeed in getting developed countries to provide such patents.

Intellectual property is complex. If nothing else, this introduction, and the chapters in this book, should have convinced the reader that the mantra of the advocates of stronger IPR—that the stronger the system of intellectual property rights, the faster the pace of innovation—has itself no intellectual basis. It is too simplistic, partly because property rights are too multifaceted to be summarized in a simple linear way (from weaker to stronger), partly because innovation is multifaceted: even if there were more patents, it doesn't mean that societal welfare is necessarily increasing, partly because it ignores the multitude of other ways in which the returns to innovation are appropriated, and it ignores the multitude of other drivers of innovation. And even if there were more innovation, somehow defined, it doesn't mean that societal welfare is increased: the innovations could be directed at enhancing and extending monopoly power, at increasing rents or seizing other firms' rents. IPR needs to be seen as part, but only part, of a country's innovation system.

Because innovation is complex, designing a good IPR system that promotes innovation is complex—and perhaps even more so in developing countries. But it should be clear that an IPR system that is appropriate for the United States and Europe (even if they had a well-designed IPR system) would not necessarily be appropriate for developing countries.

Our hope is that this book will help developing countries resist the temptation to just adopt the IPR regimes of the advanced countries, to whose innovation system they aspire. Our hope too is that the insights it provides will help them design an IPR system that enhances their growth and the well-being of their citizens.

NOTES

1. This introduction is based in part on earlier work by the authors on the issues of intellectual property, and especially Stiglitz (2004, 2006, 2008, 2013a, 2013b), Henry and Stiglitz (2010), Dosi and Nelson (2010) and Dosi, Marengo and Pasquali (2006). The authors are indebted to the participants in the IPD/Brooks World Poverty Center conference in Manchester (8–10 September 2010) and in the IPD/ECLAC conference, "Towards Inclusive Development in Latin America and Chile" (29–30 August 2011) for key insights into the issues described here, and to their

many collaborators in their work on intellectual property. We would like to acknowledge the assistance of Ritam Chaurey and the financial support of the Institute for New Economic Thinking (INET), New York, and Scuola Superiore Sant'Anna, Pisa, Italy.

2. It should be clear that the term "trade-related" was only used to enable intellectual property to be included as part of a trade agreement. The thrust of trade agreements was to open borders to the free movement of goods and services (and in some cases factors); TRIPS was designed to restrict the free flow of knowledge. Interestingly, this critical view of TRIPS is even held by strong advocates of multilateral trade agreements. For a critique of the inclusion of intellectual property rights in trade agreements, see Stiglitz (2006) and Bhagwati (2004).

3. Statement by Brazil on 30 September 2004 before WIPO General Assembly at the introduction of the proposal for a development agenda.

4. The patents on basmati rice and the medicinal uses of turmeric were eventually overthrown, but the costs of litigation were significant (see Stiglitz, 2006 and Brand, 2005). Indeed, even the U.S. courts have recognized these costs. In *United States v. General Electric Co.*, 115 F. Supp. 835, 844 (1953) the court, in arguing for compulsory licensing with zero royalties, noted that "small firms desiring to stay in or gain a foothold in the industry... may well be unequipped to engage in litigation on the validity of one patent after another at what could be incalculable expense. In order to avoid it they could be required to shoulder royalties which could prove to be the very factor that would push them out of the competitive circle of the market" (cited in Love, 2005). See Stiglitz (2006) and Perleman (2002).

5. Opposition of drug companies on this issue also underlay the reluctance of some developed countries besides the United States to ratify the bio-diversity convention. (See Henry and Stiglitz, 2010 for a brief discussion.)

6. From Stiglitz (2013a).

7. For a recent discussion of some of the controversies associated with intellectual property rights, see the winter, 2013 symposium of the *Journal of Economic Perspectives*.

8. That there is a large disparity between private and social returns has become increasingly recognized. See, for instance, Shapiro (2007) or Greenwald and Stiglitz (2014a, 2014b, 2014c).

9. In recent years, there has developed a broad critique of intellectual property within the economics literature. See, e.g. Bessen ((2008), Boldrin and Levine (2013), and Moser (2013).

10. There is, by now, a large literature not only questioning this standard wisdom, but supporting the theses which we have articulated in the previous paragraph. See, for instance, Boldrin and Levine (2010), Boyle (2003), Granstrand (2005), Scotchmer (2004), Winter (1993) and the many other references in the bibliography of this introduction and Chapter 2 in this volume.

11. Nonetheless, in much of the discussion below we shall, for simplicity, follow the conventional practice of referring to "strong" or "tight" IPR regimes. Much of the discussion here and below borrows from Stiglitz (2013a).

12. This was one of the central messages of Stiglitz (2002).

13. There is another mechanism by which patents may lead to more innovation, by facilitating a market for innovations, and thus making investments in innovation more liquid and stimulating the diffusion of knowledge. (See Arora, Fosfuri, and Gambardella, 2001 and Maskus, 2005, for detailed analyses). While it is certainly true that some IPR protection is often a necessary condition for the development of markets for technologies, there is no clear evidence that more protection means a better market for technology or that "better markets" mean more innovation. Rather, the degree to which technological diffusion occurs via market exchange depends to a great extent on the nature of technological knowledge itself, including its degree of codifiability.

14. For a brief discussion of the case, see Stiglitz (2013d).

15. Even this statement is not entirely accurate: optimal production and investment—if firms were able to define them—would then take into account the learning benefits, and thus production or investment would be greater than otherwise (provided the firm can appropriate for itself the learning benefits). See Arrow (1962b) and Greenwald and Stiglitz (2014a).

16. We will qualify this point later, showing that for some kinds of knowledge, firms are able to appropriate returns even without government action, i.e. without patents.

17. In the technical jargon, a public good faces a problem of excludability and non-rivalrous consumption (Samuelson, 1954). The notion of knowledge as a public good is discussed in Stiglitz (1987a), and the notion that knowledge is a *global* public good is discussed in Stiglitz (1995, 1999).

18. Jeremy Bentham (1839, p. 71) put the argument for patents forcefully:

    [T]hat which one man has invented, all the world can imitate. Without the assistance of the laws, the inventor would almost always be driven out of the market by his rival, who finding himself, without any expense, in possession of a discovery which has cost the inventor much time and expense, would be able to deprive him of all his deserved advantages, by selling at a lower price.

19. Some of the reasons for this are discussed below. One is that to obtain a patent, one is supposed to disclose information, information which itself might be valuable to rivals. Another is that in some sectors much relevant information is "tacit," not easily described in a patent application.

20. Stiglitz (2013c) shows that even if a stronger ("tighter") intellectual property regime resulted in a higher incentive to innovate, given the set of technological opportunities (the "knowledge pool"), a stronger intellectual property regime may result in a diminished technological pool, so that the overall level of innovation is diminished.

21. See for example the discussion in Henry and Stiglitz (2010). The far-reaching America Invents Act of 2011, which comes into force in March 2013, has significantly de-emphasized the need for disclosure in order to enforce patents. The law and related documents may be viewed at <http://judiciary.house.gov/issues/issues_patentreformact2011.html> (accessed on 8 January 2013).

22. See, for instance, Shapiro, 2001.

23. This section relies heavily on Stiglitz, 2012.

24. See, for instance, Shapiro, 2010.

25. In a perfectly functioning system, presumably there would be a deal between the patent holder and the new entrant that would avoid this wasteful expenditure, and make both parties better off. With imperfect information, the patent holder may not be able to tell who will be successful at circumventing his patent. He can't make such a deal with every possible claimant.

26. The smarthphone litigation between Samsung and Apple has exemplified the problems. See Graham and Vishnubhakat, 2013.

27. This is not true of some of the more recent theoretical work, including that focusing on weak patents, holdups and so on: cf. also the references above.

28. That is why holdups can have such an adverse effect on innovation: even a small "innovation" that is part of a new product, like a microprocessor, can extract a disproportionate share of the rents associated with the entire microprocessor.

29. See, e.g. the large literature on learning by doing, including Greenwald and Stiglitz (2014a), Stiglitz (2013b), Arrow (1962b), Pavitt (1987), Dosi and Nelson (2010) and the references cited there.

30. The suit *The Association for Molecular Pathology et al. v. United States Patent and Trademark Office et al.* provides an example of this variability. In June 2013, the Supreme Court ruled in a landmark decision that human genes could not be patented, after many contradictory rulings in lower courts, some of which had upheld Myriad Genetics' patents on a pair of genes linked to breast and ovarian cancer. See Stiglitz (2013d) for a more complete discussion. See also Harhoff, Regibeau, and Rockett (2001). For a more extensive discussion of the "law and economics" of intellectual property, see Stiglitz (2008); Maskus and Reichman (2004); Lewis and Reichman (2005); and Merges and Nelson (1994).

31. See, for instance, Dasgupta and David (1994).

32. For instance, because of increased incentives for secrecy, undermining the openness that has traditionally characterized academic settings.

33. See Farrell and Shapiro (2008).

34. In the concluding section of this paper, we note some changes in the US that may have reduced the adverse consequences of IPR.

35. In that Bayh-Dole was thus a major departure from the conception advanced by the Robert Merton (1973) of the "republic of science."

36. Though to the extent that universities share some of the royalties with researchers, the potential gain in their income may result in universities being able to recruit researchers at a lower wage than they otherwise could. We have seen no convincing evidence that this is the case.

37. For a more extensive discussion of the new regulations, see Coriat, Orsi, and Weinstein (2003). Discussion of the 1984 regulation change can be found at <http://finra.complinet.com/en/display/display_main.html?rbid=2403&element_id=754&print=1> (accessed 4 April 2013).

38. Obviously, if there were no way of appropriating returns other than patent protection, then in such a world there would be little innovation. Everyone would be a free rider. But we have emphasized that a model in which it is assumed that knowledge disseminates perfectly in the absence of patents is wrong—and so even in the absence of patent protection there will be innovation. The question is whether strengthening patent rights will increase the overall pace of innovation

from this base level, given the adverse effects that we have noted. Advocates of stronger intellectual property rights have never demonstrated that this is the case.

39. Defenders of IPR would, of course, claim that this is not a good test: technological opportunities may have been diminished, and in the absence of strong IPR, NCE would have fallen even more. But the remarkable advances in basic science would seem to suggest a rapid expansion of technological opportunities. The patent system itself may be part of the explanation of the diminution in technological opportunities. See Stiglitz 2013c.

40. The adverse effects of patents on genes were noted in the Myriad litigation mentioned above. See Huang and Murray, 2008, and Williams, 2013.

41. That is to say via capital and intermediate inputs embodied innovation that some sectors acquire from others. So, for example, the textile industry undertakes very little innovation of its own but undergoes a good deal of technical progress via the acquisition of new machinery and new fibers introduced elsewhere in the system.

42. The emerging *capability-based theory of the firm* (cf. Nelson and Winter, 1982; Teece, Pisano and Shuen, 1997; Dosi, Nelson and Winter, 2000, and Helfat et al. (2007); among many distinguished others, and the survey in Dosi, Faillo and Marengo, 2008) identifies a fundamental source of differentiation across firms in their distinct problem-solving knowledge, yielding different abilities of "doing things"—searching, developing new products, manufacturing, etc. Successful corporations derive competitive strength from their above-average performance in a small number of capability clusters where they can sustain leadership. Symmetrically, laggard firms often find it hard to imitate perceived best-practice production technologies because of the difficulty of identifying the combination of routines and organizational traits that makes *company x good at doing z*. Such barriers to learning and imitation relate to collective practices which in every organization guide innovative search, production and other corporate activities (more on all that in Chapter 16 of this book by Burlamaqui and Cimoli, and Dosi and Nelson, 2010. See also Greenwald and Stiglitz, 2014a). A critical difference among firms is thus their capabilities in learning (see Stiglitz, 1987b).

43. As we have already noted, in the context of developing countries, increased drug prices resulting from reduced access to generics means that other social objectives (including those associated with health) and spending on development projects are constrained. It is not just a matter of consumption.

44. An archetypical case to the point is the Myriad gene patent: the "innovation" would have occurred even had Myriad not done its research—the gene would have been discovered just a little later as part of the IPR-free Human Genome Project.

45. This section draws upon Stiglitz (2013a).

46. The government could (and does) undertake other roles in a country's innovation system besides funding (and in some cases, undertaking) basic research. In agriculture, its extension services have played an important role in the dissemination of knowledge, and some have proposed that government undertake similar roles in manufacturing. In pharmaceuticals, it has been argued that government could, and should, take a more active role in testing. (See Jayadev and Stiglitz, 2009, 2010 and the Conclusion to this volume). Moreover, in most countries

governments implicitly or explicitly undertake various arrays of industrial policies which deeply influence the rates and directions of innovative activities (more in Cimoli, Dosi, and Stiglitz, 2009).

47. And some of the so-called research money is really money spent on marketing: the manner in which drugs are tested is not necessarily designed to minimize cost, but to enhance drug sales after the drug is approved.

48. There are other ways by which innovation can be spurred in this instance. Just like the granting of patent can be viewed as a prize, but an inefficient one, so too can the guarantee purchase fund advocated by some for promoting innovation for medicines for diseases endemic to developing countries be viewed as a prize. In this approach, the World Bank or the Gates Foundation would guarantee one or two billion dollars to the person or people who develop a vaccine or cure for AIDS, malaria, or some other disease afflicting the developing world for the purchase of the drug. In effect, there would be a certain market. A sufficiently large guarantee would provide a clear motivation for research. These guaranteed purchase funds, however, would still maintain the inefficiency of the monopoly patent system, unless there was an accompanying commitment that would make the patent accessible to all at reasonable royalties for purchases beyond the guarantee. With the guarantee fund the discoverer still receives his "prize"—the monopoly profits—by charging monopoly prices. The poor, who get the drugs through the guaranteed purchase fund do not, of course, pay the monopoly price. But the funds are limited and when they are used up, without such a commitment, a government that wants to provide to its citizens, say, the malaria medicine that has been bought through the guarantee purchase fund, will have to pay the full monopoly price. Money spent purchasing this drug at the monopoly price is money that cannot be spent on the country's other health needs. It may be far better to use the money for the guarantee purchase fund in a way which spurs competition in the provision of the drug, to offer a prize, or to buy the patent, and to allow anyone willing to pay a limited licensing fee to produce it.

49. There may be less to this distinction than meets the eye. Within companies, there is a research board that has to approve projects, allocating funds among alternatives. Even individual entrepreneurs seeking funds for research turn to a bank, and any large project will have to be vetted by the bank. In short, research funds are never allocated by an auction mechanism; there is almost always some review board. In our diverse society, any project may be reviewed by multiple boards—there are multiple foundations to which a university research can turn, and an entrepreneur can turn to multiple corporations. Thus, in practice, decision-making involves a mixture of hierarchical (committee) and polyarchical decision-making structures. (See Sah and Stiglitz, 1985, 1986, 1988). A key distinction, however, is who bears the losses and who reaps the gains.

50. This seems to be one of the arguments that Mill used in favor of patents, arguing that it avoided "discretion." See John Stuart Mill (1862), as cited in Mennell (1999).

51. See the observation made earlier comparing expenditures on lawyers and on research.

52. The evidence is that capital markets do not fully spread risks faced by firms, because of massively imperfect information. See for example Greenwald and Stiglitz (1990) who discuss the effect of information imperfections on firm behavior and argue that informational problems in the capital market cause firms to act in a risk-averse manner. There is also considerable empirical evidence that markets do not efficiently distribute risk, i.e., firms act in a risk-averse manner, even when risks are uncorrelated with the market. See, e.g., Stiglitz, 1982.

53. They are distorted, as we have noted, because there are incentives to engage in research to innovate around a patent and to spend money in ways that extend the effective life of the patent. They are distorted too by the incentives provided for holdup innovations. These innovation distortions are in addition to the other market distortions, such as those associated with expenditures attempting to make demand curves less elastic.

54. Data from the World Intellectual Property Organizations online statistical country profile of China, available at <http://www.wipo.int/ipstats/en/statistics/country_profile/countries/cn.html> (accessed 14 January 2013).

55. In fact, the relationship between observed IPR regimes and income seems to be non-monotonic (though one should not make inferences about causality from the data) with a U-shaped relationship between the tightness of IPR regimes and per capita incomes (Maskus, 2000; Murmann, 2003; and Chapter 2 in this volume). Many low-income countries seem to have high levels of IPR—perhaps because for them it doesn't matter as they don't even have the capabilities of borrowing knowledge from others. (Alternatively, it may be because these poorer countries are more subject to pressure from the advanced industrial countries, e.g. because many are very aid dependent and are dependent on discretionary trade benefits.)

56. For a further critique of TRIPS, see Charlton and Stiglitz, 2005. For a broader discussion, see UNCTAD-ICTSD (2005).

57. *eBay Inc. v. MercExchange, L.L.C.*, 547 U.S. 388 (2006), case documents can be found at <http://www.supremecourt.gov/opinions/05pdf/05-130.pdf> (accessed on 15 January 2013).

58. Stiglitz (2012). The ITC eventually ruled in favor of Intel in February, 2013, by declaring the patents either invalid or not infringed. Matter of Microprocessors, Components Thereof, and Products Containing Same, 337–781, U.S. International Trade Commission.

REFERENCES

Angell, M. (2004), *The Truth about the Drug Companies: How They Deceive Us and What to Do about It*. New York: Random House.

Arora, A., A. Fosfuri and A. Gambardella (2001), *Markets for Technology: Economics of Innovation and Corporate Strategy*. Cambridge, MA: MIT Press.

Arrow K. (1962a), "Economic Welfare and the Allocation of Resources for Invention," in R. Nelson, ed., *The Rate and Direction of Inventive Activity*. Princeton, NJ: Princeton University Press.

—— (1962b), "The Economic Implications of Learning by Doing," *Review of Economic Studies* 29: 155–73.

Association for Molecular Pathology v. Myriad Genetics, 569 U.S. 12–398 [2013].

Avorn, J. (2004), *Powerful Medicines: The Benefits, Risks, and Costs of Prescription Drugs*. New York: Knopf.

Barton J. (2000), "Reforming the Patent System," *Science*, 287: 1933–4.

Bentham, Jeremy (1839), *A Manual of Political Economy*. New York: G.P. Putnam.

Bessen, James, and Michael J. Meurer (2008), *Patent Failure: How Judges, Bureaucrats, and Lawyers Put Innovators at Risk*. Princeton, NJ: Princeton University Press.

Bessen J. and E. Maskin (2000), "Sequential Innovation, Patents and Imitation," Working Paper 00-01, MIT Department of Economics, Cambridge, MA, available at <http://www.ftc.gov/os/comments/intelpropertycomments/jimbessenericmaskin.pdf> (accessed 14 January 2013).

—— (2004), *In Defense of Globalization*. New York: Oxford University Press.

Boldrin M. and D.K. Levine (2008), "Perfectly Competitive Innovation," *Journal of Monetary Economics*, 55 (3): 435–53.

—— (2010), *Against Intellectual Monopoly*. Cambridge: Cambridge University Press.

Boldrin, Michele, and David K. Levine (2013), "The Case against Patents," *Journal of Economic Perspectives*, 27 (1): 3–22.

Boyle, J. (2003), "The Second Enclosure Movement and the Construction of the Public Domain," *Law and Contemporary Problems*, 66 (33): 33–74.

Bradshaw, G.F. (1992), "The Airplane and the Logic of Invention," in R.N. Giere, ed., *Cognitive Models of Science*. Minneapolis, MN: University of Minnesota Press.

Brand, R. (2005), "The Basmati Patent," in E.U. von Weizäcker, O.R. Young, and M. Finger, eds, *Limits to Privatization: How to Avoid Too Much of a Good Thing*. London: Earthscan Publications.

Chang, H.J. (2002), *Kicking Away the Ladder—Development Strategy in Historical Perspective*. London: Anthem Press.

Charlton, A. and J.E. Stiglitz (2005), *Fair Trade for All*. New York: Oxford University Press.

Cimoli M., G. Dosi, and J.E. Stiglitz (eds) (2009), *Industrial Policy and Development: The Political Economy of Capabilities Accumulation*. New York: Oxford University Press.

Cohen W.M. and D.A. Levinthal (1990), "Absorptive Capacity: A New Perspective on Learning and Innovation," *Administrative Science Quarterly*, Special Issue: Technology, Organizations, and Innovation, 35 (1): 128–52.

Cohen W., R.R. Nelson, and J. Walsh (2000), "Protecting Their Intellectual Assets: Appropriability Conditions and Why US Manufacturing Firms Patent or Not," Discussion Paper 7552, NBER.

Coriat, B. and F. Orsi (2006), "The New Role and Status of Intellectual Property Rights in Contemporary Capitalism," *Competition and Change*, 10 (2): 162–79.

—— —— and C. d'Almeida (2006), "TRIPS and the International Public Health Controversies: Issues and Challenges," *Industrial and Corporate Change*, 15 (6): 1033–62.

—— —— and O. Weinstein (2003), "Does Biotech Reflect a New Science-Based Innovation Regime?" *Industry and Innovation*, 10 (3): 231–53.

Dasgupta, P. and P.A. David (1994), "Toward a New Economics of Science," *Research Policy*, 23 (5): 487–521.

—— and J.E. Stiglitz (1980), "Uncertainty, Market Structure and the Speed of R&D," *Bell Journal of Economics*, 11 (1): 1–28.

—— —— (1988), "Potential Competition, Actual Competition and Economic Welfare," *European Economic Review*, 32: 569–77.

David, P.A. (1993), "Intellectual Property Institutions and the Panda's Thumb: Patents, Copyrights, and Trade Secrets in Economic Theory and History," in M.B. Wallerstein, M.E. Mogee, and R.A. Schoen, eds, *Global Dimensions of Intellectual Property Rights in Science*. Washington, DC: National Academies Press.

—— (2002), "Does the New Economy Need All the Old IPR Institutions? Digital Information Goods and Access to Knowledge for Economic Development," Presented at Wider Conference on the New Economy in Development, Helsinki, 2002.

—— (2004a), "From Keeping Nature's Secrets to the Institutionalization of Open Science," in R.A. Ghosh, ed., *Collaborative Ownership and the Digital Economy (CODE)*. Cambridge, MA: MIT Press.

—— (2004b), "Understanding the Emergence of 'Open Science' Institutions: Functionalist Economics in Historical Context," *Industrial and Corporate Change*, 13: 571–89.

Dosi, G. (1982), "Technological Paradigms and Technological Trajectories: A Suggested Interpretation of the Determinants and Direction of Technological Change," *Reaserch Policy*, 11: 147–62.

—— (1988), "Sources, Procedures, and Microeconomic Effects of Innovation," *Journal of Economic Literature*, 26 (3): 1120–71.

—— M. Faillo and L. Marengo (2008), "Organizational Capabilities, Patterns of Knowledge Accumulation and Governance Structures in Business Firms: An Introduction," *Organization Studies*, 29 (8): 1165–85.

—— P. Llerena and M. Sylos Labini (2006), "The Relationships between Science, Technologies and Their Industrial Exploitation: An Illustration Through the Myths and Realities of the So-Called 'European Paradox'," *Research Policy*, 35 (10): 1450–64.

—— L. Marengo and C. Pasquali (2006), "How Much Should Society Fuel the Greed of Innovators? On the Relations Between Appropriability, Opportunities and Rates of Innovation," *Research Policy*, 35 (8): 1110–21.

—— and R.R. Nelson (2010), "Technical Change and Industrial Dynamics as Evolutionary Processes," in B.H. Hall and N. Rosenberg, eds, *Handbook of the Economics of Innovation*, vol. I. Burlington, MA: Academic Press.

—— R. Nelson, and S. Winter (eds) (2000). *The Nature and Dynamics of Organizational Capabilities*. Oxford and New York: Oxford University Press.

Farrell, J. and Carl Shapiro (2008), "How Strong Are Weak Patents?" *American Economic Review*, 98 (4): 1347–69.

Fink C. and K.E. Maskus (eds) (2005), *Intellectual Property and Development*, Oxford and New York: Oxford University Press.

Freeman, C. (1987), *Technology, Policy, and Economic Performance: Lessons from Japan*. London and New York: Pinter Publishers.

—— and L. Soete (1997), *The Economics of Industrial Innovation*, 3rd edn. London: Pinter.

Fudenberg, D., R. Gilbert, J.E. Stiglitz and J. Tirole (1983), "Preemption, Leapfrogging and Competition in Patent Races," *European Economic Review*, 22: 3–32.

Gallini N. (2002), "The Economics of Patents: Lessons from Recent U.S. Patent Reform," *Journal of Economic Perspectives*, 16: 131–54.

Gambardella, A. (1995), *Science and Innovation: The US Pharmaceutical Industry in the 1980's*. Cambridge: Cambridge University Press.

Gilbert, R.J. and D.G.M. Newbery (1982), "Preemptive Patenting and the Persistence of Monopoly," *American Economic Review*, 72 (3): 514–26.

Graham, S., and S. Vishnubhakat (2013), "Of Smart Phone Wars and Software Patents," Journal of Economic Perspectives, 27 (1): 67–86.

Granstrand O. (2005), "Innovation and Intellectual Property Rights," in I. Fagerberg, D. Mowery and R. Nelson, eds, *The Oxford Handbook of Innovation*. Oxford: Oxford University Press.

Greenwald, B. and J.E. Stiglitz (1990), "Asymmetric Information and the New Theory of the Firm: Financial Constraints and Risk Behavior," *American Economic Review*, 80 (2): 160–5.

—— —— (2014a), *Creating a Learning Society: A New Approach to Growth, Development, and Social Progress*, Inaugural Arrow Lecture, Columbia University. New York: Columbia University Press.

—— —— (2014b), "Industrial Policies, the Creation of a Learning Society, and Economic Development," in J.E .Stiglitz and J.Y. Lin, eds, *The Industrial Policy Revolution I: The Role of Government Beyond Ideology*. Houndmills, UK and New York: Palgrave Macmillan.

—— —— (2014c), "Learning and Industrial Policy: Implications for Africa," in J.-E. Stiglitz, J.Y. Lin, and E. Patel, eds, *The Industrial Policy Revolution II: Africa in the 21st Century*, Houndmills, UK and New York: Palgrave Macmillan.

Hagiu, A., and D. B. Yoffie (2013), "The New Patent Intermediaries: Platforms, Defensive Aggregators, and Super-Aggregators," Journal of Economic Perspectives, 27 (1): 45–66.

Hall, B. (2005), "Exploring the Patent Explosion," *Journal of Technology Transfer*, 30: 35–48.

—— and R. Ziedonis (2001), "The Patent Paradox Revisited: Firm Strategy and Patenting in the US Semiconductor Industry," *Rand Journal of Economics*, 32: 101–28

Harhoff, D.P., P. Regibeau and K. Rockett (2001), "Some Simple Economics of GM Food," Economic Policy, 16 (33): 263–99.

Helfat C., S. Finkelstein, W. Mitchell, M. Peteraf, H. Singh, D. Teece and S. Winter (eds) (2007), *Dynamic Capabilities: Understanding Strategic Change in Organizations*. Malden/Oxford: Blackwell Publishing.

Heller M. (1998), "The Tragedy of the Anticommons: Property in Transition from Marx to Markets," *Harvard Law Review*, 111: 698–701.

—— and R. Eisenberg (1998): "Can Patents Deter Innovation? The Anti-commons in Biomedical Research," *Science*, 280: 698–701.

Henry, C. and J.E. Stiglitz (2010), "Intellectual Property, Dissemination of Innovation and Sustainable Development," *Global Policy*, 1: 237–51.

Hertel, G., M. Krishnan and S. Slaughter (2003), "Motivation in Open Source Projects: An Internet-based Survey of Contributors to the Linux Kernel," *Research Policy*, 32 (7): 1159–77.

Huang, K.G. and F.E. Murray (2008), "Does Patent Strategy Shape the Long-Run Supply of Public Knowledge? Evidence from Human Genetics," Academy of Management Journal, 52 (6): 1193–221.

Jaffe A. (2000): "The US Patent System in Transition: Policy Innovation and the Innovation Process," *Research Policy*, 29: 531–57.

—— and J. Lerner (2004): *Innovation and its Discontents*. Princeton, NJ: Princeton University Press.

Jayadev, A. and Stiglitz, J.E. (2009), "Two Ideas to Increase Innovation and Reduce Pharmaceutical Costs and Prices," *Health Affairs*, 28 (1): 165–8.

—— —— (2010), "Medicine for Tomorrow: Some Alternative Proposals to Promote Socially Beneficial Research and Development in Pharmaceuticals," *Journal of Generic Medicines*, 7 (3): 217–26.

Kennedy, D. and J.E. Stiglitz (eds) (2013), *Law and Economics with Chinese Characteristics*. Oxford and New York: Oxford University Press.

Klevorick, A., R. Levin, R. Nelson and S. Winter (1995), "On the Sources and Interindustry Differences in Technological Opportunities," *Research Policy*, 24: 185–205.

Kortum S., and J. Lerner (1998), "Stronger Protection or Technological Revolution: What Is Behind the Recent Surge in Patenting?" Rochester Conference Series on Public Policy, 48: 247–307.

Landes D. (1969), *The Unbound Prometheus*. Cambridge: Cambridge University Press.

Lerner J. (2002), "150 Years of Patent Protection," *American Economic Review Papers and Proceedings*, 92: 221–5.

—— (2010), "The Patent System in a Time of Turmoil," *The WIPO Journal*, 2 (1): 28–37.

—— and J. Tirole (2002), "Some Simple Economics of Open Source," *Journal of Industrial Economics*, 52 (2): 197–234.

—— and S. Stern (eds) (2012), *The Rate and Direction of Inventive Activity Revisited*. Chicago: NBER/University of Chicago Press.

Levin, R., A. Klevorick, R.R. Nelson and S. Winter (1987), "Appropriating the Returns from Industrial R&D," *Brookings Papers on Economic Activity*, 1987 (3): 783–831.

Lewis, T. and Reichman, J. (2005), "Using Liability Rules to Stimulate Local Innovation in Developing Countries: Application to Traditional Knowledge," in K. Maskus and J. Reichman, eds, *International Public Goods and Transfer of Technology under a Globalized Intellectual Property Regime*. Cambridge: Cambridge University Press.

Love, J. (2005), "Remuneration Guidelines for Non-Voluntary Use of a Patent on Medical Technologies," working paper of the World Health Organization and United Nations Development Programme, Health Economics and Drugs TCM Series No. 18, available at <http://www.undp.org/content/dam/aplaws/publication/en/publications/poverty-reduction/poverty-website/renumeration-guidelines-for-non-voluntary-use-of-a-patent-on-medical-techologies-/RenumerationGuidelines.pdf> (accessed 15 January 2013).

Lundvall, B.-A. (ed.) (2010), *National Systems of Innovation: Toward a Theory of Innovation and Interactive Learning*. London: Anthem Press.

Machlup, F. (1958), "An Economic Review of the Patent System," Discussion paper, U.S. Congress, Washington D.C. Government Printing Office.

Maskus, K.E. (1997) "Should Core Labor Standards Be Imposed through International Trade Policy?" *The World Bank Policy Research Working Paper Series*, no. 1817.

—— (2000), "Intellectual Property Rights and Economic Development," *Case Western Reserve Journal of International Law*, 32 (3): 471–506.

—— (2005), "The Role of Intellectual Property Rights in Encouraging Foreign Direct Investment and Technology Transfer" in Fink and Maskus (2005).

—— and Reichman, J.H. (2004), "The Globalization of Private Knowledge Goods and the Privatization of Global Public Goods," *Journal of International Economic Law*, 7 (2): 279–320.

Mazzucato M. and G. Dosi (eds) (2006), *Knowledge Accumulation and Industry Evolution*. Cambridge: Cambridge University Press.

Meier, H.A. (1981), "Thomas Jefferson and a Democratic Technology," in C.W. Pursell, ed., *Technology in America: A History of Individuals and Ideas*, 2nd edn. Cambridge, MA: MIT Press.

Mennell, P.S. (1999), "1600, Intellectual Property: General Theories," in Boudewijn Bouckaert and Gerrit De Geest, eds, *Encyclopedia of Law and Economics*, available online only at <http://encyclo.findlaw.com/index.html> (accessed 5 April 2013).

Merges R. (1996), "Contracting into Liability Rules: Intellectual Property Rights and Collective Rights Organizations," *California Law Reviews*, 84: 1293–386.

—— and R. Nelson (1994), "On Limiting or Encouraging Rivalry in Technical Progress: The Effects of Patent Scope Decisions," *Journal of Economic Behavior and Organization*, 25: 1–24.

Merton R. (1973), *The Sociology of Science: Theoretical and Empirical Investigations*. Chicago: University of Chicago Press.

Mill, John Stuart (1862), *Principles of Political Economy*, 5th edn; first published 1848. New York: Appleton.

Moser P. (2005), "How Do Patent Laws Influence Innovation? Evidence from Nineteenth-century World Fairs," *The American Economic Review* 95 (4): 1214–36.

Moser, Petra (2013), "Patents and Innovation: Evidence from Economic History," *Journal of Economic Perspectives*, 27 (1): 23–44.

Mowery D., R. Nelson, B. Sampat and A. Ziedonis (2001), "The Growth of Patenting and Licensing by US Universities: An Assessment of the Effects of the Bayh-Dole Act of 1980," *Research Policy*, 30 (1): 99–119.

Murmann, J.P. (2003), *Knowledge and Competitive Advantage: The Coevolution of Firms, Technology, and National Institutions*. Cambridge: Cambridge University Press.

Murray, F.E., P. Aghion, M. Dewatrepont, J. Kolev, and S. Stern (2011), "Of Mice and Academics," MIT Sloan Working Paper.

Nelson, R.R. (1959), "The Simple Economics of Basic Scientific Research," *Journal of Political Economy*, 67 (3): 297–306.

—— (1993), *National Systems of Innovation: A Comparative Study*. New York: Oxford University Press.

—— (2004a), "The Market Economy and the Scientific Commons," *Research Policy*, 33: 455–72.

—— (2004b), "The Challenge of Building an Effective Innovation System for Catch-Up," *Oxford Development Studies*, 32 (3): 365–74.

—— (2006), "Reflections on 'The Simple Economics of Basic Scientific Research': Looking Back and Looking Forward," *Industrial and Corporate Change*, 15: 903–17.

—— and S. Winter (1982), *An Evolutionary Theory of Economic Change*. Cambridge, MA: Belknap Press of Harvard University Press.

North, D.C. (1981), *Structure and Change in Economic History*. New York: Norton.

Nuvolari, A. (2004), "Collective Invention Driving the British Industrial Revolution: The Case of the Cornish 'Pumping Engine'," *Cambridge Journal of Economics*, 28: 347–63.

Odagiri, H., A. Goto, A. Sunami and R.R. Nelson (eds) (2010), *Intellectual Property Rights, Development, and Catch Up: An International Comparative Study*. Oxford and New York: Oxford University Press.

Orsenigo L., G. Dosi, and M. Mazzucato (2006), "The Dynamics of Knowledge Accumulation, Regulation, and Appropriability in the Pharma-Biotech Sector: Policy Issues," in M. Mazzucato and G. Dosi, eds, *Knowledge Accumulation and Industry Evolution*. Cambridge: Cambridge University Press.

Ostrom, E., R. Gardner, and J. Walker (1994), *Rules, Games and Common-Pool Resources*. Ann Arbor, MI: The University of Michigan Press,

Pavitt, K. (1984), "Sectoral Patterns of Innovation: Toward a Taxonomy and a Theory," *Research Policy*, 13: 343–73.

—— (1987), "The Objectives of Technology Policy," *Science and Public Policy*, 14: 182–8.

Perleman, M. (2002), *Steal this Idea: Intellectual Property and the Corporate Confiscation of Creativity*. New York: Palgrave.

Pollack, A. (2011), "Ruling Upholds Gene Patent in Cancer Test," *New York Times*, 30 July 2011, available at <http://www.nytimes.com/2011/07/30/business/gene-patent-in-cancer-test-upheld-by-appeals-panel.html> (accessed 5 September 2013).

Pollard, S. (1981), *Peaceful Conquest: The Industrialization of Europe, 1760–1970*. Oxford: Oxford University Press.

PriceWaterhouse Coopers (2012), "2012 Patent Litigation Study: Litigation Continues to Rise amid Growing Awareness of Patent Value," available at <http://www.pwc.com/en_US/us/forensic-services/publications/assets/2012-patent-litigation-study.pdf> (accessed 9 November 2012).

Sah, R. and J.E. Stiglitz (1985), "Human Fallibility and Economic Organization," *American Economic Review*, 75 (2): 292–6.

—— —— (1986), "The Architecture of Economic Systems: Hierarchies and Polyarchies," *American Economic Review*, 76 (4): 716–27.

—— —— (1988), "Committees, Hierarchies and Polyarchies," *The Economic Journal*, 98 (391): 451–70.

Samuelson, P.A. (1954), "The Pure Theory of Public Expenditure," *Review of Economics and Statistics*, 36 (4): 387–9.

Schumpeter, J.A. (1943), *Capitalism, Socialism and Democracy*. London: G. Allen & Unwin.

Scotchmer, S. (2004), *Innovation and Incentives*. Cambridge, MA: The MIT Press.

Shapiro, C. (2001), "Navigating the Patent Thicket: Cross Licenses, Patent Pools, and Standard Setting," in A. Jaffe, Josh Lerner and Scott Stern, eds, *Innovation Policy and the Economy*. Cambridge, MA: MIT Press.

——(2007), "Patent Reform: Aligning Reward and Contribution 33–35," Working Paper No. 13141, National Bureau of Economic Research, Cambridge, MA, available at <http://papers.nber.org/papers/w13141> (accessed 5 September 2013).

——(2010), "Injunctions, Hold-Up, and Patent Royalties," *American Law and Economics Review*, 12 (2): 280–313.

Stiglitz, J. (1982), "Ownership, Control and Efficient Markets: Some Paradoxes in the Theory of Capital Markets," in K.D. Boyer and W.G. Shepherd, eds, *Economic Regulation: Essays in Honor of James R. Nelson*. East Lansing: Michigan State University Press.

——(1987a), "On the Microeconomics of Technical Progress," in J.M. Katz, ed., *Technology Generation in Latin American Manufacturing Industries*. London: Macmillan Press. (Presented to IDB-CEPAL Meetings, Buenos Aires, November 1978.)

——(1987b), "Learning to Learn, Localized Learning and Technological Progress," in P. Dasgupta and P. Stoneman, eds, *Economic Policy and Technological Performance*. Cambridge: Cambridge University Press.

——(1988), "Technological Change, Sunk Costs and Competition," *Brookings Papers on Economic Activity*, 3: 883–947.

——(1994), *Wither Socialism*. Cambridge, MA: MIT Press.

——(1995), "The Theory of International Public Goods and the Architecture of International Organizations," Background Paper No. 7, Third Meeting, High Level Group on Development Strategy and Management of the Market Economy, UNU/WIDER, 8 July, Helsinki, Finland.

——(1999), "Knowledge as a Global Public Good," in Inge Kaul, Isabelle Grunberg and Marc A. Stern, eds, *Global Public Goods: International Cooperation in the 21st Century*, United Nations Development Programme. New York: Oxford University Press.

——(2002), *Globalization and its Discontents*. New York: W.W. Norton.

——(2004), "Towards a Pro-Development and Balanced Intellectual Property Regime," keynote address presented at the Ministerial Conference on Intellectual Property for Least Developed Countries, World Intellectual Property Organization (WIPO), Seoul, 25 October, available at <http://www2.gsb.columbia.edu/faculty/jstiglitz/download/2004_TOWARDS_A_PRO_DEVELOPMENT.htm> (accessed 5 November 2012).

——(2006), *Making Globalization Work*. New York: W.W. Norton.

——(2008), "The Economic Foundations of Intellectual Property," Sixth Annual Frey Lecture in Intellectual Property, Duke University, Durham, NC, *Duke Law Journal*, 57 (6): 1693–724.

——(2012), "Rebuttal Testimony of Dr. Joseph Stiglitz on Behalf of Respondents Responding to Direct Testimony of Dr. Stern," in the Matter of Certain Microprocessors, Components Thereof, and Products Containing Same, United States International Trade Commission, Investigation No. 337-TA-781.

——(2013a), "Institutional Design for China's Innovation System: Implications for Intellectual Property Rights," in D. Kennedy and J.E. Stiglitz, eds, *Law and Economic Development with Chinese Characteristics: Institutions for the 21st Century*. New York and Oxford: Oxford University Press.

——(2013b), "Learning, Growth, and Development: A Lecture in Honor of Sir Partha Dasgupta," in (2011), C. Sepúlveda, A. Harrison and J.Y. Lin, eds., *Development Challenges in a Postcrisis World: Annual World Bank Conference on*

Development Economics. Washington, DC: The World Bank, pp. 37–88. Published in French as "Apprentissage, croissance et développement: conférence en l'honneur de Sir Partha Dasgupta," *Revue d'Économie du Développment*, 4: 19–86.

—— (2013c), "Intellectual Property Rights, the Pool of Knowledge, and Innovation," working paper, Columbia University

—— (2013d), "How Intellectual Property Reinforces Inequality," *The New York Times*, July 17, available online at <http://opinionator.blogs.nytimes.com/2013/07/14/how-intellectual-property-reinforces-inequality/> (accessed 26 September 2013).

t'Hoen, E., (2003), "TRIPS, Pharmaceutical Patents and Access to Essential Medicines: Seattle, Doha and Beyond," in J.P. Moatti et al., eds, *Economics of AIDS and Access to HIV Care in Developing Countries: Issues and Challenges*. Paris: Editions de l' ANRS.

—— (2005), "European Union Committee on International Trade: Hearings on TRIPS and Access to Medicines," Tuesday 18 January, Strassburg. As cited in Coriat, Orsi and d'Almeida (2006).

Teece, D. (1986): "Profiting from Technological Innovation: Implications for Integration, Collaboration, Licensing and Public Policy," *Research Policy*, 15: 285–305.

—— G. Pisano, and A. Shuen (1997): "Dynamic Capabilities and Strategic Management," *Strategic Management Journal*, 18: 509–33.

Tirole, J. (2002): "Protection de la propriété intellectuelle: une introduction et quelques pistes de réflexion," discussion paper, Conseil d'Analyse Economique, Paris.

UNCTAD-ICTSD (2005), *Resource Book on TRIPS and Development*. Cambridge: Cambridge University Press.

Weber, S. (2005), *The Success of Open Source*. Cambridge, MA: Harvard University Press.

Williams, H.L. (2013), "Intellectual Property Rights and Innovation: Evidence from the Human Genome," *Journal of Political Economy*, 121 (1): 1–27.

Winter S. (1982), "An Essay on the Theory of Production," in H. Hymans, ed., *Economics and the World around It*. Ann Arbor, MI: University of Michigan Press.

—— (1993), "Patents and Welfare," *Industrial and Corporate Change*, 2 (2): 211–31.

—— (2002): "A View of the Patent Paradox," slides from a presentation at LBS, 20 May 2002.

World Intellectual Property Organization (2012), "World Intellectual Property Indicators 2012," available online at <http://www.wipo.int/export/sites/www/freepublications/en/intproperty/941/wipo_pub_941_2012.pdf> (accessed 15 January 2013).

Ziedonis R.H. (2004): "Don't Fence Me In: Fragmented Markets for Technology and the Patent Acquisition Strategies of Firms," *Management Science*, 50 (6): 804–20.

Part I

IPR, Innovation and Development: Economic History and Theory

2

Innovation, Technical Change, and Patents in the Development Process: A Long-Term View[1]

Mario Cimoli, Giovanni Dosi, Roberto Mazzoleni and Bhaven N. Sampat

1. INTRODUCTION: TECHNOLOGICAL LEARNING AND ECONOMIC DEVELOPMENT

The key feature of the historical process of economic development is the "great transformation" (Polanyi, 1944) whereby the traditional organization of economic activities gives way to the systematic adoption and development of new production processes, new products and new organizational forms characterized by the prevalence of modern industries, and knowledge-intensive services. The great transformation consists first and foremost of the accumulation of various forms of knowledge and novel capabilities at the level of both individuals and organizations.

As Chris Freeman (2008) emphasizes, the pattern of development or stagnation of a national system of innovation and production is the result of co-evolutionary processes linking together several domains, including the adoption and development of new technologies, the organization of production and markets, and the changes in political and legal institutions (more on this in Cimoli, Dosi and Stiglitz, 2009). An essential aspect of "catching up" by developing countries (Abramovitz, 1986) is the emulation of technological leaders (on the notion cf. Reinert, 2007 and 2009) and the rapid accumulation by individuals and organizations of the knowledge and capabilities needed in order to sustain processes of technical learning. This process is initially imitative. It consists of the acquisition of scientific and technological knowledge as codified in the relevant literature. It also involves the acquisition of individual and organizational skills based upon various forms of experiential learning, and problem-solving knowledge embodied in organizational practices. Indeed, the latter kind of capabilities to a good extent shapes the ability to absorb the former type of knowledge. Therefore, it is particularly important to reflect upon the context within which such capabilities can develop.

The rates and patterns of development of such capabilities are fundamentally shaped by the opportunities that indigenous organizations have to enter and operate in particular markets and technology areas. In part, these opportunities reflect the intrinsic ease of imitation of technological and production knowledge. However, the ways actors exploit these opportunities are sensitive to a broad array of policies and the existence of supporting institutions, including those governing the modes though which individuals and organizations can claim the legal rights to the exclusive exploitation of their knowledge. In brief, knowledge accumulation is also influenced—in ways and to degrees that have to be determined—by the *governance of intellectual property rights (IPRs)*. The purpose of this work is to offer an assessment of such influences in the long term, beginning with the early episodes of industrialization all the way to the present regime. Are intellectual property rights conducive to knowledge accumulation? Unconditionally? Or does the effect depend on the distance from the international technological frontier? Even at the technological frontier, does the "strength" of the IPR regime map monotonically into higher rates of innovation? And finally, what influence is the current regime likely to exert on the opportunities and incentives for contemporary countries trying to catch up?

Many of the contributions to this volume focus upon some of these questions. Here, we want to provide a broad interpretative overview. In this, the history of industrialized countries, in particular of the United States, vividly illustrate the interplay between the dynamics of technological opportunities, capabilities accumulation, and the institutions governing the knowledge-related rent-seeking possibilities of individuals and organizations.

The historical record is indeed quite diverse and variegated. However, if there is a robust historical fact, it is the laxity or sheer absence of intellectual property rights in nearly all instances of successful catching up. Thus, to the extent that the emulation of the technological leaders can be identified as one of the few constants across the experience of countries which successfully caught up (Reinert, 2009), we shall argue that homogenization of patent protection onto the standards of the technological leaders is a step in the wrong direction. Moreover, the emphasis given to the role of patents and other intellectual property rights as incentives for innovation draws attention away from their potentially negative consequences for processes of knowledge and capability accumulation that are typical of latecomers to industrialization.

This chapter focuses on one form of intellectual property rights—patents. We begin in section 2 by reviewing a few theoretical arguments that economists have formulated on the effects of a system of patent protection. Our goal is not so much to offer a comprehensive survey of the literature, as to examine the economic rationale for creating or reforming patent systems in a developing economy context. We will then review the historical evidence on the roles of patents in economic development (section 3). There we also highlight the heterogeneity that has been historically common concerning the collection of laws and institutions which go under the heading of "patent systems," and the heterogeneity across nations and over time in the characteristics of these systems. Section 4 discusses at some length changes in the IPR regime that have taken place roughly over the last third of a century in the United States. The reason for focusing on the United States is that doing so will outline the broad template of patent policy reform that has been adopted by policy-makers in many other countries as a result of a varying mix of external pressures, myopia, corruption and ideological blindness. Section 5, the final part of this essay, explores the likely impact of harmonization of international patent laws—including TRIPS—on developing countries.

2. PATENTS AND INNOVATION, IN THEORY AND PRACTICE

A common argument suggests that patents are a necessary reward for inventive activities that would not take place otherwise. However, a sizeable body of scholarship points at other functions that patents might serve, which are in some cases complementary to the incentive function, and in other cases alternative to it—such as the revelation of technical information. What are the theoretical motivations for such statements, and more importantly, what does the historical evidence tell us?

In addressing these questions one should also keep in mind the fundamental distinction between the effects on countries at or near the technological frontier and those on economies that lag behind them. Indeed, the very character of innovative activities taking place among firms in a developing nation differs quite generally from what one observes in technologically leading ones. Innovations in a developing economy consist predominantly of products and processes that are new to local firms, or to the national economic context, rather than to the world. The elements of novelty, whenever present, are likely to consist of minor or incremental modifications of technologies whose basic characteristics have been defined by innovators located in other countries.

Because of these features, the rate and direction of the innovative activities carried out by local firms in developing countries might very well depend on incentive structures and appropriability mechanisms that differ from those prevailing in developed countries.[2] By the same token, the role of patents toward the disclosure and diffusion of technological information takes on somewhat different characteristics when viewed from the perspective of developing countries.

Theory

Patents as incentives for innovation

The conventional view, according to which patents are indispensable elements of the incentive structure for private profit-motivated search, is rooted in the view of knowledge as a *pure public good*. Accordingly, intellectual property rights such as patents are needed in order to create the condition of excludability that is necessary if private actors are to engage in costly innovative efforts.[3] Such theoretical orientation conflicts, as we shall see, with a substantial body of empirical evidence, and conflicts with the characterization of technological knowledge and of learning processes briefly sketched above.

There are at least two main shortcomings of the knowledge-as-public-good framework. First, the proposition that patents are necessary in order to promote inventive effort presumes that in the absence of such rights, the technological knowledge produced by the inventor would be freely available for use by third parties. On the contrary, this would not apply whenever innovative activities build upon and produce technological knowledge that is partly tacit, and rely upon capabilities that reside in complex organizational routines. Under these circumstances, knowledge related to a specific firm's innovation is not, as a rule, freely available to third parties in the absence of legal rights of exclusive control.

Second, even if, in an abstract sense, knowledge related to a specific innovation were to be made publicly available, it does not follow that every firm could use such knowledge. The use of non-excludable knowledge for the purposes of imitating or adapting an innovative technology would still depend on the initial capabilities of the imitating organization. When such capabilities are inadequate, the mere availability of knowledge is not sufficient for imitation to take place. Conversely, an organization with strong technological capabilities could not only use the publicly available knowledge, but also engage in "inventing around" the legal rights that were to be created in order to make the original invention excludable.

These two observations imply that in general, the appropriability regime governing the incentives for innovation cannot be reduced to the availability and character of patent rights on inventions. To the extent that relevant technological knowledge is opaque to third parties, the latter's capacity to imitate and compete away the innovator's rents would be only limited.

Conversely, patents can be expected to be a more important aspect of the appropriability regime whenever the relevant technological knowledge is not or cannot be protected well by virtue of its complex and tacit nature or through secrecy, and whenever the capabilities of rival firms are adequate to exploit available information (even incomplete) about the innovation in order to imitate.

The foregoing considerations apply to both "frontier" countries and countries that are catching up. From the perspective of developing countries, however, it is necessary to consider further the effect of a national patent system that recognizes the rights of foreign inventors upon the incentive for indigenous innovation. The potential restrictions created by patent rights on the diffusion and use of existing foreign-generated knowledge may well delay cumulative processes of domestic innovation and of technological learning. These obstacles can be particularly important for those firms, like most indigenous firms in a developing economy, whose technological capabilities are fragile and less likely to be capable of sustaining learning through efforts to invent around existing patents.

Patents, disclosure and diffusion

A second purported function of patents—not perfectly overlapping with the former—concerns the effects on disclosure of technological information. We note at the outset that the modern patent system was originally born as an institutional device meant *to help disclosure, not as an incentive to innovate*.[4] According to the conventional view, patent rights were offered as consideration for the disclosure of inventions that might otherwise be kept secret. Whether or not this theory is correct, virtually all existing patent systems impose a disclosure requirement on inventors and applicants. Thus, technological information will be made available through the patent system independently of the inventors' motivations for inventing and applying for a patent.

The collective economic benefits of disclosure fall into three distinct areas. First, patent disclosure could produce social benefits in the form of reducing investments in duplicative R&D. Second, the information disclosed by patents could trigger or facilitate follow-on inventive activity, or promote a broader diffusion of the technology.

That patent disclosure can promote a greater diffusion of the underlying technology, for example by licensing agreements or other forms of market-mediated technology transfer. Thirdly, patents might be argued to promote the *diffusion* of technological knowledge through licensing agreements or other forms of market-mediated technology transfer. For example, as argued by Arora, Fosfuri and Gambardella (2001), patents may encourage technology specialist firms to license their technologies in technology markets rather than trying to integrate downstream into the product markets (an issue that was also raised by Teece (1986) when arguing that a necessary, if not sufficient, condition for firms to profit from innovation via licensing is a tight appropriability regime).

Empirical evidence

A detailed assessment of the impact of different patent regimes is offered in Chapter 3 (see also Jaffe, 1998 and 2000; Merges and Nelson, 1990 and 1994; and the considerations in Dosi, Marengo and Pasquali, 2006). Here let us just sketch out some broad regularities and patterns.

Patents and incentives for R&D

While patents and other intellectual property rights are most relevant to discussion of private actors, we start by noting that most researchers at universities and public laboratories have traditionally done their work, which on occasion may result in a significant technological advance, without expectation of benefiting directly from it financially. Some inventors invent because of the challenge of it, and the sense of fulfillment that comes with solving a difficult problem. And, more importantly, in contemporary societies most scientific knowledge—of both the "pure" and "applied" nature—has been generated within a regime of *open science*. The fundamental vision underlying and supporting such a view of publicly supported open science throughout a good part of the twentieth century entailed (i) a sociology of the scientific community largely relying on self-governance and peer evaluation, (ii) a shared culture of scientists emphasizing the importance of motivational factors other than economic ones and (iii) an ethos of disclosure of search results driven by "winner takes all" precedence rules.[5] In Nelson (2006), David and Hall (2006) and Dosi, Llerena and Sylos Labini (2006), one discusses the dangers coming from the erosion of open science institutions. Advances in pure and applied sciences act as a fundamental fuel for technological advances—albeit with significant variation across technologies, sectors and stages of development of each technological paradigm.

However, the major share of inventive activities finalized to economically exploitable technologies that go on in contemporary capitalist societies is done in profit-seeking organizations with the hope and expectation of being economically rewarded if that work is successful.

The issue of how important monopolistic departures from competitive (zero profit) conditions are for incentives to innovate *even in developed countries* remains an open one, at least in theory.[6] What is the evidence on some monotonic relation between (actual and expected) returns from innovation, on the one hand, and innovative efforts, on the other?

One source of evidence in order to answer the question is the works on inter-sectoral differences in the rates of innovation. Do they stem from corresponding differences in the degrees of appropriability in general, and effectiveness of patents in particular?

Most studies on the nature and sources of technological opportunities suggest that this is unlikely to be the primary determinant of observed inter-sectoral differences (cf. Dosi and Nelson, 2010, for a critical survey). Rather, the evidence suggests that the highly uneven rates of progress among industries are shaped by differences in the strength and richness of technological opportunities.

More generally let us suggest that the widely held view that the key to increasing technological progress is in strengthening appropriability conditions, mainly through making patents stronger and wider, is deeply misconceived. Obviously, inventors and innovators must have a reasonable expectation of being able to profit from their work, where it is technologically successful and happens to meet market demands. However, in most industries this is already the case. And there is little systematic evidence that stronger patents will significantly increase the rate of technological progress. (More in Mazzoleni and Nelson, 1998a and 1998b; Jaffe, 2000; Granstrand, 1999; Dosi, Marengo and Pasquali, 2006; and the growing literature cited therein). In fact, in many instances the opposite may well be the case.

We have noted that in most fields of technology, progress is cumulative, with yesterday's efforts (both the failures and the successes) setting the stage for today's efforts and achievements. If those who do R&D today are cut off from being able to draw from and build on what was achieved yesterday, progress may be hindered significantly. Historical examples, such as those presented in Merges and Nelson (1994) on the Selden patent around the use of a light gasoline in an internal combustion engine to power an automobile, or the Wright brothers' patent on an efficient stabilizing and steering system for flying machines, are good cases to the point, showing how the patent regime may have hindered the subsequent development of automobiles and aircrafts due to the time and resources consumed by lawsuits against the patents themselves. The current debate on property rights in biotechnology suggests similar problems, whereby granting very broad claims on patents might have a detrimental effect on the rate of technical change, insofar as they preclude the exploration of alternative applications of the patented inventions.

This is particularly the case when inventions concerning fundamental techniques or knowledge are concerned. One example is the Leder-Stewart "OncoMouse"—a mouse genetically engineered to be predisposed toward getting cancer (Murray et al., 2008). This is clearly a fundamental research tool. To the extent that such techniques and knowledge are critical for further research which proceeds cumulatively on the basis of the original invention, patents could hamper further developments (Murray et al. 2008).[7]

In general, today's efforts to advance a technology often need to draw from a number of earlier discoveries and advances that build on each other. Under these circumstances patents can be a hindrance rather than an incentive to innovate. (More in Merges and Nelson, 1994; and Heller and Eisenberg, 1998). If different parties patent past and present components of technological systems, there can be an *anti-commons* problem (the term was coined by Heller and Eisenberg). While in the standard commons problem (such as an open pasture), the lack of proprietary rights is argued to lead to over-utilization and depletion of common goods, in instances like biotechnology the risk may be that excessive fragmentation of IPRs among too many owners may well slow down research activities because owners can block each other. Further empirical evidence on the negative effects of strong patent protection on technological progress is in Mazzoleni and Nelson (1998a); and at a more theoretical level, see the insightful discussion in Winter (1993) showing how tight appropriability regimes in evolutionary environments might deter technical progress (cf. also the formal explorations in Marengo et al., 2009).

Conversely, well before the contemporary movement of "open source" software, one is able to document cases in which groups of competing firms or private investors (possibly because of some awareness of the anti-commons problem) have preferred to avoid claiming patents on purpose. Instead, they prefer to operate in a weak IPR regime (involving the free disclosure of inventions to one another) somewhat similar to that of open science: see Allen (1983) and Nuvolari (2004) on blast furnaces and the Cornish pumping engine, respectively. Interestingly, these cases of "collective invention" have been able to yield rapid rates of technical change. Similar phenomena of free revelation of innovation appear also in the communities of user innovators: see von Hippel (2005).

The *second* set of questions regards the characteristics of the regimes stimulating and guiding technological advance in a field of activity. That is, *how* inventors appropriate returns. The conventional wisdom has long been that patent protection is the key to being able to appropriate them. However, a series of studies (Mansfield et al., 1981; Levin et al., 1987; Cohen et al., 2002; among others) has shown that in many industries patents are not the most important mechanism enabling inventors to appropriate returns. Thus Levin et al. (1987) reporting on the "Yale survey," find that for most industries

> Lead time and learning curve advantages, combined with complementary marketing efforts, appear to be the principal mechanisms of appropriating returns to product innovations (p. 33).

Patenting often appears to be a complementary mechanism for appropriating returns to product innovation, but not the principal one in most industries.

For process innovations (used by the innovator itself), secrecy is often important, patents seldom so.

The pharmaceuticals industry is the only where the majority of respondents rated patents more highly than other mechanisms. Other industries where patents are relatively important include organic chemicals and plastics. What is special about pharmaceuticals and chemicals? While this hasn't been completely resolved, the conjecture is that the ability to clearly define property rights through chemical nomenclature is key. This makes it easy to enforce (and difficult to invalidate) patents on new molecules. At the same time the very revelation of the composition of a molecule tells a lot about the nature of the technology one wants to protect. By contrast, in many industries "inventing around" patents is easier. On the flip side of this, the survey also found (similar to Mansfield et al., 1981) that in most industries the impact of patents on the costs of imitation is negligible, with pharmaceutical and chemical industries as outliers. These findings were largely confirmed by a follow-on study done a decade later by Wesley Cohen during his time at Carnegie Mellon University (thus, "the CMU survey"): cf. Cohen et al. (2002).

Similar results are seen in a complementary study of the Japanese patent system (Cohen, Goto et al., 2002), where the authors find that patents are of comparable effectiveness as in the U.S., and find similar differences across industry in use and effectiveness of patents. One sharp difference between the U.S and Japanese systems is on disclosure, discussed in some more detail below.

Comparing the results from the Yale and CMU surveys, one striking finding is that while patenting in "complex product" industries soared between the 1980s and 1990s (Kortum and Lerner, 1999), the effectiveness of patents in "complex" product industries was basically unchanged. Recent work suggests this "patent paradox" reflects a growth of patenting used for defensive purposes in these industries—not to appropriate returns from R&D, but rather to use as bargaining chips in negotiations, or to ward off threats of infringement from others (Hall and Ziedonis, 2001). This finds direct support in the CMU responses, where respondents from complex product industries identified "strategic" purposes rather than the appropriation of returns from R&D as their primary motives for patenting. Accumulation of large patent portfolios, even those of dubious validity, is central to this strategy (Sampat, 2009). In this respect, patenting in complex product industries—which dominates developed-country patenting—reflects a sort of socially suboptimal "red queen" dynamic: the industry (and society) would be better off in the absence of patents, but given all others are patenting, a firm is pushed to patent and increasingly so in order to match the competitors who feel compelled to do the same.

David Teece (1986) and a rich subsequent literature (cf. the Special Issue of *Research Policy*, 2006, taking stock on the advancements since his original insights) have analyzed the differences between inventions for which strong patents can be obtained and enforced, and inventions where patents cannot be obtained or are weak, in the firm strategies needed for reaping returns to innovation. A basic and rather general finding is that in many cases, building the organizational capabilities to implement and complement new technology enables returns to R&D to be high, even when patents are weak. (Note also that all of this discussion has been focused on how individual firms are able to "profit from technological innovation," not on the influence of the latter strategies upon the rates of innovation.) The bottom line is that, despite the fact that patents were effective in only a small share of the industries considered in the study by Levin et al. (1987), some three-quarters of the industries surveyed reported the existence of at least one effective method of protecting process innovation, and more than 90 percent of the industries reported the same regarding product innovations (Levin et al. 1987). These results have been confirmed by a series of other subsequent studies conducted for other countries (see for example the PACE study for the European Union cf. Arundel, van de Paal and Soete, 1995).

If there are major conclusions in this broad area of investigation, they are that, *first*, there is no evidence on any monotonic relation between degrees of appropriability and propensity to undertake innovative search, above some (minimal) appropriability threshold; *second*, appropriability mechanisms currently in place are quite sufficient (in fact, possibly overabundant); *third*, the different rates of innovation across sectors and technological paradigms can hardly be explained by variations in the effectiveness of appropriability mechanisms, and, *fourth*, even less so by differences in the effectiveness of IPR protection.

Disclosure

What about the "disclosure" role of patents? Evidence from the Carnegie Mellon survey suggests that patent documents appear to be a poor source of information for firms. This may not be surprising, given the *tacit* components of technology discussed above. At least in the U.S., another potential explanation for the limited disclosure function of patents is that many firms discourage their employees from reading patents, given much stronger penalties facing willful (not accidental) infringers (Frommer, 2009). However, recent work comparing the U.S. and Japan, based on the Carnegie Mellon Survey, suggests that the disclosure function is much stronger in Japan. This may reflect the fact that when the CMU survey was conducted, American patent applications were not published until granting, limiting the volume and speed of potential disclosure through patent documents. Moreover, Cohen et al. (2002) suggest that the existence of a pre-grant opposition system in Japan created stronger incentives there than in the U.S. to read competitors' patent documents.

In general, the empirical literature on innovation has repeatedly found that patents are *not* an important source of technological information, the most important exception being again related to firms in the pharmaceutical sector. While comparable empirical evidence from the viewpoint of innovation in developing countries is not available, it is possible to argue that the potential usefulness of patent disclosures for the purpose of preventing duplicative R&D does not seem to matter much for economies whose firms' innovative efforts are minimal, or whenever the development of technological capabilities is the main goal of firm-level R&D activities.

Although things might have been different in the past, the significance of *national* patents as a source of information about foreign technology appears today to be low, and diminishing. Thanks to the worldwide proliferation of digital databases of patent applications or grants originating from major national patent systems, access to the technological information disclosed by foreign patents is relatively easy, and it is implausible that such access would become substantially easier and cheaper thanks to the existence of a national patent system. While in some cases language barriers might still be of some importance, and thus make national patents useful for the purpose of knowledge dissemination, they are likely to be only a second-order problem relative to the obstacles that limited technological capabilities pose to making use of foreign patent disclosures. Accordingly, even if a national patent system were to be established in the putative developing economy, the technological information disclosed by patents could still largely be irrelevant for the promotion of follow-on innovation if the level of technological capabilities among indigenous firms is insufficient.

3. PATENTS AND DEVELOPMENT: HISTORICAL PERSPECTIVES

The story of industrialization has at its center the accumulation of technological capabilities by individuals and organizations, as argued at much greater length in Cimoli, Dosi and Stiglitz (2009), in that the ease of imitation of technological and production knowledge depends on both the characteristics of the knowledge itself and on the imitators' capacity for learning from available sources of knowledge. Historically, in basically all episodes of successful industrialization the process has been fuelled by many public Visible Hands promoting the development of pools of indigenous competence in various scientific and technological fields, fostering the emergence and growth of new corporate actors, and affecting directly and indirectly the allocation of resources. The creation of academic institutions has contributed to the formation of an indigenous supply of human capital that could adequately support firms' efforts at assimilating existing technologies. Likewise, early efforts at increasing the rate of absorption of existing technologies and the development of technical problem-solving capabilities can be traced to various forms of public intervention, including the creation of public research institutions (Mazzoleni and Nelson, 2009) and various other forms of "institutional engineering" involving often the active public sponsoring of selected firms, and also the creation of state-owned ones (more in Cimoli, Dosi and Stiglitz, 2009).

It is quite clear that these public interventions were aimed at promoting or accelerating processes of technological learning that would have been otherwise absent or would have occurred more slowly, attempting as they were to alter the existing patterns of comparative advantage. It is important to notice that IPRs historically had little or no influence on these developments. Not only were they irrelevant as an incentive to the accumulation of production and technological capabilities, they also proved to be only a weak constraint on access to the relevant sources of scientific and technological knowledge. An important reason for this is that a great deal of learning efforts were able to concentrate on the commons of scientific and technical knowledge that had been prospering thanks to the institutions of open science and the limited duration of private property rights on old technologies. It is also the case that relatively weak patent rights available to inventors in developing economies facilitated, in most cases, indigenous efforts at negotiating licensing agreement over technologies of interest.

Several features of the experiences of late industrializing countries in the second half of the twentieth century are by and large shared by countries that either pushed or caught up with the technological frontier during the First and Second Industrial Revolutions. Thus, the British patent system (formally in existence since 1624), it been argued convincingly, played a marginal role in providing incentives for the advances in scientific and technical knowledge that took place during the Industrial Revolution (Mokyr, 2009; David, 2004). Indeed, the legitimacy of the patent monopoly came under considerable criticism from various social groups across much of Europe during the second half of the nineteenth century (MacLeod, 1996). It was during this period that the Netherlands abolished its domestic patent system (1869), only to reinstate it under international pressure in 1912. The Dutch example and that of Switzerland—where creation of patent rights for mechanical inventions only occurred in 1888, and that for chemical inventions in 1907—have been central to Petra Moser's investigation in to the role of patents as an incentive to nineteenth-century inventive activity. Moser (2005) concludes her analysis by arguing that patents appear to have influenced the direction of inventive efforts, rather than the rate of innovation itself.

It has been argued that Swiss and Dutch inventors could still be responding to the incentives provided by patent rights, to the extent that they could secure patents rights in countries where patents were available to inventors and where their inventions could find a commercial application. While this is an important observation, it is also important to emphasize that until the principle of "national treatment" was sanctioned in the Paris Convention of 1893, many patent systems discriminated in practice if not in the letter of the law against foreign inventors. Mowery's (2012) review of the evolution of the U.S. patent system during the nineteenth century identifies several ways in which foreign inventors' protections were weakened, ranging from higher patenting fees to the denial of patent protection for imported inventions. In general, countries catching up to the frontier have historically relied upon weak protection of intellectual property as a way to secure better conditions of access to technology and other forms of knowledge for their citizens.

Recent work surveying a range of development episodes, from the U.S. to the Nordic countries to Japan, Korea, Israel, Brazil and India (Odagiri et al., 2009) shows that most examples of successful development and technological "catch up" have historically occurred under relatively lax patent regimes, and that countries have a long history of calibrating their patent systems to serve broader socioeconomic goals. For example, numerous countries (including Japan, Korea and, later, China) had so-called petty patents while they were developing. By requiring lower novelty, these systems aimed at encouraging imitation, adaptation, and diffusion.

Many countries, including Italy, Switzerland, India and Brazil, have at one time or another, barred pharmaceutical product patents. Moreover, with some rare exceptions, patents and intellectual property rights have not historically been the binding constraints to catching up.

A major exception to the general non-importance of patents is in pharmaceuticals, where numerous countries have at least on occasion *limited* the types of patents allowed, with real consequences. Note also that often these limitations were not typically aimed at promoting development of capabilities by indigenous firms; instead, they were primarily for health policy reasons, to limit monopoly pricing on drugs. We observed above that patents are particularly important in pharmaceuticals. In some countries, including Israel and India, the lack of pharmaceutical-product patents appears to have been key to the emergence of now-thriving generic industries. But also in these cases, the elimination of patents was not the only important factor: government investment in human capital and public sector laboratories, for example, were also important in each. In India, creation of an economic environment conducive to dynamic learning was also important (Sampat, 2009). Thus, *even if necessary*, a lack of product patents is not sufficient for the development of indigenous pharmaceutical industries.

Heterogeneity

Another theme from the historical record is heterogeneity. While discussions of the economic impact of patents—including ours above—tend to characterize patent systems in a dichotomous way (e.g. strong vs. weak), patent systems themselves are composed of numerous characteristics. Moreover, there has historically been considerable variation across and within countries over time, across a number of these dimensions.

One dimension is patentable subject matter: what types of things or inventions are eligible for patent protection? Within any national system of patent protection the definition of patentable subject matter is almost certain to have been altered since the time when patent rights were first recognized. These changes—typically the result of legislative reforms, but, depending on the circumstances, also of changing judicial interpretation of existing laws—have been motivated partly by the need to address the inherent novelty of specific technologies, and partly by national and international factors influencing patent policy decisions. In the U.S., for example, the definition of patentable subject matter in the Patent Act of 1793 included "any new and useful art, machine, manufacture or composition of matter and any new and useful improvement on any art, machine, manufacture or composition of matter." While this definition has survived more or less intact through many rounds of patent reform, questions concerning the scope of patentable subject matter have been answered in different ways over time both in the U.S. patent case law and in the practice of the U.S. patent office, as illustrated by the evolving views over the patentability of living things, software and business methods (we shall come back to the issue below).

Note also that while the U.S. has adhered generally to a broad characterization of patentable subject matter, many patent systems have featured specific restrictions for certain classes of inventions, including the bans on pharmaceutical patents discussed above.

A related, but different, dimension is patent standards. Today, patent standards determine how new an invention has to be, relative to information already known ("the prior art"), to warrant patent protection. Accordingly, contemporary patent offices are typically charged with determining the "inventive step," "novelty" and "non-obviousness" of patent applications in making these determinations. But the standards for doing so have changed over time (Barton, 2003), and continue to be debated in developed countries.

In the abstract, it is unclear where to put the strict boundaries between "strong" or "weak" patent systems. It is clear, however, that the definition of patent standards has made it possible in several historical instances to weaken the protection available to foreign inventors. Consider for example how the 1836 U.S. patent reform created a statutory bar against the granting of patents on inventions for which a foreign patent had been granted. This statutory bar was first revised in 1839 so that inventors could apply for a patent in the U.S. within six months of the grant of a patent abroad, provided that the inventions had not been introduced to public and common use before the application. The bar was revised again in 1870 so that inventors could apply for a patent in the U.S. for an invention covered by a foreign patent provided that the invention had not been introduced to the public and common use in the U.S. for more than two years before the date of application. This modification of the statutory bar against patenting of inventions patented abroad was accompanied by provisions setting the expiration of the U.S. patent to be the earliest expiration date among the corresponding foreign patents.[8]

These standards of patentability preserved—albeit in a different form—the discrimination against foreign inventions that earlier U.S. patent statutes realized more directly. Older statutes (e.g. the Patent Act of 1793, and subsequent revisions) denied the right to apply for a patent to foreigners who did not reside in the U.S., or had not resided in the U.S. for at least two years. Patentability standards that related to the citizenship or residence status of inventors were abolished in 1836, at the time when the statutory bar against patenting of inventions patented abroad was introduced. Moreover, the 1836 Patent Act created a discriminatory pricing structure, whereby foreigners and British inventors paid application fees equal to, respectively, ten and nearly seventeen times those required of U.S. applicants. It should be noted that during this period, the British patent laws established novelty exclusively on the basis of the publication or public use or knowledge of the invention in the UK.

Other important dimensions are the length or duration of patent terms and the scope of protection. As for many other features, the duration of patent terms has been the subject of numerous revisions in virtually every country. Many early patent statutes only declared a maximum term of protection, vesting the appropriate government officers or agents with the authority to determine the appropriate duration for any single patent. In others, the patent applicant had to select the term of patent protection among various possibilities, and pay the appropriate fees. While the trend has been toward lengthening the patent terms as a matter of statutory rights, and setting a standard term applicable to all inventions, in practice statutory patent terms (e.g. twenty years from filing) need not map to "effective" patent lives, or the number of years of market exclusivity actually provided by patents. This can be the case because market entry may not commence until well after patent terms begin (e.g. in pharmaceuticals), or because product life cycles are short enough that the whole patent term rarely binds (e.g. in semiconductors), or because "inventing around" patents is possible in some industries/contexts, as discussed above. Maintenance fee and renewal schedules also affect the economic duration of patents, as do a variety of practices concerned with the extension of patent terms on any given invention (e.g. the British patent on the Watt steam engine) and with the "ever-greening" of patent portfolios. As is the case for patent standards, policy choices about the length of patent terms defy easy characterization in terms of the "strength" of patent protection.

Similar ambiguities apply with respect to yet another dimension of patent systems, namely the range of later products that would be deemed to infringe a patented invention, or patent scope (Merges and Nelson, 1990). How close does a later use of a patented invention have to be for it to be considered infringing? How broadly should claims in a patent application be read? These determinations affect the extent to which patents can block later entrants.

Related to this, the enforcement regime also matters. Laws and the enforcement policies of the relevant governments determine what sorts of infringement are allowed *de jure* (e.g. is reverse engineering during the patent term permitted? How about for research use?), or *de facto* (Is it easy to sue infringers? Do the courts impose significant penalties for infringement?).

Laws and regulations on compulsory licensing—when the government allows others to produce products without consent of patent owners—are also part of the enforcement regime. It should be noted that compulsory licensing provisions and rules about the revocation of patent right due to the patentee's failure to work the patent in the country of issue have been commonplace in the patent statutes of most countries. These provisions served clearly the purpose of weakening the strength of protection offered to foreign inventors. Indeed, the compulsory working provisions introduced by the UK in the Patents and Design Act of 1907 marked the first time that British patent law implemented a measure clearly hostile to the interests of foreign inventors. Interestingly, it was possibly the first time that the British system of innovation *and appropriation* felt threatened by German and American innovators.

4. THE CONTEMPORARY SCENE

Since the 1980s, there has been a radical reshaping in the management and the structure of IP regimes at the global level. It is worth going into some of these details as the regime changes bear important ramifications in terms of international IPR rules and constraints. The changes have been occurring in a context where trade liberalization has been coupled with pressures—sometimes at gunpoint—to strengthen intellectual property rights on an international scale. In this regard, the changes in intellectual property regimes concern two different, although related, domains.

First, there has been quite a significant modification of prevailing norms deriving from jurisprudential rulings within the U.S. system that has influenced the *Weltgeist* in many other countries—developing and developed. Second, there is the increasing relevance of intellectual property in multilateral and bilateral trade negotiations and in international disputes between countries. In this respect, the adoption of the TRIPS agreement marked a milestone in the big push towards the homogenization of a (*quite high*) minimum standard of IP protection.

A new set of incentives in the U.S. IP laws and the "American preference"

Beginning in the 1980s, intellectual property protection has been (deliberately) intensified in the United States through various channels including: extension of patentable subject matter, extended time protection, and the growth of the range of subjects who pursue and exercise intellectual property rights over their inventions. Subsequent to these changes, there has been an upsurge in patenting activity (which, however, hardly reveals a corresponding upsurge in innovative activities; more on this in Chapter 3). A deep analysis of these issues goes beyond the scope of this chapter,[9] it suffices here to recall two major changes: (a) the extension of patent subject matter, and (b) the Bayh-Dole Act.

The extension of patentable subject matter

We have already mentioned the historical definition of patentable matter in the U.S. However, nowadays, the most probable answer to the question, "Can I patent that?" is likely to be "Yes", as Hunt (2001) argues in his critical paper on the introduction of patents for business methods in the U.S. economy. The relaxation of patentability criteria, due to some Supreme Court rulings, led to an extension of the patentable subject matter. In fact, U.S. firms increasingly use patents to protect physical inventions as well as more abstract ones, such as computer programs or business models and methods[10].

According to U.S. jurisprudential tradition, laws of nature, and hence mathematical formulas, could not be the subjects of a patent (cf. *Gottschalk v. Benson*, 1972). However, in 1981 the *Diamond v. Diehr* Supreme Court decision paved the way for computer software and business methods' patentability by asserting that "a claim drawn to subject matter otherwise statutory does not become non-statutory simply because it uses a mathematical formula, computer program or digital computer."

The Court of Appeals for the Federal Circuit (CAFC), instituted in 1982, also played a decisive role in the extension of patentable subject matter through several jurisprudential rulings that reversed the prevailing doctrine. The *State Street Bank and Trust v. Signature Financial Group* (1998) CAFC decision allowed the patentability of business methods when the claimed invention satisfies the requirements of novelty, utility and non-obviousness. This decision also made the utility requirement more lenient.

Through a re-interpretation of patentable subject matter and of previous rulings, the *State Street v. Signature* decision reversed the prevailing doctrine and allowed patenting of algorithms as long as they are "applied in a useful way," i.e. as long as they produce "a useful, concrete and tangible result." According to this decision, registrants seeking patent protection for business methods or algorithms are not required to disclose their computer methods.[11] Contrary to the previous Supreme Court ruling, a mathematical formula and a programmed digital computer *are* currently patentable subject matter (under the chapter 35, p. 101 of the U.S. Code).[12] This tendency favors the engendering of what has been called the "patent thicket" with its likely negative potential effects on future rates of innovations, especially with respect to incremental innovations. For example, in the software industry in which each application might be built upon a series of hundreds of patented algorithms (Shapiro, 2001).

The extension of the patentable domain also involved living entities. The 1980 *Diamond v. Chakrabarty* Supreme Court decision stated that "a live, human made micro-organism is patentable subject matter,"[13] paving the way for a series of rulings which led to the patentability of partial gene sequences (ESTs),[14] including genes crucial to treating illnesses (Orsi, 2002). Another decision worth mentioning is *Re Brana* 1995. This ruling established the presumption of utility and reversed the jurisprudence that supported the circumspect practice of the USPTO in granting patents in this field. *Re Brana* recognizes the validity on patent claims on discoveries not yet made or not yet materialized.

In the U.S. patent law, "utility" is an essential criterion for patentability. "Utility" refers to the industrial and commercial advances, "useful arts," enabled by the invention. Relaxing the meaning of "utility" transforms nonpatentable subject matters into patentable ones. Again, the *Re Brana* Court decision is remarkable. Partial sequences of ESTs were classified as useful due to their potential contribution to future advances in knowledge, and this sufficed for these entities' patentability, despite their value as research tools.[15] Disavowing a previous Supreme Court ruling that explicitly warned against inhibiting future research by restricting access to knowledge, *Re Brana* allowed patent applicants the right to make extensive claims with reference to "virtual" inventions, i.e. inventions that have not yet been made and that cannot be predicted. Patents were transformed from a "reward" granted to the inventor in exchange for the disclosure of the invention into a veritable hunting license.[16] Patents might thus result in a *monopolistic right of exploration* granted to the patent holder even before any invention has been made and *a fortiori* disclosed.

Subsequent rulings and Supreme Court decisions engendered a new patent regime that creates conditions for transforming research advantages into competitive advantages, guaranteeing an upstream protection of the "research product," which results in the right to exclude rival firms from benefiting from "basic" discoveries (Coriat and Orsi, 2002). The resulting fear is that the system is moving toward the dissipation of fruits of the traditional "open science" paradigm (Dasgupta and David, 1994). The new regime covers areas such as software and living entities, generic key inputs, research tools and raw materials possibly instrumental in an undefined number of "downstream" applications. In a context in which innovations are often cumulative in nature, the progressive enclosure[17] of technical knowledge, which in turn underlies subsequent advancements in science and innovation, may induce the "lockout" of potential innovators. In turn, this may offer unjustified monopoly power to small, technology-intensive "niche" firms with no physical processing or distribution capacity.

Indeed, the changes in the U.S. IP laws and jurisprudence boils down to a *de facto* industrial policy, intended to preserve competitive advantages and rents especially in a few sectors—such as the entertainment industry and biotechnology.

The Bayh-Dole Act

The inclusion of provisions that allow granting patents through *exclusive licenses* only to U.S. manufacturing firms, as it is stated in section 204 of the Bayh-Dole Act, which sets the conditions for the "American industry preference," responds to the same *de facto* industrial policy strategy. In 1980, the U.S. Congress adopted the Bayh-Dole Act, which is embedded in title 35, chapter 18, of the U.S. Code under the label of "patent rights in inventions made with federal assistance." This Act set the principles for patenting inventions realized by institutions receiving federal funds for R&D, and introduced two basic changes in the U.S. IP regime: (i) it established a new principle that gives to institutions (universities and public research laboratories) receiving public funding the right to patent their discoveries and (ii) it affirmed the right to license the exploitation of those patents as *exclusive rights* to private firms, and/or to engage in "joint ventures" with them. The literature has already extensively analyzed the impact of this act on the rate and direction of innovative activities. Scholars have stressed the fact that the enactment of the Bayh-Dole Act established a new IP regime that threatens the previously dominant open science principle.[18] The possibility of granting exclusive licenses on research findings obtained by the main centers of scientific knowledge, such as universities and public laboratories, creates a basis for appropriating basic knowledge, which should, by definition, constitute the knowledge base available to all national innovation system agents. Dasgupta and David (1994) emphasize the fact that this appropriation of knowledge is achieved through a series of "bilateral monopolies" that universities and public laboratories share with private for-profit organizations, thus contributing to the commoditization of research outcomes (Eisenberg, 2000; Orsi, 2002).[19]

In fact, the new regime also bears implications with respect to the ways in which patenting is justified. As noted in Mazzoleni and Nelson (1998a), the "incentive theory" has to fade away since the invention is made with federal financial assistance: hence inventors receive an *a priori* reward. Conversely, shifts in the U.S. patent system introduced a different (and new) type of incentive: the inducement to transfer from public research to marketable products, favoring the appropriation of research results to firms that have not been engaged in fundamental research. Firms are induced, through the benefit of exclusive licenses, to commercialize outcomes of publicly funded research even before those outcomes are obtained. In this respect, Mazzoleni and Nelson (1998a) discuss an "induced commercialization theory." Patents no longer reward the inventor *ex post*—instead, the *ex-ante* reward transmogrifies the patent's status from an exploitation right to an exploration right.

The extension of patents' domain and the 1980 Bayh-Dole Act modified the academy-enterprise links in knowledge generation and diffusion. In the decade since its passage, the number of academic patents grew dramatically. Increasingly, the outputs of publicly funded research both published and patented, and their dissemination, is governed by market mechanisms. The Bayh-Dole Act reversed the previous presumption that free access to basic research outcomes was granted equally to all firms (that profited differently from the available knowledge pool depending on their specific assets and capabilities).

International proxies for IPR protection

The multidimensional characteristics of the patent system have been addressed by numerous efforts at developing summary national measures for the strength of patent protection. Such measures provide a relatively simple basis for international comparisons and for the analysis of the determinants of patent rights, or at the very least, of the latter's correlations with various indicators of national economic development.

The construction of national indices of patent protection—exemplified by the widely cited work of Ginarte and Park (1997)—provides quantitative support to the proposition that the distribution of countries according to the strength of patent protection displays considerable and persistent heterogeneity. For a sample of 110 countries, Ginarte and Park (1997) found that both the mean and the variance of the national indices increased during every five-year period between 1960 and 1990. In light of the observed correlation between GDP per capita and strength of patent protection, this phenomenon can be obviously linked to the absence of convergence across countries in terms of their GDP per capita.

5. ...AND ALONG COMES TRIPS

TRIPs must be seen in this context. Passed in response to lobbyists from developed countries, TRIPs compels upward harmonization of patent laws. A detailed discussion of the legal changes required by TRIPs is beyond the scope of this paper (and indeed, beyond the competence of the authors). The main changes relative to the status quo discussed above are the minimum patent terms of twenty years from filing, restrictions on the ability to bar industrial patents, non-discrimination (or the requirement that domestic and foreign innovators be treated equivalently), and a set of requirements that patent laws be enforced.

By the turn of the century, most developing countries were compelled to introduce TRIPs-compliant patent laws. Countries that did not previously offer patent protection on pharmaceutical products had time until 2005 to do so, although they were required to comply with a "mailbox" provision such that patents could be filed in the country as early as 2000, even if the patent grant could not occur for at least another five years. Finally, a range of "least developed" countries were permitted to delay the timing of TRIPs implementation until 2006; this was extended to 2016 via the Doha Declaration.

There has been, interestingly, considerable variation in the timing of TRIPs implementation. Some developing countries passed legislation to adopt TRIPs-compliant patent laws well before their deadlines (e.g. Argentina, Costa Rica, the Dominican Republic, Korea), often as a result of previous or concurrent bilateral pressures (Correa, 2007). Others took full advantage of transition periods (e.g. Belize, Egypt, the Philippines) (Deere, 2009). Even a number of the least developed countries have adopted sooner than necessary (e.g. Cambodia, Chad, and Guinea).Given the importance of technological learning for catching up, and the general lack of patent protection for developing countries historically, these changes are striking. For example, Table 2.1 (reproduced from Deere, 2009, Appendix 3) suggests the widespread impact of

Intellectual Property Rights

Table 2.1 Changes in IP protection in developing and emerging countries

Country	Term of patent protection		Exemption from patent protection for pharmaceutical products	
	1988 (years)	2007 (years)	In relevant law (1988)	In relevant law (2007)
Least developed countries				
Bangladesh	16[a]	16[a]	X	X
Benin	10[a]	20	X	–
Burkina Faso	10[a]	20	X	–
Burundi	20[a]	20	–	–
Cambodia	^	20	^	X
Central Afr. Rep.	10[a]	20	X	–
Chad	10[a]	20	X	–
Ghana	10[a]	20	X	–
Mali	10[a]	20	X	–
Mauritania	10[a]	20	X	–
Nepal	7	7	X	X
Niger	10[a]	20	X	–
Rwanda	20[a]	20	–	–
Sierra Leone	20[a]	20	–	–
Swaziland	20[a]	20	–	–
Togo	10[a]	20	X	–
Uganda	20[a]	15	–	–
Tanzania	20[a]	20	–	–
Developing countries				
Argentina	5, 10, 15	20	X	–
Bolivia	15	20	X	–
Botswana	20[a]	20	–	–
Brazil	15[a]	20	X	–
Cameroon	10[a]	20	–	–
Chile	15	20	–	–
China	15[a]	20	X	–
Colombia	5	20	X	–
Congo	10[a]	20	–	–
Costa Rica	12	20	#	–
Côte d'Ivoire	10[a]	20	–	–
Cuba	10[a]	20	X	–
Dominican Republic	5, 10, 15	20	–	–
Ecuador	5	20	X	–
Egypt	15[a]	20	X	–
Gabon	10[a]	20	–	–
India	14	20	X	–
Jordan	16[a]	20	–	–
Kenya	20[a]	20	–	–
Malaysia	15	20	–	–
Mauritius	14[a]	20	–	–
Mexico	14	20	X	–
Morocco	20[a]	20	X	–
Nigeria	20[a]	20	–	–
Pakistan	16	20	–	–

Peru	5	20	X	–
Philippines	17	20	–	–
Senegal	10[a]	20	–	–
South Africa	20[a]	20	–	–
South Korea	15[a]	20	X	–
Sri Lanka	15	20	–	–
Thailand	15[a]	20	X	–
Trinidad & Tobago	14	20	–	–
Tunisia	5, 10, 15, 20[a]	20	X	–
Uruguay	15	20	X	–
Venezuela	5, 10	20	X	–
Zimbabwe	20[a]	20	X	–

[a] From filing date.
Source: Deere, 2009, Appendix 3.

two major changes to developing-country patent laws resulting from TRIPs—the upward convergence of patent terms and the requirements that pharmaceutical patents be granted.

These changes are dramatic. While it is too soon to assess their impact, for the various reasons discussed above, they are unlikely to have significant impact on domestic innovation (cf. Lerner, 2002; Lanjouw and Cockburn, 2001). Indeed, even in pharmaceuticals where patents tend to be more important, Qian (2007) finds little evidence that domestic patent laws matter for the rate of innovation. And recent work on the Indian pharmaceutical industry suggests that while the importance of R&D in the Indian drug industry has been increasing post-TRIPs, this has little to do with TRIPs per se.

Instead, the changes are likely to shift composition of patenting in developing countries towards developed country and multinational firms, who will no doubt try to use the patents to extract rents from developing-country consumers, and perhaps foreclose on developing-country firms' learning and production activities. A particular concern in India is that the new patent regime will limit production of low cost HIV-AIDS drugs by Indian generic firms, long known in public health circles as "pharmacy to the developing world" (Sampat, 2009).

There is also variation in the content of the laws. Some countries have taken significant advantage of TRIPs' flexibilities and room for maneuver. Some of these flexibilities were inherent in TRIPs, others required clarification from the WTO Declaration on TRIPs and Public Health, which affirmed the rights of countries to enact laws to prevent "evergreening" and to issue compulsory licenses to protect the public health, among other options. Thus, many developing countries have limited patents on "new uses" of existing compounds (Musungu and Oh, 2006). Most controversially, Section 3(d) of India's patent law has strong restrictions on patents on "incremental" innovations

(Sampat, 2010). Several other developing countries, including Malaysia, Indonesia and Bangladesh, are considering similar provisions.

Developed countries expected TRIPs to generate a world with patent laws mirroring the U.S. and EPO. The "counter harmonization" movement (Kapczynski, 2009) and aggressive exercise of TRIPs' flexibilities by many important countries has tempered that hope, particularly in the pharmaceutical sector where patents are most important. So far, these have been interpreted as perfectly consistent with TRIPs by the WTO.

Perhaps not surprisingly, these developments have galvanized developed countries to push again for stronger measures, now through bilateral measures. Today, the U.S. and other industrialized countries are aggressively pushing so-called "TRIPs-plus" changes in patent laws via bilateral trade agreements. The changes developed countries are lobbying for include long data exclusivity periods (which would protect innovations even where patent standards are not met), and removal on restrictions to patentable subject matter (e.g. new uses). These bilateral initiatives thus aim to ratchet up IPRs, and close the doors that TRIPs left open.

However, TRIPs flexibilities do not return us to the status quo ante: there is no doubt that most countries' patent laws are on average considerably "stronger" now than they were a decade ago. Moreover, patent laws are effectively implemented by patent examiners (Drahos and Braithwaite, 2002). In developing countries, these examiners tend to rely heavily on their developed country counterparts for their training, search manuals and databases (Drahos and Braithwaite, 2002; Kapczynski, 2009). In this context, there are questions whether there is *de facto* institutional isomorphism, with developing-country examiners following the lead of the U.S. and EPO on the same applications, rather than enforcing the nuances of their own (more restrictive) patent laws (Kapczynski, 2009; Drahos and Braithwaite, 2002).

6. CONCLUSIONS

The punch line of our discussion on the historical relations between IPR and development is that the impact of the former has been often irrelevant. Conversely, there is no convincing evidence showing that any country's development prospects are hurt by the weakness of the domestic system of IPR protection. These lessons from the historical experience inform our speculations on the consequences of the recent changes in the international IPR regime. As the discussion above suggests, the main impacts are likely to be in pharmaceuticals and chemicals. Given the limited effectiveness of patents in other fields, they may serve as nuisances and obstacles, but are unlikely to be the binding constraint on development efforts. Another reason they will have more impact in pharmaceuticals is that the difference from the pre-TRIPs era is most pronounced in that field, given the widespread restriction on product patents *ex ante*.

As discussed above, and as other contributions to this project emphasize, there are also various flexibilities, and room for interpretation, included in TRIPs, in pharmaceuticals as elsewhere. In pharmaceuticals, restrictions on patenting incremental innovations are non-trivial, since these patents dominate the pharmaceutical patent landscape in the U.S. (Kapczynski, 2009) and Europe (EC Commission Report, 2009). Thus, even in the wake of considerable harmonization there is also room to maneuver—even in pharmaceuticals. The push for "TRIPs-plus" measures is a reaction to these. To the extent that we are right about the importance of public knowledge for capability accumulation and access in developing countries, these changes toward an even tighter IPR system should be resisted. More generally, the numerous developing countries that have not yet implemented post-TRIPs patent laws should closely monitor and learn from the experiences of those that have.

Paraphrasing the conclusions of a well known review of the patent system authored by Edith Penrose (1951), we conclude by arguing that if minimum international standards of intellectual property protection did not exist, it would be difficult to make a conclusive case for introducing them. On the contrary, we believe that the findings of the empirical and theoretical literature on patents support a strong case for reforming the regime of intellectual property protection and for backing off from the global convergence toward the standards of protection that prevail in the U.S. and other advanced economies. Such reform would be in the interest not only of technological catching-up efforts by developing countries, but also in the interest of innovation in developed ones. In this respect the various chapters that follows offer important insights for institutional and policy changes.

NOTES

1. Prepared for the task force on "Intellectual Property", within the *Initiative for Policy Dialogue* (IPD), Columbia University, New York. Parts of this work draw upon Dosi and Nelson (2010), Cimoli, Coriat and Primi (2009), Cimoli, Dosi and Stiglitz (2009), Dosi, Marengo and Pasquali (2006) to which the reader is referred for further details.
2. To be sure, we do not mean to argue here that the appropriability regime is the only, or even the most important, determinant of the rate and direction of innovative activities: more in Dosi, Marengo and Pasquali (2006) and Dosi and Nelson (2010).
3. Incidentally, note that such an assumption is core within most neo-Schumpeterian models of growth, while the limited ability to appropriate returns to innovation is

often offered as the reason why the rate of technological progress is slow in some industries.

4. As early as the sixteenth century, the Venice republic was granting patents under the compulsory rule that innovators and skilled artisans from abroad were granted a temporary monopoly in exchange for their transfer of largely tacit knowledge to local artisans and firms.

5. On those points following the classic statements in Bush (1945), Polanyi (1962) and Merton (1973), see the more recent appraisals in Dasgupta and David (1994), David (2004) and Nelson (2004), and the conflicting views presented in Geuna et al. (2003).

6. Note that the possible "trade-off" discussed here is distinct from the purported, and somewhat elusive ("Schumpeterian"), trade-off referred to in the literature between propensity to innovate and market structure: more on the theoretical side in Nelson and Winter (1982), and on the empirical evidence Cohen and Levin (1989) and Soete (1979), among others.

7. It is not possible to discuss here the underlying theoretical debates: let us just mention that they range from "patent races" equilibrium models (cf. the discussion in Stoneman and Battisti, 2010) to much more empirically insightful "markets for technologies" analyses (Arora, Fosfuri and Gambardella, 2001), all the way to evolutionary models of appropriability (Winter, 1993).

8. These terms were modified again in 1903 in accordance with the Paris Convention on the Protection of Industrial Property of 1883, of which the U.S. became a member in 1887.

9. There is a remarkable body of literature analyzing the changes in IP laws and court rulings, and the boom in patenting activity. See Kortum and Lerner, 1999; Hunt, 2001; Gallini, 2002, among others.

10. The Amazon's "one click" patent granted in 1999 by the USPTO is a clear example.

11. Smets-Solanes (2000) presents evidence on several cases of patented business models that do not disclose the computer processes and algorithms involved.

12. Regarding software patentability, see Liotard (2002), Samuelson (1998) and Mergès (2001). See the Besen and Raskind (1991) survey on IP as well.

13. In Europe, in spite of the 1998 EU Directive, this process of extension of the new right regarding living entities met serious opposition.

14. *Expressed Sequence Tags* or "partial sequences" of genes. The utilization of this process constitutes an advance in the methods that can be used to identify complete sequences of genes.

15. It is worth noting that this evolution of the American law would have been impossible per se under the Continental European law, according to which a key distinction separates "discoveries" (pertaining to knowledge) and "inventions" (pertaining to applied arts), the latter being the only patentable subject matter. We should, however, further specify that even under the American law, the observed changes were neither grounded in objective fact nor even foreseeable. On this point, see the discussion in Orsi (2002).

16. This is despite the fact that the Supreme Court had specifically warned that "*a patent is not a hunting license*" in its *Brenner v. Manson* ruling. (On this point, see Orsi, 2002; and Eisenberg, 1995).

17. The idea that the new IP regime can be analyzed as a new "enclosure" movement is at the heart of a series of works and studies first introduced by Boyle. (See among others Boyle, 2003).
18. See Mowery et al. 2004; Mazzoleni and Nelson, 1998a; and Dasgupta and David, 1994 for broadly converging analyses regarding the effects of the introduction of the Bayh-Dole Act in the U.S. IP regime.
19. In this regard, we note that an important source of royalty income for universities has been represented by patents that were licensed non-exclusively, a practice that amounts to a tax on the use of the underlying knowledge.

REFERENCES

Abramovitz, M. (1986). "Catching Up, Forging Ahead, and Falling Behind," *The Journal of Economic History*, 46 (2): 385–406.

Allen, R.C. (1983). "Collective Invention," *Journal of Economic Behavior and Organization*, 4: 1–24.

Arora, A., L. Branstetter and C. Chatterjee (2008). "Strong Medicine: Patent Reform and the Emergence of a Research-driven Pharmaceutical Industry in India," Paper presented at the NBER Conference on Location of Biopharmaceuticals, Savannah, United States, 7–8 March 2008.

Arora, A., A. Fosfuri and A. Gambardella (2001). "Markets for Technology: Why Do We See Them, Why We Don't See More of Them and Why Should We Care," in A. Arora, A. Fosfuri and A. Gambardella, eds, (2001), *Markets for Technology: The Economics of Innovation and Corporate Strategy*. Cambridge, MA: MIT Press.

Arrow, K. (1962). "Economic Welfare and Allocation of Resources for Inventions," in R.R. Nelson, ed., *The Rate and Direction of Inventive Activity*. Princeton, NJ: Princeton University Press.

Arundel, A., G. van de Paal and L. Soete (1995). *PACE Report: Innovation Strategies of Europe's Largest Industrial Firms: Results of the PACE Survey for Information Sources, Public Research, Protection of Innovations, and Government Programmes, Final Report*. Prepared for the SPRINT Programme, European Commission. Maastricht, Netherlands: Merit, University of Limbourg.

Barton, J.H. (2003). "Non-Obviousness," *IDEA: The Journal of Law and Technology*, 43: 475–508.

Besen, S.M. and L.J. Raskind (1991). "An Introduction to the Law and Economics of Intellectual Property," *Journal of Economic Perspectives*, 5 (1): 3–27.

Boyle, J. (2003). "The Second Enclosure Movement and the Construction of the Public Domain," *Law and Contemporary Problems*, 66 (1/2): 33–74.

Bush, V. (1945). *Science: The Endless Frontier*. Washington, DC: U.S. GPO.

Cimoli, M., B. Coriat and A. Primi (2009), "Intellectual Property and Industrial Development: A Critical Assessment", in M. Cimoli, G. Dosi, and J.E. Stiglitz, eds, *Industrial Policy and Development: The Political Economy of Capabilities Accumulation*. New York: Oxford University Press.

Cimoli, M., G. Dosi and J.E. Stiglitz (2009). "The Political Economy of Capabilities Accumulation," in M. Cimoli, G. Dosi, and J.E. Stiglitz, eds, *The Political Economy of Capabilities Accumulation: The Past and Future of Policies for Industrial Development*. Oxford: Oxford University Press.

Cohen, W.M., A. Goto, A. Nagata, R.R. Nelson and J.P. Walsh (2002). "R&D Spillovers, Patents and the Incentives to Innovate in Japan and the United States," *Research Policy*, 31 (8–9): 1349–67.

Cohen, W. M. and R.C. Levin (1989). "Empirical Studies of Innovation and Market Structure," in R. Schmalensee and R. Willig, eds, *Handbook of Industrial Organization*, 1 (2): 1059–107 Elsevier.

Cohen, W. M. and D. A. Levinthal (1989). "Innovation and Learning: The Two Faces of R&D," *The Economic Journal*, 99: 569–96.

Cohen, W.M., R.R. Nelson and J.P. Walsh (2002). "Links and Impacts: The Influence of Public Research on Industrial R&D," *Management Science*, 48 (1): 1–23.

Coriat, B. and F. Orsi (2002). "Establishing a New Intellectual Property Rights Regime in the United States: Origins, Content and Problems," *Research Policy*, 31 (8–9): 1491–507.

Coriat, B., and F. Orsi (2006). "TRIPS, Pharmaceutical Patent and Public Health—The Case for Access to HIV Care" in K. van der Pijl, L. Assassi and D. Wigan, eds, *Global Regulation: Managing Crises After the Imperial Turn*. London: Palgrave.

Correa, C. (2007). *Trade Related Aspects of Intellectual Property Rights: A Commentary on the TRIPS Agreement*. Oxford: Oxford University Press.

Dasgupta, P. and P. David (1994). "Toward a New Economics of Science," *Research Policy*, 23 (5): 487–521.

David, P.A. (2004). "Can 'Open Science' be Protected from the Evolving Regime of Intellectual Property Rights Protections," *Journal of Theoretical and Institutional Economics*, 160 (1): 9–34.

David, P.A. and B.H. Hall (2006). "Property and the Pursuit of Knowledge: IPR Issues Affecting Scientific Research," *Research Policy*, 35 (6): 767–71.

Deere, C. (2009). *The Implementation Game*. Oxford: Oxford University Press.

Dosi, G., P. Llerena and M. Sylos Labini (2006). "The Relationships between Science, Technologies and, their Industrial Exploitation: An Illustration through the Myths and Realities of the So-called 'European Paradox'," *Research Policy*, 35 (10): 1450–64.

Dosi, G., L. Marengo and C. Pasquali (2006). "How Much Should Society Fuel the Greed of Innovators? On the Relations between Appropriability, Opportunities and the Rates of Innovation," *Research Policy*, 35 (8): 1110–21.

Dosi, G., and R.R. Nelson (2010). "Technical Change and Industrial Dynamics as Evolutionary Processes," in B.H. Hall and N. Rosenberg, eds, *Handbook of Innovation*. Amsterdam and New York: Elsevier.

Drahos, P. and J. Braithwaite (2002). *Information Feudalism*. London: Earthscan.

Eisenberg, R. (1995). "Corporate Strategies and Human Genome," in *Intellectual Property in the Realm of Living Forms and Materials*. Acte du Colloque Académie des Sciences, Technique et Documentation, 85–90.

Eisenberg, R.S. (2000). "Re-Examining the Role of Patents in Appropriating the Value of DNA Sequences," *Emory Law Journal*, 49 (3): 783–800.

European Commission Report (2009). *Pharmaceutical Sector Inquiry.* <http://ec. europa.eu/competition/sectors/pharmaceuticals/inquiry/index.html> (accessed 7 September 2013).

Freeman, C. (2008). *Systems of Innovation: Selected Essays in Evolutionary Economics.* Cheltenham, UK: Edward Elgar.

Frommer, J. (2009). "Patent Disclosure," *Iowa Law Review*, 94: 539.

Gallini, N. (2002). "The Economics of Patents: Lessons from Recent U.S. Patent Reform," *Journal of Economic Perspectives*, 16: 131–54.

Geuna, A., A.J. Salter and W.E. Steinmueller (2003). *Science and Innovation: Rethinking the Rationales for Funding and Governance.* Cheltenham, UK: Edward Elgar.

Ginarte, J.C., and W.C. Park (1997). "Determinants of Patent Rights: A Cross-National Study," *Research Policy*, 26 (3): 283–301.

Granstrand, O. (1999). "Intellectual Capitalism: An Overview," *Nordic Journal of Political Economy*, 25: 115–27.

Hall, B.H. and A. Ziedonis (2001). "The Patent Paradox Revisited: An Empirical Study of Patenting in the US Semiconductor Industry, 1979–1995," *RAND Journal of Economics*, 32: 101–28.

Heller, M.A. and R.S. Eisenberg (1998). "Can Patents Deter Innovation? The Anti-Commons in Biomedical Research," *Science*, 280: 698–701.

Hippel, E. von (2005). *Democratizing Innovation.* Cambridge, MA: MIT Press.

Hunt, R. M. (2001). "You Can Patent That? Are Patents on Computer Programs and Business Methods Good for the New Economy?" *Business Review*, Q1, 2001, Federal Reserve Bank of Philadelphia.

Jaffe, A.B. (1998). "Universities as a Source of Commercial Technology: A Detailed Analysis of University Patenting, 1965–1988," *Review of Economics and Statistics*, 80 (1): 119–27.

Jaffe, A.B. (2000). "The U.S. Patent System in Transition: Policy Innovation and the Innovation Process," *Research Policy*, 29: 531–58.

Kapczynski, A. (2009). "Harmonization and Its Limits: A Case Study of TRIPS Implementation in India's Pharmaceutical Sector," *California Law Review*, 97: 1571.

Kortum, S., and J. Lerner (1999). "What Is Behind the Recent Surge in Patenting?" *Research Policy*, 28 (1): 1–22.

Lanjouw, J.O. and I.M. Cockburn (2001). "New Pills for Poor People? Empirical Evidence after GATT," *World Development*, 29 (2): 265–89.

Lemley, M.A., D. Lichtman and B.N. Sampat (2005). "What to Do about Bad Patents," *Regulation*, 28 (4): 10–13.

Lerner, J. (2002). "150 Years of Patent Protection," *The American Economic Review*, Papers and Proceedings of the One Hundred Fourteenth Annual Meeting of the American Economic Association, 92 (2): 221–25.

Levin, R.C., A.K. Klevorick, R.R. Nelson and S.G. Winter (1987). "Appropriating the Returns from Industrial Research and Development," *Brookings Papers on Economic Activity*, 3: 242–79.

Liotard, I. (2002). "La Brevetabilité des logiciels: les étapes clés de l'évolution jurisprudentielle aux Etas Unis," *Revue d'Économie Industrielle*, 99, Numéro Spécial Les droits de propriété intellectuelle: nouvelles frontières et nouveaux enjeux.

MacLeod, C. (1996). "Concepts of Invention and the Patent Controversy in Victorian Britain," in R. Fox, ed., *Technological Change: Methods and Themes in the History of Technology*. Newark, NJ: Harwood Academic Publishers.

Mansfield, E., M. Schwartz and M. Wagner (1981). "Imitation Costs and Patents: An Empirical Study," *The Economic Journal*, 91: 907–18.

Marengo, L., C. Pasquali, M. Valente and G. Dosi (2012). "Appropriability, Patents, and Rates of Innovation in Complex Products Industries," *Economics of Innovation and New Technology*, 21 (8), 753–73.

Mazzoleni, R. and R.R. Nelson (1998a). "The Benefits and Costs of Strong Patent Protection: A Contribution to the Current Debate," *Research Policy*, 27 (3): 273–84.

Mazzoleni, R. and R.R. Nelson (1998b). "Economic Theories about the Benefits and Costs of Patents," *Journal of Economic Issues*, 32: 1031–52.

Mazzoleni, R., and Nelson R.R. (2007). "Public Research Institutions and Economic Catch-Up," *Research Policy*, 36 (10): 1512–28.

Mazzoleni, R. and Nelson R.R. (2009). "The Roles of Research at Universities and Public Labs in Economic Catch-up," in M. Cimoli, G. Dosi, and J.E. Stiglitz, eds, *The Political Economy of Capabilities Accumulation: The Past and Future of Policies for Industrial Development*. Oxford: Oxford University Press.

Merges, R. (1999). "As Many as Six Impossible Patents before Breakfast: Property Rights for Business Concepts and Patent System Reform," *Berkeley Technology Law Journal*, 14 (2): 577–93.

Merges, R. and R.R. Nelson (1990). "On the Complex Economics of Patent Scope," *Columbia Law Review*, 90 (4): 839–916.

Merges, R. and R.R. Nelson (1994). "On Limiting or Encouraging Rivalry in Technical Progress: The Effect of Patent Scope Decisions," *Journal of Economic Behavior and Organization*, 25 (1): 1–24.

Merton, R.K. (1973), *The Sociology of Science: Theoretical and Empirical Investigations*. Chicago: University of Chicago Press.

Mokyr, J. (2009). "Intellectual Property Rights, the Industrial Revolution, and the Beginnings of Modern Economic Growth," *American Economic Review: Papers & Proceedings*, 99 (2): 349–55.

Moser, P. (2005). "How Do Patent Laws Influence Innovation? Evidence from Nineteenth-century World's Fairs," *American Economic Review*, 95 (4): 1215–36.

Mowery, D.C. (2012). "IPR and US Economic Catch-up," in H. Odagiri, A. Goto, A. Sunami and R.R. Nelson, eds, *Intellectual Property Rights, Development, and Catch-Up*. Oxford: Oxford University Press.

Mowery, D.C., R.R. Nelson, B.N. Sampat and A.A. Ziedonis, (2004). *The Ivory Tower and Industrial Innovation: University-Industry Technology Transfer Before and After The Bayh-Dole Act*. Stanford, CA: Stanford University Press.

Murray, F., P. Aghion, M. Dewatripont, J. Kolev and S. Stern (2008). "Of Mice and Academics: The Role of Openness in Science," MIT Sloan Working Paper.

Musungu, S.F. and C. Oh (2006). *The Use of Flexibilities in TRIPS by Developing Countries: Can They Promote Access to Medicines?* Geneva: South Centre.

Nelson, R.R. (2004). "The Market Economy, and the Scientific Commons," *Research Policy*, 33 (3): 455–71.

Nelson, R.R. (2006). "Reflections on 'The Simple Economics of Basic Scientific Research': Looking Back and Looking Forward," *Industrial and Corporate Change,* 15 (6): 903–17.

Nelson, R.R. and S.C. Winter (1982). *An Evolutionary Theory of Economic Change.* Cambridge, MA: Belknap.

Nuvolari, A. (2004). "Collective Invention During the British Industrial Revolution: The Case of the Cornish Pumping Engine," *Cambridge Journal of Economics,* 28 (3): 347–63.

H. Odagiri et al. (eds) (2009). *Intellectual Property Rights, Development, and Catch-Up: An International Comparative Study.* Oxford: Oxford University Press.

Orsi, F. (2002). "La constitution d'un nouveau droit de la propriété intellectuelle sur le vivant aux Etats Unis: Origine et signification d'un dépassement de frontières," *Revue d'Economie Industrielle,* 99: 65–86.

Penrose, E.T. (1951). *The Economics of the International Patent System.* Baltimore: Johns Hopkins University Press.

Polanyi, K. (1944). *The Great Transformation: The Political and Economic Origins of Our Time.* Boston: Beacon Press.

Polanyi, M. (1962). *Personal Knowledge: Towards a Post-Critical Philosophy.* New York: Harper Torchbooks.

Qian, Y. (2007). "Do National Patent Laws Stimulate Domestic Innovation in a Global Patenting Environment?" *Review of Economics and Statistics,* 89 (3): 436–53.

Reichman, J. (2009). "Compulsory Licensing of Patented Pharmaceutical Inventions: Evaluating the Options," *The Journal of Law, Medicine, and Ethics,* 37 (2): 247–63.

Reinert, E.S. (2007). *How Rich Countries Got Rich . . . and Why Poor Countries Stay Poor.* London: Constable.

Reinert, E.S. (2009). "Emulation v. Comparative Advantage: Competing and Complementary Principles in the History of Economic Policy," in M. Cimoli, G. Dosi and J.E. Stiglitz, eds, *The Political Economy of Capabilities Accumulation: The Past and Future of Policies for Industrial Development.* Oxford: Oxford University Press.

Sampat, B. (2009). "The Accumulation of Capabilities in Indian Pharmaceuticals and Software: The Roles that Patents Did (and Did not) Play" in H. Odagiri et al., eds, *Intellectual Property Rights, Development, and Catch-Up: An International Comparative Study.* Oxford: Oxford University Press.

Sampat, B. (2010). "When Do Applicants Search for Prior Art?" *Journal of Law & Economics,* 53 (2): 399–416.

Samuelson, P. (2000), "Economic and Constitutional Influences on Copyright Law in the United States," available at SSRN <http://ssrn.com/abstract=234738> (accessed 10 October 2013).

Shapiro, C. (2001). "Navigating the Patent Thicket: Cross Licenses, Patent Pools and Standard Setting," in A. B. Jaffe, J. Lerner and S. Stern, eds, *Innovation Policy and the Economy,* vol. 1. Boston, MA: MIT Press.

Smets-Solanes, J.P (2000). "Stimuler la concurrence et l'innovation dans la société de l'information," document de travail, version 1.0, beta 5, polycopié.

Soete, L.L.G. (1979). "Firm Size and Inventive Activity: The Evidence Reconsidered," *European Economic Review,* 12 (4): 319–40.

Stoneman, P., and G. Battisti (2010). "The Diffusion of New Technology," in B.H. Hall and N. Rosenberg, eds, *Handbook of the Economics of Innovation*, vol. II. Burlington, MA: Academic Press.

Teece, D.J. (1986). "Profiting from Technological Innovation: Implications for Integration, Collaboration, Licensing and Public Policy," *Research Policy*, 15 (6): 285–305.

Winter, S.G. (1993). "Patents and Welfare in an Evolutionary Model," *Industrial and Corporate Change*, 2 (1): 211–31.

3

Lessons from the Economics Literature on the Likely Consequences of International Harmonization of IPR Protection

Albert G.Z. Hu and Adam B. Jaffe

1. INTRODUCTION

The interaction between intellectual property rights (IPR) and the rate and direction of technological change has been a fertile ground for economic analysis and policy debate. It has long been recognized that IPR, with the monopoly rights they grant to their holders, constitute a compromise that society endures in order to encourage invention and creation. Since Nordhaus's (1969) seminal work on optimal patent life, there has been voluminous theoretical and empirical analysis of the parameters of IPR policy from the perspective of a socially optimal trade-off between the costs of IPR and the benefits of the creations they are presumed to encourage. More recently, this debate has focused on the desirability of "harmonization," which has come to mean the extension of the IPR policies prevalent in North America, Europe and Japan to the less developed world. Since "harmonization" defined in this way involves broadening and strengthening IPR protection in developing countries, understanding its consequences must begin with understanding the consequences of IPR more generally, but the interaction of different IPR regimes through the mechanisms of international trade and investment significantly complicates the analysis.

We explore the theoretical and empirical literatures on IPR in both closed-economy and international contexts, and show that normative theoretical analysis, empirical analysis of the effects of different IPR regimes, and examinations of countries' own choices of IPR regimes at different stages of development all call into question the desirability of harmonization, suggesting that a globally efficient IPR regime will entail different IPR policies for countries with different technological capabilities and at different stages of economic development. We return to this theme in the Conclusion.

The organization of this survey is as follows. Section 2 begins with a brief overview of the patent design literature, and then proceeds to summarize the general empirical evidence on the effects of different IPR regimes. Section 3 discusses the literature that has explored the welfare implications of the international harmonization of IPR. Section 4 explores the literature that has tried to assess the impact of IPR on specific aspects of the development process, particularly trade, FDI and technology licensing. Section 5 looks at the relationship in the other direction, by examining historical and cross-sectional analysis of the determinants of IPR regimes themselves. Section 6 offers conclusions and policy implications.

2. PATENTS AND POLICY AND TECHNOLOGICAL INNOVATIONS

2.1 The patent design literature

The literature on the optimal design of the patent system is premised on the notion that patents confer an effective means to secure returns to inventions. The discussion then proceeds to analyze how the parameters of a patent system affect incentives and welfare. The parameters most frequently analyzed are patent duration, and patent breadth or scope. The early literature (Nordhaus, 1969 and Scherer, 1972) focused on patent duration. The optimal length of patent protection was obtained by weighing the balance between the deadweight loss from the static inefficiency of a patent holder's monopoly power and the cost reduction generated by the patented invention. A subsequent literature developed to bring the breadth of patent protection into the analytical framework. Klemperer (1990) differentiated two kinds of consumer welfare loss due to patents: that resulting from consumers' dropping the product from their consumption; and that generated by consumers' substituting to a less preferred variety. This analysis showed that the terms of the trade-off are likely to be sensitive to the nature of the products. Scotchmer and Green (1990), Green and Scotchmer (1995), and Scotchmer (1991, 1996) focus on the inter-temporal knowledge spillover of research and development when innovation takes place sequentially and is undertaken by different firms. The socially optimal solution to this situation turns on the nature of the bargaining between the pioneer and follower firms.

Because of the abstraction of theorizing and the richness of the strategy space in the game theoretical models, this literature has not produced many testable hypotheses that empirical economists can take to data to validate. As a result, the vast empirical literature has developed in a somewhat parallel and disjointed fashion.

2.2 Patent policy changes, patenting and innovation: empirical evidence

The last two decades of the twentieth century saw a number of major changes to the U.S. patent policy. These changes raise important questions about patent policy, but also provide, in principle, possible "experiments" regarding the effect of parameters of patent policy on the rate of invention and innovation. The major changes were (1) the creation of the Court of Appeals for the Federal Circuit (CAFC), (2) the Bayh-Dole Act and (3) the expansion of the realm of patentability. The Court of Appeals for the Federal Circuit was created in 1982 to hear appeals from district courts of patent cases. It was a procedural reform and was meant to standardize patent law across the U.S. In practice, however, the CAFC has strengthened patent protection in the U.S. Patent holders now win more often; are more likely to achieve injunctive relief shutting down their competitors; and earn larger damages, on average (Jaffe and Lerner, 2004). The Bayh-Dole Act of 1980 has allowed universities and other non-profit institutions automatically to retain title to patents derived from federally funded R&D, and encouraged technology transfer to the private sector. Finally, decisions of the CAFC and the implementation of these decisions by the Patent Office have expanded the range of inventions that are potentially patentable, to include genetically engineered bacteria, genetically altered mice, particular gene sequences, surgical methods, computer software, financial products, and methods for conducting auctions on the internet.

None of these huge changes in patent policy and practice relates directly to the parameters of patent policy that have been scrutinized by economic theory. On some level, their consequences ought to be so obvious as to be theoretically uninteresting: if you increase the probability of winning a patent case, the economic reward you receive when you win, and the number of different kinds of technologies that are eligible for patent protection, you have increased the incentive to patent and the rate of patenting should rise. To first order, the returns to invention have also risen, and so the rate of invention itself should also rise. From a policy perspective, the important question is whether this second effect is quantitatively significant.

Since the mid-1980s, U.S. patent grants and applications have been growing at an annual rate of 5 per cent, reversing a long-term secular decline in the intensity of patenting over the previous century. A number of researchers have attempted to determine whether this change can, in fact, be attributed to the approximately contemporaneous changes in policy, and to what extent the increase in *patenting* corresponds to an increase in the underlying rate of *invention*, as distinct from a change in the propensity to apply for patents on inventions that are produced.

Kortum and Lerner (1998) formulated four hypotheses that might explain the U.S. patent explosion. The "friendly court" hypothesis conjectured that the creation of the CAFC had made patents more valuable and hence increased the propensity to patent in the U.S. According to their "regulatory capture" hypothesis, large American firms are likely to be primarily responsible for the patent explosion, since they dominate the R&D process in the U.S. and therefore are a major beneficiary of pro-patent policy changes and so have the ability to influence the regulatory changes. The third hypothesis, the "fertile technology" hypothesis, postulates that newly emerged technology opportunities may have led to a higher rate of innovation and therefore more patents. The final hypothesis considered by Kortum and Lerner was that the process of R&D had become more productive. The higher R&D productivity could have been caused by the application of information technology to the process of R&D and increasing emphasis on applied research that was likely to generate patents.

They rejected the friendly court hypothesis by looking at trends in patenting by foreigners in the U.S., and by U.S. nationals abroad. If the CAFC was the source of increased U.S. patenting, this should have applied to foreigners as well as domestic inventors, and there would not necessarily have been an increase in patenting by U.S. nationals in other jurisdictions. In fact, there was no acceleration of foreign patenting in the U.S. during the friendly court period, and patenting by U.S. inventors abroad did increase during the same period. The fertile technology hypothesis was rejected because the patenting surge was widespread across patent classes instead of concentrating in some of the niche technology areas such as biotechnology and information technology that might have been most fertile. Finally, Kortum and Lerner found that the fraction of patents going to new firms and the fraction going to firms that previously had relatively few patents had both increased. This seemed to refute the regulatory capture hypothesis. Through this process of elimination, Kortum and Lerner then concluded that there must have been an increase in the productivity of R&D to account for the patenting surge.

That the explanation of the patent explosion lies outside the patent system itself received further support in the survey evidence that Cohen et al. (2000) reported. R&D managers surveyed did not perceive patents to be more effective during the 1980s than before. Cohen et al. (2000) attributed the higher rate of patenting to the increased propensity of firms using patents as a strategic tool to block products of competitors, improve bargaining position in licensing negotiations, and prevent or defend against infringement suits.

The strategic patenting hypothesis also found support in Hall and Ziedonis's (2001) study of patenting activity in the U.S. semiconductor industry. They found that large firms tended to use patents in large portfolios in negotiation of cross-licensing agreements. Two features of the semiconductor industry made it particularly amenable to such strategic use of patents. The semiconductor technology is "complex"[1] in the sense that a product usually embodies a web of interrelated and overlapping technologies that are likely to be protected by patents owned by different semiconductor firms. The need to negotiate a license and the likelihood of infringement are therefore greater than in a "simple" technology industry where products are not subject to this intricate web of patented technologies. Furthermore, semiconductor firms, particularly foundries, are capital intensive so that it is costly to shut down the production facility in the face of patent litigation threat.

China has also seen explosive growth of patent applications in recent years. Using a firm-level data set that spans the population of China's large and medium-size industrial enterprises, Hu and Jefferson (2009) find that among the multiple forces contributing to China's patent explosion, the interaction between foreign invested firms and domestic Chinese firms plays an important part: industries with larger foreign direct investment also see larger numbers of patent applications from domestic firms, which are only weakly correlated with R&D expenditure.

Following the passage of Bayh-Dole and related legislation, patenting by American universities and National Labs has increased substantially, leading to the question as to how much of this increase is a "real" increase in technology production, and how much just an increase in the fraction of technology that is patented. Henderson et al. (1998) and Mowery and Ziedonis (2002) find mixed evidence as to whether the "quality" of patents, measured by citation intensity and average licensing revenue, fell as the number of patents rose.

In one of the few studies that examined the role of economic incentives in the supply of creative work, Hui and Png (2002) examined whether the production of movies responded to changes in economic incentives. In particular they examined how variation in movie-demand shifters such as ownership of TV and video tape recorders, the population, and personal disposal income influence the production of motion pictures. Their data spanned thirty-eight countries and the period from 1990 to 2000. They conjectured that video tape recorders and movies are complements, because people watch movies on video tapes, but TV and movies are substitutes. Their results confirmed these conjectures. For example, a 1 per cent increase in video tape recorder ownership in the U.S. in 2000 would have led to a 1 per cent increase in motion pictures. They then assessed the impact of a 1998 increase in the term of copyright, or the Sonny Bono Act, on the supply of movies. This effect turned out to be insignificant. It is not clear whether this is because the duration of copyright protection is relatively unimportant, or because the 1998 extension—which added to an already long period of protection—simply had an unmeasurable marginal effect.

Kanwar and Evanson (2003) is one of the few studies that examined directly the relationship between innovation and IPR by regressing the R&D

expenditure/GDP ratio on IPR strength and other control variables. Using a cross section of twenty-nine countries from 1981 to 1990, their estimation strategy was to use a "random effects" model rather than a fixed effect one on the grounds of efficiency of the estimators, the nature of their panel data—large N and small T, and the confirmation of the result of a Hausman test. The elasticity of R&D to GDP ratio with respect to the Ginarte and Park patent index was estimated to be from 0.3 to 1.8. Therefore they concluded that IPR strength had a strong positive effect on R&D investment. As noted below, however, other authors have explored a causal relation running from the stage of economic development to the strength of IPR. Since R&D/GDP is highly correlated with other aspects of the development process, it is unclear whether the measured effect of IPR on R&D intensity is contaminated by causality running from stage of development to strength of IPR.

Lanjouw and Cockburn (2001) focused on the response of the global pharmaceutical industry to the trend of strengthening IPR that started with GATT negotiations in the mid 1980s. Their approach was to identify a potential shift of the research focus of the pharmaceutical industry as a result of the increasing strength of IPR protection in developing countries. In particular, they asked whether there had been a greater weight placed on drugs against tropical diseases, which are specific to developing countries. They surveyed pharmaceutical company executives and health researchers and collected statistical data to test their hypothesis. Their data showed that research related to malaria increased significantly from the mid 1980s. Since there was no indication that the science of developing malaria drugs was getting "easier," i.e. there did not seem to be any change in technology opportunity, the shift could only have come from the demand side, in which the strengthening of IPR could have played a role. But malaria seemed to be the only case where such a shift took place. They suggested that tropical diseases might not be the only area where strengthening IPR protection might have an effect.

Moser (2005), in a recent contribution to this literature, used a novel data set of innovations exhibited at nineteenth-century World Fairs to investigate how cross-country differences in patent law affected the nature and direction of innovations in these countries. She concluded that the adoption of patent laws had a significant effect on the direction of technological innovation by demonstrating that countries that did not have patent laws focused on a small set of industries where patents were less important.

Despite the difficulty of measuring patent scope, a small number of empirical studies have tried to relate aspects of patent scope to the rate of innovation. Examining the historical development of electrical lighting, automobiles, airplanes and radio, Merges and Nelson (1990) argued that the assertion of strong patent positions, and disagreements about patent rights, inhibited the broad development of these technologies. These case studies, while perhaps not definitive, do call into question the basic premise of much of the cumulative-innovation/patent-design literature—that initial inventors and subsequent inventors of improvements will reach agreements that can ameliorate the problems of inter-temporal knowledge spillover when innovation is sequential.

Sakakibara and Branstetter (2001) examined the effects of a change in the Japanese patent system in 1988, which effectively expanded patent protection in Japan by increasing patent scope. They hypothesized that if the increase in patent scope had increased the return to innovation, this should be reflected in both higher R&D spending and more patents produced. They found no evidence for either potential outcome.

2.3 Other theories and alternative institutions to IPR

In a provocative study, Boldrin and Levine (2008a) challenged one of the fundamental premises of the IPR literature, i.e. costless reproduction of innovation drives its *ex post* price to zero in the absence of IPR. They argued that in reality the cost of reproduction may not be costless. The capacity constraint of the imitator and the time lag that is usually observed from the time an innovation comes to fruition and when it is imitated both imply that innovators may well be able to capture enough rents to recoup the sunk costs of developing the innovation. Thus they showed that innovation survives in a perfectly competitive market.

Boldrin and Levine (2008b), after examining a large number of historical and contemporary cases and examples ranging from James Watt's invention of the steam engine to the more recent music piracy, concluded that IPR has hindered rather than encouraged innovation and that innovation has historically thrived under competition. In a more moderate critique of the recent trend of more rigorous enforcement of IPR, Lessig (2004) was more concerned with the increasingly more restrictive downstream access to existing innovations and argued for a more varied and flexible approach to the IPR system. Partly in response to the aggressive enforcement of copyright by the music industry, Romer (2002), was skeptical that the under-provision of music that might result from more liberal sharing of music would outweigh the benefit from reigning in monopoly distortions. Even when under-provision is substantial, he suggested that it might be corrected with non-IPR incentive mechanisms.

One such non-IPR scheme has been proposed by Kremer (1998). The basic idea of Kremer's patent buy-out proposal is for the government to purchase the patent from the inventor and then place the patented invention in the public domain. Thus, both the under-provision and the monopoly distortion problems can be solved. To determine the price of the patent, bids from private investors will be solicited in a sealed-bid second-price auction.

Among a number of schemes it can use to induce truthful valuations, the government will randomly select certain innovations to be sold to the bidders. Kremer (1998) argued that such a mechanism would entail less distortion compared with the patent system and less information requirement and other bureaucratic costs than *ex ante* incentive schemes such as government grant.

3. INTERNATIONAL PATENT PROTECTION HARMONIZATION AND WELFARE

Studies in this literature largely rely on models that pitch an imitative or less innovative South against an innovative North and investigate the welfare implications for both the South and the North of extending the North's IPR regime to the South.

Helpman (1993) investigated the welfare implications of international harmonization of IPR protection by examining four channels through which such effects may materialize: (1) terms of trade, (2) production composition, (3) availability of products, and (4) inter-temporal allocation of consumption. When IPR is tightened in the South, some manufacturing is relocated to the North. Thus demand for factors of production decreases in the South and increases in the North. The average price level rises in the North relative to the South. Terms of trade are therefore worsened for the South and improved for the North. With some manufacturing relocated from the low-cost South to the high-cost North, both countries lose from manufacturing inefficiency. The rate of innovation in the North responds to the tightening of IPR in the South by initially rising and then declining over time. The result is driven by the lower cost of capital in the North due to lower risk of imitation and rising cost of innovation over time. Helpman showed that this inter-temporal pattern of innovation and thus product availability hurts both the welfare of the North and the South. The bottom line of the paper is that the South clearly loses from tightening IPR in the South, whereas the welfare impact on the North is more complex and depends on the initial rate of imitation in the South and whether FDI is allowed in the South, among other factors.

FDI played a critical role in Lai's (1998) investigation of how strengthening IPR in the South affects the global rate of innovation and technology diffusion. He finds that the effects depend on whether technology diffusion takes place through FDI or imitation only. If technology diffuses to the South through Southern imitation, then strengthening IPR in the South lowers the rate of innovation and technology transfer and therefore widens the wage gap between the South and the North. On the other hand, if FDI is the primary agent of technology transfer, strengthening IPR in the South has the opposite effects.

The difference is driven by the different impacts of the two channels of technology diffusion on the cost of innovation in the North. When IPR is tightened in the South, the lives of Northern monopolies are extended. The resulting increase in demand for production labor is completely met in the South—due to its lower wage rate—and this relieves wage pressure in the North. Furthermore, as more production is moved from the North to the South, more resources in the North are freed up for innovation.

Lai and Qiu (2003) introduce a model that allows for innovation in both the South and the North. They find that having the South adopting the IPR standard of the North increases global welfare with the North gaining at the expense of the South. They recognize that strengthening IPR domestically generates an externality in the sense that the availability of more variety enhances foreign consumers' welfare, which the domestic economy does not internalize. A game-theoretic model is used to show that the Nash equilibrium level of IPR protection in the South is lower than that in the North. However, global welfare is higher under IPR harmonization. In order to make it incentive compatible for the South to adopt the North's IPR standard, they argue that the North should liberalize its traditional goods sector to the South so that both countries reap welfare gain from IPR harmonization.

In an analytical setting similar to Lai and Qiu, Grossman and Lai (2004) analyzed determinants of a country's incentive to protect intellectual property when countries interact with each other in a strategic fashion in setting their IPR policy. They showed that in non-cooperative settings countries have weaker incentives to protect IPR when they are engaged in international trade than when they are not, reflecting the international externality of IPR protection that we discussed earlier. They then defined an efficient global regime of IPR as one that provides the optimal aggregate incentives for innovation to inventors around the world. An important finding is that this efficient global regime of IPR protection can be achieved through different combinations of national IPR policies so that harmonization is neither necessary nor sufficient to achieve global efficiency. Grossman and Lai showed that the North is likely to gain at the expanse of the South in any move from the non-cooperative Nash equilibrium setting of national IPR policymaking for an efficient and harmonized global regime.

McCalman (2001) was one of the few studies that provided empirical estimates of the welfare implications of patent protection harmonization. Using data on twenty-nine mostly OECD countries, McCalman found large income transfers implicit in TRIPs: the U.S. receives a net transfer that is equal to 40 per cent of the gains of trade liberalization, while developing countries suffer losses of up to 64 per cent of the gains from trade liberalization. Transfers made by Canada, the U.K., and Japan to the U.S. would also be large.[2] It is important to note, however, that this analysis is a static one, and therefore does not include any benefits from the potentially higher incentive to innovate.

Unlike the previously discussed work, Diwan and Rodrik (1991) found that patent harmonization maximizes global welfare. A unique feature of their model is that the South and the North have different technological needs. For example, the North would like to develop drugs against cancer and heart disease, whereas the South would give priority to drugs against tropic diseases. Global R&D resources are limited, so that the South and the North have to compete for them in order for their preferred technologies to be developed. Extending IPR to the South increases the likelihood that the South's preferred technologies will be developed. A policy implication is that North–South negotiations regarding harmonization of IPR protection may proceed along product lines: concession from the South may be easier to obtain over products that are of greater importance to the South.

Lall (2003) highlighted the enormous heterogeneity among the developing countries in their innovative capability and level of economic development. Such heterogeneity is likely to produce a different impact of international IPR harmonization on these developing countries. Lall argued that TRIPs should recognize the differences in the benefits countries can expect to reap from a universal strengthening of IPR protection.

4. IPR, TECHNOLOGY DIFFUSION, TRADE, AND FDI

Much of the variation in conclusions about patent harmonization can be traced to the manner in which they treat trade and FDI as mechanisms of international technology transfer. The theoretical literature yields ambiguous predictions about the direction of the relationships among IPR, FDI and trade. The empirical literature has largely indicated a positive relationship between IPR and both trade and FDI, although the robustness of the results is not always clear.

4.1 IPR and trade

The theoretical literature, for example, the monopolistic competition model of Helpman and Krugman (1985), suggests two countervailing effects of strong IPR: market power and market expansion. Strong IPR enhances exporter's market power and induces a lower volume of sale; on the other hand, stronger IPR may open up new markets where exporters otherwise would fear to tread. The empirical analysis of the relationship between IPR and trade has investigated the monopolistic competition model as well as the simple gravity equation.

Maskus and Penubarti (1995) examined whether the distribution of bilateral trade across nations depends on the importing country's patent regime. They estimated the relationship between imports by seventy-seven developing and developed countries from twenty-two OECD countries in twenty-eight sectors and the strength of the importing country's patent regime. The patent index variable was found to have a significant and positive effect on imports, but mostly for the subgroup of large developing countries. The magnitude of the effect is, however, quite modest. Based on the information given in the paper, we calculate that if a large developing country improved its patent index from the lowest of all countries (0.902) to the highest of all countries (5.329), its imports would increase by only 3 per cent.

Smith (1999) also examined how sensitive trade was to national differences in patent regime. Her innovation was to link such sensitivity to the importing country's technological capability to imitate. She focused on exports from U.S. states to countries that she grouped into high imitation-threat countries and low imitation-threat ones. Her estimates indicated that a 1 per cent increase in the patent index would increase U.S. machine exports to the high-threat countries by 1.92 per cent, but would lead to a 6.94 per cent reduction in U.S. transportation equipment export to the weak threat group. These are enormous effects compared to what Maskus and Penubarti found. They seem to suggest that in high-threat countries the market expansion effect of IPR dominates the market power effect, whereas it is the opposite with the low-threat countries. She also constructed the counterfactual of full compliance with TRIPs by assuming that all countries brought their patent index to a certain value, 3 and 4 on a scale of 5 in her case. She found that if the high-threat countries brought their average patent index from their average of 1.27 to 4, the U.S. patent sensitive industries could increase their exports to these countries by $43.5 billion dollars (at 1992 dollar values).

In a related paper, Smith (2001) investigated whether and how U.S. firms' decision in servicing foreign markets was sensitive to the strength of the foreign country's patent regime. She examined three mechanisms through which American firms serve foreign markets: setting up affiliates, export, and licensing. She used a cross-section sample of U.S. bilateral exchange with fifty countries in 1989. Her findings showed that strong foreign patent rights increase all three kinds of foreign-market-serving activities by U.S. firms. Strong patent rights also create a location advantage in the sense that affiliate sales and licenses increase more than exports, particularly in countries with strong imitative abilities.

Liu and Lin (2005) is the only paper of which we are aware that examined the IPR and trade relationship for a newly industrialized economy. They investigated whether Taiwan's exports were related to the rigor of patent protection in the importing country. The trade partners of Taiwan were grouped into low imitative capability countries and high imitative capability ones, as in Smith (1999), with the imitative capability defined by the number of researchers per million of the population. They found that Taiwan exported more to those countries with stronger IPR protection. But unlike Smith (1999), Liu and Lin found that Taiwan exported more to those countries with a stronger R&D ability than Taiwan.

4.2 IPR and FDI

Mansfeld (1994) was the first comprehensive empirical study to investigate how IPR affects multinational firms' decision to invest in a foreign country. Mansfield's sample included ninety-four U.S. multinational corporations that reported their evaluation or perception of the rigor of IPR protection in sixteen developing and developed countries. He found that the importance of IPR for the companies' investment decision depends on the nature of the activity: 80 per cent of the firms considered IPR to be important for R&D facilities, but only 20 per cent thought it was important for sales and distribution functions.

Javorcik (2004) extended Mansfield's work to companies that reported their perception of the strength of IPR protection in Eastern Europe and the former Soviet Union for the period of 1989 to 1994. He tested two hypotheses: that the likelihood of IPR-sensitive sectors receiving FDI is related to the host country's IPR strength; and that the IPR regime affects foreign investor's choice as to whether to set up a production facility or merely engage in distribution. His findings affirmed those of Mansfeld. First, investors in sectors that rely on strong IPR tend to shun countries with a weak IPR regime. And, in all sectors, weak IPR tends to prompt FDI to focus on distribution rather than production.

McCalman (2004) investigated a similar issue to that of Javorcik (2004): whether the strength of a country's IPR regime affects the governance structure of the FDI it receives. He found that a non-monotonic relationship between IPR and FDI characterizes the behavior of Hollywood studios abroad: while Hollywood studios are likely to service a foreign market through an affiliate if the standards are either low or high, they are more likely to enter into a licensing agreement if a country offers a moderate degree of IPR protection.

4.3 IPR and licensing

The literature that investigates the relationship between IPR and technology transfer in the form of licensing largely finds that a stronger IPR regime induces more licensing. This seems to point in the direction of stronger IPR leading to more technology transfer. However, the limitation of this literature is that the magnitude of licensing is typically measured as dollars of licensing revenue. All else being equal, licensing dollars are likely to be higher where technology transfer is greater, but the increase in such revenue where IPR is stronger could simply reflect monopoly power allowing more revenue to be collected for a given amount of technology transferred.

Branstetter, Fisman, and Foley (2006) use data on U.S. affiliates in sixteen countries that have undergone IPR reform from 1982 to 1999. They found that royalty payments for technology transfer to those affiliates that used patents intensively increased by over 30 per cent after the reform. There was also a concurrent increase in R&D spending by these affiliates, although by a smaller proportion. They also reported that following the reform, non-resident patent filings at the U.S. Patent and Trademark Office had increased faster than domestic filings. While it could be that U.S. multinationals have been able to appropriate a higher rate of private return to their inventions without changing the rate of technology transfer, the evidence on R&D and patent filings suggests that at least some of the increase in royalty payments associated with IPR reform reflects an increase in technology transfer.

Branstetter et al. (2007) adopt the theoretical frameworks of Helpman (1993) and Lai (1998) to analyze the effect of strengthening IPR in developing countries on production and innovation in developing and developed countries. Their theoretical model confirms findings of the earlier literature, that is, strengthening IPR in the South reduces Southern imitation and encourages more FDI from the North and therefore more production shifting from the North to the South. They then take the prediction of their theory to data on the economic activities of foreign affiliates of U.S. multinationals. Their analysis exploits the potential impact of patent system reform in sixteen developed and developing countries and inquires whether such strengthening of IPR had led to an acceleration in the level of U.S.-multinational investment and increased production in their affiliate companies in these countries. The results show that the patent reform only boosts affiliate economic activities of those multinationals that made a larger than average technology transfer, measured by royalty payment receipts, to their affiliates before the patent reform.

The interpretation of these results is complicated by a number of issues. For example, patent reform is unlikely to be an exogenous event. Also, the patent reform may well have been undertaken as part of a trade liberalization agreement, which would affect both the shifting of affiliate activities among foreign countries by the U.S. parent and U.S. imports from these countries.

McCalman (2005) addressed the issue of whether stronger IPR regimes in destination countries leads to a faster diffusion of new products and technology. Using data on the international release patterns of sixty Hollywood movies from 1997 to 1999, he found a non-monotonic relationship between the two: moderate standards of IPR encourage the spread of movies, but very weak or very strong property rights tend to slow the speed with which American movies are released abroad.

Kim (2003) recounted Korea's experience with technology transfer in its early stage of industrialization. Without the benefit of a counterfactual analysis, Kim argued on the basis of Korea's experience that strong IPR would have hindered technology transfer to Korea. This could have further diminished indigenous learning that had been part of Korea's experience in the early stage of industrialization. He proposed that international harmonization of IPR should therefore be sensitive to the level of economic development.

Park and Lippoldt (2005) examines whether international technology transfer has responded to the strengthening of IPR in developing countries in the 1990s. Their study is different from Branstetter, Fisman, and Foley (2006) in a number of ways. They use four different indices to measure the national variation in IPR protection along four dimensions respectively. These are patent rights, copyrights, trademark rights, and enforcement effectiveness. They regressed the royalty and licensing receipts of U.S. firms from unaffiliated foreign sources on the four indicators of the strength of the foreign country's IPR regime. They did this for both different sources of royalty or licensing income (e.g. books, software) and for different industries. In addition to U.S. multinationals' licensing activities, they also used data on international alliances. They found the most robust effect of IPR in the effect of the patent rights index on licensing. The licensing–patent rights elasticity was statistically significant and ranged from 0.3 to 1.7.

5. IPR AND ECONOMIC GROWTH AND DEVELOPMENT

Most of the work reported above treats IPR as an exogenous policy choice, and then investigates its effect on economic behavior in the form of innovation, investment, and technology transfer. There is also a considerable literature that examines the political economy of IPR, looking at the economic determinants of IPR policy in the history of a country at different stages of economic development or a cross section of countries at different levels of economic development. At a low level of economic development, countries develop by bridging their technology gap through imitation. A weak IPR regime serves to reduce the cost of imitation. But as they develop indigenous innovation capability so that they start producing intellectual property, the welfare calculus changes such that countries find it in their own interest to strengthen IPR protection. This pattern of association between IPR and development has been affirmed in studies that investigate the historical relationship between the two, as well as those that use contemporary, cross-country data.

Lerner (2002) investigated determinants of the strength of patent protection in sixty countries with the highest GDP in 1997 over a 150-year period. In addition to the welfare calculus of innovation and imitation, Lerner argues that the economics of institutions suggests that administering an effective patent regime is costly to an authoritarian regime and that the evolution of institutions is path-dependent. He used four indicators to measure the rigor of a country's patent system: whether a country had a patent system, maximum duration of patent protection, time until the government could revoke or license a patent awarded to domestic applicants if it was not put to use, and the number of discriminatory provisions against foreign patent applicants. He found that the strength of patent rights is positively correlated with the level of economic development: wealthier countries are more likely to offer stronger patent protection. Democratic countries also provide stronger patent protection, all else being equal. Patent protection also varies depending on a country's legal tradition.

The correlation between IPR and economic development is confirmed in many studies using data on a cross section of countries. However, instead of the linear relationship between IPR and economic development that Lerner's analysis implied, these studies found a U-shaped relationship between the two. Using a cross section of seventy-seven developed and developing countries for 1984 and by regressing a modified version of the Rapp and Rozek (1990) patent index on the logarithm of per capita income and the square of it, Maskus (2000) found that the strength of IPR bottomed out at a per capita GNP of $523 (1984 dollar value) and the income variables explained half of the cross-country variation in the patent index. Maskus likened this to the "environmental Kuznets curve," which suggests that countries' environmental standards decline up to a certain level of development and then increase afterwards. But as Maskus acknowledged, the estimated parameters yield a U-shaped curve with a minimum that is at a very low level of development— only seventeen of the poorest countries in his sample had per capita income lower than $523.

Ginarte and Park (1997) ran similar regressions using their patent index. They included in their regressions income per capita, but not the squared term, R&D to GDP ratio, and proxies for education achievement, openness, political freedom, and market freedom. When the latter variables are added in their regressions, the coefficient of the income variable changed from positive and statistically significant to statistically insignificant. R&D intensity and market and political freedom are significant and raise the explained proportion of the variation in patent index from 0.31 to 0.51. Maskus (2000) managed to reproduce the U-shaped result using Ginarte and Park's data. But he was only able to retain the result using a different set of proxies for the other variables and obtained an R^2 of 0.37, substantially lower than Ginarte and Park's 0.51. On the other hand, the Ginarte and Park results do not necessarily negate a U-shaped relationship between IPR and economic development since per capita income and variables such as R&D intensity, and market and political freedom are likely to be highly correlated.

These results suggest a rather complex empirical interplay among income, IPR regimes, and other specific aspects of the development process such as education levels, R&D, and political/institutional variables. Chen and Puttitanun (2005) provide a structural interpretation for the U-shaped relationship between development and IPR. They present a theoretical model where the government chooses the optimal level of IPR protection balancing between the ease of imitating foreign technology and incentives for indigenous innovation. Under plausibly parameterized situations, there exists a U-shaped relationship between IPR and economic development, generated by the relative strength of the imitation motive and the innovation motive. For their empirical analysis, Chen and Puttitanun used the Ginarte and Park patent index and data for a panel of sixty-four developing countries. They estimated two equations, one for IPR and a patents production function. For the IPR equation, they regressed the patent index on GDP per capita and the squared term, tertiary education enrollment, economic freedom, international trade to GDP ratio, WTO membership dummy, and year specific effects. The inclusion of these other controls does not diminish the economic and statistical significance of the GDP per capita variables. It is not clear how well their model fits the data since they did not report R^2 of their regressions. But their point estimate suggests that the minimum level of IPR protection on the U-shaped curve occurs at a level of GDP per capita of $854 (in 1995 dollar values).

Hu and Png (2013) investigate whether stronger patent rights lead to faster economic growth using data on cross sections of up to fifty-four manufacturing industries in over seventy-two countries between 1981 and 2000. Their identification strategy is premised on the assumption that more patent-industries are likely to grow faster when national patent rights are strengthened. This research design allows them to address the issue of reverse causation from economic growth to patent regime change that plagues many earlier cross-country studies. They find that more patent-intensive industries did grow faster in countries where patent protection was stronger and the growth-promoting effect of strong patent rights was more robust in the 1990s than in the 1980s. For an industry with average knowledge intensity, a one standard deviation increase in patent rights in 1990 (equivalent to an increase from Spain to the U.S.) was associated with one-sixth of the average industry growth rate over the period. Patents "worked" through both encouraging factor accumulation and technical progress. One of the limitations of this study is that it does not identify the channel through which the growth-promoting effect of strong patent rights takes place, more rapid technology diffusion or higher level of domestic innovation. The welfare implications would be different.

The historical evolution of IPR protection in the U.S. shows that developed economies adjusted their IPR regime as they progressed through different stages of economic development. The U.S. has been a pioneer in building the modern patent system. Sokoloff and Khan (2001) and Khan (2005) provide an informative account of the early American experience with IPR. In sharp contrast with the British patent system at the time, the American patent system in the early nineteenth century was built with the goal of providing broad access to property rights on technology. One cannot help drawing a parallel between the early American patent system, which was initially a registration system, to the liberal use of "utility model" patents, also known as petty patents, in East Asian economies such as Japan, Korea, and Taiwan in their early stage of development in the twentieth century. With respect to copyrights, the U.S. statues have been protecting the rights of American citizens since 1790. But such protection was not extended to foreign citizens until 1891 when the U.S. signed the Berne Agreement. And it did so only when "the balance of trade in literary and artistic works [were] swinging in its favor" (Sokoloff and Khan, 2001). Khan (2005) concluded that in general Americans benefited from the country's disregard for foreign copyright in the nineteenth century.

Thus, overall, the history of now-developed countries' stance towards IPR belies their current stance that strong IPR medicine is good for economic development. Lall (2003) observed that: "Many rich countries used weak IPR protection in their early stages of industrialization to develop local technological bases, increasing protection as they approached the leaders."

6. CONCLUSIONS

Given the breadth and strength of the international efforts over the last fifteen years to extend U.S.-style IPR regimes to the less-developed world, it would be desirable if the economics profession could speak confidently about the consequences of such "harmonization" for the countries being asked to change their policies, and for the world at large. Unfortunately, the complex interplay of decisions regarding R&D, trade, FDI, licensing, other forms of technology transfer, and economic development make this difficult. At the risk of dangerous over-simplification, we suggest the following observations that seem to have theoretical and/or empirical support in the literature:

- Looking at the historical U.S., the post-war industrializing countries of East Asia—or today's industrializing countries, societies in the position of catching up to technological superiors—have preferred not to adopt the strongest of available IPR regimes. Though the theory of revealed preference does not strictly apply to social decisions, this certainly suggests that the process of development at this stage is not best served by harmonization to current U.S. standards.

- Analytically, the first-order effect of harmonization on developing countries is higher prices for patented goods and services. Empirical and simulation analyses indicate that this effect is significant, both in absolute terms, and relative to the magnitude of the gains that might be enjoyed by patent owners in the developed countries.

- The strongest theoretical argument for benefit to developing countries from stronger IPR is that it will encourage innovation in areas specific to their needs. Evidence for the empirical significance of this effect is extremely limited. The only real example that has been identified is research on tropical diseases. It is widely acknowledged, however, that the largest barrier to significant private investment in this area is the lack of significant buying power for any potential cures, rather than weak IPR.

- There does seem to be fairly robust evidence that a country's inbound trade, FDI, and licensing activity depends on its IPR regime, with regimes perceived as weak acting to inhibit all of these processes to some extent. Though it is difficult to quantify the distinct effects of particular mechanisms, or to identify clearly the effects of IPR separately from other aspects of a country's social, political, and economic institutions, it is likely that countries navigating the transition from middle income to fully industrialized need to pay attention to the effects of their IPR policies on their development trajectory.

- Even within the technologically advanced world, there is surprisingly little empirical evidence for the proposition that stronger IPR regimes produce faster innovation. While it is surely true that a global absence of property rights in inventions and other creations would inhibit technological advance, it does not follow that incremental strengthening of such rights, or an increase in the fraction of the world economy governed by the strongest rights, would lead to more innovation. Further, since investment in innovation is likely to be subject to decreasing returns within any given time period, extension of strong IPR to all countries is unlikely to be globally efficient.

Thus, the literature suggests overall that harmonization—defined as widespread adoption of U.S.-style IPR policies—is a policy initiative that hurts developing countries for the benefit of rich countries, with the possibility but no certainty that the global benefits exceed the global costs. If this is true, then the only defensible basis on which to pursue harmonization is for the rich countries to compensate the industrializing countries for making the change. If the compensation comes in an efficient form, such as the elimination of our own trade barriers, then it is likely that the overall initiative would be globally welfare-improving.

The most likely globally efficient IPR policy is not harmonization, but rather selective and gradual IPR reform, in which each country is allowed to devise policies that are appropriate for its particular technological situation and stage of development. For countries in the early stages of catch-up to the world technological frontier, this will mean policies that facilitate technology transfer and even a certain amount of imitation. At some point, however, countries need to recognize that movement toward fuller IPR protection will facilitate foreign FDI and licensing. Eventually, as a domestic innovation sector emerges, countries will find it in their interests to provide greater protection in order to protect their own inventions. There is nothing wrong with the rich countries encouraging such a staged process of reform, but suggestions that early adoption of our system furthers less developed countries' self-interest are at best unsupportable by the evidence and likely to be perceived as selfish and hypocritical.

NOTES

1. See Merges and Nelson (1990) for a discussion of complex vs. simple technologies.
2. The estimates of welfare implications of trade liberalization were obtained from Harrison et al. (1995).

REFERENCES

Boldrin, Michele and David K. Levine. 2008a. "Perfectly Competitive Innovation." *Journal of Monetary Economics*. 55: 435–53.

Boldrin, Michele and David K. Levine. 2008b. *Against Intellectual Property*. Cambridge: Cambridge University Press.

Branstetter, Lee, Raymond Fisman, and C. Fritz Foley. 2006. "Do Stronger Intellectual Property Rights Increase International Technology Transfer? Empirical Evidence from U.S. Firm-Level Panel Data." *Quarterly Journal of Economics*. 121 (1): 321–49.

Chen, Yongmin and Thitima Puttitanun. 2005. "Intellectual Property Rights and Innovation in Developing Countries." *Journal of Development Economics*. 78: 474–93.

Cohen, W.M., R.R. Nelson, and J. Walsh. 2000. "Protecting Their Intellectual Assets: Appropriability Conditions and Why U.S. Manufacturing Firms Patent (or Not)," National Bureau of Economic Research Working Paper No. 7552.

Ginarte, J.C. and W.G. Park. 1997. "Determinants of Patent Rights: A Cross-national Study." *Research Policy*. 26: 283–301.

Grossman, G. and Edwin Lai. 2004. "International Protection of Intellectual Property." *American Economic Review*. 94 (5): 1635–53.

Harrison, G.W., T.F. Rutherford, and D.G. Tarr. 1995. "Quantifying the Uruguay Round," in Martin, W. and Winters, L.A. (eds.), "The Uruguay Round and The Developing Economies," World Bank Discussion Paper 307.

Helpman, E. 1993. "Innovation, Imitation, and Intellectual Property Rights." *Econometrica*. 61: 1247–80.

Helpman, E. and P.R. Krugman. 1987. *Market Structure and Foreign Trade*. Cambridge, MA: MIT Press.

Henderson, R., A. Jaffe, and Trajtenberg, M. 1998. "Universities as a Source of Commercial Technology: A Detailed Analysis of University Patenting, 1965–1988." *Review of Economics and Statistics*. 80: 127–99.

Hu, Albert G.Z. and Gary H. Jefferson. 2009. "A Great Wall of Patents: What Is behind China's Recent Patent Explosion?" *Journal of Development Economics*. 90 (1): 57–68.

Hu, Albert G.Z. and Ivan P.L. Png. 2013. "Patent Rights and Economic Growth: Cross-country Evidence." *Oxford Economic Papers*. 65 (3): 675–98.

Hui, Kai-Lung and Ivan P.L. Png. 2002. "On the Supply of Creative Work: Evidence from the Movies." *American Economic Review*. 92 (2): 217–20.

Jaffe, A. and J. Lerner. 2004. *Innovation and Its Discontents: How Our Broken Patent System Is Endangering Innovation and Progress, and What to Do About It*. Princeton, NJ: Princeton University Press.

Javorcik, Beata Smarzynska. 2004. "The Composition of Foreign Direct Investment and Protection of Intellectual Property Rights: Evidence from Transition Economies." *European Economic Review*, 48: 39–62.

Kanwar, Sunil and Robert Evanson. 2003. "Does Intellectual Property Protection Spur Technological Change?" *Oxford Economic Papers*. 55: 235–64.

Khan, B. Zorina. 2005. *The Democratization of Invention*. Cambridge: Cambridge University Press.

Kim, Limsu. 2003. "Technology Transfer and Intellectual Property Rights: The Korean Experience." UNCTAD, issue paper no. 2: <http://www.ictsd.org/pubs/ictsd_series/iprs/CS_kim.pdf> (accessed 6 September 2013).

Klemperer, P.D. 1990. "How Broad Should the Scope of Patent Protection Be?" *Rand Journal of Economics*. 21 (1): 113–30.

Kortum, S. and J. Lerner. 1998. "Stronger Protection or Technological Revolution: What Is Behind the Recent Surge in Patenting?" *Carnegie-Rochester Series on Public Policy*. 48: 247–304.

Kremer, Michael. 1998. "Patent Buyouts: A Mechanism for Encouraging Innovation." *Quarterly Journal of Economics*. 113 (4): 1137–67.

Lai, Edwin L.C. 1998. "International Intellectual Property Rights Protection and the Rate of Product Innovation." *Journal of Development Economics*. 55: 133–53.

Lai, Edwin L.C. and Larry D. Qiu. 2003. "The North's Intellectual Property Rights Standard for the South?" *Journal of International Economics*. 59: 83–209.

Lall, Sanjaya. 2003. "Indicators of the Relative Importance of IPRs in Developing Countries." *Research Policy*. 32: 1657–80.

Lanjouw, Jean O. and Iain Cockburn. 2001. "New Pills for Poor People? Evidence After GATT." *World Development*. 29: 265–89.

Lerner, Josh. 2002. "The Economics of Technology and Innovation: 150 Years of Patent Protection." *American Economic Review Papers and Proceedings*. 92: 221–5.

Lessig, Lawrence. 2004. *Free Culture: The Nature and Future of Creativity*. New York: Penguin Press.

Liu, Wen-Hsien and Ya-Chi Lin. 2005. "Foreign Patent Rights and High-Tech Exports: Evidence from Taiwan." *Applied Economics*. 37: 1543–55.

Mansfeld, E. 1994. "Intellectual Property Protection, Foreign Direct Investment and Technology Transfer." International Finance Corporation discussion paper no. 19.

Maskus, Keith. 2000. *Intellectual Property Rights in the Global Economy*. Washington, DC: Institute for International Economics.

Maskus, Keith E. and Mohan Penubarti. 1995. "How Trade-related Are Intellectual Property Rights?" *Journal of International Economics*. 39: 227–48.

McCalman, P. 2004. "Foreign Direct Investment and Intellectual Property Rights: Evidence from Hollywood's Global Distribution of Movies and Videos." *Journal of International Economics*. 62: 107–23.

McCalman, Phillip. 2001. "Reaping What You Sow: An Empirical Analysis of International Patent Harmonization." *Journal of International Economics*. 55: 161–86.

McCalman, Phillip. 2005. "International Diffusion and Intellectual Property Rights: An Empirical Analysis." *Journal of International Economics*. 67: 353–72.

Merges, R. and R. Nelson. 1990. "On the Complex Economics of Patent Scope." *Columbia Law Review*. 90 (4): 839–916.

Moser, Petra. 2005. "How Do Patent Laws Influence Innovation? Evidence from Nineteenth-century World Fairs," *American Economic Review*. 95 (4): 1214–36.

Mowery. D. and A. Ziedonis. 2002. "Academic Patent Quality and Quantity Before and After the Bayh-Dole Act in the United States." *Research Policy*. 31 (3): 399–418.

Nordhaus, William D. 1969. *Invention, Growth and Welfare: A Theoretical Treatment of Technological Change*. Cambridge, MA: MIT Press.

Park, Walter G. and Douglas Lippoldt. 2005. "International Licensing and the Strengthening of Intellectual Property Rights in Developing Countries during the 1990s." *OECD Economic Studies*. 40: 7–42.

Rapp, Richard and Richard Rozek. 1990. "Benefits and Costs of Intellectual Property Rights in Developing Countries." National Economic Research Associates (White Plains, NY), working paper no. 3.

Romer, Paul. 2002. "When Should We Use Intellectual Property Rights?" *American Economic Review*. 92 (2): 213–16.

Sakakibara, Mariko and Lee Branstetter. 2001. "Do Stronger Patents Induce More Innovation? Evidence from the 1988 Japanese Patent Law Reforms." *Rand Journal of Economics*. 32 (1): 77–100.

Scherer, F.M. 1972. "Nordhaus' Theory of Optimal Patent Life: A Geometric Reinterpretation." *American Economic Review*. 62: 422–7.

Scotchmer, Suzanne. 1991. "Standing on the Shoulders of Giants: Cumulative Research and the Patent Law." *Journal of Economic Perspectives*. 5 (1): 29–41.

Scotchmer, Suzanne. 1996. "Protecting Early Innovators: Should Second-generation Products Be Patentable?" *Rand Journal of Economics*. 27 (2): 322–31.

Scotchmer, Suzanne and Jerry Green. 1990. "Novelty and Disclosure in Patent Law." *Rand Journal of Economics*. 21 (1): 131–46.

Smith, P.J. 1999. "Are Weak Patent Rights a Barrier to US Exports?" *Journal of International Economics*. 48: 151–77.

Smith, P.J. 2001. "How Do Foreign Patent Rights Affect US Exports, Affiliate Sales, and Licenses." *Journal of International Economics*. 55: 411–39.

Sokoloff, Kenneth L. and Zorina B. Khan. 2001. "Intellectual Property Institutions in the United States: Early Development and Comparative Perspective." *Journal of Economic Perspectives*. 15 (3): 233–46.

4

Intellectual Property in the Twenty-First Century: Will the Developing Countries Lead or Follow?*

Jerome H. Reichman

I. INTRODUCTION: EMERGING ROLE OF THE BRIC COUNTRIES

The precise connection between intellectual property and economic development varies over time from country to country and region to region.[1] For example, one cannot doubt that intellectual property laws played a major role in the United States' development and economic growth over the past three decades. Yet, the moment one digs deeper, one discovers that, until 1982, the United States had one of the developed world's most pro-competitive patent laws (i.e., least protective); until 1978, it had relatively weak copyright laws; and until the 1980s, it had an aggressively interventionist competition law along with a robust doctrine of patent misuse.[2] Somehow, the U.S. economy managed to survive and thrive in this relatively low protectionist, highly competitive environment.

Similarly, Japan, India, China, Korea, Malaysia, and Brazil all managed to attain relatively high levels of economic growth without strong intellectual property rights.[3] The astounding success of the Indian pharmaceutical industry that began in the 1970s was achieved by means of a state policy that largely prohibited the patenting of medicinal products as such.[4] This phenomenon reminds us that intellectual property rights are but one component of overall economic growth; that different states have different factor endowments; and that in many countries, especially those at an early stage of development, a sound agricultural policy or a sound pro-competitive industrial policy with a supportive political and legal infrastructure are more likely to stimulate economic growth than intellectual property laws.[5]

At the same time, we may confidently agree that countries such as China, India, Brazil, Korea, Malaysia, Indonesia, Argentina, Russia, South Africa, and many other emerging economies will not reach their full economic potential without suitable intellectual property regimes.[6] For example, policymakers in most Asian countries that are already committed to becoming players in the knowledge economy clearly understand they will not reach the frontiers of that economy,[7] nor will they convert their economies' intangible, nonrivalrous outputs into tradeable knowledge goods, without articulating appropriate intellectual property laws and policies, along with a whole set of interrelated economic and political foundations that are essential to maintaining a viable post-industrial economy.[8] To this end, China's third amendment of its Patent Law in 2008 expressly reflects "the needs of development of China herself," which require "the promotion of . . . independent innovation and the establishment of an innovation-oriented country."[9]

The moment one looks at Asia as a regional group, one is struck by how much the IP scenario has changed over the past twenty-five years, i.e., since the Organisation for Economic Co-operation and Development (OECD) countries began to press for higher, relatively harmonized worldwide IP standards under the aegis of what eventually became the TRIPS Agreement of 1994.[10] As many critics have observed, the TRIPS Agreement produced a regime that deliberately favored those OECD countries that already possessed developed national systems of innovation and whose multinational companies owned plenty of patented high-tech products to sell or manufacture around the world.[11] There was a built-in disposition to favor big companies seeking rents from existing innovations—or those in the pipeline—at the cost of making future innovations more difficult, especially for less technically advanced countries.[12]

Robert Ostergard recently described the "development dilemma" that TRIPS posed for poorer countries in the following terms:

> [I]f they open their domestic markets to trade, they face political and economic pressure to protect foreign IP; if they protect foreign IP, they create conditions that force them to abandon their goal to obtain IP as inexpensively as possible.[13]

Of course, these IP concessions were partly offset by trade concessions in other areas (side payments), such as textiles, agriculture, and traditionally manufactured goods, a calculus that worked differently for different countries.

Yet, as often happens in international law, efforts to rig a regime for short-term advantages may turn out, in the medium and long term, to boomerang against those who pressed hardest for its adoption. In my very first article on this subject, I warned that by reaching for high levels of international protection (that could not change in response to less-favorable domestic circumstances), technology-exporting countries risked fostering conditions that could erode their technological superiority and resulting terms of trade over time.[14] As more technology-importing countries discovered and cultivated their own innovative strengths and capacities, they would benefit both from the worldwide system of incentives and protections that the TRIPS Agreement had established, as well as from location and other endowment factors,[15] at the expense of leading developed countries that took their own technical superiority for granted.

In short, given the "incipient transnational system of innovation"[16] that had begun to emerge from the TRIPS Agreement, there was every reason to expect that the BRIC group as a whole,[17] and many other emerging economies, would gradually become major competitors in the knowledge economy itself, with growing potential to match and challenge the advanced OECD countries' preexisting comparative advantages in this area.[18]

That this transformation has been occurring all around us is too solidly evidenced for us to review here in detail.[19] What this chapter will focus on, instead, is how those developing countries with growing technological prowess should accommodate their own national systems of innovation to the worldwide intellectual property regime emerging in the post-TRIPS period, with a view to maximizing global economic welfare in the foreseeable future.[20]

II. AVOIDING PROTECTIONIST EXCESSES

High-protectionist visions of intellectual property law have become a kind of latter-day religion promoted by the special interests that have long dominated the political scene in the United States, the European Union (EU), and Japan.[21] The BRIC countries in particular will thus need to inoculate themselves against succumbing to these same high-protectionist delusions while there is still time.

If it remains true that a country cannot play in the knowledge economy without suitable intellectual property rights (IPRs),[22] experience in many OECD countries is demonstrating that badly configured, unbalanced, overprotectionist IP regimes gradually stifle innovation by making inputs to future innovation too costly and too cumbersome to sustain over time.[23] Such regimes also enable large corporations that are sometimes slothful innovators to accumulate pools of cross-licensed patents that create barriers to entry for the truly innovative small- and medium-sized firms.[24] Properly designed IPRs do, however, protect innovative small- and medium-sized firms from the predatory practices of their larger competitors.

It is widely recognized that the patent system in the United States is emerging from a period of crisis. Among other problems, the cumulative costs of litigation generated by a plethora of weak patents that increasingly pervaded the upstream research dimension threaten to exceed the aggregate returns from patented innovation, especially in the field of information technologies.[25] There is still no consensus about how to reform the patent system, despite broad agreement that reforms are needed. As time passes, the demands of different industries become more contradictory and conflictual, particularly with regard to the information technology and biotechnology sectors.[26] For these and other reasons, the European Patent Office has expressed concerns about the uncertain future of the world patent system.[27]

None of these domestic tensions deterred either the United States Trade Representative (USTR) or the European Commission (EC) from demanding that the rest of the world adopt a proposed Substantive Patent Law Treaty that, at the international level, would have locked in place most of the unsolved problems that confront the domestic system of innovation in the United States.[28] The rest of the world might logically ask which version of U.S. patent law the USTR now seeks to export, given that the U.S. Supreme Court has so profoundly changed it in a series of recent cases.[29] By the same token, one may also ask why certain Asian patent offices blindly supported these same proposals for a further upward ratcheting of international patent norms. It was as if their governments were asking the other OECD countries, "Please give us all your insoluble problems and contradictions as soon as possible, so we can undermine our own national systems of innovation too."[30]

Of course, the more that high- and middle-income developing countries become players in the knowledge economy, the more they share some of the fears and risks that usually underlie demands for higher levels of protection by powerful sectors of the advanced technology-exporting countries. For example, Asian entrepreneurs want their own exports of knowledge goods protected in the developing countries whose markets they increasingly penetrate through foreign direct investment (FDI), licensing, or sales of high-tech products. They also want to maintain flows of FDI and market-driven technology transfer into their own countries, in order to bolster their growing technological capacities.

Yet, such concerns do not necessarily add up to a compelling case for higher levels of international intellectual property protection. On the contrary, the TRIPS Agreement itself provided an unprecedented platform of IP protection for exports after 2000,[31] and there is little evidence that this platform remains insufficient for the needs of Asian exporters, or for those of other emerging economies for the foreseeable future. Meanwhile, the relation between FDI and IPRs itself remains ambiguous, given that OECD technology exporters need entry into emerging economies as much as these economies need FDI and market-driven technology transfer from the OECD countries.[32]

In China, India, and Brazil, moreover, knowledge economy skills and capacities have apparently reached the point where the stimulating effects of IPRs will influence different sectors and stakeholders quite differently, depending on the extent to which they are still driven by imitation-related innovation or investments in basic—or at least relatively original—R&D.[33] Increasingly, tensions arise between those who demand relatively strong patent protection for, say, research-driven pharmaceuticals, and those who demand a more forgiving, pro-competitive approach favoring generic pharmaceutical producers and exporters.[34] In either case, how to protect cumulative and sequential innovation—as distinct from path-breaking innovation—becomes an ever more pressing problem as more small- and medium-sized firms acquire a taste and capacity for such innovation.[35]

A parallel set of problems that the BRIC countries and other emerging economies increasingly face is how to adjust the shifting relations between private and public goods. Education, public health, agricultural improvement, scientific research, and other important areas are still heavily dependent on the public sector in most of these countries. Yet international intellectual property rights may impede the acquisition of scientific[36] and educational materials;[37] essential medicines;[38] and seeds, stocks, and fertilizers needed for economic growth.[39] The extent to which these same types of impediments will adversely affect the development and dissemination of environmental technologies still remains to be seen.[40]

Even with regard to the role of public-sector investment in basic research, which has been crucial in the most developed countries, there remains great uncertainty about the kind of regulatory regimes needed to ensure an appropriate social return from publicly funded or publicly generated research initiatives.[41]

III. DESIGNING INTELLECTUAL PROPERTY LAWS FOR THE TWENTY-FIRST CENTURY

As the high- and middle-income developing countries seek to strengthen their own national systems of innovation, they must decide how to address the challenges posed by a now highly articulated worldwide intellectual property system. This task requires policy decisions affecting the growth of a knowledge economy, rather than an economy based on physical, capital, or natural resources, which have relatively little to do with intellectual property laws as such.[42]

To the extent that intellectual property laws do play an ancillary but important role, there are, roughly speaking, two different approaches on the table. One is to play it safe by sticking to time-tested IP solutions implemented in OECD countries, with perhaps a relatively greater emphasis on the flexibilities still permitted under TRIPS (and not overridden by relevant FTAs).[43] The other approach is to embark upon a more innovative and even experimental path, with a view to addressing and perhaps solving the very problems that the advanced technology-exporting countries currently find so daunting.[44]

A. From "fair followers" to "counter-harmonization"[45]

Most technical assistance experts and many academics take the view that developing countries should stick to time-tested IP solutions while exploiting available exceptions and limitations recognized by developed countries. This approach affords the advantages of requiring relatively modest lawyering inputs (although it still requires more lawyering than one might think);[46] it may reduce internal debate about appropriate solutions; and it may deflect political and economic pressures from powerful countries whose own prior practices cast a comforting shadow.[47]

While this strategy seems politically expedient, Professor Dreyfuss and I remain skeptical for one main reason. At the end of the day, discreetly following in the technology-exporting countries' IP footsteps will merely bring the high- and middle-income developing countries face to face with the serious problems that the OECD countries have themselves failed to solve. It will place everyone in an equally unsatisfactory position, without having enhanced the governance skills of developing countries and without enriching the incipient transnational system of innovation with much-needed empirical evidence about alternative IP solutions to an array of apparently intractable problems. A deliberate policy of "counter-harmonization," instead, could "reduce the collective administrative costs of adopting an alternative patent regime, create a transnational 'counter-culture,' and increase the costs . . . of extralegal retaliation."[48]

Consider, for example, the choking and blocking effects that a proliferation of patents rooted in low non-obviousness standards increasingly produced for the software and, arguably, biotech industries in the United States and elsewhere.[49] This phenomenon elicits pressures for "quality patents" that would presumably result from higher non-obviousness standards,[50] and the U.S. Supreme Court has recently taken a first step in this direction,[51] pending further legislative reforms on the table.[52] But higher non-obviousness standards, without more, will also expose costly cumulative and sequential innovation to free-riding forms of market failure, which was the risk that induced the Federal Circuit to lower its non-obviousness standard in the first place.[53]

From this perspective, both the U.S. and foreign experiences reveal a cyclical or pendular shifting between states of under- and over-protection,[54] without policymakers ever having seriously addressed the underlying question of how appropriately to protect cumulative and sequential innovation at the core of much present-day technological progress.[55] This same question has now begun to surface in countries such as India and China.[56] For example, efforts to codify a relatively stiff standard of non-obviousness in the new Indian patent law were self-consciously aimed at freeing up space for India's thriving generic pharmaceutical industry.[57] But these same efforts elicited complaints that India's adoption of stiff eligibility standards would deprive the more research-driven pharmaceutical sector of sufficient incentives to invest in derivative applications of medicines initially developed abroad.[58]

Besides an appropriately selective non-obviousness standard, in other words, India and similarly situated developing countries need an appropriately designed domestic regime that stimulates investment in cumulative and sequential innovation. Such a regime must also avoid creating barriers to entry or unduly hindering the transformation of today's technological outputs into inputs for tomorrow's follow-on applications.[59]

Of course, the traditionalists would respond by recommending greater use of utility model laws,[60] and there has been a trend towards enacting such laws in the developing countries, including China.[61] But the limits and weaknesses of patent-like utility model laws have been well documented since the 1970s at least, as are their inherent logical and economic contradictions, even if such regimes often prove better than nothing.[62] Moreover, the Japanese experience suggests that advantages accruing from the use of utility models to surround foreign patents with tripwires of small-scale blocking effects tend to peter out once the country relying on this tactic shifts its own domestic emphasis to relatively basic research.[63] Sooner or later, utility model laws thus merely re-propose the same fundamental tensions that arise when too many patents cluster around the same rapidly developing technologies, each of which is dependent on preceding innovation and may stimulate equally dependent successive applications.[64]

In other words, the clear boundaries between property rights that are a presupposed necessary condition for efficient trading of knowledge goods have become inherently blurred and overlapping as a consequence of the patent law's struggle to keep abreast of the changing conditions of technological progress.[65] Why should the BRIC countries, for example, not address this and other related problems head on, instead of falling into the same old traps and pitfalls that undermine systems of innovation in the most developed countries?[66]

That the traditionally structured OECD innovation framework has become increasingly "brittle" over time[67] appears from even a quick review of its three main premises:

(1) Upstream scientific research, primarily theoretical in nature, was to remain immune from IPRs and to be regulated by the sharing norms of Mertonian science.[68]

(2) Routine innovation (largely cumulative and sequential in nature) was primarily protected as know-how by trade secret laws, which established

a vast semi-commons accessible to all routine engineers willing to reverse-engineer by honest means, while also providing investors with
natural lead time.[69]

(3) Legal monopolies were to be bestowed only on significant inventions,
beyond the reach of routine engineers, while competition rooted in
legally protected lead time and other comparative advantages drove the
innovation process.[70]

Today, instead, universities aggressively patent government-funded research
results.[71] Many countries protect even scientific databases as such,[72] and there
is no clear line between theoretical and applied research. The sharing norms of
science have broken down to the point where they can only be maintained by
contractually constructed scientific commons that artfully manage legal, economic, and technical restrictions on data, materials, and information.[73] At the
same time, the technical know-how underlying cumulative and sequential
innovation can seldom be kept secret for very long. Hence, trade secret
protection also breaks down, and investors faced with mounting front-end
costs suffer from a chronic shortage of natural lead time.[74]

In response, patents, copyrights, and *sui generis* laws expand in all directions to absorb cumulative and sequential innovations that lack other refuges
from free-riding appropriators and from the risk of market failure.[75] This
trend, in turn, produces mounting thickets of rights that impede both technological progress and research, while the risk of endless litigation over uncertain
legal boundaries leads to daunting litigation costs and anticompetitive, defensive patent pools held by big, but often slothful, technology distributors.[76]

B. Where developing country leadership could make a difference

The incipient transnational system of innovation emerging from the TRIPS
Agreement will simply reproduce these same unpropitious conditions if the
BRIC countries and their allies discreetly follow the models embedded in the
most developed intellectual property systems. What we need instead are new
models experimentally derived from bold attempts to deal directly with these
and other unsolved problems.

I cannot, within the confines of this short chapter, explore these problems in
depth, although more and more academic attention is being focused upon
them.[77] Let me instead put forward a partial list of initiatives that the BRIC
countries, and other emerging economies, working perhaps within the framework of a WIPO Development Agenda,[78] could consider. The list is not meant
to be exhaustive, only suggestive, but it does give an idea of the kind of
initiatives that are needed.

1. Measures Concerning Patents. In 1997, I suggested that developing countries could help to accommodate international minimum standards of patent protection to their national development goals by adopting relatively stringent eligibility standards covering subject matter, novelty, non-obviousness, and disclosure.[79]

a. Eligibility standards in BRIC countries. The one country that has most aggressively pursued this strategy so far is India, which particularly seeks to promote its pharmaceutical industry. As Professor Kapczynski's research confirms, India's patent law denies subject-matter eligibility to new uses of known substances and new forms of known substances that do not enhance "efficacy." Its stiff non-obviousness standard requires "a technical advance" or economic significance, all with a view to discouraging "me-too" and derivative patents that would circumscribe the space in which generic producers could operate.[80] Although India cannot legally vary eligibility standards to suit the needs of different industries,[81] its generally high standards are reinforced by pre-grant and post-grant opposition procedures, and by stringent disclosure requirements,[82] which other high- and middle-income developing countries would do well to consider.

The level of non-obviousness to be established under the recently enacted third revision of the Chinese Patent Law was not clear at the time of writing. Article 22 reportedly requires "prominent substantive features" and "notable" progress (as distinct from utility models that require only "substantive features" and "progress"); but the Patent Examiner's Guidelines simply invoke the "person skilled in the art" standard used in most OECD countries without further illuminating the drafters' intent.[83]

The new Chinese law definitely adopts a broader, more absolute standard of novelty than before,[84] and it will allow a prior art defense to an infringement action that "to some extent shifts [the] validity issue of a patent from . . . [the examiners] to the court."[85] The Chinese law will also require disclosure of origin for genetic resources, and may invalidate a pending patent if laws and regulations pertaining to licit procurement and use of such resources have been violated.[86]

It seems likely that the problems of low-quality patents that have recently plagued developed countries would become more pernicious if allowed to take root in high- and middle-income developing countries. In particular, low standards of non-obviousness would allow powerful foreign companies that accumulate patents on incremental innovations to block local improvers in developing countries and to maintain patent pools that could create formidable barriers to entry.

Even the United States has recently begun to elevate its eligibility standards,[87] although not as steeply as those in India. Because governments cannot discriminate against foreigners,[88] however, high standards of eligibility must apply equally to local inventors. The latter remain free to patent abroad, whatever the status of their inventions at home,[89] while "second-tier" protection may be available to stimulate local investment in small-scale innovation.[90]

Needless to say, the policy space for evaluating eligibility standards against local development needs could shrink drastically if such standards were harmonized by TRIPS-plus specifications under a Substantive Patent Law Treaty (SPLT).[91] Developing countries should accordingly continue to resist such a harmonization exercise.

b. Problems on the frontiers of science. Another reason for resisting premature harmonization exercises is that, even in developed countries, experts remain uncertain how best to resolve problems affecting cutting-edge technologies,[92] which makes evaluation of the relevant issues even more difficult in developing countries. For example, recent studies of the seminal genomic discoveries carried out at Duke University, under a grant from the National Institutes of Health and the Department of Energy, suggest a number of recurring problems on the frontiers of science that sometimes pose unresolved problems for the patent system as a whole.[93] These include:

- Broad foundational patents that can block research and downstream applications and that produce high transaction costs for would-be users.[94] For example, polymerase chain reaction (PCR) and recombinant DNA cloning were covered by a relatively small number of patents, with narrowly averted blocking effects.[95]
- An even bigger problem arises when basic research platforms are covered by multiple patents held by dispersed owners, public and private.[96]
- More generally, thickets of overlapping patents may cover a research platform or multiple components of an end product, especially in interdisciplinary research fields. This problem arises, for example, with regard to microarrays, synthetic biology (which combines life sciences, computer science, and electrical engineering), and now even nanotechnology.[97]
- With particular regard to information technology, hundreds of patents on small contributions may yield patent thickets with vague boundaries, resulting in holdups and excessive litigation.[98] A similar, if less dramatic process affects private-sector innovators in biotechnology,[99] although the extent of this problem in that sector remains controversial.[100]
- Massing of patents for defensive purposes (especially in IT) may block entry to competitors and innovators.[101]

All these problems—and the resulting transaction costs—were then worsened by the proliferation of low-quality patents, especially in the United States.

These and related problems could inhibit research and keep innovators in BRIC countries and other emerging economies from realizing their full potential in the biotechnology and information industries. They increasingly deter private-sector researchers and investors in developed countries from exploring promising routes,[102] while placing universities in a delicate legal position as academics ignore patents when conducting cutting-edge research.[103] Worse, they could eventually complicate the race for innovative climate change technology if future massive government funding were to replicate problems now experienced in biotech and IT.[104]

Generally speaking, the evidence points to the emergence of complex frontier sciences that may require integrated management in their upstream dimension (and sometimes even in the applications domain).[105] A holistic approach to intellectual infrastructure may then become essential. But the patent system operates on an ad hoc, case-by-case basis that is not designed to address or govern such complex innovation systems. There results a risk of systemic conflict between the holistic needs of frontier science (with its own corresponding innovation policy) and the methodology of traditional intellectual property laws.[106]

i. Some possible solutions. In principle, at least five primary measures, with varying degrees of nuance, can be envisioned to address these challenges.

- A broad research exemption for the experimental users of patented inventions to find new inventions, to invent around old ones, or to develop improvements.[107]
- An administrative or judicial power to require that the invention be made available on a nonexclusive license.[108]
- An anti-blocking provision, normally in the form of a compulsory license for dependent patents, that allows improvers to avoid infringing a dominant patent.[109]
- An "essential facilities" doctrine, familiar from competition law theory and practice, that would allow the pooling of overlapping patents within a platform technology.[110]
- Compulsory licensing, either for government (noncommercial) use or to enable third parties to supply the market in the public interest.[111]

In practice, the availability of these solutions, and still others that have been proposed in developed countries,[112] varies from country to country and is always somewhat problematic. Yet, nothing in the multilateral conventions prevents developing countries from implementing these and other related provisions in their domestic laws.

U.S. patent law currently lacks a bona fide research exemption, and there is little chance that legislative reform will fill this gap. The formal position in the European Union is better,[113] but actual state practice seems to have narrowed the factual availability of this exception. If so, that state of affairs would afford an obvious opportunity for "counter-harmonization"[114] where developing countries could take the lead.

The Chinese Patent Law, as amended in 2008, codifies a so-called Bolar exception, which permits generic producers to reverse-engineer patented medicines and to conduct clinical trials prior to the expiration of the patent.[115]

A WTO panel upheld the legitimacy of this exception under Article 30 of the TRIPS Agreement.[116] Whether Chinese patent law will maintain a broad exception for scientific research generally was not clear at the time of writing.[117]

There is no anti-blocking provision in U.S. patent law.[118] Hence, if a dominant patentee and an improver bargain to impasse, as occurs from time to time, the dominant patentee may keep a patented improvement off the market because its sale or use would infringe the former's patent.[119] While this result may suit a dominant patentee because it defends him or her from a serious threat of competition, it lessens social welfare by depriving the public of the improved product,[120] unless the government intervenes with a public interest compulsory license.

Many European countries have accordingly codified compulsory licenses for dependent patents,[121] which are perfectly compatible with the TRIPS Agreement,[122] although European patent authorities had, until recently, been reluctant to grant them in practice. Anecdotal evidence suggests that the authorities in Europe may now be more willing to grant such licenses and that, even in the past, parties in Italy, Germany, and the United Kingdom tended to bargain around the possible threat of such an anti-blocking measure, despite the fact that few such licenses were actually granted.[123]

While China will include a dependent compulsory license in its pending patent reform, its availability in other developing countries is not widely reported.[124] Here, in other words, one finds a relatively uncontroversial candidate for actual harmonization under TRIPS, rather than "counter-harmonization," that developing countries should wholeheartedly embrace.

Even in the absence of a patented improvement as such, the complexity of present-day inventions in which numerous overlapping patents may be combined makes it advisable that courts have the power to deny permanent injunctions for infringement in the public interest and to allow compensation instead, preferably in the form of reasonable royalties. This use of a liability rule, rather than a property rule, seems especially pertinent when the parties are not in head-to-head competition, or when one of them does not actually work the patents it owns, as cases following the Supreme Court's *eBay* decision[125] in the United States have increasingly recognized.[126] Professor Kapczynski, among others, rightly commends this approach to the developing countries, and she presents evidence that Indian case law has already begun to cite *eBay* with approval.[127]

At higher levels of technological development, moreover, the advent of platform technologies, often affecting upstream research tools, may arise suddenly out of a convergence of formerly separate interdisciplinary pursuits. Such a situation can present formidable holdout problems that can adversely affect both basic research and downstream applications, as occurred in the case of microarrays.[128] If nothing is done, a dominant aggregator may sometimes solve the problem by means of vertical integration, while leaving the progress of science in an uncertain state and possibly generating serious antitrust problems to boot.[129]

To solve this problem, when it arises, governments need the authority to override existing exclusive licenses and to grant nonexclusive licenses to additional or alternative parties in the public interest.[130] For example, governments must be able to pool or bundle platform technologies and to make the platform available as a whole to downstream applications when the platform becomes an essential infrastructure for future research and innovation.[131] In that case, all third parties who use the pooled technology should have to pay equitable compensation from their applications to the bundle or trust, for distribution to right holders.[132]

In principle, competition law can reach a comparable result by means of an "essential facilities" doctrine, which has sometimes been used in the European Union,[133] but remains in a semi-moribund state under existing case law in the United States.[134] Of course, a compulsory license for government use can also be invoked to address such a situation without a need to surmount the hurdles of competition law, and the United States has invoked government-use licenses for similar purposes in the past.[135] Both India and China have enacted comprehensive compulsory licensing schedules that appear to clearly encompass such a power.[136]

Nevertheless, developing countries with growing technological prowess should consider fashioning at least some guidelines, if not an actual codification, that would enable the authorities to intervene under an established "essential facilities" doctrine in order to rescue a platform technology when circumstances so require.[137] Such intervention becomes particularly necessary when holdouts elevate the prices charged for use of the platform to the point where both research and applications risk becoming casualties of deadweight loss.

Notice that, with regard to compulsory licenses for government use, which are widely invoked in the United States for multiple purposes, and not just national security, the TRIPS Agreement limits exports to 49.9 per cent of production.[138] So it became necessary to amend TRIPS to allow back-to-back compulsory licenses, thus enabling countries with capacity to manufacture medicines to supply poor countries that needed access to generic drugs but lacked manufacturing capacity under compulsory licenses of their own.[139] Both China and India have adopted legislation enabling them to supply generic versions of patented medicines to other countries under this scheme.[140]

There is a larger principle here of considerable importance. For example, developing countries may need to assist each other with access to essential climate change technologies, and pooled procurement strategies may become advisable.[141] So this concept of back-to-back compulsory licenses for inputs of essential technology may need to be broadened, and NGOs concerned about access to green technologies have already commissioned studies of this topic.[142]

ii. Checks and balances in the public funding of research. The developing countries that are more technologically advanced should also formulate their own approach to regulating the patenting of government-funded research results, particularly those obtained by universities and other public research centers. Although the benefits of the Bayh-Dole Act[143] are well advertised, the unresolved problems it creates are also increasingly well-documented, as are a growing list of needed reforms, which will be hard to enact in the United States.[144]

Recently, seven American experts published a detailed list of concerns about the effects of the Bayh-Dole Act in the United States,[145] and they recommended a number of minimum safeguards in the public interest.[146] Perhaps the most fundamental recommendation was that publicly funded university research results should not be exclusively licensed, unless such a license becomes essential for commercialization.[147] Because many research tools can be used off the shelf without further downstream R&D, as was the case with the Cohen-Boyer patents in DNA sequencing,[148] an exclusive license is often unnecessary and counterproductive.

Other recommendations these authors put forward are as follows:

- The governing legislation should ensure transparency in the patenting and licensing of publicly funded research results.[149]
- Where initial licensing arrangements for publicly funded research do not achieve public-interest objectives, governmental authorities must have power to override such licenses and to grant licenses to additional or alternative parties.[150]
- The government should retain an automatic right to use any invention arising from its funding.[151]
- Besides promoting commercialization of upstream research results, the government must ensure consumer access to end products on reasonable terms and conditions.[152]
- Governments should not presume that either patenting or exclusive licenses are necessarily the best options, but may instead "focus on placing by default or by strategy government-funded inventions into the public domain, creating a scientific commons, enabling collective management of intellectual property, or fostering open-source innovation."[153]
- "Where greater commercial incentives seem necessary, the benefits of nonexclusive licensing should always be weighed against the social cost of exclusive licenses."[154]

In other words, instead of simply imitating the U.S. model as it stands, the developing countries should try to formulate improved versions of the Bayh-Dole principle. Such efforts would better address both the need to ensure access to research tools for the research community and the question of abusive pricing of end products, given the extent to which relevant R&D

costs were borne by taxpayers in the first instance. In this connection, developing countries need to devise their own public-private initiatives to endow venture capital funds (and perhaps related research prize contests)[155] that might emulate or improve upon the successful models currently deployed in some OECD countries.

Unfortunately, India's hurried consideration of a Bayh-Dole-like statute without due regard to these proposed safeguards does not bode well for the future.[156] Similar statutes are under consideration in numerous other countries, including South Africa,[157] and it remains to be seen whether greater caution will be exercised there than had initially been the case in India.

iii. Smarter use of second tier regimes. While the emerging economies as a whole should maintain relatively pro-competitive markets for innovation vis-à-vis the high-protectionist regimes in the United States and the European Union, this strategy does not require developing countries to sacrifice their own domestic innovators to free-riding appropriators. Rather, these countries need to outsmart the high-protectionists by fashioning intellectual property regimes that match their own needs and capacities without violating international IP norms.[158]

In particular, they could take the lead in making sensible uses of liability rules to stimulate rapid exchanges of cumulative and sequential innovation, especially for purposes of follow-on innovation,[159] while reserving strong exclusive rights for a relatively restricted class of truly non-obvious inventions. China's second amendment to its Patent Law in 2000 may have taken a step in that direction by allowing a compulsory license when utility model owners refuse to deal on reasonable terms or conditions.[160]

As previously discussed, there are several ways developing countries could achieve this different kind of balance: by enacting and implementing compulsory licenses for dependent improvements;[161] by limiting injunctions to cases that demonstrably serve the public interest, now once again a characteristic of U.S. law and practice;[162] or by codifying an *ex ante* regime of compensatory liability rules that I have elsewhere described, which might particularly benefit commercial exploitation of traditional knowledge and related resources.[163]

iv. Incentives for promoting public health, the environment, and collaborative research. Developing countries should take the lead in revamping increasingly obsolete approaches to the use of IPRs in the field of medicine. In no other area is there a greater need for innovative approaches, with an ever-lengthening list of potential tools that could be used to increase research outputs and to achieve better distributional outcomes as well. These include:

- Proposals for pre-competitive pooling of privately owned small molecule libraries, with a view to facilitating the upstream identification of promising target molecules through university-generated assay designs.[164]

- Proposals for public-private technology pools that would undo patent thickets and stimulate investment, while preserving revenues from downstream applications for single depositors.[165]
- Proposals for government funding of clinical trial studies, with corresponding buy-ins at the international level and release of results to the worldwide scientific community.[166]
- Proposals for buy-outs and humanitarian licensing,[167] as well as for pooled procurement strategies under the amended TRIPS provisions, with a view to encouraging the distribution of essential medicines on a "high-volume, low-margin" marketing strategy.[168]
- Proposals for prizes and other novel research inducements that would help to separate the research and marketing functions in the medical sector.[169]

Were the leading developing countries to pursue their own proactive policies in this area, precisely at a time when their medical research capacity keeps growing, it could lead to novel and perhaps breakthrough solutions of benefit to the rest of the world.

Less innovative, but still worth considering, is the possibility under Article 6 of the TRIPS Agreement[170] for any country to adopt a regime of international exhaustion, with a view to permitting parallel imports of patented products from any place where the product in question was put on the market with the patentee's authorization. China's third amendment of its Patent Law in 2008 has reportedly instituted just such a regime, with an eye to obtaining "patented medicine which China has difficulty in manufacturing or otherwise obtaining."[171] Parallel imports may also help some developing countries obtain "green technologies" at more affordable prices, although this process can also exert upward pressures on the prices generally charged in developing countries, in order to avoid arbitrage through parallel imports.[172]

"Green technologies" are, of course, another area where developing countries could supply much needed leadership. Here some recent studies suggest that IPRs have so far been playing an appropriately stimulatory role.[173] The problems elsewhere observed in regard to information technology and biotechnology have not yet seriously appeared in this sector, perhaps because it remains at an incipient stage, with many small players and with relatively few large-scale capital investments.[174] Precisely because emerging economies could participate on the ground floor of future developments in environmental technologies, it behooves their governments to devise collaborative strategies to foster maximum growth and participation, without the impediments that excessive protection has caused in other sectors.[175]

Moreover, there is growing interest in new strategies to develop the so-called sharing economy, which has produced such successes as the open-source operating system and Wikipedia.[176] Considerable efforts are also underway to devise new forms of scientific cooperation that could cut through legal, technical, and economic barriers to the Mertonian sharing ethos, that could help to establish worldwide scientific networks and commons on an unprecedented scale, and that might extend "open-source" methodologies to new fields of study.[177] Here, again, developing countries should participate actively in these initiatives[178] and not sit on the sidelines waiting for others to succeed.

2. Measures Concerning Copyrights and Neighboring Rights. Another task badly in need of innovative solutions is the quest for sensible exceptions to, and limitations on, the exclusive rights of domestic copyright laws that are otherwise governed by the TRIPS Agreement and the under-theorized "three-step test" it incorporated from the Berne Convention.[179] Here, major efforts are under way in both academic and government circles to rethink the question of exceptions and limitations from a more public interest perspective than was possible in the immediate aftermath of TRIPS.[180]

Much has been written lately about the excesses of recent copyright legislation in general, and the concomitant expansion of related rights, including database protection laws, which increasingly complicate and obstruct the very creativity and innovation that intellectual property rights were originally designed to promote.[181] Nowhere are these tensions so acute[182] or so likely to generate disproportionately large social costs as in the field of basic scientific research.[183] In particular, abundant evidence now shows that science-hostile intellectual property laws, in combination with the science publishers' restrictive licensing practices, collide head-on with core advances in digitally integrated scientific research methods.[184]

a. Privatizing the scientific research commons. On one hand, new information technologies and related scientific tools, especially bioinformatics, are transforming traditional scientific fields, such as molecular biology,[185] and are spawning new fields such as genomics and proteonomics, with unlimited scientific opportunities in the digital environment.[186] The worldwide scientific community needs to develop and expand these digital opportunities, especially at public research institutes and universities, while maintaining the classical functions of certification and diffusion of research results inherited from the pre-digital print epoch.[187]

On the other hand, the digital revolution that created such promising opportunities for scientific research also generated intense fears that hardcopy publishers would become vulnerable to massive infringements online and to other threats of market failure.[188] In response, publishers pushed legislatures to recast and restructure copyright law in the online environment so as to preserve business models built around the print media.[189] In particular, as Professor Okediji and I have documented, publishers managed to curb pre-existing limitations and exceptions (L&Es) in the online environment, including those favorable to science; to embed pay-per-use machinery into electronic fences surrounding online transmissions even of scientific articles; and, particularly in the EU and increasingly elsewhere, to add new *sui generis* data protection disciplines that restrict access to the very facts, data, and information that are the lifeblood of basic scientific research.[190]

As a result, thickets of rights, backed by Technological Protection Measures (TPMs) and Digital Rights Management (DRM) restrictions in the online environment, impede effective exploitation of automated knowledge-discovery tools by blocking integrated access to scientific information and data scattered over a broad range of articles and databases that may or may not be available online.[191]

Scientists need, and traditionally depend on, a robust public domain, in which existing information and data become inputs to future knowledge assets that cannot be generated without them. Instead, successful special interest lobbying at both the national[192] and international levels[193] has overprotected existing knowledge goods at the expense of the public domain, while compromising digitally empowered scientific research opportunities with little regard for the social costs and burdens imposed on future creation and innovation.

High-level officials at the European Commission have publicly recognized the dangers to public science in this situation.[194] In 2008, the Commission itself issued a Green Paper, seeking to foster a debate about how to better promote the "free movement of knowledge and innovation" in the European Union's single market, with particular regard to the dissemination of research, science, and educational materials.[195]

Notwithstanding these initiatives, entrenched publishing interests in the European Union and the OECD countries generally have so far blocked any realistic prospects for top-down legislative reforms, despite mounting worldwide pressures for greater "access to knowledge."[196] This resistance has prodded the scientific community to make greater efforts to manage its own essential knowledge inputs by means that attempt to neutralize the impediments to upstream research that intellectual property rights increasingly spawn.[197] Some of these initiatives, particularly those spun off from the Creative Commons and Science Commons movements, have spread to developing countries, with notable success, for example, in Brazil.[198]

b. Remedial measures available to the BRIC countries. Developing countries labor under intense pressures from developed countries to duplicate the very barriers to digitally integrated scientific research that have been erected in OECD countries. Instead, the BRIC countries in particular should collectively resist these pressures and self-consciously adopt limitations and exceptions to copyright and related rights laws that would digitally empower their own scientific research communities without necessarily violating the relevant international intellectual property agreements. If these countries, and other emerging economies, marshaled the political will and governance capacity to undertake such reforms, their leadership in this area might give them a comparative advantage at a time when local scientific and technical innovation has begun to flourish in many key industrial sectors.

Accordingly, two fundamental recommendations are as follows:

- First, the BRIC countries should codify the idea-expression dichotomy (now established in the TRIPS Agreement) as a central subject matter exception,[199] and they should clarify that the legislative intent is to implement this exception at least as broadly as U.S. federal appellate courts routinely do.[200]
- Second, because the "use of automated knowledge tools in general and computational science in particular, requires scientists to reproduce entire articles from scientific journals; to extract excerpts of varying lengths from them; and to incorporate large extracts of data into their digital research tools for data mining, virtual experiments, and other forms of digital manipulation,"[201] the BRIC countries will need a broad and sweeping exemption for scientific research uses of literature and data. The clarity of such an exemption should require no gloss, no fine print, and no elaborately contrived carve-outs.[202]

The Max Planck Institute has recently proposed that a broad and general exemption of this kind should allow use and reuse of published scientific materials for virtually any scientific purpose, with express legitimatization of storage, archiving, data extraction, linking, and the like.[203] Such a reform should further clarify that scientists remain free to subject any published articles, and any scientific work made publicly available online, to "data mining procedures, data manipulation by automated knowledge tools, including virtual scientific experimentation, without any constraint other than attribution under the norms of science."[204] Any database protection laws that the BRIC countries were unwise enough to enact (by, for example, succumbing to pressures for bilateral agreements with the European Union) would have to be similarly aligned with a broad copyright exemption for uses of scientific literature.[205]

Beyond these fundamental policy positions bearing on scientific research, the BRIC countries should revise and expand their copyright exceptions for libraries and educational institutions generally, in order to fully exploit the policy space deriving from flexibilities set out in the TRIPS Agreement and other relevant treaties, especially the WIPO Copyright Treaty of 1996.[206] In this connection, the library community has been developing a plan of action to promote access to knowledge in developing countries, with particular regard to eliminating legal barriers to cross-border flows of books, periodicals, and other information in both the print media and the online environment.[207] Cooperating countries that implemented these proposals could gradually build a contractually created space in which their domestic arrangements accommodating science, education, and libraries were given mutual and reciprocal recognition.[208] Equally essential are clear legal measures to enable the bulk purchasing of foreign educational texts on reasonable terms and conditions.[209]

The BRIC countries, together with governments in other emerging economies, should also consider the potential advantages of adopting a "fair use" provision that would enable courts to deal with fact-specific situations falling outside the codified exceptions to copyright law's exclusive rights, which invariably occur in practice. A fair use option would create a buffer zone available when other provisions favoring research, education, and libraries appeared unclear or uncertain and yet the use in question served the larger public interest without undue harm to authors.[210]

Properly administered, a fair use provision could justify ad hoc awards of compensation to resolve apparent conflicts between private and public interests in hard cases. It would also help to attenuate potential conflicts between copyright law's exclusive rights and fundamental human rights, especially free speech, and the overriding "objectives and principles" of the TRIPS Agreement, as set out in Articles 7 and 8.[211]

However, implicit in any serious discussion of the trend toward adopting "fair use" regimes outside the English-speaking countries is the fundamental need to reconcile broad exceptions in domestic copyright laws with the three-step test governing limitations and exceptions in international copyright law,[212] as set out in Article 13 of the TRIPS Agreement,[213] and further elucidated in Article 10 of the WCT (together with the relevant Agreed Statement thereto).[214] Fortunately, the Max Planck Institute, following exhaustive discussions among some thirty experts, has prepared a Declaration on the Three-Step Test that seeks to accomplish this task.[215] Building on the WCT Preamble,[216] it would:

- Mandate that courts applying the three-step test of Article 13 in copyright cases take into account the interests of third parties, including individual and collective interests of the general public, and not just the interests of rights owners;[217]
- Avoid prioritizing any one step, or requiring that the answer to all steps should be "yes," but would instead require a judicial balancing of the different prongs, as occurs under U.S. fair use law;[218]
- Give particular weight to unauthorized uses that are underpinned by fundamental rights[219] and other "public interests," notably in scientific progress and cultural or economic development;[220]
- Seek to promote competition, especially in secondary markets, by a correct balancing of interests, but without making the three-step test a proxy for competition law;[221] and

- Expressly recognize that adequate compensation may be less than market pricing, where other public concerns are at stake, including third party interests or the general public interest.[222]

The BRIC countries could set an example for other developing countries by incorporating these proposals into their domestic laws, by supporting their incorporation into the WIPO Development Agenda, and, if necessary, by defending the tenets of the Declaration in WTO dispute resolution proceedings if they were challenged.[223]

Finally, no reform of the copyright laws' limitations and exceptions would be worth much in practice if the resulting provisions could not be enforced online or if publishers could simply override them by contract. In regard to the online environment, the WCT of 1996 clearly preserved a signatory state's rights to maintain all limitations and exceptions "permitted by law" when implementing international obligations to protect copyrightable works transmitted via digital networks by means of TPMs and DRMs.[224] However, the implementing legislation in the United States, i.e., the Digital Millennium Copyright Act (DMCA), declined to exercise this treaty-given power,[225] while the European Union's implementing legislation, the Infosoc Directive of 2001,[226] simply avoided the issue, which was tantamount to the same result.[227]

Developing countries should take exactly the opposite path by exercising the inherent power of WCT signatories to implement all limitations and exceptions "permitted by law" in the online environment.[228] The first step is to enact legislation that expressly applies limitations and exceptions favoring scientific research, education, and libraries to works transmitted over digital networks, irrespective of the TPMs and DRMs that otherwise regulate such transmissions. The next step is to further adopt measures that effectively enable the beneficiaries of these exceptions to enforce them despite the electronic fences and digital locks that impair access to protected works in cyberspace.[229]

This result can be achieved, for example, by means of a system of "electronic locks and keys" to break through the electronic fences for specified purposes,[230] or by resort to the less costly and burdensome "reverse notice and takedown" procedure that I and Professors Dinwoodie and Samuelson have proposed elsewhere.[231] The latter procedure enables would-be privileged users to oblige copyright proprietors to make relevant materials available without the users having to cross the electronic fence or enter the digitally locked gateway at all.[232]

Needless to say, neither approach will suffice if copyright proprietors can override applicable limitations and exceptions by contract, especially one-sided electronic contracts that regulate lawful access to digitally transmitted works. Hence, developing country legislators need to ensure that none of the key exceptions favoring research, education, and libraries can be waived or overridden by contract, especially in the online environment.[233]

Arguably, it is the BRIC countries, and other emerging economies, that have the greatest interest in treating access to scientific knowledge and educational materials as a domestic and global public good, one which should not be privatized beyond limits set by domestic law and policy.[234] While operating within the confines of existing international intellectual property laws, it behooves these countries—both at the domestic and regional levels—to play a leadership role in implementing and amplifying the flexibilities set out in the relevant international conventions, with a view to benefiting their own research and educational communities.

At the multilateral level, these countries should evaluate the extent to which their own needs for access to knowledge oblige them to support WIPO Development Agenda goals consonant with those needs, in opposition to the high-protectionist policies favored by the United States and the EU.[235] Bold legislative initiatives in domestic laws on these matters could thus help to set and define the international copyright law agenda for the next several decades.

3. Measures Concerning Competition Law and Misuse. There is nearly universal recognition of the need to redefine the border between intellectual property rights and competition law in a manner conducive to promoting worldwide markets for technology.[236] Here the high- and middle-income developing countries need to formulate competition laws and policies "to ensure that foreign technologies and know-how flow to local markets" under reasonable terms and conditions and at prices local entrepreneurs can afford.[237] In so doing, they should fully exploit the competition law exceptions available under the TRIPS Agreement[238] and draw upon solutions and proposals emanating from both past and present practices in OECD countries and elsewhere, given the political will and skill to do so.

However, resorting to competition law and policy has so far proved difficult for most developing countries. In part, this reluctance may stem from the complex economic analysis, high transaction costs, and regulatory skills associated with the practice of competition law in the most developed countries.[239] Moreover, key differences between EU practice, which emphasize measures to prevent abuse of a dominant position, and—until recently—the less aggressive stance of the U.S. authorities, who seek evidence of actual or intended monopolization,[240] may hinder clear thinking about the relevant problems in developing countries. Both the EU and U.S. regimes depend on proof of market power, although long-standing (but increasingly disfavored) common law precedents in patent law allow U.S. courts to suspend enforcement of valid patents for acts of "misuse," even in the absence of market power.[241]

Besides these technical intricacies, policymakers in developing countries that become serious about the interface between intellectual property and competition law must make high-level decisions about the goals of competition law in general, i.e., efficiency or fairness, or some combination of the two.[242] They must then reconcile their versions of competition law with the incentives to innovate that flow from the exclusive rights of intellectual property laws.[243] Here again they may be deterred by prevailing tendencies in developed countries to view competition law and intellectual property law as complementary means of mutually promoting social welfare, rather than as disparate regimes in conflict with one another.[244] The latter view more readily supports doctrines that override intellectual property rights, such as the "essential facilities" doctrine, much invoked in European scholarship and much harder to obtain in practice than in theory.[245]

Although developing countries lag behind in this field, both India and China have recently begun to formulate competition law and policy with a view to circumscribing the exclusive rights of intellectual property laws. For example, India has adopted patent misuse provisions that limit a licensee's ability to acquire or use "any article other than the patented article" or to use "any process other than the patented process," with a view to prohibiting any form of tying.[246] Refusals to deal may also trigger the grant of compulsory licenses under India's current framework,[247] as will undersupplying the market or charging excessively high prices.[248]

Similarly, China's third amendment of its Patent Law seems to have expressly codified the power to grant compulsory licenses for abusive practices with regard to both patents and utility models. Articles 48 through 54 reportedly envision a compulsory license for abuse, including failure to work within the purview of Paris Convention Article 5A, or for anticompetitive effects of the patent monopoly that "should be reduced or removed."[249] Such a license may also issue, under Article 54, for refusals to deal on reasonable terms or within a reasonable period of time.[250]

The measures adopted in India and China may serve to stimulate other emerging economies that have so far played virtually no formative role in this area at all. If so, developing countries may also discover needed self-help measures that competition law might afford if and when market failures of various kinds impede access to green technologies, as many fear will occur.[251]

Policymakers should accordingly consider early U.S. cases that emphasize fairness over efficiency.[252] They should also adopt both the "abuse of a dominant position" approach found in EU competition law and flexible doctrines of "patent misuse," which could reach refusals to deal, excessive prices, and undersupply of the market, without a showing of market power.[253] But such measures must be applied equally to domestic and foreign firms, without discrimination,[254] which could raise serious obstacles in many emerging economies.

C. Revitalizing a petrified intellectual property system

The foregoing exercise attempted to illustrate how the BRIC countries and other emerging economies could forge needed solutions to bourgeoning intellectual property problems that developed countries have either neglected or failed to resolve. In this endeavor, BRIC countries would be motivated by the greater stake they now have in what Carolyn Deere has felicitously called the "Implementation Game,"[255] owing to steadily mounting payoffs from strategic uses of locally generated knowledge goods. By carefully reevaluating their own intellectual property needs in the light of growing technological capacities,[256] they could begin to overhaul and reshape an "out of balance" system driven by ideology and power politics[257] in order to address the real conditions of creativity and innovation in today's digitally empowered universe of scientific discourse.[258]

Once embarked along such a path, policymakers in these countries would discover the growing importance of publicly accessible infrastructure in the development of new and complex technological paradigms.[259] They would profit from the problem-solving capacities of liability rules, especially when applied to upstream research outputs and tools that lack clear market values and that lend themselves to multiple downstream applications of unknown or uncertain value.[260] They would strive for more fluid and balanced interchanges between public and private goods in knowledge economies driven by both heavy public investment in basic research and by private investment in translating that research into workable commercial products.[261] And they could play a unique role in developing global administrative law norms as well.[262]

In sum, the BRIC countries, pursuing their own self-interest in economic growth with suitable coordination strategies,[263] could conceivably break the maximalists' stranglehold on intellectual property lawmaking exercises, which aims mainly to preserve a "knowledge cartel's" comparative advantage in existing technological outputs at the expense of future innovation requiring more subtle forms of nurture.[264] In so doing, the BRIC countries would devise and test new approaches and solutions that could redound to the benefit of technology-exporting countries everywhere, most of which seem incapable of reforming their increasingly dysfunctional innovation systems at the present time.[265]

IV. OBSTACLES TO IMPLEMENTING "COUNTER-HARMONIZATION" INITIATIVES

The question this optimistic portrait begs, however, is why developing countries have not already taken longer strides in this direction when implementing their responses to the challenges posed after the 1994 adoption of the TRIPS Agreement. Carolyn Deere's recent efforts to answer that very question afford a bleak and cautionary picture of the obstacles that stand in the way of autonomous intellectual property reforms.[266]

She shows, for example, that strong economic pressures, including the threat of trade sanctions and other diplomatic measures, combined with offers of future trade concessions, were more likely to produce TRIPS-plus provisions in FTAs than efforts to flesh out existing flexibilities in the TRIPS Agreement.[267] High-level lobbying by specialized knowledge communities, backed by one-sided technical assistance from WIPO and government agencies in developed countries,[268] further "shap[ed] developing country perceptions of the political climate and their room for [maneuvering] within it,"[269] although countervailing efforts by NGOs, academics, and others became more effective over time.[270]

On the domestic front, a lack of technical expertise hampered many developing countries.[271] As Professor Dreyfuss observes, "Astute lawyers should be able to utilize these [TRIPS] flexibilities. . . . The rub, however, is the need for astute lawyering . . . [which in turn depends on nurturing] a legal community capable of utilizing the Agreement's flexibilities effectively."[272]

Even when the relevant expertise emerged over time, the lack of internal government coordination among agencies affected by intellectual property law and policy left too much power in the hands of national IP offices, which were more likely to share the views of their foreign counterparts, and also left non-expert government officials more vulnerable to pressures from foreign governments.[273] In many developing countries, parliamentary debate and public discussion about intellectual property issues were negligible, which delegated policy framing to "national associations of patent and trademark agents and copyright lawyers, staff of national intellectual property offices, and national legal scholars."[274] Weak governance and widespread corruption were, of course, ancillary factors in most of the developing world,[275] with some notable exceptions in the Andean Community.[276]

One may then ask why matters should be different in the future. The answer is largely rooted in the real economic and technological capacities being attained in countries such as India, China, Brazil, and others. Such real world experience breeds, first, greater awareness of both the strengths and weaknesses of conventional intellectual property norms and policies encountered along the way, and second, a greater confidence in the ability of local entrepreneurs and policymakers to tailor future decisions and positions in their national interest.[277]

There is, of course, a countervailing risk that greater technical capacity at the national level, especially in the BRIC countries, could breed domestic lobbying pressures favoring protectionist measures that might further distort, rather than rebalance, the international intellectual property system.[278] Also relevant is the continued ability of NGO advocacy initiatives, such as the Access to Knowledge Campaign,[279] to reach policymakers in developing country capitals, despite funding cuts due to economic recession and to pressures from high-protectionist interests on foundations previously supportive of such initiatives.

Of particular importance are the lessons to be learned from the coordination and governance strategies of those BRIC countries that have most succeeded in resisting foreign pressures for TRIPS-plus agreements and legislation while maintaining an increasingly autonomous policy of their own.[280] Here empirical evidence showing the ability of Andean Community institutions to resist attempts to influence the formation of regional intellectual property laws and policies on numerous occasions sets an impressive example.[281] But regional coordination, a key aspect of Professor Kapczynski's own "counter-harmonization" strategy,[282] is often difficult to achieve and risks becoming fragile over time.[283] Moreover, that very regional process can be captured and turned against the interests of national innovation systems needing broadened TRIPS flexibilities, as Carolyn Deere documents in the case of francophone Africa.[284]

To offset these risks, Professor Kapczynski buttresses her "counter-harmonization" thesis with supplementary strategies of "fragmentation" and "mimicry."[285] Fragmentation entails "the adoption of unique or semi-unique national variations in law that create legal 'friction,' impeding the flow of the transnational circuits" that undermine local autonomy.[286] Mimicry, in contrast, entails "a dynamic reworking" of transplanted IP norms, which is cast as a process of "sharing or borrowing."[287]

For these and other related proposals to succeed, however, at least three supporting institutional factors become relevant, if not indispensable. These are: (1) the need for interagency coordination at the national, and, ideally, regional levels; (2) the need to establish facts on the ground in the domestic laws of the emerging economies; and (3) the willingness of the relevant governments to defend national variations of TRIPS flexibilities before WTO dispute resolution tribunals.

A. Interagency coordination of intellectual property law and policy

In the late 1990s, under a seed grant from a unit of UNDP, Ruth Okediji, Jayasharee Watal, and I argued that internal governmental coordination of intellectual property policy would be crucial to formulating appropriate domestic strategies to implement international intellectual property standards under the TRIPS Agreement.[288] Because, in our view, these new IP standards would affect all of a country's creative and industrial sectors in different ways, depending on its specific national assets and liabilities in each sector, there could be no internal "one size fits all" solutions, despite external pressures for such an approach.[289] Rather, the challenge for governments was to take stock of those same national assets and liabilities and then to fashion implementing strategies that would enable each developing country to maximize potential gains from intellectual property protection over time while minimizing the social costs.[290]

Our central recommendation was accordingly that developing country governments needed to form and staff ongoing interagency coordinating committees on intellectual property law and policy, in order to advise policy-makers about the implications for economic and social welfare as a whole of every proposed legislative or administrative decision concerning compliance with the TRIPS Agreement and related issues.[291] Above all, it seemed essential that these local coordinating committees would oversee the activities of national intellectual property offices, while pooling their resources at the regional level, in order to maintain coherent and effective negotiating positions in the relevant multilateral fora, including WIPO, WTO, WHO, UNCTAD, and UNESCO.[292]

To their credit, UNCTAD sponsored a conference in Ghana at which some sixteen delegations from different countries evaluated these proposals. Notwithstanding the attending delegations' enthusiastic endorsement of these proposals, and UNCTAD's strong commitment to promoting their implementation, further UNDP funding was denied. The project was soon abandoned, in part because some high-level UNDP officials thought that developing countries should work to repeal the TRIPS Agreement rather than to comply with it, and in part—one suspects—due to pressures on UNDP from key donor countries to steer clear of controversial intellectual property matters.

In retrospect, both Carolyn Deere's and Laurence Helfer's empirical findings demonstrate the validity of the proposals for interagency coordination that were put forward in the late 1990s and the extent to which such recommendations still remain relevant to today's counter-harmonization strategies, including efforts to implement the WIPO Development Agenda. Deere's study shows that those BRIC countries that were most successful in defining and maintaining autonomous intellectual property policies and positions over time, especially India and Brazil, despite enormous pressures from foreign governments, were precisely those countries that had highly developed interagency coordination mechanisms in place early on.[293]

In this connection, it is worth noting that China's third amendment of its Patent Law in 2008, which self-consciously seeks to balance incentives to innovate with the larger public interest, was the product of a high-level policymaking group charged with the formulation of a National Intellectual Property Strategy.[294]

Elsewhere, Professor Helfer's research team shows that the Andean Community's own intellectual property rules significantly influenced the expectations and behavior of private actors.[295] By the same token, the Andean

Tribunal of Justice (ATJ) not only created the kind of procedures and standards familiar in well-functioning legal systems, it "helped to rebuff pressure by the United States and multinational corporations to circumvent Andean IP rules, leading to different behavior by national actors from what it would have been in the absence of the Andean legal system."[296]

In contrast, most other governments delegated the task of responding to TRIPS and drafting the relevant laws to a small staff of technocrats located in national intellectual property offices.[297] Carried to the regional level in Africa, for example, this meant that national intellectual property policies were largely delegated to the African Intellectual Property Organization (OAPI) and to the African Regional Intellectual Property Organization (ARIPO) (English-speaking countries). Both entities worked closely with WIPO and left few countries at the national level with sufficient "capacity . . . to critically review patents granted," among other policy issues.[298]

Of course, the successes attained in India, Brazil, and China were also due to the economic opportunities their large markets offered to foreign investors, irrespective of their own intellectual property laws and policies.[299] Nevertheless, it seems clear that without effective interagency coordination of these issues at the domestic level, developing countries will not attain the leadership role in intellectual property policymaking at the international level to which they otherwise could and should aspire.[300]

B. Establishing facts on the ground

The Development Agenda, now officially established at WIPO[301] and analogous forums at other institutions, such as the IGWG deliberations at WHO[302] and their progeny,[303] have changed the policy climate at the international level. They elevate the concerns of developing countries, as well as the broader constituencies in developed countries that they indirectly represent, to a level of importance that cannot be ignored.[304] They make the implementation of the flexibilities set out in the TRIPS Agreement and in other intellectual property conventions as much a matter of legitimate multilateral concern as compliance with proprietors' exclusive rights.

In this respect, users' rights and other third-party interests, including the larger public interest in research, education, and access to knowledge, have become an integral part of the relevant international intellectual property standards set out in these conventions.[305] Moreover, by linking the larger development component to questions of enforcing intellectual property standards at the international level, the Development Agenda and IGWG-related consultations make it mandatory for both IGOs and national delegations to take into account the countervailing demands of the human rights conventions,[306] as well as the expressly designated objectives and principles codified in Articles 7 and 8 of the TRIPS Agreement.[307]

Yet, nothing is cheaper than talk at IGOs. The prospects of top-down multilateral legislation mandating hard law provisions favoring the interests of developing countries are virtually nil at the present time, given the governance structure of these organizations and the hostility of the United States, European Union, and Japan to any such initiatives. Whether soft law reforms stand a better chance of approval remains to be seen,[308] including the social costs of any trade-offs that would have to be made in order to win the assent of the aforementioned developed countries.[309]

Meanwhile, secret provisions likely to be incorporated into the pending Anti-Counterfeiting Trade Agreement (ACTA) negotiations[310] could undo key provisions of the Doha Declaration on the TRIPS Agreement and Public Health.[311] EU customs officials are further undermining access to medicines by intercepting shipments of unpatented generic pharmaceuticals from India to developing countries in other continents.[312] And proposals for both bilateral and regional free trade agreements multiply further proprietary restraints on access to knowledge.[313]

What must occur, instead, if the WIPO Development Agenda is to produce more than talk,[314] is that leading developing countries, especially the BRIC countries, take steps to implement model TRIPS-compliant flexibilities in their own domestic laws, while championing these same positions in the relevant international fora. China, for example, has articulated the "public order" exception to patentability under Article 27.2 of the TRIPS Agreement to exclude "any invention-creation that is contrary to the laws of the State or social morality or that is detrimental to the public interest."[315] Building on this provision, China's third revision of its Patent Law regulates access to genetic resources for the first time;[316] imposes a "prior informed consent regime" consistent with the Convention on Biological Diversity;[317] and makes disclosure of origin a precondition for the granting of any patented invention "depending on genetic resources."[318] These provisions were adopted to deal with the problem of "biopiracy" and modeled on similar legislation in the Andean Community and India.[319]

In contrast with these palpable concerns about protecting potentially valuable genetic resources, the BRIC countries as a group lag behind in recognizing impediments to computational research methods and innovation that lie hidden in obsolete copyright regimes.[320] For example, nothing prevents Brazil, India, and China from proceeding on their own to codify broad limitations and exceptions for digitally integrated scientific research, education, and libraries in their domestic laws, as stepping stones to broader international action.[321] By the same token, courts or legislatures in these and other countries could begin to implement the Max Planck Institute's Declaration on the Three-Step Test in their domestic laws,[322] along with selected other "ceilings" on intellectual property rights that have emerged from parallel initiatives in the Nordic countries.[323]

Only if leading developing countries begin to enact suitable reforms of intellectual property law and policy at home will it become realistically possible to foresee these reforms spreading to the regional and multilateral levels, where both positive and negative results of such experiments could be evaluated. Just as the AIPPI forums in the nineteenth and early twentieth centuries shed a comparative light on state practice in developed countries and led to the progressive harmonization of inventors' rights over time,[324] so, too, can the WIPO Development Agenda become a focal point for comparing and contrasting diverse state actions on the road to achieving a new and better equilibrium between private and public goods at the national, regional, and multilateral levels.

Meanwhile, still other worthwhile initiatives can be rooted in state practice without formal acquiescence at IGOs. For example, there are now real prospects for an international treaty providing greater access to literature for the blind,[325] a process that is long overdue and worthy of strong support by all WIPO member countries. At the same time, nothing stops the developing countries from immediately codifying key provisions of this proposed treaty in order to create "facts on the ground" that would benefit the blind now and pave the way for future enactment in the WIPO framework.

Similarly, if a prize fund to promote research on a vaccine for Chagas disease is a good idea, as the evidence suggests,[326] then the Latin American countries should establish such a fund now, with their own contributions, and shame the developed countries into joining them later. In other words, the more that the developing countries are willing to stand up for their own intellectual property needs, the more likely they are to ensure that those needs will be respected in future international intellectual property lawmaking exercises.

C. Defending the TRIPS flexibilities at the WTO

Moving beyond talk will not become feasible unless developing countries are willing to defend their rights to implement the TRIPS flexibilities in their own domestic laws without undue interference from powerful states that espouse conflicting interpretations of international IP standards. The more that single states, such as the BRIC countries, or regional coalitions, take steps to fully implement limitations and exceptions to the exclusive rights covered by the TRIPS Agreement, for example, the more likely it becomes that governments in developed countries will contest the legality of such actions through diplomatic representations and threats of retaliatory measures.

The USTR has repeatedly used actions under Section 301 of the Trade Act of 1974[327] to challenge developing country governments' interpretations of the TRIPS Agreement, in combination with threats to withdraw GSP privileges in reprisal.[328] These tactics aimed to keep developing countries from using compulsory licenses to persuade pharmaceutical companies to market patented medicines on a "high-volume low-margin" basis[329] rather than at prices only the affluent can afford.[330]

Unless public officials in developing countries are willing to stand up for their rights under the TRIPS Agreement and related conventions before the TRIPS Council[331] and, where necessary, in WTO dispute-resolution proceedings,[332] they will not retain the full policy space in which to maneuver that these conventions actually afford.[333] Conversely, governments that do stand up for such rights stand a good chance of persuading the WTO Appellate Body that unilateral actions taken against them violate fundamental WTO precepts.

Article 23 of the WTO's Dispute Settlement Understanding (DSU) obliges members to seek redress for alleged violations of the WTO Agreement, including its TRIPS component, by means of specified multilateral venues and procedures.[334] Under this provision, the U.S. authorities can challenge a developing country's interpretation of its TRIPS obligations by initiating litigation before a dispute settlement panel, with a right of appeal to the WTO Appellate Body. But the USTR cannot unilaterally adjudicate disputes over matters covered by the TRIPS Agreement, nor can it legally impose sanctions for the loss of its expected trade benefits.[335] Freedom from unilateral action of this kind is one major reason that developing countries signed onto the 1994 agreement establishing the WTO in the first place.[336]

In 1999, a WTO panel convoked by European Union officials criticized the United States for unilaterally applying Section 301 to TRIPS-related matters, and it warned that sanctions would be in order if such violations continued in the future.[337] If developed countries continue to engage in unilateral retaliations of this sort, they run the further risk of other countervailing measures that aggrieved countries could invoke:

> Because such action constitutes a violation of the DSU and of the framework Agreement Establishing the WTO, it would entitle the aggrieved party to all the remedies that the Vienna Convention on the Law of Treaties provides for breach of the relevant agreements. A primary remedy thus provided is the age-old right of self-help implicit in the power of an aggrieved party to suspend its obligations under the treaty in question, pending compensation for breach.[338]

Developing countries that win dispute settlement cases against developed countries may also invoke cross-collateral trade sanctions in the event that damages based on sanctions against imports of knowledge goods alone were insufficient to cover the actual trade losses caused by the defendant country's violations of the WTO Agreements.[339]

Those developing countries willing to defend their interpretations of the TRIPS Agreement before WTO dispute settlement panels have already made significant contributions to our understanding of international intellectual property law. For example, in the very first WTO TRIPS case concerning a dispute between the United States and the European Union on one side and India on the other, the Appellate Body, while finding against India on the merits, rejected the interpretation put forward by the plaintiffs.[340] Instead, the Appellate Body stressed the need for deference to the manner in which states undertook good faith implementation of TRIPS obligations within their domestic legal systems, in keeping with Article 1.1 of the TRIPS Agreement itself.[341]

More recently, in a dispute about the enforcement of intellectual property rights between China and the United States, the panel's decision on the merits went both ways, depending on the specific issues.[342] Nevertheless, as Professor Dreyfuss points out, the panel gave China "extensive leeway to determine how to dispose of infringing goods and where to set the threshold for criminal enforcement," while stressing that "TRIPS is a *minimum* standards regime . . . that gives members freedom to determine the most appropriate method of implementing their obligations."[343] Professor Dreyfuss thus predicts that greater participation of the emerging countries in the WTO adjudication process would likely push both panels and the Appellate Body to more carefully scrutinize the balancing factors favoring developing country interests that are already built into the TRIPS Agreement than has so far occurred in cases where the only antagonists are developed country members.[344]

V. CONCLUDING OBSERVATIONS

While much of the recent literature continues to focus on two fundamental tenets of the high-protectionist rhetoric, namely that stronger IPRs necessarily lead to more innovation and more transfer of technology and that they are essential for attracting FDI,[345] other studies have demonstrated that technology exporters need access to emerging Asian and Latin American markets as much as these countries need FDI, licensing, and up-to-date high-tech goods.[346] So long as the general level of IP protection in emerging markets affords technology exporters the minimum standards and entrepreneurial options available under the TRIPS Agreement, these exporters will find ways to reach attractive markets, and would-be purchasers in developing countries can usually meet their needs through sound procurement strategies.

Specific bottlenecks are more likely to arise from refusals to deal, excessive pricing, territorial restraints on outputs, and other restrictive business practices that suitable competition laws and policies could help to resolve than from gaps or inadequacies in local intellectual property laws.[347] Even so, the weak enforcement of IP laws that impede counterfeit goods may have detrimental effects on both local and foreign producers.[348] Meanwhile, innovative firms benefiting from a pro-competitive environment in developing countries can also profit from high-protectionist IP regimes abroad—under the independence of patents doctrine[349]—without aping the protectionist excesses of those regimes.

As Keith Maskus has explained, IP regimes are but one component of a healthy development-oriented economy. Without an appropriate infrastructure that includes corporate law, bankruptcy law, and a solid educational system, among other variables, IP protection may add little to either FDI or economic growth in its own right.[350] Moreover, as the relations between IPRs and innovation in knowledge economies become better scrutinized, the proper role of IPRs as such in overall development policies remains far less clear and more complex than the IP literature normally recognizes.[351]

Policies favoring the formation of scientific research commons, as well as open access to knowledge initiatives, may become as important in the BRIC countries, especially for sustainable upstream knowledge outputs, as strategic reliance on exclusive rights to stimulate downstream commercial applications of basic research.[352] Unless these countries actively adapt the TRIPS Agreement's flexibilities to their own development needs, with a view to maximizing the benefits and minimizing the social costs of harmonized international IP standards,[353] they may end up "financing not just or even primarily their own growth, but promoting the economic growth of developed countries, possibly to the detriment of their own economic development."[354]

Against this background, the high- and middle-income developing countries, as a group, are well positioned to undertake a leadership role in adapting traditional intellectual property law to the new technological conditions and challenges that the OECD countries have increasingly failed to address.[355] To the extent that these emerging economies avoid the pitfalls that have begun to undermine markets for technology in the United States and the European Union, fashioning a more flexible, balanced, and modern approach to intellectual property law could in fact enable them to boost their growing comparative advantages in cutting-edge technologies well beyond current levels.[356] To achieve this result, however, will require developing country governments to self-consciously adopt disciplined legal and political strategies that preserve the policy space in which to devise and test their own intellectual property institutions and to stimulate a vigorous and concerted debate about the proper design of those same institutions.[357]

Legal circles in the emerging economies will also have to study and master the relevant WTO jurisprudence, as the Japanese did at an earlier period,[358] in order to steer clear of obvious legal obstacles and to defend national autonomy at the TRIPS Council or, when necessary, in actual dispute settlement cases. These countries should also avoid further multilateral and bilateral standard-setting negotiations likely to limit their own autonomy and governance capacities, while at the same time seeking to forge regional understandings on these same issues that could attenuate the pressures from abroad.[359] Above all, most developing countries still need to establish solid interagency review mechanisms that can exercise oversight of their intellectual property bureaus and ensure that the latter properly implement national innovation policies established at the highest levels of government.[360]

From a broader perspective, any uniquely developing country effort to fashion appropriate intellectual property regimes for the twenty-first century must necessarily seek a new equilibrium between public and private goods. Because the last half of the twentieth century was so consumed with conflicts between public-centered and private-centered economies, insufficient thought was given to evaluating the proper and ever-evolving interrelationship between private and public goods, which the rise of knowledge economies has made so critically important.[361] In this context, Joseph Stiglitz's call to recognize the role of "knowledge as a global public good"[362] has generated an important literature whose practical implementation should become a primary goal of forward-looking policymakers in all developing countries.[363]

These countries should also build ever stronger connections to the worldwide flow of scientific and technical information, a task that will require sharing locally generated scientific data with the rest of the world (as China has begun to do),[364] while resisting legal, economic, and technological restraints on the dissemination of such data.[365] A particularly forward-looking policy would, for example, lead developing countries to support open access and other sharing mechanisms at the level of scientific enquiry,[366] while taking steps to better ensure downstream support for innovative applications flowing from cooperative public-private upstream research initiatives.

If, at the end of the twentieth century, we learned that access to knowledge was as important for economic growth and human welfare as stimulating investment in the production of knowledge goods, it could be the developing countries as a group that lead us out of certain blind alleys that currently pit these two essential policy goals against one another. It is, as Professor Dreyfuss and I have recently argued, precisely a time for experimentation, and not a time to copy or codify obsolete approaches that are likely to boomerang against the long-term interests of the very developed countries that are most avidly pushing the harmonization buttons at the international level.[367]

To be sure, charting one's own course is never easy, especially when powerful countries and knowledge cartels apply countervailing pressures at every step. Nevertheless, I continue to believe that, with enlightened leadership, buttressed by "skillful lawyering, political determination and coordinated planning,"[368] the intellectual property institutions inherited from the Industrial Revolution can evolve into a worldwide system of innovation that will benefit countries at every stage of economic development.

NOTES

* Earlier versions of this paper were presented at the Conference on the Future of Intellectual Property Law, University of Illinois at Urbana-Champaign, 6–8 March 2008; at the International Conference to Celebrate the Foundation of the Institute of Legal Studies, Sungkyunkwan University College of Law, South Korea, 16 May 2008; and at the Global Forum on Intellectual Property Law 2009, Singapore Academy of Intellectual Property Law, Singapore, 8–9 January 2009.

Later versions were presented at the Conference on Intellectual Property in International Perspective, University of Houston Law Center, Santa Fe, NM, 5–7 June 2009; (Symposium Issue, 46 *Houston L. Rev.* 1–1256 (2009)); at the Conference on Intellectual Property Rights and Development, sponsored by the Initiative for Policy Dialogue (Columbia University) and the Brooks World Poverty Institute, University of Manchester, 22–23 June 2009; at the Meeting of the China Task Force on Regulation after the Crisis, sponsored by the Initiative for Policy Dialogue (Columbia University) and the Research Center for Property Exchange, Peking University, Beijing, China, 29–30 October 2009; and at the Conference on Promoting Strategic Responses to Globalization, National Institute for Science and Technology on Public Policies, Strategies and Development, Federal University, Rio de Janeiro, Brazil, 3–6 November 2009.

The author sincerely thanks the organizers of these events and the participants, and is especially indebted to James Boyle, Leonardo Burlamaqui, Heping Cao, Ana Celia Castro, Peter Evans, Daniel Gervais, Laurence Helfer, Craig Joyce, David Kennedy, Jay Kesan, Ruth Okediji, Henning Grosse Ruse-Khan, Ken Shadlen, Joseph Stiglitz, Craig Vetner, Brian Wright, Peter Yu, and Lei Zhen for helpful comments, criticism, and moral support. He is also particularly grateful to Professors Rochelle C. Dreyfuss and Amy Kapczynski who have been independently writing on similar topics and who have graciously shared their views with him. A final acknowledgement is due for the support of the National Human Genome Research Institute and the Department of Energy (5P50H-G003391-01).

1. See, e.g., Meir Pugatch, "The Process of Intellectual Property Policy-Making in the 21st Century: Shifting from a General Welfare Model to a Multi-Dimensional One," 31 *Eur. Intell. Prop. Rev.* 307 (2009). See generally Keith E. Maskus, *Intellectual Property Rights in the Global Economy*, 2–3 (2000); Meir P. Pugatch, Stockholm Network, "If It Ain't Broke, Don't Fix It: A Discussion Paper on the Benefits of the Voluntary Market-Driven Approach to Innovation" (2008) ("[I]nnovation both influences, and is influenced by, a number of exogenous or external factors—social, cultural and demographic trends, for example").

2. See Christopher May & Susan K. Sell, *Intellectual Property Rights: A Critical History*, 139–42 (2006); James Boyle, "The Second Enclosure Movement and the Construction of the Public Domain," *Law & Contemp. Probs.*, Winter/Spring 2003, at 33, 37–40; Keith E. Maskus & Jerome H. Reichman, "The Globalization of Private Knowledge Goods and the Privatization of Global Public Goods," in *International Public Goods and Transfer of Technology under a Globalized Intellectual Property Regime* (K.E. Maskus & J.H. Reichman eds., 2005); see also Herbert Hovenkamp, "The Intellectual Property-Antitrust Interface," in 3 *Issues*

in Competition Law and Policy 1979, 1980–86 (examining the historic interplay between antitrust and intellectual property law and policy).

3. See, e.g., Rochelle C. Dreyfuss, "The Role of India, China, Brazil and Other Emerging Economies in Establishing Access Norms for Intellectual Property and Intellectual Property Law Making," 11 Institute for Int'l Law & Justice, 2–4, Working Paper 2009/5, 2009), available at <http://ssrn.com/abstract=1442785> (accessed 13 September 2013) (suggesting that some developing countries are now in a unique position to exercise their increasing influence to advance "pro-access views" and "contribute to the harmonization and integration" of international intellectual property norms).

4. See, e.g., Amy Kapczynski, "Harmonization and Its Discontents: A Case Study of TRIPS Implementation in India's Pharmaceutical Sector," 97 *California Law Review*, 1571 (2009).

5. See Daniel Gervais, "Of Clusters and Assumptions: Innovation as Part of a Full TRIPS Implementation," 77 *Fordham L. Rev.* 2353, 2371 (2009).

6. See, e.g., Dreyfuss, *supra* note 3, at 6, 11; Gervais, *supra* note 5, at 2360–1.

7. (UNESCO), *Towards Knowledge Societies*, 27–56 (2005) [hereinafter *Towards Knowledge Societies*]; See also Mary-Louise Kearney, UNESCO, "Research in the Knowledge Society: Global and Local Dimensions," Concept Paper for the International Experts Workshop (19–21 March 2009), available at <http://unesdoc. unesco.org/images/0018/001821/182189e.pdf> (accessed 13 Septermber 2013) (discussing the benefits of and obstacles to obtaining access to knowledge in developing countries).

8. See generally Daniel Gervais, "TRIPS and Development," in *Intellectual Property, Trade and Development* 3 (Daniel J. Gervais ed., 2007); Peter Yu, "Intellectual Property, Economic Development, and the China Puzzle," in *Intellectual Property, Trade and Development* (Daniel J. Gervais ed., 2007) at 173, 195.

9. Xiaoqing Feng, "The Interaction Between Enhancing the Capacity for Independent Innovation and Patent Protection: A Perspective on the Third Amendment to the Patent Law of the P.R. China," *U. Pitt. J. Tech. L. & Pol'y*, Spring 2009, at 1, 6; See also Andrea Wechsler, "Intellectual Property in the P.R. China: A Powerful Economic Tool for Innovation and Development" 42 (Max Planck Inst. for Intellectual Prop., Competition & Tax Law, Research Paper No. 09-02, 2008) ("China continues to realize the importance of both the unhampered influx of knowledge and intellectual property into China and the promotion of domestic innovation . . . [and] it has come to embed its IP policy into the framework of an overall pro-innovation industrial policy which protects domestic S&T innovations").

10. Agreement on Trade-Related Aspects of Intellectual Property Rights, 15 April 1994, Marrakesh Agreement Establishing the World Trade Organization, Annex 1C, Legal Instruments-Results of the Uruguay Round, 33 I.L.M. 1125 (1994) [hereinafter TRIPS Agreement]. See generally Jerome H. Reichman, "Universal Minimum Standards of Intellectual Property Protection Under the TRIPS Component of the WTO Agreement," in *Intellectual Property and International Trade: The Trips Agreement*, 23 (Carlos M. Correa & Abdulqawi A. Yusuf, eds., 2nd edn, 2008).

11. See, e.g., May & Sell, *supra* note 2, at 187; Gervais, *supra* note 5, at 2357–8.

12. See Peter Drahos with John Braithwaite, *Information Feudalism: Who Owns the Knowledge Economy?* 125–6 (2002); Jerome H. Reichman & Rochelle Cooper Dreyfuss, "Harmonization without Consensus: Critical Reflections on Drafting a Substantive Patent Law Treaty," 57 *Duke L.J.* 85, 94–6 (2007) (reasoning that high rents charged by technology exporters hamper developing countries' abilities to preserve their own comparative advantages).

13. Robert L. Ostergard, Jr., "Economic Growth and Intellectual Property Rights Protection: A Reassessment of the Conventional Wisdom," in *Intellectual Property, Trade and Development*, *supra* note 8, at 115, 155.

14. J.H. Reichman, "Intellectual Property in International Trade: Opportunities and Risks of a GATT Connection," 22 *Vand. J. Transnat'l L.* 747, 891 (1989). For evidence that this inversion is occurring within the Indian pharmaceutical industry, see Kapczynski, *supra* note 4 (noting that, instead of pushing Indian competitors out of the low-value Indian markets, multilateral pharmaceutical firms "may have also pushed Indian companies *into* the U.S. and EU markets on which their profits much more substantially rely").

15. See Yu, *supra* note 8, at 176–9.

16. Maskus & Reichman, *supra* note 2, at 44.

17. "BRIC" refers to those developing countries with fast-growing economies, especially Brazil, Russia, India and China. See Dominic Wilson & Roopa Purushothaman, "Dreaming with BRICs: The Path to 2050," at 3 (Goldman Sachs, Global Economics Paper No. 99, 2003), available at <http://www2.goldmansachs.com/ideas/brics/book/99-dreaming.pdf> (accessed 13 September 2013).

18. Maskus & Reichman, *supra* note 2, at 44; See also Jerome H. Reichman, "Richard Lillich Memorial Lecture: Nurturing a Transnational System of Innovation," 16 *J. Transnat'l L. & Pol'y* 143, 147–8 (2007).

19. See Carsten Fink & Keith E. Maskus, "Why We Study Intellectual Property Rights and What We Have Learned," in *Intellectual Property And Development* 1, 7–8 (Carsten Fink & Keith E. Maskus, eds., 2005); Wechsler, *supra* note 9 (case of China); Ricardo Machado Ruiz, "Technological Leadership and Market Leadership: Expected Convergences or Structural Differences?" Paper presented at the International Seminar INCT-PPED: Promoting Strategic Responses to Globalization, Rio de Janeiro, Brazil (5 November 2009) (case of Brazil).

20. See Gervais, *supra* note 5, at 2361–71 (emphasizing adaptation problems of national systems of innovation and citing authorities).

21. See, e.g., *Information Feudalism*, *supra* note 12, at 11–12; Michael P. Ryan, *Knowledge Diplomacy*, 85–9 (1998) (noting the influence of special interest groups on U.S. bilateral intellectual property diplomacy and citing specific examples). But see generally European Patent Office, *Scenarios for the Future* (2007) (evaluating four competing scenarios for the evolution of patent law regimes with very different and conflicting premises and outcomes).

22. See Gervais, *supra* note 8, at 33–6; Wechsler, *supra* note 9, at 42–3 (stressing that China's new patent law was not the outcome of external pressure but was intended "to allow China's domestic firms to compete effectively with their foreign counterparts").

23. See James Bessen & Michael J. Meurer, *Patent Failure: How Judges, Bureaucrats, and Lawyers Put Innovators at Risk*, 218 (2008) (describing the prohibitive costs of

obtaining and litigating patents); James Boyle, *The Public Domain: Enclosing the Commons of the Mind*, 113 (2008); Reichman & Dreyfuss, *supra* note 12, at 102–8; See also Jerome H. Reichman & Ruth L. Okediji, "When Copyright Law and Science Collide: Empowering Digitally Integrated Research Methods on a Global Scale," 96 *U. Minn. L. Rev.* 1362–480 (2012).

24. See, e.g., Geertrui van Overwalle, "Of Thickets, Blocks and Gaps: Designing Tools to Resolve Obstacles in the Gene Patents Landscape," in *Gene Patents and Collaborative Licensing Models*, 383 (Geertrui van Overwalle, ed., 2009); Carl Shapiro, "Navigating the Patent Thicket: Cross Licenses, Patent Pools, and Standard Setting," in *Innovation Policy and the Economy*, (Adam B. Jaffe et al., eds., 2001), at 1, 119, 130–1.

25. See Bessen & Meurer, *supra* note 23, at 218; Michael Heller, *The Gridlock Economy*, 52–3 (2008); Adam B. Jaffe & Josh Lerner, *Innovation and Its Discontents*, 4–5 (2004). Studies by the Federal Trade Commission and the National Academy of Sciences have also confirmed the diminishing returns that an unbalanced patent system has been producing in the United States. Heller, *supra*, at 65.

26. Reichman & Dreyfuss, *supra* note 12, at 103–4.

27. See European Patent Office, *supra* note 21, at 8–11 (evaluating four competing scenarios for the evolution of patent law regimes with very different and conflicting premises and outcomes); See also Paul Edward Geller, *An International Patent Utopia?* 25 *Eur. Intell. Prop. Rev.* 515 (2003).

28. See, e.g., World Intell. Prop. Org. [WIPO], "Standing Comm. on the Law of Patents," *Report*, at 4–5, 19–21, WIPO Doc. SCP/10/11 (1 June 2005); WIPO, Standing Comm. on the Law of Patents, *Information on Certain Recent Developments in Relation to the Draft Substantive Patent Law Treaty (SPLT)*, at 1–3, WIPO Doc. SCP/10/8 (17 March 2004) (discussing the efforts of the standing committee to draft a Substantive Patent Law Treaty that can be quickly adopted and later supplemented once consensus is reached on controversial provisions).

29. See, e.g., *Quanta Computer, Inc., v. LG Elecs., Inc.*, 128 S. Ct. 2109, 2122 (2008) (holding that the doctrine of patent exhaustion applies to the sale of components of a patented system); *MedImmune, Inc., v. Genentech, Inc.*, 549 U.S. 118, 124–5 (2007) (holding that a patent licensee does not have to terminate its license agreement before it can seek a declaratory judgment that the patent is invalid); *KSR Int'l Co. v. Teleflex Inc.*, 550 U.S. 398, 426–8 (2007) (expanding the rules governing the inquiry into whether a patent claim is "obvious" in light of prior art, admonishing that such an analysis "must not be confined within a test or formulation too constrained to serve its purpose"); *Microsoft Corp. v. AT&T Corp.*, 550 U.S. 437, 441–3 (2007) (holding that patent infringement occurs when one supplies a patented invention's components from the United States and the product is reproduced; however, this rule does not apply to software exported but not installed overseas); *eBay Inc. v. MercExchange, L.L.C.*, 547 U.S. 388, 391 (2006) (holding that the generally applicable four-factor test for permanent injunctive relief applies to disputes arising under Patent Act); See also *In re* Bilski, 545 F.3d 943, 956 (Fed. Cir. 2008) (en banc), *cert. granted sub nom. Bilski v. Doll*, 129 S. Ct. 2735 (2009) (holding the machine-or-transformation test to be the applicable test for determining patent eligibility of process claims in business method patent applications).

30. For the view that "transnational legal culture" may link developing-country patent offices into epistemic communities detached from broader policy considerations, see Peter Drahos, *The Global Governance of Knowledge: Patent Offices and Their Clients* (Cambridge U. Press (2010)). See also Kapczynski, *supra* note 4. Carolyn Deere, *The Implementation Game*, 314–20 (2009) (studying the sources of the wide variation found in developing countries' use of TRIPS flexibilities and intellectual property enforcement in general).

31. See TRIPS Agreement, *supra* note 10, art. 65.2 (setting the year 2000 as the end of the transition period for developing countries). For pharmaceuticals, the effective transition period ended in 2005. *Id.* art. 65.4. For some of the thirty-two least-developed countries, the transition period for patents in general need not end until 2013 and for pharmaceuticals, until 2016. *Id.* art. 66.1; World Trade Organization, Declaration on the TRIPS Agreement and Public Health, WT/MIN(01)/DEC/2 (20 November 2001), 41 I.L.M. 755 (2002) [hereinafter Doha Public Health Declaration]; Council for Trade-Related Aspects of Intellectual Property Rights, "Extension of the Transition Period Under Article 66.1 of the TRIPS Agreement for Least-Developed Country Members for Certain Obligations with Respect to Pharmaceutical Products," IP/C/25 (1 July 2002); Council for Trade-Related Aspects of Intellectual Property Rights, "Extension of the Transition Period under Article 66.1 for Least-Developed Country Members," IP/C/40 (30 November 2005).

32. See Yu, *supra* note 8, at 177–80 (emphasizing that stronger IP protection may not be necessary to attract FDI for countries that possess large and dynamic markets).

33. See, e.g., Yu, *supra* note 8, at 181–4 (discussing the relationship between FDI and IPRs in China's economic system); Kapczynski, *supra* note 4 (case of Indian pharmaceutical industries); Machado Ruiz, *supra* note 19; See also Pedro Nicoletti Mizukami & Ronaldo Lemos, "From Free Software to Free Culture: The Emergence of Open Business," in *Access to Knowledge in Brazil* (Lea Shaver, ed., 2008), 25, 29–32 (describing the relationship between FDI and IPRs in Brazil's economic system).

34. See, e.g., Janice M. Mueller, "The Tiger Awakens: The Tumultuous Transformation of India's Patent System and the Rise of Indian Pharmaceutical Innovation," 68 *U. Pitt. L. Rev.* 491, 539–41 (2007) (noting the divergent views of the pharmaceutical companies in India).

35. See, e.g., Reichman & Dreyfuss, *supra* note 12, at 118–20.

36. See, e.g., Reichman & Okediji, *supra* note 23, at 29–30 (arguing that broad exceptions for scientific uses are needed under current IP rules); J.H. Reichman & Paul F. Uhlir, "A Contractually Reconstructed Research Commons for Scientific Data in a Highly Protectionist Intellectual Property Environment," *Law & Contemp. Probs.*, at 315, 461–2 (Winter/Spring 2003); Jacques Warcoin, "'Patent Tsunami' in the Field of Genetic Diagnostics: A Patent Practitioner's View," in *Gene Patents and Collaborative Licensing Models*, *supra* note 24, at 331. See generally Boyle, *supra* note 23.

37. Margaret Chon, "Intellectual Property 'from Below': Copyright and Capability for Education," 40 *U.C. Davis L. Rev.* 803, 821–9 (2007); Ruth L. Okediji, "Sustainable Access to Copyrighted Digital Information Works in Developing Countries," in

International Public Goods and Transfer of Technology under a Globalized Intellectual Property Regime (Keith E. Maskus & Jerome H. Reichman eds., 2008), *supra* note 2, at 142, 184–5.

38. Frederick M. Abbott & Jerome H. Reichman, "The Doha Round's Public Health Legacy: Strategies for the Production and Diffusion of Patented Medicines under the Amended TRIPS Provisions," 10 *J. Int'l Econ. L.* 921, 928 (2007); Kevin Outterson, "Pharmaceutical Arbitrage: Balancing Access and Innovation in International Prescription Drug Markets," 5 *Yale J. Health Pol'y, L. & Ethics* 193 (2005).

39. Michael Blakeney, "Stimulating Agricultural Innovation," in *International Public Goods and Transfer of Technology under a Globalized Intellectual Property Regime*, *supra* note 2, at 367, 381; Robert E. Evenson, "Agricultural Research and Intellectual Property Rights," in *International Public Goods and Transfer of Technology under a Globalized Intellectual Property Regime, supra* note 2, at 188, 212–13; Timothy Swanson & Timo Goeschl, "Diffusion and Distribution: The Impacts on Poor Countries of Technological Enforcement within the Biotechnology Sector," in *International Public Goods and Transfer of Technology under a Globalized Intellectual Property Regime*, *supra* note 2, at 669, 674–5; See also Michael Halewood, "Agriculture and the Global Crop Commons," paper presented at the Task Force on Intellectual Property Rights and Development, Manchester, United Kingdom (23 June 2009).

40. See, e.g., Frederick M. Abbott, "Innovation and Technology Transfer to Address Climate Change: Lessons from the Global Debate on Intellectual Property and Public Health," 27–8 (Int'l Ctr. for Trade & Sustainable Dev., Issue Paper No. 24, 2009), available at <http://ictsd.org/downloads/2009/07/innovation-and-technol ogy-transfer-to-%20address-climate-change.pdf> (accessed 13 September 2013); Jerome Reichman, Arti K. Rai, Richard G. Newell, & Jonathan B. Wiener, "Intellectual Property and Alternatives: Strategies for Green Innovation," 7–8 (Chatham House Energy, Env't & Dev. Program Paper, Preliminary Working Paper No. 08/ 03, 2008); Keith E. Maskus & Ruth L. Okediji, "Intellectual Property Rights and International Technology Transfer to Address Climate Change: Risks, Opportunities, and Policy Options," 16–17 (November 2009) (unpublished manuscript, on file with *Houston Law Review*).

41. See, e.g., Bhaven N. Sampat, "The Bayh-Dole Model in Developing Countries: Reflections on the Indian Bill on Publicly Funded Intellectual Property" (United Nations Conference on Trade & Dev., Int'l Ctr. for Trade & Sustainable Dev., Policy Brief No. 5, 2009); Anthony D. So et al., "Is Bayh-Dole Good for Developing Countries? Lessons from the US Experience," 6 *PLOS Biology* 2078, 2080–2 (2008); Arti K. Rai & Rebecca S. Eisenberg, "Bayh-Dole Reform and the Progress of Biomedicine," *Law & Contemp. Probs.* at 289, 313–14 (Winter/Spring 2003) (arguing that funding agencies should be given more authority over universities to restrict patenting of publicly funded research).

42. See, e.g., Gervais, *supra* note 5, at 2361–71 (discussing strategies for research and education, for the clustering or networking of centers of innovation, for steering innovation in suitable directions, for inculcating social norms conducive to innovation, and for a suitable regulatory infrastructure); Leonardo Burlamaqui, "IPRs and Development Policy: From Intellectual Property to Knowledge

Governance," paper presented at the International Seminar INCT-PPED: Promoting Strategic Responses to Globalization, Rio de Janeiro, Brazil (5 November 2009).

43. See Daniel J. Gervais, *Epilogue:* "A TRIPS Implementation Toolbox," in *Intellectual Property, Trade and Development, supra* note 8, at 527, 529–30; J.H. Reichman, "From Free Riders to Fair Followers: Global Competition under the TRIPS Agreement," 29 *N.Y.U. J. Int'l L. & Pol.* 11, 13–16 (1997) (recommending strategies for developing and developed countries to implement TRIPS differently); See also Deere, *supra* note 30, at 2.

44. See Reichman & Dreyfuss, *supra* note 12, at 93, 102–8; See also John F. Duffy, "Harmony and Diversity in Global Patent Law," 17 *Berkeley Tech. L.J.* 685, 691–2 (2002). The notion of nation states as conductors of experimental IP laboratories goes back to Stephen Ladas's discussion of the Paris Convention for the Protection of Industrial Property (1883). See Stephen P. Ladas, *Patents, Trademarks, and Related Rights*, 9–13 (1975).

45. Professor Kapczynski has coined the felicitous term, "counter-harmonization," which I gratefully adopt here. See Kapczynski, *supra* note 4.

46. See Gervais, *supra* note 43, at 529–31 (providing examples of bilateral agreements that, while adopting TRIPS norms, require nation-specific variations); Carlos M. Correa, "TRIPS and TRIPS-Plus Protection and Impacts in Latin America," in *Intellectual Property, Trade and Development, supra* note 8, at 221, 225.

47. Cf. Laurence R. Helfer, Karen J. Alter & M. Florencia Guerzovich, "Islands of Effective International Adjudication: Constructing an Intellectual Property Rule of Law in the Andean Community," 103 *Amer. J. Int'l L.* 1, 16–36 (2009) (evidencing intense IP pressures on Latin American countries and collective response by the Andean Group); Robert C. Bird, "Developing Nations and the Compulsory License: Maximizing Access to Essential Medicines while Minimizing Investment Side Effects," 37 *J.L. Med. & Ethics* 209, 219 (2009) (stressing retaliatory pressures on developing countries that adopt compulsory licensing schemes in order to maximize public health benefits under current IP regimes).

48. Kapczynski, *supra* note 4; See also Reichman & Dreyfuss, *supra* note 12, at 121. Professor Gervais observes that "many developing countries also want a system that is simpler than some of the doctrines" in more technologically advanced countries, although he concedes that complexity is less of a problem for BRIC countries and other emerging economies. E-mail from Daniel Gervais, Professor of Law, Vanderbilt University Law School, to Jerome Reichman, Professor of Law, Duke University School of Law (14 September 2009) (on file with author).

49. See, e.g., Rebecca S. Eisenberg, "Noncompliance, Nonenforcement, Nonproblem? Rethinking the Anticommons in Biomedical Research," 45 *Hous. L. Rev.* 1059, 1079 (2008) (evaluating the argument that upstream patents may prevent projects in the biomedical field from getting off the ground); M.A. Heller & R.S. Eisenberg, "Can Patents Deter Innovation? The Anticommons in Biomedical Research," 280 *Science* 698, 699 (1998) (recognizing the increased cost associated with bundling patent licenses together); Arti K. Rai, John R. Allison & Bhaven N. Sampat, "University Software Ownership and Litigation: A First Examination," 87 *N. C. L. Rev.* 1519, 1554 (2009) (arguing that certain university-owned patents

allowed the right holders to "extract rents and perhaps even hold up development efforts"); See also Warcoin, *supra* note 36, at 331, 332–3.

50. See, e.g., Heller, *supra* note 25, at 65 (outlining the Federal Trade Commission and National Academy of Sciences's recommendation for reforming and strengthening non-obviousness standards).

51. See Heller, *supra* note 25, at 65–6 ("[T]he Court raised the bar for 'obviousness' . . . and reduced the ease with which patent holders can threaten other innovators with business-killing injunctions." (citing *KSR Int'l Co. v. Teleflex Inc.*, 550 U.S. 398 (2007))); See also *In re* Bilski, 545 F.3d 943, 997 (Fed. Cir. 2008) (en banc), *cert. granted sub nom. Bilski v. Doll*, 129 S. Ct. 2735 (2009) (revising eligibility criteria for business method patents).

52. Patent Reform Act of 2009, S. 610, 111th Cong.; Patent Reform Act of 2009, H.R. 1260, 111th Cong. However, legislative efforts to further refine the non-obviousness standard are no longer apparent in the pending bills, after the Supreme Court's decision in KSR. See generally Jay Thomas, Keynote Address at the Seventh Annual Hot Topics in Intellectual Property Law Symposium, Duke University School of Law, Durham, North Carolina: Progressive Patent Policy in the Post-Reform Era (29 February 2008).

53. See J.H. Reichman, "Of Green Tulips and Legal Kudzu: Repackaging Rights in Subpatentable Innovation," 53 *Vand. L. Rev.* 1743, 1772–6 (2000); See also Douglas Gary Lichtman, "The Economics of Innovation: Protecting Unpatentable Goods," 81 *Minn. L. Rev.* 693 (1997) (demonstrating difficulties of recouping development costs under current competitive conditions).

54. J.H. Reichman, "Legal Hybrids between the Patent and Copyright Paradigms," 94 *Colum. L. Rev.* 2432, 2519 (1994) [hereinafter Reichman, "Hybrids"]; J.H. Reichman, "Charting the Collapse of the Patent-Copyright Dichotomy: Premises for a Restructured International Intellectual Property System," 13 *Cardozo Arts & Ent. L.J.* 475, 515 (1995).

55. See J.H. Reichman, "Saving the Patent Law from Itself: Informal Remarks Concerning the Systemic Problems Afflicting Developed Intellectual Property Regimes," in *Perspectives on the Properties of the Human Genome Project* (F. Scott Kieff & John M. Olin, eds., 2003), 289, 295–301 (suggesting that an alternative set of liability rules that requires second-comers to compensate first-comer improvers is necessary to protect cumulative innovation).

56. Janice M. Mueller, "Biotechnology Patenting in India: Will Bio-Generics Lead a 'Sunrise' Industry to Bio-Innovation?" 76 *Umkc L. Rev.* 437, 446 (2007) (detailing India's efforts to promote biotechnology research through intellectual property protection, including the creation of a Biotechnology Patent Facilitating Cell aimed at facilitating the filing of patent applications); Janice M. Mueller, "Taking TRIPS to India-Novartis, Patent Law, and Access to Medicines," 356 *New Eng. J. Med.* 541, 542 (2007) [hereinafter Mueller, "Taking TRIPS to India"] (highlighting increased patent protection measures taken by India since becoming a WTO member and resulting concerns); R.A. Mashelkar et al., "Report of the Technical Expert Group on Patent Law Issues" (2009), available at <http://www.patentoffice.nic.in> (accessed 22 December 2009) (expressing concerns that high standards for judging non-obviousness will adversely affect cumulative innovation); See also Yu,

supra note 8, at 195–7 (noting that China initially overhauled its IPR system for admittance into the WTO).

57. Mueller, "Taking TRIPS to India", *supra* note 56, at 541.
58. See, e.g., Mueller, "Taking TRIPS to India", *supra* note 56, at 541 (highlighting the controversy surrounding the Indian Patent Office's rejection of Gleevec's patent application for a leukemia drug); Mashelkar et al., *supra* note 56.
59. See e.g., Reichman, *supra* note 53 (suggesting alternative intellectual property protection approaches that would deter free-riding appropriation of small-scale innovations without diminishing access to small-scale technical knowhow). See generally United Nations Conference on Trade and Development (UNCTAD) *Using Intellectual Property Rights to Stimulate Pharmaceutical Production in Developing Countries—A Reference Guide* (U.N. Press 2011) [prepared by C. Spennemann and J. H. Reichman].
60. See Reichman, "Hybrids", *supra* note 54, at 2457–9 (explaining that utility model laws are designed to provide shorter term protection than patent laws through weaker non-obviousness standards and a narrower scope of protection); See also Lichtman, *supra* note 53 (advocating use of state *sui generis* regimes for a similar purpose).
61. Lulin Gao, "The Third Amendment of Patent Law and Its Implementation Regulations in China," paper presented at the Second Global Forum on Intellectual Property, Singapore Academy of Intellectual Property Law (8–9 January 2009); See also Feng, *supra* note 9, at 19 (stressing limited innovation ability in China and the corresponding need to encourage "invention creation" of utility models).
62. See Reichman, "Hybrids", *supra* note 54, at 2459 (citing authorities).
63. See Reichman, "Hybrids", at 2455–59.
64. See Eisenberg, *supra* note 49, 1063–64; Brett M. Frischmann, "An Economic Theory of Infrastructure and Commons Management", 89 *Minn. L. Rev.* 917 (2005).
65. See Bessen & Meurer, *supra* note 23, at 46–7; Eisenberg, *supra* note 49, at 1076–84 (discussing the possible dampening impact of patents and the accompanying due diligence on research especially in industrial settings); Reichman & Dreyfuss, *supra* note 12, at 103–4.
66. Cf. Feng, *supra* note 9, at 15 (observing that one aim of China's patent laws is to "define the space where the public is free to exploit technology for invention-creations").
67. Geoffrey Yu, Remarks at the Second Global Forum on Intellectual Property, Singapore Academy of Intellectual Property Law (8–9 January 2009).
68. Rebecca S. Eisenberg, "Property Rights and the Norms of Science in Biotechnology Research," 97 *Yale L.J.* 177, 181–4 (1987); Arti Kaur Rai, "Regulating Scientific Research: Intellectual Property Rights and the Norms of Science," 94 *Nw. U. L. Rev.* 77, 89–91 (1999).
69. Reichman, *supra* note 55, at 289, 291–3; See also Lichtman, *supra* note 53, at 727–8 (stressing the chronic inability of lead time to recoup R&D costs).
70. See Reichman, "Hybrids", *supra* note 54, at 2521–2.
71. David C. Mowery et al., *Ivory Tower and Industrial Innovation* 92–5 (2004); So et al., *supra* note 41, at 2078–9.

72. See, e.g., Paul A. David, "Koyaanisqatsi in Cyberspace: The Economics of an 'Out-of-Balance' Regime of Private Property Rights in Data and Information," in *International Public Goods and Transfer of Technology under a Globalized Intellectual Property Regime*, supra note 2, at 81, 103 (detailing the implications of the European Union Directive on the Legal Protection of Databases); J.H. Reichman & Pamela Samuelson, "Intellectual Property Rights in Data?" 50 *Vand. L. Rev.* 51, 76–7 (1997) (explaining the origins of the EU's decision to allow the *sui generis* protection of databases). See generally Estelle Derclaye, *The Legal Protection of Databases: A Comparative Analysis* (2008).

73. See, e.g., John Wilbanks & James Boyle, "Introduction to Science Commons," 5 (2006), available at <http://sciencecommons.org/wp-content/uploads/ScienceCommons_% 20Concept_Paper.pdf> (accessed 22 December 2009) (describing the launch of Science Commons, a project designed "to ease unnecessary legal and technical barriers to sharing, to promote innovation, [and] to provide easy, high quality tools that let individuals and organizations specify the terms under which they wished to share their material"); Peter Lee, "Contracting to Preserve Open Science: Consideration-Based Regulation in Patent Law," 58 *Emory L.J.* 889, 940–2 (2009) [hereinafter Lee, "Contracting to Preserve"] (blaming the proliferation of patenting in university research for the decrease in sharing of research findings); Reichman & Uhlir, *supra* note 36, at 329–31 (advocating a new system of contractually created public access to scientific data as the solution to the increasing problem of hoarding); Peter Lee, "Toward a Distributive Commons in Patent Law" 33–4 (U.C. Davis Sch. of Law, Legal Studies Research Paper Series, Research Paper No. 177, 2009) [hereinafter Lee, "Distributive Commons"] (advocating a commons to solve the problems in technology distribution); Jerome H. Reichman, Paul F. Uhlir & Tom Dedeurwaerdere, *Governing Digitally Integrated Genetic Resources, Data, and Literature: Global Intellectual Property Strategies for the Microbial Research Commons* (Cambridge University Press, forthcoming).

74. Reichman, *supra* note 53, at 1747–8; See also Lichtman, *supra* note 53, at 727–8.

75. See, e.g., Reichman, "Hybrids", *supra* note 54, at 2525, 2531–4; Pamela Samuelson et al., "A Manifesto Concerning the Legal Protection of Computer Programs," 94 *Colum. L. Rev.* 2308, 2339–40 (1994) (highlighting the necessity of legal proscription against copying in order to encourage innovation in the software industry and "cure the market failure that unconstrained copying would cause").

76. See Shapiro, *supra* note 24; Eisenberg, *supra* note 49, at 1087–8 (exploring the "burden of inertia" regarding intellectual property rights and the resulting distribution of responsibility for the removal of access restrictions); See also Birgit Verbeure, "Patent Pooling for Gene-Based Diagnostic Testing. Conceptual Framework," in *Gene Patents and Collaborative Licensing Models*, supra note 24, at 3.

77. See, e.g., van Overwalle ed., *Gene Patents and Collaborative Licensing Models*, *supra* note 24 (discussing existing models designed to render patented genetic inventions accessible for use in research and exploring further alternatives); *supra* notes 49, 73; See also European Patent Office, *supra* note 21.

78. See, e.g., Jeremy de Beer, "Defining WIPO 'Development Agenda,'" in *Implementing the World Intellectual Property Organization's Development Agenda* (Jeremy

de Beer ed., 2009), 1, 1–2, 6–8; Peter Yu, "A Tale of Two Development Agendas," 35 *Ohio N.U. L. Rev.* 465 (2009).

79. See Reichman, *supra* note 43, at 26–42.

80. See The Patents Act, 1970, No. 39, Acts of Parliament, 1970, § 3(d)–(f), *as amended by* The Patents (Amendment) Act, 2005, No. 15, Acts of Parliament, 2005; Kapczynski, *supra* note 4.

81. See TRIPS Agreement, *supra* note 10, art. 27.1 ("[P]atents shall be available and patent rights enjoyable without discrimination as to the place of invention, the field of technology and whether products are imported or locally produced."); Dreyfuss, *supra* note 3, at 12 (explaining how India's system adapted in order to meet the neutrality standard in TRIPS, while ensuring that the public will continue to have access to generic drugs).

82. See Mueller, *supra* note 34, at 567–74; Kapczynski, *supra* note 4.

83. See, e.g., Gao, *supra* note 61; e-mail from Jia Hua, PhD candidate, Pennsylvania State University, to Jerome Reichman, Professor of Law, Duke University School of Law (17 November 2009) (on file with author).

84. See, e.g., Gao, *supra* note 61 (discussing pending Articles 23 and 24); See also Wenting Cheng, "Third Revision of Patent Law in China (Part I)," *Intell. Prop. Watch,* 8 September 2009, <http://www.ip-watch.org/weblog/2009/09/08/third-revision-of-patent-law-in-china/> (accessed 13 September 2013) (discussing Article 22 of the Chinese Patent Law (as amended 2009), which extends disclosure of prior use or any other means "from domestic (relative) to international (absolute)").

85. Gao, *supra* note 61 (discussing pending art. 63).

86. See *infra* notes 316–19 and accompanying text.

87. See *KSR Int'l Co. v. Teleflex Inc.*, 550 U.S. 398, 427 (2007) ("[T]he results of ordinary innovation are not the subject of exclusive rights under the patent laws."); *In re* Bilski, 545 F.3d 943, 952 (Fed. Cir. 2008) (en banc), *cert. granted sub nom. Bilski v. Doll*, 129 S. Ct. 2735 (2009).

88. See TRIPS Agreement, *supra* note 10, arts. 2.1, 3–4; Paris Convention for the Protection of Industrial Property art. 2(1), 20 March 1883, *revised* 14 July 1967, 21 U.S.T. 1583, 828 U.N.T.S. 305 [hereinafter Paris Convention].

89. TRIPS Agreement, *supra* note 10, art. 2.1; Paris Convention, *supra* note 88, art. 4*bis*(1).

90. See *supra* notes 59–66 and accompanying text; *infra* text accompanying notes 158–63.

91. See Reichman & Dreyfuss, *supra* note 12, at 98–102.

92. See Reichman & Dreyfuss, *supra* note 12, at 103.

93. Jerome H. Reichman & Jennifer Giordano-Coltart, "A Holistic Approach to Patents Affecting Frontier Sciences: Lessons from the Seminal Genomic Discovery Studies," paper presented at the CEER Retreat, Duke University Center for Genetics, Ethics & Law (April 2008) and at the European Patent Forum: Inventing a Cleaner Future: Climate Change and the Opportunities for IP, Ljubljana, Slovenia (May 2008).

94. See Eisenberg, *supra* note 49, at 1084–5.

95. Reichman & Giordano-Coltart, *supra* note 93, at 4–6 (discussing Cohen-Boyer patents), 5–6 (discussing PCR, which largely emerged from the private sector).

96. See Frischmann, *supra* note 64, at 995–7 (asserting that competition among downstream users for exclusive licenses favors uses reasonably expected to generate appropriate returns, leaving "socially valuable research paths . . . fallow and unexplored"); Lee, "Contracting to Preserve", *supra* note 73, at 903.

97. See Sapna Kumar & Arti Rai, "Synthetic Biology: The Intellectual Property Puzzle," 85 *Tex. L. Rev.* 1745, 1747 (2007); Mark A. Lemley, "Patenting Nanotechnology," 58 *Stan. L. Rev.* 601, 618–22 (2005); Tim Lenoir & Eric Giannella, "The Emergence and Diffusion of DNA Microarray Technology," *J. Biomedical Discovery & Collaboration*, 22 August 2006, available at <http://www.j-biomed-discovery.com/content/pdf/1747-5333-1-11.pdf> (accessed 13 September 2013).

98. See Bessen & Meurer, *supra* note 23, at 51–4 (attributing the "poor performance of the notice function in the patent system" to "fuzzy and unpredictable" patent boundaries, the ease with which patent boundary information can be hidden from the public, the disconnect between patent rights and possession of an invention, and the failure of systemic safeguards against patent proliferation); Rai, Allison & Sampat, *supra* note 49, at 1551–4.

99. Eisenberg, *supra* note 49, at 1072; Warcoin, *supra* note 36, at 331–2 (describing a "patent tsunami" in diagnostics and related fields).

100. Eisenberg, *supra* note 49, at 1081–4 (summarizing studies of the experiences of research-performing institutions regarding the effects of intellectual property restrictions); John P. Walsh, Ashish Arora & Wesley M. Cohen, "Effects of Research Tool Patents and Licensing on Biomedical Innovation," in *Patents in the Knowledge-Based Economy* (Wesley M. Cohen & Stephen A. Merrill eds., 2003), 285, 292–3 (finding little empirical evidence of "constraints" on scientific research and considerable evidence of widespread infringement by academic scientists who ignore patents); See also Christopher M. Holman, "The Impact of Human Gene Patents on Innovation and Access: A Survey of Human Gene Patent Litigation," 76 *UMKC L. Rev.* 295 (2007) (finding little evidence that gene patents adversely impact research and public health in contrast to biomedical patents on key pathways and patents on information technologies).

101. See Shapiro, *supra* note 24, at 120–1; Verbeure, *supra* note 76, at 4–7.

102. See, e.g., Eisenberg, *supra* note 49, at 1080; Warcoin, *supra* note 36, at 331–2; See also Fiona Murray & Scott Stern, "Do Formal Intellectual Property Rights Hinder the Free Flow of Scientific Knowledge? An Empirical Test of the Anti-Commons Hypothesis" 25, 27 (Nat'l Bureau of Econ. Research, Working Paper No. 11465, 2005).

103. See, e.g., Walsh et al., *supra* note 100.

104. See Reichman et al., *supra* note 40, at 7–8.

105. See Frischmann, *supra* note 64, at 998–1003 (advocating a hybrid of various possible solutions to revive the information commons); van Overwalle, *supra* note 24, at 385–90.

106. Reichman & Giordano-Coltart, *supra* note 93, at 19.

107. See, e.g., Convention on the Grant of European Patents art. 64(1), 5 October 1973, 1065 U.N.T.S. 255, 274; Rudolph J.R. Peritz, "Freedom to Experiment: Toward a Concept of Inventor Welfare," 90 *J. Pat. & Trademark Off. Soc'y* 245 (2008).

108. See *eBay Inc. v. MercExchange*, L.L.C., 547 U.S. 388, 396–7 (2006) (Kennedy, J., concurring) (explaining that in the current system, injunctions can be used as a bargaining chip to charge licensees exorbitant fees).

109. See TRIPS Agreement, *supra* note 10, art. 31(*l*) (stating the conditions under which a compulsory licence for a dependent patent may be granted); Gustavo Ghidini, *Intellectual Property and Competition Law*, 44–5 (2006) (advocating the use of compulsory licensing where the subject of an existing patent "has been developed through an entirely different and more advanced process").

110. See Brett Frischmann & Spencer Weber Waller, "Revitalizing Essential Facilities," 75 *Antitrust L.J.* 1, 10–21 (2008) ("Essential Facilities, Infrastructure, and Open Access"); Herbert Hovenkamp, Mark Janis & Mark A. Lemley, "Anticompetitive Settlement of Intellectual Property Disputes," 87 *Minn. L. Rev.* 1719, 1744–5 (2003) (promoting the idea of cross-licenses that allow parties to use each other's technology without fear of liability); Allen Kezsbom & Alan V. Goldman, "No Shortcut to Antitrust Analysis: The Twisted Journey of the 'Essential Facilities' Doctrine," 1996 *Colum. Bus. L. Rev.* 1, 1–2 ("[W]hen a monopolist or near-monopolist controlling what is deemed an 'essential facility' denies an actual or potential competitor access to that facility, where the facility cannot reasonably be duplicated and where there is no valid . . . justification for denying access, then the doctrine is applied"). But see *Verizon Commc'ns Inc. v. Law Offices of Curtis V. Trinko*, LLP, 540 U.S. 398, 410–11 (2004) (declining to recognize or repudiate the essential facilities doctrine but suggesting that it would not mandate complete cooperation between competitors even if recognized).

111. See TRIPS Agreement, *supra* note 10, art. 31; Jerome H. Reichman with Catherine Hasenzahl, "Non-Voluntary Licensing of Patented Inventions: Historical Perspective Under TRIPS, and an Overview of the Practice in Canada and the USA" 10, 24 (Int'l Ctr. for Trade & Sustainable Dev., Issue Paper No. 5, 2003), available at <http://ictsd.org/downloads/2008/06/cs_reichman_hasenzahl.pdf> (accessed 13 September 2013) (chronicling the history of compulsory licenses and the situations in which such licenses can be used most effectively).

112. See generally *Gene Patents and Collaborative Licensing Models*, *supra* note 24 (exploring proposals and experience with patent pools, clearing houses, open source models, and liability regimes).

113. See *Madey v. Duke Univ.*, 307 F.3d 1351, 1360–62 (Fed. Cir. 2002) (narrowly construing the experimental use defense to patent infringement); Peritz, *supra* note 107; Convention for the European Patent for the Common Market (Community Patent Convention), art. 31(b), 1976 O.J. (L 17) 1, 9; Agreement Relating to Community Patents, art. 27(b), 1989 O.J. (L 401) 1, 15 (not yet in force).

114. See *supra* note 48 and accompanying text.

115. See Feng, *supra* note 9, at 109 & n.190 (arguing that Article 69(5) of the Chinese Patent Law (as amended 2008) "helps to balance the relationship between the interests of the patentee and the public . . . and to prevent the abuse of patent rights").

116. Panel Report, *Canada-Patent Protection of Pharmaceutical Products*, 7.45, WT/DS114/R (17 March 2000).

117. See, e.g., Feng, *supra* note 9, at 109 n.190 (noting the existence of an "exception for the purpose of scientific research and experiment" in prior law without further comment on its scope).

118. See Robert Merges, "Intellectual Property Rights and Bargaining Breakdown: The Case of Blocking Patents," 62 *Tenn. L. Rev.* 75, 84–5 (1994).

119. Ghidini, *supra* note 109, at 36–7.

120. Ghidini, *supra* note 109, at 37–41.

121. See Reichman with Hasenzahl, *supra* note 111, at 12.

122. See TRIPS Agreement, *supra* note 10, art. 31(*l*).

123. Interviews with Professors Ghidini, Anderman, and Hanns Ullrich.

124. See Gao, *supra* note 61. It seems likely, but not certain, that a compulsory license for a dependent patent could be justified under Article 84 of the Indian patent law as it exists. See Kapczynski, *supra* note 4.

125. *eBay Inc. v. MercExchange*, L.L.C., 547 U.S. 388, 393 (2006) (determining that a patent holder's lack of commercial activity in working a patent should not automatically preclude the granting of a permanent injunction, nor does a finding of infringement automatically entitle the holder to such an injunction).

126. See, e.g., *Christopher Phelps & Assocs. v. Galloway*, 492 F.3d 532, 543 (4th Cir. 2007) (applying the *eBay* holding and rejecting the plaintiff's argument that it is entitled to injunctive relief to remedy a copyright infringement).

127. Kapczynski, *supra* note 4; Amy Kapczynski, "Innovation Policy for a New Era," 37 *J.L. Med. & Ethics* 264, 267–8 (2009).

128. See, e.g., Lenoir & Giannella, *supra* note 97; Kumar & Rai, *supra* note 97; Frischmann, *supra* note 64.

129. See, e.g., Audio tape: Suzanne Scotchmer, "A Non-obvious Discussion of Patents," held by the 7th Annual Meredith and Kip Frey Lecture in Intellectual Property, Duke University Law School (3 April 2008), available at <http://www.law.duke.edu/webcast/%20podcast/?match=Suzanne+Scotchmer> (accessed 22 December 2009) (discussing the dominant aggregatory outcome); Frischmann & Weber Waller, *supra* note 110, at 10–28.

130. See, e.g., So et al., *supra* note 41; Peter Lee, "The Evolution of Intellectual Infrastructure," 83 *Wash. L. Rev.* 39, 102–20 (2008); Reichman et al., *supra* note 40.

131. See, e.g., So et al., *supra* note 41, at 2081; Verbeure, *supra* note 76, at 16–20 (case studies), 21–9 (application to diagnostic testing); Frischmann, *supra* note 64; Robert P. Merges & Richard R. Nelson, "On the Complex Economics of Patent Scope," 90 *Colum. L. Rev.* 839, 890–1 (1990) (demonstrating that a government-imposed patent pool enabled the manufacture of airplanes for use in World War I).

132. See, e.g., Reichman, Uhlir & Dedeurwaerdere, *supra* note 73, ch. 4 (proposing pooled semicommons for upstream microbial research materials, with liability rules for downstream applications); See also Lee, *supra* note 130, at 112–16 (showing the critical role of liability rules in preserving access to intellectual infrastructure); Arti K. Rai, Jerome H. Reichman, Paul F. Uhlir & Colin Crossman, "Pathways Across the Valley of Death: Novel Intellectual Property Strategies for Accelerated Drug Discovery," 8 *Yale J. Health Pol'y L. & Ethics* 1, 20–30 (2008) (proposing the pooling of pre-competitive small molecule libraries, with liability rule option); Reichman et al., *supra* note 40, at 28–33 (identifying

technical tools under the TRIPS Agreement for breaking obstacles to transfer of green technologies). See generally Reichman, *supra* note 53, at 1776–7 (proposing a compensary liability regime in place of a model that favors hybrid exclusive rights).

133. See, e.g., Case T-201/04, *Microsoft Corp. v. Comm'n*, 2007 E.C.R. II-3601; Emanuela Arezzo, "Intellectual Property Rights at the Crossroad between Monopolization and Abuse of Dominant Position: American and European Approaches Compared," 24 *J. Marshall J. Computer & Info.* L. 455, 486–7 (2006) (noting that the European Court of Justice has never formally recognized the "essential facilities" doctrine); Rita Coco, "Antitrust Liability for Refusal to License Intellectual Property: A Comparative Analysis and the International Setting," 12 *Marq. Intell. Prop. L. Rev.* 1, 14–17 (2008) (discussing the evolution of the "exceptional circumstances" doctrine as applied by the European Court of Justice to create an "essential facilities" paradigm).

134. *Verizon Commc'ns Inc. v. Law Offices of Curtis V. Trinko*, LLP, 540 U.S. 398, 410–11 (2004) (declining to recognize or repudiate the "essential facilities" doctrine). But see Frischmann & Weber Waller, *supra* note 110 (making the case for revitalizing this doctrine to promote access to intellectual infrastructure).

135. Reichman with Hasenzahl, *supra* note 111, at 5.

136. See, e.g., Feng, *supra* note 9, at 29–31; Kapczynski, *supra* note 4; Gao, *supra* note 61.

137. Frischmann & Weber Waller, *supra* note 110, at 17–28.

138. TRIPS Agreement, *supra* note 10, art. 31(f) ("[A]ny such use shall be authorized *predominantly* for the supply of the domestic market of the Member authorizing such use." (emphasis added)); Reichman with Hasenzahl, *supra* note 111, at 5.

139. See Doha Public Health Declaration, *supra* note 31, ¶6 ("WTO Members with insufficient or no manufacturing capacities in the pharmaceutical sector could face difficulties in making effective use of compulsory licensing under the TRIPS Agreement."); World Trade Organization, General Council Decision of 30 August 2003, "Implementation of Paragraph 6 of the Doha Declaration on the TRIPS Agreement and Public Health," ¶2, WT/L/540 (2 September 2003); World Trade Organization, General Council Decision of 6 December 2005, "Amendment of the TRIPS Agreement, Annex," WT/L/641 (8 December 2005) (pending ratification by members); Abbott & Reichman, *supra* note 38, at 942 (explaining the requirements for granting compulsory licenses to exporting members under paragraph 6 of the Doha Public Health Declaration).

140. See Abbott & Reichman, *supra* note 38, at 969; Feng, *supra* note 9, at 100–1 (discussing Article 50 of the Chinese Patent Law (as amended 2008)). See generally Jerome H. Reichman, "Compulsory Licensing of Patented Pharmaceutical Inventions: Evaluating the Options," 37 *J.L. Med. & Ethics* 247 (2009) (tracing the relevant legislative history pertaining to compulsory licensing of patented pharmaceuticals and the effect of the waiver to, and amendment of, Article 31 of the TRIPS Agreement).

141. Abbott & Reichman, *supra* note 38, at 973–9 (advocating pooled procurement strategies when seeking essential medicines under compulsory licenses enabled by the waiver to TRIPS art. 31(f)).

142. See Abbott, *supra* note 40, at 26; Reichman et al., *supra* note 40, at 25–8 (suggesting cooperative methods for transfer of clean technology from developed countries to developing countries).

143. 35 U.S.C. §§ 200–12 (2006 & Supp. 2009).

144. Rai & Eisenberg, *supra* note 41, at 310–11 (recommending reforms to the Bayh-Dole Act that would allow more latitude for funding agencies and would maximize the social value of federally funded inventions and discoveries); So et al., *supra* note 41, at 2079–80 (analyzing recent studies showing that the Bayh-Dole Act has not significantly increased revenues earned by academic institutions from patent licensing and noting the tax-like effect that the law has on institutions with licenses on the resulting patents).

145. So et al., *supra* note 41, at 2078. Besides Anthony So, the authors included Bhaven Sampat, Arti K. Rai, Robert Cook-Deegan, Jerome H. Reichman, Robert Weissman, and Amy Kapczynski.

146. So et al., *supra* note 41, at 2081.

147. So et al., *supra* note 41, at 2081.

148. So et al., *supra* note 41, at 2079 (demonstrating that nonexclusive licensing did not deter the commercialization of the Cohen-Boyer patents for recombinant DNA, which produced $255 million in licensing revenues while reportedly contributing to 2,442 new products and $35 billion in sales).

149. So et al., *supra* note 41, at 2081.

150. So et al., *supra* note 41, at 2081.

151. So et al., *supra* note 41, at 2081.

152. So et al., *supra* note 41, at 2081.

153. So et al., *supra* note 41, at 2082; See also Boyle, *supra* note 23 (chapter on Science Commons); Janet Hope, "Open Source Genetics: Conceptual Framework," in *Gene Patents and Collaborative Licensing Models, supra* note 24, at 171; Esther van Zimmerman, "Clearinghouse Mechanisms in Genetic Diagnostics," in *Gene Patents and Collaborative Licensing Models, supra* note 24, at 63.

154. So et al., *supra* note 41, at 2078.

155. See, e.g., James Love & Tim Hubbard, "The Big Idea: Prizes to Stimulate R&D for New Medicines," 9 (2007), available at <http://www.keionline.org/misc-docs/%20bigidea-prizes.pdf> (accessed 22 December 2009) (discussing the development of a prize system as an alternative to exclusive marketing rights); Audio tape: Thomas Pogge, The AstraZeneca Lecture of 2008, held by the Federation of European Pharmacological Societies (13–17 July 2008), available at <www.ephar2008.org/downloads/TPoggePublicEthicsRadioLatest.pdf> (accessed 22 December 2013).

156. The Protection and Utilisation of Public Funded Intellectual Property Bill, 2008, Bill No. LXVI of 2008 (India); See also Sampat, *supra* note 41; Rahul Vartak & Manish Saurastri, "The Indian Version of the Bayh-Dole Act," *Intell. Asset Mgmt.*, March/April 2009, at 62–4 (noting concerns that the proposed Indian law was hastily drafted without public debate and fails to protect the public interest but insisting that the bill "is a step in the right direction").

157. So et al., *supra* note 41, at 2078.

158. See Reichman, *supra* note 53, at 1754–6 (advocating a liability rule for small-scale innovation to avoid the social costs of hybrid regimes of exclusive property rights); see also Lichtman, *supra* note 53.

159. Jerome H. Reichman & Tracy Lewis, "Using Liability Rules to Stimulate Local Innovation in Developing Countries: Application to Traditional Knowledge," in *International Public Goods and Transfer of Technology under a Globalized Intellectual Property Regime*, *supra* note 2, at 337, 356–8 (proposing a compensatory liability regime to advance the interests of developing countries without impeding follow-on innovation or creating barriers to entry).

160. See Feng, *supra* note 9, at 30 (citing Articles 48 and 51 of the Chinese Patent Law 2000). Actual use of this provision was not known at the time of writing.

161. See *supra* notes 121–2 and accompanying text.

162. See *supra* notes 125–6 and accompanying text; Kapczynski, *supra* note 4 (discussing *F. Hoffman-La Roche Ltd. v. Cipla Ltd.*, (2008) 642 I.A., in which the Indian tribunal referenced the U.S. Supreme Court's *eBay* decision when denying an injunction to promote access to medicine).

163. See *supra* notes 53, 159 and accompanying text.

164. See Rai et al., *supra* note 132, at 21–2.

165. See Roy Widdus, "Product Development Partnerships on 'Neglected Diseases': Intellectual Property and Improving Access to Pharmaceuticals for HIV-AIDS, Tuberculosis and Malaria," in *Negotiating Health: Intellectual Property and Access to Medicines* (Pedro Roffe et al. eds., 2006), 205, 211–14; See also Carmen E. Correa, "The SARS Case: IP Fragmentation and Patent Pools," in *Gene Patents and Collaborative Licensing Models*, *supra* note 24, at 42; Verbeure, *supra* note 76 (diagnostic testing).

166. See Jerome H. Reichman, "Rethinking the Role of Clinical Trial Data in International Intellectual Property Law: The Case for a Public Goods Approach," 13 *Marq. Intell. Prop. L. Rev.* 1, 52–3 (2009); Tracy R. Lewis, Jerome H. Reichman & Anthony D. So, "The Case for Public Funding and Public Oversight of Clinical Trials," *Economists' Voice* at 1, 1–2, January 2007. Available at <www.bepress.com/ev/vol4/iss1/art3> (accessed 13 September 2013).

167. See Amy Kapczynski et al., "Addressing Global Health Inequities: An Open Licensing Approach for University Innovations," 20 *Berkeley Tech. L.J.* 1031, 1109 (2005) (detailing a "neglected disease exemption" to advance access to biomedical technology in low- to middle-income countries); James Love, "Four Practical Measures to Enhance Access to Medical Technologies," in *Negotiating Health: Intellectual Property and Access to Medicines*, *supra* note 165, at 241, 243 (showing that the flexibilities in the TRIPS Agreement allow for humanitarian licensing to address public health crises); Kevin Outterson, "Patent Buy-Outs for Global Disease Innovations for Low and Middle-Income Countries," 32 *Am. J.L. & Med.* 159, 171 (2006).

168. Abbott & Reichman, *supra* note 38, at 973–83.

169. Love & Hubbard, *supra* note 155, at 2–4.

170. TRIPS Agreement, *supra* note 10, art. 6.

171. Feng, *supra* note 9, at 104–6 (assessing the impact of parallel import as authorized by Article 69 of the Chinese Patent Law (as amended 2008)).

172. See Reichman et al., *supra* note 40, at 33–7.
173. See John H. Barton, "Mitigating Climate Change through Technology Transfer: Addressing the Needs of Developing Countries," 9–10 (2008), available at <http://www.chathamhouse.org.uk/files/12357_1008barton.pdf> (accessed 13 September 2013); John H. Barton, "Intellectual Property and Access to Clean Energy Technologies in Developing Countries" 18 (Int'l Ctr. for Trade & Sustainable Dev., Issue Paper No. 2, 2007), available at <http://www.iprsonline.org/New%202009/CC%20Barton.pdf> (accessed 22 December 2009).
174. See Maskus & Okediji, *supra* note 40, at 2–3; Reichman et al., *supra* note 40, at 7–8.
175. See Chatham House, "Changing Climates: Interdependencies on Energy and Climate Security for China and Europe," 61 (2007), available at <http://www.chathamhouse.org.uk/research/eedp/papers/view/-/id/580> (discussing the bilateral establishment of standards to encourage trade and investment between China and the European Union); "Int'l Ctr. For Trade & Sustainable Dev., Geneva Annual China Dialogue: China, Trade and Climate Change," 7 (2008), available at <http://ictsd.net/downloads/2009/03/geneva-annual-china-dialogue-on-trade-and-cliamte-change-meeting-report1.pdf> (accessed 13 September 2013) (summarizing different approaches to promote research on climate change in developing countries).
176. See, e.g., Yochai Benkler, *The Wealth of Networks*, 70–1 (2006) (examining the development of Wikipedia); Boyle, *supra* note 23, at 197–8.
177. Reichman, Uhlir & Dedeurwaerdere, *supra* note 73, chs. 2, 5 (proposing a digitally integrated microbial research commons covering materials, literature, and data). See generally Reichman & Uhlir, *supra* note 36 (proposing contractually reconstructed research commons for scientific data); Jonathan M. Barnett, "Sharing in the Shadow of Property: Rational Cooperation in Innovation Markets" 57–68 (Univ. S. Cal. Ctr. in Law, Econ. & Org., Research Paper No. C08-22, 2008), available at <http://ssrn.com/%20abstract=1287283> (accessed 13 September 2013) (discussing the evolution of open source software in the United States); Lee, "Distributive Commons", *supra* note 73, at 918–19 (demonstrating that open source methods provide a model for the contractual creation of a biomedical science research commons); Michael J. Madison, Brett M. Frischmann & Katherine J. Strandburg, "Constructing Commons in the Cultural Environment" 95 *Cornell L. Rev.* 657 (2010) (proposing a research framework for the analysis of constructed cultural commons in the context of intellectual property).
178. See, e.g., Mizukami & Lemos, *supra* note 33, at 46–7 (analyzing Brazil's *tecnobrega* industry to show that innovation can thrive without a system of intellectual property enforcement); Alessandro Octaviani, "Biotechnology in Brazil: Promoting Open Innovation," in *Access to Knowledge in Brazil, supra* note 33, at 127, 134–6 (discussing the Genoma Program in Brazil to show that a decentralized network approach to biotechnology can be successful in a developing country); Minna Allarakhia, "Open Source Biopharmaceutical Innovation: A Mode of Entry for Firms in Emerging Markets," 6 *J. Bus. Chemistry* 11, 11 (2009).
179. See, e.g., TRIPS Agreement, *supra* note 10, art. 13 ("Members shall confine limitations or exceptions to exclusive rights to certain special cases which do

not conflict with a normal exploitation of the work and do not unreasonably prejudice the legitimate interests of the right holder"); Berne Convention for the Protection of Literary and Artistic Works art. 9(2), 9 September 1886, as revised at Paris on 24 July 1971, and amended on 28 September 1979, S. Treaty Doc. No. 99-27 (1986) ("It shall be a matter for legislation in the countries of the Union to permit the reproduction of such works in certain special cases, provided that such reproduction does not conflict with a normal exploitation of the work and does not unreasonably prejudice the legitimate interests of the author").

180. See, e.g., P. Bernt Hugenholtz & Ruth L. Okediji, Open Soc'y Inst., "Conceiving an International Instrument on Limitations and Exceptions to Copyright," 19 (2008) (emphasizing the need to ensure that copyright laws are "effectively harnessed for the public good"); Christophe Geiger et al., Max Planck Institute for Intell. Prop., Competition & Tax Law, "Declaration on a Balanced Interpretation of the "Three-Step Test" in Copyright Law," 39 *Int'l Rev. Intell. Prop. & Competition L.* 707 (2008) [hereinafter "Three-Step Test"] (emphasizing the need to consider not only the interests of right holders, but also the public); Marianne Levin, "Intellectual Property Rights in Transition: Legal Structures and Concepts in Adaptation to Technological Challenges towards an Intellectual Property System for the 21st Century," 42 *Scandinavian Stud. L.* 83, 88 (2002) (highlighting the importance of safeguarding investments with public interests); Henning Grosse Ruse-Khan, "Time for a Paradigm Shift? Exploring Maximum Standards in International Intellectual Property Protection," 1 *Trade L. & Dev.* 56 (2009); See also WIPO, "Proposal for the Establishment of a Development Agenda for WIPO," Annex, WIPO Doc. PCDA/1/5 (17 February 2006) (noting developing countries' proposal for the adoption of a Treaty on Access to Knowledge); *infra* note 195 and accompanying text (CEC Green Paper (2008)). See also Rochelle Cooper Dreyfuss, "TRIPS-Round II: Should Users Strike Back?" 71 *U. Chi. L. Rev.* 21, 22–7 (2004) (suggesting ways to combat the "one-way ratchet" of intellectual property protection without regard to the public interest); Jerome H. Reichman, Graeme B. Dinwoodie & Pamela Samuelson, "A Reverse Notice and Takedown Regime to Enable Public Interest Uses of Technically Protected Copyrighted Work," 22 *Berkeley Tech. L.J.* 981, 984–5 (2007); Knowledge Economy Int'l, Proposal for Treaty on Access to Knowledge art. 3.1, <http://www.cptech.org/a2k/a2k_treaty_may9.pdf> (accessed 13 September 2013) stressing the need for limitations to copyrights when the public use value outweighs the cost to the copyright holder).

181. See generally Benkler, *supra* note 176, at 470–1 (discussing the difficulty that will be involved in passing the needed reforms); Boyle, *supra* note 23, at 26; David L. Lange & H. Jefferson Powell, "No Law: Intellectual Property in the Image of an Absolute First Amendment," 157 (2008) (discussing the failure of copyright law to protect freedom of expression and freedom of the press); Lawrence Lessig, "Free Culture: The Nature and Future of Creativity," 188–94 (2005) (providing specific examples of the barriers to innovation resulting from current copyright law); James Boyle, "The Second Enclosure Movement and the Construction of the Public Domain," *Law & Contemp. Probs*, at 33, 43–4 (Winter/Spring 2003); Paul Edward Geller, "Beyond the Copyright Crisis: Principles for Change," 55

J. Copyright Soc'y U.S.A. 165, 168 (2008), available at <http://ssrn.com/abstract= 1114372> (accessed 13 September 2013) ("The growth of copyright law has inexorably impinged on basic interests in freedom of expression and privacy").

182. See, e.g., Reto Hilty, "Copyright Law and Scientific Research", in *Copyright Law: A Handbook of Contemporary Research* (Paul Torremans ed., 2007), 315, 318 [hereinafter Hilty, "Copyright Law and Scientific Research"] ("[Scientists] have suddenly become aware that copyright is not only capable of providing them with protection for their achievements, but also that under certain circumstances it can become an obstacle . . . ."); Reto M. Hilty, "Five Lessons about Copyright in the Information Society: Reaction of the Scientific Community to Over-Protection and What Policy Makers Should Learn," 53 *J. Copyright Soc'y U.S.A.* 103, 116–18 (2006) [hereinafter Hilty, "Five Lessons"]; Reichman & Uhlir, *supra* note 36, at 396–415 (evaluating social costs of a disintegrating scientific research commons); Pamela Samuelson, "Anticircumvention Rules: Threat to Science," 293 *Science* 2028, 2028 (2001) ("Recent legislation in the United States and Europe whose ostensible purpose is to protect copyrighted works from pirates is being used to inhibit science and stifle academic research").

183. See, e.g., Paul David, "The Economic Logic of 'Open Science' and the Balance between Private Property Rights and the Public Domain in Scientific Data and Information: A Primer," in *The Role of Scientific and Technical Data and Information in the Public Domain* (Julie M. Esanu & Paul F. Uhlir eds., 2003), 19, 27 (discussing how the proliferation of intellectual property rights is inhibiting access to information in several areas, including basic research); Reichman & Okediji, *supra* note 23.

184. See generally Reichman, Uhlir & Dedeurwaerdere, *supra* note 73, chs 5–7; Reichman & Okediji, *supra* note 23, 1414–25 (discussing the problem of data protection disciplines that "restrict access to the very facts, data, and information that are the lifeblood of basic scientific research").

185. Reichman, Uhlir & Dedeurwaerdere, *supra* note 73, ch. 5.

186. [T]he use of computational methodologies within the life sciences, such as bioinformatics, in the building of global collections of articles and data in microbiology, and in the integration of relevant research results makes it possible to build accumulative, field-specific knowledge repositories that capture reams of relevant scientific and technical information and data about micro-organisms. . . . [S]toring, curating, maintaining and making this huge accumulation of genomic data of interest to microbiology presents unique problems as well as unique opportunities. Once available, there is a pressing need to develop general data-mining tools for automated knowledge discovery in the chosen environment and to establish dynamically updated and flexible portals for disseminating research results. Reichman, Uhlir & Dedeurwaerdere, *supra* note 73, ch. 5 (citations omitted).

187. See Reichman, Uhlir & Dedeurwaerdere, *supra* note 73, ch. 5.

188. Reichman & Okediji, *supra* note 23, 1372–1425.

189. See Pamela Samuelson, "The U.S. Digital Agenda at WIPO," 37 *Va. J. Int'l L.* 369, 405–6 (1997); See also Geller, *supra* note 181, at 166 ("Copyright law is in crisis . . . it has become more and more complicated and less and less reliable, while losing legitimacy").

190. See Reichman & Okediji, *supra* note 23; See also J.H. Reichman & Pamela Samuelson, "Intellectual Property Rights in Data?" 50 *Vand. L. Rev.* 51, 95 (1997); See also Derclaye, *supra* note 72.

191. See, e.g., Nancy L. Maron & K. Kirby Smith, "Current Models of Digital Scholarly Communication," 31 (2008), available at <http://www.arl.org/bm-doc/current-models-report.pdf> (accessed 22 December 2009); Hilty, "Copyright Law and Scientific Research," *supra* note 182, at 315; Paul A. David, "New Moves in 'Legal Jujitsu' to Combat the Anti-commons: Mitigating IPR Constraints on Innovation thru a "Bottom-up" Approach to Systemic Institutional Reform" (Dynamics of Insts. & Mkts. in Europe, Working Paper No. 81, 2008), available at <http://www.dime-eu.org/files/active/0/WP81-IPR.pdf> (accessed 13 September 2013).

192. See, e.g., Digital Millennium Copyright Act, Pub. L. No. 105-304, 112 Stat. 2860 (1998) (codified as amended in scattered sections of 17 U.S.C.); Council Directive 2001/29/EC, 2001 O.J. (L 167) 4, 9 (EC); Council Directive 96/9/EC, 1996 O.J. (L 77) (EC); See also Hilty, "Five Lessons", *supra* note 182, at 112 (attributing the passage of the DMCA to "sustained pressure from the entertainment industry's powerful lobbying efforts").

193. See, e.g., WIPO Copyright Treaty, *adopted* 20 December 1996, S. Treaty Doc. No. 105-17 (1997) [hereinafter WCT] (an international treaty enacted in 1996 concerning digital copyright issues); WIPO Performances and Phonograms Treaty, *adopted* 20 December 1996, S. Treaty Doc. No. 105-17 (1997) (international treaty enacted in 1996 governing so-called neighboring rights of performers and producers of sound recordings). Very restrictive domestic implementation of these treaties is then re-exported to developing countries by means of bilateral or regional Free Trade Agreements (FTAs). See, e.g., Bryan Mercurio, "TRIPS-Plus Provisions in FTAs: Recent Trends," in *Regional Trade Agreements and the WTO Legal System* (Lorand Bartels & Federico Ortino eds., 2006), 215, 217–19 (describing the process of enacting international agreements governing copyright issues).

194. See, e.g., Tilman Lüder, Copyright Expansion: Can We Have Too Much?, Remarks at the Second Global Forum on Intellectual Property, Singapore Academy of Intellectual Property Law (8–9 January 2009); Tilman Lüder, Remarks at the Workshop on Creation and Innovation, Seventeenth Annual Fordham Intellectual Property Law Institute Conference, Cambridge, United Kingdom (15–16 April 2009); "Commission First Evaluation of Directive 96I9IEC on the Legal Protection of Databases," 23–4 (12 December 2005), available at <http://ec.europa.eu/internal_market/copyright/docs/databases/%20evaluation_report_en.pdf> (last visited 20 November 2009) (discussing the danger of *sui generis* protection inhibiting innovation and growth).

195. "Commission Green Paper on Copyright in the Knowledge Economy," at 3, COM (2008) 466/3, available at <http://ec.europa.eu/internal_market/copyright/docs/copyright-infso/greenpaper_en.pdf> (accessed 22 December 2009).

196. Amy Kapczynski, "The Access to Knowledge Mobilization and the New Politics of Intellectual Property," 117 *Yale L.J.* 804 (2008); Amy Kapczynski, "Linking Ideas to Outcomes: A Response," *Yale L.J. Pocket Part* 289, 289–90 (2008); James Love, "Risks and Opportunities for Access to Knowledge," in *Vision or Hallucination?* 187, 189 (Soledad Bervejillo ed., 2005).

197. See Minna Allarakhia, D. Marc Kilgour & J.D. Fuller, "Game Models of the Defection Dilemma in Biopharmaceutical Discovery Research," 7 (2008), <http://orion.uwaterloo.ca/-hwolkowi/henry/reports/mitacs.d/pdf/David/pub1. pdf> (accessed 22 December 20093) ("Fully disclosing knowledge facilitates future collaboration while appropriating knowledge strengthens a researcher's bargaining position for trade in knowledge."); Peter Lee, "Contracting to Preserve" Open Science: Consideration-Based Regulation in Patent Law, 58 *Emory L.J.* 889, 963–74 (2009); Reichman & Uhlir, *supra* note 36, at 416–60 ("A Contractually Reconstructed Research Commons for Science and Innovation"); See also Creative Commons, <http://www.creativecommons.org> (last visited 16 November 2009) (providing free copyright licenses to various works and allowing the creator to choose among several levels of access); Science Commons, <http://www.sciencecommons.org> (last visited 16 November 2009) (providing a similar service for scientific works aimed at "[i]dentifying and lowering unnecessary barriers to research"); Wilbanks & Boyle, *supra* note 73, at 5 (describing Science Commons as a project designed "to ease unnecessary legal and technical barriers to sharing, to promote innovation, [and] to provide easy, high quality tools that let individuals and organizations specify the terms under which they wished to share their material").

198. Pedro Paranagua, "A Comprehensive Framework for Copyright Protection and Access to Knowledge: From a Brazilian Perspective and Beyond," in *South Perspective—How Developing Countries Can Manage Intellectual Property Rights to Maximize Access to Knowledge* (Carlos M. Correa & Xuan Li eds., 2009), 103, 106; Mizukami & Lemos, *supra* note 33, at 44–8.

199. See TRIPS Agreement, *supra* note 10, art. 9.2.

200. Reichman & Okediji, *supra* note 23, at 1432 (citing authorities).

201. Reichman & Okediji, *supra* note 23, at 28; see, e.g., Victoria Stodden, "Enabling Reproducible Research: Open Licensing for Scientific Innovation," 13 *Int'l J. Comm. L. & Pol'y*, at 1, 24–5 (Winter 2009) ("How far the fair use exception extends into entire research compendia is not clear since the contours of fair use of copyrighted scientific material are not clearly delineated.").

202. Reichman & Okediji, *supra* note 23, at 1439–41. See also Reichman & Okediji, at 1441–52 ("Breaking the Digital Locks," "Disciplining Contractual Overrides," and "Aligning Database Protection Laws").

203. Reto M. Hilty et al., "Comments by the Max Planck Institute for Intellectual Property, Competition and Tax Law on the European Commission's Green Paper: Copyright in the Knowledge Economy" (Max Planck Inst. for Intellectual Prop., Competition & Tax Law, Research Paper No. 08-05, 2008), available at <http://papers.ssrn.com/sol3/papers.cfm?abstract_id=1317730> (accessed 14 September 2013).

204. Reichman & Okediji, *supra* note 23, at 1440. For further nuances concerning derivative works and possible downstream applications to commercial products justifying use of compensatory liability rules, see *id.* at 1450–1.

205. Reichman & Okediji, *supra* note 23, at 1449–52.

206. See WCT, *supra* note 193, pmbl. & art. 10. The accompanying Agreed Statement concerning Article 10 enables contracting parties "to carry forward and

appropriately extend into the digital environment limitations and exceptions in their national laws which have been considered acceptable under the Berne Convention . . . [and] to devise new exceptions and limitations that are appropriate in the digital network environment."

207. See Electronic Information for Libraries (eIFL), eIFL Handbook on Copyright and Related Issues for Libraries, <http://www.eifl.net/cps/sections/services/eifl-ip/issues/%20handbook/handbook-e> (last visited 20 November 2009) (listing Recommendations for a Development Agenda in WIPO in order to foster "a greater understanding of the importance of flexibilities, especially for developing and least-developed countries, and balanced IP education to include copyright exceptions and limitations, library copyright issues, the public domain, fair use model laws and pro-competitive licensing regimes").

208. Cf. Grosse Ruse-Khan, *supra* note 180 (proposing ceilings on exclusive rights of authors); Reichman & Uhlir, *supra* note 36, at 429 (discussing possible "treaties" between universities to regulate the sharing of government-funded research data); Peter K. Yu, "Access to Medicines, BRIC Alliances, and Collective Action," 34 *Amer. J.L. & Med.* 345, 345–87 (2008) (proposing coordination strategies for BRIC countries to increase access to medicines).

209. See, e.g., Okediji, *supra* note 37, at 178–86.

210. Reichman & Okediji, *supra* note 23, at 1434–9.

211. Reichman & Okediji, *supra* note 23, at 1434–9; Peter K. Yu, "The Objectives and Principles of the TRIPS Agreement," 46 *Hous. L. Rev.* 979, 1006 (2009) (describing how these provisions may be interpreted to facilitate development and to protect the public interest).

212. Ruth Okediji, "Toward an International Fair Use Regime," 39 *Colum. J. Transnat'l L.* 75, 149 (2000).

213. TRIPS Agreement, *supra* note 10, art. 13.

214. WCT, *supra* note 193, art. 10 (reiterating the three-step test of TRIPS art. 13). The accompanying Agreed Statement of the diplomatic conference that adopted the WCT confirms that Article 10 allows signatories to "devise new" limitations and exceptions for the digital environment. See *supra* note 206.

215. "Three-Step Test", *supra* note 180, at 711–12.

216. WCT, *supra* note 193, pmbl. ("Recognizing the need to maintain a balance between the rights of authors and the larger public interest, particularly education, research and access to information, as reflected in the Berne Convention").

217. "Three-Step Test", *supra* note 180, at 712; cf. TRIPS Agreement, *supra* note 10, art. 30 (exceptions to exclusive rights of patentees).

218. "Three-Step Test", *supra* note 180, at 709, 711. U.S. copyright law provides: "In determining whether the use made of a work in any particular case is a fair use the factors to be considered shall include-

(1) the purpose and character of the use, including whether such use is of a commercial nature or is for nonprofit educational purposes;

(2) the nature of the copyrighted work;

(3) the amount and substantiality of the portion used in relation to the copyrighted work as a whole; and

(4) the effect of the use upon the potential market for or value of the copyrighted work."

17 U.S.C. § 107 (2006). But see Mihaly Ficsor, *The Law of Copyright and the Internet*, 91–2 (2002) (arguing that the legislative history of the Berne Convention prohibits this approach).

219. "Three-Step Test", *supra* note 180, at 712; See Hugenholtz & Okediji, *supra* note 180, at 21 (describing some decisions in European courts that have allowed unauthorized uses); Lange & Powell, *supra* note 181, at 126 (analyzing the tensions between the First Amendment and copyright protection); Laurence R. Helfer, "Toward a Human Rights Framework for Intellectual Property," 40 *U.C. Davis L. Rev.* 971, 1017 (2007) ("In particular, there have been a number of decisions in the field of copyright in which the freedom of expression has been invoked to justify a use that is not covered by an exception provided for in the law." (quoting Christophe Geiger, "Fundamental Rights, a Safeguard for the Coherence of Intellectual Property Law?" 35 *Int'l Rev. Intell. Prop. & Competition L.* 268, 277 (2004))).

220. "Three-Step Test", *supra* note 180, at 712; See Chon, *supra* note 37, at 820.

221. "Three-Step Test", *supra* note 180, at 709–10.

222. "Three-Step Test", *supra* note 180, 710.

223. See *infra* text accompanying notes 331–4.

224. See WCT, *supra* note 193, art. 11.

225. 17 U.S.C. §§ 1201–5 (2006).

226. Council Directive 2001/29/EC, art. 6(4), 2001 O.J. (L 167) (EC).

227. Reichman, Dinwoodie & Samuelson, *supra* note 180, at 1042–5.

228. WCT, *supra* note 193, art. 11.

229. See Mark A. Lemley & R. Anthony Reese, "Reducing Digital Copyright Infringement without Restricting Innovation," 56 *Stan. L. Rev.* 1345 (2004) (advocating administrative measures to enforce limitations and exceptions online); Reichman, Dinwoodie & Samuelson, *supra* note 180, at 1003 (discussing the importance of a commitment to ensuring that copyright limitations and exceptions are as available when copyrighted works are protected by TPMs as when they are not).

230. Reichman & Okediji, *supra* note 23, at 1443.

231. Reichman, Dinwoodie & Samuelson, *supra* note 180, at 1032–8 (proposing judicially enforceable measures to extract privileged matter without the user having to enter digitally locked gateways).

232. Reichman, Dinwoodie & Samuelson, *supra* note 180, at 1032–8.

233. See, e.g., Hilty et al., *supra* note 203, at 3; Reichman & Okediji, *supra* note 23, at 1447–52.

234. See Mario Cimoli, Giovanni Dosi & Joseph E. Stiglitz, "The Political Economy of Capabilities Accumulation: The Past and Future of Policies for Industrial Development," in *Industrial Policy and Development: The Political Economy of Capabilities Accumulation* (Mario Cimoli et al. eds., 2009), 1, 4–5; Joseph E. Stiglitz, "Knowledge as a Global Public Good," in *Global Public Goods* 308 (Inge Kaul et al. eds., 1999) (advocating the perspective that knowledge is a public good that should be protected by the state); cf. Maskus & Reichman, *supra* note 2, at 41–4.

235. See *supra* text accompanying note 78; *infra* notes 301–3 and accompanying text.

236. See, e.g., Josef Drexl, "The Critical Role of Competition Law in Preserving Public Goods in Conflict with Intellectual Property Rights," in *International Public Goods and Transfer of Technology under a Globalized Intellectual Property Regime, supra* note 2, at 709, 717–18; Eleanor M. Fox, "Can Antitrust Policy Protect the Global Commons from the Excesses of IPRs?" in *International Public Goods and Transfer of Technology under a Globalized Intellectual Property Regime, supra* note 2, at 758, 767 ("In a world of global markets and world ramifications of local action, both antitrust and intellectual property law cry out for global conceptions"); see also Sean Flynn, Aidan Hollis & Mike Palmedo, "An Economic Justification for Open Access to Essential Medicine Patents in Developing Countries," 37 *J.L. Med. & Ethics* 184, 191–3 (2009) (suggesting that developing countries adopt legal standards, especially competition law doctrines, to drive down prices in competitive markets).

237. Reichman, *supra* note 18, at 161.

238. TRIPS Agreement, *supra* note 10, arts. 8.2, 40. See Mark D. Janis, "'Minimal' Standards for Patent-Related Antitrust Law under TRIPS," in *International Public Goods and Transfer of Technology under a Globalized Intellectual Property Regime, supra* note 2, at 774, 776–80; Hanns Ullrich, "Expansionist Intellectual Property Protection and Reductionist Competition Rules: A TRIPS Perspective," in *International Public Goods and Transfer of Technology under a Globalized Intellectual Property Regime, supra* note 2, at 726, 730; see also Shubha Ghosh, "Comment II: Competitive Baselines for Intellectual Property Systems," in *International Public Goods and Transfer of Technology under a Globalized Intellectual Property Regime, supra* note 2, at 793, 807–11 (concentrating on the possibilities afforded to members to limit intellectual property rights through competition law and policy indirectly under Articles 6, 13, 30 and 31 of the TRIPS Agreement).

239. See, e.g., Hovenkamp, *supra* note 2, at 1979–2007 (examining the complex historical enforcement of antitrust laws to protect intellectual property rights in the United States).

240. See Arezzo, *supra* note 133, at 458–65 (analyzing the differences between EU and U.S. antitrust laws).

241. Hovenkamp, *supra* note 2, at 1991–2 (explaining that the U.S. Supreme Court's diminishing hostility toward tying arrangements and "reduced concern about anticompetitive effects" resulted in an "increasing insisten[ce] that market power be explicitly proven"); See *Ill. Tool Works Inc. v. Indep. Ink, Inc.*, 547 U.S. 28, 42–3 (2006) (replacing the presumption of illegality in a tying arrangement involving a patented product with the requirement of proof of power in the relevant market). See generally Thomas F. Cotter, "Misuse," 44 *Hous. L. Rev.* 901 (2007) (tracing the development of the misuse doctrine).

242. See Fox, *supra* note 236, at 768–9 (describing U.S. antitrust laws as being guided by efficiency rather than fairness principles and suggesting that the goals would coincide upon limiting immunities); Ullrich, *supra* note 238, at 747–8 (detailing the shift of competition law enforcement toward efficiency-based innovation).

243. See Ghidini, *supra* note 109, at 114–15.

244. See Drexl, *supra* note 236, at 716–17 ("In principle, IPRs and competition laws . . . are two complementary instruments for the establishment and preservation of competitive markets."); Fox, *supra* note 236, at 764 (asserting that many nations' antitrust laws are ineffective in policing monopolies granted by IPRs because they neither prohibit excessive pricing nor recognize the refusal to license intellectual property as an offense); Hovenkamp, *supra* note 2, at 1979 (explaining that while both IP and antitrust policy seek to promote economic welfare, they do so in different ways, causing the relation between the two to be "unstable and problematic").

245. See Coco, *supra* note 133, at 20; Frischmann & Weber Waller, *supra* note 110, at 57–64 (discussing the European cases).

246. Kapczynski, *supra* note 4 (quoting The Patents Act, 1970, No. 39, Acts of Parliament, 1970, § 140(iii)); Einer Elhauge, "Tying, Bundled Discounts, and the Death of the Single Monopoly Profit Theory," 123 *Harv. L. Rev.* 397 (2009) (rejecting efficiency claims and demonstrating how tying generally harms consumer welfare).

247. The Patents Act, 1970, No. 39, Acts of Parliament, 1970, § 84(6)(ii), (iv), *as amended by* The Patents (Amendment) Act, 2002, No. 38, Acts of Parliament, 2002.

248. The Patents Act, 1970, No. 39, Acts of Parliament, 1970, § 84, *as amended by* The Patents (Amendment) Act, 2002, No. 38, Acts of Parliament, 2002; Kapczynski, *supra* note 4.

249. See Feng, *supra* note 9, at 99–102.

250. Feng, *supra* note 9, at 100.

251. See, e.g., Abbott, *supra* note 40, at 20; Maskus & Okediji, *supra* note 40, at 7–8; Reichman et al., *supra* note 40, at 28–33.

252. See Fox, *supra* note 236, at 760–1.

253. See Paris Convention, *supra* note 88, art. 5A; G.H.C. Bodenhausen, *Guide to the Application of the Paris Convention for the Protection of Industrial Property as Revised at Stockholm in 1967*, at 70–1 (1968) (pointing out flexibilities in the Paris Convention allowing nations to define and legislate against abuses which might result from the exercise of the exclusive rights conferred by a patent); Cotter, *supra* note 241, at 908–9; See also Reichman with Hasenzahl, *supra* note 111, at 21 (noting U.S. practice of nonenforcement, used to correct misuses of exclusive rights).

254. See TRIPS Agreement, *supra* note 10, arts. 3, 4, 8.2, 40 (requiring members to accord no less favorable treatment to other members with regard to the protection of intellectual property); Paris Convention, *supra* note 88, art. 2(1) (declaring that nationals of any country of the Union shall have the same protection and legal remedy with regard to industrial property as in any of the other countries of the Union).

255. See Deere, *supra* note 30, at 3.

256. See Dreyfuss, *supra* note 3, at 7 (stressing policy space within TRIPS flexibilities to promote local creative and technological skills).

257. For evidence of the Andean Community's successful efforts in this regard, see Helfer et al., *supra* note 47, at 16–36.

258. See David, *supra* note 72, at 82 (arguing that the Hopi word *koyaanisqatsi,* meaning "life out of balance," can be used to describe the international regime of intellectual property rights due to the "dangerously altered . . . balance between private rights and the public domain in data and information").

259. See, e.g., Frischmann, *supra* note 64, at 923–6 (developing a theory that strong economic arguments exist for managing and sustaining openly accessible intellectual infrastructure); Lee, "Contracting to Preserve", *supra* note 73, at 893–4 (suggesting that public institutions have freedom to effectuate norms favoring wide dissemination of research technologies through a new model of "consideration-based patent regulation"); Lee, "Distributive Commons", *supra* note 73, at 21–2 (comparing health technologies to infrastructure). See generally Benkler, *supra* note 176, at 3 (claiming that the information economy is entering a new stage, which he calls the "networked information economy").

260. See, e.g., Reichman, Uhlir & Dedeurwaerdere, *supra* note 73, ch. 4 (proposing compensatory liability regime for commercial applications of microbial genetic materials deposited for research purposes in culture collections); Victoria Henson-Apollonio, "The International Treaty on Plant Genetic Resources for Food and Agriculture (ITPGRFA): The Standard Material Transfer Agreement as Implementation of a Limited Compensatory Liability Regime," in *Gene Patents and Collaborative Licensing Models, supra* note 24, at 289, 289–3 (describing recent efforts to facilitate the exchange of crop germ plasm for commercial food and agricultural purposes through compensatory liability regimes); Rai et al., *supra* note 132, at 26 (proposing liability rule for pre-competitive pooling of small molecule libraries for high throughput screening); Reichman & Lewis, *supra* note 159, at 345–8 (proposing use of liability rules to stimulate investment in traditional knowledge). See generally Reichman, *supra* note 53, at 1776–7 (proposing compensatory liability regime for small-scale innovation).

261. See, e.g., Rai & Eisenberg, *supra* note 41, at 300–1; So et al., *supra* note 41, at 2078–82 (describing the Bayh-Dole Act of 1980 and examining the potential problems for developing countries modeling legislation on the Act); V.C. Vivekanandan, "The Public-Private Dichotomy of Intellectual Property: Recommendations for the WIPO Development Agenda," in *Implementing the World Intellectual Property Organization's Development Agenda, supra* note 78, at 131, 132–4.

262. Dreyfuss, *supra* note 3, at 21–5.

263. See, e.g., Yu, *supra* note 208, at 370–83 (stressing coordination strategies such as South-South Alliances, North-South Cooperation, and use of the WTO Dispute Settlement Process); See also Dreyfuss, *supra* note 3, at 17–21 (stressing importance of coordination in international lawmaking exercises concerning IPRs in general).

264. Maskus & Reichman, *supra* note 2, at 3, 19.

265. Reichman & Dreyfuss, *supra* note 12, at 122–9.

266. See generally Deere, *supra* note 30 (revealing the international pressures and national political dynamics which resulted in the variation of responses to TRIPS in developing countries).

267. Deere, *supra* note 30, at 164–7.

268. See, e.g., Sisule F. Musungu & Graham Dutfield, "Multilateral Agreements and a TRIPS-Plus World: The World Intellectual Property Organisation (WIPO)," 16–17 (2003), available at <http://www.quno.org/geneva/pdf/economic/Issues/Multilateral-Agreements-in-TRIPS-plus-English.pdf> (accessed 13 September 2013).

269. Deere, *supra* note 30, at 167–8, 180 (emphasizing ideational power as an explanation for the varying actions of developing countries and describing capacity-building as the area of clearest intersection between economic and ideational power in the TRIPS implementation game); see also Drahos with Braithwaite, *supra* note 12, at 90–93; Graham Dutfield, *Intellectual Property Rights, Trade and Biodiversity*, 12 (2000) (attributing the adoption of the TRIPS Agreement, "given the ambivalent if not hostile stance of many developing countries," to the promise of favorable agreements in areas such as textiles and agriculture); Peter Drahos, "BITS and BIPS: Bilateralism in Intellectual Property," 4 *J. World Intell. Prop.* 791, 803–4 (2001) (revealing the danger of developing countries "being led into a highly complex multilateral/bilateral web" that is eroding their ability to set and interpret intellectual property standards domestically).

270. Deere, *supra* note 30, at 172–9; See also Laurence R. Helfer, "Regime Shifting: The TRIPS Agreement and New Dynamics of International Intellectual Property Lawmaking," 29 *Yale J. Int'l L.* 1, 23–7 (2004) (observing that NGOs and developing countries began to regard TRIPS as a "coerced agreement" and describing how, in the wake of TRIPS, NGOs aided developing nations in intellectual property lawmaking).

271. Deere, *supra* note 30, at 197. In Africa, this lack of expertise at the national level led to the delegation of intellectual property matters to regional entities that were particularly susceptible to high-protectionist pressures from WIPO and OECD countries generally. See Deere, *supra* note 30, at 219–20.

272. Dreyfuss, *supra* note 3, at 7.

273. See Deere, *supra* note 30, at 211–20; See also Helfer et al., *supra* note 47, at 16–32 (documenting more successful regional coordination efforts in the Andean Community).

274. Drahos, *supra* note 30; *see also* Deere, *supra* note 30, at 207. Professor Gervais points to the perception of arcane "club" rules beyond the written word of the treaties, with the risk that the intellectual property club can create distance between policymakers and their country's larger public interest. E-mail from Daniel Gervais, Professor of Law, Vanderbilt University Law School, to Jerome Reichman, Professor of Law, Duke University School of Law (14 September 2009) (on file with author).

275. See Deere, *supra* note 30, at 198 (noting the impact of weak public administration and corruption on TRIPS implementation in developing countries).

276. See Helfer et al., *supra* note 47, at 16–32.

277. See, e.g., Gordon C.K. Cheung, *Intellectual Property Rights in China*, 63–82 (2009) (describing the quantitative and legal measures taken by the Chinese government to counteract rampant counterfeiting of intellectual property); Al-larakhia, *supra* note 178, at 11 ("As economies in emerging markets enter the biopharmaceutical arena, it is essential that developed economies share not only

technological expertise, but also their experiences regarding knowledge production and dissemination."); Mizukami & Lemos, *supra* note 33, at 44–5 (analyzing the *tecnobrega* industry in Brazil and its implications for intellectual property protection); Yu, *supra* note 208, at 346–8 (exploring how the BRIC countries can "promote access to essential medicines in the less developed world" through collaboration with other developing countries); See also Shamnad Basheer & Annalisa Primi, "The WIPO Development Agenda: Factoring in the "Technologically Proficient" Developing Countries," in *Implementing the World Intellectual Property Organization's Development Agenda, supra* note 78, at 100, 101–4 (cautioning against a polarized view of developing countries in the context of technological capability); Pedro Paranagua, "Strategies to Implement WIPO's Development Agenda: A Brazilian Perspective and Beyond," in *Implementing the World Intellectual Property Organization's Development Agenda, supra* note 78, at 140, 140–2 (focusing on the role of NGOs in implementing the WIPO Development Agenda).

278. I am indebted to Laurence Helfer for this cautionary note.
279. See, e.g., Kapczynski, "Access to Knowledge," *supra* note 196; Paranagua, *supra* note 277.
280. See, e.g., Deere, *supra* note 30, at 199, 211–18 (describing Brazil as "the country that exhibited the highest degree of coordination domestically on IP policy matters and that also achieved the greatest coordination of its external IP relations").
281. See Helfer et al., *supra* note 47, at 16–32.
282. Kapczynski, *supra* note 4; See also Reichman & Dreyfuss, *supra* note 12, at 177–82 (suggesting new approaches to existing IP problems rather than premature patent harmonization efforts).
283. For example, the Andean Community has lost Venezuela and Bolivia, and may be disintegrating. See Helfer et al., *supra* note 47.
284. See, e.g., Deere, *supra* note 30, at 240–86 (describing experience of the African Organization for Intellectual Property (OAPI)).
285. Kapczynski, *supra* note 4.
286. Kapczynski, *supra* note 4.
287. Kapczynski, *supra* note 4; See also Paul Edward Geller, "Legal Transplants in International Copyright: Some Problems of Method," 13 *UCLA Pac. Basin L.J.* 199 (1994).
288. See Jerome Reichman, Jayasharee Watal & Ruth Ghana Okediji, "Flagship Project on Innovation, Culture, Biogenetic Resources, and Traditional Knowledge," U.N. Development Programme (2000) (unpublished manuscript, on file with author).
289. See generally Basheer & Primi, *supra* note 277.
290. Reichman, Watal & Okediji, *supra* note 288; See also Chon, *supra* note 37, at 806–20 (probing the relationship between IP law and social justice); Maskus & Reichman, *supra* note 2, at 24 ("These countries can hardly absorb the unknown social costs of new intellectual property burdens when the real costs of the last round of legislative initiatives are still making themselves felt.").
291. See Reichman, Watal & Okediji, *supra* note 288.

292. See Peter K. Yu, "Building Intellectual Property Coalitions for Development," in *Implementing the World Intellectual Property Organization's Development Agenda, supra* note 78, at 79, 90–3 ("Regional or pro-development fora are particularly effective means for coordinating efforts by less developed countries in the areas of public health, IP, and international trade.").

293. "With the exception of a handful of countries, like Brazil and India, the prospect of tailored approaches to TRIPS implementation was curtailed by the absence of a broader policy framework setting out national needs and priorities through which reform options could be considered.... Among developing countries, Brazil stood out for having a strategic approach to TRIPS implementation based on a broad policy framework for development and associated industrial policies. India also worked to place IP issues within a broader policy framework through its five-year plans." Deere, *supra* note 30, at 199.

294. Feng, *supra* note 9, at 10–11.

295. Helfer et al., *supra* note 47, at 17–32.

296. Helfer et al., *supra* note 47, at 17.

297. Deere, *supra* note 30, at 199; see, e.g., Drahos, *supra* note 30; "Integrating Intellectual Property Rights and Development Policy," 5, Commission on Intellectual Property Rights (2003), available at <http://www.iprcommission.org/pa pers/pdfs/final_report/CIPRfullfinal.pdf> (accessed 22 December 2009); Carlos Correa, "Formulating Effective Pro-development National Intellectual Property Strategies," in *Trading Knowledge: Development Perspectives on TRIPS, Trade and Sustainability* (Christophe Bellman et al. eds., 2003), 209, 214 ("Due to their limited domestic capacity, developing countries are strongly dependent on technical assistance, and rely for expert advice and commentary on new draft legislation on the [WIPO] and the [WTO], especially to conform consistency of draft legislation with international obligations.").

298. Deere, *supra* note 30, at 219.

299. See Yu, *supra* note 8, at 177–80.

300. For the view that the United States' own interagency review mechanisms no longer meet today's needs for a vibrant and effective innovation policy, see Stuart Minor Benjamin & Arti K. Rai, "Fixing Innovation Policy: A Structural Perspective," 77 *Geo. Wash. L. Rev.* 1, 3–8 (2008) (highlighting "certain well-established pathologies of the regulatory state").

301. WIPO, "General Report Adopted by the Assemblies of the Member States of WIPO," at 135–47, WIPO Doc. A/43/16 (12 November 2007), available at <http://www.wipo.int/edocs/%20mdocs/govbody/en/a_43/a_43_16-main1.pdf> (accessed 22 December 2009); see, e.g., Denis Borges Barbosa, Margaret Chon & Andres Moncayo von Hase, "Slouching towards Development in International Intellectual Property," 2007 *Mich. St. L. Rev.* 71, 120–3 (addressing the purpose and constraints of the WIPO Development Agenda); de Beer, *supra* note 78, at 1–2.

302. World Health Org. [WHO], "Global Strategy and Plan of Action on Public Health, Innovation and Intellectual Property," WHO Doc. WHA 61.21 (24 May 2008), available at <http://apps.who.int/gb/ebwha/pdf_files/A61/A61_ R21-en.pdf> (accessed 13 September 2013) (building upon the report of the

Intergovernmental Working Group on Public Health, Innovation and Intellectual Property).

303. See, e.g., WHO, "Draft Global Strategy and Plan of Action on Public Health, Innovation and Intellectual Property: Mapping the Funding for Research and Development for Neglected Diseases," WHO Doc. A/PHI/IGWG/2/INF.DOC./2 (28 August 2007), available at <http://apps.who.int/gb/phi/pdf/igwg2/PHI_IGWG2_ID2-en.pdf> (accessed 13 September 2013) (reporting on the funding for health research and development of research related to neglected diseases); WHO, "Strengthening Health Systems to Improve Health Outcomes: Who's Framework for Action," 1–5 (2007), available at <www.who.int/healthsystems/strategy/everybodys_business.pdf> (accessed 13 September 2013) (noting the unacceptable health outcomes across the developing world and providing a framework to strengthen health systems to reverse this trend); WHO, "Equitable Access to Essential Medicines: A Framework for Collective Action," 1–6 (2004), available at <http://archives.who.int/tbs/ndp/s4962e.pdf> (accessed 13 September 2013) (proposing actions for policymakers to take to improve access to existing essential medicines and vaccines).

304. See, e.g., Carolyn Deere, "Reforming Governance to Advance the WIPO Development Agenda," in *Implementing the World Intellectual Property Organization's Development Agenda, supra* note 78, at 43, 43–46 (critically evaluating WIPO's governance); Xuan Li, "A Conceptual and Methodological Framework for Impact Assessment under the WIPO Development Agenda (Cluster D)," in *Implementing the World Intellectual Property Organization's Development Agenda, supra* note 78, at 34, 40; See also E. Richard Gold & Jean-Frederic Morin, "From Agenda to Implementation: Working outside the WIPO Box," in *Implementing the World Intellectual Property Organization's Development Agenda, supra* note 78, at 57, 64–6 (encouraging WIPO to outsource the implementation of the Development Agenda).

305. See Hugenholtz & Okediji, *supra* note 180, at 9–15 (suggesting that international harmonization of limitations and exceptions in copyright law would enhance the benefits of substantive rights harmonization); Dreyfuss, *supra* note 180, at 22 (making a case for adding explicit user rights to the TRIPS Agreement); Annette Kur & Henning Grosse Ruse-Kahn, "Enough is Enough: The Notion of Binding Ceilings in International Intellectual Property Protection," 19–25 (Max Planck Inst. for Intellectual Prop., Competition & Tax Law Research Paper Series, Paper No. 09-01, 2008), available at <http://ssrn.com/abstract=1326429> (accessed 14 September 2013); "Three-Step Test", *supra* note 180, at 1 (observing the need for the "Three-Step Test" to be interpreted "so as to ensure a proper and balanced application of limitations and exceptions").

306. See Laurence R. Helfer, "Human Rights and Intellectual Property: Conflict or Coexistence?" 5 *Minn. Intell. Prop. Rev.* 47, 55–7 (2003) (discussing the "antagonistic approach to TRIPS" taken by the UN Sub-Commission on the Promotion and Protection of Human Rights in Resolution 2000/7 on Intellectual Property Rights and Human Rights); Helfer, *supra* note 219, at 1009–14; See also Joost Pauwelyn, *Conflict of Norms in Public International Law*, 304–305, 309 (2003) (discussing the Vienna Convention's objective of prohibiting agreements that

affect the rights or obligations of third parties, which extends to those agreements that "detract . . . from substantive human rights"); Thomas Cottier, Joost Pauwelyn & Elisabeth Biirgi, "Introduction" to *Human Rights and International Trade* (Thomas Cottier et al. eds., 2005).

307. TRIPS Agreement, *supra* note 10, arts. 7–8; See generally Yu, *supra* note 211.

308. See Hugenholtz & Okediji, *supra* note 180, at 49–50 (expounding the benefits of a soft-law modality).

309. For example, while expanded protection for Geographical Indications and perhaps some forms of traditional knowledge might become acceptable to both sides, proposals for database protection or deep patent law harmonization would almost certainly cost developing countries far more than any gains from greater recognition of so-called user rights. See Reichman & Dreyfuss, *supra* note 12, at 93–4.

310. See generally Charles R. McManis, "The Proposed Anti-Counterfeiting Trade Agreement (ACTA): Two Tales of a Treaty," 46 *Hous. L. Rev.* 1,235 (2009) (describing what is known of the closed-door trade negotiations surrounding ACTA, an agreement ostensibly aimed at fighting the proliferation of counterfeit and pirated goods in international trade).

311. See Doha Public Health Declaration, *supra* note 31.

312. Posting of Tom Bollyky, "Terminology Matters: The Dispute between India and EU over Generic Drug Transshipments," to Global Health Policy Blog (12 August 2009), <http://blogs.cgdev.org/globalhealth/2009/08/terminology-matters-the-dispute-between-india-and-eu-over-generic-drug-transshipments.php> (accessed 14 September 2013); Kaitlin Mara, "Drug Seizures in Frankfurt Spark Fears of EU-wide Pattern," *Intell. Prop. Watch*, 5 June 2009, <http://www.ip-watch.org/weblog/2009/06/05/drug-seizures-in-frankfurt-spark-fears-of-eu-wide-pattern> (accessed 14 September 2013); See also Abbott & Reichman, *supra* note 38, at 966 (reporting that the EU had been "effectively seeking to burden" countries with "the duty to implement the terms of its Intellectual Property Enforcement Directive," by ordering provisional measures such as "the physical seizure of infringing goods").

313. See Brian Mercurio *supra* note 193.

314. See Pedro Paranagua, "The Development Agenda for WIPO: Another Stillbirth? A Battle between Access to Knowledge and Enclosure," 41–2 (1 July 2005) (unpublished LLM thesis, Queen Mary & Westfield College), <http://ssrn.com/abstract=844366 > (accessed 14 September 2013) (criticizing long discussions as irrelevant to the main goals of the Development Agenda).

315. See Wenting Cheng, "Third Revision of Patent Law in China (Part II)," *Intell. Prop. Watch*, 1 October 2009, <http://ip-watch.org/weblog/2009/10/01/third-revision-of-patent-law-in-china-part-ii> (accessed 14 September 2013).

316. Cheng, *supra* note 315. Draft regulations define "genetic resources" as any material that "is obtained from the human body, animals, plants or micro-organism, contains a genetic functional unit, and is of actual or potential value." Inventions subject to the provision "make . . . use of the genetic function of genetic resources." *Id.*

317. Cheng, *supra* note 315; See Convention on Biological Diversity arts. 1, 15–16, 5 June 1992, 1760 U.N.T.S. 79, 143 (promoting the "sharing in a fair and

equitable way the results of research and development and the benefits arising from the commercial and other utilization of genetic resources").

318. Cheng, *supra* note 315.

319. See Feng, *supra* note 9, at 63–4. In China, unauthorized exports of genetic materials from wild soybeans, local gooseberry varieties, "and even the famous Beijing duck" had allegedly led to the development of hybrids patented abroad that were subsequently imported into China. Cheng, *supra* note 315.

320. See *supra* text accompanying notes 200–5 (suggesting that developing countries adopt broad exemptions aimed at promoting scientific research uses of literature and data). See generally Reichman, Uhlir & Dedeurwaerdere, *supra* note 73, chs. 6–7.

321. See, e.g., Reichman & Okediji, *supra* note 23, at 1428–51; "Three-Step Test", *supra* note 180, at 3 (prefacing that individual states should have flexibility to shape their own copyright laws and stating that the three-step test should not undermine European legislation on limitations); See also Andrew Rens, "Implementing WIPO's Development Agenda: Treaty Provisions on Minimum Exceptions and Limitations for Education," in *Implementing the World Intellectual Property Organization's Development Agenda*, *supra* note 78, at 158, 160–1 (pointing out that "[e]xceptions and limitations already exist in the laws of most developed countries and many developing countries" and, in particular, arguing for copyright exceptions for educational purposes). But lobbying pressures against change in the pending Brazilian copyright reform are reportedly fierce, according to confidential top-level sources.

322. See "Three-Step Test", *supra* note 180, at 3 ("[T]he Test may be incorporated directly or it may function exclusively as an aid to the interpretation of domestic legislation.").

323. See Kur & Grosse Ruse-Khan, *supra* note 305, at 26 n.89.

324. See Ladas, *supra* note 44, at 63–94 (chronicling the development of the Paris Convention).

325. WIPO, "Treaty for Improved Access for Blind, Visually Impaired and Other Reading Disabled Persons," Annex, WIPO Doc. SCCR/18/5 (25 May 2009), available at <http://www.wipo.int/edocs/mdocs/copyright/en/sccr_18/sccr_18_5.pdf> (accessed 13 September 2013) (proposal put forward by Brazil, Ecuador, and Paraguay based on recommendations of the World Blind Union); William New, "Proposed WIPO Treaty on Visually Impaired Access Gets Deeper Look," *Intell. Prop. Watch*, 29 May 2009, <http://www.ip-watch.org/weblog/2009/05/29/proposed-wipo-treaty-on-visually-impaired-access-gets-deeper-look> (accessed 13 September 2013).

326. See Sara E. Crager & Matt Price, "Prizes and Parasites: Incentive Models for Addressing Chagas Disease," 37 *J.L. Med. & Ethics* 292, 300–1 (2009).

327. Trade Act of 1974, Pub. L. No. 93-618, § 301, 88 Stat. 1978, 2041–2 (1975) (codified as amended at 19 U.S.C. § 2411 (2006)).

328. Office of the U.S. Trade Representative, "2009 Special 301 Report" 3, 17, 23 (2009), available at <http://www.ustr.gov/sites/default/files/Full%20Version%20of%20the%202009%20SPECIAL%20301%20REPORT.pdf> (accessed 22 December 2009) (noting that Argentina and Brazil appear on the Priority Watch

and Watch Lists, respectively, as targets for enforcement through trade preference programs such as the Generalized System of Preferences (GSP)).

329. See Bird, *supra* note 47, at 210, 214 ("[L]icenses invite scrutiny by wealthy governments ready to defend their multinationals through trade sanctions.... Evidence
certainly exists that compulsory licensing, or even the threat of compulsory licensing, can lower drug prices dramatically."); Kristina M. Lybecker & Elisabeth Fowler,
"Compulsory Licensing in Canada and Thailand: Comparing Regimes to Ensure
Legitimate Use of the WTO Rules," 37 *J.L. Med. & Ethics* 222, 233 (2009); See also
Abbott & Reichman, *supra* note 38, at 929–30; Bryan C. Mercurio, "TRIPs, Patents,
and Access to Life-Saving Drugs in the Developing World," 8 *Marq. Intell. Prop.
L. Rev.* 211, 224 (2004); Outterson, *supra* note 38, at 229–30.

330. See Flynn, Hollis & Palmedo, *supra* note 236, at 186 (describing the use of
monopoly pricing in under-developed pharmaceutical markets).

331. See TRIPS Agreement, *supra* note 10, art. 68; Agreement Establishing the World
Trade Organization art. IV, 15 April 1994, Marrakesh Agreement Establishing
the World Trade Organization, Legal Instruments-Results of the Uruguay
Round, 33 I.L.M. 1125 (1994) (designating the roles and duties of the TRIPS
Council).

332. Understanding on Rules and Procedures Governing the Settlement of Disputes,
15 April 1994, Marrakesh Agreement Establishing the World Trade Organization, Annex 2, Legal Instruments-Results of the Uruguay Round, 33 I.L.M. 1125
(1994) [hereinafter DSU].

333. See Reichman, *supra* note 140, at 254 (observing that developing countries are
hesitant to employ legitimate legal tools and flexibilities contained in the TRIPS
Agreement when faced with threats of retaliation by powerful countries); Yu,
supra note 208, at 350 (discussing Brazil's request for consultation following a
dispute settlement process with developed countries). But see Gregory Shaffer,
"Recognizing Public Goods in WTO Dispute Settlement: Who Participates? Who
Decides? The Case of TRIPS and Pharmaceutical Patent Protection," in *International Public Goods and Transfer of Technology under a Globalized Intellectual
Property Regime*, *supra* note 2, at 884, 895–901 (describing impediments), 901–7
(prescribing strategies to overcome them).

334. DSU, *supra* note 332, art. 23.1.

335. The USTR has revoked the GSP privileges against several Latin American
countries in the past (notably Argentina and Brazil), see *supra* note 328, and it
has threatened Thailand with similar actions. Because GSP concessions are
voluntary, and not required under the General Agreement on Tariffs and
Trade (GATT 1994), they may normally be revoked at will; however, revoking
GSP privileges as retaliation for a unilaterally determined violation of a TRIPS
obligation would seem to violate both the letter and spirit of Article 23 of the
DSU. Michael J. Trebilcock & Robert Howse, "The Regulation of International
Trade" 434 (3rd edn, 2005); Abbott & Reichman, *supra* note 38, at 980.

336. See UNCTAD-ICTSD, *Resource Book on TRIPS and Development*, 4–5, 8, 10, (2005).

337. Panel Report, "United States-Sections 301–310 of the Trade Act of 1974," WT/
DS152/R (22 December 1999). At the time, the USTR promised to exercise its
power in conformity with the DSU.

338. Reichman, *supra* note 140, at 259 (footnotes omitted); see Vienna Convention on the Law of Treaties art. 60, 23 May 1969, 1155 U.N.T.S. 33 (permitting suspension of treaty obligations when one party materially breaches a multilateral treaty).

339. See, e.g., UNCTAD-ICTSD, *supra* note 336, at 682 (discussing cross-retaliation in the form of trade sanctions by suspension of concessions); Henning Grosse Ruse-Khan, "A Pirate of the Caribbean? The Attractions of Suspending TRIPS Obligations," 11 *J. Int'l Econ. L.* 313, 316–18 (2008) (recounting a WTO Panel decision allowing Antigua to request suspension of its TRIPS obligations in response to the United States' refusal to comply with a prior DSB order to cease interference with Antigua's gambling and betting services); see also Catherine Saez, "WTO Ruling on Brazil-US Cotton Opens Door to Cross-Retaliation Against IP Rights," *Intell. Prop. Watch,* 7 September 2009, <http://www.ip-watch. org/weblog/2009/09/07/wto-ruling-on-brazil-cotton-opens-door-to-cross-retaliation-against-ip-rights> (accessed 13 September 2013) describing the DSB's authorization of Brazil to take cross-collateral trade sanctions against the United States for illegal cotton subsidies.

340. Appellate Body Report, "India-Patent Protection for Pharmaceutical and Agricultural Chemical Products," ¶58, 84, WT/DS50/AB/R (19 December 1997).

341. Appellate Body Report, supra note 340, ¶46, 59; TRIPS Agreement, *supra* note 10, art. 1.1 ("Members shall be free to determine the appropriate method of implementing the provisions of this Agreement within their own legal system and practice."); see Jerome H. Reichman, "Securing Compliance with the TRIPS Agreement after *US v India,*" 1 *JIEL,* 585, 596 (1998) ("Deference to local law and strict construction of treaties have thus become the pedestal on which the Appellate Body's TRIPS jurisprudence rests."); see also Dreyfuss, *supra* note 3, at 15–16.

342. Panel Report, "China-Measures Affecting the Protection and Enforcement of Intellectual Property Rights," ¶8.1–4, WT/DS362/R (26 January 2009) [hereinafter "China Enforcement of IP"].

343. Dreyfuss, *supra* note 3, at 16; See "China Enforcement of IP", *supra* note 342, ¶7.236.

344. Dreyfuss, *supra* note 3, at 17.

345. See Cheung, *supra* note 277, at 8; Gervais, *supra* note 5, at 2371–2; Yu, *supra* note 8, at 176–8; *supra* note 21 and accompanying text.

346. See Daniel C.K. Chow, "Counterfeiting in the People's Republic of China," 78 *Wash. U. L.Q.* 1, 47, 49 (2000) (asserting that foreign brand owners invest in China's economy, in part due to the market for counterfeit products); Yu, *supra* note 8, at 175, 180 (arguing that foreign investors are attracted to China because of low production costs and market potential). See generally Keith E. Maskus, "The Role of Intellectual Property Rights in Encouraging Foreign Direct Investment and Technology Transfer," 9 *Duke J. Comp. & Int'l L.* 109 (1998) (noting the large amount of foreign investment in Latin American countries, in part due to tax and operating advantages).

347. See *supra* notes 239–43, 253–4 and accompanying text.

348. See, e.g., Cheung, *supra* note 277, at 26, 31; Chow, *supra* note 346, at 51.

349. See Paris Convention, *supra* note 88, art. 4*bis* ("Patents applied for . . . shall be independent of patents obtained for the same invention in other countries, whether members of the Union or not."); TRIPS Agreement, *supra* note 10, art. 2.1 (incorporating substantive provisions of the Paris Convention).
350. Maskus, *supra* note 1, at 200–3.
351. See, e.g., Margaret Chon, "Substantive Equality in International Intellectual Property Norm Setting and Interpretation," in *Intellectual Property, Trade And Development, supra* note 8, at 475, 488–91 ("[L]ittle . . . reflection takes place within intellectual property about its relationship to development law. . . . [T]he international intellectual property framework must begin to incorporate the alternate model of development as freedom."); Stiglitz, *supra* note 234, at 318–19.
352. See, e.g., Allarakhia, *supra* note 178, at 12; Hope, *supra* note 153, at 186–7; Octaviani, *supra* note 178, at 133 (predicting downstream research benefits of collaborative and open practices in biotechnology); Reichman & Uhlir, *supra* note 36, at 11 ("[G]overnment agencies will have to find ways of coping with bilateral data exchanges with other countries that exercise intellectual property rights in their own data collections."). See generally Benkler, *supra* note 176, at 130–1 (emphasizing the importance of networked information on economic opportunity and access to knowledge for both advanced and developing economies).
353. See Reichman, *supra* note 43, at 28 (noting the "wiggle room" that the TRIPS Agreement gives to developing countries in implementing intellectual property policies).
354. See Ostergard, Jr., *supra* note 13, at 155.
355. See Dreyfuss, *supra* note 3, at 2–3 (referring to India, Brazil, and China as the "emerging Middle" countries positioned to "move into a leadership position in establishing new practices").
356. Translating nascent technical advantages into competitive advantages on world markets is said to be an explicit goal of the Chinese Patent Law (as amended 2008). Feng, *supra* note 9, at 6–9.
357. See, e.g., Pedro Nicolletti Mizukami et al., "Exceptions and Limitations to Copyright in Brazil: A Call for Reform," in *Access to Knowledge in Brazil, supra* note 33, at 67, 114 (concluding that Brazilian citizens must address the "inadequate state of the law" in order to deal with both copyright infringement problems and users' rights).
358. Professor Akio Shimizu, "Japan's Evolving International Trade Law" lecture delivered at Duke University School of Law (March 2008).
359. See Maskus & Reichman, *supra* note 2, at 36, 38 (calling for a moratorium on stronger international standards in order to give developing countries "breathing room" to adapt); Reichman & Dreyfuss, *supra* note 12, at 102 ("Developing countries cannot succeed if, at the international level, a new round of multilateral intellectual property negotiations threatens to raise the technological ladder once again.").
360. See *supra* notes 290–4 and accompanying text.
361. See Maskus & Reichman, *supra* note 2, at 15–18 (noting that the knowledge goods sector "is the most dynamic of all in terms of potential growth and yet

partially resistant to any consensus-based economic analytical framework"). See generally Peter Drahos, "The Regulation of Public Goods," in *International Public Goods and Transfer of Technology under a Globalized Intellectual Property Regime, supra* note 2, at 46, 62.

362. Stiglitz, *supra* note 234, at 308.

363. See, e.g., *Towards Knowledge Societies, supra* note 7, at 27, available at <http://unesdoc.unesco.org/images/0014/001418/141843e.pdf> (accessed 13 September 2013) ("[T]he emerging global information society only finds its *raison d'etre* if it serves to bring about a higher and more desirable goal, namely the building, on a global scale, of *knowledge societies* that are a source of development for all, first and foremost for the least developed countries."); Cimoli, Dosi & Stiglitz, *supra* note 234, at 3–6.

364. See, e.g., Guan-Hua Xu, "Open Access to Scientific Data: Promoting Science and Innovation," 6 *Data Sci. J. (Open Data Issue)* 21 (2007).

365. See *supra* notes 36–41 and accompanying text; Reichman & Uhlir, *supra* note 177, at 8.

366. See, e.g., So et al., *supra* note 41, at 2081–2; John Wilbanks, Vice President, Creative Commons, "The Digital Commons: Infrastructure for the Data Web," Keynote Address at the Second COMMUNIA Conference on Global Science and the Economics of Knowledge-Sharing Institutions at Turin University (30 June 2009) (overviewing the models needed to utilize the data generated by worldwide research); Mizukami & Lemos, *supra* note 33, at 50–2 (suggesting that legal scholarship will be important to prepare lawmakers and enforcers "in mapping the territory of possible interactions between copyright law and other fields of the law, to provide solutions for potential controversies").

367. Reichman & Dreyfuss, *supra* note 12, at 86, 102–3.

368. Abbott & Reichman, *supra* note 38, at 921.

Part II

Knowledge Appropriation
and Development

5

Ethical Incentives for Innovation[1]

Sarah Chan, John Harris, and John Sulston

INTRODUCTION

In discussions of the economics of IP regimes, underlying assumptions which guide thinking on the social and economic justifications for IPRs often remain unidentified and unexamined, with wider ethical considerations considered to be externalities. The current consideration of innovation in the broader context warrants an analysis of these assumptions from an ethical perspective, supported by explicit articulation of normative ethical principles.

Specifically, we are interested in the relationship between what we might describe as the morally legitimate justifications for science and innovation, the motivations for pursuing these activities, and the way in which systems of IPRs interact with these, in theory and in practice. If criticism is to be made of particular aspects of the current IPR system for failing to fulfill their purposes with respect to science and innovation and with respect to ethics, we will need an adequate account first of what those purposes are, but also an account of how and why they are justified ethically, or of their ethical deficiencies. This in turn will require us to examine the motivations for science and innovation, both theoretical and actual; and consider whether and why these motivations are "legitimate," morally speaking.

For example, a criticism often leveled at IPRs in their current form is that they prevent access to the benefits of research. Implicit in this criticism are many assumptions: that science ought to produce benefits; that those benefits ought to be made accessible; and that part of the purpose of IPRs is to facilitate this process. While these are not unreasonable assumptions per se, the normative claims underlying them require some moral explanation. What is the purpose—or rather, what are the purposes—of science; how are these purposes fulfilled through the process of innovation; and what is or should be the role of IPRs in supporting this?

In this chapter we will analyze the motivations for scientific endeavor and innovation from an ethical and policy perspective. We examine the moral justifications for science and the implications of these for ethical innovation in order to provide an ethical basis for cross-disciplinary discussions regarding IPRs and ownership of knowledge and innovation. Finally, we consider some implications of this analysis for global innovation and development.

SCIENTIFIC MOTIVATION AND INCENTIVES FOR INNOVATION

There are two sorts of scientific motivation, and both are important. One is motivation for doing science, and the other is motivation for funding science.

The two motivations may coincide, but they don't have to. In particular, we need to draw a distinction between financial motivation for funding, with which economics seems chiefly to concern itself, and exploratory or philanthropic motivation which is less amenable to mathematical analysis and for that reason is largely neglected.

Now, at one level this neglect can be justified in terms of society's needs. Exploration can be dismissed as "mere curiosity," and not-for-profit activity does not contribute directly to GDP. A marketing executive can always hire a scientist to produce novel goods—the key attribute for the company is the executive's ability to market them competitively. This view, that the market reigns supreme and all else is subservient to it, has spread widely through the developed world in recent years. For that reason, there is much discussion about the detailed management of financial reward for innovation, and about the limitations of existing mechanisms, but on its own this picture is incomplete.

Motivations for doing science

People go into science in the first place mostly because they like the challenge, they enjoy doing it, and commonly because they see it as beneficial to society. They like finding out new things, following their curiosity with the excitement of discoverers exploring unknown terrain, and devising new methods to measure, probe, and alter the world around them. For the majority of scientists, motivation is independent of the higher echelons of financial reward, though the ability to secure a decent and reasonably secure living is important to them as it is to everyone. In addition, scientific equipment is often expensive, so there is a need for adequate resourcing—in most fields research costs are considerably greater than salary costs. Beyond these basic necessities, however, high financial reward is of interest only to a minority of scientists. Even for those who are financially ambitious, this is typically not their primary reason for doing science: rather, they got into science because they liked it and then were successful.

Scientists, like everyone, come with many different attitudes and motivations. Like everyone else they have to chase the money, taking on the protective coloration of the age in which they find themselves, in order to do what they enjoy. Their jobs range from the extremely creative to the extremely mundane, and from constant variety to meticulous repetition. However, we can identify two key characteristics of successful scientists.

First, to make progress there is a requirement in practice to be fairly obsessive, to narrow one's perspective enough to make time for dedicated interest in the problem at hand, and to be disinclined to take short cuts, all of which is rather antipathetic to those engaged in more worldly pursuits, and frustrating to marketing departments, which pressure researchers into exaggerated claims and sometimes outright falsification (in turn causing mistrust of science by the public). Second, there is an ability to perceive, and a willingness to pursue, novel findings. This perhaps seems at odds with the first characteristic, but in practice the two activities go along beside each other, with a switch from time to time into preoccupation with a fresh line of enquiry. The combination is the basis for real innovation, which is unpredictable and so is not susceptible to planning. In addition to her advertising skills our iconic executive depends on the advances thrown up by scientific research, to be exploited as they arise. So from a strictly pragmatic perspective we can ask: is it broadly effective, or alternatively counterproductive, to treat all scientists as business people?

Science as a process works because it has a system for combining all inputs (whatever the messy human reasons were in the first place) into a dynamically growing model of everything. This system depends on a high degree of openness, and where IPRs conflict with this, progress is impeded. The open access movement is trying to reduce the barriers to communication that have been erected by the ever increasing strength of copyright, reinforced both by the longevity of rights in law and by the ease of policing electronic media. Access to knowledge is a vital requirement for development, and so the removal of barriers for less developed countries is of particular importance.

Motivations for funding science

We can think of science funding as coming from two sources—public and private. Public funding—usually government or charity—does not seek financial return on its investment, and is motivated by a combination of goodwill and the expectation of usually unpredictable long-term rewards. Private funding is motivated by financial return, often in the short term. Insofar as funding is profit motivated, science is channeled into marketable commodities. This is not a problem in itself, and indeed is often seen as a win-win situation, but it leads to the exclusion of areas of knowledge and production of social goods that are believed not to be immediately marketable. The more detached the funder is from the science the more this is true. Companies owned by shareholders tend to be more detached than those in private hands, and share-owning by mutuals, which account for a large part of investment, leads to still greater detachment.

During the last few decades there has been a progressive increase in the proportion of privately funded science. The line between public and private has always been blurred, in that any funder may have a mixture of motives, but the blurring has increased of late. For example, governments may seek profit from academic research (a trend that can be traced back to the Bayh-Dole Act in the U.S. and its counterparts in other countries), and long-term funding of "blue skies research" by companies is commonplace. But in either case, the increasing attention paid to IPRs causes channeling into profitable areas, and the zone of true public funding is being squeezed out.

For good or ill, the current system is now being exported massively to developing countries. Indian students have commented to us that they need more IPRs; they have taken on board the whole system without much criticism, because for them the plus of catching up outweighs the caveats. Acquiring revenue from patents is a way of funding their labs. Freedom to fund in this way is arguably beneficial, given that even if adequate public resources are available review processes may be flawed, slow, or unfair. We have heard the same sentiments expressed by scientists in China. The role of international organizations, such as UNESCO and ICSU, to maintain a framework of open communication is more important than ever.

THE MORAL FOUNDATIONS OF SCIENCE

An examination of the different motivations for doing and funding science tells us much about what drives science, what makes science work; but it does not provide us with normative reasons as to why science itself is a good thing or which motivations we should seek to encourage. To develop an ethical analysis of the processes that contribute to science and innovation, we need first to construct an account of morality with respect to science. What are the moral justifications for science, and therefore which motivations for science align with these justifications and are morally justified. Which motivations might be at cross-purposes?

In this section we will discuss the moral foundations of science, moving from the personal to the impersonal, and argue that at both of these levels there are good moral reasons to support science.

Virtue and consequence?

Science may be said to have its own internal morality in terms of the values that are shared by scientists and the normative ideals of scientific culture. The idea, common to the scientific community in general, of what makes "good science" includes values such as openness; freedom of inquiry and communication; objectivity; rationality; truthfulness; non-self-interestedness and so forth. These and similar principles are laid out in numerous codes of conduct, recommendations on research integrity, and other formulations of aspirational norms for science; and are inculcated into scientists-in-training as part of the culture of science.

This construction of scientific ideals can be interpreted as a normative concept of "scientific virtue," not only what makes good science but by implication what makes a good scientist and what the actions of a good scientist should be. By way of analogy, we may compare the evolution of an internal morality of science with the medical ethos developed from the Hippocratic ideal. Just as we as a society have ideas as to what doctors ought to do and this is reinforced by the intra-professional ethos, we also have a concept of what scientists ought to do, shaped in part by the scientific community themselves.

The notion of scientific virtue stems in some ways from innate curiosity as a motivation for science, in that those who value the pursuit of knowledge tend to favor mechanisms that support the acquisition and dissemination of knowledge. It has also been argued, however, that the development of a set of scientific norms incorporating these values was an attempt deliberately to construct an ideology of science that would preserve the institutional *status quo* in the face of a changing culture with respect to science.[2]

Whatever the origins of the ethos of scientific virtue, it is certainly the case that certain principles are seen as important in "good science," and it may well be that this has created a sort of ideology of scientific virtue by which to assess the moral character of scientific actions.

Equally important, if not more so, are the consequences for science of acting in accordance with these principles, or of flouting them. Such principles of "scientific virtue" as may be identified are important to the working of science itself: if they were not upheld, the institution of science would cease to function. If science and its outputs are morally worthwhile, therefore, there are good consequential reasons to support the system and the values that sustain science.

Be that as it may, the culture of scientific research seems to be shifting, allowing more and more compromises to be made to the values that once formed the heart of scientific ideology.

The movement of society towards a more market-driven economy is entraining successive generations of researchers, who adapt to the change simply in order to do science. Indeed, many now feel that this is normal, because they know no other way. Paucity of public funding and strings attached are not questioned—people are busy, they accept the system as it is.

This trend can be regarded as a reinstatement of old norms. Over most of scientific history, scientists have been either entrepreneurial or amateur. The increase of state funding in the mid-twentieth century may prove to have been a transient phase, but it led to flowering in many areas. In terms of biology, for example, public funding was highly successful. The first green revolution was largely public domain. The first vaccines were public domain. When Jonas Salk was asked in 1955 whether he had patented his polio vaccine, the world's first, he replied rhetorically: "Could you patent the sun?" The answer now is yes of course we could (and while we're about it, let's patent the idea of a sun, and get those aliens to pay rent for their starlight).

Where does this take us? The fact is that most people have goodwill towards their fellows, but are being educated out of that to be more ambitious and competitive in a worldly sense than they actually want to be. Studies of societal attitudes show a shift away from community-oriented values and decreasing faith in the ability of institutions such as science to serve the public interest, and a corresponding rise in self-interested concerns such as increasing personal wealth.[3] This is causing destructive large- and small-scale effects. As much as thinking about how to attribute credit and reward enterprise, we should be thinking about socioeconomic changes that result in more social solidarity. It may be that in paying too much attention to detail and inventing ingenious fixes to the present system we are propping up something that is intrinsically broken. Fixes are fine in themselves, but equal time should be spent on the big questions, and in looking to the motivation of the people.

Science and its uses

In his *Life of Galileo*, Bertolt Brecht gives a memorable insight into the justification of science to Galileo. Talking to Andrea Sarti, his former student and colleague who is about to smuggle the *Discorsi*, Galileo's heretical treatise on mechanics and local motion, out of Italy, Galileo says:

> The battle for a measurable heaven has been won thanks to doubt; but thanks to credulity the Rome housewife's battle for milk will be lost time and time again. Science, Sarti, is involved in both these battles. To what end are you working?

Presumably for the principle that science's sole aim must be to lighten the burden of human existence. If the scientists, brought to heel by self-interested rulers, limit themselves to piling up knowledge for knowledge's sake, then science can be crippled. You may in due course discover all that there is to discover, and your progress will nonetheless be nothing but a progress away from mankind.[4]

We agree with Brecht that science should necessarily not only be conducted ethically, in accordance with both the internal ethos of science and the requirements of ethical treatment of research participants, but also embody a moral purpose. It is undoubtedly true that we human persons are quintessentially curious beings, indeed this could be part of our species-typical description; we want to know the why and how about everything. The enlargement of human understanding is one of the best answers to the question "Why are we here?" and so the contribution of science to knowledge is a justifiable end in itself. But the justification for science that we address here is about the benefits that such a pursuit can bring.

We do not always know and sometimes cannot even anticipate the applications of scientific enquiry. For this reason too it is necessary to defend and indeed actively to promote not only goal-oriented research but also research which investigates fundamental problems. Of course the costs which it would be rational to bear, when we have no idea about possible outcomes, may be proportionally more modest than when specific goals are in mind.

There is a universal moral responsibility to pursue the good, for ourselves, the Rome housewife, and her "brothers and sisters." Without the recognition of and alertness to the possibilities of doing good that science and innovation generate, they are surely jobs half done.

We have already discussed the commercial exploitability of science and noticed that much of the funding of science is directed towards the possibility of marketing its products. This possibility depends on the utility of those products, on the fact that they are useful, needed, or desired. Of course meeting the needs and responding to the desires of people is part of a social institution of mutual dependence and respect which, whatever else it is, is essentially ethical. It is well known, however, that such desires can be "manufactured" by advertising and hype of various sorts, and these wishes and desires can be undesirable.[5]

This is not the place for a full discussion of the difference between basic needs (shelter, food, healthcare, liberty, etc.) and manufactured "needs," or between authentic and inauthentic desires. We note that even frivolous desires or ambitions have their place. Given that we are talking of that part of science and its products that are plausibly conducive to, or at least not incompatible with, the public good and which might attract funding because of their social utility and importance, such concerns are perhaps less important. There is, however, one circumstance in which seeking to fulfill manufactured needs is contrary to the moral purpose of science. This is where the artificial creation of such needs directly obstructs attention to, or frustrates greater fulfillment of, a basic need. This, unfortunately, is sometimes the case with the marketing of innovation. When more money is spent on marketing—to convince the public that they need something that will not truly benefit (or may in some cases harm) them[6]—than is spent on research and development into ways of addressing pressing basic needs that already exist, the market model of innovation oversteps the bounds of morality.

THE DUTY TO RESEARCH

As we have argued, science is important for three powerful and importantly related reasons.

1. It is quintessentially human, expressing and satisfying our innate curiosity, as individuals and as a species.
2. It is essentially moral, its practice and products contributing substantially to the public good.
3. It is very useful at producing knowledge and products that are valued and valuable, independently of their contribution to the public good.

For these reasons we have powerful, ethical, practical, and prudential reasons for pursuing and supporting science. But these reasons are so powerful that we believe that in certain circumstances they also amount to a powerful obligation to pursue, support, and participate in science.[7]

Two separate but complementary lines of argument underpin a powerful obligation to pursue, support, and participate in scientific research.

The first is one of the most powerful obligations that we have: the obligation not to harm others. Where our actions will probably prevent serious harm, then if we can within reason (given the balance of risk and burden to ourselves and benefit to others), we clearly should act, because to fail to do so is to accept responsibility for the harm that then occurs.[8] This is the strong side of a somewhat weaker, but still powerful duty of beneficence, our basic moral obligation to help other people in need. This is sometimes called "the rule of rescue."[9] We tend to think of rescues as dramatic events with heroes snatching victims from the jaws of death. However, rescue occurs whenever people faced with threats to their lives or health or liberty receive assistance which mitigates these needs or their effects. Most if not all diseases create needs, in those who are affected, and in their relatives, friends, and carers, and indeed in society. Where research is likely to prove a necessary component of relieving those sorts of need, as well as in the more dramatic (fire, police, ambulance) cases, furthering research becomes a moral obligation. This obligation involves supporting research in many ways, for instance economically, at the personal, corporate, and societal levels, and indeed politically; it can also involve physical participation in research projects, for example, as a research subject.

There is a continuum, an overlap or potent analogy, between treating or curing dysfunction and enhancing function. This continuum has two dimensions. In one sense the withholding of a benefit that could be conferred harms the potential recipient. It is always in our interests to receive a benefit, against our interests not to receive a benefit. If the potential recipient knows about the possibility of benefit she will probably wish to receive it, so that not only are her interests but also her desires, wants, and choices engaged by this possibility. Often, the very same actions or procedures that constitute therapies for some will offer enhancement to others. These two dimensions of the continuum between ameliorating dysfunction and enhancing function mean that a decision to withhold benefit is always damaging, always something a decent person has a moral reason not to do. Whether those moral reasons are decisive will of course depend on many other things including an assessment of the risks and costs of conferring the benefit.

Second, the obligation also flows from an appeal to basic fairness. This is sometimes expressed as an appeal to the unfairness of being a free-rider. We all benefit from the existence of the social practice of medical and scientific research. Many of us would not be here if infant mortality had not been brought under control, or antibiotics had not been discovered and made usable. Most of us will continue to benefit from these and other medical advances (and indeed other advances such as clean drinking water and sanitation). Since we accept these benefits, we have an obligation in justice to contribute to the social practice which produces them. We may argue that since we could not opt out of advances that were made prior to our becoming capable of autonomous decision-making we are not obliged to contribute. But it may still be unfair to accept their benefits, and opting out would also imply that we should forego the fruits of any future advances.[10] For example, we bear duties of reciprocity to our parents for their care of us although we did not choose our parents nor the care they gave us in early life. Few, however, are willing to reject benefits to which they have not contributed, and even fewer are willing to forgo benefits that have been created through the sacrifices of others when their own hour of need arises![11]

Reciprocity, however, is not confined to circumstances in which a direct return can be made to those who have previously contributed. Reciprocity is not merely repayment, it is more akin to mutuality, solidarity, or fellowship. The idea is one of a community which accepts mutual responsibility, not least because such mutuality has been accepted by others and because all have benefited from the actions or forbearance of others.

To sum up, we all benefit from living in a society, and, indeed, in a world in which serious scientific research is carried out and which utilizes the benefits of past research. We all also benefit from research into diseases or conditions from which we do not currently suffer or into problems the solution of which have protective or beneficial implications for us, for example into genetics or stem cells, climate change, poverty, or clean energy. Science gives us security for the future, for ourselves and our descendants, and others for whom we care. Ultimately, we have an interest in these benefits being extended to all of humanity. Apart from humanitarian concerns that we may individually feel, how else can we arrive at a happy and peaceful world?

These obligations of beneficence, fairness, and solidarity combine to create an overall moral obligation on all of us as citizens to support research. These same lines of reasoning also imply certain moral imperatives with respect to how this research is carried out and how its products are used.

The obligation of beneficence imposes not only a duty to support research that may lead to benefits, but also to ensure that the benefits stemming from science should be made available where they will do good—there is an obligation to pursue science that will lead to benefits, but this obligation does not end with the research but extends to seeing that the benefits are realized.

In terms of the obligation from fairness and solidarity, this implies that current and future research should contribute back to science, including by sharing knowledge and research findings. As science and scientists today have benefited from the availability of knowledge generated by science in the past, they should in fairness make the benefits of further knowledge available in return. The sharing of knowledge also serves to promote solidarity both within the scientific community and between science and the wider public, as it supports relationships of mutual communication and benefit and increases trust.

THE PUBLIC GOOD OF SCIENCE

The above conclusions about the benefits of research and the moral obligations based on beneficence and fairness that follow from it rely on the assumption that research actually will produce these benefits; that it will contribute towards improving the welfare of persons and that it is an institution that operates for the good of the public and which we, therefore, as members of the public, have a duty of reciprocity to support. An important question, therefore, is how IPRs (particularly narrow or restrictive IPRs) might affect this.

Private research delivers many public goods, albeit incidentally to its primary goal of profit. It has the substantial advantage of using money raised from the people's interest in investing in the stock market, rather than money derived from taxation. Such money is perhaps more readily available, for certain sorts of research at least, but comes with motivations different from those applying to public research funding: the downside of course is that private commercial money demands profit, which correspondingly restricts the range of uses to which it can be put.

We would probably agree that the moral duty to participate in research which will contribute directly to improvements in welfare—through, for example, development of new disease therapies made widely available—is considerably clearer than a similar duty to participate in research that goes only inefficiently towards the same goal via the more pressing drive for profit. This is so firstly because the benefit, the good done by the latter, is much less evident; but also because it is rather less clear that research with the primary aim of private profit achieves the kind of social goods that we ought to be supporting. In the absence of any relationship of mutuality or solidarity between for-profit science and society, the cycle of discovery and innovation becomes solely financially driven.

We might suppose that this means simply that we have a lesser duty to support science when it is for private profit rather than public benefit, and that we should continue to participate in the latter while leaving the former to progress or not as it may.

It is misleading, however, to think that profit-driven science can simply be segregated from public research in this way. The potential effects of private research on the progress of science as a whole may well be inimical to public benefit, for at least two reasons. Science that is driven by profit rather than by concern for the public good and interest in knowledge is liable to erode public trust in science generally and therefore threatens the solidarity of the public science–society relationship. Furthermore, by limiting research and innovation through restrictive IPRs, and by diverting scientific talent from public uses, it can act as a direct impediment to the kind of beneficial public science we want to support. If this is the case, then not only do we not have a duty to support and participate in private science, perhaps we ought morally speaking to oppose it, or at least to oppose its current method of operation.

When we turn to considering fairness and the "free rider" problem in terms of research protected by highly restrictive IPRs, there is even less justification to support such research. Is it fair that private science may build on the knowledge acquired through centuries of public (or charitable) research but does not in general give back in kind? In fact, this is worse than free riding, since in effect it is taking knowledge/goods acquired through collective effort and not only making use of them in a way that does not support the whole, but using them for private gain at the expense of the whole.

It is in this manner that the application of restrictive IPRs creates a distinction between morally legitimate incentives for research, that align with our obligations to support research and the moral reasons we have to do so, and those that are at cross-purposes. This divergence of research, into the private arena driven by profit and into the public arena driven by concern for human welfare as well as curiosity, is liable to be detrimental to science as a whole and because of that, to society.

This can be demonstrated empirically as well as in theoretical ethical analysis, by studies examining the effect of IPRs in practice. There is considerable evidence from economic analysis of the effect of introducing market relations into a system, showing that the predicted negative consequences in terms of disruption of social relations and of the institution itself do indeed manifest.

This is not to say that privately funded research can never be of any benefit to the public; indeed, it produces many benefits, as we have acknowledged. The obligation to support research, however, and what we should do in view of that obligation, takes on a different form when it comes to private research enterprise.

One issue that has been noted with regard to determining the scope of the duty to support research is that as well as the obligation to produce benefits through research, there are many other ways in which we can benefit others. How are we then to prioritize between the many beneficent deeds we could perform?[12] In terms of government money for research, allocation decisions must be made between using these funds to support science and investing them in other public institutions which the state has a duty to maintain for the benefit of its citizens, such as education, health care, and basic welfare. Ethical policymaking with respect to public and charitably funded research hence involves some element of deciding what balance between the various means of producing benefits, including research and other activities, is most fruitful or worthwhile; and thus whether funds ought to be allocated to research or elsewhere.

But for privately funded science, precisely because it is motivated by profit first and benefit second, the moral dilemma over resource allocation is largely absent. The money is not, by and large, available for other beneficent purposes; it is there to do research that the funders hope will lead to profit and that may also be of some public benefit—but whether the public benefit is more or less depends on how this research is done and how its fruits are disseminated. What morality requires of us in this context, therefore, involves ensuring insofar as is possible that the potential benefits of the research that this money funds are realized and maximized. The proper and ethically sound management of IPRs is crucial to this process.

IPRS AND MORAL RIGHTS

Before we come to discuss the implications of these arguments for ethical innovation in policy and practice, it is fitting, in a moral and ethical analysis of

IPRs, to make some brief comments on the nature of rights and the place of intellectual property rights specifically in a moral world.

Rights involve moral and legal claims that we make on one another and on society. IPRs are a subclass of such rights claims but they are not the only or the most important sorts of rights with which we should be concerned. As such, IPRs are subject to the same rational self-interest and the same powerful moral reasons as other claims. As Shakespeare had Brutus famously say, "Good reasons must, of force, give way to better,"[13] and unless IPRs are to be fetishized outrageously, they must compete on their merits with other conflicting rights claims.

It is crucial that the powerful moral reasons for conducting science research are not drowned by the motivations we and others might have for protecting IPRs. There is a balance to be struck here, but it is not a balance that must always and inevitably be loaded in favor of the protection of IPRs.

Moral rights are never the premises of a moral argument but are established, if at all, as some of the conclusions of moral arguments; legal rights follow from these insofar as they have a moral basis. So if we are interested in the questions: What should we do? or How should the world be? thought of as moral questions, we are asking what should we do to make this person's life better or the world a better place. If the answers to such questions are constrained by what the law happens to be or what habits or social practices currently pertain, we will never be able to see or rationally consider possible alternatives. Here there is an obvious science equivalent. At any given time science might appear to be governed by fixed, established laws, Newton's Laws, God's Laws, but these are always open to revision in the light of evidence and argument.

It is therefore necessary to leave all questions open. The church said to Galileo, the Earth is fixed at the centre of the universe so what you are seeing cannot mean that it is moving. The law concerning IPRs says this company or this individual has these property rights in processes or products, and this constrains what you may do. But if we want to know either what it is correct to believe or best to do, we have to treat all questions as open. Is it right to uphold the legal rights established by current IP law and practice—do these have a valid moral basis, and how should we balance competing, perhaps overriding, moral rights concerning science and innovation? This is a question requiring serious ethical consideration backed by empirical evidence.

IMPLICATIONS FOR ETHICAL INNOVATION

In this chapter we have addressed the motivations and the moral justifications for science, and examined how these interact in the context of science that is privatized, commercialized, or subjected to restrictions of use or access by various means—IPRs among them. In the process, we have outlined what we propose are some important moral principles or rules for both the doing and the use of science.

How do these moral rules apply to impoverished populations in developing countries? Do different circumstances lead to different moralities, or just different moral priorities?

The operation of the free market takes advantage of existing inequalities but exacerbates them, makes things worse not better. Top scientists from developing countries get the opportunity to come to the developed world for research, further reinforcing the research strength of the already-strong, while at the same time weakening research in developing nations where it is most needed. Those scientists should not be blamed for such an outcome: they face an invidious choice between a successful and fulfilling career in a rich country versus struggling with inadequate infrastructure and resources in a poor country where they are limited to working on urgent development needs.

How to address and control these problems? How to reverse the "brain drain"? Is the moral importance of fundamental research less when the moral need for humanitarian science and innovation is greater? But why should the burden of doing the latter be borne primarily or solely by scientists in countries that need it the most? Surely this situation raises questions about global justice in science and research.

The way forward is to increase support for training, infrastructure, and ongoing research in developing countries. Progress must occur through encouragement rather than coercion—not denying scientists from the developing-world visas or work opportunities, but by making it more feasible and rewarding to do research in a developing country. China is moving in this direction, for example. Promotion of international cooperation and trust to overcome national boundaries in research is of great value, as is funding to establish centers of excellence in developing countries. Both governmental organizations and national and international NGOs have an important role to play in this process.

None of this, however, is helped by the current system of IPRs. Trade agreements and resource needs are being used to shore up advantageous positions with respect to IPRs for the rich, thereby increasing rather than reducing global inequalities. More global cooperation is required in the development and diffusion of innovation, rather than the current trend of international competition and insular safeguarding of national interests via stronger and stronger IPRs.

The moral imperative for greater global cooperation with respect to innovation is not only for the benefit of scientists and citizens in developing nations, however. Increasingly, we face problems at a global level that will require collective action at an international level—climate change being an obvious example. Nor is it only scientific applications, the end products of innovation, that are required to address these problems. In the context of climate change, for example, science functions as a diagnostic tool as well as potential cure; if it were not for science we would not even know there was a problem to be solved. We therefore need knowledge in order to make moral, social, and political decisions, so that even if we were to choose *not* to use science to attempt to "fix" climate change, we need the knowledge with which science provides us in order to make that choice in an optimally autonomous manner; in short, in order for that choice to be "evidence based" and "fully informed."

Thus, the knowledge that science generates and the international system of science research and education which produces and disseminates the results of science research is not only an essential precursor to innovation and the products it generates, but is essential for the evaluation of that knowledge and those products. Science in pursuit of knowledge, even blue skies research, is inseparable from science in pursuit of good. It is therefore crucial that any consideration of the effects of IPRs on science and innovation takes into account the importance of pure research in this process, as well as the more obvious aspects of access to the end products of innovation.

CONCLUSIONS

Science and innovation have both public and private dimensions and their motivations are manifold. Science is not a single-minded activity, and may be variously aimed at gathering knowledge, achieving humanitarian gains, or profit. The legitimate moral motivations for science extend far beyond simple market relations: the business of science and innovation is not just business. It is important that IPRs or whatever other methods we may have of managing and disseminating the fruits of science recognize this truth.

NOTES

1. The authors wish to acknowledge the members of the iPD Task Force on Intellectual Property Rights and Development, Manchester, 22–23 June 2009, for their helpful input and discussion at the Task Force; and in particular Lea Schafer for her stimulating comments which contributed to the development of this chapter.
2. Michael J. Mulkay (1976) "Norms and Ideology in Science," *Social Science Information*, 15 (4/5): 637–56.
3. See Robert Putnam (2000) *Bowling Alone: The Collapse and Revival of American Community*. New York: Simon & Schuster, 259–61.

4. Bertolt Brecht (1994) *Life of Galileo*, tr. John Willett. London: Methuen, scene 14, 108–9.

5. "Desired" means "actually desired"; "desirable" means "worthy of being desired."

6. Examples of this include the development and subsequent marketing of drug variants that will remain under patent longer but have no greater therapeutic efficacy, perhaps at the expense of genuine R&D into new, more effective forms of treatment; and the marketing of direct-to-consumer genetic tests.

7. John Harris (2005) "Scientific Research Is a Moral Duty," *J. Med. Ethics*, 31 (4): 242–8.

8. The arguments for and the basis of this duty are set out in John Harris, *Violence & Responsibility*, London: Routledge & Kegan Paul, 1980.

9. See Brian Barry, *Justice as Impartiality*. Clarendon Press: Oxford, 1995, p. 228.

10. Hans Jonas (1972) "Philosophical Reflections on Experimenting with Human Subjects," in P.A. Freund, ed., *Experimentation with Human Subjects*. London: Allen and Unwin.

11. The argument here follows lines developed in John Harris (2009) "Scientific Research Is a Moral Duty," *Journal of Medical Ethics*, 31 (4): 242–8, and Sarah Chan and John Harris (2009) "Free Riders and Pious Sons: Why Science Research Remains Obligatory," *Bioethics*, 23 (3) 161–71.

12. A question raised in, for example, Iain Brassington (2007) "John Harris' Argument for a Duty to Research," *Bioethics* 21 (3): 160–8. This problem is one of scope but does not, as we have argued previously, negate the existence of the obligation towards research *as well as* other obligations of beneficence: see Sarah Chan and John Harris (2009) "Free Riders and Pious Sons: Why Science Research Remains Obligatory," at note 11, *supra*.

13. William Shakespeare, *Julius Caesar*: IV.3.233. In W.J. Craig, (ed.) *The Complete Works of William Shakespeare*. London: Oxford University Press, 1914.

6

Is Bayh-Dole Good for Developing Countries? Lessons from the U.S. Experience

Anthony D. So,* Bhaven N. Sampat, Arti K. Rai,
Robert Cook-Deegan, Jerome H. Reichman, Robert Weissman,
and Amy Kapczynski

Recently, countries from China and Brazil to Malaysia and South Africa have passed laws promoting the patenting of publicly funded research,[1,2] and a similar proposal is under legislative consideration in India.[3] These initiatives are modeled in part on the United States Bayh-Dole Act of 1980.[4] Bayh-Dole (BD) encouraged American universities to acquire patents on inventions resulting from government-funded research and to issue exclusive licenses to private firms,[5,6] on the assumption that exclusive licensing creates incentives to commercialize these inventions. A broader hope of BD, and the initiatives emulating it, was that patenting and licensing of public sector research would spur science-based economic growth as well as national competitiveness.[6,7] And while it was not an explicit goal of BD, some of the emulation initiatives also aim to generate revenues for public sector research institutions.[8]

We believe government-supported research should be managed in the public interest. We also believe that some of the claims favoring BD-type initiatives overstate the Act's contributions to growth in U.S. innovation. Important concerns and safeguards—learned from nearly thirty years of experience in the U.S.—have been largely overlooked. Furthermore, both patent law and science have changed considerably since BD was adopted in 1980.[9,10] Other countries seeking to emulate that legislation need to consider this new context.

OVERSTATING CLAIMS

On a positive note, the BD Act required different agencies that funded U.S. research and development to adopt more consistent policies about ownership of patents arising from federal funding.[5] One of BD's intended virtues involved transferring default patent ownership from government to parties with stronger incentives to license inventions. BD assigned ownership to institutions, such as universities, nonprofits, and small businesses, although it could just as easily have opted for individual grant and contract recipients.

Nevertheless, many advocates of adopting similar initiatives in other countries overstate the impact of BD in the U.S. Proponents note *The Economist*'s 2002 claim that the Act was "[p]ossibly the most inspired piece of legislation to be enacted in America over the past half-century."[11] They also cite data (originally used by U.S. proponents of the Act) on the low licensing rates for the 28,000 patents owned by the U.S. government before BD to imply that the pre-BD legal regime was not conducive to commercialization.[12] But as Eisenberg[5] has argued, that figure is misleading because the sample largely comprised patents (funded by the Department of Defense) to which firms had already declined the option of acquiring exclusive title. Moreover, these figures are of questionable relevance to debates about public sector research institutions, because most of the patents in question were based on government-funded research conducted by firms, not universities or government labs.[13] Finally, and most importantly, the narrow focus on licensing of patented inventions ignores the fact that most of the economic contributions of public sector research institutions have historically occurred without patents—through dissemination of knowledge, discoveries, and technologies by means of journal publications, presentations at conferences, and training of students.[6,14,15]

Throughout the twentieth century, American universities were the nation's most powerful vehicles for the diffusion of basic and applied research results,[16] which were generally made available in the public domain, where industry and other public sector researchers could use them. These activities were central to the rise of American technological success broadly and to the growth of knowledge-based industries, such as biotechnology and information technology, in particular.

Public sector research institutions also relied on generous public funding for academic research—from a highly diverse group of federal funding agencies—which grew dramatically after the Second World War, and on the availability of venture capital to foster the development of early-stage ideas.[6] These and other unique features of the U.S. research and development system explain much more about innovation in the U.S. after BD than the rules about patenting that BD addressed.

In the pre-BD era, discoveries emanating from public research were often commercialized without patents, although academic institutions occasionally patented and licensed some of their publicly funded inventions well before BD, and these practices became increasingly common in the 1970s.[17] Since the passage of the Act in 1980, U.S. academic patenting, licensing, and associated revenues have steadily increased. BD accelerated this growth by clarifying ownership rules, by making these activities bureaucratically easier to administer, and by changing norms towards patenting and licensing at universities.[6] As a result, researchers vested with key patents sometimes took advantage of exclusive licenses to start spin-off biotechnology companies. These trends, together with anecdotal accounts of "successful" commercialization, constitute the primary evidence used to support emulating BD in other countries. However, it is a mistake to interpret evidence that patents and licenses have increased as evidence that technology transfer or commercialization of university technology has increased because of BD.

Although universities can and do patent much more in the post-BD era than they did previously, neither overall trends in post-BD patenting and licensing nor individual case studies of commercialized technologies show that BD facilitated technology transfer and commercialization. Empirical research suggests that among the few academic patents and licenses that resulted in commercial products, a significant share (including some of the most prominent revenue generators) could have been effectively transferred by being placed in the public domain or licensed non-exclusively.[6,18]

Another motivation for BD-type legislation is to generate licensing revenues for public sector research institutions. In the U.S., patents are indeed a source of revenue for some universities, but aggregate revenues are small. In 2006, U.S. universities, hospitals, and research institutions derived $1.85 billion from technology licensing compared to $43.58 billion from federal, state, and industry funders that same year,[19] which accounts for less than 5 per cent of total academic research dollars. Moreover, revenues were highly concentrated at a few successful universities that patented "blockbuster" inventions.[20]

A recent econometric analysis using data on academic licensing revenues from 1998 to 2002 suggests that, after subtracting the costs of patent management, net revenues earned by U.S. universities from patent licensing were "on average, quite modest" nearly three decades after BD took effect. This study concludes that "universities should form a more realistic perspective of the possible economic returns from patenting and licensing activities."[21] Similarly, the head of the technology licensing office at MIT (and former President of the Association of University Technology Managers) notes that "the direct economic impact of technology licensing on the universities themselves has been relatively small (a surprise to many who believed that royalties could compensate for declining federal support of research) . . . [M]ost university licensing offices barely break even."[22]

It is thus misleading to use data about the growth of academic patents, licenses, and licensing revenues as evidence that BD facilitated commercialization in the

U.S. And it is little more than a leap of faith to conclude that similar legislation would automatically promote commercialization and technology transfer in other, very different, socioeconomic contexts.

SOURCES OF CONCERN

What have we learned from the U.S. experience with BD? Because the Act gives recipients of government research funds almost complete discretion to choose what research to patent, universities can patent not only those inventions that firms would fail to commercialize or use without exclusive rights, but also upstream research tools and platforms that do not need patent protection and exclusive licensing to be adopted by industry.[6,9,10]

For example, while the patented technologies underlying recombinant DNA were fundamentally important for biotechnology and generated ample revenues for Stanford, the University of California, Columbia University, and City of Hope Medical Center,[6] the patenting and licensing of these research platforms and technologies were not necessary for commercialization. Both the Cohen-Boyer patents for recombinant DNA and the Axel patents on co-transformation were rapidly adopted by industry even though neither invention came with the BD "carrot" of an exclusive right. The Cohen-Boyer patents reportedly contributed to 2,442 new products and $35 billion in sales. Its licensing revenues to Stanford University and the University of California, San Francisco were $255 million.[23] With thirty-four firms licensing the technology, the Axel patents earned $790 million in royalties for Columbia University over the patent period (Colaianni and Cook-Deegan, unpublished data). While the patenting and licensing of these inventions clearly enriched the universities involved, there is no reason to believe that nonexclusive licensing (as opposed to simple dedication to the public domain) deterred commercialization of the invention(s). In fact, Columbia University justified efforts to extend the life of its Axel patents not because such extension would improve commercialization, but rather because it protected royalty income that would be channeled back into its educational and research mission.

While BD gave those conducting publicly funded research the discretion to patent fundamental technologies, changes in U.S. patent law since 1980 provided the means, by expanding eligibility standards to include basic research and research tools. These trends have been notable in the biotechnology and information technology sectors.[24,25] A widely watched, recent consequence of this shift involves the suite of University of Wisconsin patents on embryonic stem cell lines.[26–28] Biotechnology firms eager to do research on stem cells have complained about the excessive licensing fees that

Wisconsin charges (as well as about "reach through" provisions that call for royalties on any product developed from research on embryonic stem cells, and impose restrictions on use.)[29] Rather than promote commercialization, these patents on basic research platforms constitute a veritable tax on commercialization.[30] Nor were these efforts to tax future innovation unprecedented, as the example of recombinant DNA shows. The Wisconsin Alumni Research Foundation's extension of licensing terms to academic research institutions[31] and its imposition of restrictions on use became especially controversial because these measures went beyond the Cohen-Boyer precedent. The manager of recombinant DNA licensing at Stanford quipped, "[W]hether we licensed it or not, commercialization of recombinant DNA was going forward . . . a non-exclusive licensing program, at its heart, is really a tax . . . But it's always nice to say 'technology transfer'."[32]

The broad discretion given to publicly funded research institutions to patent upstream research raises concern about patent thickets, where numerous patents on a product lead to bargaining breakdowns and can blunt incentives for downstream R&D.[33,34] Barriers to bundling intellectual property necessary for R&D become higher in frontier interdisciplinary research areas, such as synthetic biology, microarrays, and nanobiotechnology, because they draw upon multiple fields, some of which may be likelier than others to form thickets over time.[9,10,32,35] Although there is some evidence that biotechnology and pharmaceutical firms may be able to avoid thickets through secret infringement or by "off-shoring" research to countries with fewer patent restrictions,[36] secret infringement and the transfer of R&D to other countries are hardly tactics that government policy should encourage.

The problems that BD has raised for the biopharmaceutical industry are dwarfed by the problems it has raised for information technology. Universities may too often take a "one size fits all" approach to patenting research results, notwithstanding the evidence that patents and exclusive licensing play a much more limited role in the development of information technology than they do in the pharmaceutical sector.[37] In testimony to the U.S. Congress, a prominent information technology firm complained that aggressive university patenting impeded both product development and university–industry collaboration, which encouraged companies to find other university partners, often outside the U.S.[38] Expressing similar concerns in a proposal to explore alternatives to the BD model, officials from the Ewing Marion Kauffman Foundation (the leading U.S. foundation supporting entrepreneurship research) recently argued that "Technology Transfer Offices (TTOs) were envisioned as gateways to facilitate the flow of innovation but have instead become gatekeepers that in many cases constrain the flow of inventions and frustrate faculty, entrepreneurs, and industry."[39]

These problems have not escaped the attention of funding agencies, most notably the U.S. National Institutes of Health (NIH), which has issued guidelines stating that patents should be sought, and exclusive licenses should be restricted, only when they are necessary for purposes of commercialization.[40,41] Beyond such hortatory guidelines, however, U.S. funding agencies retain very limited authority to guide the patenting and licensing practices of publicly funded research institutions. Under BD, agencies can declare particular areas off-limits to patenting only when they find "exceptional circumstances." Moreover, they must present this decision to the Department of Commerce, the primary administrator of BD. The "exceptional circumstances" authority has only rarely been used.[30] However, when exclusive licensing demonstrably impeded commercialization, the funding agencies did not intervene by exercising their authority to mandate additional licensing. Their reluctance to take such action stems in part from the realization that, under the BD regime as enacted, any mandate could immediately be challenged (and its effect stayed) pending the outcome of protracted litigation.[30]

Some of the top U.S. universities have themselves begun to recognize the difficulties that overly aggressive proprietary behavior can engender, as demonstrated by their March 2007 declaration highlighting "Nine Points to Consider in Licensing University Technology."[42] How this declaration will affect university behavior is difficult to predict. Moreover, the "Nine Points" declaration focuses almost entirely on licensing and fails to address how universities should determine whether patents are necessary for commercialization in the first instance.

BD has also led to downstream concerns. The BD framework makes minimal reciprocal demands from licensees of government-funded technologies, and neither universities nor government agencies have sought to include requirements that products derived from these inventions be sold to consumers on reasonable terms.[43] Nor do funders require either disclosure of follow-on investments, so that prices might reflect the private contribution to development or the avoidance of abusive or anticompetitive marketing practices.[43–47]

Some have raised concerns that the Act contributed to a change in academic norms regarding open, swift, and disinterested scientific exchange.[48,49] For example, in a survey to which 210 life science companies responded, a third of the companies reported disputes with their academic collaborators over intellectual property, and 30 per cent noted that conflicts of interest had emerged when university researchers became involved with another company.[50] Nearly 60 per cent of agreements between academic institutions and life science companies required that university investigators keep information confidential for more than six months—considerably longer than the thirty to sixty days that NIH considered reasonable—for the purpose of filing a patent.[50] Similarly, in a survey of life-science faculties at universities receiving the most NIH funding, nearly a third of the respondents receiving a research-related gift (e.g., biomaterials, discretionary funds, research equipment, trips to meetings, or support for students) reported that the corporate donor wanted pre-publication review of any research articles generated from the gift; and 19 per cent reported that the companies expected ownership of all patentable results from the funded research.[51]

Although the surveys discussed above were conducted in the early to mid 1990s, their findings appear robust over time. In a more recent survey of university geneticists and life scientists, one in four reported the need to honor the requirements of an industrial sponsor as one of the reasons for denying requests for post-publication information, data, or materials.[52] This finding is also corroborated by a survey of U.S. medical school faculty. In these settings, researchers most likely to report being denied research results or biomaterials by others were "those who have withheld research results from others" or who had patented or licensed their own inventions.[53] So the practices of patenting and licensing clearly encumber the openness of scientific exchange in universities.

INSTITUTING SAFEGUARDS

Countries seeking to enhance the contributions of universities and public sector laboratories to social and economic development have numerous policy options. Many of these policies do not involve intellectual property rights at all, but rather look to provide funds for basic and applied research; subsidize scientific and engineering education; strengthen firms' ability to assimilate university research; and invest in extension, experimentation, and diffusion activities.[39,54,55] But even policies focused on intellectual property management need not presume that patenting and exclusive licensing are the best options. For example, they may instead focus on placing by default or by strategy government-funded inventions into the public domain, creating a scientific commons, enabling collective management of intellectual property, or fostering open-source innovation.[56–60] Where greater commercial incentives seem necessary, the benefits of non-exclusive licensing should always be weighed against the social cost of exclusive licenses.

The appropriate array of policies will vary from country to country: there is no "one size fits all" solution. Based on our review above, we believe it is doubtful that the benefits of legislation closely modeled on BD would outweigh their costs in developing counties. For those countries that nonetheless decide to implement similar laws, the U.S. experience suggests the crucial importance, at a minimum, of considering a variety of safeguards (see Box 6.1).

Box 6.1. Safeguards Serving the Public Interest

Governments adopting laws styled after the U.S. BD Act should be vigilant to ensure that the public's interests are served. In commercializing publicly funded research, a number of safeguards on patenting and licensing practices should be built into any law or its regulatory implementation.

No exclusive licensing unless necessary for commercialization
Any BD-style legislation should be founded on the principle that publicly funded research should not be exclusively licensed unless it is clear that doing so is necessary to promote the commercialization of that research. Public sector institutions should not, for example, exclusively license research tools that were developed with public funding if those tools can instead be used off the shelf by others. Where exclusive licenses are not required for commercialization, one may ask whether universities and public sector labs should be patenting research at all. Will encouragement of patenting and nonexclusive licensing, as in the Cohen-Boyer model discussed above, help or hurt researchers, firms, and the public in developing countries? Even nonexclusive licenses will tax downstream users, although presumably with lower rents and transaction costs and more pro-competitive effects. As suggested above, revenues from licensing academic inventions are likely to be minuscule for most institutions, and aggressive university patenting can have other deleterious effects. A robust research exemption can ward off some of the problems potentially associated with restrictive licensing of upstream inventions.[62]

Transparency
The legislation should ensure transparency in the patenting and licensing of publicly funded research. Public accountability should follow public funding. Institutions that engage in patenting and licensing should be required to report or make public all information that is necessary to determine whether they are reasonably serving the public interest. Such information may include the number of patents and licenses obtained, the funds expended on patenting and licensing activities, licensing revenues, and the key terms (e.g., exclusive or non-exclusive, humanitarian access, research exemption, definition of market segmentation or field of use, performance milestones, and march-in rights) of licenses. The lack of a transparency mandate is a key flaw of the BD Act that should not be replicated.

Government authority to issue additional licenses
Where licensing arrangements for publicly funded research do not achieve public interest objectives, governmental authorities must have power to override such licenses and to grant licenses to additional or alternative parties.[9,10,43] In the U.S., this authority is formally embodied in the government's "march-in" rights under BD, but this power has never been exercised. Petitions to invoke it have been made a few times,[46,47,63,64] but they have never been granted, and because of the administrative disincentives built into BD, this power is unlikely ever to be used.[30] To avoid this result, legislatures must develop standards to ensure that march-in rights or comparable authority will be exercised when public interest objectives are not otherwise attained.

In evaluating licensing options, those receiving government research funding could also be required to consider the option of licensing patented inventions to a "technology trust," that is, a commons that would ensure designated inventions remained available to all interested parties on predetermined terms. Such a commons could enable the pooling of socially useful bundles of technology, particularly research tools and health technologies for neglected or rare diseases. Governments might also consider reducing or waiving patent application and maintenance fees for such inventions when they are made broadly available for research and humanitarian application, without royalty, for a specific geographical area or field of use.

Government-use rights

The government should retain an automatic right to use any invention arising from its funding. Under BD, the U.S. government has an automatic "nonexclusive, nontransferable, irrevocable, paid-up license"[65] to use any invention developed with government funds. Typically, however, it does not invoke such a license and often pays monopoly prices for products that it funded. The U.S. experience shows the importance both of establishing that the government should be provided with an automatic license in products resulting from its funding and of elaborating standards to ensure such licenses are actually exercised in appropriate circumstances.

From a broader perspective, governments retain the right to use any invention, whether or not it arises from public funding, under international law.[66] Governments may choose to use patented inventions to promote public health,[67] national security,[66] or comparable objectives, while public-interest compulsory licenses may sometimes be granted to avoid abusive licensing practices or to ensure access to patented research products on reasonable terms and conditions.[43,66] Where publicly funded grantees fail to commercialize a technology appropriately or to foster its availability, the trigger for government use—under any enabling provision adopted in domestic law—must work better than the march-in right has under BD.

Access to end products

Besides promoting commercialization, the government must ensure consumer access to end products. The public is entitled to expect that the inventions it paid for will be priced fairly. The U.S. experience shows that a BD system that lacks mandatory rules concerning the affordability of end products will not deliver on this reasonable expectation.[43-47] As a condition of receiving a license to a government-funded invention, parties should be required to ensure that end products are made available to the public on reasonable terms and conditions. What constitutes "reasonable" will vary by national context, but it is important to ensure that the term is defined with enough precision to be enforceable.

Licenses to government-funded inventions should presumptively include access-oriented licensing provisions that address humanitarian needs in other countries.[68] One such provision is an open license for production and sale of end products in (or to) developing countries in exchange for a fair royalty.[69] At the very least, when inventions have foreseeable applications in resource-poor regions, a plan for access in those regions should be explicitly incorporated into technology licensing.

CONCLUSION

While policies supporting technological innovation and diffusion contribute to economic growth and development, the appropriate sets of policies to harness public sector R&D are highly context-specific. Much depends on factors such as the level of publicly funded research, the focus of such research on basic versus applied science, the capabilities of industry partners, and the nature of university–industry linkages.[54,55]

Recognizing these difficulties, reasonable minds may disagree about the likely impact of BD-type legislation elsewhere. Nevertheless, the present impetus for BD-type legislation in developing countries is fueled by overstated and misleading claims about the economic impact of the Act in the U.S., which may lead developing countries to expect far more than they are likely to receive. Moreover, political capital expended on rules of patent ownership may detract from more important policies to support science and technology, especially the need for public funding of research. Given the low level of public funding for research in many developing countries, for example, the focus on royalty returns at the expense of public goods may be misplaced.[61] Furthermore, it is unclear whether any of the positive impacts of BD in the U.S. would arise in developing countries following similar legislation, absent the multi-agency federal pluralism, the practically oriented universities, and other features of the U.S. research system discussed above.

In any event, both the patent laws and patterns of scientific collaboration have changed substantially since BD was passed in 1980. To the extent that legislation governing the patenting and licensing of public sector research is needed in developing countries at all, it should reflect this new context rather than blindly importing a U.S. model that is thirty years old.

NOTES

* This work was originally published under the citation: So, A.D., Sampat B.N., Rai A. K. Cook-Deegan R., Reichman J.H., et al. (2008) "Is Bayh-Dole Good for Developing Countries? Lessons from the US Experience." *PLoS Biol* 6 (10): e262. Doi: 10.1371/journal/pbio.0060262.

This is an open-access article distributed under the terms of the Creative Commons Attribution License, which permits unrestricted use, distribution, and reproduction in any medium, provided the original authors and source are credited.

This work emerged from "Emulating the BD Act: Steps to ensure innovation and access for health in developing countries," a meeting organized on 29 May 2008 by the Program on Global Health and Technology Access at Duke University's Sanford School of Public Policy. All of the authors contributed to the writing of the paper. The authors particularly appreciate the capable research assistance of Corrina Moucheraud, Chris Manz, and Amy Forrestel.

1. Graff G.D. (2007) "Echoes of Bayh-Dole? A survey of IP and technology transfer policies in emerging and developing economies," Krattiger A., Mahoney R.T., Nelsen L., Thompson J.A., Bennett A.B., et al., eds, *Intellectual Property Management in Health and Agricultural Innovation: A Handbook of Best Practices.* Oxford: MIHR, and Davis, CA: PIPRA, pp. 169–95.
2. Republic of South Africa (2008) "Intellectual Property Rights from Publicly Financed Research and Development Bill" [B46B-2008]. Available: <http://www.pmg.org.za/bill/20080815-intellectual-property-rights-publicly-financed-research-and-developmen-0> (accessed 16 September 2008).
3. Jishnu L. (2008) "Does India need a Bayh-Dole Act? Patently absurd," *Business Standard.* Available: <http://www.business-standard.com/india/storypage.php?autono=328187> (accessed 16 September 2008).
4. United States Code (1980) The Patent and Trademark Act of 1980. Public Law 96–517. §6(a), 94 Stat. 3015, 3019–28.
5. Eisenberg R.S. (1996) "Public research and private development: Patents and technology transfer in government-sponsored research," *Va. Law Rev.* 82: 1663–727.
6. Mowery D.C., Nelson R.R., Sampat B.N., and Ziedonis A.A. (2004) *Ivory Tower and Industrial Innovation: University-Industry Technology Transfer before and after Bayh-Dole.* Stanford, CA: Stanford University Press, p. 241.
7. Mowery D.C. and Sampat B.N. (2005) "The Bayh-Dole Act of 1980 and university-industry technology transfer: A model for other OECD governments?" *Journal of Technology Transfer*, 30: 115–27.
8. Pathak K. (2008) "Varsities may soon own patent rights," *Business Standard.* Available: <http://www.business-standard.com/india/storypage.php?autono=317122> (accessed 16 September 2008).
9. Reichman J.H. and Giordano-Coltart J. (2008) "A holistic approach to patents affecting frontier science: Lessons from the seminal genomic technology studies," paper presented to the European Patent Forum 2008; 6–7 May 2008, Ljubljana, Slovenia.
10. Mackey T.M. (2009) "Nanobiotechnology, synthetic biology, and RNAi: Patent portfolios for maximal near-term commercialization and commons for maximal long-term medical gain," *Marquette Intellect Prop Law Rev*, 123 (2009). Available: <http://scholarship.law.marquette.edu/iplr/vol13/iss1/3> (accessed 9 September 2013).
11. [No authors listed] (2002) "Innovation's golden goose," *The Economist* 365: 3.
12. Pitroda S. (2007) "Letter to Indian prime minister from the National Knowledge Commission." Available: <http://knowledgecommission.gov.in/downloads/recommendations/LegislationPM.pdf> (accessed 16 September 2008).
13. Sampat B.N. (2006) "Patenting and US academic research in the 20th century: The world before and after Bayh-Dole," *Research Policy*, 35: 772–89.
14. Cohen W.M., Nelson R.R., and Walsh J.P. (2002) "Links and impacts: The influence of public research on industrial R&D," *Management Science*, 48: 1–23.

15. Agrawal A. and Henderson R. (2002) "Putting patents in context: Exploring knowledge transfer from MIT," *Management Science*, 48: 44–60.

16. Nelson R.R. (2004) "The market economy, and the scientific commons," *Research Policy*, 33: 455–71.

17. Mowery D.C. and Sampat B.N. (2001) "University patents and patent policy debates in the USA, 1925–1980," *Industrial and Corporate Change*, 10: 781–814.

18. Colyvas J., Crow M., Gelijns A., Mazzoleni R., Nelson R.R., et al. (2002) "How do university inventions get into practice?" *Management Science*, 48: 61–72.

19. Association of University Technology Managers (2007) "AUTM U.S. licensing activity survey: FY2006 survey summary." Available: <http://www.autm.net/events/file/AUTM_06_US%20LSS_FNL.pdf> (accessed 16 September 2008).

20. Mowery D.C., Nelson, R.R., Sampat, B.N., and Ziedonis A.A. (2001) "The growth of patenting and licensing by U.S. universities: An assessment of the effects of the Bayh-Dole Act of 1980," *Research Policy*, 30: 99–119.

21. Bulut H. and Moschini G. (2006) "U.S. universities' net returns from patenting and licensing: A quantile regression analysis," Center for Agricultural and Rural Development at Iowa State University, Working Paper 06-WP 432. Available: <http://www.card.iastate.edu/publications/DBS/PDFFiles/06wp432.pdf> (accessed 16 September 2008).

22. Nelsen L. (1998) "The rise of intellectual property protection in the American university," *Science*, 279: 1460–1.

23. Feldman M.P., Colaianni A., and Liu C.K. (2007) "Lessons from the commercialization of the Cohen-Boyer patents: The Stanford University licensing program," in Krattiger A., Mahoney R.T., Nelsen L., Thompson J.A., Bennett A.B., et al., eds, *Intellectual Property Management in Health and Agricultural Innovation: A Handbook of Best Practices*. Oxford: MIHR, and Davis, CA: PIPRA. pp. 1797–807.

24. United States Supreme Court (1972) *Gottschalk v. Benson*. 409 U.S. 63, No. 71–485. Available: <http://www.altlaw.org/v1/cases/398051> (accessed 16 September 2008).

25. Reichman J.H. and Cooper Dreyfuss R. (2007) "Harmonization without consensus: Critical reflections on drafting a substantive patent law treaty," *Duke Law Journal* 57: 85–130.

26. Thomson J.A., inventor; Wisconsin Alumni Research Foundation, assignee (1998) Primate embryonic stem cells. U.S. Patent 5843780. Available: <http://www.patentstorm.us/patents/5843780.html> (accessed 16 September 2008).

27. Thomson J.A., inventor; Wisconsin Alumni Research Foundation, assignee (2001) Primate embryonic stem cells. U.S. Patent 6200806. Available: <http://www.patentstorm.us/patents/6200806.html> (accessed 16 September 2008).

28. Thomson J.A., inventor; Wisconsin Alumni Research Foundation, assignee (2006) Primate embryonic stem cells. U.S. Patent 7029913. Available: <http://www.patentstorm.us/patents/7029913.html> (accessed 16 September 2008).

29. Holden C. (2007) "U.S. Patent office casts doubt on Wisconsin stem cell patents," *Science* 316: 812.

30. Rai A.K. and Eisenberg R.S. (2003) "Bayh-Dole reform and the progress of biomedicine," *Law and Contemporary Problems*, 66: 289–314.
31. Abrams I. (2006) "Human embryonic stem cells: A review of the intellectual property landscape," *Journal Association of University Technology Managers*, 8: 1–14.
32. Reimers N. (1998) "Stanford's Office of Technology Licensing and the Cohen/Boyer cloning patents: An oral history" conducted in 1997 by Sally Smith Hughes, PhD Regional Oral History Office, The Bancroft Library, University of California, Berkeley. Available: <http://content.cdlib.org/view?docId=kt4b69n6sc&brand=calisphere&doc.view=entire_text> (accessed 16 September 2008).
33. Heller M.A. and Eisenberg R.S. (1998) "Can patents deter innovation? The anticommons in biomedical research," *Science* 280: 698–701.
34. Lemley M.A. (2008) "Are universities patent trolls?" *The Fordham Intellectual Property, Media & Entertainment Law Journal*, 18: 611–31.
35. Kumar S. and Rai A. (2007) "Synthetic biology: The intellectual property puzzle," *Texas Law Review*, 85: 1745–68.
36. Walsh J.P., Arora A., and Cohen W.M. (2003) "Working through the patent problem," *Science* 299: 1021.
37. Rai A.K. (2007) "The role of federally-funded university research in the patent system." Hearing before the United States Senate Committee on the Judiciary, 110th Congress. Available: <http://www.law.duke.edu/news/pdf/rai_testimony.pdf> (accessed 16 September 2008).
38. Johnson W. (2007) "Bayh-Dole: The next 25 years." Hearing before the Subcommittee on Technology and Innovation of the United States House of Representatives Committee on Science & Technology. Available: <http://science.house.gov/publications/Testimony.aspx?TID=7129> (accessed 16 September 2008).
39. Litan R.E., Mitchell L., and Reedy E.J. (2007) "Commercializing university innovations: A better way." National Bureau of Economic Research working paper. Available: <http://www.brookings.edu/papers/2007/05_innovations_litan.aspx?rssid=education> (accessed 16 September 2008).
40. Department of Health and Human Services, National Institutes of Health (1999) "Principles and guidelines for recipients of NIH research grants and contracts on obtaining and disseminating biomedical research resources: Final notice." Fed Regist 64: 72090–96. Available: <http://ott.od.nih.gov/policy/rt_guide_final.html> (accessed 16 September 2008).
41. Department of Health and Human Services, National Institutes of Health (2005) "Best practices for the licensing of genomic inventions: Final notice." Fed Regist 70: 18413–15. Available: <http://ott.od.nih.gov/policy/genomic_invention.html> (accessed 16 September 2008).
42. Stanford News Service (2007) "In public interest: Nine points to consider in licensing university technology." Available: <http://news-service.stanford.edu/news/2007/march7/gifs/whitepaper.pdf> (accessed 16 September 2008).
43. Reichman J.H. (2004) Testimony before the NIH Public Hearing on March-In Rights under the Bayh-Dole Act, National Institutes of Health. Available: <http://

www.ott.nih.gov/policy/meeting/Jerome-Reichman-Duke-Univ.pdf> (accessed 16 September 2008).

44. U.S. Office of Technology Assessment (1992) "Federal and private roles in the development and provision of alglucerase therapy for Gaucher disease." Publication OTA-.BP-H-104. Available: <http://www.princeton.edu/~ota/disk1/1992/9214/9214.PDF> (accessed 16 September 2008).

45. United States General Accounting Office (2003) "Technology transfer: NIH-Private sector partnership in the development of Taxol." Report to the Honorable Ron Wyden, GAO-03-829. Available: <http://www.gao.gov/new.items/d03829.pdf> (accessed 16 September 2008).

46. Love J. and Flynn S. (2004) "Petition to use authority under Bah-Dole Act to promote access to Latanoprost." Letter to Thomas Thompson, Secretary of United States Department of Health and Human Services. Available: <http://www.essentialinventions.org/legal/xalatan/xalatan-29jan04petition.pdf.> (accessed 16 September 2008).

47. Love J. and Flynn S. (2004) "Petition to use authority under Bayh-Dole Act to promote access to Norvir." Letter to Thomas Thompson, Secretary of United States Department of Health and Human Services. Available: <http://www.essentialinventions.org/legal/norvir/norvir-29jan04petition.pdf> (accessed 16 September 2008).

48. Washburn J. (2005) *University Inc.: The Corporate Corruption of Higher Education.* New York: Basic Books, p. 352.

49. Greenberg D.S. (2007) *Science for Sale: The Perils, Rewards, and Delusions of Campus Capitalism.* Chicago: University of Chicago Press, p. 288.

50. Blumenthal D., Causino N., Campbell E., and Louis K.S. (1996) "Relationships between academic institutions and industry in the life sciences: An industry survey," *The New England Journal of Medicine*, 334: 368–74.

51. Campbell E.G., Louis K.S., and Blumenthal D. (1998) "Looking a gift horse in the mouth: Corporate gifts supporting life sciences research," *The Journal of the American Medical Association*, 279: 995–9.

52. Campbell E.G., Clarridge B.R., Gokhale M., Birenbaum L., Hilgartner S., et al. (2002) "Data withholding in academic genetics: Evidence from a national survey," *The Journal of the American Medical Association*, 287: 473–80.

53. Campbell E.G., Weissman J.S., Causino N., and Blumenthal D. (2000) "Data withholding in academic medicine: Characteristics of faculty denied access to research results and biomaterials," *Research Policy*, 29: 303–12.

54. Mazzoleni R. and Nelson R.R. (2007) "Public research institutions and economic catch-up," *Research Policy*, 36: 1512–28.

55. Mowery D.C. and Sampat B.N. (2005) "Universities in national innovation systems," in Fagerberg J., Mowery D.C., and Nelson R.R., eds, *The Oxford Handbook on Innovation.* New York: Oxford University Press, pp. 209–39.

56. Marshall E. (2001) "Bermuda Rules: Community spirit, with teeth," *Science* 291: 1192.

57. International AIDS Vaccine Initiative (2007) An interview with Dennis Burton. IAVI Report 11. Available: <http://www.iavireport.org/Issues/Issue11-1/Burton.asp> (accessed 16 September 2008).

58. Atkinson R.C., Beachy R.N., Conway G., Cordova F.A., Fox M.A., et al. (2003) "Public sector collaboration for agriculture IP management," *Science* 301: 174–5.

59. von Hippel E. and von Krogh G., (eds) (2003) "Open source software development," *Research Policy*, 32: 1149–291. doi:10.1016/S0048-7333(03)00054-4.

60. Reichman J. and Uhlir P. (2003) "A contractually reconstructed research commons for scientific data in a highly protectionist intellectual property environment," *Law and Contemporary Problems*, 66: 315–462.

61. Maskus K.E. and Reichman J.H. (2003) "The globalization of private knowledge goods and the privatization of global public goods," in Maskus K.E., Reichman J.H., eds, *International Public Goods and Transfer of Technology under a Globalized Intellectual Property Regime*. Cambridge: Cambridge University Press, pp. 3–45.

62. Dreyfuss R. (2004) "Protecting the public domain of science: Has the time for experimental use defense arrived?" *Arizona Law Review*, 458: 457–72.

63. Bar-Shalom A. and Cook-Deegan R. (2002) "Patents and innovation in cancer therapeutics: Lessons from CellPro," *Milbank Quarterly*, 80: 637–76.

64. McGarey B.M. and Levey A.C. (1999) "Patents, products, and public health analysis of the CellPro march-in petition," *Berkeley Technology Law Journal*, 14: 1095–116.

65. United States Patent and Trademark Office (1980) "March-in rights." U.S. Code title 35, part II, chapter 18, §203. Available: <http://uspto.gov/web/offices/pac/mpep/documents/appxl_35_U_S_C_203.htm#usu35s20.3> (accessed 16 September 2008).

66. Reichman J.H. and Hasenzahl C. (2002) "Non-voluntary licensing of patented inventions: Historical perspective, legal framework under TRIPS, and an overview of the practice in Canada and the USA." UNCTAD-ICTSD Project on IPRs and Sustainable Development Series. Available: <http://www.ictsd.org/pubs/ictsd_series/iprs/CS_reichman_hasenzahl.pdf> (accessed 25 September 2008).

67. Abbott F.M. and Reichman J.H. (2007) "The Doha Round's public health legacy: Strategies for the production and diffusion of patented medicines under the amended TRIPS provisions," *Journal of International Economic Law*, 10: 921–87.

68. Outterson K. (2006) "Patent buy-outs for global disease innovations for low- and middle-income countries," *American Journal of Law & Medicine*, 32: 159–61.

69. Kapczynski A., Chaifetz S., Katz Z., and Benkler Y. (2005) "Addressing global health inequities: An open licensing approach for university innovations," *Berkeley Technology Law Journal*, 20: 1031.

Part III

Experiences from Public Health, Agriculture, and Green Technology

7

IPRs, Public Health and the Pharmaceutical Industry: Issues in the Post-2005 TRIPS Agenda

Benjamin Coriat and Luigi Orsenigo

1. INTRODUCTION

Pharmaceuticals is an industry in which the debate on the role and effects of patent protection is virulent. This sector brings the trade-offs and issues involved in patent theory and practice to their extreme consequences. The pharmaceuticals industry is one of the few in which patents are recognized as being key instruments for privately appropriating the economic benefits of innovation and, therefore, serving as an important incentive for innovation. In this sector competition is largely based on innovation, and basic science is becoming increasingly crucial for the discovery and development of new products. Pharmaceuticals occupy an extremely socially sensitive sector: large parts of the population increasingly perceive health care as a fundamental human right. The very definition of what a just society should look like increasingly involves references to health care. For developing countries in particular, health has become a major issue, magnified by the tragedies of pandemics like HIV/AIDS. Controversies about the welfare implications of patents have characterized this industry ever since its inception. But in the last thirty years or so, the establishment of a strong tendency towards an extremely tight IP at the global-level regime has made this debate even more heated, especially but not exclusively for developing countries.

In this chapter we begin by succinctly reviewing the main problems and the available evidence concerning the relationships between IPRs, innovation and welfare in pharmaceuticals. Section 2 summarizes the main theoretical arguments in favor and against (strong) IPRs in pharmaceuticals and presents the little direct available empirical evidence, concerning innovation and drug prices respectively. Section 3 focuses on TRIPS and access to care in developing countries, with particular reference to the case of HIV (the most emblematic example of the problems generated by enforcement of the TRIPS agreement) and the post-2005 issues. A brief conclusion summarizes the main points.

2. IPRs, INNOVATION AND WELFARE IN THE PHARMACEUTICAL INDUSTRY

2.1 Patents as an incentive to innovation: the background

Patents are considered to be a key factor sustaining innovativeness and growth in the pharmaceutical industry. At the same time, the very nature of the product of this sector—drugs and health—magnifies the social costs involved by patent protection. Critiques, arguing that the monopoly power granted by patents leads to excessive prices and profits, have been recurrently advanced. For example, in the USA the Kefauver Commission debated this claim in the 1960s, and suggested that patent protection should be considerably shortened (Comanor, 1986). But these suggestions were never transformed in law and it was felt at the time that the patent system was sufficiently balanced: if anything, its negative implications should be countervailed by inducing competition after patent expiry or—as in many European countries—by price controls.

The debate has become even more heated in the last decade, following the tendency towards the establishment of a very tight IPR regime, first in the USA and then in other industrialized countries and—through the TRIPS—at the global level. The main steps of these processes have already been discussed in this volume (see Chapter 2) and we shall not recall them again.

To organize the discussion of these issues, it might be worthwhile to remind instead the two basic arguments for (strong) patent protection. First, patents provide an incentive for profit-motivated agents to engage in innovative activities: absent patents, the outcome of research would have the characteristics of a public good, with consequent underinvestment. Public funding of research would then become necessary. Second, patents disclose information and may induce the commercialization of innovation and the development of markets for technology, allowing for an "ordered" path of exploitation of such knowledge and avoiding the wasteful duplication of efforts (Arora et al. 2001).

The first argument is certainly relevant for the pharmaceutical industry which has been—especially after World War II—highly innovative (and profitable): it is one of the most R&D-intensive sectors (with the R&D to sales ratio approximating 15 per cent in recent years).[1] The costs of R&D are substantial and they have been soaring in recent years. Moreover, innovation is an extremely uncertain process, which—as Sutton (1998) suggests—can be usefully described as a lottery. In addition, it is worth being reminded that innovations tend not to build on preceding work: technological progress is only mildly cumulative and firms find it difficult to use the knowledge accumulated in developing one product for developing a truly different one. Thus, large R&D portfolios allow firms to pool the risk of promising molecules failing at one point in the R&D process. Profits from the sale of products that succeed on the market can cover the costs of unsuccessful R&D undertakings (Fink, 2008). Conversely, imitation is relatively easy and marginal costs of production are comparatively low. Thus, without patents, the product of the pharmaceutical industry—i.e. the knowledge embodied in the drugs—would be a public good.

These features contribute to define the patterns of competition in the industry and its market structure. Firms compete first by trying to discover and develop new drugs. If and when a new molecule is discovered, it is patented and then it goes through a lengthy period of development which may take up to a decade and entails dramatic rates of attrition: the "real" life of a patent is thus much shorter than the statutory duration. After the introduction of a new drug, innovators, mainly thanks to patent protection, obtain a dominant position and enjoy high profits. As patent expiry approximates, innovators engage in developing variants of the original product, trying to obtain new patents and/or extensions to further indications. These strategies of patent "evergreening" have become increasingly important (and controversial), as the generics segment of the industry grows and consolidates. Innovators also try to defend their market power through marketing strategies, which often result in even higher prices of the branded drug (Pammolli et al., 2002).

2.2 Patents as an incentive to innovation: the evidence

However, it is not clear how much patent protection actually stimulates innovation in the pharmaceuticals industry. The empirical evidence on these issues is surprisingly thin. There is extremely robust evidence—mainly obtained by surveys—that in the pharmaceutical industy patents are deemed by managers to be an important tool for privately appropriating the economic benefits of innovation and that R&D would be substantially reduced in the absence of patent protection (Mansfield et al., 1981; Levin et al., 1987, Cohen et al., 2002. Yet, innovative pharmaceutical companies have historically used instruments other than patents to extract profits from their innovations: for example, advertising, direct foreign investment, and licensing.

Moreover, throughout the history of pharmaceuticals, the scope and efficacy of patent protection has varied significantly over time and across countries. Many European countries offered protection only for processes, not products. France introduced product patents in 1960; Germany in 1968; Japan in 1976; Switzerland in 1977; Italy, Netherlands, and Sweden in 1978; and Canada and Denmark in 1983. In many cases, the absence of this protection did not seem to produce negative effects on innovation.

Last, it is worth being reminded that the remarkable performance of this sector has been sustained by the combination of different factors, other than patents. Heroically summarizing a complex story (see for instance, Henderson et al., 1998, two fundamental factors have to be emphasized. First, public support to biomedical research. Second, the development of the welfare state—especially of national healthcare systems—provided a rich market for drugs in the developed world—even if their features varied drastically across countries—which sustained industry growth on the demand side.

The role of public support to biomedical R&D can hardly be overestimated. It boomed after World War II and—especially in the USA—it continued to grow steadily thereafter. Nowadays, it is estimated that almost 50 per cent of biomedical R&D is funded in the USA by public sources—mainly the National Institutes of Health (NIH) (De Francisco and Matlin, 2006)—and according to other estimates Federal-Government-sponsored health-related research was even larger than the whole sum spent by the industry (CBO, 2006). Similarly, Lazonick and Tulum (2011) calculate that from 1978 through 2004, NIH spending on life sciences research totaled $365 billion in 2004 dollars, providing a continuously growing and stable flow of funds to biomedical research. This research is primarily directed towards more basic science, although there are many instances of new drugs being developed almost entirely through NIH support: whilst it is difficult to estimate—both conceptually and statistically— the shares of basic and applied research, an overwhelming share of basic research leading to new molecules is certainly performed in public institutions and financed by public funding.

Public research creates the opportunities for the discovery and development of new drugs and hence for private R&D investment. Indirectly, it raises the productivity of private R&D by supporting the training of researchers working in the private sector. More generally, public funding is essential for developing the fundamental knowledge base and infrastructures that allow the industry to prosper and to attract further funding through the financial markets, venture capital and public equity funds which have sustained the development of biotechnology.

On the demand side, the health of the pharmaceutical industry depends quite obviously on the ability of consumers to pay for the products they are offered, especially when patent protection makes drugs very expensive. In this respect, a crucial role is again played by governments, which to different degrees and in widely different fashions contribute to the cost of drugs. To give an example, even in the USA the share of national health expenditures borne by public funds has increased from around 25 per cent in 1960 to almost 40 per cent in 1970 (following the introduction of Medicare and Medicaid in 1965) to reach 46.2 per cent in 2007. And an increasing proportion of national health expenditures is spent on prescription drug expenditures, reaching more than 10 per cent in recent years.

Given the basic preconditions, only a few studies have tried to measure directly the impact of patent protection on innovation in the pharmaceutical industry. Indeed, these exercises are made difficult to carry on and to interpret because of both the paucity of data and the existence of complex—often non-linear—relations between measures of patent protection, innovation, and other crucial variables like technological opportunities and size of the market. Thus, Schankerman (1998) estimated the value of patent rights using data on patent renewal rates and fees for France, and computed the equivalent cash subsidy to R&D, obtaining a value of only 4 per cent. However, this result might depend on the fact that, in France, drug prices are very low. Indeed, a similar exercise for Germany yielded a value of 15.2 per cent (Lanjouw, 1998b).

These studies focus on the impact of patents on R&D or on innovation as measured by patents themselves. Arora et al. (2008) use survey data to estimate the so-called patent premium—that is, the proportional, incremental increase in the value of an innovation that is realized by patenting it. A value of the premium less than one would, therefore, imply a loss. Results indicate an expected patent premium around 1.3 in biotechnology and 1.05 for drugs. However, these values increase considerably—to 2.45 and 2.3, respectively—if the patent premium is computed conditionally on having actually patented the innovation. These results imply that a 10 per cent increase in the patent premium increases R&D by 10.6 per cent in biotech and by 8.9 per cent in drugs, corresponding to an equivalent subsidy rate equal to 22 per cent. Moreover, a 10 per cent increase in patent premium increases patent applications by 14.3 per cent in biotech and by 12.5 per cent in drugs.

These results are broadly in line with the findings by Acemoglu and Linn (2004), who estimate that, in pharmaceuticals, a 1 per cent increase in the size of the market for pharmaceutical products raises the number of new drugs by 4–6 per cent implying an elasticity of innovations to R&D ranging from 0.8 to 0.85.

2.3 Strenghtening patent regimes

A slightly different question concerns the strengthening of patent regimes. First, it has been noted that reforms of patent laws do not appear to have had a significant impact on the innovative capabilities of industries like the Italian or Japanese pharmaceuticals industries. If anything, patent protection to drugs might have had a negative effect, further weakening national industries mainly composed of generic producers (Scherer and Weisburst 1995). Conversely, the cases of India, Israel, and partially Brazil are examples where vibrant domestic production of generics has been developed in the absence of patent protection (see, among others: Lanjouw, 1998a; Ramani and Maria, 2005; and Chaudhuri, 2005). Here, the little evidence available so far suggests that the introduction of TRIPS might have deleterious effects, without promoting indigenous innovative activities. A few Indian companies are actually trying to enter the club of innovative firms, with mixed results thus far. On the other hand, while evidence does not yet show any dramatic shake-out of local producers of generics, most analysts seem to agree that a substantial restructuring is bound to occur. Similarly, data concerning the Brazilian case show a marked increase in domestic patenting activities, which is, however, due almost exclusively to foreign multinationals (Laforgia et al., 2008).

These insights are confirmed by other studies, which suggest that the relationship between innovation and the strength of the IPR regime has an inverted U-shape. With specific reference to pharmaceuticals, Qian (2007) examines the effects of patent protection on pharmaceutical innovations for twenty-six countries that established pharmaceutical patent laws during the period 1978 to 2002. Controlling for country characteristics through matched sampling techniques she finds that national patent protection alone does not stimulate domestic innovation. Domestic innovation accelerates in countries with higher levels of economic development, educational attainment, and economic freedom. But, if anything, above a threshold further enhancement of IPRs actually reduces innovative activities.

In sum, there are strong reasons to doubt that strengthening IPRs— especially in developing countries—would have a positive impact on domestic innovative activities. Such an effect presumes sufficient scientific and technological capabilities, access to knowledge and active participation in research networks, and large domestic markets and/or the ability to export. Conversely, stronger IPRs might possibly make life more difficult for local brands and generics producers, especially if data-exclusivity agreements and patentability for second-use provisions are enforced. Similarly, there is so far no evidence that stronger IPRs in developing countries have introduced incentives for developing drugs for local diseases—for example, malaria. Decisions concerning the direction of innovative activities are still influenced by considerations of profitability, both by local and foreign innovators (Ramani and Maria, 2005).

Finally, it is important to notice that over the last two decades the productivity of R&D and the innovative performance of the industry have been falling. Despite the enormous opportunities opened by the "molecular biology revolution" since the mid 1970s and in a period when the patent regime was becoming increasingly stronger, R&D expenditures have increased tenfold while patenting output increased only sevenfold since 1978 (Nightingale and Martin, 2004). The number of New Chemical Entities (NCE) approved by the FDA in the USA has been declining since the early 1990. Similarly, Pisano (2006) shows that the number of compounds developed by commercial organizations that have progressed at least to human clinical testing has not increased significantly since the advent of the biotechnology revolution. Moreover, only a half of NME approvals result from "priority" NMEs—those judged by the FDA to provide "a significant therapeutic or public health advance" over existing drugs—and only about one-third of new-drug applications submitted to the FDA are for new molecular entities. Most of the rest are either for reformulations or incremental modifications of existing drugs or for new "on-label" uses. The issue remains, however, hotly contested, given that these kinds of drugs do sometimes entail significant benefits.

Various explanations have been suggested to explain the "falling productivity" paradox. Some interpretations are relatively optimistic, emphasizing that the production of new drugs is characterized by strong cyclical components. The current downswing might therefore be considered as a temporary phenomenon. Other explanations point to either more stringent regulation,[2] or to an intrinsic difficulty in discovering new drugs for increasingly complex pathologies (signalling an incumbent "maturity" of the industry, see Nightingale and Martin, 2004). In a more radical stance, it is suggested that large pharmaceutical companies have moved away from truly innovative research, either developing compounds originating from basic research conducted at universities, hospitals and biotechnology companies (one third of new drugs) or concentrating on the development of me-too drugs and minor improvements upon existing products. According to this interpretation, now big pharma does little more than serve as a manufacturing and especially marketing organization, exploiting knowledge generated by public research and biotechnology firms.

The question remains open: while drug discovery and development now rely on a dense web of interactions between universities, biotech companies, hospitals, firms organizing trials and so forth, large corporations still maintain key positions as integrators of the whole process (Orsenigo et al., 2001). Also, it is not possible to draw from these observations any strong inference about the relationships between the strength of the patent regime and innovative performance. One might suggest that the recent performance of the industry would have been much worse with a milder IPR regime. Yet, if anything, these trends confirm at least that no simple relation exists between patent protection and innovativeness.

2.4 Patents as incentives to commercialize innovations

The second set of arguments supporting (strong) patents conceives IPRs as a mechanism for inducing the development and commercialization of inventions and for creating markets for technologies (Arora et al., 2001). The Bayh-Dole Act is clearly based on these assumptions.

Here, again, as discussed in Chapter 2 of this volume, both the theory and the empirical evidence are far from conclusive.

First, the development of the biotechnology industry is customarily considered as one of the best examples of the positive role of patents in this respect. Indeed, there is evidence that markets for technology have grown rapidly in the last two or three decades and that patenting has favored the creation of new, specialized "knowledge-base" companies who sell or license their patents to larger corporations. The boom in university patenting and in the creation of biotech companies (often founded by university scientists) are typically cited as examples of the positive effects of the "new" IPR regime on the commercial exploitation of basic scientific research.

Yet, according to some analysts the picture is not unambiguously rosy. First, it must be simply noted that as universities and public research institutes have adopted aggressive strategies for patenting and commercializing their research efforts, the taxpayers pay twice for medical R&D: first through government-sponsored scientific research and then through above-marginal-cost pricing of patented medicines (Fink, 2008). Second, the performance of the biotechnological segment looks disappointing in terms of both operating profits and new drugs and it is argued that the business model which has emerged in this sector—based on strong patents on the results of basic research, venture capital and knowledge transactions between specialized biotechnology firms and larger companies developing and marketing the resulting drugs—might not be economically and socially efficient. A more effective organizational architecture should imply free basic research and more integrated and long-term oriented firms (Pisano, 2006, Coriat et al., 2003).

Third, as discussed in other chapters of this book, various studies have shown that the effects of the Bayh-Dole Act on technology transfer from university to industry are largely overestimated. Fourth, there is contrasting evidence that university scientists have shifted their focus from basic to applied research. Much of the research conducted in universities is located in the so-called Pasteur's quadrant (i.e., it is at the same time basic and use-inspired (Stokes, 1997)), and, if anything, the evidence seems to indicate strong correlations between patenting and publishing (Agrawal and Henderson, 2002; Azoulay et al., 2004; Geuna and Nesta, 2006; and Breschi et al., 2005). Walsh et al. (2003), in a survey of biomedical researchers in universities and private companies, find no major delays or abandonment of projects due to transaction costs, but some evidence of increasing obstacles and delays in securing material transfer agreements for research purposes. Other studies, however, find evidence for a quantitatively modest, but statistically significant, anti-commons effect (Murray and Stern, 2007 and document solid evidence on publication restrictions for sponsored research in the life sciences (Thursby, Fuller and Thursby, 2007). More generally, though, costs of litigation have been soaring and industry increasingly complains about the negative effects of very aggressive patenting policies by universities.

In the case of developing countries, stronger IPRs might hinder the development of domestic scientific capabilities if royalties on basic research tools are too expensive. However, for these countries, it has been sometimes argued that well-defined IPRs may attract foreign direct investment (FDI) and, possibly, related R&D. This argument has some empirical support (Maskus et al., 2004), particularly as it concerns clinical trials and market-development activities. Yet, it is widely recognized that IPRs are only one of the motivations leading to FDI. Other considerations—the availability of local skills, research infrastructures and capabilities, and demand characteristics, as well as other institutional and legal preconditions—are usually more important.[3] Moreover the recognition of patent protection in developing countries with small domestic markets may push large pharmaceutical companies to concentrate their production facilities in one country—to benefit from economies of scale—and use that country as an export base for the others. In that case the extension of strong IPR regime may hinder FDI.

2.5 The costs of IPRs: distortions on research directions and effects on prices

Jointly with the potential benefits on innovation, patents entail directs costs to society.

First, they can distort the directions of innovative activities: research focuses on diseases whose patients are typically rich enough to pay for prescriptions, and, more generally, on patentable cures and treatments (excluding, for example, nutrition, exercise, environment, etc.). Diseases which are rare and/or hit disproportionately poor countries are neglected: for example, patenting related to tropical diseases account for around 0.5 per cent of overall pharmaceutical patents (Lanjouw and Cockburn, 2000).

Second, patents imply higher prices due to monopoly power. In the case of pharmaceuticals, this cost is magnified by the intrinsic properties of the market for drugs. Given the value that users attribute to the product, demand elasticity tends to be low. Moreover, most consumers are insured (privately or publicly) against at least a part of the cost of prescription drugs, so they are only partially interested in drug prices. The prescribing physicians alike are not completely sensitive to prices, both because they will not pay for the prescribed drugs, and because the respect of professional norms makes them more attentive to the safety and therapeutic value of medicines. Patients are not completely informed about the properties of a drug. Also, the physicians' prescribing behavior is heavily affected by advertising and brand loyalty, and follows routinary patterns: much of the information available to physicians is provided by the companies themselves. Thus, producers exploit these asymmetries and the low demand elasticity by charging prices much higher than marginal costs.

For these reasons and also for considerations related to the containment of public health expenditures, in many countries (the USA and Germany being notable exceptions), drug prices are subject to various forms of control.

Once again, it is very difficult to evaluate, in general, the effects of stronger IP protection on drug prices. Scarcity of data and the extreme difficulties in computing comparable price indexes (Danzon and Kim, 1998) prevent systematic analysis. Clearly, such effects will be different across countries. Some estimates suggest that patents increase prices by an average of 300–400 per cent above the competitive market price, and in some cases by more than 1,000 per cent (Baker, 2004). Price increases after the introduction of patents were estimated by Watal (2000) and Fink (2000) to range from 50 per cent to 200 per cent in India, while Baker and Chatani (2007 suggest that the average increase in price for pharmaceuticals due to patent protection is probably close to 400 per cent (see Maskus, 2001, for a survey).

Three issues deserve specific attention. First, higher prices induced by patent protection stimulate further excessive marketing expenses and political lobbying. Second, price regulations may limit price increases. However, patent holders may choose not to supply the local market at the regulated prices. Conversely, when prices are defined on the basis of reference indexes of prices in other markets, firms have an incentive to bargain for the highest possible prices in the low-price economies in order to gain a higher set of global reference prices (Maskus 2001). Third, price discrimination is often considered as a possible counterbalance to unaffordable drug prices in poor countries. However, this implies banning parallel imports, an important source of low price drugs in many countries (and a source of exports for producers in developing countries). Further, price discrimination is often viewed as anticompetitive because it allows firms to set prices according to market power in each country. Indeed, Maskus (2001) shows that prices are often higher in developing nations than would be expected under a simple price-discrimination equilibrium and, indeed, are at times higher than in the rich nations.

3. THE SIGNING OF THE TRIPS AND THE NORTH/SOUTH CONFLICT ON PUBLIC HEALTH ISSUES

3.1. The changes introduced by the signing of the TRIPS

If the effects of strong drug-patenting regimes are fiercely debated in industrialized countries, it is hardly surprising that the signing of the TRIPS agreement in 1994, extending to Southern countries the same type of IPR regime that was designed in the North, should renew the controversy.

In substance, TRIPS heralded the enforcement of the new, stricter patent regime introduced in the Northern countries on a worldwide scale (Reichman and Lange, 1998; Coriat and Orsi, 2002; and Cimoli et al., 2009). By implementing so-called "minimum standards," this treaty insured a dramatic worldwide upward harmonization and introduced a radical break with some of the foundations and rules which had hitherto shaped international IPR protection. With specific reference to drugs, two main new "minimum standards" were introduced: the patentability of molecules became mandatory in all member countries, and the length of patent protection was extended to twenty years (see Coriat et al., 2006 for a broader discussion).

Two different deadlines were fixed for compliance to the new requirements: 2005 for the majority of DCs, 2011 for LDCs.[4] In practice, however, few countries could resist the pressure exerted by developed countries to anticipate the date of compliance. Thus Brazil modified its IP law to comply with the TRIPS as early as 1996 (Orsi et al., 2003) and Thailand even earlier, in 1994–95. India is a remarkable exception, since it extensively used its right to copy existing molecules right up until the end of the deadline (2005), thus playing a crucial role in the supply of low-cost generic drugs. India thus became until 2005 "the pharmacy of the third world."

It should be recalled that before the signing of the TRIPS agreement, international relations in these matters were governed by *very loose common rules*. International relations in the field of IP protection were governed by only two important treaties (Berne and Paris) which imposed few constraints on the signatory countries: before TRIPS, international treaties recognized *the right of different countries to implement different systems of IP protection, according to their level of economic development* and the products concerned. Among these products, essential drugs, considered "basic needs," were ranked of the highest importance (Scherer and Watal, 2002). Thus, a number of countries dispensed *with any form of IPR for drugs*, while many others dispensed only with patenting therapeutic molecules.[5] As mentioned before, in many cases (Brazil, India, Thailand, just to mention the most important generic drug producers) this made it possible to establish a large local industry for the low-cost production of generic drugs as a means to ensure access to treatment for the poorer segments of the population (Orsi et al., 2003).

It has to be noticed that in addition to TRIPS, bilateral and regional free trade agreements between the USA, Europe and developing countries are currently introducing further restrictions:

(a) requirements to extend the patent term for delays in obtaining author-
    izations to market new drugs and to make patents available for new uses
    of known products;
(b) provisions that prevent marketing approval of a generic drug during the
    patent term without the consent of the patent holder;
(c) protection of test data submitted to regulatory agencies for marketing
    approval through exclusive rights lasting at least five years, creating in
    effect a huge barrier to entry for generic suppliers (who should generate
    their own test data) and conferring market exclusivity even if a patent
    has not been granted in a particular country.

The developing countries were quick to bring the issue of the impact of the TRIPS on public healthcare to the forefront. The main preoccupation was the access to drugs in developing countries (Roffe, 2006), particularly in relation to the generic drugs hitherto produced at low cost by certain Southern countries. Since the pandemic was at that time exploding all over the world, with a concentration in the poorest countries of the South (and above all in sub-Saharan countries), the debate has been centred on the question of access to HIV/AIDS treatments. Before generic ARVs came into the market in the early 2000s, the price of ART[6] was around $10,000 to $12,000 per person per year. Obviously, this prohibited access to care for almost all people living with HIV (PLWHIV) in Southern countries, where no health insurance system, even when there is one, can support such a cost for each patient.[7]

In this context, following the pressures by Southern countries, in November 2001 the fourth Ministerial Conference of the WTO in Doha adopted a Declaration on TRIPS and Public Health.[8] This "Doha Declaration" explicitly acknowledges that IPR can damage public health through their effect on the price of drugs and it affirms the right of countries to interpret and apply the TRIPS in the best way to protect public health. Thus:

> We agree that the TRIPS Agreement does not and should not prevent Members
> from taking measures to protect public health. Accordingly, while reiterating our
> commitment to the TRIPS Agreement, we affirm that the Agreement can and
> should be interpreted and implemented in a manner supportive of WTO Mem-
> bers' right to protect public health and, in particular, to promote access to
> medicines for all (The Doha Declaration, 2001, Article 4).

However, the legal status of this declaration is rather weak, since none of its stipulations were ever introduced into the TRIPS agreement itself.

The legal provisions of which Southern countries can make use involve certain exceptions to exclusive patent rights (TRIPS, 1994, Articles 30 and 31), known as "TRIPS Flexibilities", relating mainly to the use of compulsory licenses.

Despite those flexibilities contained in the agreement, the signing of the TRIPS established a new legal "global order," where the right to "learn by imitating and copying"—abundantly exploited by today's developed countries as long as they needed it, is now denied to the newcomers (See Maskus, 2003 and Maskus et al., 2004).

Regarding access to drugs, it has to be noted that until 2005, solutions could be found to cope with the AIDS pandemic. Since many of the active substances used against HIV/AIDS were available on the market before the signing of the TRIPS (or for some countries, notably India, up until the deadline for TRIPS compliance), generic producers could supply Southern countries at very low costs. This fact, combined in certain cases with "preferential pricing" for Southern countries offered by big pharmaceutical firms within the framework of the ACCESS programme,[9] generated competition not only between generic producers and the big pharmas, but also between the generic producers themselves, ultimately leading to substantial reductions in the prices of the most widely used tritherapies: less than $100 per person per year (for a standard 3TC/d4T/NVP combination) today. At the same time, international aid really started to take off in 2003, notably with the setting up of the GFTAM, a multilateral organization whose annual budget has now reached several billion dollars a year.[10]

All these elements help to explain the significant results that were achieved during the first half of the 2000s.

3.2 Threats posed by the post-2005 scenario and the new situation wrought by the financial and environmental crisis

However, the second half of the 2000s got off to a much worse start. Prospects were considerably darkened by the convergence of a number of factors.

As stated above, 2005 was the deadline for those developing countries that had not already done so to make their national laws compliant with TRIPS. The essential effects of full application of the agreement concern the most recent drugs, those that were not produced in generic form before 2005—or for which generic producers had not yet made significant investments. In practice, this involved almost all the second-line anti-retroviral drugs.[11] The consumption of these drugs is already substantial and is certain to grow strongly over time. It has been estimated by the Clinton Foundation that each year 10 per cent of any given cohort of patients on first-line treatments will have to move to second-line treatments. Since the purchase cost of second-line drugs is seven to twelve times higher than that of first-line drugs (depending on the countries and the combinations administered to patients), the impact of 2005 TRIPS compliance in this domain has been staggering.[12] The graph below illustrates the differences in prices between first- and second-line treatments (Figure 7.1). In some middle-income countries that cannot access the generic products because of patent protection, the price hike could be as much as seventeen-fold.

The situation is all the more worrying because second-line treatments are not the only drugs affected. Already, and even for countries with limited resources, WHO treatment guidelines include some of the "new" ARVs, the production and sale of which are therefore subject to the restrictions entailed by full application of the TRIPS. In recent years, the WHO has twice modified its treatment guidelines for poor countries (2006 and 2009). To take into account the experience acquired in terms of the tolerance and toxicity of the first-generation ARV and the contribution made by new drugs (and the new combinations they make possible), the new WHO guidelines now include a number of new important drugs, none of which can be produced in generic form (except under exceptional circumstances).

This trend is bound to intensify over time. In the future, good medical practice will include an increasing proportion of new-generation ARV, even in first-line regimens for treatment-naive patients. As a result, the framework that allowed mass access to treatment (about 5 million patients at the end of 2010) at low cost is rapidly disintegrating.

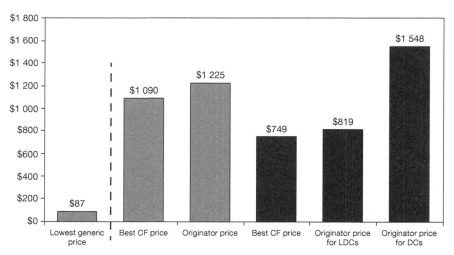

Figure 7.1 The impact of switching to second-line regimens on the price of ARV treatment

CF is put for drugs combining in one pill two or three ARV.

Source: MSF compilation based on WHO "Price Reporting Mechanism" and WHO report, available at <http://www.msfaccess.org/resources/key-publications/> (accessed 9 September 2013).

The situation can only be aggravated by the fact that the cost of ARV is not the only factor that is going to weigh more heavily on budgets. The follow-up care of patients (for the early detection of treatment failure, due to virus mutation for other reasons), requires regular monitoring of their immuno-logical and virological status. Every six months (according to the standard WHO guidelines for developed countries) patients must be tested to measure their viral load. The cost of buying the equipment, conducting the tests and training staff to carry out and interpret the tests or to manage and maintain the equipment constitutes a considerable extra burden. All the more so since this type of equipment (and the personnel capable of using it) are lacking in most Southern countries.

Furthermore, unlike the ARV market, which is relatively transparent and competitive, the market for tests and monitoring equipment is very opaque and oligopolistic: as a consequence, the cost of monitoring assays and install-ing laboratory networks capable of using them are inflated.

Last but not least, while huge extra investments are now needed, there are serious threats hanging over the funding of public health budgets. First, the international financial crisis is prompting donor countries to tighten their purse strings. Thus, for the first time ever, the Global Fund to Fight AIDS, Tuberculosis and Malaria (GFATM) has reported a funding deficit of more than \$4 billion for the 2009–2010 period.[13,14] Finally the campaign for the third replenishment of the GFTAM (covering the period 2011–2013) ended with very disappointing results. With only \$11.7 billion collected for three years the fund didn't even reach its lowest expectations.[15]

Thus, at the very moment when the cost of access to healthcare is doubly burdened by the shift to new drugs—now protected by patents over which competition cannot exert any moderating influence—and by the need to set up monitoring networks and purchase the vast amounts of equipment required, there is a grave risk that international funding of public health will be cut.

3.3 The reaction of Southern countries: the case of Thailand and Brazil

To deal with the new situation, after 2005 the Southern countries most involved in the fight against AIDS had to find new solutions. After refraining from doing so for a long time, Thailand, soon followed by Brazil, have started issuing compulsory licenses. Although Thailand was not the first country to issue compulsory licenses,[16] the initiative taken by this country was crucially important, because it is both a large producer of generics and heavily engaged in the fight against AIDS at a national level. It was only after lengthy deliber-ations inside the country, leading to the establishment of a powerful coalition of social forces in favor of generics that the country finally took the plunge

(Tantivess et al., 2008 and Krikorian, 2008). After several unsuccessful attempts to negotiate price reductions with the patent-holder companies, the Ministry of Health proceeded in two stages, issuing two series of compulsory licenses.[17] The first, in November 2006, was for Efavirenz, and the second—two months later—was for Lopinavir/r. These licenses were issued for "governmental use," on the grounds of public interest, a "flexibility" provided for in the TRIPS. The effect on the procurement costs of these two ARVs was an immediate reduction of 44 per cent for Efavirenz and even more for Lopinavir/r. The production of these generics was entrusted to the GPO, the national public laboratory in Thailand.

Drawing on the experience of Thailand, the Brazilian Ministry of Health issued a compulsory license for Efavirenz in April 2007. Like Thailand, Brazil entrusted the production of generics to its public laboratory, Far Manghinos. While waiting for the latter to enter into full production,[18] the generics were to be imported from India. The reduction in procurement costs was huge, falling from $1.59, (price per unit at which Merck sold its proprietary drug) to $0.43, the price of the generic (d'Almeida et al., 2008).

Yet, the evidence shows that these measures are not enough. A detailed and exhaustive study of the issuing of compulsory licenses (d'Almeida et al., 2008) highlights the limits of these initiatives:

- the process of issuing such licenses is long, expensive and politically very sensitive;
- even if significant reductions are obtained for the drugs produced under compulsory license, the impact on the overall cost of treatment remains slight, because of the very small number of ARVs produced under compulsory license;
- lastly, the process is subject to dispute and legal challenge; in practice the provision of drugs depends on the vagaries of legal procedures and court rulings, creating a situation of uncertainty that is unacceptable when tens of thousands of patients need to be supplied with different types of drug combinations on a daily basis.

All in all, compulsory licensing is therefore ill-adapted to dealing with a disease like AIDS. Because it is a chronic disease caused by a virus capable of mutation, changes in treatment are regularly needed to take into account the evolution of the epidemic and the continual arrival of new drugs. But each time such a change is needed, the flexibilities currently codified in TRIPS require governments to issue new licenses, to locate producers, to negotiate the terms of the contract and to place the necessary orders—without any guarantee that they will not, at one stage or another, encounter obstacles that compromise the procurement.

For all these reasons, the use of compulsory licenses—under the conditions currently governing their issue—is an unwieldy, expensive and ultimately ill-adapted process. Clearly, if the issue is to face the pandemic, more appropriate tools are needed, and the TRIPS flexibilities need to be significantly enlarged.

4. CONCLUSION

The IPR system governing pharmaceuticals has become increasingly dysfunctional—even in countries like the USA. Thus, the efficacy and desirability of extending strong IPR protection in the rest of the world raises very legitimate doubts. The consequences of the TRIPS as regards access to care in developing countries—as illustrated by the case of the fight against the HIV/AIDS pandemics—could be dramatic.

Strong patent laws do indeed confer an advantage to innovators in the pharmaceuticals industry, but the magnitude and even the shape of such effects is difficult to assess, both theoretically and empirically. In any case, they may not be enough to promote innovation in contexts where innovative capabilities are low or missing altogether. Conversely, excessively tight IPRs have strong negative effects on prices and access to health, especially in developing countries.

How can the negative effects of stronger patent protections be offset? Or alternatively should we think to redesign the whole system of IP protection currently enforced in the pharmaceutical sector?[19] A series of measures (like advanced purchase commitments and product development partnerships) have been introduced and several schemes for the design of alternative incentive mechanisms to innovation (e.g., prizes) have been proposed. Their efficiency and feasibility remains controversial. Key research questions—with strong practical implications—are urgent on the agenda.

NOTES

1. Estimates vary drastically according to different sources and methodologies. For example, the Pharmaceutical Research and Manufacturers of America (PhRMA) provides a figure of around 19 per cent in the USA, whereas according to the National Science Foundation R&D intensity is around 8–10 per cent. Though it is worth reminding readers that marketing expenditures have been also increasing rapidly reaching a ratio to sales ranging between 20–25 per cent in the USA according to different sources (Gagnon and Lexchin, 2008).
2. However, in more recent years, regulations have become more relaxed and approval times shortened (due to the Prescription Drug User Fee Act in 1992 and the FDA Modernization Act in 1997).

3. A counter-argument is that increased foreign direct investment might produce a crowding-out effect on skilled labour and local researchers for domestic companies.

4. For LDCs this deadline was subsequently extended to 2016.

5. According to a recent survey by UNCTAD, before the signing of the TRIPS, no less than fifty-three countries did not recognize any form of protection for therapeutic molecules in their IP laws and codes (UNCTAD-ICTSD 2005).

6. ART: Antiretroviral Therapy denotes the different combinations of three ARVs (tritherapies) used since 1996 in the fight against AIDS.

7. In fact, it was only in the early 2000s, with the arrival of generic copies (proposed by the Indian manufacturers) that this cost fell to around $140 per person per year. For certain drugs this price has continued to fall ever since.

8. WTO document number: WT/MIN(01)/DEC/2 available at <www.wto.org/eng lish/thewto_e/minist_e/min01_e/mindecl_trips_e.htm> (accessed 9 September 2013).

9. The ACCESS programme (also known as the Accelerated Access Initiative) was launched in the early 2000s. Under the aegis of major international organizations (the United Nations Population Fund, UNICEF, the World Health Organization, the World Bank and UNAIDS) a partnership was set up with large pharmaceutical companies (Boehringer, BMS, Glaxosmithkline, Merck, Roche and later joined by Abbott) with the aim of offering access to treatment to developing countries. Within this framework, and using a classification based on the human development indicator, countries classified as "developing" or "least developed" are eligible for different but significant reduction in the price of ARVs. However, each pharmaceutical company sets its own restrictions on eligibility, determining on a case-by-case basis the nature and price of the drugs offered. These idiosyncratic distinctions account for the large price discrepancies observed for the same drug in different countries. They also explain the weak final impact of the ACCESS programme on price reductions observed after 2000. For more details on this issue, see (Lucchini et al., 2003).

10. The setting up of the GFTAM (Global Fund against Tuberculosis, AIDS and Malaria) in 2003 is the most emblematic and visible of the initiatives taken by the international community to fund access to health care in Southern countries. The same period (the beginning of the 2000s) also saw the reorganization of the World Bank AIDS programme, at the level of multilateral aid, and the launching of the PEPFAR initiative in the United States, which was, however, a bilateral aid programme marked by severe restrictions (details in Coriat, 2008).

11. The so-called first-line treatments are recommended for "treatment-naive" patients. They all entail a triple combination of ARV, which may vary according to the patient's viral load, profile and tolerance to the treatment. But in the event of treatment failure or virus mutation (which occurs regularly after a number of years of first-line treatment), new drugs must be prescribed. Hence, the second-line and even third-line treatments.

12. The arguments presented in this chapter are an update of those set out in Orsi et al. (2007).

13. Global Fund against AIDS, TB and Malaria (GFATM). Report of the Executive Director, Twentieth Board Meeting, Addis Ababa, Ethiopia.

14. The prospects for the future are even more worrying. The big NGO *Médecins Sans Frontières* notes in a recent document that: "The most glaring sign of the decreasing political commitment to HIV/AIDS is a major funding deficit. The Global Fund to Fight AIDS, Tuberculosis and Malaria Board is considering a motion to cancel the funding round (Round 10) for 2010; if accepted, no new proposals will be considered until 2011. Similarly, the US President's Emergency Plan for AIDS Relief (PEPFAR) plans to "flat-fund" its programs for the next two years, reneging on promises made last year to support expanded treatment access." In "Punishing Success? Early Signs of a Retreat from Commitment to HIV/AIDS Care and Treatment," 5 November 2009. Available at <www.msfaccess.org/resources/key-publications/> (accessed 9 September 2013).

15. The lowest expectations (known as "scenario 1") was designed to allow for the continuation of funding of existing programs. New programs could only be funded at a significantly lower level than in recent years. The resources required for this scenario were estimated at $13 billion.

16. In fact, several African and Asian countries "with limited resources" or classified as "intermediate" issued compulsory licenses before 2005. They include Zimbabwe (2002), Indonesia, Malaysia, Mozambique and Swaziland (2004). Ghana, Guinea and Taiwan issued such licenses during 2005.

17. ARVs are not the only drugs concerned by such licenses. They have also been issued for other drugs of public interest, notably anti-cancer drugs.

18. At the same time as the compulsory license was issued, local public-private partnerships were set up as a means to ensure the relatively rapid production of the active principles required to manufacture the Efavirenz.

19. Among the contributions focusing on this issue, two may deserve particular attention. The first one emanates from the US National Academy of Science, (Merril et al., 2004), the second from a group of developing countries led by Argentina and Brazil aiming at opening a discussion inside the WIPO arena on IP issues (WIPO, 2004).

REFERENCES

Acemoglu, Daron and Joshua Linn. 2004. "Market Size in Innovation: Theory and Evidence from the Pharmaceutical Industry," *Quarterly Journal of Economics*, 119 (3): 1049–90.

Agrawal, A. and R. Henderson. 2002. "Putting Patents in Context: Exploring Knowledge Transfer from MIT," *Management Science*, 45 (7): 905–17, <http://www.cepr.net/documents/publications/intellectual_property_2004_09.pdf> (last accessed 10 October 2013).

d'Almeida, C., L. Hasenclever, G. Krikorian, et al. 2008. "New Antiretroviral Treatments and Post-2005 TRIPS Constraints. First Moves towards IP Flexibilization in Developing Countries," in Coriat (ed.) 2008, 25–51.

Arora, Ashish, Marco Ceccagnoli, and Wesley M. Cohen. 2008. "R&D and the Patent Premium," *International Journal of Industrial Organization*, 26 (5): 1153–79.

Arora, Ashish, Andrea Fosfuri, and Alfonso Gambardella. 2001. *Markets for Technology: The Economics of Innovation and Corporate Strategy.* Cambridge, MA: MIT Press.

Arora, Ashish, Marco Ceccagnoli, and Wesley M. Cohen. 2005. "R&D and the Patent Premium," *NBER Working Paper Series*, No. 9431.

Azoulay, Pierre, Waverly Ding, and Toby Stuart. 2004. "The Effect of Academic Patenting on (Public) Research Output," in *Academic Science and Entrepreneurship: Dual Engines of Growth?* Cambridge, MA: NBER Books.

Baker, Dean. 2004. "Financing Drug Research: What Are the Issues?" Center for Economic and Policy Research, Washington, DC.

Baker, Dean and Noriko Chatani. 2007. "Promoting Good Ideas on Drugs: Are Patents the Best Way?" Center for Economic and Policy Research, <http://www.cepr.net/docu ments/publications/Promoting_Good_Ideas_on_Drugs.pdf> (accessed 9 September 2013).

Breschi, Stefano, Francesco Lissoni, and Fabio Montobbio. 2005. "From Publishing to Patenting: Do Productive Scientists Turn into Academic Inventors?" *Revue d'Economie Industrielle*, 110 (2): 75–102.

Chaudhuri, Sudip. 2005. *The WTO and India's Pharmaceutical Industry.* Oxford: Oxford University Press.

Cimoli, M., B. Coriat, and A. Primi. 2009. "Intellectual Property and Industrial Development," in M. Cimoli, G. Dosi, and J.E. Stiglitz (eds), *The Political Economy of Capabilities Accumulation: The Past and Future of Industrial Policies for Development.* Oxford: Oxford University Press.

Cohen, Wesley M., Richard R. Nelson, and John P. Walsh. 2002. "Links and Impacts: The Influence of Public Research on Industrial R&D," *Management Science*, 48: 1–23.

Comanor, W.S. 1986. "The Political Economy of the Pharmaceutical Industry," *Journal of Economic Literature*, 24: 1178–217.

Congressional Budget Office. 2006. "Research and Development in the Pharmaceutical Industry," Washington DC, October.

Coriat, B. (ed.) 2008. *The Political Economy of HIV/AIDS in Developing Countries.* Cheltenham, UK. Edward Elgar.

Coriat, B. and F. Orsi. 2002. "Establishing a New Intellectual Property Rights Regime in the United States: Origins, Content, Problems," *Research Policy*, 31: 1491–507.

Coriat, B., F. Orsi, and C. d'Alameida. 2006. "TRIPS and the International Public Health Controversies: Issues and Challenges," *Industrial and Corporate Change*, 15 (6): 1033–62.

Coriat, B., F. Orsi, and O. Weinstein. 2003. "Does Biotech Reflect a New Science Based Regime," *Industry and Innovation*, 10 (3): 231–53.

Danzon, Patricia M. and Jeong Kim. 1998. "International Price Comparisons for Pharmaceuticals: Measurement and Policy Issues," *Pharmacoeconomics*, 14: 115–28.

De Francisco, Andrés and Stephen Matlin (eds). 2006. "Monitoring Financial Flows for Health Research 2006: The Changing Landscape of Health Research for Development," Global Forum for Health Research, Geneva.

Fink, C. 2000. "How Stronger Patent Protection in India Might Affect the Behavior of Transnational Pharmaceutical Industries." Policy Research Paper, World Bank, no. 2352.

Fink, C. 2008. "Intellectual Property and Public Health: An Overview of the Debate with a Focus on U.S. Policy." Working Paper 146, Center for Global Development.

Food and Drug Administration. 2005. "CDER NDAs Approved in Calendar Years 1990–2004 by Therapeutic Potential and Chemical Type," <www.fda.gov/cder/rdmt/pstable.htm> (accessed 9 September 2013).

Gagnon M.A. and J. Lexchin. 2008. "The Cost of Pushing Pills: A New Estimate of Pharmaceutical Promotion Expenditures in the United States," *PLoS Med*, 5 (1): e1. doi:10.1371/journal.pmed.0050001.

Geuna, Aldo and Lionel Nesta. 2006. "University Patenting and its Effects on Academic Research: The Emerging European Evidence," *Research Policy*, 35: 790–807.

Henderson, Rebecca, Luigi Orsenigo, and Gary P. Pisano. 1998. "The Pharmaceutical Industry and the Revolution in Molecular Biology: Exploring the Interactions Between Scientific, Institutional and Organizational Change," in D. Mowery and R. Nelson, eds, *The Sources of Industrial Advantages*. Cambridge: Cambridge University Press, 267–311.

Krikorian, G. 2008. "New Trends in IP Protection and Health Issues in FTA Negotiations" in Coriat (ed.) 2008, 52–77.

Laforgia, Francesco, Fabio Montobbio, and Luigi Orsenigo. 2008. "IPRs, Technological and Industrial Development and Growth: The Case of the Pharmaceutical Industry," in N. Netanel, ed., *The Development Agenda: Global Intellectual Property and Developing Countries*. Oxford: Oxford University Press.

Lanjouw, Jean O. 1998a. "The Introduction of Pharmaceutical Product Patents in India: Heartless Exploitation of the Poor and Suffering?" *NBER Working Papers Series*, No. 6366.

Lanjouw, Jean O. 1998b. "Patent Protection in the Shadow of Infringement: Simulation Estimations of Patent Value," *The Review of Economic Studies*, 65: 671–710.

Lanjouw, J.O. and I. Cockburn. 2000. "Do Patents Matter? Empirical Evidence After GATT," *NBER Working Papers Series*, No. 7495.

Lazonick, W. and Ö Tulum. 2011. "US Biopharmaceutical Finance and the Sustainability of the Biotech Business Model," *Research Policy*, 40: 1170–87.

Levin, Richard C., Alvin K. Klevorick, Richard R. Nelson, and Sidney G. Winter. 1987. "Appropriating the Returns from Industrial Research and Development," *Brookings Papers on Economic Activity*, (3): 783–820.

Lucchini, S., B. Cisse, S. Durand, and J.-P. Moatti. 2003. "Decrease in Prices of Antiretroviral Drugs for Developing Countries: From Political 'Philanthropy' to Regulated Markets?" in J. P. Moatti, B. Coriat, Y. Souteyrand, et al., eds, *Economics of AIDS and Access to HIV Care in Developing Countries: Issues and Challenges*. Paris: Editions de l' ANRS.

Mansfield, E., M. Schwartz, and S. Wagner. 1981. "Imitation Costs and Patents: An Empirical Study," *Economic Journal*, 91: 907–18.

Maskus, K.E. 2001. "Parallel Imports in Pharmaceuticals: Implications for Competition and Prices in Developing Countries," Final Report to World Intellectual Property Organization, <http://www.wipo.int/export/sites/www/about-ip/en/studies/pdf/ssa_maskus_pi.pdf> (last accessed 10 October 2013).

Maskus, K.E. 2003. "Transfer of Technology and Technological Capacity Building," WP UNCTAD-ICTSD, <http://www.iprsonline.org/unctadictsd/bellagio/docs/Maskus_Bellagio2.pdf> (last accessed 10 October 2013).

Maskus, K.E, K. Saggi, and T. Puttitanun. 2004. "Patent Rights and International Technologuy Transfer Through Direct Investment and Licensing," WP UNCTAD-ICTSD.

Merril, S.A., R. Levin, and M.B. Myers. 2004. *A Patent System for the 21st Century.* Washington, DC: National Research Academy, The National Academies Press.

Murray, Fiona and Scott Stern. 2007. "Do Formal Intellectual Property Rights Hinder the Free Flow of Scientific Knowledge? An Empirical Test of the Anti-Commons Hypothesis," *Journal of Economic Behavior & Organization*, 63: 648–87.

Nightingale, Paul and Paul Martin. 2004. "The Myth of the Biotech Revolution," *Trends in Biotechnology*, 22 (11): 564–9.

Orsenigo, Luigi, Fabio Pammolli, and Massimo Riccaboni. 2001. "Technological Change and the Dynamics of Networks of Collaborative Relations: The Case of the Bio-pharmaceutical Industry," *Research Policy*, 30: 485–508.

Orsi, F., et al. 2007. "Trips Post-2005 and Access to New Antiretroviral Treatments in Southern Countries: Issues and Challenges," *AIDS*, 21: 1997–2003.

Orsi, F., L. Hasenclever, B. Fialho, P. Tigre, and B. Coriat. 2003. "Intellectual Property Rights, Anti-Aids Policy and Generic Drugs: Lesson from the Brazilian Public Health Program," in J.P. Moatti, B. Coriat, Y. Souteyrand, et al., eds, *Economics of AIDS and Access to HIV Care in Developing Countries: Issues and Challenges.* Paris: ANRS Editions.

Pammolli, F., L. Magazzini, and L. Orsenigo. 2002. "The Intensity of Competition after Patent Expiry in Pharmaceuticals: A Cross-Country Analysis," *Revue d'Economie Industrielle* 99: 107–31.

Pisano, Gary. 2006. *Science Business: The Promise, the Reality and the Future of Biotech.* Cambridge, MA: Harvard Business School University Press.

Qian, Y. 2007. "Do National Patent Laws Stimulate Domestic Innovation in a Global Patenting Environment? A Cross-Country Analysis of Pharmaceutical Patent Protection, 1978–2002," *The Review of Economics and Statistics*, 89 (3): 436–53.

Ramani, Shyama V. and Augustin Maria. 2005. "TRIPS: Its Possible Impact on Biotech Segment of the Indian Pharmaceutical Industry," *EPW Special Articles*, February 12–18: 675–83.

Reichman, J. and D. Lange.1998. "Bargaining around the TRIPS Agreement: The Case for Ongoing Public-Private Initiatives to Facilitate Worldwide Property Transactions," *Duke Journal of Comparative & International Law*, 9 (11): 11–68.

Roffe, P. 2006. *Negotiating Health.* London: Earthscan Publishers.

Schankerman, Mark. 1998. "How Valuable is Patent Protection? Estimates by Technology Field," *Rand Journal of Economics*, 29 (1): 77–107.

Scherer, F. M. and Watal, J. 2002. "Post-TRIPS Options for Access to Patented Medicines in Developing Nations," *Journal of International Economic Law*, 5: 913–39.

Scherer, F.M. and S. Weisburst. 1995. "Economic Effects of Strengthening Pharmaceutical Patent Protection in Italy," *International Review of Industrial Property and Copyright Law* 6: 1009–24.

Stokes, Donald. 1997. *Pasteur's Quadrant: Basic Science and Technological Innovation.* Washington, DC: Brookings Institution Press.

Sutton, J. 1998. *Technology and Market Structure.* Cambridge, MA: MIT Press.

Tantivess, S., et al. 2008. *Introducing Government Use of Patents on Essential Medicines in Thailand, 2006–2007: Policy Analysis with Key Lessons Learned and Recommendations*. Thailand: International Health Policy Program.

Thursby, Jerry G., Anne Fuller, and Marie C. Thursby. 2007. "U.S. Faculty Patenting: Inside and Outside the University," *NBER Working Paper Series*, No. 13256.

UNCTAD-ICTSD. 2005. *Resource Book on TRIPS and Development*. Cambridge: Cambridge University Press.

Walsh, John P., Wesley M. Cohen, and Ashish Arora. 2003. "Patenting and Licensing of Research Tools and Biomedical Innovation," in S. Merrill and M. Meyers, eds, *Innovation in a Knowledge-Based Economy*. Washington, DC: National Academies Press.

Watal, Jayashree. 2000. "Pharmaceutical Patents, Prices and Welfare Losses: A Simulation Study of Policy Options for India under the WTO TRIPS Agreement," *The World Economy*, 23: 733–52.

WIPO. 2004. "Proposal by Argentina and Brazil for the Establishment of a Development Agenda for WIPO," presented at the WIPO General Assembly, 2004, WIPO pub. WO/GA/31/11.

8

Innovation, Appropriability and Productivity Growth in Agriculture: A Broad Historical Viewpoint

Alessandro Nuvolari and Valentina Tartari

1. INTRODUCTION

The introduction and diffusion of innovations in agriculture has been one of the fundamental drivers of economic and social change on a world scale. This appears very clearly when we consider that the most common periodization adopted by economic historians regards the history of mankind as marked by two fundamental turning-points, both of them related to the introduction of innovations in agriculture: the Neolithic agricultural revolution and the industrial revolution (Cipolla, 1962).

The Neolithic agricultural revolution consisted in the transition from the hunter-gatherer lifestyle to a sedentary way of life based on the domestication of plants and animals. This transition first took place in about 8,500 BC in the regions of the Fertile Crescent of the Near East. Somewhat later, a sedentary lifestyle based on the domestication of plants and animals emerged also in other locations such as China, and possibly Mexico (Diamond, 1997: 100). From these early centers, the domestication of plants and animals spread at uneven rates but inexorably throughout most of the world, progressively becoming the predominant lifestyle. Furthermore, the emergence of agriculture permitted the formation of larger, denser and socially differentiated communities.

Interestingly enough, the predominant consensus today is that the emergence and diffusion of agriculture did not include among its effects a sustained improvement in per-capita material living standards. In fact, some historians have even suggested that the adoption of agriculture brought about an actual deterioration in material living standards, in terms of quantities and qualities of calories consumed, frequency of diseases and amount of leisure time (see Clark, 2007 for a particular "strong" version of this view). Material living standards began to rise steadily only at a much later date, with the industrial revolution, which is, obviously, the second fundamental turning-point mentioned above.

One of the classic definitions of the industrial revolution is that of a structural shift from an economic system in which the majority of the population is employed in agricultural activities to an economic system in which this proportion is less than 5–10 per cent of the total. So it is clear that the transformation of the agricultural sector played a critical role also for the origins, consolidation and spread of industrialization in the world economy (Bairoch, 1973).

The aim of this chapter is to provide an historical survey of long-term patterns of innovation in agriculture and explore their relationship both with the dynamics of productivity growth and with the evolution of intellectual property rights regimes. We shall concentrate mostly on the experience of the Western world.

Both economists and economic historians have frequently suggested that in contexts of weak appropriability of economic returns of inventions, there will be a systematic underinvestment in inventive activities and as a result productivity will stagnate (see, for example, North (1981: 163–6) and Jones (2002: 196–7) for two authoritative formulations of this view and Chapter 2 in this volume for a thorough critical reassessment).[1] In this perspective, the historical development of agriculture is of particular interest, because it is a human activity that for a long time was characterized by a very weak appropriability regime, at least in terms of the existence of formal institutional arrangements conferring private property rights for inventions. Still, the evidence shows that agriculture during its approximately 11,000 years of history, most of them taking place in a context of extremely weak intellectual property protection, has witnessed the introduction of major innovations that have contributed to an increase in productivity of several orders of magnitude (Boldrin and Levine, 2008: 79). Concerning the rate of technological change in the most recent period, Federico (2005: 74–82) estimates that over the period 1800–2000, in most countries of the world, the rate of agriculture's total factor productivity growth (which is the index most commonly used by economists for gauging the rate of technical change) was positive (the average for the world is 0.58 per cent per year). Furthermore, in many countries, the rate of growth of total factor productivity in agriculture outperformed that of their manufacturing sector and that of the overall economy for significant periods (Federico, 2005: 79–80).

2. INNOVATION AND TRANSFORMATION OF AGRICULTURE: THE MAIN TRENDS

For schematic purposes, innovations in agriculture have been frequently classified in four main categories: (i) biological innovations (i.e., "new" types of plants and animals), (ii) improvements or transformations of practices of cultivation, (iii) mechanization, and (iv) chemical products (fertilizers and pesticides).

On the basis of this classification, historians have also frequently put forward a schematic chronology of the long-term innovation trends in agriculture: until the industrial revolution, innovations in agriculture were mostly belonging to the first two categories (biological innovations and improvements in cultivation), afterwards mechanization and chemical inventions assumed a predominant role. This state of affairs lasted until the 1930s, when biological innovation gained new momentum stimulated by developments in biological sciences (for example, the rediscovery of Mendelian genetics) and supported in many Western countries by a robust public research infrastructure. Interestingly enough, Olmstead and Rhode (2008) have recently challenged this view, arguing, in a rather compelling way, that biological innovation remained the fundamental form of innovation for the agricultural sector also throughout the entire nineteenth century and that previous accounts have largely exaggerated the primacy of mechanical innovation in this period.

2.1 Crop transfers and improvements in cultivation practices

If we take a long-run view, agriculture before the industrial revolution experienced two major transformations. The first is the great "Colombian exchange": that is the exchange of crops and livestock species between America and Europe with potato, maize, tobacco, tomato, hemp and turkeys going from America to Europe, and wheat, barley, grapes, cattle, sheep and chickens going from Europe to America (Federico, 2005: 85, see also Nunn and Qian, 2010 for a general reassessment).[2] The systematic introduction of foreign plant and animal varieties was particularly important in the development of the agricultural sector in the United States throughout the nineteenth century (Olmstead and Rhode, 2008: 390–5). This type of biological innovation taking place in the form of the transfer of crops and livestock from one location to another has clearly progressively diminished in significance, as over time all known types of crops and animals were systematically tried in most locations. According to Federico (2005: 86), this "saturation point" was probably reached at the end of the nineteenth century. Afterwards, the introduction of new plants and animals took the form of hybridization of pre-existing species, and more recently by means of genetic engineering.

The second and surely the most significant transformation of agriculture taking place before the industrial revolution, was the so-called "agricultural revolution" of the seventeenth and eighteenth century. Traditionally, this agricultural revolution is conceived as the introduction of a number of improvements in the practices of cultivation, in particular the introduction of the system of "continuous rotation." This practice consisted in the introduction in the rotation system of a number of new crops (such as turnips, legumes or clover) capable of reintegrating the fertility of the soil, in combination with heavy manuring. These innovations permitted the elimination of fallow completely. It is not known the exact year in which these practices were adopted for the first time in Europe. However, the two locations in which "continuous rotation" was systematically introduced and refined were England and the Low Countries. By the middle of the eighteenth century the Norfolk rotation (turnips, barley, clover and wheat) had been widely recognized as "best-practice" (R. C. Allen, 2004: 110). Allen estimates that in England between 1300 and 1800 the average yield of wheat increased from twelve bushels to twenty bushels per acre. Approximately half of this 66 per cent increase in yields was attained mostly after 1600 by virtue of the introduction of nitrogen fixing plants in the rotation system (Allen, 2008).

Recent research has also recognized that the improvements in cultivation practices of the agricultural revolution were intertwined with a steady stream of biological innovations. In England, from the seventeenth century, farmers systematically collected seeds from the best plants (either exemplars that were high-yielding or resistant to disease) and cultivated them separately (R. C. Allen, 2004: 108). Similarly, the systematic adoption of various methods of selective breeding was responsible for a significant growth in the size and quality of the livestock (R. C. Allen, 2004: 109).

2.2 Mechanization and chemical products

Many historians, following an original cue of Douglass North (North, 1981: 163–6), consider the English patent system emerging from the Statute of Monopolies of 1623 as the first attempt at creating an institutional arrangement capable of establishing enforceable property rights for inventions (see MacLeod, 1988 for an history of the English patent system to 1800 and again, Chapter 2 of this volume for an overview of the development of patent systems in the major industrialized countries). It is, then, interesting to remark that most of the inventions of the agricultural revolution (consisting in the introduction of new crops and in improvements in cultivation practices) have instead left no trace in the patent records. Sullivan estimates that only 3 per cent of the English patents granted over the period 1711–1850 covered agricultural inventions (Sullivan, 1990). This share is probably even lower for the seventeenth century (MacLeod, 1988: 98–102). Of course, the chief explanation is that biological innovations and improvements in cultivation practices were in general considered as not amenable to patenting, as patents in the Statute of Monopolies were reserved for the "working or making of new manufactures" (MacLeod, 1988: 17).[3] Some inventors adopted the strategy of trying to appropriate the returns for the introduction of improvements in cultivation practices by describing them in detail in agrarian treatises and securing copyrights on them. This was the case of Jethro Tull with his treatise, *The Horse-Hoeing Husbandry* (MacLeod, 1988: 98).

During the nineteenth century, in most European countries and in the U.S. the bulk of patents in agriculture were represented by patents covering agricultural implements such as improved ploughs, seed-drills, etc. and machinery (threshing and winnowing machines). In fact, it is possible to trace back to the last decade of the eighteenth century the emergence of a modern industry specialized in the production of industrial machines and implements (MacLeod, 1988: 98). Since the industrial revolution, the agricultural sector in the Western world has been characterized by a trend towards the increasing mechanization of processes previously done by hand. Historians of technology have traditionally produced accounts of the contours of agricultural innovation in the nineteenth century that seem actually in line with the dominant role that mechanical inventions have in patent statistics for agriculture.[4] These accounts emphasize the role of inventions such as the cotton gin (1793), the threshing machine (1786), the reaping machine (1830s) and other later types of harvesting and picking machines in accounting for the substantial increase of agricultural productivity during the nineteenth century. Furthermore, the mechanization of agricultural operations was further stimulated by the advent and improvement of the gasoline tractor, which provided a small-scale and moveable source of power and that could be very effectively integrated into the agricultural production system (Olmstead and Rhode, 2003).

Chemical innovations contributed significantly to agricultural productivity from the late nineteenth century when chemical fertilizers began to be increasingly adopted (the key breakthrough in this area was achieved in 1909 with the development of the Haber-Bosch process for producing ammonia). Nitrogen fertilizers provided a very effective way of reintegrating soil fertility, without resorting to complicated systems of rotations and they were responsible for a very significant share of the productivity increase attained in agriculture over the twentieth century. Some scholars even claim that given its major contribution to the increase of yields, the Haber-Bosch process ought to be considered the most important invention of the nineteenth century (Erisman et al. 2008). The second contribution of chemical innovations to agriculture was the development of chemical substances that could be used effectively to fight pests and weeds. Also in this area, the first important results can be dated to the end of the nineteenth century.

The account we have outlined so far regards agriculture as a sector that, since the nineteenth century, has "received" innovations from other industries, in particular from machinery and chemicals. These two industries, in most Western countries, could rely on patent protection (although in some countries only chemical processes could be patented). Hence, at least at first glance, it would appear that for the agricultural inventions generated by these two industries, inventors could appropriate economic returns in a straight-forward way using patents. In fact, patents feature prominently in the biographies of inventors such as Eli Whitney (cotton gin), Andrew Meikle (threshing machine) and Cyrus McCormick (reaping machine), the heroic inventors of the early mechanization of agriculture. All three used patents, albeit with different fortunes to reap economic returns from their innovations.

However, more recent evidence points to the existence of a large volume of inventive activities undertaken in the field of agricultural machinery without patent protection. Even if we consider agricultural implements such as ploughs, we find that inventors frequently preferred not to use patents, but either kept innovative plough designs as trade secrets or made them publicly available in order to enhance their own reputations (Brunt, 2003: 451; Mokyr, 2009: 183). Petra Moser (2012) provides a very interesting snapshot on the volume of inventions outside the coverage of the patent system by looking at how many inventions exhibited at the Crystal Palace exhibition in 1851 were not covered by patents. Moser shows that only 19.9 per cent of the British exhibits and 37 per cent of the American exhibits in the category of "agricultural machinery" were patented. Overall, these low patenting rates indicate that, even in a field like agricultural machinery where patents could be used most effectively, inventors preferred to adopt mechanisms of appropriability and did not contemplate the use of patents for protecting their inventions. Moser's findings of a low patenting rate in the area of agricultural machinery are fully corroborated by a more recent exercise carried out by Brunt et al. (2012) who look at the prize competition for agricultural machinery and agricultural implements organized by the Royal Agricultural Society of England. They find that only a share of about 20 per cent of the inventions that entered into the competition were patented. Additionally, Brunt et al. (2012) also show that, at least in the area of agricultural machinery, prizes (in particular prestigious non-pecuniary prizes) represented a very powerful inducement for inventive activities.

Similar considerations also hold for chemical inventions. This is clearly another domain in which patents can be used most effectively as a tool for appropriating returns from innovations. However, even in this field, patents were not used in isolation. For example, the Haber-Bosch process for the production of ammonia was protected by a number of patents, but at the same time the details of the catalyst system were protected as a trade secret (Arora et al., 1999: 227). It is also interesting to notice that some scholars have also argued that the innovative performance of the emerging German chemical industry was also stimulated by the very limits of patent protection in chemicals. German patent law allowed only process, but not product patents: in this way, German firms were stimulated to systematically search every possible way to obtain specific compounds. Furthermore, this limitation in patent scope had also the effect of enhancing the technological competition among German chemical manufacturers with positive reverberations on their innovative performance (Dutfield and Suthersanen, 2005: 136–8).

2.3 Innovation without patents?

As we have seen the agricultural revolution of the seventeenth and eighteenth centuries was essentially constituted by a stream of biological innovations and of improvements in cultivation practices that remained completely outside the scope of patent protection. The historical significance of the agricultural revolution then raises the question of why inventive activities were not discouraged in a context of relatively weak appropriability. A tentative answer to this question has been recently attempted by Allen (2009: 67–74). Allen suggests that the agricultural revolution was actually based on two co-existing innovation models: (i) the "experimental" landlord model and (ii) the collective invention model. In the landlord model the owners of large estates acted as experimental stations introducing new crops and cultivation practices. Successful innovations were adopted by the landlords' tenants and, subsequently, spread further by means of imitation. An example of this model is the case of the introduction of the turnip and of the four-field crop rotation system. These practices were the outcomes of the experiments of Charles Townshend in his estate of Raynham. Landlords could appropriate some returns from their inventive efforts by means of higher rents. However, it seems that non-pecuniary motives such as reputation also played a role. Several country gentlemen assumed that agricultural research was one of their civic duties: for example, the famous experimental agricultural station of Rothamstead was created and funded by Sir John Bennet Lewes (Hayami and Ruttan, 1985: 207). The spread of the agricultural innovations developed in these estates was enhanced by the detailed description of cultivation practices in agricultural treatises, which became a very popular literary genre during the eighteenth century. Agricultural improvers also keep abreast of novelties by means of public discussions in agricultural societies and of correspondence networks, sharing information on the relative success of new crops and cultivation methods in different conditions (Fussell, 1932 and Mokyr, 2009: 185–97).

Intensive knowledge-sharing was also a feature of the second model of innovation identified by Allen. Concerning this second model, most of the literature has regarded open-field farmers as retrograde and unwilling to introduce novelties. Instead, on closer inspection, the evidence shows that open-field farmers engaged in what Allen has called "collective invention." In collective-invention settings, a group of competing actors prefers to share the innovations they have introduced, rather than protecting them by means of patents or other instruments or keeping them secret. Collective invention was first recognized for industrial technologies such as blast furnaces (Allen, 1983) or steam pumping engines (Nuvolari, 2004). In these cases of complex industrial technologies where the understanding of the different factors affecting the performance of the artifact can be understood only after prolonged experimentation, collective invention was found to be a particularly effective way of organizing inventive activities, because by sharing information, inventors can build on each other's experiences and fruitful lines of technological advance can be promptly identified and pursued (Allen, 1983; Bessen and Nuvolari, 2011).

Allen (2009: 69–74) contends that seventeenth-century open-field farmers also adopted the collective invention model. This is indeed not surprising because the successful introduction of new crops and new rotation practices always requires a prolonged phase of experimentation in order to adapt the crop to specific local circumstances.[5] Thus, new crops such as sainfoin, clover or turnips were first tried and perfected on small portions of land and if successful adopted on a larger scale by open-field farmers.[6] A later example of this collective invention model is perhaps provided by Moser and Rhode (2012) in their recent study of the development of rose breeding in the United States. Moser and Rhode show that hobbyists developed a significant number of new high-quality rose varieties before 1930. Interestingly enough, hobbyist rose breeders in this period typically shared these advances freely, without restrictions, sometimes within the framework of formalized institutions such as the American Rose Society (Moser and Rhode, 2012: 430).

From the second half of the nineteenth century, the English model of innovation that we have outlined here was superseded by the German model. This model is essentially geared around the systematic public funding of agricultural research. The chief objective was the application of scientific knowledge in the sphere of agriculture. For this purpose, the German system was based on the creation of publicly funded agricultural experimental stations, where scientific insights (in particular from chemistry) could be systematically tried and assessed. The advantage of the public system was that individual farmers have often limited resources for carrying out systematic experimentation. The efficacy of the system was obviously dependent on the spread of the innovations developed by the publicly supported research institutions. Hence, public support involved not only research, but also diffusion policies and education.

The United States substantially imitated the German system. However, besides publicly funded research stations, the American system was based on the creation of specialized colleges and universities for both agricultural research and training, funded by means of the donation of federal lands (for a detailed account of the American public research system in agriculture, see Huffman, and Evenson, 1993). The major success of the U.S. public research system pertained to the area of biological innovations, in particular the development of scientific hybridization of corn varieties around the

1920s (Hayami and Ruttan, 1985: 218–19). The success of hybrid corn, developed mainly by publicly funded agricultural experiment stations, seems indeed to confirm the notion that biological innovations, because of their weak appropriability, were dependent on public research funding. More recently, public research efforts at an international level have also been geared towards the creation of broadly accessible clearinghouses of crop genetic resources. In fact, on a more general level, it should be noted that plant breeding is inherently based on what already exists and, for this reason, inventive activities in this field require free access and use or sharing of materials. One of the main motivations leading to the creation of the International Board on Plant Genetic Resources (IBPGR) in 1973 was precisely the constitution of an international clearinghouse for the conservation of plant germplasm in order to make it available for future research (see Chapter 10 of this volume).

3. THE EVOLUTION OF THE INTELLECTUAL PROPERTY REGIME FOR BIOLOGICAL INNOVATIONS

3.1 The twentieth-century history of intellectual property rights for plant varieties

As we have seen, during the twentieth century, biological innovations were developed by virtue of the fundamental contribution of public research funding. However, the legal framework was not static and from the beginning of the twentieth century the case for introducing some systematic form of protection for private breeders for the creation of new plant varieties gained momentum. Overall, the picture emerging is that of a progressive deepening and extension of intellectual property over biological innovations in agriculture. This trend is mostly visible in the U.S., but it is also traceable in Europe and, via TRIPS, at a global level. The extension of intellectual property in the realm of biological innovation grew out of the strong lobbying actions of inventors and companies involved in chemical and biotechnological research. Dutfield (2009: 47) argues that a significant component of these lobbying activities were aimed at securing not only a favorable rearticulation of intellectual property legislation, but also what he calls the "interpretive custody" of the patent system. This means that the lobbying strategies of the companies were not limited to obtaining support for specific reforms, but were also aimed at shaping the conventional wisdom of both government and society on the nature of biological innovation and, in particular, at removing from the public eye many of the ambiguities arising from the establishment and enforcement of intellectual property rights in this area, so that many critical questions could be perceived as merely technical matters to be left to the decisions of experts. Only recently, with the debate over TRIPS this "interpretative custody" of the patent system by chemical, pharmaceutical and biotechnology companies has been explicitly challenged by alternative viewpoints (Dutfield, 2009).

In the U.S., during the second half of the nineteenth century, the reduction of transport costs and the consequent formation of larger national markets generated a pressure from animal breeders and nurserymen for the creation of some form of intellectual property protection. When markets were local, breeders and nurserymen competed by relying chiefly on reputation. This became more difficult in a large national market where transactions became more impersonal. In order to protect their innovative assets, animal breeders developed systems of registration certifying the pedigrees of the animals in publicly available studbooks (Kevles, 2007).[7] Leading nurseries instead lobbied to obtain some specific form of federal intellectual protection for plants.[8] A first attempt was made in 1906 with the proposal of a trademark approach to protect plant varieties (this is, for example, the case of the "Stark Delicious" apple). The attempt failed, partly because of the patent-like goal embedded in the proposal: protection of a product was obtained by protection of a registered name (Bugos and Kevles, 1992). Moreover, "trademarking protected only the name: it did little to defend the breeder against the fact that the same rose by any other name might be marketed to smell as sweet" (Bugos and Kevles, 1992: 98).

European countries were also experimenting with a similar approach: in France, Germany and the Netherlands a de facto protection of breeders' rights was in place by means of a system of *catalogue* and *certification*. The United Kingdom was very late in adopting any form of legislation to ensure the purity of the seeds on the market and the government approach to this issue was shaped by strong anti-interventionist concerns.[9] Between 1912 and 1921, several plant-breeding research institutes were established with public funding in the UK. They had the mission of developing better seeds for the market (this was of course accompanied by huge concern from the private seed traders), and they were founded in the belief that Mendelian genetics would drastically transform plant-breeding practice (this belief was not shared by all the biologists). The principal institutes were the Plant Breeding Institute at Cambridge (1912), the Welsh Plant Breeding Station in Aberystwyth (1919), and the Scottish Plant Breeding Station in Corstorphine (1921). The organization claimed as a model for these institutes was the Swedish Seed Association, which provided varieties for a joint stock seed company, whose profits were, in turn, used to finance research, with any residue shared among the shareholders. Although acceptable in Sweden, this model was not accepted by the British seed trade. This was not the only problem related to the plant-breeding research institutes: they were in fact characterized by a very poor performance in adoption and commercial terms. Virtually all new varieties produced in the UK were not considered profitable by farmers, who were looking for greater quantity than quality. This failure was the result of a lack of communication channels between agricultural scientists and farmers (Palladino, 1990).

Formal attempts to introduce patent protection for plant varieties started literally a few weeks after the failed effort to introduce plant breeding in the U.S. trademark system. Congress was presented with a proposal to amend the utility patent statute to accommodate plant innovation. This attempt also failed and two main motives were put forward. First, there was the "natural products" objection against patenting living subject matter. In fact, plant patenting had been already discouraged in 1889 by the U.S. Commissioner of Patents, when an application for a patent covering a fibre created using the needles of a pine tree was rejected. The commissioner regarded it as "unreasonable and impossible" to allow patents upon the plants of the earth (Bugos and Kevles, 1992). This position was somewhat softened in 1891, when the respected plant scientist Liberty Hyde Bailey of Cornell stated that "when the time comes that men breed plants upon definite laws and produce new and valuable kinds, then plant patents may possibly become practicable" (cited in Bugos and Kevles, 1992: 80). Moreover, the proposed amendment to patent law required disclosure of the new plant varieties just in terms of identification and not of replications as is required for standard utility patents.

Despite this unpromising start, the U.S. was still the first country to offer patent protection for new plant varieties. With the Townsend-Purnell Plant Patent Act of 1930, patent-like protection (*sui generis*) was offered to new plant varieties asexually reproduced, explicitly excluding plants reproduced via seeds.[10] Two main factors can account for the introduction of this distinction between asexual and sexual reproduction. Plants that reproduce asexually are essentially ornamentals and fruits: this Act was indeed heavily pushed forward by the lobby of the flower nursery operators (led by Paul Stark of the Stark Brothers Nursery, the largest breeder in the country). Moreover patent protection for plants of critical importance for food supply was not felt politically acceptable during the Great Depression. The idea of food as a scarce resource still had strong roots in public opinion, so that policymakers were extremely reluctant to allow the establishment of, even a temporally limited, monopoly power in this area. The gloomy economic landscape of the Depression on the other side facilitated the passage of the Bill, as the prevailing conventional wisdom on how to respond to the recession was to stimulate private investments and to reduce public expenditure. Protection for plants was further strengthened in 1939 with the Federal Seed Act which imposed standards on seeds sold in interstate commerce: this certification not only protected consumers against unreliable seeds but also defended high-quality seed from competition from low-quality alternatives.

In a recent contribution, Moser and Rhode (2012) have provided an appraisal of the effects of the Plant Patent Act of 1930 on the rates of innovation in plant variety looking at the evolution of the U.S. rose-breeding industry over the period 1930–70 (nearly 45 per cent of the plant patents granted between 1931 and 1970 were for roses). Moser and Rhode found also that in this period the patentees who were granted most patents were all connected with major companies. Additionally, Moser and Rhode also established that the majority of rose patents were systematically assigned to commercial breeders. These two pieces of evidence may perhaps suggest that the Plant Patent Act exerted a favorable impact on inventive activities stimulating the creation of new rose varieties suitable for commercialization. However, Moser and Rhode (2012) provide a different interpretation. In their view, large U.S. commercial breeders were forced to use plant patents for protecting new varieties to shield themselves from the threat of litigation rather than for directly appropriating economic returns from the breeding activities. In fact, comparing rose patents with the variety of roses registered with the American Rose Society (breeders use these type of registrations not as tool for direct appropriation, but rather as authors' rights, i.e. for establishing the name of the new variety of rose they had created and for claiming reputational credit), they estimate that only 16 per cent of the new rose varieties created between 1931 and 1970 were patented. Hence, on closer scrutiny, the Plant Patent Act did not actually provide a significant stimulus to inventive activities in this field. Furthermore, registration data also indicate that European and not U.S. breeders developed the majority of new rose varieties introduced in the U.S. in the period 1930–70.

European countries also moved towards the developing of *sui generis* forms of intellectual property protection for plant varieties. These systems were harmonized in 1961 with the establishment of the International Union for the Protection of New Varieties of Plants (or UPOV). The system supported by UPOV included protocols to describe and evaluate the characteristics of new varieties in order to guarantee their distinctiveness, uniformity and stability. It required member states to provide protection for plant breeders' rights for at least twenty years. The system also contained important limitations to the monopoly right: breeders could use protected seeds without authorization to create new varieties, and compulsory licensing was possible in case public interest required the use of the plant (Dutfield, 2009: 206). The underlying idea was to protect breeders' efforts without disadvantaging farmers or jeopardizing the food supply.

In the same years, and under the stimulus of UPOV, the U.S. Congress started considering the possibility of legislation to extend patent rights to seed-grown plants. New aspects had emerged in the breeding landscape that forced congressmen to revise the status quo in terms of plant protection. First of all, the promises of hybridization as a mean to protect varieties were falling short for several plants, notably wheat. Moreover, the seed market was becoming increasingly globalized and demand for seeds was increasing not only in the developed countries, but also in developing countries, as shown by the Green Revolution. European agriculture had recovered from the Second World War and returned to the international markets as a strong competitor of the U.S. Finally, the extremely high post-war demand for U.S. agricultural products (which meant that quantity was preferred over innovation) was declining (Bugos and Kevles, 1992). In 1971, the Plant Variety Protection (PVP) Act was passed, which guaranteed *sui generis* protection for sexually reproduced (i.e. through seeds) plants. The criteria for protection were novelty, distinctiveness, uniformity and stability.[11] Moreover, when filing an application for a patent protecting a plant variety, a seed deposit was required (this is a way to manage the issue of public disclosure). However, there remain fundamental differences between the PVP regime and the utility patent regime: first, in the PVP there is no requirement of non-obviousness; moreover, the disclosure requirements are not comparable to the ones found in general patent law. Furthermore, PVP contains two limitations that are not present in patent law: the research exemption (as long as it is *bona fide*) and the saved seed exemption (farmers are allowed to save part of their harvest to extract seeds for the next season) (Janis and Kesan, 2002; Williams, 1984).

In the U.S. a further step towards the strengthening of intellectual property protection was made with the well-known *Diamond v. Chakarabarty* decision of the U.S. Supreme Court in 1980 (which ruled that a live, human-made micro-organism is a patentable subject matter). After this decision, genetically modified plant varieties were more likely to be protected using a utility patent rather than a PVP certificate. In the U.S., the legislative landscape became even more favorable to granting patents for living organisms in 1988, with the OncoMouse (or Harvard Mouse) patent. The protected mouse is a genetically modified mouse engineered to carry a specific gene (an activated oncogene) which increases the mouse's susceptibility to develop cancer, making the animal particularly suitable for cancer research. The patent granted in the U.S. explicitly excluded humans, in order to address widespread concerns about patents on human beings and on the human genome (Kevles, 2002). In Europe, the history of this patent is more complex. The Examining Division of the European Patent Office (EPO) initially refused to grant a patent for the OncoMouse, as the European Patent Convention (EPC) excludes animals from patentability (art. 53b). This decision was however appealed, as the convention in article 53b excludes plant and animal varieties from protection, but not animals as such. Following this appeal, an EPO patent for the OncoMouse was granted in 1992. This patent was then opposed on the grounds of another article of the EPC, which excludes from patentability inventions contrary to public order or morality (art. 53a). The opposition took place in 2001 and the patent was maintained in an amended form, limiting claims to mice. In order to address the exception contained in article 53a, the EPO employed a utilitarian balancing test, weighting the potential benefits of the invention (in this case the expected medical benefits to humanity) against negative aspects (in this case the suffering of the mouse). Another appeal took place in 2004, which was unsuccessful, and the patent is thus maintained in the amended form.

Until the beginning of the 1990s, the protection of plant varieties has been essentially an exclusive characteristic of developed countries. However, following the Uruguay Round of the WTO, the international efforts to harmonize intellectual property protection systems have also accelerated the diffusion of plant variety protection systems in other countries. Article 27.3(b) of the TRIPS agreement states indeed that vegetable varieties can be excluded from patent protection but they must be granted an effective *sui generis* protection (Srinivasan, 2005). Table 8.1 contains a summary overview of the historical evolution of the intellectual property regime for biological inventions.[12]

Table 8.1 The historical evolution of intellectual property protection for biological inventions

Year	Country	Key facts
1889	U.S.	Rejection of the application for a patent on a fibre obtained from pine tree needles.
1906	U.S.	Proposal of a trademark approach to protect plant varieties: failed.
1906	U.S.	Proposal to amend the utility patent statute to incorporated creation of new plant varieties: failed.
1912–1921	UK	Establishment of publicly funded plant-breeding research institutes.
1930	U.S.	Townsend-Purnell Plant Patent Act: patent-like (*sui generis*) protection offered to asexually reproduced plants.
1939	U.S.	Federal Seed Act: setting of standards on seed sold in interstate commerce.
1961	Europe	International Convention for the Protection of New Varieties of Plants: creation of the Union for the Protection of New Varieties of Plants (UPOV).
1971	U.S.	Plant Variety Protection (PVP) Act *sui generis* protection offered to sexually reproduced plants.
1978	U.S.	Ratification of the Convention for the Protection of New Varieties of Plants (accompanied by major revisions).
1981	U.S.	*Chakrabarty v. Diamond*: first patent on a living human-made micro-organism).
1988	U.S.	OncoMouse patent (1992 in Europe).
1986–1994	Worldwide	TRIPs Agreement: plant varieties must be granted at least *sui generis* protection.

3.2 The impact of plant variety protection on productivity

Since the enactment of the PVP Act, there have been claims that this reform increased the number of plant varieties available on the market. Several studies (Butler and Marion, 1985; Perrin et al., 1983) found that the PVP Act has had a significant impact on private variety research in terms of the number of new varieties introduced in the market. However, it is important to take into account that one of the effects of the Act was also to increase the incentive of breeders towards the production of varieties with a shorter lifespan, in order to induce farmers to adopt new varieties every year. In fact, the empirical evidence on the quality of PVP-protected varieties is still not conclusive.

Clearly, the overall assessment of the impact of plant variety protection on the performance of the agricultural sector is a very difficult one. Seeds are a peculiar factor of production because, at least potentially, a farmer could produce his own seed by withdrawing a small portion of his crop from the market. This procedure is usually quite easy and not very costly. Of course, seed companies need to convince the farmer not to do so, and to buy new seeds every year. There are then two possible strategies for the seed producer. The first involves economies of scale: the producer should be able to produce seeds of the appropriate quality cheaper than the farmer, which is not often the case. The second consists in reaping monopoly profits by creating seeds that have a very short lifespan or are consumed in the production process, in other words, that are not self-reproducing (see Chapter 9 of this volume for a more extensive discussion).

There are two possible ways to do so: the first is by hybridization, which already started at the beginning of the twentieth century, the second is through the employment of genetic use-restriction technologies (GURTs). These technologies come in two broad types: variety-level (they are designed so that a seed producer can inoculate the seed with a specific regulator that renders the plant infertile, thus making it pointless to save seeds) or trait-specific (in this case seeds can be saved for reproduction but the valuable trait, such as disease resistance, must be activated with a highly specific and proprietary compound) (Wright et al., 2007). The profits derived from the employment of such technologies can be considerably high, especially in a commodity market like the one for seeds, and this has had a strong influence on the direction of breeding research, especially in Europe and in the U.S., and on the concentration of the market (Berland and Lewontin, 1986). For example, the protection via hybridization was strong enough in the U.S. to foster the creation of a profitable private seed industry in the 1930s (Wright et al., 2007).

For these reasons, the assessment of the impact of intellectual property reforms in this area requires an approach which can properly take into account these specificities: the legislation which grants intellectual property rights over plants, the level of enforcement of such legislation, the specific biological characteristics of the crop, the state of the technology used and the actions of both seed producers and farmers. If we analyze the trend of granting PVP certificates from 1973, we note that more than 60 per cent of all certificates have been awarded after 1990, while the majority of certificates are withdrawn before the end of the protection period (Srinivasan, 2005). The total number of certificates is increasing, but this is mainly due to new countries entering the UPOV agreement. In Europe and in the U.S. the situation is stagnant: European countries have indeed opted for a community certificate (CPVO), while the protection in the U.S. is shifting towards utility patents. The decline in UPOV certificates in the U.S. is accompanied by a large increase in the number of patents granted to plant varieties (Srinivasan, 2005). A study conducted by Frey (1996) in the U.S. highlighted that the PVP Act of 1971 has been beneficial only for some specific varieties. Other studies pointing to empirical evidence support the claim that the strength of the intellectual property system is positively correlated with the number of PVP certificates granted (Pardey et al., 2003; Srinivasan et al., 2002).

These studies, however, do not take into account the impact of the introduction of plant varieties protection on overall welfare and productivity. Indeed, it is not surprising that the introduction of a stronger form of intellectual property protection for plants has induced more private research investment in this field. Interestingly enough, studies which have tested the effect of the PVP Act on agricultural productivity, found that the Act's effect on yield improvement was not statistically significant (Perrin et al., 1983; Babcock and Foster, 1991; Alston and Venner, 2002). Concerning overall welfare, even studies pointing to a positive impact of stronger appropriability (comparing hybrid and non-hybrid crop varieties) on the increase of yields, note the detrimental impact of stronger appropriability on the spread of innovations (see again also Chapter 9 of this volume).

An example of the importance of diffusion for a developing country is represented by the case of the soybean in Argentina. Argentina introduced legislation for plant breeders' rights following the UPOV guidelines in 1994, but still refrained from allowing full patent protection for plant varieties. Thus, the transgenic variety of Roundup Ready soybean patented by Monsanto in the U.S. and Europe was not recognized as patentable subject matter in Argentina. This resulted in a particularly rapid diffusion of this particular variety and in a sustained growth of soybean output establishing Argentina as one of the world-leading producers of this crop (López, 2009). In 2004 Monsanto withdrew completely from the Argentinian market blaming infringement of intellectual property and black market competition. Later, Monsanto adopted the strategy of starting infringement actions against importers of Argentine soy in Europe where the transgenic seed by Monsanto had been patented in 1996 (Kranakis, 2007: 723–4). To date, both a UK court and the European Court of Justice ruled against Monsanto, while holding that patent protection on the gene was extendable to soy by-product imports (see Cohen and Morgan, 2008 for an analysis of the UK court decision).

Finally, we should add that several scholars have pointed out that stronger intellectual property protection for new plant varieties may degenerate in what in the literature is called the "anti-commons" tragedy, that is a situation in which inventions are underutilized because they are subjected to multiple, fragmented property rights. In order to avoid the risk of the anti-commons tragedy several "open-source" initiatives aimed at facilitating the sharing of knowledge in the field of agricultural biotechnology have recently emerged (Wright et. al., 2007 and Chapter 10).

4. CONCLUSIONS

We think that our review of the literature warrants two important conclusions. The first is that innovation processes in agriculture rely on the exploitation of different knowledge bases such as mechanical and chemical technologies, biology, etc. As a result, the institutional arrangements supporting inventive activities are extremely variegated, with a number of different actors involved. It is clearly important to take this specificity into account in the design of future intellectual property reforms. Secondly, it is also clear that in agriculture a large share of inventive activities has been carried out for very long spans of time in regimes of weak intellectual property protection. This is clearly the case for biological innovations. The recent contribution of Olmstead and Rhode (2008) has the merit of bringing to our attention the dramatic rate of progress attained in plant and animal breeding in the U.S. throughout the nineteenth century, well before the introduction of formalized intellectual property protection. It is worth quoting from the conclusions of their study:

> [W]ell before plants received patent protection there was a plethora of private sector inventive activity, where leading farmers and seed companies made significant contributions to plant improvement. State and federal agencies added to this brew. Animal breeders were at least as active, and many developed national markets for their creations. A large and important literature has identified inventions with patents. The absence of patent records for a large class of biological activities has led to the inference that little has happened. However, a search of the press, farm journals, Patent Commission reports, and various state and federal commission reports suggests that innovators were making great strides in the introduction of new and more productive plants and animals.
>
> (Olmstead and Rhode, 2008: 400–1)

To this we should add, that even in areas where patents were available and could be used effectively such as agricultural machinery, it is frequently possible to find examples of inventors using successful appropriability strategies that do not rely on formalized intellectual property rights. When the recent discussions on intellectual property protection reform for agriculture are considered in this light, one cannot avoid the impression that excessive emphasis has been put on the implementation of strong intellectual property regimes and that, instead, a more sober and pragmatic approach to this issue is in order. In this respect, our historical survey of agriculture resonates well with the broader concerns emerging from the analysis by Cimoli et al. in Chapter 2 of this volume.

NOTES

1. "Strong" and "weak" appropriability in this chapter refers to the degree of enforceability of intellectual property rights.
2. A major invention, greatly enhancing the transportation of plants over long distances, was the so-called "Wardian case" invented by the Englishman Nathaniel Bagshaw Ward (1791–1868) in the 1830s. The "Wardian case" was an almost airtight glass case in which plants could be kept alive for very long periods of time. Interestingly enough, Nathaniel Ward did not patent his invention, rather he published a detailed description of it in 1842, *On the Growth of Plants in Closely Gazed Cases* (D. E. Allen, 2004). Using portable Wardian cases, in 1851 Robert Fortune was able to transfer more than 2,000 plants and 17,000 seedlings from China to India (Boulger and Baigent, 2004).
3. The non-patentability of plants in the framework of the early English patent system was not really clear and MacLeod was able to identify three patents for "new crops" granted during the second half of the seventeenth century (MacLeod, 1988: 98).
4. Parker and Klein (1966) is a classic growth-accounting exercise of the sources of productivity growth in American agriculture during the second half of the nineteenth century showing that "mechanization was the strongest direct cause of productivity growth" (Parker and Klein, 1966: 543). For a revision of Parker and Klein's estimates which, instead, emphasizes the predominant contribution of biological innovation, see Olmstead and Rhode (2008: 57–62).
5. It is interesting to note that in most cases, given the atomistic structure of most agricultural markets, the quantity produced by each farmer has a negligible impact on price. Hence, the sharing of technical know-how with neighbours is not likely to determine a competitive backlash. Further, in this context, if knowledge sharing is reciprocated, this may lead to a generalized welfare improvement. These characteristics of agriculture can account for many cases of the cooperative approach taken by farmers with respect to the introduction of inventions that are highlighted in the literature. See Braguinsky and Rose (2009) for a discussion and formalized treatment.
6. Havinden (1961) contains a detailed case study of the introduction of sainfoin and turnips in Oxfordshire open-fields.
7. Bugos (1992) contains a detailed case study showing that US chicken breeders, even without resorting to patent protection, could effectively appropriate economic returns from innovation using a variety of methods such as the establishment of quality standards, trade secrets, etc.

8. According to Boldrin and Levine (2008: 53), the lobbying activities for IP protection of plant breeders suggests a slowing down of the innovative dynamism of the industry with respect to its early years: "Innovative and dynamic industries emerge because intellectual monopoly is not present or because it can be easily bypassed. They grow rapidly because competition and imitation allow and force their firms to innovate or perish. In fact, in the early stage, agricultural innovators often would provide their customers with incentives to copy and reproduce their seeds, as a tool to spread their use. However, as the industry grows more powerful and opportunities for further innovation diminish, the value of monopoly protection for insiders increases, and lobbying efforts multiply and most often succeed."

9. Charnley (2013) shows that, even in late nineteenth-century England, i.e., a context without formalized intellectual property rights and limited public funding, a system based on reputation (which he terms "moral economy of plant breeding") provide plant breeders with significant incentives for engaging in inventive activities.

10. Thomas Edison also provided support to the Plant Patent Act of 1930 in congressional debates. He argued that plant patents "would give us many Burbanks." Luther Burbanks was a successful breeder who had successful developed many plant varieties and was a personal friend of Edison. To this statement, Fiorello La Guardia retorted that "Luther Burbank did very well without patent protection" (both passages cited in Moser and Rhode, 2012).

11. A variety must be (i) "distinct, in the sense that the variety is clearly distinguishable from any other variety the existence of which is publicly known or a matter of common knowledge at the time of the filing of the application," (ii) "uniform, in the sense that any variations are describable, predictable and commercially acceptable," (iii) "stable, in the sense that the variety, when reproduced, will remain unchanged with regard to the essential and distinctive characteristics of the variety with a reasonable degree of reliability commensurate with that of varieties of the same category in which the same breeding method is employed."

12. For a recent overview of the evolution of intellectual property rights for plant varieties in global perspective see Campi and Nuvolari (2013).

REFERENCES

Allen, D. E. (2004), "Ward, Nathaniel Bagshaw (1791–1868)," *Oxford Dictionary of National Biography*. Oxford: Oxford University Press, online edn, <http://www.oxforddnb.com/view/article/28701> (accessed 10 September 2013).

Allen, R. C. (1983), "Collective Invention," *Journal of Economic Behavior and Organization*, 4: 1–24.

Allen, R. C. (2004), "Agriculture during the Industrial Revolution, 1700–1850," in Floud, R. and Johnson, P. (eds.), *The Cambridge Economic History of Modern Britain*. Cambridge: Cambridge University Press.

Allen, R. C. (2008), "The Nitrogen Hypothesis and the English Agricultural Revolution: A Biological Analysis," *Journal of Economic History*, 68: 182–210.

Allen, R. C. (2009), *The British Industrial Revolution in Global Perspective*. Cambridge: Cambridge University Press.

Alston, J. M. and Venner, R. J. (2002), "The Effects of the US Plant Variety Protection Act on Wheat Genetic Improvement," *Research Policy*, 31: 527–42.

Arora, A., Landau, R. and Rosenberg, N. (1999), "Dynamics of Comparative Advantage in the Chemical Industry," in Mowery, D. C. and Nelson, R. R. (eds.), *Sources of Industrial Leadership*. Cambridge: Cambridge University Press.

Babcock, B. A. and Foster, W. E. (1991), "Measuring the Potential Contribution of Plant Breeding to Crop Yields: Flue-Cured Tobacco, 1954–1987," *American Journal of Agricultural Economics*, 73: 850–59.

Bairoch, P. (1973), "Agriculture and the Industrial Revolution," in Cipolla, C. M. (ed.), *The Fontana Economic History of Europe. Vol. 3. The Industrial Revolution*. London: Collins/Fontana.

Berland, J. P. and Lewontin, R. (1986), "Breeders' Rights and Patenting Life Forms," *Nature*, 322: 785–88.

Bessen, J. and Nuvolari, A. (2011), "Knowledge Sharing among Inventors: Some Historical Perspectives," LEM Working Paper no. 2011–21.

Boldrin, M. and Levine, D. K. (2008), *Against Intellectual Monopoly*. Cambridge: Cambridge University Press.

Boulger, G. S. and Baigent, E. (2004), "Fortune, Robert (1812–1880)," *Oxford Dictionary of National Biography*. Oxford: Oxford University Press, online edn, <http://www.oxforddnb.com/view/article/9953> (accessed 10 September 2013).

Braguinsky, S. and Rose, D. C. (2009), "Competition, Cooperation and the Neighbouring Farmer Effect," *Journal of Economic Behavior and Organization*, 62: 361–76.

Brunt, L. (2003), "Mechanical Innovation in the Industrial Revolution: The Case of Plough Design," *Economic History Review*, 56: 444–57.

Brunt, L., Lerner, J. and Nicholas, T. (2012), "Inducement Prizes and Innovation," *Journal of Industrial Economics*, 60: 657–96.

Bugos, G. E. (1992), "Intellectual Property Protection in the American Chicken-Breeding Industry," *Business History Review*, 66: 127–68.

Bugos, G. E. and Kevles, D. J. (1992), "Plants as Intellectual Property: American Practice, Law, and Policy in World Context," *Osiris*, 7: 74–104.

Butler, L. J. and Marion, B. W. (1985), *The Impacts of Patent Protection on the U.S. Seed Industry and Public Plant Breeding*. Research Division, College of Agricultural and Life Sciences, University of Wisconsin-Madison.

Campi, M. and Nuvolari, A. (2013), "Intellectual Property Protection in Plant Varieties: A New Worldwide Index (1961–2011)," LEM Working Paper no. 2013–09.

Charnley, B. (2013), "Seeds without Patents: Science and Morality in British Plant Breeding in the Long Nineteenth Century," *Revue Economique*, 64: 69–87.

Cipolla, C. M. (1962), *The Economic History of World Population*. Harmondsworth: Penguin.

Clark, G. (2007), *A Farewell to Alms: A Brief Economic History of the World*. Princeton: Princeton University Press.

Cohen, S. and Morgan, G. (2008), "*Monsanto Technology LLC v. Cargill*: A Matter of Construction," *Nature Biotechnology*, 26: 289–91.

Diamond, J. (1997), *Guns, Germs and Steel*. London: Vintage.

Dutfield, G. (2009), *Intellectual Property Rights and the Life Science Industries: Past, Present and Future*. Singapore: World Scientific.

Dutfield, G. and Suthersanen, U. (2005), "Harmonisation or Differentiation in Intellectual Property Protection? The Lessons of History," *Prometheus*, 23: 131–47.

Erisman, J. W., Sutton, M. A., Galloway, J., Klimont, Z. and Winiwarter, W. (2008), "How a Century of Ammonia Synthesis Changed the World," *Nature Geoscience*, 1: 636–9.

Federico, G. (2005), *Feeding the World: An Economic History of Agriculture, 1800–2000*. Princeton: Princeton University Press.

Frey, K. J. (1996), "National Plant Breeding Study I: Human and Financial Resources Devoted to Plant Breeding Research and Development in the United States in 1994," Ames, Iowa Agriculture and Home Economics Experiment Station, Iowa State University, Special Report 98.

Fussell, G. E. (1932), "Early Farming Journals," *Economic History Review*, 3: 417–22.

Havinden, M. A. (1961), "Agricultural Progress in Open Field Oxfordshire," *Agricultural History Review*, 9: 73–83.

Hayami, Y. and Ruttan, V. W. (1985), *Agricultural Development: An International Perspective*. Baltimore: Johns Hopkins University Press.

Huffman, W. E. and Evenson, R. E. (1993), *Science for Agriculture: A Long-Term Perspective*. Ames: Iowa University Press.

Janis, M. D. and Kesan J. P. (2002), "U.S. Plant Variety Protection: Sound and Fury . . . ?" *Houston Law Review*, 39: 727–78.

Jones, C. I. (2002), *Introduction to Economic Growth*. New York: W. W. Norton.

Kevles, D. J. (2002), "Of Mice and Money: The Story of the World's First Animal Patent," *Daedalus*, 131: 78–88.

Kevles, D. J. (2007), "Patents, Protections, and Privileges: The Establishment of Intellectual Property in Animal and Plants," *Isis*, 98: 323–31.

Kranakis, E. (2007), "Patents and Power: European Patent System Integration in the Context of Globalization," *Technology and Culture*, 48: 689–728.

López, A. (2010), "Innovation and IPR in a Catch Up-Falling Behind Process: The Argentine Case," in Odagiri, H., Goto, A., Sunami, A. and Nelson, R. (eds.), *Intellectual Property Rights, Development, and Catch Up: An International Comparative Study*. Oxford: Oxford University Press.

MacLeod, C. (1988), *Inventing the Industrial Revolution*. Cambridge: Cambridge University Press.

Mokyr, J. (2009), *The Enlightened Economy: An Economic History of Britain, 1700–1850*. New Haven: Yale University Press.

Moser, P. (2012), "Innovation without Patents: Evidence from the World's Fairs," *Journal of Law and Economics*, 55: 43–74," NBER Working Paper no. 13294.

Moser, P. and Rhode, P. W. (2012), "Did Plant Patents Create the American Rose?" in Lerner, J. and Stern, S. (eds.), *The Rate and Direction of Inventive Activity Revisited*. Chicago: University of Chicago Press.

North, D. C. (1981), *Structure and Change in Economic History*. New York and London: W. W. Norton.

Nunn, N. and Qian, N. (2010), "The Columbian Exchange: A History of Disease, Food and Ideas," *Journal of Economic Perspectives*, 24: 163–88.

Nuvolari, A. (2004), "Collective Invention during the British Industrial Revolution: The Case of the Cornish Pumping Engine," *Cambridge Journal of Economics*, 28: 347–63.

Olmstead, A. L and Rhode, P. W. (2003), "Reshaping the Landscape: The Impact and Diffusion of the Tractor in American Agriculture, 1910–1960," *Journal of Economic History*, 61: 663–98.

Olmstead, A. L. and Rhode, P. W. (2008), *Creating Abundance: Biological Innovation and American Agricultural Development.* Cambridge: Cambridge University Press.

Palladino, P. (1990), "The Political Economy of Applied Research: Plant Breeding in Great Britain, 1910–1940," *Minerva*, 28: 446–68.

Pardey, P.G., Koo, B. and Nottenburg, C. (2003), "Creating, Protecting, and Using Crop Biotechnologies Worldwide in an Era of Intellectual Property," Paper presented at the WIPO-UPOV Symposium on Intellectual Property Rights in Plant Biotechnology, Geneva, 24 October 2003, Document WIPO-UPOV/SYM/03/4.

Parker, W. N. and Klein, J. V. (1966), "Productivity Growth in Grain Production in the United States, 1840–1860 and 1900–1910," in Brady, D. S. (ed.), *Output, Employment and Productivity in the United States after 1800.* New York: Columbia University Press.

Perrin, R. K., Hunnings, K. A. and Ihnen, L. A. (1983), "Some Effects of the U.S. Plant Variety Protection Act of 1970," Econ. Res. Rep. no. 46, North Carolina State University.

Srinivasan, C. S. (2005), "International Trends in Plant Variety Protection," *Journal of Agricultural and Development Economics*, 2: 182–220.

Srinivasan, C. S., Shankar, B. and Holloway, G. (2002), "An Empirical Analysis of the Effects of Plant Variety Protection Legislation on Innovation and Transferability," Paper presented at the meeting of the European Association of Agricultural Economists, Zaragoza, Spain, August 2002.

Sullivan, R. J. (1990), "The Revolution of Ideas: Widespread Patenting and Invention during the English Industrial Revolution," *Journal of Economic History*, 50: 349–62.

Williams, S. B. (1984), "Protection of Plant Varieties and Parts as Intellectual Property," *Science*, 225: 18–23.

Wright, B. D., Pardey, P. G., Nottenburg, C. and Koo B. (2007), "Agricultural Innovation: Investments and Incentives," in R. Evenson and P. Pingali (eds.) *Handbook of Agricultural Economics, Vol. 3.* North Holland: Elsevier.

9

The Distributive Impact of Intellectual Property Regimes: A Report from the "Natural Experiment" of the Green Revolution[1]

Timothy Swanson and Timo Goeschl

1. INTRODUCTION

Over the past half-century there has been an important difference in the manner in which information and innovation is able to be packaged and sold in regard to different agricultural plant varieties. Some plants come complete with the capacity to reproduce any innovation inherent within them, while others do not have this capacity. This difference provides the setting for a "natural experiment" of the most obvious sort—in which the impact of the *impactedness* of information may be tested. Is general growth and social welfare advanced if the innovator's innovations are easily and fully protected, or is it better for growth and welfare if those innovations diffuse more readily?

We will use this natural experiment to explain how intellectual property regimes determine how benefits are distributed. We argue that differences in the information-impactedness of innovations can explain in part the way in which agricultural yields have evolved across the globe, thereby determining the distribution of benefits from innovation in this sector. This argument is based on the idea that the observed variance in yields across countries is best analyzed as a problem in the diffusion of innovations from an expanding productivity frontier to the set of infra-marginal receiver countries. Innovations contribute both to the general growth of the productivity frontier, but also diffuse from the frontier to all other countries to generate growth there as well. We will use this model to consider how this natural impactedness affects the welfare of both the frontier and the infra-marginal states.

We believe that this experiment in information-impactedness is also a good analogy for the way in which different intellectual property right (IPR) regimes work in general. Property right regimes may be viewed as existing along a spectrum of "information-impactedness": open access regimes enable free diffusion while strong IPR regimes provide for full impactedness of information (non-diffusion). This is because a strong regime will attempt to halt any unlicensed diffusion, thereby keeping information impacted within the products sold. In fact, it would be expected that such strong property regimes would be important for purposes of internalizing the value of information, and enhancing the incentives to invest in innovation. Hence, strong property right regimes over innovations have two predicted effects, advancing the rate of innovation at the frontier but also slowing the rate at which these innovations diffuse to parties off that frontier (Maskus, 2000). This implies a clear trade-off inherent within strong intellectual property right protection, that varies with the vantage point of the particular party concerned. Here we wish to estimate these two effects and calculate the implied trade-off in growth and welfare between those states at the technology frontier and those within the frontier. In doing so, we demonstrate how the perceived benefits of strong intellectual property right protection are dependent upon the country's initial positioning with respect to the technological frontier.[2]

We examine these questions on the basis of a panel study of the yield development of the eight major crop varieties across developing countries from 1961 to 1999.[3] These crops can be distinguished on the basis of the mode of property right protection that innovations enjoy within the crop, with two varieties (HYV hybrids) enjoying technological (or extremely "strong" property right) protection and six experiencing legal (or relatively "weak" property right) protection under domestically enforced plant variety legislation.[4] Thus the crop varieties themselves provide the context for a "natural experiment" on the impacts of IPR regimes. Some varieties exhibit strong and the others weak property right protection, and the effects of this difference may be viewed across both space and time. Which form of IPR regime is more conducive to the creation of and sharing of benefits across the global industry?

In the following sections we look at the development and diffusion of agricultural innovation across the globe during the progress of the "green revolution" (1960–2000). In section 2 we develop the nature of the puzzles resulting from that period of rapid technological change; how did growth rates occur and where were they concentrated? We discover that although there was pronounced agricultural growth throughout the world, much greater benefits were received in the developed world than in the developing. This is contrary to the theory-backed expectations about "convergence" in development, and much of the remainder of the paper is focused on explaining this counter-intuitive result. In section 3 we explore the precise nature of the growth and diffusion process in global agriculture over this period, and find that there is both a positive rate of growth within the data but also some evidence of a cost of diffusion. It is this friction within the diffusion of innovations that is skewing the benefits from innovation toward developed countries. We show that this cost of diffusion is dependent on the agricultural crop concerned; in particular, maize and sorghum show the greatest rates of friction. In section 4 we discuss the likely explanations underlying this evidence, and relate the evidence to the respective property rights regimes. We show that stronger forms of property right protection are more likely to produce higher levels of growth in those sectors in which they are applied, but that they also have the effect of impeding the diffusion of innovations to those societies far from the technological frontier. Simulations demonstrate that stronger property right regimes both skew benefits relatively and (over some time scale) even absolutely toward the developed countries. Section 5 concludes the chapter.

In general, this is a study looking back at the green revolution to find out how the benefits from that major era of change were distributed, and also looking forward to demonstrate how institutional changes can be expected to distribute their benefits in future. One major observation emerges—it pays to be on or near the technological frontier.

2. THE FAILURE OF CONVERGENCE IN AGRICULTURE DURING THE GREEN REVOLUTION

2.1 The evidence on distribution and growth of benefits in agriculture

Our aim in this paper is to review the evidence on the patterns of diffusion of innovation, and in doing so to provide a case study for the broader questions of innovation, property rights, diffusion and global welfare impacts. In situating its inquiry in the context of agriculture, it follows a tradition in the literature on the economics of technological change that originated with Griliches' seminal work on the diffusion of innovations (1957), Schmitz and Seckler's work on the social welfare impacts of mechanized production (1970), and Evenson et al. on the economic benefits from R&D (1979).

We commence with a review of the basic evidence regarding agricultural yield developments in the eight major crop varieties (in use globally) over much of the "green revolution." During this period, the average global growth in agricultural yields exceeded 2 per cent by most measures, and few parts of the world remained outside of this global phenomenon of growth and advancement. In fact, many in the industry advanced claims that some of the

Table 9.1 Acreage, global distribution, growth, and relative yield gap in eight major crops

Crop	Global acreage in million ha in 1999	Average growth rate in developed countries, 1961–1999	Average growth rate in developing countries, 1961–99	Relative yield gap in 1961	Relative yield gap in 1999
Barley	58.6	1.53%	1.03% (40)	−57%	−59.9%
Cotton	34.3	2.45%	1.54% (60)	−24%	−47.4%
Maize	**139.2**	**2.27%**	**1.42% (95)**	**−65%**	**−72.4%**
Millet	37.2	0.93%	0.41% (46)	−49%	−57.4%
Rice	153.1	0.85%	1.24% (60)	−64%	−57.9%
Sorghum	**44.8**	**2.08%**	**0.54% (64)**	**−48%**	**−67.2%**
Soybeans	72.1	1.24%	1.58% (32)	−46%	−40.0%
Wheat	214.2	1.75%	1.89% (54)	−60%	−54.5%

primary beneficiaries from the agricultural advancements of this era were the poorest societies on Earth. Growth in agricultural production eliminated food security as a major concern in many parts of the world.

Table 9.1 tells a slightly more complicated story. It shows the general picture on the growth as well as the distribution of growth within this industry during the period 1960–1999. The poorer parts of the world were improving their agricultural production during this time, but not relative to the developed parts of the world. In five of the crops listed above, the average growth rate evinced across developing countries was significantly below that demonstrated in developed countries. The gap between levels ("yield gap," or difference between average yields) in developed and developing countries actually worsened significantly in the case of four of these crops. So, it was in fact the case that average growth rates were positive for all crops in almost all parts of the world, and so the benefits from agriculture were increasing everywhere, but it was not the case that the distribution of the benefits from global agriculture were becoming less skewed in favor of the developed world. In fact, more of the benefits from global agriculture (for the majority of these crops) were flowing to the developed world during the green revolution than was the case before 1960. The changes that occurred in agriculture were benefiting the developed countries more (or at least earlier) than those still developing.

2.2 The lack of convergence

Why was it the case that the large amount of change occurring in global agriculture was systematically favoring the developed world over the developing? The answer to this question must lie in a failure of *convergence*: the developing countries were not adopting the innovations in agriculture at a rate

Table 9.2 Regressions for convergence of crop yields, 1961–1999

Crop	Barley	Cotton	Maize	Millet	Rice	Sorghum	Soy	Wheat
b	−0.0409	−0.0930	−0.0046	−0.0417	−0.0607	−0.0002	−0.0383	−0.0501
	(0.0143)**	(0.0150)**	(0.0134)	(0.0124)**	(0.0114)**	(0.0105)	(0.0112)**	(0.0204)*
R^2(number	0.180	0.399	0.016	0.203	0.265	0.000	0.280	0.104
of observ.)	(39)	(60)	(75)	(46)	(80)	(63)	(32)	(54)

* indicates significance at the 5% level.
** at the 1% level.
Note: Figures in parentheses are standard errors.

that was sufficient to enable them to catch up to the developed countries. In general, economists expect a process of "catching up" to occur on account of the relative ease of imitation in comparison to innovation. Those countries on the technological frontier must innovate to generate growth while those within the frontier need only imitate. This difference leads to the expectation that convergence will occur in those sectors where a significant number of innovations are available for imitation. This is a very general claim within growth theory, viz. that we would expect countries with lower productivity to experience more rapid productivity growth than the countries at the frontier on account of the availability of innovations for diffusion.

This would have been the case for agriculture in the context of the green revolution. Significant rates of innovation were occurring in the agricultural and plant-breeding industries centered in the developed world, providing a large stock of innovations available for imitation. The expectation would then be that the ready imitation of these innovations would lead to higher rates of growth in the developing world, and a reduced gap in average yields. In fact, it would even be the case that the further from the frontier, the greater the stock of innovations available for imitation, and so the higher the expected rate of growth. For this reason, *convergence* on the technological frontier is the expected result in growth theory, with the highest growth rates expected in those countries furthest from the frontier.

A very basic analysis demonstrates that this expectation is not upheld by the experience across all crop varieties. Some supported the theory of convergence reasonably well, while others did not. Table 9.2 reports the regression results from a study of productivity growth rates in developing countries that regresses the average growth rate in country yields on the country's initial productivity value across all countries for each crop. Figures 9.1 through 9.4 give a graphical representation of the procedure for the cases of maize, sorghum, wheat and rice respectively.

In this exercise, we are estimating a model of the standard form

$$AVG = c + b \cdot \log(Y_{1961}) + \varepsilon \tag{1}$$

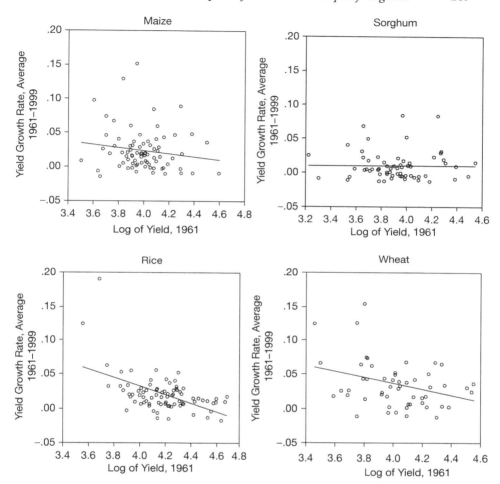

Figure 9.1–9.4 A graphical representation of the procedure for the cases of maize, sorghum, wheat and rice

where AVG is the average growth rate over the observation period (1961–99) and Y_{1961} is the yield level in 1961. This estimation simply ascertains whether there is any evidence of general convergence: the existence of an increased average growth rate being correlated with an initially low level of production.

Table 9.2 gives the resulting estimations for b for each of the eight crops we have studied. These are all negative in sign (indicating that a lower initial level correlates with a higher average growth) but only some of the coefficients are statistically significant (** representative of significance at the 1 per cent level).

For most crops, the convergence hypothesis bears out from this basic analysis of the data. This relationship is particularly strong in the case of cotton, rice and wheat, somewhat less so in millet, soybeans and barley. In short, countries that started out "further back" from the frontier made more progress toward it.

What is striking is that there are two crops for which convergence is rejected by the data, namely sorghum and maize. These results indicate that there is little evidence that developing countries have experienced any catching-up in the yields of these two crops. Interestingly, this result is somewhat counter-intuitive: In maize and sorghum, yield growth at the frontier has been at the higher end of the distribution (see Table 9.1). This would indicate that there is a higher rate of innovation, and thus an imitation-friendly environment conducive to catching-up by those developing countries off the frontier.[5]

These general relationships are demonstrated graphically in Figures 9.1–9.4. These scatterplots show the relationship between initial yield and subsequent growth for each of the developing countries in the database. The lines represent the observed relationship. Clearly the two "convergence crops" shown here (rice and wheat) demonstrate the anticipated relationship much more clearly than do the other two (sorghum and maize).

Our discussion of the empirical account of yield growth at the frontier and of the catching-up process has two major implications: The first is that there is evidence that the differences in the yield gaps between crops presented in Table 9.1 reflects (to some extent) a problem of failed convergence. Some crops have demonstrated little or no convergence whatsoever. In general, convergence has not been sufficiently present to close the yield gaps for many of the crops in global agriculture. The second implication is that there are significant differences between crops and the diffusion process occurring across them. This raises questions about why innovations move so much more slowly in some contexts than in others. The cases of maize and sorghum indicate that there exist crucial determinants of the rate of convergence (other than the yield gap) that ensure that developing countries can benefit from technological change.

The remainder of this paper aims to provide an answer to this puzzle of differential convergence. It is an important puzzle because, when the context is one of change and growth, the process of diffusion is the method by which innovation's benefits are distributed.

3. THE DIFFUSION OF INNOVATIONS

In this section, we estimate the rates of diffusion of innovations for different crops in order to resolve the puzzle of the relative gaps and of conditional convergence (Griliches, 1957). The crop specificity of technological protection enables us to compare the performance of each of these regimes with respect to diffusion. A particular feature of this analysis is that it enables us to decompose the development of the yield gaps in each of the crops into its three basic components: (1) innovation at the frontier, (2) the diffusion process of these innovations to developing countries, and (3) the country-specific factors that impact on the capacity for yield growth such as specific agro-ecological conditions. The first will tend to increase yields as the set of technological possibilities expands. The second will decelerate the speed at which these gains reach developing countries, and the third sector will determine the long-run capacity of a country to experience yield growth in a particular crop at a rate above or below the growth rate at the frontier.

3.1. A simple model of technological diffusion

Barro and Sala-i-Martin (1995) provide a simple model of technological diffusion in which the source of technological progress is the constant returns to scale to innovation in intermediate goods in the spirit of Romer (1990). The particular multi-economy setting that we explore here is a leader–follower model in which there is a technological frontier at which innovations occur that are imitated by countries off the frontier. Countries have different endowments of inputs that enable them to produce final output and to generate new products through innovation (by the leader) or imitation (by the follower). As Barro and Sala-i-Martin (1995) show, this setting allows a straightforward estimation of a model with suitable convergence characteristics: an economy's rate of growth varies proportionately in the distance from its steady-state. Barro and Sala-i-Martin then formulate the result as a log-linear approximation that explains the growth rates for a country off the frontier (a follower) as the growth at the technological frontier (a leader country) minus the "friction" induced by the fact that imitation is costly.

In the context of diffusion of innovations in crops, there are structural factors that inhibit the diffusion of innovations and that are likely to remain constant over time (Evenson and Kislev, 1973; Evenson, 1974). The most important structural factor is agro-ecological barriers to diffusion that will limit the amount of innovation useful in a follower country. One way to interpret this barrier is to see it as equivalent to the intrinsic productivity differences between leader and follower countries in a particular crop. Differences in the growth path of crop yields can then originate from two sources: (1) inherent and persistent problems in the follower country to keep up with the yield dynamics in the leader country, to be captured in a country fixed effect, and (2) problems in the diffusion of innovations from the leader to the follower country, to be captured by a catch-up parameter. Barro and

Sala-i-Martin interpret the catch-up rate as a measure of the costs of imitation in the follower country.

There are two fundamental assumptions that underlie this model. One is that innovations take place only in those countries that make up the frontier. Our claim is that even though total expenditures on agricultural R&D in the developing countries combined are roughly the same as those in developed countries combined (Alston et al., 1998),[6] technological factors result in the developed countries' R&D production function being significantly more efficient than that of developed countries. In sum, the vast majority of yield-enhancing innovations have been generated in the developed countries. The second fundamental assumption is that we do not allow country-specific factors to influence the coefficient that estimates the rate of diffusion.

3.2. Estimating the econometric model

In order to assess the diffusion patterns in each crop, we conducted a study of the development of agricultural yields in developing and developed countries for the eight crops chosen based on FAO data covering thirty-nine years, from 1961 to 1999. The amount of data available for each crop differs due to varying cultivation areas and completeness of data over the entire estimation period. This means that for soybeans, we have 38 observations from 27 countries available, while for maize we have 38 observations from 82 countries.[7]

The method we use is a fixed-effect panel estimation model that allows for heterogeneity among the countries through variable intercepts (Hsiao, 1986). In order to estimate the Barro-Sala-i-Martin diffusion model consistently, we convert the model into a form that presumes that all developing countries are subject to the same exogenous stochastic shock, in this case the event of an innovation that sets countries back in their relative yields. It then estimates for each crop the rate at which this shock is compensated for, allowing for heterogeneity in the intrinsic "rate of recovery" between countries. The model has the form

$$\varDelta G_{it} = a_i + \beta \cdot G_{i,t-1} + \varepsilon \qquad (2)$$

where $G_{i,t}$ is the gap in growth rates between the specific country i and the lead country in year t, $\varDelta$ signifies the observed change in the gap for country i in year t, and ε is a normally distributed random variable with $E(\varepsilon) = 0$ and a known variance. The intercept term a denotes the long-term difference in productivity growth in equilibrium. As laid out in section 1, the interpretation of a is to regard it as a country-specific intercept that captures the agro-ecological and institutional factors that influence the overall productivity development of the country. In this it captures the content of the hypotheses that claim country-specific factors are responsible for the disproportionate yield gap that exists in the case of maize and sorghum. The coefficient β that is to be estimated then reports the diffusion coefficient of the particular crop.

Empirically, we enter the growth rates of the frontier and the country i in the form of $log(y_{it})$ with y denoting the yield of country i. Then we estimate the diffusion coefficient β according to the model above as a GLS-regression correcting for the residuals being cross-section heteroskedastic by down-weighting each pool equation by an estimate of the cross-section residual standard deviation.[8] Table 9.3 reports the result for different crops.

3.3. Econometric results

Each of the estimations delivers a coefficient β that is statistically highly significant and we also report a parameter $\tilde{a}$ that denotes the *average* intercept for all countries in the estimation. Since we have restricted the model to a common slope coefficient, a high number of observations can be expected to result in a low R-squared. The Durbin-Watson coefficients indicate that serial correlation is not a particular problem for this estimation, thus strengthening our claim that the results provide an analysis that is independent from the trends at the frontier.

Before interpreting the results, it is convenient to perform some algebra in order to bring the model into a simpler form. Re-arranging the above equation, we arrive at the following equation for the growth rate of yield, $\Delta \hat{y}_t$ in the average developing country:

$$\Delta \hat{y}_t = \Delta y_t^* - (1 + \beta) \cdot G_{t,t-1} + \hat{a} + \varepsilon \tag{3}$$

This formulation reveals the separate components that drive the growth rate of yields in the average developing country: The first component is the yield gain

Table 9.3 Regressions for diffusion of innovations in different crops

Crop	Barley	Cotton	Maize	Millet	Rice	Sorghum	Soy	Wheat
β	−0.326	−0.318	−0.249	−0.335	−0.254	−0.283	−0.469	−0.387
	(0.0203)**	(0.0150)**	(0.0117)**	(0.0184)**	(0.0142)**	(0.0138)**	(0.0271)**	(0.0184)**
A	−0.339	−0.294	−0.365	−0.294	−0.230	−0.369	−0.291	−0.384
R^2(number of observ.)	0.171 (35)	0.166 (54)	0.135 (82)	0.172 (44)	0.154 (71)	0.160 (62)	0.244 (27)	0.234 (48)
DW-Statistic	2.40	2.26	2.40	2.45	2.23	2.42	2.27	2.30

* indicates significance at the 5% level.
** at the 1% level.
Note: The figure in parentheses is the standard error.

Intellectual Property Rights

at the frontier Δy^*. This reflects the expansion of the set of technological possibilities. The second component captures the extent to which an innovation can diffuse in the country. We define the gap G to take on positive values. Therefore, we would expect that the coefficient β is negative (indicating that innovations do not have a negative effect on growth) and that the closer the coefficient is to -1, the more rapid the gains dissipate from the frontier to the average developing country. The third parameter, $\hat{a}$, summarizes the country-specific growth lags as an average. A positive value would indicate that on average, developing countries have a higher "intrinsic" rate of yield growth in this crop.

3.4. Interpreting the results: diffusion

The results indicate considerable differences regarding the diffusion coefficients in the crops under examination. One can identify roughly three different groups of crops with respect to diffusion. Rapid diffusion happened only in the case of soybeans with a diffusion coefficient well below -0.45 (in absolute terms), and moderate diffusion (below -0.3) in wheat, millet, barley and cotton. In sorghum, rice and maize, diffusion has been slow (above -0.3) such that gains from innovation have taken a relatively long time to reach developing countries.

To get a more concrete impression of the differences in the rates of diffusion, Table 9.4 displays the results of a simulated diffusion situation. It shows the process of catching-up in different crops after an innovation at the frontier in period 0. The graphs demonstrate how differently diffusion occurs in these crops.

After one period, the "best" diffusing crop has made up 47 per cent of the initial shock while the "worst" diffusing crop has only compensated for 25 per cent. While the absolute difference becomes smaller over time as the slower crops catch up, in relative terms the difference widens. After ten periods, when the yield in the "best" crop, soybeans, has essentially converged back to the frontier yield, the "worst" crop, maize, still lags by more than 5 per cent. Eventually, of course, all crops catch-up to the frontier.

Table 9.4 Projected rates of convergence (i.e. remaining yield-gaps) after specified number of years for specified crops

Time since shock	Soy	Wheat	Millet	Barley	Cotton	Sorghum	Rice	Maize
1 year	−53.1	−61.3	−66.5	−67.4	−68.2	−71.7	−74.6	−75.1
5 years	−4.2	−8.7	−13.0	−13.9	−14.8	−19.0	−23.1	−23.9
10 years	−0.2	−0.8	−1.7	−1.9	−2.2	−3.6	−5.3	−5.7

3.5. Other effects: country-specific lags

A second set of important differences arises from the country-specific data on "individual growth capacity." This reveals firstly that, on average, developing countries would experience slower growth in all crop yields as the coefficient (â) is below zero for all crops. However, these impediments to growth are quite different between crops, ranging from rice, a crop with good intrinsic growth potential in developing countries at $\hat{a} = -0.230$, to wheat, with high average barriers to growth at $\hat{a} = -0.384$. This captures the history-dependent nature of diffusion for each crop. The level of the coefficient indicates whether the pattern of diffusion has brought it to countries where the local conditions are either more beneficial or more adverse to the successful cultivation of the plant.[9] Interestingly, there is no correlation between parameter estimates of â and β, which indicates that the processes of diffusion are disjoint from the effects of local conditions.[10]

Another informative statistic is how diverse countries are in their experience. It shows that with sorghum, cotton and soy there is a wide dispersion of local coefficients, indicated by the variance-to-mean ratio $r = \sigma_i^2 / \mu_i > 5$, while the experiences are fairly similar between countries for the other crops, where $r < 4$.

In general, the other factors explored in this regard generate little more explanatory value.[11] It seems that the rate of innovation at the technological frontier, and the rate of diffusion of innovation within the frontier, explain the vast majority of the pattern of yield growth across the developing world.

4. TESTING FOR THE ROLE OF IP REGIMES IN GROWTH AND DIFFUSION

This paper has put forward three sets of observations on crop yield developments across developing countries. The first observation set out the average yield gaps between developed and developing countries. The yield gaps are large across the entire range of crops (developing country yield gaps between 40 and 60 per cent) but the two outliers in the group are clearly maize (72 per cent gap) and sorghum (67 per cent gap). The second observation consisted of a test for "absolute convergence" across all varieties—a test for whether countries with lower yields at the beginning of the period of observation (in 1961) have experienced higher average growth rates over the ensuing period (between 1961 and 1999). This exercise showed that sorghum and maize are the only crops that do not exhibit this absolute convergence property, indicating the presence of convergence-limiting factors for these two species. We then examined the rates of diffusion from the technological frontier to developing countries. This part of the study found significant differences in the rates of diffusion of innovation between crops, and that diffusion had been particularly slow in maize, sorghum and rice. Based on a standard innovation-diffusion model (Barro and Sala-i-Martin, 1995), this can be interpreted as evidence for higher imitation costs in these two crops.

In each part of the study, maize and sorghum have been highlighted as the distinctive crops in the relationship between developed and developing-country crop yields. In this section we set out our hypothesis concerning the reasons underlying these observations on these crops' relative performances.

In the context of the diffusion model by Barro and Sala-i-Martin (1995), differences in the diffusion coefficients are indicative of differences in the cost of imitation, i.e. the costliness of transferring an innovation from its developed country of origin to its developing country context. An important determinant of the cost of imitation in the context of crops is how readily the value-adding traits in a novel variety from the leader country can be identified and extracted by the follower. This in turn is significantly influenced by the form of property right protection afforded to the value-adding traits within the innovative variety.

There is no question that property rights may be claimed in innovative plant varieties,[12] but the capacity to protect these claims varies. At present, there are two principal forms of protection for claims of property rights to innovations in plant varieties: (1) "legal protection," which is dependent for effect on the resources expended on monitoring and enforcement by the follower country; and (2) "technological protection," which is independent of the resources expended by the follower for effectiveness. It is probably fair to assert that—over the past 40 years—there has been little legal protection afforded to intellectual property rights claims to innovations in plant varieties throughout most of the developing world. Since most developing countries have had little to gain from expending resources on the implementation or enforcement of property rights for the benefit of innovators situated primarily overseas, there have been minimal incentives for such expenditures.[13] Therefore, it is likely that the primary route available for the effective protection of intellectual property right claims in developing countries has been technological.

Currently, technological protection is available only in the form of modern hybrid varieties, and thus limited in practice to the "outbreeding crops": maize and sorghum. Hybridization affords protection to improved plant varieties of these species, because the seed from them that is sold to farmers represents a relatively diverse gene pool and subsequent re-plantings generate widely divergent varieties. The other crop species reproduce in such as manner as to guarantee that the parents and offspring are identical in genetic structure. Sales of improved varieties from these species may be copied perfectly (and almost costlessly) from purchased seed, unless national laws effectively prevent such practices.

It is for this reason that we are able to claim that the technologically protected species act in effect as a case study on the impact of effective or "strong" property rights in innovation. They are to be contrasted with the impacts of innovations in the non-technologically protected species that act, in developing countries, as "weakly" protected innovations. In short, maize and sorghum are distinguished by their unique capacity for the technological protection of innovations in their sectors.[14] They present a unique context in which to conduct a "natural experiment" on the impacts of different IPR regimes on different countries' experience of growth and development in this sector.

4.1 Modeling diffusion under varying property right regimes

We test for the presence of a difference in the rate of diffusion through a dummy variable for observations involving the two hybrid crop varieties. The model then estimates for each category the rate at which this shock is compensated for, allowing for heterogeneity in the intrinsic "rate of recovery" between countries. The model has the form

$$\Delta G_{it} = a_i + \beta \cdot G_{i,t-1} + \gamma \cdot D \cdot G_{i,t-1} + \varepsilon \qquad (4)$$

where G_{it-1} is the gap in logarithm between the yields in a specific country i and the lead country in year t-1 and ΔG_{it} signifies the change in that gap from year t-1 to year t. The intercept term a_i denotes the long-term difference in productivity growth in equilibrium and is to be interpreted as before: It captures country-specific factors responsible for the disproportionate yield gap that exists in the case of maize and sorghum. The coefficient β that is to be estimated then reports the diffusion coefficient across all crops and γ is the diffusion rate differential for hybrid crops identified through the dummy variable D which is set to $D = 1$ in case of hybrid crops. Fixed effects for country and crop complete the model. Empirically, we perform Fisher's test as a panel data unit root test. We then estimate the diffusion coefficient β and the diffusion rate differential γ according to equation (2) as a GLS-regression.

4.2 Econometric results

The estimation delivers coefficients β and γ that are statistically highly significant. We also report the **average** intercept for all countries in the estimation denoted by $\hat{a}$. Before interpreting the results, it is convenient to perform some algebra in order to bring the model into a simpler form. Re-arranging (1), we arrive at the following equation for the growth rate of yield, $\Delta \hat{y}_t$ in the average developing country

$$\Delta \hat{y}_{it} = \Delta y_{it}^* - (1 + \beta + \gamma \cdot D) \cdot G_{it,t-1} + \hat{a}_i + \varepsilon \qquad (5)$$

with the analogous interpretation of the components as before. The new component, γD is the effect of hybridization on the growth rate. The fourth parameter, â, summarizes the country-specific growth lags as an average. A positive value would indicate that on average, developing countries have a higher "intrinsic" rate of yield growth in this crop and vice versa.

Table 9.5 shows the results of the econometric estimation of equation (1). The most important result is that hybridization has a measurable impact on the rate of diffusion. The coefficient of the hybrid dummy variable is highly significant, despite allowing for fixed effects both by country and by crop. The rate of diffusion of innovations from the frontier to developing countries across all crops was such crops carried over roughly 69 per cent of the gap opened by an innovation into the next year. The "diffusion penalty" involved in having innovations predominantly occur in hybridized crops is about 7.1 per cent per year. This means that developing countries retained about 7 per cent more of the yield gap each year in hybrids than in non-hybrids. This explains an important part of the cumulative yield gap that has developed in hybrids. The results also indicate that there is merit to the idea that structural effects, such as agro-ecological conditions, have contributed to inhibiting yield growth of hybrids in developing countries. The parameter $\hat{a}$ is the mean of the individually estimated parameters a_i. The means computed for hybrids and non-hybrids indicate that in hybrids, the average developing country has had a greater negative long-term deviation from the growth rate of the frontier than in non-hybrids. The combination of structural and diffusion effects is

Table 9.5 Regressions for diffusion of innovations in different crops

Coefficient	
β	−0.313
	(0.008)***
γ	0.071
	(0.011)***
a	−0.33611
R^2 (number of observ.)	0.16
	(14858)
DW-statistic	2.39

The figure in parentheses is the standard error. * indicates significance at the 5% level, ** at the 1% level.

therefore responsible for the significant gap in yields that persists between developed and developing countries in hybrid crops.

We believe that the observed differences in yield growth and diffusion across crop varieties noted in the previous sections are attributable to the distinctive property right regimes that were available for claiming rights to innovation in these varieties. The observations are consistent with the idea that strong property right regimes have resulted in varying costs of imitation across countries, which increase with the distance of the country from the technological frontier. This increasing cost of imitation translates into the observed consequence that innovations are impacted and slow to diffuse, especially for the two crops afforded effective protection. The ultimate outcome is that the two crops in which strong property rights exist are the only two which do not exhibit absolute convergence. The poorer countries fail to "catch up," only for those crops where strong intellectual property rights regimes prevail. Finally, this failure to catch up is captured in aggregate terms in the relative lags between the yields in developing and developed countries. All of the observations on crop yields and changes across the past forty years are consistent with the hypothesis that strong property rights protection over innovations inhibits their diffusion across the developing world.

If this is the case then it provides significant evidence in the general debate about the global impact of enhanced property right regimes. These observations imply that the receipt of benefits from strong property rights protection is inversely related to the distance of the particular country from the technological frontier. This would imply that, even if innovation occurs more rapidly under strong property rights protection, countries far from the frontier might prefer the combined rate of innovation/diffusion inherent within a weaker form of property rights regime. All intellectual property rights regimes would entail an inherent trade-off between innovation and diffusion, and the preferred regime would depend upon the perspective (i.e. the technological level) of the country concerned. (Krugman, 1979; Lai, 1999)

4.3 Simulating the impacts of different IPR regimes

To illustrate the impact of the different regimes on different countries, we now conduct a series of simulations that demonstrate how the impact of two distinct IPR regimes would impact the growth and development of agriculture in differing countries (post green revolution), when these countries differ in their starting points regarding the technological frontier. We have conducted simulations demonstrating how we would expect agricultural yields to develop from the year 2000 forward, given where each of these countries stood as of that date and under the assumptions of two distinct possible IPR regimes. One IPR regime would diffuse innovations in a manner similar to the weak regime represented by that used in the previous years for all non-hybrid varieties, and the other would operate like the strong regime with use restriction apparent in the hybrid varieties. The growth and diffusion rates estimated in the previous section are thus applied to a number of different countries and their starting positions.

The first figure appended illustrates how a stronger IPR regime generates a higher rate of growth for those countries at or near the technological frontier. Figure 9.5 demonstrates that, given the higher rate of growth that use restriction enables, the growth in general agricultural yields in the twenty years post-2000 is in aggregate almost 25 per cent greater than it would be without stronger IPR. This is the direct effect of information-internalization—greater rates of innovation and growth are expected to occur by reason of the strengthened IPR.

The other figures appended illustrate the manner in which diffusion confuses this impact of internalization. While countries at the frontier are innovating more rapidly and thus growing more rapidly (by reason of the direct effect of stronger IPR), the countries within the frontier are receiving those innovations at a slower rate. So, while the technology frontier is moving out at a more rapid rate, and there is a flow of innovations between that frontier and those countries not on it, the rate of flow between frontier and non-frontier is reduced by stronger IPR. This is the second—or indirect—effect of stronger IPR: a reduced rate of diffusion.

The combination of the two effects is different for different countries. For those countries on the technological frontier there is no indirect effect, as imitation is nearly instantaneous. For this reason the impact of stronger IPR on developed countries is wholly positive. Increased internalization results in increased rates of investment in innovation, thereby increasing innovation and growth.

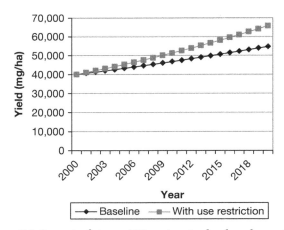

Figure 9.5 Impact of strong IPR regime in developed countries

For those countries off the technological frontier (the so-called developing countries) the indirect effect may subtract quite a bit from the positive impact of stronger IPR. The size of the indirect effect will depend upon the distance of the country from the technological frontier. If the initial position of the country is very near the technological frontier, then the diffusion of innovation continues to be nearly instantaneous and there is a very low cost to the country resulting from increased internalization. An example of one such country is China (*c.*2000), which sat just off the technological frontier in agriculture. For this country it would be expected that this slight distance would occasion a small cost of diffusion, but the general result would remain the same as in the developed world: stronger IPR would be conducive to greater growth. Figure 9.6 bears out this intuition, and shows that the impact of stronger IPR is positive for China but at a reduced rate. The additional growth over the forecast period represents a positive increase of 12.5 per cent, about half that of those countries on the technological frontier. So, stronger IPR regimes are a positive improvement for China, but not as much as they are for the developed countries. This results in the distributional effect noted for much of the green revolution. Even when technological change results in positive growth for both developed and developing countries, it is skewed more toward developed than developing. China's projected experience of IPR strengthening is consonant with this observation.

Figure 9.7 demonstrates a more complicated picture. In this case we examine Ethiopia, a country that is a fair distance off the technological frontier, and so the increased growth coming from the increased rate of innovation at the frontier is significantly reduced by reason of the increased time it takes to reach countries off the frontier. This is the meaning of the reduced rate of diffusion—increased internalization comes at the cost of reduced rates of flow of innovation to those countries off the frontier. Although technology is

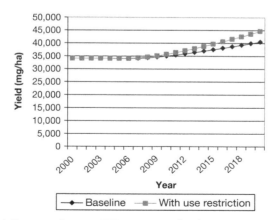

Figure 9.6 Impact of strong IPR regime in developing countries (China)

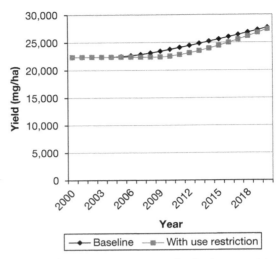

Figure 9.7 Impact of strong IPR regime in developing countries (Ethiopia)

moving at a more rapid pace on the frontier, those countries off the frontier are kept from receiving the benefits from this rate of change by reason of their "technological distance" from the frontier countries. It is as if they are standing too far away from the noise of innovation to be able to hear or understand what is happening at a distance. Nevertheless, the increased activity at the frontier means that the world is rapidly changing, and the countries at a distance ultimately receive benefits from this, but it might be some time before these innovations are able to close across the space between them.

Figure 9.7 demonstrates that Ethiopia would be largely indifferent concerning the institutional changeover to stronger IPR. The trade-off between direct effect (increased growth) and indirect effect (reduced diffusion of the innovations generating that growth) largely nullifies the impact of IPR institutions over the twenty-year period being examined. the impact of IPR strengthening (increased restriction) is largely neutral from an isolated perspective, but clearly Ethiopia is falling much farther behind relative to those states actually on the frontier. The distributional impacts are pronounced.

Finally, we come to an example of a country far off the frontier: Tanzania. For states such as Tanzania, the crucial feature of any innovation policy is how well and how quickly it facilitates the movement of innovations from the frontier to those far from it. These countries benefit very little from enhanced rates of activity in places far away from them. In Figure 9.8 it is apparent that the changeover to a policy of strong IPR has a very strong and negative indirect effect—which swamps the always-present positive impact at the frontier. Over the twenty-year period of the simulation, Tanzania loses ground on where it would be in the absence of institutional change. There is a 12.5 per cent

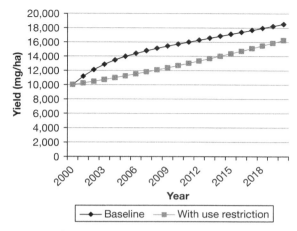

Figure 9.8 Impact of strong IPR regimes in developing countries (Tanzania)

loss in growth as a result of the enhanced IPR regime. For this country and over this time period, the adoption of a strong IPR regime is a bad thing, both absolutely and relatively.

Overall, these simulations explain the nature of the anomalies we saw in the original data on growth and gaps in the green revolution. The general lessons to be learned from technological change in agriculture are that its benefits are not unalloyed nor indiscriminate. Some countries are doing much better within this environment of rapid change, while others are doing better but not by much. This differential rate of improvement is one of the things that leads to the large distributional impacts resulting from technological change. Even more striking is the fact that institutional impacts are not just skewed, but negatively biased. The effect of enhanced internalization—stronger property rights—is clearly positive for those countries on the technological frontier or just off it. However, stronger property rights can have a negative impact for those countries furthest from the frontier over a reasonably long period of time. This comes across in the data as another factor affecting benefit distribution in aggregate, but it is also an indication that it cannot be assumed that all institutional changes have positive impacts for all countries just because they have positive impacts for some.

5. CONCLUSION

This paper has examined the growth and IPR implications of the green revolution: the development of yields in developing and developed countries in the eight most important agricultural crops over a period of almost forty years. This was a period worth examining as a great "natural experiment" during which rapid technological change worked its way across the globe subject to some very different regimes for innovation and internalization.

The results of our study indicate that although growth has been impressive in this period of rapid technological change, problems in the global distribution of agricultural productivity over this era persist and give cause for concern. Our results also indicate that there are significant differences in both the dynamics of yield growth in the developed countries and the diffusion of these gains to developing countries between crops that require explanation. Evidence on the convergence of yields in developing countries shows that convergence occurs in all crops examined with the exception of maize and sorghum. We explore the reasons for this difference further by estimating the diffusion coefficients of innovations from the yield frontier to developing countries. We conclude that the failure of convergence in maize and sorghum can be explained by the exceptionally low rate of diffusion applying to these two crops alone.[15]

Maize and sorghum are exceptional among crops because they have been the only varieties for which hybrid use restriction is available. This is a very strong form of IPR regime. This has led to higher than average growth of yields in these crops through the mobilization of private R&D efforts, investment and innovation. At the same time, our results indicate that the technological protection of enhanced property rights afforded by hybridization has had a negative effect on the rate of diffusion of these innovations. The existence of this innovation-diffusion trade-off highlights the problematic international welfare implications inherent in choosing a particular regime of intellectual property protection. Based on the empirical data, we are able to exactly quantify this trade-off in the case of crop varieties and to decompose the growth of yield in the average developing country as a combination of innovation at the frontier, diffusion to the developing country and structural factors in the adoption of new varieties.

The case of agriculture is a possibly unique setting within which the debate over the impacts of enhanced property right regimes might be tested. This initial evidence from the green revolution indicates that there is an inherent trade-off between enhanced rates of innovation (and thus growth) and enhanced rates of diffusion (and hence distribution). This means that there are frictions within the system of technological dissemination that inhibit the flows of beneficial information, and that enhanced property rights regimes will work most prominently against the interests of those states furthest from the frontier. Whenever this is the case, enhanced IPR regimes will have the impact of skewing the distribution of benefits towards those states on or near the technological frontier. In the case of those countries furthest from the frontier, it is probable that the impact of heightened IPR is likely to be negative over any reasonable time horizon.

NOTES

1. This research has its origins in a research grant from the UK Department for International Development. We are grateful to Robert Carlisle for encouraging us to explore this area. We are particularly grateful to James Symons and Hashem Pesaran for helpful discussions on the econometrics and comments, and grateful to Mark Rogers and Keith Maskus for helpful discussions and comments without implicating them in any way in the remaining errors.

2. This paper thus falls in the theoretical line established by Krugman (1979) and leading to Lai (1999); however, its approach is empirical. The distributional implications of this paper's arguments are more fully simulated and expounded in Goeschl and Swanson (2000) and Goeschl and Swanson (2003).

3. The argument presented here does not rule out that there are other factors that impinge on the transferability of innovations in agricultural technology, such as agro-ecological factors or crop-specific complementary inputs that are biased against developing countries. These are the points commonly put forward to explain this diversity of gaps. By abstracting from these factors, this paper points instead to a broader problem in the area of agricultural R&D, namely the conflict between stimulating an optimal amount of R&D and ensuring optimal diffusion of the resulting innovations.

4. This distinction between strong and weak property right regimes is discussed in greater detail in two other publications by ourselves: Swanson (2002) and Swanson and Goeschl (2004).

5. Support for this intuition comes from a significantly positive correlation between the growth rate at the frontier and the convergence coefficient β for all other crops except maize and sorghum. The correlation coefficient between the growth rate at the frontier and β is -0.01 when based on the estimates of all eight crops. When omitting maize and sorghum, it jumps to 0.67, suggesting a significantly positive correlation.

6. In 1991, agricultural R&D expenditures in 131 developing countries combined were $8,009 million 1985 international dollars and in 22 developed countries combined, $6,941 million (both at 1985 U.S. dollar value). For 1981, the data were $5,503 million and $5,713 million, and for 1971 2,984 million and $4,298 million respectively (Alston et al., 1998). So over the entire period, R&D expenditures were of roughly comparable size.

7. The country yield data suffers from several deficiencies. The most obvious one is that the yield data for some countries does not appear particularly reliable. Fortunately, this tends to be more the case the smaller the production. Another one is the fact that some crops were only introduced into countries during the observation period. Here we adopt the rule that only those countries that cultivated the crop in 1961 should be included in the sample as adopters are likely to underperform at early stages of cultivation and thus to bias the estimation. In the case of soybeans, this led to a fairly high number of observations being discarded.

8. The presence of heteroskedasdicity tends to lead to higher diffusion coefficients. This weighting procedure corrects for that. The White test for cross-section heteroskedasticity is performed for all estimations and reports consistent parameters for all crops.

9. For each crop there are countries in which the intrinsic growth rate of the yield is basically equal or above that prevalent in the frontier countries. In the case of barley, this holds for Zimbabwe; in the case of cotton, for Israel and Syria; in the case of maize, for Chile; in the case of millet, for China; in the case of rice, for Egypt and Korea; in the case of sorghum, for Egypt and Israel; in the case of soybeans, for Ethiopia; and in the case of wheat, for Egypt and Zimbabwe.

10. The correlation coefficient between $\hat{a}$ and β is 0.02.

11. The authors also investigated the importance of increased allocations of land, and of agro-ecological circumstances, and found these factors to be either of no significance or much lower impact than the factors discussed here.

12. The so-called UPOV Convention provides that each member state should provide property right protection in innovative plant varieties. It is also possible to take traditional forms of patent rights in innovative seeds.

13. Maskus (2000) cites two types of evidence for this proposition. First, there is the generally observed positive correlation between national income and adoption of IPR regimes. Second, there is the positive correlation between national income and perceived effectiveness of IPR regimes, as demonstrated in the World Economic Forum's surveys of perceived strength of IPR enforcement (index for 21 developed countries 50 per cent greater than that for 18 developing countries).

14. An interesting issue in future will be the impact of technological change that affords technological protection to other crop species, so-called genetic use restriction technologies, and the welfare implications for various countries. Goeschl and Swanson (2000).

15. At the same time, we show that agro-ecological factors are likely to affect diffusion, but cannot explain the exceptional cases of maize and sorghum.

REFERENCES

Alston, J.M., P.G. Pardey and Vincent H. Smith (1998) "Financing Agricultural R&D in Rich Countries: What's Happening and Why?" *The Australian Journal of Agricultural and Resource Economics* 42 (1): 51–82.

Barro, R. and X. Sala-i-Martin (1995) *Economic Growth.* Boston: MIT Press.

Evenson, R.E. (1994) "Analyzing the Transfer of Agricultural Technology," in J.R. Anderson (ed.) *Agricultural Technology: Policy Issues for the International Community.* Wallingford: CABI, 165–79.

Evenson, R. and Y. Kislev (1973) "Research and Productivity in Wheat and Maize," *Journal of Political Economy* 81 (6): 1309–29.

Goeschl, T. and T. Swanson (2000) "Genetic Use Restriction Technologies and the Diffusion of Yield Gains to Developing Countries," *Journal of International Development* 12: 1159–78.

Goeschl, T. and T. Swanson (2003) "The Development Impact of Genetic Use Restriction Technologies: A Forecast Based on the Hybrid Crop Experience," *Environment and Development Economics* 8: 149–65.

Griliches, Z. (1957) "Hybrid Corn: An Exploration in the Economics of Technological Change," *Econometrica* 48: 501–22.

Hsiao, C. (1986) *The Analysis of Panel Data.* Econometric Society Monographs No. 11. Cambridge: Cambridge University Press.

Krugman, P. (1979) "A Model of Innovation, Technology Transfer, and the World Distribution of Income," *Journal of Political Economy* 87: 253–66.

Lai, E. L-C. (1999) "International Intellectual Property Rights Protection and the Rate of Product Innovation," *Journal of Development Economics*, 55: 133–53.

Maddala, G.S. and Shaowen Wu (1999) "A Comparative Study of Unit Root Tests with Panel Data and a New Simple Test," *Oxford Bulletin of Economics and Statistics*, 61: 631–52.

Maskus, Keith E. (2000). *Intellectual Property Rights in the Global Economy.* Washington, DC: Institute of International Economics.

Romer, P. (1990) "Endogenous Technological Change," *Journal of Political Economy* 98 (5): part II, S71–S102.

Swanson, T. (ed.) (2002) *Biotechnology, Agriculture and the Developing World.* Cheltenham: Edward Elgar.

Swanson, T. and T. Goeschl (2004): "Diffusion and Distribution: The Impacts of Technological Enforcement on Poor Countries," in K. Maskus and J. Reichman (eds.) *International Public Goods & Transfer of Technology Under a Globalised Intellectual Property Regime.* Cambridge: Cambridge University Press.

10

International Efforts to Pool and Conserve Crop Genetic Resources in Times of Radical Legal Change

Michael Halewood

1. INTRODUCTION

Since the earliest days of settled agriculture, crop domestication and improvement efforts have generally taken place within open systems of innovation. As a result, the basic building blocks of these activities—plant genetic resources—have generally been exchanged and used in an open-access manner. The maintenance of collaborative systems to collect, conserve, and provide access to plant genetic resources in support of crop science and plant breeding distinguishes agricultural innovation systems from those associated with pharmaceutical, cosmetic, and industrial research and development. Section 2 of this chapter examines the historical patterns of use of plant genetic resources for food and agriculture (PGRFA) highlighting the extent to which all countries in the world have become interdependent on these resources.

In recent years, there has been a disturbing trend towards the "hyper-ownership" of genetic resources through the exercise of intellectual property rights, restrictive contracts, and access and benefit-sharing laws. This trend is examined in section 3 of this chapter. Literature in the field generally focuses on the (actual or potential) negative impact of these relatively new forms of exclusive control on long-standing agricultural innovation. What appears to be largely unremarked upon, however, is the fact that, at the same time that these exclusive forms of control have proliferated, there have also been unprecedented levels of international policy support for the collective pooling and sharing of PGRFA, as reflected, ultimately, in the negotiation and coming into force of the International Treaty on Plant Genetic Resources for Food and Agriculture (ITPGRFA).[1]

At first blush, these developments—the proliferation of exclusive legal controls over PGRFA and the confirmation of international rules for their common pooling and sharing—are hard to reconcile. Section 4 of this chapter argues, however, that they are actually very closely related. In short, early efforts to consolidate internationally rules that were legally binding on countries regarding pooling, conserving, and sharing benefits from PGRFA floundered when they were based on conceptions of PGRFA as part of the public domain and/or common heritage of humankind. Ultimately, the collective political will to formalize rules could only be purchased by abandoning earlier concepts of PGRFA and recognizing instead—at different times and in different intergovernmental fora—the primacy of intellectual property rights and national sovereignty over genetic resources. In essence, countries and legal individuals were only willing to agree to rules for pooling (some subsets of) PGRFA after their "deeper" rights of exclusive control over those resources had been conclusively established. In this way, the "poolers" ended up embracing and using the same tools that were being promoted by the "controllers," but for a different purpose.

Section 5 of the chapter examines the current architecture of the global crop commons, focusing primarily on the ITPGRFA's multilateral system of access and benefit sharing and as its supporting components. The chapter reveals how the resolution (or lack of resolution) of controversial issues in the pre-treaty period influenced the multilateral system's scope and modus operandi. It also highlights how unresolved issues from the pre-treaty period continue to present challenges to the present day.

2. HISTORICALLY OPEN SYSTEMS OF INNOVATION AND INTERDEPENDENCE

Crop domestication began independently in a number of parts of the world between 10,000 and 2,000 years ago (Smith, 2006; Harlan, 1992). Thereafter, planting materials from the crops in question, and knowledge about how to use them, spread relatively quickly across continents and even from one continent to another. Their dispersal can be partly attributed to the opportunistic relationships that crops developed with peoples who engulfed their neighbours. Yam, for example, was originally domesticated in what is now Nigeria and Cameroon, and later it accompanied (and fueled) the Bantu expansion across southern Africa (Diamond, 1997). The diffusion of crops can also be attributed to the fact that once people acquired them and adapted them to their own settings and needs, they allowed them to be passed on for use by others. While largely unplanned and taking place over thousands of years, these pre-historical crop-development "projects" involved "technology uptake" and "livelihood impacts" that are beyond the wildest dreams of today's development research planners. Consider the cultural diversity of the peoples involved in the domestication/improvement of einkorn and emmer wheat and barley as they were passed on from Mesopotamia, to North Africa, to Crete, to mainland Greece, and, from there, to eastern, western, and northern Europe—a voyage that took about six thousand years. Then factor in the equally impressive voyage that these same crops made as they traveled eastward to India and China about six and a half thousand years ago (Solbrig and Solbrig, 1994; Harlan, 1992).

The "Columbian exchange" that attended the early contact, and subsequent colonial conquest, of the Americas by European powers, represented an enormous "leap forward" in terms of global crop diffusion (Crosby, 1972, 1986). An enormous range of crops that had already made their way to Western Europe from Africa, Asia, and other parts of Europe were introduced to the Americas, and an extremely important portfolio of new world crops were introduced to Europe. For example, apples, bananas, barley, coffee, lettuce, millet, oats, onions, rice, tea, soya, beans, sugar cane, and wheat were introduced to the 'New World', while beans, bell peppers, chili peppers, cocoa, maize, manioc (cassava), peanuts, potatoes, pumpkin, squash, sunflower, tobacco, tomatoes, and sunflowers were brought back for the first time to Europe—and then, on to Africa and Asia.

The enthusiasm for these new crops was, and continues to be, surprising when one considers how static many peoples' "traditional" or national diets sometimes seem. Maize was introduced into Africa for the first time in the early sixteenth century (Andrews, 1993). It is now sown on 27 million hectares, yields 51 million tonnes of grain, and accounts for one-third of the mean caloric intake of sub-Saharan Africans (CGIAR, 2009). Wheat is now the world's most widely planted crop, with over 220 million hectares planted in 2005 and a yield of 631 million tonnes (CGIAR, 2009). Rice, which was originally domesticated approximately 6,700 years ago (Fuller et al. 2009) is now grown in over one hundred countries. In 2005, 621 tonnes of rice was harvested from 154 million hectares. One of the end results of this mass diffusion of crops is that a very small number have gained extraordinary global importance. It is estimated that just four crops—rice, wheat, maize, and sugar—are the source of 60 per cent of calories currently consumed by humans worldwide (Palacios, 1997).

Since the 1960s, publicly funded international agricultural research organizations, in concert with national agricultural research organizations, have been the main pumps for the global movement of plant genetic resources for food and agriculture. The International Board on Plant Genetic Resources for Food and Agriculture (IBPGR) was created in 1974 to coordinate the collection and conservation of plant germ plasm for future research and production

(Pistorius, 1997). It was hosted by the Food and Agriculture Organization (FAO) and supported by the Consultative Group on International Agricultural Research (CGIAR). Between 1974 and 1988, the IBPGR coordinated 300 collecting missions in 90 countries through which 120,000 new accessions were collected (Pistorius, 1997). IBPGR made agreements with gene banks around the world to hold collected materials in a network of base collections, on the understanding that if "material stored is not available from an active collection, it will be made freely available from the base collection to any professionally qualified institution or individual interested in it" (Engels and Thormann, 2005). As shall be highlighted below, the international nature of these efforts to collect and conserve plant genetic resources and to make them available—and some dissatisfaction with respect to how those activities were carried out (Mooney, 1983)—gave rise to many of the policy developments that are addressed in this paper. By 1990, IBPGR had such agreements with 42 national institutes and eight CGIAR centers' (Engels and Thormann, 2005). Since then, the international agricultural research centers of the CGIAR have continued to acquire materials. As of 2009, the gene banks of these centers held over 650,000 accessions in crop and forage collections. Most of the emphasis in assembling these collections has been focused on obtaining an infra-specific diversity of a relatively small group of crops and forages that play the largest role in agricultural production systems around the world. For example, International Rice Research Institute hosts 100,000 accessions of *Oryza sativa*, and the International Maize and Wheat Improvement Center's (CIMMYT) international wheat collection includes 96,000 accessions, while its international maize collection includes 26,000 accessions.

Each year, the CGIAR centers facilitate the transfer of approximately 450,000 samples of PGRFA internationally. Of this material, approximately 75 per cent is improved by the centers themselves, and 80 per cent of the transfers were to developing countries (and countries with economies in transition), while approximately 5 per cent goes to developed countries, 15 per cent is transferred between centers, and 95 per cent is sent to public sector organizations (SGRP, 2009). Table 10.1 shows the extent to which different regions accessed materials that were originally collected from other regions over a twenty-year period by way of the CGIAR gene banks (not including the centers' breeding programs). The percentages of requests for foreign germ plasm are even higher when one considers materials accessed from other countries within the same region. For example, on average, 90 per cent of the beans, finger millet, groundnut pigeon pea, and forages accessed from the CGIAR center gene banks by Kenya and Uganda from 1980 to 2002 were originally collected from other countries (Halewood, Gaiji, and Upadyaya 2004).

Table 10.1 PGRFA from other regions accessed through the CGIAR gene banks, 1980–2000

Region	No. of accessions held in CGIAR gene banks originally collected from the region	No. of samples sent to the region from the CGIAR gene banks	% of materials received that were originally collected from other regions
South Asia	128,679	448,288	54
Sub-Saharan Africa	124,168	134,233	57
South America	62,303	43,423	61
South-west Asia	58,574	47,168	46
Europe	32,711	82,396	92
Meso-America	29,944	39,312	67
East Asia	20,996	45,804	87
North Africa	18,313	37,720	75
North America	13,965	57,872	95
Oceania-Pacific	1,671	14,592	100

Sources: CGIAR-SINGER 2006, Gaiji, Samy personal communication.

Table 10.2 illustrates the same point—namely, that countries are extremely interdependent on PGRFA to support their breeding and research efforts—but it does so in a different way and without focusing on the role of the CGIAR centers. It presents the results of an analysis of the geographical origin of the landrace ancestors in the pedigrees of 1,709 improved rice varieties that were released, starting in the early 1960s, in 15 countries (Gollin 1998, Gollin and Evenson 1998). The table dramatically demonstrates the extent to which almost all of the countries were heavily reliant on landrace ancestors from other countries.

Improved materials from the CGIAR centers have been dispersed widely throughout the world. While countries sometimes introduce center-improved materials directly into their production systems, they more often make crosses between those improved materials and locally adapted varieties. Worldwide, 35 per cent of the approximately 8,000 modern varieties of 11 crops released between 1960–2000 have been based on crosses with materials developed by the CGIAR centers (Evenson, 2005). In the Middle East and Africa, 50 per cent of the modern varieties released between 1960 and 2000 had ancestors released from CGIAR centers (Evenson and Gollin, 2003). By the mid 1990s, one-fifth of the wheat, and three-quarters of the rice grown in the United States had ancestors bred by CGIAR centers (Pardey et al., 1996). Heisey et al. (2003) estimate that, by the 1990s, one half of all wheat varieties released in developing countries were CIMMYT crosses, and a further 25 per cent had a CIMMYT parent. In terms of productivity, the national agricultural research programs were up to 40 per cent more productive over the last forty years as a

Table 10.2 Countries' dependence on foreign rice germ plasm

Country	Total landrace progenitors in all released varieties	Own landraces	Borrowed landraces
Bangladesh	233	4	229
Brazil	460	80	380
Burma	442	31	411
China	888	157	731
India	3,917	1,559	2,358
Indonesia	463	43	420
Nepal	142	2	140
Nigeria	195	15	180
Pakistan	195	0	195
Philippines	518	34	484
Sri Lanka	386	64	322
Taiwan	20	3	17
Thailand	154	27	127
United States	325	219	106
Vietnam	517	20	497

Source: Fowler and Hodgkin, 2004, based on a table originally included Gollin, 1998.

result of their use of advanced breeding lines from the CGIAR centers (Evenson, 2003). It has been estimated that in the absence of these centers' global contributions to crop genetic improvement, world grain prices would be 12 per cent higher and overall food production would be 7 per cent lower in developing countries (Evenson and Rosegrant, 2003).

CGIAR centers are not, of course, the only organizations facilitating the international movement of germ plasm. During the 1990s, the United States distributed approximately 16,000 samples of ten crops on an annual basis. Gene banks from the Netherlands, Brazil, Canada, and Scandanavia each distributed between 1,500 and 2,500 samples per year during the same period (Fowler and Hodgkin, 2004). Half of Brazil's commercially successful varieties of soya are the result of crosses with improved materials that were introduced from the United States in the 1960s and 1970s (Pardy et al., 2002). In addition, the private sector has also benefited from public research and the availability of germ plasm.

As a result of the way in which crops have been domesticated, improved, and diffused, all countries of the world are highly reliant on genetic resources for crops that were originally from other parts of the world. For example, Ximena Palacios (1997) estimates that central African countries are dependent on "foreign" crops for 67–93 per cent of people's daily caloric intake. Countries on the Indian and Pacific Oceans are 93–100 per cent dependent on foreign crops, and North American countries are about the same. Furthermore, it seems that, with climate change, countries will become more interdependent on plant genetic resources. Even by conservative estimates, the climate will change in many parts of the world at rates that exceed the adaptive capacity of the crops currently being grown there. As a result, countries will be required to either give up crop production or search for climate adaptive traits in genetic resources from other countries (Fujisaka, Williams, and Halewood, 2009).

3. RECENT ENCROACHMENTS

Up to this point, I have been focusing on collaborative efforts to conserve, share, and improve PGRFA. Of course, this is not the entire story. There are trends towards what Sabrina Safrin (2004) calls "hyperownership," whereby various actors are striving to exert forms of exclusive control over genetic resources, including PGRFA. From the mid 1990s to 2010, the numbers of new accessions that countries have provided to the centers with permission to provide global access dropped precipitously. (Between 2010 and 2012 the numbers increased, largely as a result of the regeneration project coordinated by the Global Crop Diversity Trust. More details about this program are provided below.) Given the central role of the CGIAR gene banks as "pumps" for the international movement of PGRFA in support of agricultural research, this trend was, and continues to be potentially disturbing. While there are a number of factors contributing to this phenomenon, the gene bank curators cite access and benefit-sharing issues related to the implementation of the Convention on Biological Diversity (CBD) as one of the leading causes.[2] In general, countries have tended to approach the implementation of the CBD by putting in place relatively rigid, process-heavy access and benefit-sharing regulations that are designed to ensure no unregulated "leakage" of genetic resources from the country with a concomitant loss of opportunities to negotiate benefit-sharing terms with access seekers (Nijar et al. 2009). Generally, these systems require access applications to be considered on a case-by-case basis, involving potentially complex negotiations, and the development of novel contracts to reflect agreements reached. In addition, most such laws also require the involvement of competent authorities from national governments to approve and possibly sign the agreements (Moore and Tymowski, 2005).

Transaction costs associated with the CBD are not limited to the operation of the laws that are in place. The CBD has contributed to such a heightened sensitivity within countries about potential losses of improperly regulated, unauthorized access that otherwise competent authorities are reluctant to authorize access without explicit authorization by national laws (Wambugu and Muthamia, 2013). The cumulative effect can lead to significant delays or total cessation of research, conservation, and economic development programs. Some CGIAR gene-bank managers reported that when they have made requests for new material to add to their international collections, they have experienced: multiple deferrals of their requests to alternative authorities without any definitive response being provided; indefinite delays in responses to applications; outright refusals; agreements to send materials that have not been honoured; and reversals of assurances by national technical experts by higher, political-level authorities citing access and benefit-sharing concerns (Halewood et al., 2013). The situation deteriorated in the late 1990s to the point that some centers adopted policies to stop asking countries to make new materials available until the negotiations of the ITPGRFA were finished in the hope that the treaty would help break the deadlock (Halewood et al., 2013).

The link between access and benefit-sharing laws and frustrated research and conservation projects has been remarked upon by a number of commentators (Jinna and Jungcourt, 2009; Fowler, 2002; Correa, 2005; Nijar et al., 2009; Evenson, 2005). In 2006, a group of 200 scientists from across Latin America considered the impact of access and benefit-sharing laws on their research efforts. Their report states that "[b]asic biological research is seriously hampered by many of the current national ABS regimes," and "[d]istrust, rather than trust, is presently dominating the situation in many countries, hampering biological research. This holds for national as well as international research." The meeting further recommended that "[a]ll countries are encouraged to review their processes for permits on research, collection, import, and export of specimens to rationalize and streamline the ABS process. In addition, rules and regulations need to be practicable" (UNEP 2006).

Concerns have also been expressed about the impact of intellectual property rights (IPRs), and particularly patents, on the availability of PGRFA for use in plant breeding. As Nuvolari and Tatari point out in Chapter 8 of this volume, until very recently, the high level of inventiveness in the agriculture sector has been characterized by "weak appropriability" and virtually no intellectual property protection, particularly in the area of crop improvement. Plant breeders' rights, as embodied in the 1968 International Convention for the Protection of New Varieties of Plants (UPOV Convention), and its subsequent revisions in 1978 and 1991, preserve exemptions for breeders to use protected varieties for plant breeding, including incorporation of protected varieties into the pedigrees of new varieties.[3] Patents have considerably more potential to restrict downstream innovators' use of technologies associated with plant breeding. In the United States, the research exemption has been interpreted extremely narrowly. In France and Germany, the research exemption for patents is wider but not as broad as the research exemption provided by the UPOV Convention. For example, while patented materials can be used for research purposes, the new inventions that incorporate patented material cannot be commercialized (Correa, 2009).[4]

Patenting has become increasingly common in the plant-breeding sector— a phenomenon directly linked to the combined emergence of biotechnological applications in plant breeding, adaptations to national patents laws to cover living matter, and increased participation of the private sector in the plant-breeding field. In the United States, at the beginning of the twentieth century, two-thirds of expenditure on agricultural research was public; by 2000, the situation had become reversed, with the private sector making two-thirds of the overall investment (Evenson, 2005). At the same time, there has been a trend towards universities behaving more like private sector counterparts and seeking patents over their innovations—a trend that was kicked off in the United States with the University and Small Business Patent Procedures Act (Baye-Dohl Act), and followed in numerous countries in the developed world (Toenniessen and Delmer, 2006).[5] Universities have granted exclusive licenses to companies over important enabling technologies (Graff et al., 2003).

A considerable body of literature has emerged decrying the potential impact of the patenting on plant breeding in general (Plantum NL, 2009) and on the development and diffusion of appropriate technologies for developing countries in particular (Toenniessen and Delmer, 2006). In this context, commentators have expressed concerns about unjustifiably broad patents or "patent thickets" that reduce the freedom of public sector breeders to operate (Correa, 2009; Atkinson et al., 2003); the growing dependence of public sector organizations on proprietary technologies (Toenniessen and Delmer, 2006); and the need for public organizations to develop commercially viable technologies (Taylor and Cayford, 2003).[6] On the other hand, empirical evidence to date concerning the net impact of increased patenting on biotechnologies is inconclusive (Spence, 2008; Rai, 2008). And there is some evidence that, up to this point, public-private partnerships, while still limited, appear to be facilitating important technology transfers (Rangnekar, 2004).

At the very least, IPR restrictions on direct use and, more controversially, on research and plant breeding will interrupt the immediate cycling back of improved materials into innovations systems as openly accessible PGRFA. While some commentators note occasional disregard for patent restrictions by universities and public research and non-for-profit organizations (Wesley, Cohen, and Walsh, 2010; van Zeebroeck et al., 2008; Nottenburg et al., 2002),[7] it seems inevitable that the increased use of patents will ultimately increase the costs of research, especially in those cases where the incorporation of protected materials is involved. It is possible that owners of proprietary materials will make these proprietary materials available for downstream research on reasonable terms through licenses (including humanitarian licenses for uses in developing countries), cross-licensing, and patent pooling. While there have been a number of initiatives to encourage the pooling of patents or to create royalty clearing houses in order to facilitate public research with development objectives, they have been slow to take off, suggesting that either the problem of gaining access to proprietary technologies has not been as difficult as originally forecasted (G. Barry, personal communication) or that it is more complicated than one might think to make such systems actually work (Spence, 2008).[8]

Some technologies have been developed that make it difficult, if not impossible, for farmers to grow harvested seed. The seed of hybrid maize varieties, for example, which were commercialized in the United States as early as the 1920s, does not grow-out well, thereby compelling farmers to return to commercial sources for each planting/harvest cycle (see Chapter 9 in this volume). Furthermore, given that considerable investment is required to develop the inbred parental lines that are used to develop the hybrids, there is an incentive for producers of commercial hybrid varieties to not share those PGRFA as well. Hybridization has since been extended to other crops, including sorghum, rice, cotton, wheat, and peanuts.

Transgenic genetic use restriction technologies have recently been developed that have the potential to extend the quality of producing non-viable seed to all crops. These technologies would (and do) make IPR prohibitions against unauthorized direct use largely redundant. Tim Swanson and Timo Goeschl (Chapter 9) predict that the widespread use of genetic use restriction technologies will have considerable negative impact on the diffusion of useful technologies to developing countries. Like restrictive IPRs, these technical restrictions prohibit the cycling back of PGRFA products into research and breeding efforts by others.

The ITPGRFA was negotiated while these trends were developing. The "solution" that the treaty embraces, vis-à-vis PGRFA pooling and collective management, attempts to meet "head on" access and benefit-sharing challenges by carving out policy and legal space for the multilateral system of access and benefit sharing, and, much less directly, by working around intellectual property and technology-based restrictions on the use of PGRFA for downstream research. There has not been enough time for the treaty's multilateral system of access and benefit sharing to establish a track record (Wambugu and Muthamia, 2013), which is why I have not attempted to include an account of its impact on the emerging trends in PGRFA pooling and or its exclusive uses. In section 5 below, I examine the treaty in more detail. Yet before doing so, I will take a step backwards in time and examine how the efforts to secure international legal support for pooling PGRFA "played out" over the 20 years leading up to the adoption of the treaty. In this context, I will examine how these efforts have been affected by contemporaneous international agreements concerning IPRs, and access and benefit sharing. Ultimately, much of what occurred during those 20 years, in the relatively obscure backwater of the FAO's Commission on Plant Genetic Resources, determined the shape and modus operandi of the recently minted multilateral system of the ITPGRFA.

4. EFFORTS TO SECURE INTERNATIONAL LEGAL SUPPORT FOR POOLING PGRFA FROM 1983 TO THE PRESENT: SEA CHANGES IN THE UNDERLYING LEGAL CONCEPTS

The year 1983 is an appropriate starting point for this analysis because it is the year in which the international community created the Commission on Plant Genetic Resources, which provided an intergovernmental forum for the consideration of PGRFA policy issues. It is also the year in which the international community adopted an international legal instrument—the International Undertaking on Plant Genetic Resources—that attempted to provide international legal support for the collective pooling and management of PGRFA.[9]

The objective of the International Undertaking was "to ensure that plant genetic resources . . . particularly for agriculture, will be explored, preserved, evaluated and made available for plant breeding and scientific purposes." The International Undertaking sought to realize this objective by supporting the creation of an "internationally coordinated network of national, regional and international centers . . . under the auspices or the jurisdiction of FAO, that have assumed the responsibility to hold, for the benefit of the international community and on the principle of unrestricted exchange, base or active[10] collections of PGR."[11] This network was supposed to include the international network of base collections coordinated by IBPGR, to replace the loose formality of IBPGR arrangements with legally binding agreements between FAO and participating institutions or preferably governments" (Frankel, 1988: 35). It was anticipated that the number of centers would be "progressively increased so as to achieve as complete a coverage as necessary, in terms of species and geographical distribution."[12] Furthermore, the International Undertaking recognized the central importance of developing a "global information system . . . related to plant genetic resources maintained in the aforementioned collections . . . linked to systems established at the national, subregional and regional levels."[13] The International Undertaking also anticipated the establishment of an international financial mechanism to secure funds to support conservation and sustainable use of PGRFA in developing countries.[14]

These few clauses encapsulated a basic vision that has motivated champions of the global crop commons until the present day. What has changed completely since 1983, however, is the underlying concept of the legal status of PGRFA, and the kind of international agreement that has been considered necessary to support their common pooling and collective management. Interestingly, one of the most divisive, unresolved issues—levels of support for developing countries through the international fund—has persisted, more or less unaffected by the sea-changes in the legal and political status of PGRFA. Unfortunately, this unresolved tension has turned out to be one of the most significant ties that binds the pre- and post-ITPGRFA efforts to secure the global crop commons. In the following subsections, I analyze how efforts within the Commission to secure the global network were affected by combined uncertainties concerning sources and levels of funding for developing countries, benefit sharing from use of PGRFA, intellectual property rights, and national sovereignty.

4.1 Money Problems

At its first meeting in 1985, the Commission noted that some developing countries did not have resources to support conservation programs in line with the International Undertaking. It called on developed countries to make funds available to support those activities, and recommended consideration of the development of an international fund for this purpose. Developed countries expressed "reservations in principle" to establishing such a fund arguing that existing funding mechanisms were adequate. On the other hand, most developing countries argued that they did not have adequate resources to implement their responsibilities under the International Undertaking. Here, in the earliest Commission meeting, we see the nascent expressions of a divisive issue that continues to challenge internationally coordinated efforts to conserve, pool, and share genetic resources under the ITPGRFA. Not suprisingly, almost immediately, discussion of the international fund was linked to discussions of benefit sharing by users. For example, during the Commission's second session some countries raised the possibility of "a levy on the trade in improved seeds" as a means to support the fund (CPGR, 1987). The concept of farmers' rights[15] endorsed by the FAO Council in 1989 (see section 4.2) reflected the idea that it was necessary to support continuation of farmers' contributions to conserving, improving, and making plant genetic resources available, as well as the attainment of the overall purposes of the International Undertaking. While an International Fund on Plant Genetic Resources was eventually established, it has never received substantial contributions, fueling resentment by developing countries who considered themselves to be both the source of most genetic diversity, and the least able to commercially exploit that diversity. In response, a number of developing countries have demonstrated reluctance to move ahead with making more of their genetic resources available. If developed countries stood to gain the most, but were unwilling to make contributions to the fund, why should developing countries sign-away their controls over those resources? Their unease with this situation was aggravated, as is shown below, by developed countries' pressure to advance intellectual property rights.

4.2 Recognizing the Primacy of Plant Variety Protection

The International Undertaking explicitly stated that it was based on "the universally accepted principle that plant genetic resources are a heritage of mankind and consequently should be available without restriction."[16] The principle was not, however, universally accepted. From the very beginning, the principle was under assault because it did not recognize the primacy of IPRs over the principle of unrestricted availability. When it appeared that no more discussion would break the impasses between delegations on the issue, the majority decided to go ahead and adopt the International Undertaking, departing from the FAO tradition of adopting policies by consensus (Esquinas-Alcazar Hilmi & López Noriega, 2013; Kloppenberg, 1988). Eight developed countries registered reservations concerning the impact of the heritage of human kind concept on plant breeders' rights. (Mekouoar, 2002).

Ultimately, however, the existence of the reservations was widely appreciated as less-than-desirable, and by its first meeting, the Commission initiated a long, concerted effort to make accommodations to appease the reluctant countries. The Commission considered three possibilities: doing nothing, revising the text of the International Undertaking, or negotiating a resolution that would address the issue. The Commission opted for the latter approach and charged a working group with the responsibility of addressing this issue prior to the next session. It is interesting to note that by this time the issue seems to have been largely resolved. The report of the second session states that the "Commission recognizes that . . . plant breeders" rights would be a legitimate interest and would not necessarily constitute an impediment to access to protected varieties for the purpose of research and the creation of new varieties and therefore would be consistent with the International Undertaking (CPGR, 1987: para. 20). Those who, despite this interpretation, remained opposed in spirit to the recognition of plant breeders' rights used the opportunity to push for recognition of farmers' rights as part of an overall compromise deal. Ultimately, at its third session in 1989, the Commission agreed to the texts of resolutions recognizing both "Plant Breeders Rights, as provided for under the UPOV" and Farmers' Rights[17] within the International Undertaking framework. Both resolutions were subsequently unanimously adopted by the FAO conference as Resolutions 4/89 and 5/89 respectively. The compromise reached in the Commission in 1985 concerning the relationship of IPRs and commonly pooled plant genetic resources has remained more or less unchallenged to the present day (an issue which I revisit below).

In retrospect, it is interesting to note that, compared to the present time, there were relatively few countries with intellectual property laws extending to plant genetic resources. The UPOV Convention had only 17 members in 1989, and, at that time, there was no effective means by which developed countries could encourage developing countries to join. Such pressure would come later in the form of the Agreement on Trade-Related Aspects of Intellectual Property Rights (TRIPS Agreement), which transformed the relatively rare practice of creating IPR laws to protect plant varieties into a global obligation. In 1989, the Uruguay Round of Multilateral Trade Negotiations had been launched, and intellectual property had been included in the mix of issues to be considered. However, the negotiating mandate with respect to IPRs was still understood to be relatively narrow (Gervais, 1998). While there was considerable resistance to Resolution 4/89 by a number of countries, one can only imagine it would have been much stronger if developing countries could have known in advance just how substantive the outcomes of the Uruguay Round were going to be concerning IPRs. That said, it is worth noting that Resolution 4/89 does not extend its recognition of IPRs to patents. This is significant given the fact that by 1989, in the United States, the landmark case of *Diamond v. Chakrabarty* (1980) and *ex parte Hibberd* (1985) has already established the patentability of living organisms, and seed, plants, and tissue cultures respectively. In Europe, *In re Ciba Geigy* (1983) confirmed the patentability of plant propagating material (though not plant varieties per se). Furthermore, commentators were already sounding warnings that patents posed a much bigger threat to PGRFA-based innovation systems than plant variety protection laws (Barton and Christensen, 1988; Frankel, 1988).

4.3 Recognizing the Primacy of National Sovereignty

Another issue that clearly challenged the International Undertaking's vision of a global system based on the principle of "unrestricted availability" was the simple fact that some countries were not actually making materials available on that basis. For example, considerable publicity was generated by revelations that pursuant to American law, the IBPGR base collections hosted by the National Seed Storage Laboratory in Fort Collins, Colorado would be considered the property of the USA government, and that USA had refused access to recipients in countries with whom it had poor political relations, (Kloppenburg, 1988; Mooney, 1983). The first session of the Commission on Plant Genetic Resources in 1985 noted that while "the present informal, bona fide system in germ plasm exchange generally worked satisfactorily," it "did not provide all legal guarantees many considered necessary to ensure unrestricted exchange of material from base collections" (CPGR 1985, para. 29). As part of its strategy to address this situation, the Commission requested that the Director General of the FAO conduct a study "examining the present legal situation related to ex situ base collections" and to make recommendations on "any provisions necessary to further the objectives of the Undertaking" (CPGR 1985, para. 29). The Director General was also asked to explore governments' and international organizations' willingness to be included in the international network of base collections under the auspices of the FAO, noting that "this would imply that the material in the base collections would be available to all, through relevant active collections, for unrestricted mutual exchange" (CPGR 1985, para. 21). The Commission's Secretariat also commissioned a study concerning the options for legal agreements to include materials within the global network of base collections.

By its second session in 1987, the Commission had noted that, as far as PGRFA in national public organizations was concerned, "ownership and control were vested, to all intents and purposes, in the state" (CPGR, 1987: para. 17).[18] In addition, the Commission "considered that no legal guarantees existed at the international level for free exchange of such resources" (CPGR, 1987: 21). This latter opinion might simply reflect the fact that the International Undertaking was not a legally binding agreement. Or it might be read to betray a deeper acceptance of the fact that international recognition of PGRFA as a heritage of mankind was not, on its own, compelling enough to guide countries to act in the spirit of the International Undertaking. Firmer guidelines would be necessary, working at the level of particular collections, to ensure that those collections were managed in ways that were consistent with the principles set out in the International Undertaking. Consequently, it became increasingly important to move forward with the development of agreements for governments and/or organizations so that they could formally include their collections in the international network of base collections.

The Commission considered four model agreements. It described one option as involving "complete control over the collections being exercised by FAO" (CPGR, 1987: para. 25). Pursuant to this model (model B), the organization or government concerned would transfer "unconditionally to FAO the designated germplasm" and "renounces the right to subject the designated germplasm to national legislation." The FAO would then "determine all policies in respect of activities related to the designated germplasm" (CPGR, 1991: Appendix J). Other model agreements (models C and D) involved looser arrangements, whereby the concerned organization or country would "retain ownership of the resources of the designated germplasm" and would make it "available when necessary for the purpose of scientific research, plant breeding or genetic resource conservation, without restriction, either directly to users or though FAO, either on mutually agreed terms or free of cost" (CPGR, 1991: Appendix J).

Progress developing these model agreements was slow. By the fourth session of the Commission in 1991, most countries had expressed their preference for models whereby they "retained ownership" of the designated genetic resources, rejecting the transfer of "total control" to the FAO. However, none of the models were complete; there was still considerable uncertainty on key issues such as how much latitude signatories had to negotiate the terms of supply. The models stated that signatories would make germ plasm available "without restriction... either on mutually agreed terms or free of cost" (CPGR, 1991: Appendix J). Given ongoing dissatisfaction with the amount of support that was being made available to developing countries through the international fund, either from developed countries or commercial users, developing countries were loathe to surrender the concept of mutually agreed terms. Tensions that were associated with low levels of contribution to the international fund were exacerbated by the way other issues were being resolved (or not) under the Commission. For example, in 1987, it was decided that the Commission should develop a Code of Conduct on Biotechnology as it affected the conservation and use of plant genetic resources. The negotiations of the code highlighted the contrasting potential of developed and developing countries to exploit the commercial benefits associated with the use of plant genetic resources. And in those negotiations as well, developed countries successfully resisted the introduction of mechanisms to redistribute some of the benefits gained from biotechnological exploitation of genetic resources.

Developments in other international fora would have heightened developing countries' concerns still further. By this time, the negotiations of the Uruguay Round with respect to IPRs had broken considerably more ground than many would have expected at the outset, not because developing countries were suddenly more interested in developing intellectual property laws but rather, because they were interested in finding a "trade-off" to obtain concessions in other areas of the negotiations. By 1990, in preparation for the ministerial round that was scheduled to conclude the negotiations, most of the current text of the TRIPS Agreement had been agreed to, with just a few particularly controversial issues left unresolved (for example, compulsory licensing) (Gervais, 1998). Another development that would have added to the intellectual property-related concerns of developing countries was the 1991 revision of the UPOV Convention that strengthened plant breeders' rights. In light of these developments, some Commission members may have been increasingly dissatisfied, retroactively, with the "carve out" for IPRs in Resolution 5/89. Furthermore, the negotiations of the CBD, which had been ongoing since 1987, were drawing to a close at this time, with a heavy emphasis on national sovereign rights to regulate access to genetic resources to protect against unfair exploitation. There was little or no focused discussion during those negotiations of mechanisms to support pooling genetic resources in research and development.

In light of the way things were proceeding, it is not surprising that in 1991 the Commission recommended a resolution for the adoption by the FAO conference recognizing "that nations have sovereign rights over their genetic resources."[19] Like Resolutions 4/89 and 5/89 before it, 3/91 was meant to constitute an interpretation of the International Undertaking. However, it is hard to accept that the wording: "nations have sovereign rights over their genetic resources" *can* be an interpretation of the International Undertaking's "universally acknowledged principle that PGRFA are a heritage of mankind and should be available without restriction." Indeed, it appears that, through the resolution, the former was really intended to displace the latter.[20] Since there was not the political will to renegotiate the International Undertaking, and actually delete any reference to common heritage, the document, read together with Resolution 3/91, ended up looking somewhat schizophrenic, espousing two very different principles at the same time.

The adoption of Resolution 3/91 was not attended by anywhere near the same intensity of debate that preceded Resolutions 4/89 and 5/89. Indeed, the Commission's own record of events does not betray any dissention among the countries concerned. As the developments outlined in this section make clear, by 1991 it had already been clear for quite some time that countries' exercise of national sovereignty with respect to genetic resources was the de fato state of affairs, despite their *de jure* commitment to the principle of the heritage of mankind espoused in the International Undertaking.

4.4 Exercising National Sovereignty to Pool Genetic Resources

Very importantly, the effective end of the "heritage of mankind" principle did not signal an end to the efforts within the Commission to develop legal support for international cooperation to conserve, pool, and share PGRFA. The Commission continued to work on the model agreements to include collections in the international network of base collections. Indeed, in 1991, 32 countries indicated to the Commission that they were willing to sign variants of the model agreements (CPGR, 1991), though ultimately none were signed by countries or national organizations. The Commission continued to work on the model agreements for countries and national organizations until 1997, when it was noted that further work should be postponed until the ongoing negotiations of the ITPGRFA—which started in 1994—were concluded. In 1994, twelve International Agricultural Research Centers of the CGIARs signed variants of these agreements and agreed to hold their *ex situ* PGRFA collections "in trust" for the international community (Halewood, 2010). As international organizations with long histories of making the collections they hosted globally publicly available, the centers were not engaged in the ongoing discussions about asserting national sovereignty or preserving IPR rights over materials in trust for the benefit of the international community, and won't seek IPRs over it. The agreements also stated that the materials in the collections were originally donated to be made globally available.

Ultimately, the ITPGRFA rendered further work on the model agreements for countries and national organizations redundant since it adopted a formula whereby many of the PGRFA collections that would have been subject to model agreements were automatically included in the multilateral system of access and benefit sharing supported by the treaty (see below). The ITPGRFA negotiators did not attempt to revisit the issue of the legal status of PGRFA as it is described in Resolution 3/91—subject to national sovereign rights of control. Instead, like the members of the Commission who continued to work on the model agreements after 1991, the ITPGRFA negotiators constructed their system of internationally pooled genetic resources based on the affirmation of national sovereignty over those resources, and in full recognition of the primacy of IPRs.

Experiences within the Commission and, later, during the negotiations of the ITPGRFA, demonstrate that an international genetic resources commons can be populated with materials of various legal statuses, subject to a range of different legal controls, including genetic resources in the public domain, genetic resources that are considered to belong to everyone and genetic resources which are recognized to be subject to prior, deeper rights of control or ownership vested in individuals, or countries who voluntarily enter into agreements to pool, share, and co-manage those resources. Indeed, the crop commons, as it exists today, includes materials of very different legal status, as defined by a range of norms developed at local, national, regional, and global levels.

Interestingly, despite representing a crucible of the geopolitical and legal tensions concern plant genetic resources at the time, Resolution 3/91 is rarely examined in depth in the literature. This phenomenon can largely be attributed to the fact that it was eclipsed by the CBD, which also emphasized (albeit later) the primacy of national sovereignty. There are several factors contributing to the CBD's higher visibility. The CBD was adopted at the end of a highly publicized process, as part of a package of instruments designed to address environmental issues of widespread public concern. Furthermore, unlike the International Undertaking, the CBD is legally binding and it applies to a much broader range of genetic resources. It is also possible that the CBD has received more attention because it is much more widely associated with actual, significant changes in states' behaviour than Resolution 3/91. The paradigm shift from "PGRFA as heritage of mankind" to "PGRFA as subject to national sovereignty and intellectual property rights" in the context of the Commission's implementation of the International Undertaking did not deter efforts within the Commission to create policy to support the collective pooling, conservation and sharing of genetic resources on an international scale. The parties continued their efforts in this regard, despite the sea-change in the underlying legal status of PGRFA. Indeed, Resolution 3/91 seemed to be no more than a confirmation of the de facto operation of national sovereign control over PGRFA collections. The CBD, on the other hand, has clearly had an impact on the way countries have approached access and benefit sharing. As highlighted in section 3 above, the CBD is widely associated with empowering countries to dramatically tighten controls over foreigners' access to genetic resources within their borders. The CBD has generally not been implemented in ways that are consistent with, or supportive of, the kinds of efforts that were being made within the Commission to pool and share genetic resources. Indeed, a recent study conducted for the Twelfth Session of the Commission on Genetic Resources for Food and Agriculture (previously the Commission on Plant Genetic Resources) notes that, of the 23 national access and benefit-sharing laws, policies, and guidelines examined in the study, none mention food security as one of its objectives and none include special measures related to genetic resources for food and agriculture, other than, in some cases, exempting materials in the ITPGRFA's multiltateral system from the scope of the law in question (Nijar et al., 2009).

The Conference of the Parties to the CBD has not explored or provided any guidance with respect to the possibility of countries exercising their sovereignty to create common pools of genetic resources in support of research or development. The Bonn Guidelines, which were adopted by the CBD's Conference of the Parties in 2002, do not even mention such a possibility, much less encourage countries to investigate the means of supporting such practices with access and benefit-sharing laws (other than mentioning the need to implement the guidelines in harmony with the ITPGRFA).[21]

The Nagoya Protocol[22] on access and benefit sharing, which was adopted by the CBD Conference of the Parties in October 2010 states that,

> Parties shall consider the need for and modalities of a global multilateral benefit-sharing mechanism to address the fair and equitable sharing of benefits derived from the utilization of genetic resources and traditional knowledge associated with genetic resources that occur in transboundary situations or for which it is not possible to grant or obtain prior informed consent.[23]

While this explicit mention of multilateralism may represent a new development in the collective thinking of the Conference of the Parties, it is important to note that the emphasis is entirely on benefit sharing; not on multilaterally constructed access mechanisms (such as that which has been created by the Treaty, and which the CPGR tried to formalize from 1985 onwards). It appears that the Conference of the Parties of the CBD is still not actively interested in considering the development of systems through which countries (and their constituents) could give advance informed consent to provide access through multilaterally constructed systems of pooling and use of genetic resources.[24] That said, the parties are still in the very early stages of exploring what can be done under article 10 of the Protocol, perhaps they will consider such options in the future.

The very different approaches by countries to the exercise of their national sovereignty vis-à-vis genetic resources in these two different United Nations' sponsored processes attest to the depth of the cultural and institutional divide between environmentalists and national environment ministries (who lead national delegations at the CBD), on one hand, and farmers and ministries of agriculture (who lead delegations at the Commission on Genetic Resources for Food and Agriculture[25] (CGRFA)), on the other.

The adoption of the CBD text in 1992 did, however, provide an opportunity for some creative "crossover" between the two bodies. The Nairobi Final Act, which was the instrument used to adopt the text of the CBD in 1992, included a few ancillary resolutions. Resolution 3, entitled "The Interrelationship between the Convention on Biological Diversity and the Promotion of Sustainable Agriculture" states that contracting parties need to "seek solutions to outstanding matters concerning plant genetic resources within the Global System, in particular access to *ex situ* collections not acquired in accordance with the CBD, and farmers' rights."[26] In 1993 the FAO conference seized on the opportunity presented by the resolution and requested the FAO enable the CGRFA to host intergovernmental negotiations to revise the International Undertaking in harmony with the CBD and to consider the issues of farmers' rights and access to plant genetic resources, including *ex situ* collections that are not addressed by the CBD. This new mandate provided a boost to the efforts of Commission members working on the model agreements. Indeed, it provided them with the opportunity to "leapfrog" over that process and create a new, legally binding international agreement that would automatically include many of the collections for which they were developing model agreements. Seven years later—much longer than anyone imagined it would take—the FAO conference adopted the text of the ITPGRFA.

As the next section will highlight, the ITPGRFA represents an enormous breakthrough by providing a sound legal basis for internationally coordinated efforts to conserve, pool and share PGRFA, at least as far as the world's most widely used crops are concerned. In doing so, the ITPGRFA has, on the one hand, successfully "lowered the tone" of debates related to the legal status of PGRFA collections and access and benefit-sharing terms. On the other hand, some of the debates that characterized the pre-ITPGRFA period persist in this new setting with some of the same potential to frustrate progress under the ITPGRFA.

5. THE ITPGRFA AND SUPPORTIVE COMPONENTS

The ITPGRFA was adopted by the FAO conference in 2001. It came into force in 2004. As of January 2010, 123 state parties (including the European Community) had ratified or acceded to it. Most importantly, for the purposes of this chapter, the treaty creates the "multilateral system of access and benefit-sharing."[27] The multilateral system is a virtual, international pool of PGRFA of 35 crops and 29 forage species as well as related information. The criteria for selecting these crops and forages were that countries must be interdependent upon them, and they must be important for food security. The content of the list was highly contentious, and its scope fluctuated dramatically over the course of the negotiations, from including all PGRFA to including just a handful of species (Lim and Halewood, 2008). Countries and regions made last-minute deals agreeing to leave crops on the list and engaged in retaliations if countries took crops off that others wanted on (Lim and Halewood, 2008). Ultimately, most of the world's most-used food crops are included in the list. Among the species and genera notably absent are: soybean, tomato, okra, fonio (a millet), a range of tropical forages, and most industrial crops such as coffee, oil palm, and *Hevea brasiliensis* (rubber trees). A wide range of lesser known, locally used crops were also not included on the list.

The pooled materials in the multilateral system are to be made available for "utilization and conservation for research, breeding and training for food and agriculture."[28] Natural and legal persons in contracting parties have access to the pool, either free of charge or for minimal administrative fees.[29]

The multilateral system includes PGRFA from three principle sources.[30] The first source is PGRFA that are "under the management and control of Contracting Parties and in the public domain."[31] This material is automatically included in the multilateral system upon ratification of the treaty by the country concerned. It is currently difficult to say how much material from the contracting parties has been automatically included in the system by this means. Comparatively few countries are able to provide exhaustive accession-level information about their *ex situ* collections. Even fewer—perhaps none—are able to account for all of the diversity of Annex 1 materials that they may have in in situ conditions. In addition, it appears that some countries are having difficulty interpreting "under management and control" and "in the public domain" within their own national contexts. As of the date this chapter was written, only 23 of the 127 member states have sent such notifications to the ITPGRFA secretariat confirming what materials within their countries are in the multilateral system, to publish on their behalf on the treaty website. However, it is reasonable to expect that more notifications will be made soon.

The second source of PGRFA is from individuals and corporate entities. The ITPGRFA anticipates that natural and legal persons will voluntarily place materials in the multilateral system. Few such contributions have been reported to the ITPGRFA's governing body. The treaty has a built-in mechanism to address this situation—namely, the governing body may decide to discontinue the access of natural and legal persons to the multilateral system if they do not include voluntary materials in it.[32]

The third source is international organizations that sign agreements with the governing body of the treaty and thereby voluntarily place their collections within the treaty's framework. These collections make up the vast majority of the identified material in the multilateral system. The eleven CGIAR centers holding PGRFA collections signed such agreements in 2006, placing 650,000 accessions in the multilateral system. Four other additional international organizations have signed such agreements,[33] and it seems likely that others will move towards similar agreements in the future.

All transfers of material in the multilateral system are made using the single, unalterable, standard material transfer agreement (SMTA), which was adopted by the governing body in 2006 (GB/ITPGRFA, 2006: Appendix G).[34] Recipients of materials under the SMTA may pass them on, but they must do so under the SMTA. The SMTA states that recipients "shall not claim any intellectual property or other rights that limit the facilitated access to the Material provided under this Agreement, or its genetic parts or components, in the form received from the Multilateral System" (GB/ITPGRFA, 2006: Article 6.2). It is unclear if the clause permits recipients to patent, for example, genes that it isolates from the material received. The clause is purposefully vague. It was not possible for countries to agree on this issue during the negotiations of the treaty. Later, during the negotiations of the SMTA, the issue proved to be equally divisive, so the treaty's vague language was incorporated into the SMTA, thereby postponing resolution of the issue to another time, perhaps through international arbitration, if a dispute concerning the clause ever arises (Halewood and Nnadozie, 2008).

Importantly, the SMTA anticipates that recipients may eventually want to commercialize and/or seek IPRs over new products that incorporate materials from the multilateral system. When the new products are subject to either technical or legal restrictions that make them unavailable for research and breeding, the recipient/commercializer is required to pay 1.1 per cent of the gross sales of that product (minus 30 per cent of the 1.1 per cent) to the international benefit-sharing fund created by the ITPGRFA. If, instead, the commercializing party takes out a form of IPRs that allows downstream users to use the new product for research and breeding without restriction, they are only encouraged to make a voluntary payment. This recognition of the importance of access to PGRFA (including new products that are themselves PGRFA) reflects the patterns of use and sharing of PGRFA in agricultural innovation over millennia. It also echoes the resolution of the struggle between "heritage of mankind" and plant variety protection rights in Resolution 4/87.

Recipients may select an alternative financial benefit-sharing option, whereby they agree to pay 0.5 per cent of the gross sales, over a ten-year period, of *all* of the products belonging to the same crop as the material accessed from the multilateral system. The payment would be made even if the products were made available for breeding and regardless of whether they incorporated the material received. Given that this option does not turn on establishing incorporation, or tracing whether a recipient seeks IPRs, it would involve lower transaction costs for the operation of the system overall. However, to date, recipients are not selecting this option. Given that it applies to a much wider range of products than the default benefit-sharing clause, it probably should have required a comparatively lower level of payment, such as between 0.1 and 0.3 per cent.

This second benefit-sharing option is reminiscent of another approach to benefit sharing that was considered in the early period of the treaty negotiations. Under this approach, the multilateral system would have been implemented by countries adopting legislation that would have required, among other things, commercial companies to pay percentages of overall sales to the international fund (as was considered as early as 1987 in the Commission). It was only after negotiations got under way that some developed countries, with support from the seed industry, successfully promoted the multilateral system's private contractual modus operandi—namely, tying benefit sharing to the actual incorporation of material from the multilateral system in particular products and in the sales of those products. During the negotiations of the SMTA, developed countries and the seed industry pushed for a further extension of this approach, arguing that benefit sharing should not be triggered unless material received from the multilateral system constitutes at least 25 per cent of the new product by pedigree. Inclusion of any level of incorporation (as opposed to a minimum percentage) in the benefit-sharing formula was considered to be a major compromise by industry groups, and they continue to militate against it to the present day (International Seed Federation, 2007). Some companies have indicated that they will only take materials from the multilateral system if they cannot find other sources (SGRP, 2007).

Financial benefits raised through the operation of these clauses are not channeled back to the countries or persons who first provided the material to the multilateral system. Instead, such benefits go back to the multilateral system itself, to an international benefit-sharing fund established by the treaty. These funds are distributed, pursuant to the rules and priorities determined by the governing body, to support conservation and use-related activities, primarily in developing countries. In light of the fact that multilateral system providers are not direct recipients of financial benefits, presumably they will have less incentive to ensure that recipients comply with the benefit-sharing conditions. To address this possibility, the SMTA (not the ITPGRFA) includes provisions that allow a representative of the third-party beneficiary interests of the multilateral system to initiate legal actions against recipients who do not comply with the SMTA. The FAO has been invited to act as this representative.

Since it takes several years to breed, certify, and market new plant varieties, no funds based on gross sales—pursuant to either of the mandatory monetary benefit-sharing schema—have been directed to the international fund. However, in the meantime, some governments have made direct contributions to the fund. Demands for considerably more financial support from developing countries, and developed countries' refusal to provide it, has created tension since the first meeting of the governing body in 2006. The spokesperson for one developing region stated at the second meeting of the governing body in 2007 that developing countries would be reluctant to move forward with the implementation of the multilateral system as long as there were inadequate funds for activities in developing countries. Following the same logic, developing countries within the governing body have been unwilling to complete negotiations for treaty compliance rules (including the means to address countries that were not, in practice, providing access to materials that are in the multilateral system) until agreement was reached on the funding strategy. The third meeting of the governing body in June 2009 finally agreed to a funding strategy target of $116 million to support activities over the course of five years (GB/ITPGRFA 2009). It is not clear where the funds will come from or how developing countries will react if the target is not reached. The Fourth Session in March 2011 finally agreed to rules for compliance. One organization that is making considerable contributions to meeting the costs of the multilateral system is the Global Crop Diversity Trust. This trust was established with support from the CGIAR centers and the FAO, with the objective of developing a multimillion-dollar endowment fund to provide support, in perpetuity, for gene banks conserving important PGRFA. The trust has signed a "relationship agreement" with the governing body of the ITPGRFA, which recognizes the trust as an "essential element of the Funding Strategy of the International Treaty in relation to ex situ conservation and availability of PGRFA."[35] The GCDT is projected to raise hundreds of millions of dollars for an endowment fund, from which it has already provided grants to support the long-term conservation of 18 crop collections. It also provides support for the operations of the Svalbard Global Seed Vault, which provides back-up safety duplication for materials from all over the world (GCDT, 2011). It has also entered into contracts with over 86 institutes in 72 countries, to support the regeneration of approximately 90,000 accessions of unique, "at risk" materials (GCDT, 2011). Duplicates of these materials will be saved in long-term storage facilities and will be made available using the SMTA. While the countries concerned are partly motivated by financial support from the trust, and partly motivated by their own interest in conserving and sharing the "at risk" germ plasm, they probably would not have agreed to making those materials available in the absence of the legal certainty (and benefit-sharing provisions) of the multilateral system and the SMTA. (This program is largely responsible for the reversal in the declining trend of acquisitions of PGRFA by the CGIAR centers' genebanks from 2010–12, mentioned above. Now that the program is finished, it will be interesting to monitor future trends.) Despite its early successes, the GCDT, with its focus on *ex situ* conservation, is not in a position to ease tensions associated with the demands from developing countries for support for in situ conservation and the sustainable use of PGRFA in local agro-ecosystems.

Like the International Undertaking before it, the ITPGRFA calls for a global information system that will allow users to know what materials are available, from where, and to get access to important information about those materials to facilitate their utilization, such as passport data (from where it was collected originally, when, and under what agro-ecological conditions) and non-confidential evaluation and characterization data. Getting less well-developed gene banks to adopt computerized data management systems and integrating the plethora of different information systems that have developed around the world is an enormous undertaking. Yet there are ongoing efforts to develop such an integrated system, and it might be possible to have the governing body of the treaty eventually adopt such a system. In 2010 a prototype umbrella portal of this nature called Genesys was developed by Bioversity International (one of the CGIAR Centers) in collaboration with the Global Crop Diversity Trust and the ITPGRFA Secretariat. As of January 2011, Genesys includes the CGIAR's system-wide accession level information system (SINGER), the European Plant Genetic Resources Search Catalogues (EURISCO) accession level information system, and the system currently used by the United States' Department of Agriculture. So far, Genesys includes information on about approximately 2.3 million accessions of PGRFA and nearly 5 million records of characterization and evaluation data.[36] A number of countries are "pilot testing" the information system with the view to providing information about the material that they are making available through the multilateral system. (Arnaud et al., 2009). It is not yet clear if the global information system will evolve into a highly centralized system, or a loosely federated network of information systems.

The treaty did not come into force until 2004, and the SMTA—without which the multilateral system certainly could not operate—was not adopted until 2006. Rules for the operation of the third party beneficiary and a treaty funding strategy were not adopted until mid 2009. One could argue that in the absence of these components, the international architecture for the operation of the multilateral system was not in place. From this point onwards, however, it is reasonable to expect that the multilateral system should start to serve the function for which it was designed. Certainly, some of the early signs have been positive. In their first three years operating under the treaty, the CGIAR centers have distributed over a million samples of PGRFA under the SMTA (SGRP, 2011). With support from the GCDT, countries are agreeing to regenerate and make available, through the multilateral system, a significant range of PGRFA that would be otherwise at risk of being lost. After the treaty came into force, the IRRI gene bank received confirmation from 20 countries that they could make approximately 20,000 accessions available, under the SMTA, which IRRI had previously agreed to hold on a restricted basis (Halewood et al. 2013). Despite these positive signs, it remains to be seen how far countries will go as participants in the multilateral system. For example, will they initiate or permit the organization of new collecting missions within their borders and make new materials available to the CGIAR centers for global distribution on the same scale as before the mid 1990s? Or will they step into the role of global suppliers themselves? Either way, the most important early test of the health of the multilateral system in the next few years will be if increased quantities of PGRFA are available and transferred through the multilateral system.

The ITPGRFA's multilateral system of access and benefit sharing stands in contrast to the way many countries are approaching the regulation of access and benefit sharing under the CBD. Countries that ratify the ITPGRFA will need to consider whether their access and benefit-sharing policies to implement the CBD leave "legal space" to implement the multilateral system. If not, those laws will need to be repealed or revised. The ITPGRFA's relationship to intellectual property law is more accommodating. It does not offer an alternative intellectual property protection system. Instead, the ITPGRFA picks its way among intellectual property law developments, tacitly favoring laws that permit use of PGRFA for breeding and "punishing" those that use IPRs to restrict the use of new PGRFA inventions for breeding. On the one hand, accommodating IPRs in this way was clearly a *sine qua non* for the conclusion of decades of effort to develop an international agreement in support of

PGRFA pooling. On the other hand, this accommodation continues to fuel resentment, particularly on the part of some developing countries. Developed and developing countries (with the growing exception of the "BRICS") are unequal in their technical capacities to generate inventions that can be patented. Naturally then, developing countries will place greater importance on the operation of the benefit-sharing provisions of the SMTA, especially given that they are triggered in part by highly restrictive IPRs. Thus, another test for the operation of the multilateral system will be if it generates financial benefits that can be channeled through international benefit sharing. If not, it is clear that funds from other sources will be required as part of a package that will be acceptable to developing countries.

Of course, it possible to imagine reforms to the multilateral system that would significantly lower transaction costs, give rise to more funds for the international benefit-sharing fund, and erase reservations that companies might have about receiving materials from the multilateral system. For example, one could return to a version of the option raised in the Commission in 1987, where benefit sharing was not tied to sales of products that actually incorporate material from the multilateral system; where it was not necessary to keep records of actual use, and it was irrelevant whether or not they were available for further research. Financial benefit sharing would take the form of a royalty on gross sales of all PGRFA (by all PGRFA sellers).[37] Such a system could be implemented by national governments through executive or legislative enactments,[38] doing away with the need to encapsulate all benefit-sharing conditions in material transfer agreements between providers and recipients (and the subsequent need to keep track of them all). Of course, it is relatively easy to imagine such a system. Obtaining international support for such reforms, however, is another matter. It took a long time to negotiate the treaty, and then the SMTA, and all sides had to make compromises for the process to be able to draw to a close. It is reasonable to be careful about making recommendations to recommence negotiations.

6. CONCLUSIONS

Internationally pooled PGRFA plays an extremely important role in agricultural research, and in plant breeding in particular. Their direct and spillover benefits to all countries have been enormous. Nonetheless, efforts to develop norms at international levels in support of PGRFA pooling and collective management have met with numerous challenges. By the mid to late 1990s, the international community appeared to reach the nadir of distrust and uncertainty with respect to how PGRFA should be regulated and managed.

Over the course of efforts to establish a firm legal basis for conserving, pooling, and sharing PGRFA, the international community has shifted from conceiving of those resources as part of the public domain, to heritage of mankind, to recognizing them as subject to national sovereignty and intellectual property rights. In retrospect, the apparent advantage of these shifts is that they provided counties and many of their constituents with the confidence to finally endorse an international legal agreement—the ITPGRFA—that supports the conservation and virtual collective pooling of PGRFA for agricultural research and plant breeding.

The ITPGRFA represents an extremely important breakthrough. Nonetheless, it is clear that some would-be participants in the multilateral system are still being "held back" by dissatisfaction about the quantum of financial benefits that are being generated to support their participation in fulfilling other Treaty objectives. These tensions are not new; they have existed in various forms since the earliest sessions of the Commission on Plant Genetic Resources and have animated many or all of its meetings, and those of the governing body of the ITPGRFA ever since. The multilateral system has only recently been enabled to start functioning, and it will take time to gather evidence about whether it has finally struck a sufficiently balanced treatment of the relevant actors' interests to provide a sound, long-term foundation for collective pooling and management of PGRFA on an international scale. While the ITPGRFA clearly represents an enormous step in that direction, there are also signs that the international community will likely need to periodically revise aspects of the multilateral system including the standard material transfer agreement to address outstanding concerns and new issues that could arise in the future as a result of technological, political, and economic developments.

NOTES

1. International Treaty on Plant Genetic Resources for Food and Agriculture, 3 November 2001, <http://sedac.ciesin.org/pidb/texts-menu.html> (accessed 1 February 2010) [ITPGRFA].
2. Convention on Biological Diversity, 5 June 1992, 31 I.L.M. 818 (1992).
3. *International Convention for the Protection of Plant Varieties*, 23 October 1978, (revised 10 November 1972, 23 October 1978, and entered into force 8 November 1981) U.K.T.S. 11 (1984), <http://www.upov.int/upovlex/en/conventions/1991/act1991.html> (accessed 1 February 2014).
4. Interestingly, developing countries are generally not fully exploiting the flexibility in the WTO Agreement on Trade-Related Aspects of Intellectual Property Rights to implement these sorts of research exemptions. See WTO Agreement on Trade-Related Aspects of Intellectual Property Rights, 15 April 1994, Annex 1C of the Marrakech Agreement Establishing the World Trade Organization, 15 April 1994, 33 I.L.M. 15.

5. University and Small Business Patent Procedures Act, 35 U.S.C. para. 200–12.
6. The most recent, potentially troubling trend has been the granting of patents over conventionally bred varieties that have relied on biotechnologically assisted methods, such as marker-assisted breeding, but that have not included biotech-assisted genetic transformation per se (Then and Tippe, 2009; Correa, 2009).
7. It is important to note that universities, public sector and not profit organizations may be more carefully scrutinized that their counterparts in biomedical research (Clift, 2007). Wright and Pardey (2006) note that "the effects on research of lack of access to needed technology have been more serious on average for biotechnologists working on agriculture than for those focused on human health. This might reflect the smaller set of promising technologies in agriculture and the lower level of resources available to help scientists surmount or invent around roadblocks."
8. Michael Spence (2008, 161) writes that "[t]he notion of a royalty clearinghouse for biotech patents is beguilingly simple."
9. International Undertaking on Plant Genetic Resources, 1983, <ftp://ftp.fao.org/ag/cgrfa/iu/iutexte.pdf> (accessed 1 February 2010) [International Undertaking].
10. The International Undertaking defines "base collection of plant genetic resources" as a collection of seed stock or vegetative propagating material (ranging from tissue cultures to whole plants) held for long-term security in order to preserve the genetic variation for scientific purposes and as a basis for plant breeding. It defines "active collection" as "a collection which complements a base collection, and is a collection from which seed samples are drawn for distribution, exchange and other purposes such as multiplication and evaluation." (Article 2)
11. International Undertaking, *supra* note 8, Article 7a.
12. International Undertaking, *supra* note 8, Article 7b.
13. International Undertaking, *supra* note 8, Article 7e.
14. International Undertaking, *supra* note 8, Article 8.
15. Resolution 5/89 defines Farmers Rights as: "rights arising from the past, present and future contributions of farmers in conserving, improving, and making available plant genetic resources, particularly those in the centres of origin/diversity. These rights are vested in the International Community, as trustee for present and future generations of farmers, for the purpose of ensuring full benefits to farmers, and supporting the continuation of their contributions, as well as the attainment of the overall purposes of the International Undertaking in order to:

   (a) ensure that the need for conservation is globally recognized and that sufficient funds for these purposes will be available;

   (b) assist farmers and farming communities, in all regions of the world, but especially in the areas of origin/diversity of plant genetic resources, in the protection and conservation of their plant genetic resources, and of the natural biosphere;

   (c) allow farmers, their communities, and countries in all regions, to participate fully in the benefits derived, at present and in the future, from the improved use of plant genetic resources, through plant breeding and other scientific methods."

16. International Undertaking, *supra* note 9, Article 1.
17. See note 15 and accompanying text.

18. Commentators were drawing similar conclusions in the literature at the time. For example, Jack Harlan wrote in 1988 that "Sovereign nations are *de facto* owners of national germplasm collections and can do with them what they please" (Harlan, 1988: 361).

19. International Undertaking, *supra* note 8, Resolution 3/91.

20. The same argument could be made about Resolution 4/89 and even Resolution 5/89. However, their incursions into the principles of the "heritage of human kind" and the imperative of making PGRFA available without restriction were less complete. Intellectual property rights (IPRs) can only subject a fraction of PGRFA to private ownership. National sovereignty, arguably, subjects all PGRFA to public control. Furthermore, as the Commission was at pains to point out, UPOV-style plant variety protection laws do not restrict access for research and breeding. Of course, they do create restrictions on availability-protected materials for direct use in cultivation, but then the International Undertaking only mentions availability for plant breeding and scientific research as its objective.

21. The Bonn Guidelines on Access to Genetic Resources and Fair and Equitable Sharing of Benefits Arising out of their Utilization, part of COP-VI/Decision 6/24, available at <http://www.cbd.int/decision/cop/?id=7198> (accessed 10 September 2013).

22. Nagoya Protocol on Access to Genetic Resources and the Fair and Equitable Sharing of Benefits Arising from their Utilization (ABS) to the Convention on Biological Diversity, available at <http://www.cbd.int/abs/text/> (accessed 10 September 2013).

23. Nagoya Protocol, Article 10.

24. On the other hand, Article 4.2 states that: "Nothing in this Protocol shall prevent the Parties from developing and implementing other relevant international agreements, including other specialized access and benefit-sharing agreements, provided that they are supportive of and do not run counter to the objectives of the Convention and this Protocol." While the article does not explicitly mention specialized agreements that are multilateral in nature, at least it provides room for introduction of such considerations in the future. Certainly it was with multilaterally-inspired international agreements in mind that the Systemwide Genetic Resources Programme of the CGIAR circulated a policy brief highlighting the importance of maintaining flexibility for future development of specialized access and benefit agreements (SGRP, 2010).

25. The Commission on Plant Genetic Resources (CPGR) was renamed the Commission on Genetic Resources on Food and Agriculture (CGRFA) in 1995 to reflect a broader mandate.

26. Nairobi Final Act of the Conference for the Adoption of the Agreed Text of the Convention on Biological Diversity, 1992 (UNEP 2007).

27. ITPGRFA, *supra* note 1 at Part 4.

28. The ITPGRFA, *supra* note 1, Article 12.3.a, and the Standard Material Transfer Agreement (SMTA) (GB/ITPGRFA 2006, Appendix G, Article 6.1), also explicitly state that the materials cannot be used for "chemical, pharmaceutical and/or other non-food/feed industrial uses."

29. Nothing in the ITPGRFA actually prevents contracting parties from providing access to materials in the multilateral system, under SMTA, to non-contracting parties (and to natural and legal persons within them). The same is true for

international organizations placing their materials under the framework of the treaty. To this end, after signing agreements with the ITPGRFA governing body, the CGIAR centers stated that they would continue to make materials available to recipients in non-contracting parties. It has been noted that providing PGRFA material to non-parties in this way may undermine some of their incentive for ratifying the ITPGRFA (Altoveros et al 2013.).

30. Another source is PGRFA resulting from projects funded by the International Benefit-Sharing Fund. The funding strategy adopted by the governing body states that such materials shall also be available according to the terms and conditions of the multilateral system along with related information (GB/ITPGRFA 2009).

31. ITPGRFA, *supra* note 1, Article 11.2.

32. ITPGRFA, *supra* note 1, Article 11.4.

33. The full texts of all of the Article 15 agreements signed by international organizations and the governing body are available on the website maintained by the treaty secretariat at <http://www.planttreaty.org/inclusions> (accessed 17 October 2013). While the non-Annex 1 materials held by Article 15 organizations are under the treaty's framework, they are not formally part of the multilateral system as it is restricted to Annex 1 crops and forages. However, at its second session in 2007, the governing body decided that the centers should also distribute non-Annex 1 materials under the same legal terms as Annex 1 materials—that is, using the SMTA (GB/ITPGRFA, 2007).

34. It took years to negotiate the SMTA because the ITPGRFA left a few difficult issues to be resolved as part of the SMTA negotiations. For example, the treaty's Article 13.2.d.ii left it to the first meeting of the governing body to "determine the level, form and manner of the payment" of mandatory financial benefit sharing.

35. Relationship Agreement between the Global Crop Diversity Trust and the Governing Body of the International Treaty on PGRFA, available at <http://www.croptrust.org/documents/Signed%20Relationship%20Agreement.pdf> (accessed 11 September 2013).

36. Genesys can be viewed at <http://www.genesys-pgr.org> (accessed 11 September 2013).

37. It would also be possible to discriminate between patent and PBR holders (in keeping with Resolution 4/89 and the ITPGRFA) at aggregate levels, with a royalty rates corresponding to the proportion of products a company or public institution subjects to more or less restrictive forms of intellectual property or technical restrictions.

38. Norway has recently passed a national regulation whereby the government undertakes to contribute 0.1 per cent of national seed sales to the treaty's International Benefit-Sharing Fund.

REFERENCES

Nestor, C. et al. 2013. In I. López Noriega, M. Halewood, and I. Lapena, eds, *The Multilateral System of Access and Benefit-Sharing: Case Studies on Implementation in Kenya, Morocco, Philippines and Peru*. Rome: Bioversity International.

Andrews, J. 1993. "Diffusion of the Mesoamerican Food Complex to Southeastern Europe." *Geographical Review* 83: 194–204.

Atkinson, R. et al. 2003. "Public Sector Collaborations for Agricultural Intellectual Property Management." *Science* 301: 174

Arnaud, E. et al. 2009. "A Global Portal Enabling Worldwide Access to Information on Conservation and Use of Biodiversity for Food and Agriculture." In L. Maurer and K. Tochtermann, eds, *Information and Communication Technologies for Biodiversity Conservation and Agriculture*. Aachen, Germany: Shaker Verlag.

Barton. J. and E. Christensen. 1988. "Diversity Compensation Systems: Ways to Compensate Developing Nations for Providing Genetic Materials." In J. Kloppenburg, ed, *Seeds and Sovereignty: The Use and Control of Plant Genetic Resources*. Durham and London: Duke University Press.

Clift, C. 2007. "Patenting and Licensing Research Tools." In A. Krattiger et al., eds, *Intellectual Property Management in Health and Agricultural Innovation: A Handbook of Best Practices*. Oxford: MIHR; Davis, CA: PIPRA; Rio de Janeiro: Oswaldo Cruz Foundation; and Ithaca, NY: bioDevelopments-International Institute.

CPGR. 1985. *Report of the First Session of the Commission on Plant Genetic Resources*. Rome, 11–15 March 1985, Doc. CPGR/85/REP.

——1987. *Report of the Second Session of the Commission on Plant Genetic Resources*. Rome, 16–20 March 1987, Doc. CPGR/87/REP.

——1989. *Report of the Third Session of the Commission on Plant Genetic Resources*. Rome, 17–21 April 1989, Doc. CPGR/89/REP.

——1991. *Report of the Fourth Session of the Commission on Plant Genetic Resources to the Ninety-Ninth Session of the UNFAO Council*. Rome, 10–21 June 1991, Doc. CL 99/16.

CGIAR. 2009. *Research and Impact: Areas of Research*, available at <http://www.cgiar.org/impact/research/index.html> (accessed 11 September 2013).

Correa, C. 2005. "Do National Access Regimes Promote Use of Genetic Resources and Benefit Sharing?" *International Journal of Environment and Sustainable Development* 4 (4): 444–463.

——2009. *Trends in Intelletual Property Rights Relating to Genetic Resources for Food and Agriculture*. Background Study no. 49. Commission on Genetic Resources for Food and Agriculture. Rome: United Nations Food and Agriculture Organization.

Crosby. A. 1972. *The Columbian Exchange: Biological and Cultural Consquences of 1492*. Westport, CT: Greenwood Publishing.

—— 1986. *Ecological Imperialism: The Biological Expansion of Europe, 900–1900*. Cambridge: Cambridge University Press.

Diamond, J. 1997. *Guns, Germs and Steel: The Fate of Human Societies*. New York: Norton.

Engels, J. and I. Thormann. 2005. IBPGR/IPGRI Register of Base Collections. Unpublished.

Evenson. R. 2003. "Modern Variety Production: A Synthesis." In Evenson and Gollin, eds, (2003).

——2005. "Agricultural Research and Intellectual Property Rights." In K. Maskus and J. Reichman, eds, *International Public Goods and Transfer of Technology under a Globalized Intellectual Property Regime*. Cambridge: Cambridge University Press.

——and D. Gollin (eds). 2003. *Crop Variety Improvement and Its Effect on Productivity: The Impact of International Agricultural Research.* London: CAB International.

——and M. Rosegrant. 2003. "The Economic Consequences of Crop Genetic Improvement Programmes." In Evenson and Gollin, eds, (2003).

Esquinas-Alcazar, J., A. Hilmi, and I. Lopez-Noriega. 2013. "A Brief History of the Negotiations of the International Treaty on Plant Genetic Resources for Food and Agriculture." In M. Halewood, I. Lopez Noriega, and S. Louafi, eds, *Crop Genetic Resources as a Global Commons: Challenges in International Governance and Law.* Oxford: Routledge.

Fowler, C. 2002. "Sharing Agriculture's Genetic Bounty." *Science* 297 (5579): 157.

—— and T. Hodgkin. 2004. "Plant Genetic Resources for Food and Agriculture: Assessing Global Availability." *Annual Review of Environmental Resources* 29: 143–179.

Fujisaka, S., D. Williams, and M. Halewood. 2009. "The Impact of Climate Change on Countries' Interdependence on Genetic Resources for Food and Agriculture." Background Paper no. 48. Available at <ftp://ftp.fao.org/docrep/fao/meeting/017/ak532e.pdf> (accessed 11 September 2013).

Fuller, D. et al. 2009. "The Domestication Process and Domestication Rate in Rice: Spikelet Bases from the Lower Yangtze." *Science* 323 (5921): 1607–10. DOI: 10.1126/science.1166605.

Frankel, O. 1988. "Genetic Resources: Evolutionary and Social Responsibilities." In J. Kloppenburg, ed., *Seeds and Sovereignty: The Use and Control of Plant Genetic Resources.* Durham and London: Duke University Press.

Gaiji, Samy. 2005. Coordinator of the System-wide Information Network on Genetic Resources, personal communication, 15 January 2009.

GCDT. 2011. "Report of the Executive Board of the Global Crop Diversity Trust to the Governing Body of the International Treaty on Plant Genetic Resources for Food and Agriculture." Appendix 1 to Report from the Global Crop Diversity Trust, Fourth Session of the Governing Body, Bali, Indonesia, 14–18, 2001, IT/GB-4/11/20. Available at <http://www.itpgrfa.net/International/sites/default/files/gb4w20e.pdf> (accessed 11 September 2013).

Gervais. D. 1998. *The TRIPS Agreement: Drafting History and Analysis.* London: Sweet and Maxwell.

Gollin, D. 1998. "Valuing Farmers' Rights." In R.E. Evenson, D. Gollin, and V. Santaniello, eds, *Agricultural Values of Plant Genetic Resources.* London: CAB International.

——and R.E. Evenson. 1998. "Breeding Values of Rice Genetic Resources." In Evenson and Gollin, eds, (2003).

GB/ITPGRFA. 2006. *First Session of the Governing Body of the International Treaty on Plant Genetic Resources for Food and Agriculture.* Madrid, Spain, 12–16 June 2006, Doc. IT/GB-1/06/Report. Available at <ftp://ftp.fao.org/ag/cgrfa/gb1/gb1repe.pdf> (accessed 1 February 2010).

——2007. *Second Session of the Governing Body of the International Treaty on Plant Genetic Resources for Food and Agriculture.* Rome, Italy, 29 October–2 November 2007, Doc. IT/GB-2/07/Report. Available at <ftp://ftp.fao.org/ag/agp/planttreaty/gb2/gb2repe.pdf> (accessed 11 September 2013).

———2009. *Third Session of the Governing Body of the International Treaty on Plant Genetic Resources for Food and Agriculture.* Tunis, Tunisia, 1–5 June 2009, Doc. IT/GB-3/09/Report. Available at <ftp://ftp.fao.org/ag/agp/planttreaty/gb3/gb3repe.pdf> (accessed 11 September 2013).

Graff, D., S. Cullen, K. Bradford, D. Zilberman, and A. Bennett. 2003. "The Public-Private Structure of Intellectual Property Ownership in Agricultural Biotechnology." *Nature Biotechnology* 21 (9): 989–995.

Halewood, M. 2010. "Governing the Management and Use of Pooled Microbial Genetic Resources: Lessons from the Global Crop Commons." *International Journal of the Commons* 4 (1): 404–36. Available at: <http://www.thecommonsjournal.org/index.php/ijc/article/view/152/114> (accessed 11 September 2013).

———and K. Nnadozie. 2008. "Giving Priority to the Commons: The International Treaty on Plant Genetic Resources for Food and Agriculture." In G. Tansey and T. Rajotte, eds., *The Future Control of Food: A Guide to International Negotiations and Rules on Intellectual Property, Biodiversity and Food Security.* Cambridge, Ottawa, and Geneva: Earthscan, International Development Research Center, and Quaker International Affairs Programme.

———et al. 2013. "Changing Rates of Acquisition of Plant Genetic Resources by International Genebanks: Setting the Scene to Monitor an Impact of the International Treaty." In M. Halewood, I. López Noriega, and S. Louafi, eds, *Crop Genetic Resources as a Global Commons: Challenges in International Law and Governance.* London: Routledge.

Heisey, P.W., M.A. Lantican, and H.J. Dubin, 2003. "Wheat." In Evenson and Gollin, eds, (2003).

Harlan. J. 1992. *Crops and Man*, 2nd edition. Madison, WI: American Society of Agronomy.

———1988. "A Critical Review." In J. Kloppenburg, ed., *Seeds and Sovereignty: The Use and Control of Plant Genetic Resources.* Durham and London: Duke University Press.

International Seed Federation. 2007. *ISF Position Paper on Access to Plant Genetic Resources for Research and Breeding.* Available at <http://www.worldseed.org/cms/medias/file/PositionPapers/OnSustainableAgriculture/Plant_Genetic_Resources_for_Food_and_Agriculture_20070523_(En).pdf> (accessed 1 February 2010).

Jinna, S. and S. Jungcourt. 2009. "Could Access Requirements Stifle Your Research?" *Science* 323: 464.

Kloppenburg, J. 1988. *First the Seed: The Political Economy of Plant Biotechnology. 1492–2000.* Cambridge: Cambridge University Press.

Lim, E. and M. Halewood. 2008. "A Short History of the Annex 1 List." In G. Tansey and T. Rajotte, eds, *The Future Control of Food: A Guide to International Negotiations and Rules on Intellectual Property, Biodiversity and Food Security.* Cambridge, Ottawa, and Geneva: Earthscan, International Development Research Center, and Quaker International Affairs Programme.

Mekouar, A. 2002. *A Global Instrument on Agrobiodiversity: The International Treaty on Plant Genetic Resources for Food and Agriculture.* Food and Agriculture Organization Legal Paper. Available at <http://www.fao.org/Legal/default.htm> (accessed 1 February 2010).

Mooney, P. 1983. "The Law of the Seed: Another Development and Plant Genetic Resources." *Development Dialogue* 1–2: 1–172.

Moore, G., and W. Tymowski. 2005. *Explanatory Guide to the International Treaty on Plant Genetic Resources for Food and Agriculture.* Gland, Switzerland: International Union for the Conservation of Nature.

Nijar, G.S., Gan Pei Fern, Lee Yin Harn, and Chan Hui Yun. 2009. *Framework Study for Food Security and Access and Benefit Sharing for Genetic Resources for Food and Agriculture.* Background Study no. 42. Rome: United Nations Food and Agriculture Organization.

Nottenburg, C., P. Pardey, and B. Wright. 2002. "Accessing Other People's Technology for Non-Profit Research" *Australian Journal of Agricultural and Resource Economics* 46: 289–416. Available at: <http://ssrn.com/abstract=320462> (accessed 11 September 2013).

Palacios, X.F. 1997. *Contribution to the Estimation of Countries' Interdependence in the Area of Plant Genetic Resources.* Background Study no. 7. Rome: Food and Agriculture Organization, available at <http://www.fao.org/ag/cgrfa/docs.htm#bsp> (accessed 1 February 2010).

Pardy, P.J., J. Alston, J. Christian, and S. Fan. 1996. *Hidden Harvest: U.S. Benefits from International Research Aid.* Washington, DC: International Food Policy Research Institute.

——J. Alston, C. Chan-Kang, E. Magalhaes, and S. Vosti. 2002. *Assessing and Attributing from Varietal Improvement Research: Evidence from Embrapa, Brazil.* Washington, DC: International Food Policy Research Institute.

Pistorius. R. 1997. *Scientists, Plant and Politics: A History of the Plant Genetic Resources Movement.* Rome: International Plant Genetic Resources Institute.

Plantum N.L. 2009. *Plantum NL Position on Patent- and Plant Breeders' Rights,* available at <http://www.plantum.nl/pdf/Standpunt_octrooi_kwekersrecht_extended_UK.pdf> (accessed 11 September 2013).

Rai, A. 2008. "Proprietary Rights and Collective Action." In K. Maskus and J. Reichman, eds., *International Public Goods and Transfer of Technology under a Globalized Intellectual Property Regime.* Cambridge: Cambridge University Press.

Rangnekar, Dwijen. 2004. *Demanding Stronger Protection for Geographical Indications: The Relationship between Local Knowledge, Information and Reputation.* Discussion Papers no. 11. United Nations University, Institute for New Technologies.

Safrin, S. 2004. "Hyperownership in a Time of Biotechnological Promise: The International Conflict to Control the Building Blocks of Life." *American Journal of International Law* 98: 641.

Smith. B. 2006. "Eastern North America as an Independent Center of Plant Domestication." *Proceedings of the National Academy of Science* 103 (33): 12,223–12,228.

Solbrig, O.T., and D.J. Solbrig. 1994. *So Shall You Reap: Farming and Crops in Human Affairs.* Washington, DC: Island Press.

Spence, M. 2008. "Comment on the Conceptual Framework for a Clearinghouse Mechanism." In G. van Overwalle, ed., *Gene Patents and Collaborative Licensing Models: Patent Pools, Clearinghouses, Open Source Models and Liability Regimes.* Cambridge: Cambridge University Press.

SGRP. 2010. *Booklet of CGIAR Center Policy Instruments, Guidelines and Statements on Genetic Resources, Biotechnology and Intellectual Property Rights.* Available at <http://www.sgrp.cgiar.org/sites/default/files/Policy_Booklet_Version3.pdf> (accessed 11 September 2013).

——2010. "The In-Trust Germ Plasm Collections." Available at <http://sgrp.cgiar.org/?q=node/31> (accessed 11 September 2013).

——2010. "Leaving Room in the Cbds ABS Protocol for the Future Development of Specialized Access and Benefit-Sharing Arrangements: The Example of Agricultural Microbial Genetic Resources." Available at: <http://www.sgrp.cgiar.org/sites/default/files/SGRP%20Policy%20Brief_Microbials_10_41_FINAL.pdf> (accessed 11 September 2013).

——2011. "CGIAR Centers." Their experience with the implementation of their Agreements with the Treaty's Governing Body, with particular reference to the use of the SMTA for Annex 1 and non-Annex 1 materials. Available at: <http://www.itpgrfa.net/International/sites/default/files/gb4i05e.pdf> (accessed 11 September 2013).

Taylor, M. and J. Cayford. 2003. *American Patent Policy, Biotechnology, and African Agriculture: A Case for Policy Change.* Washington, DC: Resources for the Future.

Then, C. and R. Tippe. 2009. *The Future of Seeds and Food under the Growing Threat of Patents and Market Concentration: Berne Declaration, Greenpeace, Kein patent ouf Leben, Swissaid.* Available at <http://www.no-patents-on-seeds.org> (accessed 11 September 2013).

Toenniessen, G. and D. Delmer. 2006. "The Role of Intermediaries in Maintaining the Public Sector's Essential Role in Crop Varietal Improvement." In *CGIAR Research Strategies for IPG in a Context of IPR.* Available at <http://www.sciencecouncil.cgiar.org/fileadmin/user_upload/sciencecouncil/SC_4_Meeting/SPPSintermed.pdf> (accessed 11 September 2013).

UNEP. 2006. *Outcomes and Recommendations of the Meeting of "Biodiversity—The Megascience in Focus."* Doc. UNEP/CBD/COP/8/INF/46.

——2007. *Handbook on the Convention on Biological Diversity,* 3rd edition. London: Earthscan. Available at <http://www.cbd.int/doc/handbook/cbd-hb-09-en.pdf> (accessed 11 September 2013).

Nicolas van Zeebroeck, N., B. van Pottelsberghe de la Potterie, and D. Guellec. 2008. "Patents and Academic Research: A State of the Art." *Journal of Intellectual Capital* 9 (2): 246–63.

Wambugu, P. and Z. Muthamia. 2013. "Incentives and Disincentives for Kenya's Participation in the Multilateral System of Access and Benefit-Sharing." In I. López Noriega, M. Halewood, and I. Lapena, eds, *The Multilateral System of Access and Benefit-Sharing: Case Studies on Implementation in Kenya, Morocco, Philippines and Peru.* Rome: Bioversity International.

Wesley, M., W. Cohen, and J.P. Walsh. 2010. "Access—or Not—in Academic Biomedical Research." In R.C. Dreyfuss, H. First, and D.L. Zimmerman, eds, *Working within the Boundaries of Intellectual Property: Innovation Policy for the Knowledge Society.* Oxford: Oxford University Press.

Wright, B. and P. Pardey. 2006. "Changing Intellectual Property Regimes: Implications for Developing Country Agriculture." *International Journal of Technology and Globalisation* 2: 93–114.

11

Mode of Entry for Emerging Markets: An *ex ante* and *ex post* Perspective of the Open Source Development and Management of Biotechnology Knowledge Assets

Minna Allarakhia

INTRODUCTION

The Human Genome era has emphasized the notion that biological knowledge is complex. Discovery research no longer simply focuses on individual units of knowledge, but considers the behavior and relationships of all units of knowledge in a particular biological system from a functional perspective (Kitano, 2001, 2002). Genomes are now being described as consisting of complex, intersecting systems rather than unitary collections of separately functioning structures (Hood, 2000; Dutfield, 2003). In this sense, it is possible to observe many similarities to software development. Software is a complex system, developed from many intersecting components (lines of code). Several developers may be required to generate these intersecting lines of code so that the associated processes can emerge and function. Demarcating the lines of ownership in this case can be an onerous task. It has been argued then that the open source software model evolved as a reaction to the challenges associated with proprietary software (Lakhani and von Hippel, 2003; Chesbrough et al., 2006).

As biological knowledge has become increasingly high in complementarity, high in applicability, but low in substitutability, open source innovation, particularly when knowledge exists in disembodied form during the upstream phases of research, can provide multiple firms with the opportunity to pursue downstream product-development activities. From a mode of entry perspective, open source strategies can further enable firms from emerging markets to enter a technological arena without the onerous upfront costs associated with exporting, developing subsidiaries, pursuing acquisitions or forming joint ventures, as well as encountering transactions costs associated with the sourcing of and contracting for proprietary knowledge (Antonelli, 2003; Malhotra, 2003).

NEW BIOLOGY

The pharmaceutical industry, traditionally dominated by large firms who relied on their own chemical research, is now increasingly faced with a new drug discovery reality which includes biology, nanotechnology, computational as well as chemical sciences—with knowledge more often than not developed outside of the walls of large pharmaceutical companies (Newbert et al., 2009; van der Valk et al., 2009). Suddenly, knowledge management is not as simple as before (Allarakhia and Walsh, 2011).

The catalyst

The Human Genome Project (and its successful completion) is the catalyst of this technological and legal change (Coccia and Rolfo, 2008; Bianchi et al., 2011). Since the completion of the Human Genome Project, new technology in this industry is often generated at the intersection between bio-pharmacology, chemistry, nanotechnology, and computational sciences, and is occurring outside the boundaries of pharmaceutical firms with intellectual property rights (IPR) assigned throughout the research value chain including university entrepreneurial activity (Reppy, 2008; Hoyle and Pries, 2009). The Human Genome Project emphasized the need for interdisciplinary researchers. Completing the sequence map of the Human Genome required breakthroughs in understanding computational sciences, measurement technologies, statistics, and data management. Tools enabling high-throughput quantitative measurements of biological information were developed from this collective understanding. Computer science, mathematics, and statistics were also employed to handle, store, disseminate as well as analyze biological information (Allarakhia and Walsh, 2011).

Discovery at the interface

The new industry paradigm of "discovery at the interface" rather than the traditional research paradigm of discovery based on a silo chemical monomer drug discovery approach has created new norms of intellectual property ownership and dispersion (Allarakhia and Walsh, 2011). These new norms—supported by current legislation, enable a researcher to secure royalties on an invention and funding from a possible private sector collaborator for future work (Atkinson et al., 1998; Blumenthal, 1992; Blumenthal et al., 1997; Boardman, 2008). Powell and Owen-Smith (1998) argue that the separation of the scientist in the academic world and the technologist in the private arena no longer holds in the life sciences. Universities have therefore become much more oriented to the commercialization of research (Walsh, 2004). Analysts have explained that legislative changes such as the Bayh-Dole Act (BD) sparked a considerable upsurge in licensing, as well as the growth in the number of university-industry research centers, consortia, and agreements (Kautt et al., 2007). This focus on commercialization by public institutes was anticipated to provide private firms with the incentive to invest in the downstream development of any resulting commercial products (Rai and Eisenberg, 2003). However, this legislation provided no distinction between downstream knowledge that leads directly to commercial products and fundamental knowledge that serves as an input into downstream research and is in itself far removed from commercial product development (Kieff, 2003; Foray, 2004).

Innovation proliferation problems arise when intellectual property rights and exclusive licenses are assigned to partner companies especially for fundamental technologies, as fewer opportunities remain open for other downstream inventors (Thumm, 2004).

Furthermore, as collaborations cross institutional and national boundaries, the parceling out of intellectual property rights will be a daunting if not an impossible task. With the assignment of property rights, the role of the patent holder in providing broad versus narrow access to the knowledge will then depend on the original incentives for producing the knowledge and the differing countries' intellectual property rights legal systems (Kieff, 2003; Romig et al., 2007).

NEW BIOLOGY AND INTELLECTUAL PROPERTY COMPLEXITIES

Existing patent law allows a researcher who has discovered a new, non-obvious, and useful process, machine, article of manufacture, or composition of matter to receive patent protection (Kieff, 2003; Foray, 2004; www.uspto.gov, 2010). Traditionally, the pharmaceutical industry had built its patent fence around not only chemical compositions of matter, but also around methods of synthesis, formulations, dosing, methods of treatment, and drug delivery systems. Commercialization in the pharmaceutical industry was based on chemical compositions as articles of manufacture. As the industry develops and uses biologics, biological materials, and new biological information in addition to genomic-based tools and diagnostics, patent examiners are increasingly finding it difficult to apply the chemical patent law doctrines to the current paradigm (Drews, 1998; Dutfield, 2003; Kieff, 2003). Consequently, the industry has been forced to change their strategy and re-evaluate the current patent system to not only accommodate new processes associated with the current paradigm, but also new categories of "biological" goods (Foray, 2004; David, 2009; Woodcock, 2010). With the move toward "synthetic biology," that is, the creation of new life forms by starting at the genetic level, this re-evaluation has reached a stage of urgency (Kaiser, 2007; Rai and Boyle, 2007). In parallel, researchers discuss that in the emerging bioconvergence paradigm, unlike other industries in which patentees are actual or potential participants in the downstream market, a significant number of corporate patentees will own rights not just in the industry in which they participate, but other industries as well (Lemley, 2005). Analysts fear that over-patenting alongside the large shadow of such patents, could not only fragment technology, but could discourage stakeholders in a number of industries from attempting to enter a domain to develop products incorporating infringing technologies (Lemley, 2005; David, 2009).

Knowledge complexities

The suggested re-evaluation of appropriation strategies needs to consider that drug discovery is fraught with knowledge complexities. First, drug discovery research has become associated with a much higher level of knowledge complexity as the sources of knowledge are diverse and derive from a wide variety of scientific fields and technological competencies. Generating new knowledge and embodying knowledge in products or processes are often conditional on the ability to access and then piece together a significant variety of research inputs (Scotchmer, 1991; Foray, 2004; Grant and Baden-Fuller, 2004; Cimoli et al., 2009). In this case, it will be necessary to pool knowledge from the public domain or from licensors willing to trade at a reasonable cost. Second, the ability to invent around knowledge will determine whether or not new knowledge can be generated and then embodied by follow-on researchers that do not directly own the knowledge. The discovery of facts from nature, as is associated with many of the informational, upstream research inputs in genomics, cannot be substituted (Kieff, 2003; Walsh et al., 2003). If follow-on inventors cannot develop or obtain substitute knowledge, first innovators can potentially extract high rents for rights to access and use their knowledge (Thumm, 2004). Finally, product development is characterized by even higher appropriability risks. Research activities are characterized by high levels of risk and uncertainty in terms of both generating knowledge and then in terms of applying knowledge in downstream activities. As patent holders may not be aware *ex ante* what knowledge will be key in disease development or drug intervention, patent holders should be willing to provide access to this biological knowledge at a fair price (Merges, 1994; Heller and Eisenberg, 1998; Scherer, 2002; Kieff, 2003).

Finding the transition point

These new realities necessitate finding the correct "transition point" (Allarakhia and Walsh, 2011). The transition point is defined as the point in discovery research as the moment when researchers come to believe that unilateral gains from private management of knowledge including appropriation activities are greater than shared gains from open or shared knowledge (Allarakhia and Walsh, 2011). If this transition point occurs too far upstream, holdouts and bargaining failures associated with licensing technology may preclude downstream development by making knowledge unavailable. Specifically, the placement of the transition point upstream in the drug discovery and development pipeline may include the appropriation of disembodied knowledge that is often high in complementarity, non-substitutable, and high in applicability. The placement of the transition point downstream in the drug discovery and development pipeline will likely include the appropriation of embodied knowledge that is often high in complementarity and applicability, but often substitutable. Finally, given the placement of the transition point, upstream or downstream, the characteristics of knowledge will determine the appropriate innovation management strategy—open access non-exclusive or exclusive licensing—and the resulting transaction costs (Allarakhia and Walsh, 2011). Hence, shifts in the transition point are of consequence to firms operating in similar research or product domains.

Learning from the past

As evidence of the need to cautiously manage the transition point are the hearings before the U.S. Court of Appeals for the Federal Circuit in a landmark case centering on whether human genes should be patentable. The argument at hand was whether or not, genes, as products of nature, fall outside the domain of patentable material. In 2010, the U.S. District Court for the Southern District of New York invalidated the Myriad patents on two genes linked to breast and ovarian cancer, ruling that they were barred by laws preventing the patentability of natural phenomena. The court also overturned another patent held by Myriad on a testing method that determines a patient's risk for breast and ovarian cancers. Myriad appealed. In June of 2013, the Supreme Court, in a unanimous ruling indeed indicated that the genes Myriad isolated were products of nature, and are not eligible for patents (Kendall, 2013). The case could have far-reaching implications. About 20 per cent of human genes have been patented and products have been built atop the intellectual property rights that the patents grant (Schwartz and Pollack, 2010). Complicating the matter is the hierarchical nature of biological know-ledge. At any level of the hierarchy, patents may exist. Depending on the breadth of patents filed at a particular level—in this case at the genomic level— these patents can dominate other hierarchical levels of biological information including downstream diagnostics and medical entities. Dominance of patents filed earlier in time, at the lowest levels of the biological information hierarchy, can therefore significantly hinder the incentive to conduct research into the higher levels of the hierarchy where appropriation may not be possible (Allarakhia and Wensley, 2005; David, 2009). Alternatively, if patents filed at the lower levels of the hierarchy are rendered invalid, at stake could be products built atop these patents—in this case several diagnostic tests built on the basis of gene patents.

Cause for concern for emerging markets

Emerging markets have serious cause for concern and should look to these lessons of the past. Recently, countries from China and Brazil to Malaysia and South Africa have passed laws promoting the patenting of publicly funded research and a similar proposal is under legislative consideration in India (Jishnu, 2008; Graff, 2007; So et al., 2008). These initiatives are modeled in part on the U.S. Bayh-Dole Act of 1980 (So et al., 2008). The original Act gives recipients of government research funds almost complete discretion to choose what research to patent; universities can therefore patent not only those inventions that firms would fail to commercialize or use without exclusive rights, but also upstream research tools and platforms that may not benefit from patent protection (So et al., 2008; Allarakhia et al., 2010). The BD framework further makes minimal reciprocal demands from licensees of government-funded technologies, and neither universities nor government agencies have sought to include requirements that products derived from these inventions be sold to consumers on reasonable terms (Reichman, 2004). Some have raised concerns that the Act contributed to a change in academic norms regarding open, swift, and disinterested scientific exchange (Washburn, 2005; Greenberg, 2007). In light of the fact that both the patent laws and patterns of scientific collaboration have changed substantially since BD was passed in 1980, policy analysts strongly advocate that any attempt to pass laws promoting the protection of federally funded research, should reflect the "current biological paradigm" including joint knowledge production and knowledge access rather than "blindly importing a US model that is 30 years old" (So et al., 2008). These analysts suggest that governments adopting such laws should be vigilant to ensure that the public's interests are served. In commercializing publicly funded research, proposed are a number of safeguards on patenting and licensing practices including: licensing terms, government authority to issue additional licenses, government use rights, and provisions to ensure responsible access to end products (So et al., 2008).

Cimoli et al. (2009) equivalently discuss that while the rate and direction of the innovative activities carried out by local firms in developing countries will likely depend on incentive structures and available appropriability mechanisms, these structures and mechanisms should differ from those prevailing in developed countries (Cimoli et al., 2009; and Chapter 2 in this volume). Cimoli et al. (2009) contend that innovative activity will be shaped by the opportunities to enter and operate in particular markets and technology areas. Furthermore, as a consequence of a differential capacity for innovation (resource availability, learning ability, technological capability) in particular markets or arenas and the differential ability to exploit knowledge and intellectual property, Cimoli et al. (2009) advocate that it is necessary to consider the effect of a national patent system (that not only recognizes the rights of local inventors but also the rights of foreign inventors) upon the incentive for indigenous innovation in a developing country.

Interestingly, Hu and Jaffe (2009) suggest that the most likely globally efficient intellectual property rights policy is not harmonization, but rather a selective and gradual reform process with policies devised to meet the needs of each individual country based on its particular technological situation and stage of development (see Chapter 3 in this volume). For example, for countries in the early stages of technological innovation—the catch-up phase—this will entail policies that facilitate technology transfer and a certain amount of imitation. At some point, however, countries will need to recognize that stronger and more comprehensive IPR protection will facilitate foreign direct investment and licensing. Finally, as a domestic innovation sector emerges, countries will find it in their interests to provide greater protection in order to safeguard their own inventions. While developed countries are encouraging this reform, Hu and Jaffe (2009) suggest that the notion of early adoption of the developed world's IPR system as furthering less developed countries' own systems of innovation are neither supportable by the available evidence, and could be perceived as simply self-serving. Clearly then, developing countries should cautiously engage in reform and harmonization of IP systems targeting both publicly and privately developed indigenous innovation.

RESPONSE TO NEW BIOLOGY

Mergers, acquisitions, and strategic alliances such as joint ventures, as well as new structures such as knowledge-based networks will represent alternative strategies that may be used to create, access, or acquire knowledge-based resources in the current paradigm (Child and Faulkner, 1998; Kogut, 1998; Das and Teng, 2000). Such alliances will contribute to the efficient utilization of knowledge including the integration of knowledge into products (Grant and Baden Fuller, 2004). These efficiencies are critical when there is uncertainty as to the role of future knowledge requirements for new product development—with varied types and forms of knowledge—and where there are early-mover advantages associated with rapid knowledge access and product development (Grant and Baden Fuller, 2004).

Knowledge-based networks

Preliminary research provides evidence of changing firm strategy with respect to R&D activities in the emerging bioconvergence era including the increased use of knowledge-based networks (Allarakhia and Walsh, 2011). Knowledge-based networks are communities or consortia of individuals and/or organizations such as universities, government laboratories, and private sector firms with the objectives of producing and disseminating knowledge (Powell et al., 1996; Staropoli, 1998; Reid et al., 2001; Rampersad et al., 2010). These networks of collaboration are often supported by information and communication technologies and are enabling researchers from a variety of disciplines and laboratories to generate and validate knowledge as well as develop the associated tools needed to conduct research and development. At a national level, several governments have recognized the importance of knowledge-based networks to develop innovation capacity and compete on an international level. Consequently, policies are now providing more R&D funding and incentives encouraging the formation of multi-sectoral networks including those from emerging markets. For example, Brazil's Organization for Nucleotide Sequencing and Analysis (ONSA) Network's Genoma Program, India's Open Source Drug Discovery initiative (OSDD) adopt an open collaborative approach to basic research and drug discovery respectively. Moving further downstream are the Drugs for Neglected Diseases initiative (DNDi) and the Distributed Drug Discovery (D3) project. Working in partnership with industry, academia, and non-profit organizations (NGOs): DNDi has built the largest ever R&D portfolio for neglected diseases and currently has seven clinical and four preclinical projects underway (www.dndi.org, 2011). Finally, the premise of the D3 project is that if simple, inexpensive equipment and procedures are developed for each of the core scientific drug discovery disciplines (computational chemistry, synthetic chemistry, and biochemical screening): large research problems can be broken down into manageable, smaller units and carried out by students at multiple academic sites throughout the developing and developed world (Scott and O'Donnell, 2009).

Knowledge dissemination

With the formation of knowledge-based networks, knowledge-based assets jointly created must then be disseminated. Allarakhia and Walsh (2011) broadly categorize knowledge access strategies as including five distinct models: the open access model, the common pool model, the non-exclusive licensing model, the exclusive licensing model, and the integration model. While all of these systems are serviceable they have accompanying issues. In open access systems, for example, no one has the legal right to exclude others from using a resource (Ostrom et al., 1994). However, in common property regimes, members of a clearly defined group can legally exclude non-members from using the resource (Ostrom et al., 1994). With the assignment of property rights and the ability to license knowledge, knowledge can be valued as a good itself and sold in disembodied form in the market for technological knowledge or embodied into tools, diagnostics, or drugs (Antonelli, 2003; Foray 2004). The choice of exclusively licensing or non-exclusively licensing a patent is a function of the characteristics associated with the knowledge, the desire of the patent holder to maximize revenue from the disembodied versus embodied knowledge, and the desire to diffuse the knowledge versus develop the knowledge (Arora and Fosfuri, 2003; Foray, 2004).

The decision to sell disembodied knowledge in the form of patents and licenses can complement or substitute for the sale of embodied knowledge in the form of products. Substitution may occur when the value attained from the sale of disembodied knowledge is greater than that from the sale of embodied knowledge (Antonelli, 2003; Arora and Fosfuri, 2003). When the costs of internal coordination of the knowledge are larger than the transaction costs associated with the market for technical knowledge, or when special assets are required to progress further downstream, the patent holder may pursue a licensing strategy, specifically an exclusive licensing strategy (Antonelli, 2003; Arora and Fosfuri, 2003; Teece, 1986). Complementarity between the sale of disembodied knowledge and internal embodiment occurs when knowledge possesses high applicability and it is possible to operate in different, exploitable markets from other licensees of the knowledge (Teece, 1986; Arora and Fosfuri, 2003; Foray, 2004; Scotchmer, 2004). In this case, a non-exclusive licensing strategy can ensure that multiple participants can pursue multiple streams of research. Furthermore, cross-licensing is a useful innovation management strategy when knowledge exhibits high levels of complementarity (Shapiro, 2001). With downstream activities dependent on the recombination of a variety of knowledge, the cost of the coordination including accumulation of the full range of required knowledge may be too high for one innovator (Allarakhia and Walsh, 2011; Antonelli, 2003; Burk and Lemley, 2003). Specifically, the capabilities of the one innovator may only cover a portion of the research domain. Innovators may therefore find it profitable to engage in cross-licensing for knowledge. As such, the ability for each innovator to access knowledge depends on the amount and type of proprietary knowledge each one is able to contribute in any bargaining event (Allarakhia and Walsh, 2011; Antonelli, 2003).

As products are developed, patents can protect against future loss of profit through imitation and can be used to prevent competitors from entering the market. Patents can also protect the future right to pursue downstream development in a technological arena. Increasingly, as patents are being filed on upstream disembodied knowledge assets, the intent is to protect the right to downstream research and/or product development—in some cases through internal development and in other cases (including jointly) through licensing agreements. Clearly then, the strategic intent of an innovator with respect to patent rights will determine the knowledge assets targeted and then the innovation management strategy adopted (Allarakhia and Walsh, 2011).

OPEN SOURCE: A RESPONSE TO IP COMPLEXITIES

Despite the accompanying issues, open source drug discovery is one solution that is increasingly being sought to manage product development complexities. Upstream knowledge-based complexities associated with complementary assets, technological complexities given the scale of research and interdependencies between disciplines, and downstream commercialization complexities are all drivers encouraging the use of this strategy. Mirroring the efforts of the open source community that developed Linux, open knowledge networks and other cooperative strategies (classified as open source discovery initiatives) are enabling stakeholders to access knowledge-based resources critical to downstream drug development.

Expansion of the open source domain

While the Human Genome Project catalyzed the open source movement in genomics and proteomics-based research, Allarakhia et al. (2010) discuss that increasingly open-source-based alliances seek to provide broad access to research-based tools—including microarrays, assays, software, preclinical samples—including biological models and tissue samples, and downstream compounds. Furthermore, the emergence of open source alliances appear to have shifted from the public sector to the private sector—in some cases, with private sector stakeholders singularly encouraging open source discovery. As evidence, Eli Lilly, Merck, and Pfizer recently announced their commitment to launch a research group in Asia focusing on new therapies and diagnostics for Asia's most common cancer types. The Asian Cancer Research Group's (ACRG) formation represents an example of a growing trend in pre-competitive collaboration in which biopharmaceutical companies combine their resources and expertise to rapidly increase knowledge of disease and disease processes (Weigelt, 2009; Munos, 2010; www.lilly.com, 2010) The three pharmaceutical companies hope to create one of the most extensive pharmacogenomic cancer databases over the next two years using the open source approach (www.lilly.com, 2010). Likewise, GlaxoSmithKline (GSK) announced that it would make 13,500 compounds that could lead to the development of new and innovative treatments for malaria, including the chemical structures and associated assay data, freely available to the public via leading scientific websites (Hunter and Stephens, 2010; www.gsk.com, 2010). The release of these data and creation of a powerful public repository of knowledge are thought to parallel the scale of human genome data release (www.gsk.com, 2010). Through the Eli Lilly Phenotypic Drug Discovery (PD2) Initiative, Lilly works with research universities, institutes, and biotechnology companies to uncover compounds that may become future medicines targeting cancer, neurological disorders, and metabolic diseases. Using the PD2 website, external investigators can access Lilly's phenotypic assays. As part of the PD2 business model, promising compounds can be further advanced through optimization. The goal of PD2 is not to promote a random, high-volume compound submission, but rather to stimulate the testing of compounds that represent novel chemical diversity and molecular hypotheses that are strategically considered in light of the biology associated with each assay (Hunter and Stephens, 2010; www.pd2.lilly.com, 2010). Keeping in mind the complexities associated with transferring technologies to underdeveloped markets, the Open Source Drug Discovery (OSDD) is a consortium that provides a global and open platform for collaborative discovery work into novel therapies for neglected tropical diseases including malaria, tuberculosis, and leishmaniasis (www.osdd.net, 2010). The OSDD provides an online platform for stakeholders with diverse expertise to participate in open drug discovery. Through this platform, the entire drug discovery process is divided into problems that are open for the community to contribute to and benefit from (Munos, 2010; www.osdd.net, 2010).

A framework for understanding open source strategies

The need then exists to understand innovative designs for multi-organizational research collaborations. In this paper, an initial framework is designed with a focus on the type of participant as impacting the motivation to participate in an open source initiative, the objective of any open source strategy as impacting the structural model adopted, and the structure of knowledge produced as impacting its management. An *ex ante* and *ex post* perspective are adopted to understand how open source strategic alliances and open licensing respectively can be used as modes of entry into the industry by firms in emerging markets. Case examples include Brazil's Organization for Nucleotide Sequencing and Analysis (ONSA): Network's Genoma Program, India's Open Source Drug Discovery (OSDD) initiative both of which adopted an open collaborative approach to basic research and drug discovery respectively, and CAMBIA's Biological Innovation for Open Society initiative (BiOS) enabling a new way to share the capability to use patented technology. The case studies are used to provide a basis for the development of *ex ante* and *ex post* models of knowledge generation and then management. Recommendations for institutional design and knowledge governance are discussed in the context of the case analyses and model development. Ultimately, the success of such initiatives will rest on the correct assessment of the transition point and then the choice of most effective governance strategy once knowledge is appropriated.

THE *EX ANTE* AND *EX POST* PERSPECTIVES TO OPEN SOURCE STRATEGIES

The *ex post* view analyzes strategies for enabling intellectual property assignment and transfer as a means of providing access to and then enabling downstream knowledge use in product development. In contrast, the *ex ante* view analyzes other mechanisms available, either prior to patent assignment or during patent assignment, to ensure access to and use of knowledge for product development. In this paper, the focus is on *ex ante* and *ex post* open strategies to manage knowledge assets—namely the use of open strategic alliances and open licensing as a mode of entry for firms from emerging markets. While several collaborative alliances (including open-source based alliances) previously discussed, target upstream discovery research, many are increasingly focused on the health needs of emerging markets—chronic and neglected diseases. Consequently, I consider the need for biotechnology-based open source strategies from the perspective of emerging markets as a proactive measure from such stakeholders to address local, emerging market health and technological needs, particularly as we enter the bioconvergence paradigm.

The decision to participate *ex ante* in open source initiatives is affected by the degree of accessibility to the associated knowledge. Open access ensures that knowledge is available to all researchers for downstream activities regardless of participation in the initiative. In this case, the possibility of free-riding exists by outside firms who can enjoy the disclosed knowledge at little or no cost (Gintis et al., 2001). Closed access in contrast ensures that knowledge is only available to those contributing members within the alliance; therefore, the ability for a researcher or firm outside of the alliance to pool internal knowledge with that from the closed pool may not be possible or at a cost that will vary with the market power of the closed group. The ability to join is further tempered by informal and formal rules of participation. With formality, entrance costs may be used to facilitate research and development activities as well as to signal cooperation and commitment to the initiative (Gulati et al., 1994; Kollock, 1998; Gintis et al., 2001).

In terms of mode of entry into the biotechnology arena, firms from emerging markets can enjoy many of the benefits associated with participation in an open-source-based initiative. These benefits include early access to knowledge, absorptive capacity development, and cost sharing during knowledge production activities. However, firms from emerging markets may have limited resources available and should be aware of the structure and rules associated with the initiative before committing these resources. The objectives in terms of knowledge production and dissemination will determine both the most effective organizational structure and the types of participants that will join. The organization of any knowledge production activities will impact not only accessibility to knowledge but also the learning experience for any firm.

An awareness of participant type—public or private sector—can provide an indication of motivation with respect to participation and likely adherence to the open source model including: the need to develop a collegial reputation; the need to create general reciprocity obligations; the need to enable the adoption of a technology standard; the improvement of industry performance; and/or the pre-emption of rivals (Foray, 2004). The objectives and rules for participation should be understood at the outset; these rules can determine which firms wish to and/or are able to join the initiative as a function of resource availability. Then depending on the knowledge access policy—open access for members only, open access for members and the public at large, or open licensing—a firm may be forced to join the initiative in order to access critical knowledge, a firm may choose to free-ride and access knowledge without any resource commitments, and/or choose to access knowledge as a licensee (Grant and Baden-Fuller, 2004; Chokshi et al., 2006) (see Figure 11.1).

As discussed earlier, the *ex post* choice of exclusively licensing or non-exclusively licensing a patent is a function of the characteristics associated with the knowledge, the desire of the patent holder to maximize revenue from disembodied versus embodied knowledge, or the desire to diffuse the knowledge versus develop the knowledge (Arora and Fosfuri, 2003; Foray, 2004). I contend in Figure 11.2 that both knowledge type—disembodied versus embodied—as well as participant type—private or public sector—will subsequently impact the intellectual property rights management strategy adopted (Blumenthal et al., 1997; Walsh et al., 2003). Open or non-exclusive licensing with or without royalties will encourage multiple firms to enter and/or stay within a technological arena. In contrast, exclusive licensing will enable one firm to enter and possibly maintain control of a technological arena (Walsh et al., 2003). Worth noting, in the case of cross-licensing, only firms with tradable knowledge assets may be able to bargain for other knowledge assets and in turn, enter or stay within the technological arena. It is important to consider that the ability to enter and stay in a technological arena will also depend on the substitutability of knowledge

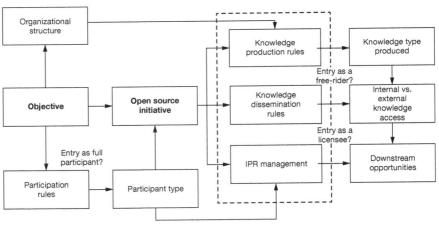

Figure 11.1 Open-source-based model and mode of entry options[A]

[A] Flow: The objectives of the open source initiative determine both organizational structures to manage knowledge development activities, as well as the necessary participation rules. Participation rules determine the types of organizations that can join including the ability for firms from emerging markets to join as full participants. Rules may be established to manage knowledge production (learning in this case is determined by the established organizational structures): knowledge dissemination, and the management of any associated intellectual property. Knowledge production rules determine the type of knowledge produced. Knowledge dissemination rules determine which participants can access the knowledge including emerging market firms inside and outside the initiative. Intellectual property rights (IPR) management rules impact which firms can pursue downstream product development opportunities including the ability for firms from emerging markets to license knowledge/technology (Allarakhia, 2009).

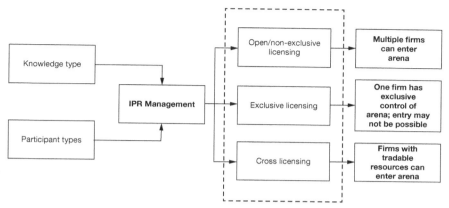

Figure 11.2 Impact of IPR management on entry options[B]

[B] Flow: The characteristics of knowledge and participant types (including their motives) will impact how intellectual property rights are managed. Options include open licensing, exclusive licensing, or cross licensing. Each option has an associated impact on the opportunity for firms to pursue downstream product development opportunities (Allarakhia, 2009).

assets. For example, the existence of non-infringing work-around solutions will encourage a licensor to provide open or non-exclusive licenses (Antonelli, 2003; Allarakhia et al., 2010).

EX ANTE AND *EX POST* CASE ANALYSES

The case examples that follow include the ONSA, the OSDD, and the BiOS initiative. The case studies are used to provide a basis for the previous *ex ante* and *ex post* models of knowledge generation and management. The first case study—the ONSA Network's Genoma Program—discusses the success of upstream genomic research via the development of a virtual research center. The second case study—that of the OSDD—discusses an open drug discovery platform to address neglected diseases. And finally, the third case study— CAMBIA's BiOS—discusses the development of an *ex post* legally enforceable framework to enable the sharing of the capability to use patented technology, including materials and methods. Each case study adopts a governance strategy perspective with the intention of uncovering patterns across the case studies in terms of knowledge production, dissemination, and intellectual property rights management. It is worth noting that I progress from upstream research to downstream product development as we move through the three chosen case studies.

Brazil's Organization for Nucleotide Sequencing and Analysis (ONSA) Network's Genoma Program

Brazil was applauded for completion of the first genome sequence of a plant pathogen following the development of a virtual research center—a collaborative network of laboratories throughout the state of São Paulo, bringing together scientific community and investment from both the government and the private sector (Camargo and Simpson, 2003). Brazil—a developing country with a reasonably well developed scientific infrastructure, used the strategy of the collaborative research network to enhance its genomic expertise (Simpson and Perez, 1998; Simpson et al., 2000). In contrast to the traditional model for enabling genomics research—that is by establishing a single national genomics research facility, the Brazilian experiment sought to coordinate the efforts of many smaller laboratories. This decentralized production model was facilitated by the contributions of a distributed network of researchers linked to a central data repository through the Internet. In this way, the founders sought to build comparable genomics research capabilities in Brazil, but at a lower cost and shorter start-up time (Macilwain and Neto, 2000).

The São Paulo State Foundation for Research Assistance—Fundação de Amparo à Pesquisa do Estado de São Paulo (FAPESP)—established the Genoma Program in 1997. The program had two objectives: first, to discover new biotechnological methods for improving local agriculture; and second, to develop expertise in genomics in the State of São Paulo (Dal Poz, 2000; O Estado de São Paulo, 1997). To achieve these goals, FAPESP established a network of thirty university laboratories. These laboratories acted as "a virtual genomics institute" to collaborate in sequencing the complete genome of xylella fastidiosa—a bacteria responsible for significant damage to the region's citrus crops (Shaver, 2008).

Participants: The X. fastidiosa genome project quickly became the largest and most widely known scientific project in Brazil, receiving financial support of approximately US$12 million and involving laboratories spread throughout the state of São Paulo. The network was composed of one coordination laboratory, one bioinformatics laboratory, and 30 sequencing centers functionally linked by the Internet (watson.fapesp.br, 2010; Camargo and Simpson, 2003).

Ex ante Rules for Knowledge Production: The Genoma Program's work was guided by a five-member steering committee—composed of three international experts in genome sequencing and two scientists from the state of São Paulo. A single project DNA coordinator was charged with generating the fragments of the genome to be assigned to each laboratory for sequencing and coordinating the flow of completed sequences from the laboratories to the bioinformatics center. Individual laboratories were responsible for their own project management (Shaver, 2008). Laboratories received a specified payment per base pair of finished sequence. This was set at R$4 per base pair in the initial research stage to cover start-up costs. Of this payment, 70 per cent was advanced before the service was rendered, and 30 per cent was paid upon delivery of the sequence to the center (Shaver, 2008). To support the collaboration between distant laboratories, new communications protocols were developed to enable faster information dissemination. Centralized support for bioinformatics was made the responsibility of the Computing Institute of the State University of Campinas—Universidade Estadual de Campinas (UNI-CAMP) (Shaver, 2008).

Ex ante *Rules for Knowledge Dissemination*: Membership in the network was granted by means of a contract between the participating laboratory and the São Paulo State Foundation for Research Assistance (FAPESP). Under the terms of the contract, sequencing laboratories received DNA material, equipment, and training. In return, they were obligated to sequence assigned DNA fragments at a prescribed standard of quality, within one year. The resulting mapped information would be deposited back into a common repository associated with the project, which could then be accessed by any interested party. As soon as a laboratory successfully delivered a sequence, it could apply for a second assignment (Shaver, 2008).

Outcomes with Respect to Market Entry: Several other collaborative research networks have since been established in Brazil. These include a functional genomics network to study phytopathogens, an initiative to complete the coding sequences of expressed human genes, a viral-genetics network to monitor the genotype of endemic viral pathogens, and a significant effort to record and register the complete range of fauna and flora in the state of São Paulo (www.biota.org.br, 2010). The research network is now a firmly established model throughout the country and in many different fields (Camargo and Simpson, 2003).

The ONSA Network enabled peripheral laboratories in two ways. First, participation in the project was open to laboratories with no previous experience in DNA sequencing. The project therefore, enabled such laboratories to purchase state-of-the-art DNA sequencing machines, and to train their student technicians on these sequencing machines—encouraging the development of relevant expertise to develop within the state university system (Shaver, 2008). At the beginning of the program, few members of the ONSA Network had ever sequenced DNA. Five years later, more than four hundred and fifty researchers had training and experience in DNA sequencing (Camargo and Simpson 2003). Second, because the participating laboratories were encouraged to work in tandem on a common project, the joint accomplishments were of a scope that none of the laboratories could have achieved independently. The scale of these accomplishments helped Brazil to develop a reputation in the associated scientific disciplines previously held by researchers in more developed countries (Camargo and Simpson 2003; Shaver, 2008).

The open research model relied on a different incentive system, wherein contributors received payment according to their research output, as well as developed valuable skills training and gained reputational benefits. This incentive structure did not require excluding others from accessing knowledge produced through the granting of intellectual property rights, but rather rewarded researchers for their contributions to a shared knowledge pool (Shaver, 2008; see Figure 11.3). Shaver (2008) discusses that companies in the Brazilian biotechnology sector may see open source approaches as an opportunity to free themselves from transaction costs and successfully compete with more established foreign players. Discoveries that are patented will likely be subject to open licenses—alleviating concerns that Brazil's natural resources and government-funded research will end up unfairly appropriated by foreign biotechnology companies (Shaver, 2008).

India Open Source Drug Discovery (OSDD)

Open Source Drug Discovery (OSDD) is a Council of Scientific and Industrial Research (CSIR) Team India Consortium that provides a global platform for collaborative discovery work into novel therapies for neglected tropical diseases including malaria, tuberculosis, and leishmaniasis (www.osdd.net, 2010). OSDD provides a platform for scientists, medical

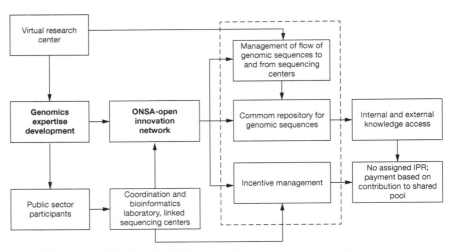

Figure 11.3 The Brazil ONSA network *ex ante* open innovation strategy

and software professionals, students and others with diverse expertise to facilitate the drug discovery process. The OSDD portal is the platform supporting this collaboration effort. The challenges are well-defined and problems are posted on the website. Each of the solutions to these problems is then peer-reviewed. Appropriate rewards are assigned for the respective contributions; in this sense, the OSDD model appears to be emulating the InnoCentive model. (www.innocentive.com, 2010; www.osdd.net, 2010) Based on the points accrued by contributors, four levels of membership cards are awarded. Each type of card entails a certain set of rights, privileges, and responsibilities in the entire process.

Participants: OSDD is a community of public and private stakeholders—all committed to the open source discovery of drugs. The OSDD project is managed online. All project documents and tracking are done through the OSDD portal. Principal investigators report directly to the project director through this portal. In addition, the core OSDD team meets monthly. The chief mentor further reviews the progress of the platform on a quarterly basis along with the board of mentors (www.osdd.net, 2010).

As of the early part of 2013, OSDD had more than seven thousand registered participants. These participants post innovative projects online, actively engage in ongoing scientific projects, share positive and negative results, as well as participate in the review process of other projects posted on the OSDD portal (www.osdd.net, 2010).

Ex ante *Rules for Knowledge Production*: The OSDD's objective is to create a collaborative online platform for the exchange of ideas, data, and resources including: a Wiki-based genome annotation service; a platform for open source tools for drug discovery; integrative genomic maps; an open access document repository; and a metadata archive and search engine for open access to theses and dissertations. Contribution can be made in the form of database, molecular library or other biological resource donations, laboratory access or the sharing of technological capabilities, computing time, bandwidth or other computation resource access, and monetary or in-kind rewards for contributions themselves. Collaboration spaces enable participants to post ideas, to discuss methodologies and possible solutions to the problems, bookmark web-based resources for drug discovery, and share experimental data (www.osdd.net, 2010).

The process of drug discovery is divided into problems that are open for the entire community to contribute to. Larger, complex problems are broken into simpler, smaller sets of activities which have clear and well-defined scope and deliverables. The smaller sets of activities are termed work packets or work packages (WPs). Work packages include: target analysis at a computational level including systems biology research and setting up networks;

experimental expression of protein targets bringing together experimental reagents and chemicals into the open space; screening of targets discovered using large chemical libraries often involving the participation of contract research organizations; *in silico* docking and identification of a library of chemicals for specific screening—another computation activity; microarray gene expression analysis on human cells and tissues with the most optimal inhibitors; lead optimization of non-toxic hits—an essential stage of the drug discovery process; medicinal chemistry including the synthesis of analogues; proteomics-based lead affinity experiments to check for human cellular protein binding; preclinical toxicity analysis of lead compounds—in order to develop a pharmacological profile of the investigational drug; and finally, clinical development of new molecular entities—to establish safety, tolerability, and efficacy of the entities (OSDD, 2009).

Ex ante *Rules for Knowledge Dissemination*: In formulating the terms and conditions of knowledge access and use, the OSDD explicitly addresses the potential problem of other parties filing, and being awarded intellectual property rights based on the information, data, ideas or other materials available on its website, either pre-existing or generated by the OSDD community (www.sysborgtb.osdd.net, 2010).

Hence, all participants are required to partially assign their right(s) pertaining to the resources they contribute, to CSIR acting on behalf of OSDD, for the sole purpose of taking action against any potential infringement. Such an assignment is partial and only for the purpose of protecting the intellectual property generated by OSDD. This step seeks to prevent the IPR based on the information, ideas, and intellectual property generated by the OSDD users from being misappropriated. Thus OSDD/CSIR holds the intellectual property over the content generated as protected commons. Information available on the OSDD website in any form is confidential information and the proprietary right of the OSDD. Any appropriation of the information to acquire intellectual property rights, without an explicit license of OSDD, is considered misappropriation of the protected commons and liable to legal action under the applicable laws (www.sysborgtb.osdd.net, 2010). Donors may retain their rights over the patents except to the extent that they may be used in the drug discovery process or for selling any product or process arising out of any invention (www.sysborgtb.osdd.net, 2010). By submitting a patented invention for OSDD, donors agree not to place any encumbrances on products or processes arising out of the use of the patented contribution (www.sysborgtb.osdd.net, 2010). I could argue that OSDD has adopted both an *ex ante* and *ex post* strategy for the management of contributed knowledge assets.

Outcomes with Respect to Market Entry: An example of an outcome from the OSDD is the drug discovery project for tuberculosis. For life-style diseases, OSDD indicates that pharmaceutical companies actively scouted advances in basic research in search of new and potentially lucrative drug targets. This is not the case with TB which is mainly a disease affecting developing and poverty-stricken countries. Hence, this project leveraged the world's largest Mycobacterium tuberculosis (MTB) database (hosted by OSDD) to bring together 13 researchers across India to decode 400 of the 4,000 genes of MTB in less than six months—this constitutes years of work for a single researcher (Menon, 2009). Dr. Anshu Bharadwaj, a scientist at the Institute of Genomics and Integrative Biology (IGIB): recently published results of the project having decoded 400 of the 4,000 genes of MTB. Another researcher has published the targets for several genes; and yet another project has shortlisted compounds that are to be tested against the biological targets (Menon, 2009).

As is the case for the TB project, the OSDD platform brings together both public and private stakeholders with the goal of bringing down the cost of drug discovery for such neglected diseases via open knowledge sharing and constructive collaboration (Figure 11.4). Drug discovery in the context of a market greatly affected by TB should allow for a local understanding of the disease and product requirements. Likewise, the training provided and lessons learned can then lend themselves to the discovery of other drugs for neglected diseases such as malaria and leishmaniasis. The associated knowledge production, knowledge dissemination, and IPR management rules specifically seek to ensure that multiple downstream product development opportunities are exploited for affected markets.

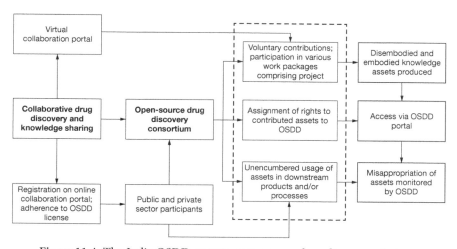

Figure 11.4 The India OSDD *ex ante* open-source drug discovery strategy

CAMBIA's Biological Innovation for Open Society (BiOS)

BiOS is an initiative of the Centre for Applications of Molecular Biology in Agriculture (CAMBIA) with the objectives to develop new means for cooperative innovation, improvement, and dissemination of life sciences technologies. The BiOS initiative serves as a clearinghouse and exists to administer and certify Biological Open Source (BiOS) agreements, and provides a forum to increase open access to patented and patentable technologies for public benefit (Thomas, 2005; Sulston, 2006; www.bios.net, 2010). The BiOS initiative operates in two main areas: intellectual property informatics and analysis through the Patent Lens; and innovation-system structural reform through the BiOS licenses (www.bios.net, 2010).

Participants: The BiOS license is available to research institutions, private sector firms, as well as hospitals or landowners providing clinical or field-test data. Private sector stakeholders are often requested to provide part of the costs of providing services in which improved protocols, descriptions of improved materials, implementation, and regulatory data are being supplied and documented, and of the costs of providing materials for downstream use. Support requested from private sector firms based in non-OECD countries, however, are oriented more to in-kind provision than financial support (www.bios.net, 2010).

Ex post *Patent Data Management*: The Patent Lens is an open source and open access patent search navigation system. The Patent Lens tools are useful to help innovators determine *ex post* their freedom to operate in downstream development activities. Users can search and retrieve the full-text of more than nine million patent documents from the U.S., Europe, Australia, and WIPO, including their status and counterparts in up to 70 countries. The recently launched Initiative for Open Innovation (IOI) builds on the platform of the Cambia Patent Lens. Over the next few years, IOI will add the full text of worldwide patents and applications in all languages, associated DNA and protein sequences and chemical structures, and will integrate business and regulatory data and scientific and technical literature into the Patent Lens. New web applications will then enable users to build public maps of intellectual property in any field (www.patentlens.net, 2010).

Ex post *Licensing*: BiOS provides an *ex post* legally enforceable framework to enable the sharing of the capability to use patented and patentable technology, which may include materials and methods. Those who join BiOS agree not to assert intellectual property rights against each others' use of the technology to conduct research, or in the development of products. Consequently, BiOS-compatible agreements support both the freedom to operate and the freedom to cooperate (www.bios.net, 2010).

Under a BiOS-compliant agreement, users must agree to conditions that encourage cooperation and development of the technology in order to obtain the right to use the technology, instead of royalties or other conditions that discourage the creation of products (Sulston, 2006).

The conditions include a provision that licensees cannot exclusively appropriate the fundamental essence of the technology or improvements (www.bios. net, 2010). The base technology remains the property of the entity that developed it, but improvements can be shared with others that support the development of a protected commons around the technology. Participants who agree to the same terms obtain access to improvements and other information, such as regulatory and biosafety data (www.bios.net, 2010). To maintain legal access to the technology, users must agree not to prevent others who have agreed to the same terms from using the technology and any improvements in the development of varied products (see Figure 11.5).

Licensing Targets: Versions of the first BiOS license, developed for plant molecular enabling technologies, have been executed by a range of companies and non-profit organizations based in many countries in the developing and developed world. BiOS is drafting a similar license for health-related technologies (www.bios.net, 2010).

The first BiOS license covers plant molecular enabling technologies including Transbacter, GUSPlus, and know-how related to these and other plant molecular enabling technologies. A second BiOS license is also available, covering genetic resources technologies, but not limited to plants. BiOS licenses are further being developed to cover certain health technologies including technology that can be used for cancer diagnostics and stem cell research, and technology based on glucuronidase-related enzymes that can be used for various types of diagnostics and medical devices (www.bios.net, 2010).

Outcomes with Respect to Market Entry: The licensing strategy promoted by BiOS hopes to encourage entry into a technological arena with a focus on those researchers and firms in neglected markets. Specifically, it is anticipated that open source agricultural research will enable innovation by small

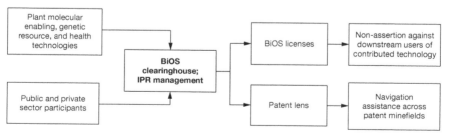

Figure 11.5 The CAMBRIA BiOS *ex post* intellectual property right management strategy

biotechnology companies. This will permit the development of locally suited technologies, reduce dependence on giant agribusiness conglomerates, and facilitate research on crops suited for local conditions in developing countries (Thomas, 2005).

The ONSA project founders sought to build comparable genomics research capabilities, but at a lower cost and shorter start-up time. The ONSA incentive structure did not require excluding others from accessing knowledge produced through the granting of intellectual property rights, but rather rewarded researchers for their contributions to a shared knowledge pool. The capacity developed in genomic sequencing, as well as open access strategy, provided a signal of the quality of research emerging from the Brazilian biotechnology sector and should enable multiple paths to be pursued for downstream development and market entry. Similarly, the OSDD platform brings various stakeholders via a decentralized web-based community portal with the objective of bringing down the cost of drug discovery and market entry for neglected diseases through open knowledge sharing and constructive collaboration. Appropriate rewards are assigned for the respective contributions to the OSDD community, with a further agreement to provide unencumbered access to contributed knowledge assets for downstream development activities. In contrast, the BiOS patent lens and license framework seek to enable stakeholders to navigate *ex post* across any patent minefields and provide an *ex post* legally enforceable framework to ensure the sharing of the capability to use technology, including non-assertion for downstream use. The anticipation is once again: entry into key agriculture and health markets with a focus on product localization and open opportunities for the smaller biotechnology companies. Table 11.1 outlines the knowledge production and governance strategies adopted by each initiative.

Table 11.1 Comparing *ex ante* and *ex post* knowledge management strategies

Open-source initiative	Participant type	Knowledge management	Incentive/IPR management
Brazil ONSA network	Public sector	Common repository for genomic sequences	Rewards for contribution to shared pool; no IPR
India OSDD	Public and private sector	Collaborative discovery/ knowledge management through virtual portal	Rewards for contribution; OSDD license for the management of contributed assets
CAMBIA's BiOS	Public and private sector	Patent repository; clearinghouse for contributed technologies	*ex post* sharing of patented technologies

DISCUSSION

One's ability to join an open source initiative will be tempered by informal and formal rules of participation. With formality, entrance costs may be used to facilitate research and development activities as well as to signal cooperation and commitment to the initiative (Kollock, 1998; Gintis et al., 2001). The role of such entrance costs or rules for participation is to create trust through a visible signal. For example, committing resources in advance including monetary fees makes other participants in the initiative, and future researchers who are considering participation, aware of a researcher's cooperative intentions (Gulati et al., 1994). The decision to participate in any initiative is also affected by the degree of accessibility to the associated knowledge. Open access ensures that knowledge will be available to all participants in future downstream research regardless of participation (Gintis et al., 2001). Closed access in contrast, ensures that knowledge is available only to contributing members within the initiative.

In terms of property rights, Ostrom (2006) argues these rights do not emerge spontaneously from a common property system. Private property rights depend on the existence and enforcement of rules that define who has a right to pursue which activities involving a resource and how the returns from that activity will be allocated (Ostrom, 2006). For example, the use of binding agreements can ensure cooperation during knowledge dissemination. Therefore, in the management of open source initiatives, the research outcomes to be disseminated, the format for dissemination, and the knowledge to be privatized should be clearly understood by all the participants. Internal rules or mechanisms used to promote cooperative behavior can include: formalizing the requirements to join the knowledge network; ensuring frequent interactions; encouraging communication between participants; punishing defection; and setting the boundary for access to knowledge. An authority that regulates access to knowledge can ensure that a fair and efficient knowledge governance strategy is indeed used (Ostrom et al., 1994).

If and when knowledge is appropriated through the filing of patents, rules should further encourage licensing that provides the greatest collective value to the initiative members and/or the public at large. For example, many of the open source initiatives analyzed by Allarakhia et al. (2010) advocated the use of royalty-free non-exclusive licenses. Where technology can be substituted through non-infringing work-around solutions, a patent holder will also have an incentive to offer a non-exclusive license, rather than face competition without any possible compensation for his/her initial discovery. Alternatively, in cases where the market for technology is relatively small with technology having zero standalone commercial value, a patent holder may need to offer a non-exclusive license to ensure that a downstream developer will use the

Table 11.2 Managing open-source-based innovation

Open-source management issue	Rules, options, solutions
Participation in an open source initiative	Participation rules; entrance costs to signal commitment
Structure of initiative—open or closed access	Participation rules; binding agreements
Organization of knowledge production activities	Project, technology, and/or geographic-based teams
Encouraging cooperation during knowledge production	Enabling frequent interactions and communication; punishing defection e.g. costs associated with defection; regulating authority
Encouraging cooperation during knowledge dissemination	Public databases; internal rules and external guidelines regarding appropriation and licensing; patent pools; clearinghouses to manage knowledge and technology

technology in products, thereby enabling the patent holder to reap the rewards of his/her original discovery.

From a mode of entry perspective, open source initiatives can level the playing field for new entrants into a technological arena. Organizations from emerging markets adhering to the open source model should equally ensure that the public domain of knowledge is not only sustained, but also augmented. Public sector and private sector organizations from such economies can institute policies that preserve the public domain of knowledge, enable the formation of open source initiatives for standard or technology development, encourage the use of open licensing strategies for appropriated knowledge, and promote the use of clearinghouses that can manage knowledge and technological assets—ensuring broad dissemination and adoption of these assets. Table 11.2 outlines these issues and the rules or associated solutions that can be used to manage open-source-based initiatives.

CONCLUSION AND POLICY RECOMMENDATIONS

Rising costs, technological complexities, and shorter life cycles have put pressure on companies and their internal innovation processes. Chesbrough (2003, 2007) discusses that open business models can enable biopharmaceutical companies to leverage external resources and human capital to save time and money during the innovation process. The open business model equally ensures the generation of revenue through the licensing of technologies that cannot be fully exploited within an organization and through the in-licensing of technologies that are discovered outside the boundaries of the organization

(Chesbrough, 2003, 2007). Therefore, managers of firms in developed and in emerging markets alike should seek out these opportunities presented by open innovation—including participating in open-source-based innovation.

As new paradigms and knowledge structures emerge, we should also keep in mind that developing markets and new industries will offer once isolated firms the opportunity to develop products. Here, governments including public funding agencies and patent systems, may need to work together in order to establish an equitable opportunity for these weaker players to enter research arenas. Beyond North–South partnerships and local capacity building, it is necessary that researchers and technology transfer officers take greater caution in the patenting and licensing of technologies that have significant application in developing and under-developed markets. Maintaining and building the public domain with particular attention to knowledge that is of benefit to these economies can provide researchers with rapid and cost-effective access to knowledge. Open licensing, geographic-based licensing, assigning fair royalties are all options being employed to assist researchers in developing economies to access technologies that address, for example, local health and food needs as well as, increasingly, local energy needs. Patent systems can provide support as paradigms and knowledge structures evolve in terms of (1) breadth of claims approved in patent applications—ensuring that high standards of utility, obviousness, and written enablement are used, (2) the pre-grant and post-grant review processes used to contest new patent applications—ensuring that uncertainty surrounding patents is resolved earlier in time, and (3) the information available to patent officers regarding the characteristics of knowledge underlying patent applications.

Several funding agencies, including the National Institutes of Health (NIH) and the Wellcome Trust, have played a significant role in enabling the creation of large-scale collaborative projects. For example, the National Institute of General Medical Sciences Glue Grant provides resources for the formation of research teams to tackle complex problems that are of central importance to biomedical science but beyond the means of any one research group. Investigators request resources to form a consortium to address the research problem in a comprehensive and highly integrated fashion (www.nigms.nih.gov, 2010). By supporting such collaborations, funding agencies also indirectly encourage the norm of disclosure (NHGRI, 1996). Guarantees of disclosure and descriptions of mechanisms for knowledge dissemination are often components of an application.

Firms in emerging markets can then use the experience gained from participation in open-source-based innovation to make an informed decision regarding the investment into downstream product development—particularly in the convergence era bringing together the biological, information, and devices disciplines. In the biotechnology industry, as product development includes expensive clinical trial or field testing and regulatory approvals, an informed decision needs to be based on the firm's resource availability across the value chain as a function of a particular technological opportunity—perhaps even the need to continue participating in open innovation during product development. Initiatives such as the OSDD will provide valuable feedback as to the decision to continue pursuing open source strategies as members progress into downstream clinical studies and product development. Here the transition-point model provides value, permitting participants to determine the effective timing of appropriation activities and exit from an open source alliance. Understanding the impact of knowledge-based structures on this timing can prevent members from engaging in *ex post* holdups.

In terms of future research, it is essential to analyze new case studies involving emerging market firms and their participation in open innovation communities. These case studies should seek to look at the evolving models of open innovation as the number and type of participants change, as the objectives with respect to innovation evolve, and as the complexities associated with knowledge structures increase so that knowledge management becomes paramount (as will be the case in the emerging bioconvergence paradigm). This analysis should further seek to understand any geographic-based issues hampering technological innovation by firms in emerging markets and how to eventually position these firms to meet both global and local product needs through open innovation. I advocate that a repository of governance strategies including any licensing templates be created, as has been created by BiOS and the Creative Commons, so that stakeholders can effectively manage knowledge-based assets from the outset of any collaborative development effort. The case studies included in this chapter provide a starting point for the creation of this repository and lessons learned (www.bioendeavor.net, 2011; see Table 11.3).

Table 11.3 Future policy recommendations

Strategic issue	Policy implications
Enabling large-scale global research projects	Federal policy encouraging the development of global teams with participants from the public and private sectors including North-South and South-South partnerships
Encouraging open-source innovation in large-scale global research projects	Development of federal funding proposals with dissemination clauses
Careful crafting of and management of intellectual property rights	Pre-grant/post-grant patent reviews; open licensing, geographic-based licensing, assigning fair-royalties
Learning from past governance strategies	Creation of a repository of governance strategies and licensing templates used by previous open source initiatives

REFERENCES

Allarakhia, M. (2009) "Open Source Biopharmaceutical Innovation: A Mode of Entry for Firms in Emerging Markets," *Journal of Business Chemistry*, 6(1): 11–30.

Allarakhia, M., Kilgour, D.M., and Fuller, D. (2010) "Modeling the incentive to participate in open source biopharmaceutical innovation," *R&D Management*, 40 (1): 50–66.

Allarakhia, M., and Walsh, S. (2011) "Managing knowledge assets under conditions of radical change: The case of the pharmaceutical industry," *Technovation*, 31 (2–3): 105–17.

Allarakhia, M., and Wensley, A. (2005) "Innovation and intellectual property rights in systems biology," *Nature Biotechnology*, 23: 1485–8.

Antonelli, C. (2003) "Knowledge complementarity and fungeability: Implications for regional strategy," *Regional Studies*, 37 (6–7): 595–606.

Arora, A., and Fosfuri, A. (2003) "Licensing the market for technology," *Journal of Economic Behavior & Organization*, 52 (2): 277–95.

Atkinson, P., Batchelor, C., and Parsons, E. (1998) "Trajectories of collaboration and competition in a medical discovery," *Science, Technology and Human Values*, 23: 259–84.

Bianchi, M., Cavaliere, A., Chiaroni, D., Frattini, F., and Chiesa, V. (2011) "Organizational modes for open innovation in the bio-pharmaceutical industry: An exploratory approach," *Technovation*, 31 (1): 22–33.

Blumenthal, D. (1992) "Academic-industry relationships in the life sciences: Extent, consequences, and management," *Journal of the American Medical Association*, 268: 3344–9.

Blumenthal, D., Causino, N., and Campbell, E.G. (1997) "Academic-industry research relationships in genetics: A field apart," *Nature Genetics*, 16 (1): 104–8.

Boardman, P. (2008) "Beyond the stars: The impact of affiliation with university biotechnology centers on the industrial involvement of university scientists," *Technovation*, 28: 291–7.

Burk, D.L., and Lemley M.A. (2003) "Biotechnology's Uncertainty Principle," in F. Scott Kieff, ed., *Perspectives on Properties of the Human Genome Project*. San Diego, CA: Elsevier Academic Press, 305–54.

Camargo, A.A., and Simpson, A.J.G. (2003) "Collaborative research networks work," *The Journal of Clinical Investigation*, 112 (4): 468–71.

Chesbrough, H.W. (2003) "The Era of Open Innovation," *MIT Sloan Management Review*, 44 (3): 35–41.

Chesbrough, H.W. (2007) "Why Companies Should Have Open Business Models," *MIT Sloan Management Review*, 48 (2): 22–8.

Chesbrough, H.W., Vanhaverbeke, W., and West J. (2006) *Open Innovation: Researching a New Paradigm*. Oxford: Oxford University Press.

Child, J., and Faulkner, D. (1998) *Strategies of Cooperation: Managing Alliances, Networks and Joint Ventures*. Oxford: Oxford University Press.

Chokshi, D.A., Parker, M., and Kwiatkowski, D.P. (2006) "Data sharing and intellectual property in a genomics epidemiology network: Policies for large-scale research collaboration," *Bulletin of the World Health Organization*, 84 (5): 382–7.

Cimoli, M., Dosi, G., Mazzoleni, R., and Sampat, B. (2009) "Innovation, technical change and patents in the development process: A long term view," for task force on "Intellectual Property," within the Initiative for Policy Dialogue (IPD): Working paper series, March 2011, Columbia University, New York.

Coccia, M, and Rolfo S. (2008) "Strategic change of public research units in their scientific activity," *Technovation*, 28: 485–94.

Dal Poz, M.E.S. (2000) "Da dupla à tripla hélice: o projeto genoma Xylella," Dissertação (Mestrado em Geociência): Campinas, IG-Unicamp.

Das, T.K., and Teng, B.S. (2000) "A resource-based theory of strategic alliances," *Journal of Management*, 26: 31–61.

David, P.A. (2009) "Mitigating damages to global science from 'the anti-commons,'" draft chapter for The Intellectual Property Rights Task Force Conference, Manchester.

Drews, J. (1998) *In Quest of Tomorrow's Medicine*. New York: Springer-Verlag.

Dutfield, G. (2003) *Intellectual Property Rights and the Life Sciences Industries: A Twentieth-Century History*. Burlington, VT: Ashgate Publishing.

Foray, D. (2004) *The Economics of Knowledge*. Cambridge, MA: MIT Press.

Graff. G.D. (2007) "Echoes of Bayh-Dole? A survey of IP and technology transfer policies in emerging and developing economies," in Krattiger, et al., eds, *Intellectual Property Management in Health and Agricultural Innovation: A Handbook of Best Practices*. MIHR, and Davis, CA; and PIPRA, Oxford, p. 169–95.

Gintis, H., Alden Smith, E., and Bowles, S. (2001) "Costly signaling and cooperation," *Journal of Theoretical Biology*, 213: 103–19.

Grant, R.M., and Baden-Fuller, C. (2004) "A knowledge accessing theory of strategic alliances," *Journal of Management Studies*, 41 (1): 61–84.

Greenberg, D.S. (2007) *Science for Sale: The Perils, Rewards, and Delusions of Campus Capitalism*. Chicago, IL: University of Chicago Press.

Gulati, R., Khanna, T., and Nohria, N. (1994) "Unilateral commitments and the importance of process in alliances," *MIT Sloan Management Review*, 35 (3): 61–9.

Heller, M.A., and Eisenberg, R.S. (1998) "Can patents deter innovation? The anti-commons in biomedical research," *Science*, 280: 698–701.

Hood, L.E. (2000) "The university office of technology transfer: The inventor/researcher's view," CASRIP Symposium Publication Series, No. 5. Seattle, WA: CASRIP, University of Washington.

Hoyle, K. and Pries, F. (2009) "Repeat commercializers, the habitual entrepreneurs of the university-industry technology transfer," *Technovation*, 29: 682–9.

Hu, A.G.Z., and Jaffe, A.B. (2009) "Lessons from the Economics Literature on the Likely Consequences of International Harmonization of IPR Protection," draft chapter for task force on Intellectual Property, within the Initiative for Policy Dialogue (IPD): Columbia University, New York.

Hunter, J., and Stephens, S. (2010) "Is open innovation the way forward for big pharma?" *Nature Review Drug Discovery*, 9: 87–8.

Jishnu, L. (2008) "Does India need a Bayh-Dole Act? Patently absurd," *Business Standard*, 9 July 2008.

Kaiser, J. (2007) "Synthetic biology: Attempt to patent artificial organism draws a protest," *Science*, 316: 1557.

Kautt, M., Walsh, S., and Bittner, K. (2007) "Global distribution of micro–nano technology and fabrication centers: A portfolio analysis approach," *Technology Forecasting and Social Change*, 74: 1697–717.

Kieff, S.F. (ed.) (2003) *Perspectives on Properties of the Human Genome Project*. San Diego, CA: Academic Press.

Kitano, H. (2001) "Systems biology: Toward systems-level understanding of biological systems," in Kitano, H. (ed.) *Foundation of Systems Biology*. Cambridge, MA: MIT Press, 1–29.

Kitano, H. (2002) "Systems biology: A brief overview," *Science*, 295 (5560): 1662–4.

Kogut, B. (1998) "Joint ventures: Theoretical and empirical perspectives," *Strategic Management Journal*, 9: 319–32.

Kollock, P. (1998) "Social dilemmas: The anatomy of cooperation," *Annual Review of Sociology*, 24: 183–214.

Lakhani, K.R., and von Hippel, E. (2003) "How open source software works: Free user-to-user assistance," *Research Policy*, 32 (6): 923–43.

Lemley, M.A. (2005) "Patenting nanotechnology," *Stanford Law Review*, 58: 601–30.

Macilwain, C., and Neto, R. (2000) "A springboard to success," *Nature*, 407: 440.

Malhotra, N. (2003) "The nature of knowledge and the entry mode decision," *Organization Science*, 24 (6): 935–59.

Menon, S. (2009) "Researchers sans borders," *Business Standard*, 1 March 2009.

Merges, R. (1994) "Intellectual property rights and bargaining breakdown: The case of blocking patents," *Tennessee Law Review*, 62: 75–106.

Munos, B. (2010) "Can open-source drug R&D repower pharmaceutical innovation?" *Clinical Pharmacology and Therapeutics*, 87 (5): 534–6.

Newbert, S.L., Gopalakrishnan, S., and Kirchhoff, B.A. (2009) "Looking beyond resources: Exploring the importance of entrepreneurship to firm-level competitive advantage in technologically intensive industries," *Technovation*, 28: 6–19.

NHGRI (1996) Policy Regarding Intellectual Property of Human Genomic Sequence, *NHGRI*, 9 April.

O Estado de São Paulo (1997) "Fapesp quer reunir os melhores cérebros," *NetEstado*, 11 October.

Open Source Drug Discovery (OSDD), "What Is OSDD," <http://www.osdd.net/about-us/what-is-OSDD>, 21 January 2014.

Ostrom, E., Gardner, R., and Walker, J. (1994) *Rules, Games and Common-Pool Resources*. Ann Arbor, MI: University of Michigan Press.

Ostrom, V. (2006) "Some developments in the study of market choice, public choice and institutional choice," in Jack Rabin, W. Bartley Hildreth, and Gerald J. Miller, eds, *Handbook of Public Administration*. New York: CRC Press.

Powell, W.W., Koput, K.K., and Smith-Doerr, L. (1996) "Inter-organizational collaboration and the locus of innovation: Network of learning in biotechnology," *Administrative Science Quarterly*, 41: 116–45.

Powell, W.W., and Owen-Smith, J. (1998) "Universities and the market for intellectual property in the life sciences," *Journal of Policy Analysis and Management*, 17: 253–77.

Rai, A.K., and Boyle, J. (2007) "Synthetic biology: Caught between property rights, the public domain, and the commons," *PLoS Biology*, 5: 389–92.

Rai, A.K., and Eisenberg, R.S. (2003) "Bayh-Dole reform and the progress of biomedicine," *Law and Contemporary Problems*, 66: 289–314.

Rampersad, G., Quester, P., and Troshani, I. (2010) "Managing innovation networks: Exploratory evidence from ICT, biotechnology and nanotechnology networks," *Industrial Marketing Management*, 39: 793–805.

Reichman J.H. (2004) *Testimony before the NIH Public Hearing on March-In Rights under the Bayh-Dole Act*. Washington, DC: National Institutes of Health.

Reid, D., Bussiere, D., and Greenway, K. (2001) "Alliance formation issues for knowledge-based enterprises," *International Journal of Management Reviews*, 3: 79–100.

Reppy, J. (2008) "A biomedical military–industrial complex?" *Technovation*, 28 (12): 802–11.

Romig, A. et al. (2007) "An introduction to nanotechnology policy: Opportunities and constraints for emerging and established economies," *Technological Forecasting and Social Change*, 74: 1634–42.

Scherer, F.M. (2002) "The economics of human gene patent," *Academic Medicine*, 77: 1348–67.

Schwartz, J., and Pollack, A. (2010) "Judge invalidates human gene patent," *New York Times*, 29 March 2010.

Scotchmer, S. (1991) "Standing on the shoulders of giants: Cumulative research and the patent law," *The Journal of Economic Perspectives*, 5: 29–41.

Scotchmer, S. (2004) *Innovation and Incentives*. Cambridge, MA: MIT Press.

Scott, W., and O'Donnell, M.J. (2009) "Distributed drug discovery, part 1: Linking academia and combinatorial chemistry to find drug leads for developing world diseases," *Journal of Combinatorial Chemistry*, 11 (1): 3–13.

Shapiro, C. (2001) "Navigating the patent thickets: Cross-licenses, patent pools, and standard-setting," in A. Jaffe, J. Lerner, and S. Stern, eds, *Innovation Policy and the Economy*. Cambridge: MIT Press. pp. 119–50.

Shaver, L. (2008) *Access to Knowledge in Brazil: New Research on Intellectual Property, Innovation and Development*. New Haven, CT: Information Society Project.

Simpson, A.J., and Perez, J.F. (1998) "ONSA, the Sao Paulo Virtual Genomics Institute: Organization for Nucleotide Sequencing and Analysis", *Nature Biotechnology*, 16: 795–96.

Simpson, A.J., et al. (2000) "The genome sequence of the plant pathogen Xylella fastidiosa," *Nature*, 13: 151–7.

So, A.D. et al. (2008) "Is Bayh-Dole good for developing countries? Lessons from the US experience," *PLoS Biology*, 6 (10): e262.

Staropoli, C. (1998) "Cooperation in R&D in the pharmaceutical industry: The network as an organizational innovation governing technological innovation," *Technovation*, 18: 13–23.

Sulston, J. (2006) "Staking claims in the biotechnology Klondike," *Bulletin of the World Health Organization*, 84 (5): 412–13.

Teece, D.J. (1986) "Profiting for technological innovation: Implications for integration, collaboration, licensing and public policy," *Research Policy*, 15 (6): 785–805.

Thomas, Z. (2005) "Open source agricultural biotechnology," *Current Science*, 88 (8): 1212–13.

Thumm, N. (2004) "Patents for genetic inventions: A tool to promote technological advance or a limitation for upstream inventions?" *Technovation*, 25: 1410–17.

van der Valk, T., Moors, E.H.M., Meeus, M.T.H. (2009) "Conceptualizing patterns in the dynamics of emerging technologies: The case of biotechnology developments in the Netherlands," *Technovation*, 29: 247–64.

Walsh, S. (2004) "Roadmapping a disruptive technology: A case study—the emerging microsystems and top-down nanosystems industry," *Technological Forecasting and Social Change*, 71: 161–85.

Walsh, J.P., Arora, A., and Cohen, W.M. (2003) "Effects of research tool patents and licensing on biomedical innovation," in *Patents in the Knowledge-Based Economy*. Wesley M. Cohen and Stephen A. Merrill, eds, Washington, DC: The National Academies Press, 285–340.

Washburn J. (2005) *University Inc.: The Corporate Corruption of Higher Education*. New York: Basic Books.

Weigelt, J. (2009) "The case for open-access chemical biology," *EMBO Reports*, 10 (1): 941–5.

Woodcock, J. (2010) "Precompetitive research: A new prescription for drug development?" *Clinical Pharmacology and Therapeutics*, 87 (5): 521–3.

www.bioendeavor.net (accessed 04/2011).

www.bios.net (accessed 10/2010).

www.biota.org.br (accessed 10/2010).

www.dndi.org (accessed 04/2011).

www.fapesp.br (accessed 10/2010).

www.gsk.com (accessed 10/2010).

www.innocentive.com (accessed 10/2010).

www.lilly.com (accessed 10/2010).

www.nigms.nih.gov (accessed 10/2010).

www.osdd.net (accessed 10/2010).

www.Pd2.lilly.com (accessed 10/2010).

www.patentlens.net (accessed 10/2010).

www.sysborgtb.osdd.net (accessed 10/2010).

www.uspto.gov (accessed 10/2010).

www.watson.fapesp.br (accessed 10/2010).

12

Intellectual Property and Alternatives: Strategies for Green Innovation

Jerome H. Reichman, Arti K. Rai, Richard G. Newell,
and Jonathan B. Wiener

This chapter was originally prepared for Chatham House as a Discussion Paper in 2008. It has not been updated since then. The authors are grateful to Chatham House for the opportunity to explore these issues and to further disseminate this Discussion Paper.[1]

INTRODUCTION

There is widespread agreement that achieving the very substantial reductions in greenhouse gas (GHG) emissions necessary to stabilize GHG concentrations at 450 to 750 parts per million (ppm) will require innovation and large-scale adoption of GHG-reducing technologies throughout the global energy system.[2] The associated policy debate is therefore not so much over the importance of new technology per se in solving the climate problem, but rather over what the most effective policies and institutions are for achieving the dramatic technological changes and associated emission reductions necessary for stabilization.

Although many policies and institutions relevant to green innovation have been discussed, one area to which relatively little attention has been paid until recently is intellectual property rights (IPRs). The absence of attention may stem from the reality that IPRs are, by design, decentralized, market-driven incentives that presume appropriate market signals on the demand side. In the area of green innovation, by contrast, the primary problem has been the absence of appropriate greenhouse gas (GHG) pricing and hence the absence of an appropriate demand side signal. However, assuming the demand side problem is fixed (through interventions such as carbon taxes or cap and trade systems)[3] then the issue of how IPRs—and various alternatives to IPRs—can most usefully play a role in fostering the supply of green innovation will necessarily come to the fore.

In this report, we provide an analysis of how IPRs, and alternatives to IPRs, might operate in green innovation. Section I of the paper discusses the economics of green innovation, including the important role that will need to be played by the private sector. Because of the critical role of the private sector, demand side issues will need to be fixed in order for there to be an appropriate level of green innovation. Section II discusses the IPR issues, principally involving patents, that may arise if and when GHG externalities are addressed through the appropriate pricing of greenhouse gases. Because these problems will primarily arise in the future (if at all), we rely heavily in this part on analogies to current technological sectors (and sections thereof) that are currently experiencing difficulties. Section III addresses alternatives to traditional patents and exclusive licenses, including patent pools, liability rules, and prizes.

Currently, more than 95 per cent of global R&D takes place in OECD countries. Thus Sections II and III primarily address IPR difficulties for R&D in these countries. However, if climate change is going to be addressed successfully, clean technology must be adopted globally. Thus, in section IV, we examine at some length the international context. Section IV focuses on intellectual property buyouts, the potential for international R&D treaties, impediments to technology transfer that may be posed by IPRs, and the use of IPRs to stimulate indigenous innovation in developing countries.

I. ECONOMIC BACKGROUND

While the idea of balancing the atmospheric GHG stock by reducing the net GHG flow to zero seems simple enough, the technological reality of what it will take to do this is far from simple. Currently 69 per cent of global anthropogenic GHG emissions come from fossil fuels, such as oil, coal, and natural gas, which satisfy 81 per cent of global energy supply.[4] The remainder of global energy is supplied by renewable energy (13 per cent) and nuclear power (6 per cent).[5] Stabilizing GHG concentrations will therefore require large-scale and widespread substitution toward energy technologies with low-to-zero net GHG emissions throughout the global energy system. New technologies may also be needed in other sectors to reduce GHG emissions, such as improved agricultural methods or crop varieties to reduce the conversion of forests (which sequester carbon) to farmland; improved technologies for biofuels that avoid raising corn prices and thereby spurring deforestation;

and improved agricultural techniques to produce crops and raise ruminant animals with reduced emissions of methane and nitrous oxide.

To gauge, in economic terms, the magnitude of the innovation challenge presented by climate change, it is helpful to consider possible targets for GHG reduction and the projected costs of achieving these targets.[6] These projected costs, most commonly measured in terms of reduced Gross Domestic Product (GDP), indicate the scale of the benefit that could come from innovations that significantly reduce (or eliminate) the cost disadvantage of climate-friendly technologies relative to the competition. Many proposals, and most analyses, have centered on reduction paths that are consistent with ultimate stabilization targets in the range of 450–550 ppm CO_2. Modeling scenarios of cost-effective global climate-mitigation policy suggest that, for targets in this range, the cost of GHG mitigation through 2050 is trillions or tens of trillions of dollars of discounted GDP, or an annualized cost in the tens to hundreds of billions per year. Longer-term total costs through 2100 are approximately double this amount. While these estimates are based on numerous economic and policy assumptions, they give a sense of the magnitude of the payoff from innovations that could significantly lower the cost of achieving various GHG reduction goals.

Many studies demonstrate the central role that the availability and cost of advanced energy technologies plays in determining the cost of achieving various GHG reduction goals.[7] Virtually all studies find that a cost-effective technology solution entails a mix of energy efficiency, low-GHG energy supply, as well as emission reductions in non-CO_2 GHGs. Thus, R&D supporting such a transition must also be broad-based, covering a wide range of technological opportunities. For example, one study finds that if we were limited to technologies available in 2005, the present value cost of achieving stabilization at 550 ppm CO_2 would be over \$20 trillion greater than with expected developments in energy efficiency, hydrogen energy technologies, advanced bioenergy, and wind and solar technologies.[8] While it is not typically made explicit in these models, they presume a significant degree of innovative effort in the form of R&D, learning, and diffusion of new technologies that would have to underpin these assumed technological improvements.

Other studies have found that accelerated technology development offers the potential to dramatically reduce the costs of stabilization, with advanced technology scenarios reducing the cumulative costs of stabilization by 50 per cent or more, yielding economic benefits of hundreds of billions to trillions of dollars globally (see Figure 12.1).[9] While one might reasonably argue over detailed modeling assumptions, these and other results demonstrate that technological advances have the potential to significantly decrease the costs of attaining societal goals for climate change mitigation. The challenge is to structure policy to maximize the likelihood that we will harness these technological opportunities as effectively and efficiently as possible.

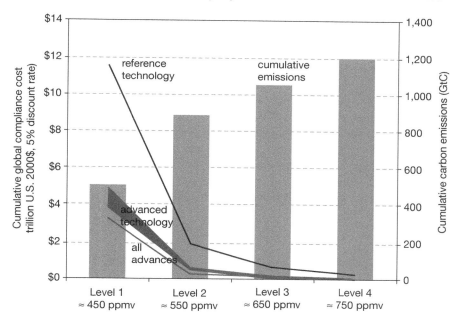

Figure 12.1 Cumulative global mitigation costs under alternative technology scenarios

Source: Clarke et al. (2006, p. 65).

With respect to technological innovation, both the public and private sector play a critical role. However, in terms of scale, the private sector is currently the major actor. One useful indicator of innovative activity is R&D spending. Industry is by far the largest player in R&D spending, funding over 60 per cent and performing almost 70 per cent of R&D globally in 2006 (the most recent year for which complete data were available at the time of writing). This industrial R&D is stimulated by market demand for technologically advanced products and processes. Establishing a GHG emission price (through policies such as cap-and-trade and emission taxes) is thus essential from a technology perspective: such pricing creates a demand-driven, profit-based incentive for the private sector to gain from selling low-GHG products that are currently available and, more importantly, to invest effort in developing new, lower-cost climate-friendly innovations.

If private-sector profit incentives are not clearly aligned with societal GHG reduction goals, then any public R&D spending will likely push against an insurmountable tide. Conveniently, as discussed further in section IV, the most global innovative effort currently takes place in the developed countries that are expected to take the most significant initial steps towards implementing GHG emission pricing.

For GHG emission policy to provide an effective inducement to innovation, however, it is critical that the policy be credible to the private sector over the long term. Given the sometimes substantial time lags between initial discovery and profitable market penetration, companies must be confident that there will indeed be sufficient demand once their innovations reach the market. Such confidence would be increased by domestic policies and international agreements that put in place GHG emission targets whose stringency is spelled out for many decades in advance, and that provide stable financial incentives across a wide array of technological solutions.

Of course, government funding of relevant basic research does exist and could grow beyond its current levels. Thus the discussion below addresses at some length the special IPR issues raised by publicly funded research.

II. GREEN TECHNOLOGY AND INTELLECTUAL PROPERTY: A SURVEY OF THE CENTRAL QUESTIONS

As discussed in section I, innovation in the climate-mitigation arena faces an environmental externality problem not raised by other types of innovation. The GHG externality must be addressed on the technology demand side, by putting a price on greenhouse gases. But the GHG externality does not represent the only potential barrier to innovation. In this section, we address IPR issues that need to be thought through, particularly as the GHG externality is increasingly addressed.

In recent years, a few analysts have begun to address how IPRs might affect the development of green technologies. Given the early stage of research in certain areas, and in the absence of appropriate GHG pricing in most of the world, this analysis is necessarily quite speculative. Nonetheless, some analysts have suggested reasons why patenting and associated restrictive practices might pose impediments to creation and diffusion of climate-friendly technologies. In contrast, others have seen little current evidence of dysfunction and have suggested that strong patent rights may assist in the development and dissemination of environmentally friendly technologies. Unfortunately, given the relatively nascent stage of much of the technology, there is little compelling empirical evidence to support either point of view.

At the moment, green technology looks too heterogeneous to be subject to any across-the-board generalizations. Unlike other heterogeneous technologies, moreover, (e.g. nanotechnology), the U.S. Patent and Trademark Office (PTO) does not recognize green technology as a class. Thus, it is not necessarily easy to find reliable quantitative information about patent rights in green technology.

However, there is considerable evidence that the patent system is not functioning effectively in some other areas of technology, particularly information technology and to some extent biotechnology.[10] Controversy over the existing system has spurred concerted efforts to implement patent reform in the United States. It has also blocked attempts to further harmonize substantive patent law norms in a proposed WIPO treaty.[11]

Accordingly, we begin this section by examining the operation of the patent system with respect to other technologies for which we have considerable evidence. Because of the possibility that a significant percentage of green innovation may eventually have a publicly funded component, we pay special attention to the role of IPRs in areas such as biotechnology that rely substantially on public funding of relevant, basic research. We then discuss green innovation, both generally and in particular sectors. In each of the major sectors, we suggest scenarios for the future by drawing upon the roles, both positive and negative, that IPR is playing in other, more developed areas of innovation.

a. The existing evidence for other technologies

1. Innovation generally

The economic and legal literature on IPRs has long recognized the positive role that such rights (and particularly patents) can play in the innovation context. The most obvious positive role involves the incentive effects that should emerge if the innovator can capture a substantial percentage of the very significant positive externalities associated with innovation (as defined to include initial invention, further development, and ultimate commercialization/diffusion). Economists have estimated that social rates of return from innovation can be 30 per cent or more.[12] Although innovators should be able to capture some of this return through mechanisms such as head-start advantages and trade secrecy, patents also represent a powerful mechanism.[13]

A related, potentially positive effect is the role patents can play in creating small-firm-driven "markets for technology." Economic theory suggests that patents should help to ensure that information retains its value even when it is disclosed outside the boundaries of the firm.[14] In other words, patents should allow innovation rents to be appropriated even when a firm is not vertically integrated and thus cannot itself participate in all stages of the R&D process. To the extent that a system of industrial organization that includes small firms and markets is likely to yield more innovation (particularly cumulative innovation) than a system that comprises only large, vertically integrated firms,[15] patents' role in promoting the former type of industrial organization is important.

To some extent, the available empirical evidence backs these propositions on the positive role played by patents. In particular, for small firms, patents do appear to play a positive role in attracting venture capital, particularly in the biotechnology industry. One study reports that 50 per cent of biotechnology firms that received venture capital (VC) backing in the late 1990s held patents;[16] moreover, this 50 per cent is probably an underestimate, because (as discussed further below) many biotechnology firms receive exclusive licenses on university-backed research.[17]

For large, publicly traded firms, by contrast, the evidence indicates that in the 1990s, U.S. patents had significant private value (i.e. value for appropriating returns from innovation) primarily in the chemical and pharmaceutical sectors.[18] In the pharmaceutical and medical device sectors, the cost of regulatory approval for end products make patent protection for such products (or marketing exclusivities that resemble patent protection, such as those provided by the Orphan Drug Act) a virtual *sine qua non*.

Patents can also pose obstacles for innovation. Many of these obstacles consist of transaction cost problems that can arise in the licensing necessary for follow-on innovation. For example, as a historical matter, progress in the automobile and aircraft industries was hampered by problems in licensing broad patents on foundational platforms.[19] In other areas, problems associated with broad patents on research platforms were narrowly averted. In the area of computer hardware, the threat of broad patents loomed large until government action forced licensing of the AT&T transistor patent as well as patents obtained by Texas Instruments and Fairchild Instruments on integrated circuits. As for software, it was already a robust industry before software patents became available, at least in any widespread fashion.

A relatively small number of broad patents on foundational research do not represent the only potential difficulty. There is also the possibility that a follow-on inventor will be deterred by the need to clear rights on a "thicket"[20] of overlapping patents[21] that cover either a research platform or individual components of an end product. In this regard, it bears mention that a 2003 IP survey of IP managers found that 23 per cent said that competitor patents played an important role in decisions to abandon development of otherwise promising technologies.[22] Currently, these problems appear to be most salient in the area of information and communications technology (ICT).[23] Not only do products in information technology represent combinations of dozens if not hundreds of patented components, but patent claims in this area often do not give clear notice of their boundaries.

Even where patent thickets do not prevent projects from going forward,[24] they create the potential for inefficient holdup. If a follow-on improver has to clear rights on a plethora of patents with vague boundaries, it may either miss certain patents or simply not bother with the rights-clearing exercise. The patent holder can then sue for infringement after the improver has already invested. And to the extent that the patent holder is able credibly to assert the threat of injunctive relief, it may be able to appropriate from the improver far more than the value of their patent.

Holdup problems are particularly salient in the related context of standard-setting, where substantial investments in standards are often made prior to a patent holder's coming forward to assert its claim. Although these types of problems are usually associated with the ICT industries, they can arise in other industries. Indeed, one prominent recent case of alleged patent abuse in a standard setting context directly involved environmental technology. In this 2003 case, the Federal Trade Commission alleged that the Union Oil Company of California ("Unocal") violated Section 5 of the FTC Act in falsely representing to the California Air Resources Board that it did not have relevant patent interests when it participated in a standard-setting exercise involving the composition of low-emissions gasoline. In fact, according to the FTC, Unocal had begun the process of obtaining relevant patents. After the standard had been adopted, and other refiners had made investments to comply with the standard, Unocal obtained and disclosed the patents. When other refiners filed suit to have the patents declared invalid and not infringed, Unocal counterclaimed with a charge of infringement. The court found Unocal's patents valid and infringed and ordered the other refiners to pay royalties that could exceed $500 million.

In certain cases the potential problems caused by patents do not involve transaction cost difficulties associated with licensing foundational research for follow-on work or negotiating patent thickets. Rather, the prospect of patents may lead to "too much" R&D—that is, rent-dissipating races.[25] Moreover, because patent law sometimes allows multiple parties to own overlapping patents over what is essentially the same technology, some races may have multiple victors. In that case, the overlapping patents held by multiple parties may lead to substantial, and expensive, litigation. A case in point is microarray technology. Microarrays are a powerful genomic research platform that involves depositing short DNA sequences on a support medium as a mechanism to test for gene expression. Over the past decade, multiple firms (including Affymetrix, Hyseq, Incyte, and Oxford Gene Technologies) that raced to dominate the platform have tangled in court with respect to patents they hold on this platform.[26] Although many of these suits have resulted in settlements involving cross-licensing, with the result that no firm is currently a monopoly provider, it is unclear whether microarray patents have, on balance, been beneficial.

In the case of microarray technology, the overlapping patents held by multiple firms were arguably the consequence of an inefficient race. In other cases, particularly in the information technology industry, firms may amass patent portfolios that overlap heavily with those of their competitors and are used almost exclusively for defensive purposes. Although this defensive accumulation of patents appears at best inefficient, and at worst can be used to exclude competitors that do not have such patents, eliminating defensive use poses an obvious collective action problem.

Problems with foundational patents, patent thickets, races, and patent portfolios, are exacerbated when patents are of low quality. Low quality can stem from patentability standards that are too lax or from the PTO's failure to mandate compliance with those standards. Low-quality patents may cover inventions that are obvious. Alternatively, they may claim too much inventive territory or fail to specify exactly what territory they cover. In recent years, problems with low-quality patents have been particularly salient in the ICT industries.

At least in the United States, some recent decisions by the Supreme Court may alleviate some of the problems caused by low-quality patents. The court's 2007 decision in *KSR v. Teleflex*[27] raises the patentability requirement of "non-obviousness" in a manner that calls into question many patents that represent combinations of previously known information. Additionally, the court's 2006 decision in *eBay v. MercExchange* reverses prior patent law that appeared to mandate injunctive relief once a patent had been proved valid and infringed. Under the court's current new standard, district courts have discretion to award monetary damages rather than injunctions barring use of the patented invention, particularly when the patent in question covers only a small piece of the defendant's product, and the patent holder is not a direct competitor of the infringer.[28]

Interestingly, one of the first Federal Circuit cases to address a district court's handling of damages post-*eBay* arises in the area of green technology. In *Paice v. Toyota*, the patentee, a non-manufacturing entity, had sued Toyota for manufacturing cars that infringed patents covering a drive train for hybrid electric vehicles. The Federal Circuit affirmed the district court's decision to deny permanent injunctive relief and instead order Toyota to pay Paice an "ongoing royalty."[29] The potentially significant effects of these Supreme Court decisions illustrate that assessments regarding whether patents are likely to hinder or promote innovation are subject to ongoing revision.

On the other hand, even with new decisions from the courts, administrative processes are likely, for the foreseeable future, to continue to produce questionable patents. In the United States, the available evidence indicates that the PTO struggles to keep quality at acceptable levels. The PTO has fewer than 6,000 examiners for the more than 400,000 patent applications filed each year. So the typical examiner has only a few days to examine an application on which the applicant may have spent many months. The examiner also bears the burden of proving a patent application is invalid. Moreover, under the complex incentive-based compensation regime for patent examiners, accumulating disposal credits (or "counts") may be easier if the examiner grants a patent application rather than denying it.[30] Similarly, the president of the

European Patent Office has expressed concern that the patent system is "drifting towards dysfunctionality."[31]

In addition to false positives in the form of improperly granted patents, there is also some possibility of false negatives. There are anecdotal reports that, in the last few years, the U.S. PTO has responded to complaints that it grants "too many" patents by routinely (and arbitrarily) denying patent applications the first time they are filed. Certainly, the evidence indicates that the percentage of first applications that are denied has gone up in the last few years.[32]

Finally, in both the U.S. and Europe, there are very serious concerns about increasing time delays in patent examination. In the U.S., total pendency for a first application rose from 25.9 months in 2003 to 31.9 months in 2007. Overall, the U.S. has a backlog of over 750,000 patent applications. The delays caused by this backlog have particularly severe implications for small firms that may use patents to attract venture capital.

2. The case of biotechnology

For purposes of thinking about green technology, biotechnology represents a particularly interesting area in which to investigate in some detail the effect of patents. Not only will green technologies, such as second- and third-generation biofuels, be based on biotechnology but the green technology sector, like the biotechnology sector, is likely, in the long run, to rely heavily on complex interactions between publicly and privately funded research.

The history of publicly funded research in biotechnology suggests several key lessons. First, where the invention in question is a publicly funded research platform that can be adopted by industry without transfer of tacit knowledge or follow-on investment, the conventional rationale for patenting publicly funded research—that patents provide incentives for such knowledge transfer and investment—does not apply. Many of biotechnology's most useful and widely diffused platform technologies—including monoclonal antibodies and Maxam-Gilbert sequencing—were generated through public funding and were not patented. Second, if the publicly funded platform invention does happen to be patented, nonexclusive licensing should be used to ensure maximum diffusion. For example, although the Cohen-Boyer recombinant DNA technologies were patented, the University of California voluntarily converted its exclusive right into a liability rule—a non-exclusive "take and pay" rule—under a standard form contract.[33] Although such nonexclusive licensing increases costs relative to free technology transfer, modest licensing fees should not impose an undue burden on commercialization.

Unfortunately, at least in the U.S., the available empirical evidence indicates that institutions that make decisions on whether to seek patents on their publicly funded research, and on how to license patents that they have secured, do not always make these decisions in a manner that comports with the public interest in efficient technology transfer.[34] Thus, there is reason to consider modifying laws such as Bayh-Dole that govern the patenting of publicly funded research, at least to the extent that they confer unfettered discretion over patenting to institutions that receive public funding.

In the case of research tools and platforms that are privately developed, patents are likely to be necessary. As noted, small firms that develop such platforms appear to need patents to attract venture capital. Thus, for example, patents on polymerase chain reaction (PCR) technology may have been critical to the business model of the small firm, Cetus, that initially developed the technology. But such patents may also pose problems. Given the lack of an exemption for academic research in U.S. patent law,[35] academics who cannot afford to pay commercial licensing fees for a key patent must rely on the hope that the patent holder will refrain from suing academics. Essentially, academics must hope that the patent holders engage in an informal regime of price discrimination. This price discrimination ultimately arose in the case of PCR but only after some uncertainty.[36] More generally, although academics appear routinely to ignore patents with impunity,[37] routine lawbreaking is not necessarily a stable equilibrium.

While biotechnology platforms, such as PCR and recombinant DNA, were covered by a few patents with a single owner, other research platforms may be covered by multiple patents held by dispersed owners, public and private. Such thickets may become particularly salient in interdisciplinary research areas of biotechnology, such as synthetic biology, that draw not only upon the life sciences but also upon computer science and electrical engineering.[38] Although there is evidence that biotechnology and pharmaceutical firms may be able to avoid thickets through infringement that is secret (e.g. infringement of a research tool or process that is discovered only after the statute of limitations for lawsuits has expired) or by "off-shoring" research to countries with fewer patent restrictions,[39] these are not necessarily strategies that should be encouraged. In addition, secret infringement may not always be possible: for example, if (as discussed further below) synthetic biology's goal of producing standardized biological parts is realized, the use of such standards may be apparent. In that case, synthetic biology may be subject to the same possibility of holdup that we see in the information technology industries.[40] Notably, even those analysts who are relatively optimistic about the transaction cost difficulties associated with thickets note that "even if patents do not stop ongoing research, the very prospect of a thicket or restricted access may dissuade researchers from choosing particular projects and limit lines of attack in that way."[41]

As with the legal picture in innovation generally, the legal picture in biotechnological innovation is not stable. The *KSR* decision on non-obviousness may raise the bar for patents in interdisciplinary research: to the extent such research simply combines well known knowledge in different fields, it may no longer be patentable. The *KSR* decision may also lead to case law that makes it more difficult to secure gene patents.

b. Green technologies

With this overview of how patents work in other, more developed, technological areas, we can now consider how they may work in different sectors of green technology. Key technological areas[42] in which there is some emerging evidence regarding the influence of patents include: (1) second- and third-generation biofuels; (2) thin-film (photovoltaic) solar; (3) transportation, specifically hybrid cars and fuel cells; and (4) wind energy. These sectors are at different stages of technological development. For example, while third-generation biofuels are still at a relatively early stage of development, wind energy and hybrid cars are already at the commercialization stage. Not surprisingly, the areas in which we see some evidence of IPR-related problems—for example, wind and hybrid cars—are both further along commercially than others and the number of patents have increased in recent years (see Figure 12.2). But even in areas where we do not currently see difficulties, the situation may change as recent research results in patents and as R&D escalates in response to appropriate GHG pricing.

1. Second- and third-generation biofuels

As a purported green technology, the "first-generation" biofuel of corn-based ethanol remains controversial: it necessarily creates a conflict between the use of plants for food and fuel, and it has a carbon emissions profile similar to that of fossil fuels.

In contrast, second-and third-generation biofuels are more promising. Second-generation biofuels include cellulosic ethanol, which is made from non-food crop residues such as corn stover and wheat straw, or from timber and lumber residues. In the area of cellulosic ethanol, a major challenge is the phenomenon of "biomass recalcitrance," a term that refers to the natural resistance of plant cell walls to microbial and enzymatic decomposition.[43]

It appears that small firms are finding, and patenting, novel enzymes that catalyze such decomposition. Then, in a pattern reminiscent of the bio-pharmaceutical industry, they are collaborating with large firms in a manner that develops the technology.[44] To date, patents do not appear to have posed problems in this context. On the contrary, there are multiple joint ventures working on different enzymes, and patents on enzymes appear to have fostered markets for technology driven by small firms. More generally, as Figure 12.1 shows, the number of patents granted in the biofuels area (as in the

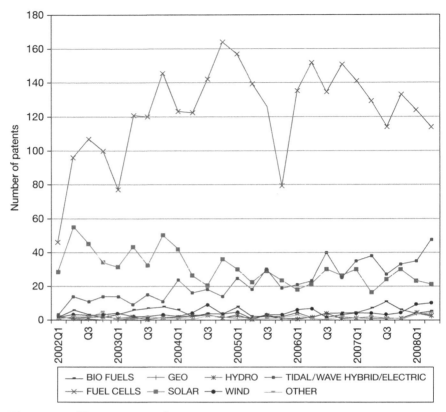

Figure 12.2 All sector patents by quarter 2002–2008

Source: Clean Energy Patent Growth Index (U.S.).

biopharmaceutical industry) appears to be relatively small.[45] Nevertheless, the situation could change dramatically in the future, as more recent research in this area has not yet resulted in issued patents.

Patents in the area of third-generation biofuels, such as those produced by synthetic biology, may also become a concern. Unlike traditional recombinant DNA, which simply transfers one or more genes from one organism to another, synthetic biology aims to create standard, modular DNA parts that can be mixed and matched in different ways within a standard "chassis" organism. In the biofuels context, the organisms created through mixing and matching would be designed to take cellulosic feedstock and produce fuel. At the moment, synthetic biology is sufficiently removed from commercial end products that patent applications on items such as microbial chasses (Craig Venter's firm, Synthetic Genomics, had applications pending on several such chasses at the time of writing)[46] were not likely to cover the inventions that would ultimately become the standard. But to the extent that standard-ization is achieved in the future, the prospect of patents on synthetic biology standards raises the same concerns as existing patents on various ICT stand-ards.[47] Perhaps most notably, secret infringement, which (as discussed earl-ier)[48] is currently one prominent strategy for avoiding patent thickets in biotechnology, may be less feasible when relevant platforms are standardized.

2. Photovoltaic solar

Photovoltaic technology involves the use of panels to produce electricity when the panel is exposed to sunlight. While the first generation of this technology used crystalline silicon, the improvement process has involved applying thin films of semiconductors to the surface of materials such as glass. Another important piece of PV technology involves the inverter used to convert the DC power produced by the panels to AC power. According to John Barton's study of the photovoltaic industry in 2007, the industry was only moderately concentrated, which allowed choice among patented products that were substitutes for each other.[49]

In terms of aggregate patent numbers, the trends do not appear particularly dramatic. In the U.S., the number of patents issued annually in the solar area appeared to be holding relatively steady at the time of writing (see Figure 12.2). In the EPO, patent applications in the solar area grew about 11 per cent between 1998 and 2007, lower than the 16 per cent increase for alternative energy technologies generally.

3. Transportation: hybrid cars and fuel cells

As shown in Figure 12.2, many U.S. patents were being issued in the area of fuel cells at the time of writing. Similarly, in the EPO, patent applications in the area of fuel cells grew 22 per cent between 1998 and 2007. In both this area and the area of wind energy (discussed next), many patents may represent relatively incremental improvements. Thus, as with the information technol-ogy industries, an end product could conceivably be covered by a large number of patents, each of which contributes only a small percentage to the total value of the invention. Indeed, the *Paice v. Toyota* case, discussed above, represented precisely this situation.[50]

4. Wind

Because certain types of wind technology (e.g. windmills) have been available for decades, patenting in this space can also represent incremental innovation. Additionally, as shown in Figure 12.2, the number of issued U.S. patents in this area has been increasing in recent years. Similarly, in the EPO, patent applications in the area of wind power increased 31 per cent from 1998 to 2007.

There have been increasing tensions between key wind power companies in recent years.[51] The wind turbine industry is also quite concentrated, with the top four firms accounting for almost 75 per cent of the market. In the U.S. market, General Electric is the major player, and it has a reputation for enforcing its patents aggressively. For example, in February 2008 GE asked the U.S. International Trade Commission to bar imports of wind turbines made by Japan's Mitsubishi Heavy Industries Ltd., arguing that Mitsubishi's turbines infringe on its patents.

5. *Proprietary rights beyond patents*

There is more at stake here than patents alone. Green technologies, particularly in the area of second- and third-generation biofuels, are likely to be heavily dependent on access to microbial materials and associated data that will have to be processed as part of the overall research trajectory.[52] The challenge is to enable scientists to access vast amounts of materials and data for upstream research, without compromising the possibilities of downstream commercial applications that may be patented.

In other words, if all we focus on are potential patent problems, we may miss problems caused by data protection techniques under copyright and *sui generis* laws (especially the EU Database Law, which now applies in some 50 countries) as well as restrictions on access to genetic resources in material transfer agreements. Our solutions would thus be incomplete because they would fail to address the risk that the scientific system, even when rendered compatible with traditional patent law, might be deprived of necessary data (covered perhaps by crown copyrights or crown database rights in the EU) or deprived of access to essential resource inputs, such as microbial strains held by repositories that restrict access to their holdings even for public scientific purposes. Hence efforts to design a worldwide microbial research commons could significantly affect the pace and direction of patented technologies, including green technologies.[53]

III. ALTERNATIVES TO TRADITIONAL PATENTING AND LICENSING

We have already alluded to the need for legal change—perhaps most notably changes to administrative processes that currently do a poor job of granting high-quality patents in a timely manner. But even without such legal change, which may be difficult to achieve, much can be done to avert patent difficulties.

a. Technology pools

A standard mechanism for addressing certain types of patent thickets is technology pools. These pools function particularly well when multiple complementary patents owned by different parties cover a platform technology or standard. Once the patents are pooled, licenses to the pool can then be made available both to contributors of relevant patents and to outsiders.

The MPEG-2 pool, which comprises patents essential for compliance with the MPEG-2 digital compression technology standard, illustrates well the central features of a pro-competitive pool. Contributing members of the pool agree to license the patent portfolio on a nondiscriminatory basis to all firms that request a portfolio license. Owners of portfolio patents are also free to license their own patents independent of the portfolio. The entity that administers the MPEG-2 pool is known as MPEG LA, and it receives an administrative fee out of royalties collected. The MPEG LA model has been adopted in a large number of similar situations involving patent thickets.

As a conceptual matter, a package of innovations licensed under a non-exclusive license of this kind invites the world to make use of the package at will, while organizing the contributors to the package as de facto partners of all subsequent users, who labor under a contractually specified obligation to pay reasonable royalties for follow-on applications. The more successful the package becomes, the more follow-on users it generates, and the greater are the "lottery-effect" royalties paid to those who contribute to the package.[54]

In certain contexts, royalty-free licensing might be adopted. In February 2008, various firms launched the Eco-Patent Commons, which aims to pool clean technology patents for royalty-free licensing. Thus far, the Commons is limited in scale. It includes 47 patents, 27 owned by IBM and 12 by Xerox. Other contributors include Nokia, Pitney Bowes, and Dupont. Whether firms will have incentives to contribute significant numbers of patents to this type of commons, and whether it will include patents that are ultimately useful for reducing carbon emissions, remains to be seen. In the context of other firm donations of patents to a commons (e.g. IBM's donation of patents relevant to the Linux operating system), the firms in question have had a financial incentive to contribute, as they make products complementary to the platforms covered by the patents in the commons.

b. Prizes

In addition to the traditional approaches of using patents and related licensing or basic research funding administered via grants, another option is to offer inducement prizes for achieving specific advances in GHG-reducing science and technology.[55] The idea here is to offer financial or other rewards for achieving specific innovation objectives that have been specified in advance.[56] Prize-like approaches have also gained traction within the private sectors. Firms such as Innocentive match "seekers" (organizations with challenging problems) with "solvers" (innovators with solutions) by offering them cash awards. Among other things, Innocentive has a philanthropic subprogram devoted to "clean tech and renewable energy" offering prizes supported by a private foundation.

Although inducement prizes are not suited to all research and innovation objectives, they have the potential to play a larger role alongside research contracts and grants. In contrast to these other instruments, prizes target and reward innovation outputs rather than inputs: the prize is paid only if the objective is attained. This can help to encourage maximal research effort per dollar of public research funding. Prizes or awards can also help to focus efforts on specific high-priority objectives, without specifying how the goal is to be accomplished. Because prize competitors select themselves based on their own knowledge of their likelihood of success—rather than being selected in advance by a research manager—prizes can also attract a more diverse and potentially effective range of innovators from universities, other research institutions, and the private sector.

The detailed process of selecting appropriate prize topics and crafting prize-specific rules (e.g. the type of contest, size of award, criteria for winning, method of choosing winner, whether patents will be sought on the targeted invention)[57] requires extensive consultation with experts and potential participants. Identification of particular technical and scientific challenges in GHG mitigation that might be fruitfully addressed through an inducement prize approach could become a part of the above systematic assessment. Then the best institutional arrangements for administering the prize would need to be determined. Consideration would then be given to the treatment of intellectual property arising from associated innovations (as with any joint R&D project), and to the development of terms for related licensing.

IV. INTERNATIONAL CONTEXT

Thus far, we have focused on the intellectual property situation in the OECD context (and particularly the U.S. context). This focus is justifiable to the extent that more than 95 per cent of global R&D currently takes place in OECD countries. However, reduction of GHG emissions will necessarily be a global effort. Thus, in this section we explicitly consider issues of technology transfer to developing countries as well as prospects for innovation in developing countries.

a. Prizes and other funding in the international context

Prizes could be particularly useful for advancing innovation specifically relevant to developing-country climate-mitigation and adaptation-technology needs, given the relatively low market-driven inducement for innovation that may be present in those countries.[58] For similar reasons, the use of innovation prizes has been advocated for medical advances particularly relevant to developing countries (e.g. anti-malaria drugs).[59] One advantage of a prize approach relative to research grants in an international context is that it would not require choosing the winner of R&D funding in advance, which can become politically charged when researchers and research institutions reside in particular countries.

An internationally coordinated climate technology prize fund could be established for these purposes. While contributions to such a fund could be sought on an as-needed basis for specific projects, it would probably be advantageous to have larger-scale general funds that could then be prioritized to specific prize topics.

In addition to a prize fund, a fund that provided peer-reviewed research grants could also be established. A portion of this fund could be set aside for scientists and innovators in developing countries and thus provide them with opportunities and outlets for innovative proposals that do not otherwise exist at the present time.[60]

b. Buying out and pooling intellectual property

Parties to the United Nations Framework Convention on Climate Change (UNFCCC) and WIPO administrators could also consider establishing a "global fund" within the WIPO for the potential purchase of intellectual property.[61] The UNFCCC, adopted at Rio in 1992, already contains provisions for technology transfer and financial assistance for agreed incremental costs to developing countries. Its Kyoto Protocol added further assistance provisions. And the demand-side incentives in a global regime that used a tax or cap and trade system to limit GHG emissions could spur a flow of funds and technology to developing countries in allowance sale transactions. But the parties to the climate-change treaties could go further to address IPRs through forms of collaboration with WIPO that we are now sketching.

Specifically, a global fund could "buy out" selected intellectual property rights and then make the innovation available to others, especially developing countries, as if it were in the public domain or at least a semi-commons. An earlier proposal to this effect for pharmaceuticals was made by Professor Kevin Outterson, who pointed out that the aggregate value of the rights to poor-country markets may be relatively small, in which case significant public health impact could be achieved with such an investment.[62] Because the inventors will normally have recouped R&D expenses and made the bulk of their profits in OECD countries, such a strategy provides them with an extra source of income while relieving them of concerns about the enforcement of IPRs in the countries for which rights have been purchased. However, thought must be given to the possibility of restricting re-exports of the products developed under such arrangements back into OECD countries under various theories of exhaustion, lest they undermine the innovators' returns from investments in their primary markets.

An organization that administered buy-outs might also arrange to pool technologies or inputs to essential technologies, with a view to making them available as a package to innovators, especially innovators in developing countries. This strategy looks promising and has already produced positive results in the pharmaceutical sector. For example, public-private partnerships have successfully pooled patented technologies under the auspices of DNDi, with a view to introducing two new malaria drugs onto the market.[63]

c. Technology transfer and international R&D agreements

At least in the near term, much of the relevant R&D for clean technology will occur in the developed world. Transferring the resulting technological knowledge and equipment to developing countries—and ensuring that future technologies are appropriate—will require additional actions at an international level. While technology-transfer strategies must address typical impediments to technology adoption, such as information availability, technological maturity, and the absorptive capacity of importing countries they also must address financing barriers specific to developing countries. The degree of intellectual property rights protection, rule of law, regulatory transparency, and market openness are also critical conditions and potential impediments bearing on technology transfer.

Activities undertaken under knowledge sharing and coordination agreements can include meetings, planning, exchange of information, the coordination and harmonization of research agendas and measurement standards, and some degree of integrated, cooperative R&D.[64] In addition to increasing international exchanges of scientific and technical information, joint R&D can more directly increase cost-effectiveness through cost-sharing and reduced duplication of effort. The largest number of existing international agreements relevant to climate-mitigation technology have been developed as so-called Technology Implementing Agreements under the auspices of the IEA.[65] IEA Implementing Agreements use two primary mechanisms: task-sharing and cost-sharing. In task-sharing, a joint program is pursued within participating countries, but each country funds and implements its own contribution to the project. In cost-sharing, participating countries pool funding for a single contractor to perform a research task. There are 41 existing IEA Implementing Agreements, all of which incorporate task-sharing and about half of which adopt cost-sharing mechanisms. They cover the fields of renewable energy and hydrogen (10), end-use energy efficiency (13), fossil-fuel technologies (6), nuclear-fusion energy (9), and cross-cutting activities (3). Membership in these agreements is not restricted to governments or to IEA or OECD countries, and a number of organizations from non-OECD countries have participated.

Activities under these agreements are funded and conducted primarily through domestic R&D programs and budgets. Pooled funds often go to the bundling of research results and provision of a platform for information exchange and learning (i.e. desk studies rather than primary research).

In addition, other agreements have also been developed in recent years, including the Carbon Sequestration Leadership Forum, the Asia Pacific Partnership on Clean Development and Climate, and the International Partnership for a Hydrogen Economy. Energy science and technology agreements that feature a higher degree of joint, collaborative R&D are less common, and appear to be most successful in research that is more fundamental and that has not yet accumulated commercial interests. Examples include the ITER fusion reactor and European Organization for Nuclear Research (CERN).

Invigorated and expanded international agreements on climate technology mitigation via R&D coordination could be very valuable, particularly as countries increase R&D efforts and seek maximal impact in addressing this global problem.[66] The IEA is the best-positioned international institution to administer any such agreement(s) related to energy technology, although other international institutions may be more appropriate to engage for non-energy technologies. One concern with the existing IEA implementing agreements, however, is that they each have their own secretariats and operate independently. While this approach eases the need for more central administration, it may also suffer from overlap across agreements, and a lack of overall coordination and strategic vision.

G8, other major R&D-performing countries, and likely major developing-country technology users, could therefore consider agreeing to an overall framework for knowledge-sharing and coordination of climate-mitigation R&D efforts.[67] This framework could include a process whereby parties make regular submissions of a climate technology development plan, including R&D funding levels, current and future program plans, pertinent R&D policies, and other relevant information. In addition to such national submissions, the process could include an evaluation of existing climate-technology agreements—with an eye toward identifying best practices and expanding, integrating, or suspending particular agreements—and draw from other related national and international efforts by the European Union,[68] Japan,[69] the United States,[70] and IEA work in support of G8 and other processes.[71]

At a minimum, those implementing such a project would monitor progress, share information on individual national efforts in an integrated manner, and identify where overlaps and gaps exist across countries.[72] One mechanism under this framework could also include the development of roadmaps to assess the current development status of particular technologies, systems, and relevant areas of underlying science, including the identification of appropriate milestones and necessary R&D funding levels. The framework would also provide a more systematic means for improving the cost-effectiveness of R&D by identifying particular areas where it makes sense for individual countries to focus on sub-parts of an integrated overall package and areas where joint funding is sensible. An agreement could also set out general guidelines for expectations for the magnitude of task-sharing and cost-sharing across countries for collaborative R&D projects. This framework could highlight the importance of human talent to both knowledge development and transfer, by helping to identify high-priority areas for scholarly exchange—including from developing to developed countries.

An international agreement could also be fashioned to increase domestic funding of climate technology R&D, analogous to internationally agreed emission targets for each country.[73] International agreement concerning the necessary level and reasonable burden-sharing of R&D effort across parties could be valuable. Such an agreement could, for example, target a level of climate technology R&D as a percentage of GDP, or as a percentage increase from recent levels, with those levels set with the intention of significantly expanding R&D. The general idea is not without precedent: in 2002 the European Union set the goal of increasing its relatively low level of overall R&D intensity—currently 1.7 per cent of GDP—to 3 per cent of GDP by 2010.[74] The goal is EU-wide rather than country-specific and applies jointly to both public and private R&D funding. However, there was little evidence of measurable progress toward the goal at the time of writing, although ongoing discussions among government representatives and major R&D-performing companies have illuminated many of the key impediments.

A more detailed example—albeit in the medical rather than climate arena— is the 2005 proposal to the World Health Organization for a Treaty on Medical Research and Development.[75] The core country obligations in the proposal are for minimum levels of support for qualified medical R&D (both general and "priority" areas), measured as a share of GDP, according to a schedule varying by national income. Among other things, the proposal also identifies methods of qualified R&D financing (e.g., direct public support, tax expenditures, philanthropic expenditures, and certain business R&D).

Specifically with regard to energy, the IEA already collects annual data on public energy R&D spending by IEA countries, a process that could be adjusted if necessary to serve a more formal purpose.[76] Such an agreement could incorporate a "pledge and review" structure, and the necessary reporting on funding levels integrated with the regular climate technology development plan submissions described above. Targets could be structured as a share of GDP, as a percentage increase from recent levels, or some other metric. The IEA could serve as the review body—either directly or as an assistant to a UNFCCC Expert Group on Technology Development. The process could also include a broader energy innovation policy review element: the IEA already conducts regular reviews of the energy policies, including energy technology policies, of IEA member countries and other major energy consumers and producers[77]

d. Impediments to technology transfer, with particular regard to intellectual property rights

As we have discussed, IPRs provide incentives to invest in R&D and operate as modalities for recouping those investments and turning a profit, despite the intangible and essentially non-rivalrous character of intellectual creations in the raw state of affairs. To this end, the TRIPS Agreement of 1994, by harmonizing international minimum standards of intellectual property protection within the confines of the Agreement Establishing the World Trade Organization, aimed to improve the baseline conditions for the transfer of knowledge and technology in a global marketplace.[78] The "incipient transnational system of innovation"[79] emerging from this Agreement has created incentives and opportunities for entrepreneurs in developing countries once they become capable of producing and exporting knowledge goods to an increasingly competitive global market.

In principle, this worldwide intellectual property system should encourage the transfer of climate-change technology to and from developing countries. Even if returns generated by IP protection in these countries are relatively small, the availability of such protection should stimulate some transfer as well as foreign direct investment (FDI). Thus, developing-country governments should give careful thought to mechanisms for addressing the fears of foreign innovators regarding lax protection of their IPRs. Besides implementing their enforcement obligations under TRIPS,[80] governments should consider devising ways and means outside of their intellectual property and administrative laws to reassure companies that are willing to cooperate in transfers of essential technologies. While states may not discriminate against other states with regard to such laws, a long GATT tradition does allow governments to make better deals with cooperative companies than with others who may drag their heels.

On the negative side, however, there is evidence that the TRIPS Agreement has produced an adverse impact on access to essential public goods, especially in areas such as public health and agriculture. And when thinking about potential problems in advance of their becoming acute in the environmental sector, it is well to remember that although the TRIPS agreement sets up a baseline of protection, it also has a variety of provisions that give developing countries some flexibility in addressing access issues. Thus, it is worth emphasizing that governments in developing countries can under TRIPS maintain relatively stiff standards of patentability. Of course, stiff standards of eligibility must apply without discrimination to both national and foreign innovators. But these same standards might widen the space in which local companies could reverse-engineer foreign innovations that fail to qualify and still obtain, say, utility model rights or "compensatory liability" rights in incremental innovations of their own.[81] These same regimes might also serve to protect small-scale innovations held by foreigners, without generating the thickets of rights and other barriers to entry that too many patents can produce.

Even when foreign companies qualify for patent protection under suitably exigent domestic patent laws, the existence of second-tier regimes provides incentives to local firms to adapt such inventions to local circumstances and to improve upon them. Moreover, the Japanese experience demonstrates that local firms that obtain second-tier rights of this kind in improvements then possess tradable rights that can become bargaining chips when dealing with large transnational corporations. By the same token, the fact that a local company can obtain, say, only a utility model right or a liability regime at home, in no way affects the patentability of its innovation in other countries, especially OECD countries. This is an important advantage of the "independence of patents" doctrine, incorporated into TRIPS,[82] which developing countries could leverage in the environmental sector so as to generate more significant profits in countries with larger markets.

Should tensions surrounding access in the environmental sector mount as they have in the pharmaceutical sector, the primary defensive options for developing countries would reside in article 31 of the TRIPS Agreement, which allows compulsory licenses to be issued on patented inventions for almost any reason, subject to the payment of compensation and certain other technical prerequisites.[83] Here developing countries have a wide array of defensive options that must be carefully evaluated and duly supported by legislative and administrative provisions.

For example, one of the most relevant and least studied of these options is the right to enact compulsory licenses for so-called dependent patents.[84] These licenses kick in when second comers develop patented improvements on existing dominant inventions, and they permit the improver to exercise his or her patent, despite its infringing posture, in exchange for a cross-license to and from the holder of a dominant patent. In effect, this compulsory license avoids blocking effects by manufacturing a liability rule solution for improvers.

Compulsory licenses for anticompetitive practices and behavior afford developing countries another set of options, especially when foreign firms refuse to deal with local firms or refuse to make technologies available at prices that local firms can afford.

While U.S. competition law would not necessarily support compulsory licenses on such grounds, they are fully established in international patent law and are increasingly invoked under the European Commission's own competition law and policy, which closely regulates potential "abuses of a dominant position" by holders of IPRs. Compulsory licenses issued for anti-competitive behavior under articles 8, 31(k) and 40 of the TRIPS Agreement are subject to minimum restrictions and prerequisites, other than some administrative or judicial procedures, and even the right to compensation may be virtually nullified by such behavior.

Another compulsory license likely to be relevant in the environmental sector is the government use license. Under a government use license, a private contractor may be made an agent of the government for purposes of manufacturing the patented product and making it available to the public at large. Such activity is immunized against an infringement action in the courts. Instead, the patentee must seek adequate compensation from the government itself, which can be measured in terms of local conditions. Government use licenses are also subject to very few prerequisites, they can be rapidly issued for virtually any reason, and the relevant transaction costs are low.

Still another form of compulsory license widely used in the EU and elsewhere is the so-called "public interest" compulsory license. On this approach, the government may enable third-party private contractors to produce the patented goods without a license from the patentee, if the public interest requires the goods in question to be made available in greater quantities or at lower prices than the patentee is willing to accept. Such licenses do require notice and prior negotiations with right holders, and prior negotiations themselves usually suffice to break the bottleneck in question without actual need to issue the compulsory license in the end. Recently, in the context of public health needs, both France and Belgium have enacted laws allowing the issuance of expedited public interest compulsory licenses for public health purposes.[85]

It needs to be stressed, moreover, that the existence of these defensive measures gives rise to certain offensive possibilities if planning and coordination problems are otherwise properly managed. Here we refer to the possibility of pooled procurement strategies that can enable poor countries to boost their bargaining power with respect to foreign suppliers of needed technologies.[86] From this perspective, there are gains of trade to be made when small countries coordinate their procurement strategies, especially when the objective is to stimulate foreign producers to lower the price of technologies or even to establish local production facilities in a given region. By pooling their purchasing requirements, countries may achieve economies of scale and scope that will entice foreign suppliers to deal on more favorable terms. Moreover, coordinated procurement strategies toughen the threat of compulsory licenses— if all the participating governments are willing to issue them—while sweetening the carrots of cooperative behavior by offering originators (or willing producers of substitutes) a larger market in which to establish their trademarks, sell their products, or even establish local production. Pooled procurement strategies with or without compulsory licenses look ever more promising in the pharmaceutical sector[87] (where, however, special enabling legislation already exists),[88] and they should be carefully evaluated for application in the environmental sector as well.

However, most of these defensive measures are subject to certain technical, legal, and political constraints. For example, a threat to issue a compulsory license may be meaningless if the country possesses no capacity to reverse-engineer the product or process in question, unless it can obtain similar products from other countries where they are off patent or available under the doctrine of exhaustion. Similarly, most compulsory licenses under article 31(f) of the TRIPS Agreement must be made "predominantly for the supply of the local market," which means no more than 49.9 per cent of the production can be exported to another country (unless such exports can conceivably be justified as an "exception" within article 30).[89] These restrictions can also hinder implementation of pooled procurement strategies, at least to the extent that they depend on compulsory licensing.

Of course, climate-mitigation technology is quite different from the pharmaceutical sector, in which many of these defensive measures have been used. Because pharmaceutical products are generally quite inexpensive at marginal cost, developing countries have eagerly embraced such products (and have resisted attempts to raise the cost through patent restrictions). In contrast, absent GHG pricing, certain green technology can be more expensive than conventional technology even when sold at marginal cost. Nonetheless these measures demonstrate that there are means for the international community to address threats to the public good if and when IPRs become an impediment.

e. Indigenous innovation in developing countries

The international climate negotiations, as well as the academic literature, have largely assumed that green climate-friendly technologies will primarily or exclusively be developed in wealthy countries, and will then need to be transferred to poor countries through private or public mechanisms. This model of innovation in wealthy countries and diffusion to poor countries has characterized other fields of technology, especially pharmaceuticals (as previously discussed). It is buttressed by the fact that 95 per cent of global R&D spending currently takes place in wealthy countries.

But there is evidence that indigenous innovation of green climate-friendly technology may become feasible in a number of developing countries. If so, the global pattern of climate-related R&D would look different from that of prior technologies, and the need for technology transfer from OECD countries to others might be somewhat reduced. At the same time, the prospects for indigenous innovation in developing countries will depend upon the incentive systems operating within those countries. Choices and debates about the design of and limits on IPRs and alternative incentive instruments, discussed above in the context of wealthy countries, would then become applicable to developing countries.

There are several reasons for expecting developing countries to supply more indigenous technological innovation in the green energy or climate change sectors than in other fields of R&D. First, the impetus for climate-friendly innovation will be greatest in the wealthiest developing countries, not the poorest. Unlike in the case of essential medicines, where the countries most in need are also the poorest and those with the least capacity to innovate, in the case of energy and climate technology the major developing countries most in need—that is, the largest emitting countries that will be hard pressed to reduce their emissions—are also the wealthiest with the greatest capacity to innovate. Growing greenhouse gas emissions usually (though not inevitably) correlates with rising energy use, electrification, vehicle ownership and distances traveled, and wealth.

Notably, China, India, and Brazil are three of the largest greenhouse gas emitters in the world (China having surpassed the U.S. in 2007 to become the world's largest CO_2 emitter).[90] They are also three of the wealthiest developing countries and, indeed. emerging great powers. Although they still have significantly lower per capita income than most OECD countries, their aggregate GDP is rising to the point where it equals or surpasses that of many OECD countries. GDP in Europe and the U.S. has been growing at about 2 or 3 per cent per year over the past decade; China's GDP has been growing at over 10 per cent annually over that same period. (On present forecasts, China may become the world's largest economy within a decade or two, although the 2008 economic crisis will have reduced growth rates in both China and OECD countries.)

Other major emitters among the developing countries, such as Indonesia and South Africa, are less wealthy with slower rates of economic growth, but they still rank among the better-off developing countries and are thus capable of supporting some indigenous innovation. The only large GHG emitters among the very poor developing countries are those experiencing rapid deforestation, such as countries in central Africa. Technical innovation in agriculture and cooking could slow deforestation and thus reduce GHG emissions in those very poor countries (by reducing demand for converting forests to farmland, and for clearing forests for fuelwood, respectively). Even if some of this innovation may originate elsewhere and be transferred to poor countries, there remain prospects for indigenous innovation in farming and cooking methods.

Another consideration is that the wealthier developing countries already have large communities of well-educated professionals working in R&D. China and India now host a large percentage of the world's scientists and engineers. Brazil has become a world leader in liquid fuel technologies. This human capital advantage in high GHG-emitting developing countries contrasts with the human capital deficit in poor countries seeking pharmaceuticals for destitute populations.

Still another positive factor is the credit available to finance indigenous R&D. At least some of these emerging powers, most obviously China, have large pools of available credit. China created a new sovereign investment fund in 2007, endowed with approximately $400 billion, and in early November 2008 announced a new domestic infrastructure investment initiative of $586 billion over the next two years.[91] Foreign investors will add to these financial markets. This trend may be reinforced if the current credit market problems in the U.S. and Europe continue, in which case investment opportunities in China, India, and Brazil would seem relatively more attractive.

There is also a nascent community of venture capital firms already at work in China and other major developing countries. This source of financing and entrepreneurial insight can be critical to small start-up firms.

Moreover, there is already at least domestic demand for innovation to reduce emissions in these countries. As China adds a new coal-fired electric power plant each week (and India adds one about every other week), their coal combustion yields not only CO_2 but also SO_2, NOx, fine particulates, and black carbon.[92] The public health damage from these co-pollutants is serious (in China, up to 750,000 deaths per year).[93] Moreover, this public health burden is increasingly recognized by those countries' leaders as both a drag on economic growth[94] and a source of political unrest.[95] As a result, political leaders in these countries have incentives to promote domestic public R&D spending to reduce emissions; and domestic pollution control policies in these countries may spur private investment in relevant domestic innovation.

If the demand-side market failure of climate change was corrected with a price on carbon (via carbon taxes or a cap and trade regime), and if that policy became applicable to the major developing countries, then there would be real incentives for innovation within those countries to reduce GHG emissions. For example, there would be incentives to reduce CO_2 emissions from coal combustion (e.g., via carbon capture and storage), and CH^4 emissions from natural gas pipelines, ruminant animals and rice cultivation. If indigenous innovation in any given country could reduce these emissions at lower cost than reliance on imported external innovation, that country would benefit from lower abatement costs (as well as from the opportunity to sell emissions allowances on the world market, if a cap and trade regime was adopted).

In this context, some countries may serve as role models for others because they have recently succeeded in stimulating indigenous technological innovation as part of their vault from poor to wealthy, including admission to OECD membership. For example, in the last three decades, South Korea and Taiwan have demonstrated that indigenous innovation in manufacturing, electronics, biomedicine, and related industries can be part of rapid economic growth in Asia as a whole.

All the above-mentioned factors are already spurring increased innovation in the energy sector in major developing countries. In China, innovation has accelerated in recent years.[96] This trend is publicly associated with President Hu Jintao's commitment to "harmonious society" and the "scientific concept of development."

To be sure, future progress in green or climate-friendly indigenous innovation in developing countries will depend on several additional factors. One is the effective demand for new methods of reducing GHG emissions as a result of policies to raise the price of emissions. A second is the reach of this demand across diverse sectors in which several GHGs are emitted, including electricity generation, vehicles, buildings, agriculture, and forests. A third is the role of IPRs or alternatives available within these countries in stimulating the supply of new technologies, as discussed in prior sections of this paper.[97] A fourth is the general ease of doing business within these economies.[98]

It will accordingly be important to study the design of IPRs or alternatives to encourage green climate-friendly technological R&D in major developing countries, as well as in wealthy countries.[99] Lessons from the performance of IPRs in the energy and agricultural sectors of wealthy countries may prove useful in this regard, provided that the different economic and social contexts of each developing country is taken into account.

V. CONCLUSION

In this report, we provide an analysis of how IPRs, and alternatives to IPRs, might operate in stimulating green innovation. Because IPR challenges are likely to arise (if at all) only after sufficient levels of innovation have been generated by a combination of appropriate GHG pricing policies and public funding, we rely heavily on analogies to existing technological sectors that are currently experiencing difficulties. Because over 95 per cent of global R&D is currently generated in OECD countries, we focus primarily on these countries in our discussion of IPR challenges. Nevertheless, if climate change is going to be addressed successfully, clean technology must be adopted globally. Our paper thus concludes by examining at some length the international context, with particular regard to prospects for indigenous innovation in developing countries.

NOTES

1. Chatham House is independent and owes no allegiance to government or to any political body. It does not hold opinions of its own; the views expressed in this chapter are the responsibility of the authors.
2. Intergovernmental Panel on Climate Change (IPCC), Climate Change 2007: Synthesis Report (R.K. Pachauri and A. Reisinger, eds. 2007), available at <http://www.ipcc.ch/pdf/assessment-report/ar4/syr/ar4_syr.pdf> [hereinafter IPCC] (accessed 24 October 2013).
3. For reviews of the policy options to limit greenhouse gas emissions, including the effect of such policies on private sector innovation, see e.g., Architectures for Agreement: Addressing Global Climate Change in the Post-Kyoto World (Cambridge University Press, Robert N. Stavins and Joseph Aldy, eds. 2007); Richard B. Stewart and Jonathan B. Wiener, Reconstructing Climate Policy: Beyond Kyoto (American Enter. Inst. Press 2003).
4. Int'l Energy Agency (IEA), World Energy Outlook 2007: China and India Insights (2007), available at <http://www.worldenergyoutlook.org/media/weowebsite/2008-1994/weo_2007.pdf> (accessed 24 October 2013) [hereinafter IEA (2007)]. IEA, *CO₂ Emissions from Fuel Combustion: Emissions of CO₂, CH₄, N₂O, HFC, PFC, FS6*, vol. 2007, release 01 (Paris: OECD/IEA).
5. IEA (2007), *supra* note 4.
6. Richard G. Newell, A U.S. Innovation Strategy for Climate Change Mitigation (Brookings Inst. Press 2008), available at <http://dspace.cigilibrary.org/jspui/bitstream/123456789/25395/1/A%20US%20Innovation%20Strategy%20for%20Climate%20Change%20Mitigation.pdf?1"> (accessed 24 October 2013).
7. IPCC, *supra* note 2.
8. J.A. Edmonds et al., Global Energy Technology Strategy: Addressing Climate Change (Battelle Memorial Inst. 2007).
9. Newell, *supra* note 6.
10. James Bessen and Michael Meurer, Patent Failures: How Judges, Bureaucrats and Lawyers Put Innovation at Risk (Princeton University Press 2008); Michael Heller, Gridlock Economy: How Too Much Ownership Wrecks Markets, Stops Innovation and Costs Lives (Basic Books, 2008); European Patent Office (EPO), Scenarios for the Future—How Might IP Regimes Evolve by 2025? What Global Legitimacy Might Such Regimes Have? (2007); Adam B. Jaffe and Josh Lerner, Innovation and Its Discontents: How Our Broken Patent System Is Endangering Innovation and Progress and What to Do About It (Princeton University Press 2011).
11. See, e.g., Jerome H. Reichman and Rochelle C. Dreyfuss, *Harmonization Without Consensus: Critical Reflections on Drafting a Substantive Patent Law Treaty*, 57 Duke L.J. 85 (2007).
12. See, e.g., Charles I. Jones, *Sources of U.S. Economic Growth in a World of Ideas*, 92 Am. Econ. Rev. 220 (2002) (giving this estimate).
13. In general, empirical studies have found that social rates of return from private firm research and development are at least twice private rates of return. Charles I. Jones and John Williams, *Measuring the Social Return to R&D*, 113(4) Q. J. Econ. 1119–35 (1998).

14. See, e.g., Ashish Arora et al., Markets for Technology: The Economics of Innovation and Corporate Strategy (MIT Press 2001).

15. Joseph Schumpeter, Capitalism, Socialism and Democracy (1942) (making the theoretical point that entrepreneurial firms may be more likely than large firms with vested interests in existing products to be able to move outside routine tasks into "untried technological possibilit[ies]"); see also William J. Baumol, The Free-Market Innovation Machine: Analyzing the Growth Miracle of Capitalism (Princeton University Press 2002); Zoltan Acs and David Audretsch, Innovation and Small Firms (MIT Press 1990); David Audretsch, Innovation and Industry Evolution (MIT Press 1995) (presenting empirical data on the extent to which significant innovations in biotechnology and information technology have been driven by small firms).

16. Ronald J. Mann and Thomas W. Sager, *Patents, Venture Capital, and Software Start-ups*, 36(2) Research Pol'y 193–208 (2007).

17. Additionally, the late 1990s represented a time when venture capital markets were relatively robust.

18. James Bessen and Michael Meurer, Patent Failure: How Judges, Bureaucrats, and Lawyers Put Innovators at Risk chs. 5 and 6 (Princeton University Press 2008) (collecting existing research data based on patent renewal statistics and market value regressions and presenting new data); see also Wesley Cohen, Richard Nelson, and John Walsh, *Protecting Their Intellectual Assets: Appropriability Conditions and Why Manufacturing Firms Patent (or not)* (Nat'l Bureau of Econ. Research (NBER) Working Paper Series No. 7752, Feb. 2000), available at <http://www.nber.org/papers/w7552.pdf> (accessed 24 October 2013) (finding, based on survey conducted in 1990s, that R&D managers in the chemical and pharmaceutical industries ranked the effectiveness of patents higher than managers in other industries). In fact, according to one analysis that relied on renewal data, market value regressions, and event studies in attempting to calculate both the private value of patents and the private costs of patent litigation, the net private incentive provided by the patent system outside the chemical and pharmaceutical industries had, by the late 1990s, turned negative. Bessen and Meurer, *supra* ch. 6.

19. Robert P. Merges and Richard R. Nelson, *On the Complex Economics of Patent Scope*, 90 Colum. L. Rev. 839 (1990).

20. Carl Shapiro, *Navigating the Patent Thicket: Cross Licenses, Patent Pools, and Standard Setting*, in 1 Innovation Policy and the Economy 119–50 (Nat'l Bureau of Econ. Research, Adam B. Jaffe et al. eds., 2001).

21. Patent law explicitly allows for overlapping, or blocking, patents.

22. Iain M. Cockburn and Rebecca Henderson, Survey Results from the 2003 Intellectual Property Owners Association Survey on Strategic Management of Intellectual Property, p. D.2 (Oct. 2003), available at <http://www.ipo.org/wp-content/uploads/2013/04/survey_results_revised.pdf> (accessed 24 October 2013).

23. As discussed further below, the situation in biotechnology is less clear.

24. For example, there is some dispute about the extent to which firms in the information technology industries bother to examine the patent landscape. To the extent that they do not do such an examination, they may not be deterred by patent thickets.

25. Edmund Kitch bases his famous argument for granting broad patent rights very early in the R&D process on the idea that later grants would lead to such rent-dissipating races. Edmund W. Kitch, *The Nature and Function of the Patent System*, 20 J. L. & Econ. 265 (1977).

26. Richard Rouse and Gary Hardiman, *Microarray Technology: An Intellectual Property Retrospective*, 4 (5) Pharmacogenomics 623–32 (2003).

27. *KSR Int'l Co. v. Teleflex, Inc.*, 550 U.S. 398 (2007).

28. *eBay Inc. v. MercExchange*, L.L.C., 547 U.S. 388 (2006).

29. *Paice v. Toyota Motor Corp.*, 504 F.3d 1293 (2007). The CAFC did, however, remand for the district court to reevaluate the royalty rate, as the opinion had given no reason for the decision to impose a fee of $25 for every Prius II, Toyota Highlander, or Lexus RX400h manufactured during the remaining life of the infringed patent.

30. The question is not entirely clear because an examiner can also accumulate "counts" if a patent denial results in the applicant coming back with a repeat (or "continuation") application.

31. Alison Brimelow [then-President of the European Patent Office] closing remarks delivered at the European Patent Forum: Inventing a Cleaner Future, Ljubljena, Slovenia (6–7 May 2008).

32. Evidence of this percentage is a bit misleading because, under current U.S. rules, there is no such thing as a final denial of a patent application—rather, the applicant can file the same patent application as many times as they wish. But even taking account of these continuation applications, the percentage of applications granted appears to have decreased in recent years. At some point, applicants appear to abandon their quest for a patent. Mark A. Lemley and Bhaven Sampat, *Is the Patent Office a Rubber Stamp?*, 58 Emory L. J. 157 (2008), available at <http://www.law.emory.edu/fileadmin/journals/elj/58/58.1/Lemley_Sampat.pdf> (accessed 24 October 2013).

33. Jerome H. Reichman, *Of Green Tulips and Legal Kudzu: Repackaging Rights in Subpatentable Innovation*, 53 Vand. L. Rev. 1743 (2000), available at <http://scholarship.law.duke.edu/cgi/viewcontent.cgi?article=1403&context=faculty_scholarship> (accessed 24 October 2013).

34. For a review of this evidence, see, e.g., David Mowery et al., Ivory Tower and Industrial Innovation (Stanford University Press 2004).

35. See *Madey v. Duke University*, 307 F.3d 1351, 1362 (Fed. Cir. 2002).

36. Jerome H. Reichman and Jennifer Giordano-Coltart, "A Holistic Approach to Patents Affecting Frontier Sciences: Lessons from the Seminal Genomic Discovery Studies," paper presented at the CEER Retreat, Duke University Center for Genetics, Ethics & Law (April 2008) and at the European Patent Forum: Inventing a Cleaner Future, Ljubljana, Slovenia (6–7 May 2008).

37. John P. Walsh, Wesley M. Cohen, and Charlene Cho, *Where Excludability Matters: Material Versus Intellectual Property in Academic Biomedical Research*, 36 Research Pol'y 1184 (2007); John P. Walsh, Charlene Cho, and Wesley M. Cohen, *The View from the Bench: Patents, Material Transfers and Biomedical Research*, 309(5743) Science 2002 (2005).

38. Reichman and Giordano-Coltart, *supra* note 36.

39. John P. Walsh et al., *Working Through the Patent Problem*, 299(5609) Science 1021 (2003).

40. Arti K. Rai and Sapna Kumar, *Synthetic Biology: The Intellectual Property Puzzle*, 85 Texas L. Rev. 1745–68 (2007), available at <http://scholarship.law.duke.edu/faculty_scholarship/1628/> (accessed 24 October 2013).

41. Wesley M. Cohen and John P. Walsh, *Real Impediments to Academic Biomedical Research*, in 8 Innovation Policy and the Economy 11 (Nat'l Bureau of Econ. Research, Adam B. Jaffe et al. eds., 2008).

42. These are areas particularly important for developing countries.

43. Michael E. Himmel et al., *Biomass Recalcitrance: Engineering Plants and Enzymes for Biofuels Production*, 315(5813) Science 804 (2007). See further A. Dechezleprêtre et al., Invention and Transfer of Climate Change Mitigation Technologies on a Global Scale: A Study Drawing on Patent Data (CERNA Research Programme on Tech. Transfer & Climate Change, Dec. 2008), <http://www.nccr-climate.unibe.ch/conferences/climate_policies/working_papers/Dechezlepretre.pdf> (accessed 24 October 2013).

44. Steve Suppan, *Patents: Taken for Granted in Plans for a Global Biofuels Market* (Inst. Agric. & Trade Pol'y, Working Paper, Oct. 17, 2007), available at <http://www.iatp.org/documents/patents-taken-for-granted-in-plans-for-a-global-bio fuels-market> (accessed 24 October 2013); see also John H. Barton, Intellectual Property and Access to Clean Energy Technologies in Developing Countries: An Analysis of Solar Photovoltaic, Biofuel and Wind Technologies (Int'l Ctr. for Trade & Sustainable Dev. (ICTSD) Programme on Trade & Envt. 2007), available at <http://ictsd.org/i/publications/3354/?view=document> (last accessed Oct. 8, 2013).

45. See also Todd Miller, James Peterson and T. Christopher Tsang, *Patent Trends in the Cleantech Industry*, Intell. Prop. & Tech. L. J. (July 2008), available at <http://www.jonesday.com/files/Publication/8d04d8da-5094-4d63-a490-a2d840e6282d/Presentation/PublicationAttachment/70a0eecb-8ed3-4d7b-9788-aa837805097d/7_08%20-%20IPT%26LJ%20Article.pdf> (accessed 24 October 2013) (noting that there has been no "noticeable increase" in the number of U.S. patents issuing in the biofuels/synfuels area).

46. Jocelyn Kaiser, *Attempt to Patent Artificial Organism Draws a Protest*, 316(5831) Science 1557 (2007).

47. See *generally* Rai and Kumar, *supra* note 40.

48. See text accompanying notes 39–40, *supra*.

49. See John H. Barton, *supra* note 44.

50. See *generally* Matthew Rimmer, Intellectual Property and Climate Change: Inventing Clean Technologies (Elgar Publishing 2011), 197–236.

51. Bernice Lee et al., Who Owns Our Low Carbon Future? Intellectual Property and Energy Technologies (London, Chatham House 2009), available at <http://www.chathamhouse.org.uk/files/14699-roqoq-lowcarbonfuture> (accessed 24 October 2013).

52. Jerome H. Reichman, Paul F. Uhlir, and Tom Dedeurwaerdere, Governing Digitally Integrated Genetic Resources, Data, and Literature: Global Intellectual Property Strategies for the Microbial Research Commons (Cambridge University Press, forthcoming).

53. Reichman, Uhlir, and Dedeurwaerdere, *supra* note 52.

54. On the use of these types of non-exclusive licenses, also known as liability rules, see Reichman, *supra* note 33. A concept related to liability rules (in the sense that it creates markets for technology with low transaction costs) is a clean-tech patent clearinghouse. One such site, called Lynxstreet, was recently launched. Membership on the site allows companies to list patents, view what others are offering, and also specify their own technology needs. A clearinghouse site might be particularly useful for small inventors. See Geertrui Van Overwalle, Gene Patents and Collaborative Licensing Models: Patent Pools, Clearinghouses, Open Source Models and Liability Regimes (Cambridge University Press 2009).

55. Newell, *supra* note 6.

56. Richard G. Newell and Nathan E. Wilson, *Technology Prizes for Climate Mitigation*, (Resources for the Future, Discussion Paper No. 05-33, June 2005), available at <http://www.rff.org/documents/RFF-DP-05-33.pdf> (accessed 24 October 2013). Recently proposed prizes relevant to energy and climate policy include Prizes for Achievement in Grand Challenges of Science and Technology authorized in the U.S. Energy Policy Act of 2005, the H-Prize (for hydrogen) and Bright Tomorrow Lighting Prizes authorized in the U.S. Energy Independence and Security Act of 2007, the privately-funded Progressive Automotive X-Prize, and the Earth Challenge Prize announced by British financier Richard Branson. Only the last two private prizes were funded at the time of writing.

57. See Nat'l Research Council, Innovation Inducement Prizes at the National Science Foundation (Nat'l Acads. Press 2007), available at <http://www.nap.edu/catalog. php?record_id=11816> (accessed 24 October 2013).

58. See Richard Newell, *International Climate Technology Strategies*, (Harvard Project on Int'l Climate Agreements, Discussion Paper No. 2008-12, Oct. 2008).

59. James Love and Tim Hubbard, *The Big Idea: Prizes to Stimulate R&D for New Medicines*, 82(3) Chi-Kent L. Rev. 1519 (2007).

60. For analogous proposals in regard to medical research, see Frederick M. Abbott and Jerome H. Reichman, *The Doha Round's Public Health Legacy: Strategies for the Production and Diffusion of Patented Medicines under the Amended TRIPS Provisions*, 10 J. Int'l Econ. L. 921, 983–4 (2007), available at <http://scholarship. law.duke.edu/cgi/viewcontent.cgi?article=2490&context=faculty_scholarship> (accessed 24 October 2013).

61. See Newell, *supra* note 58.

62. Kevin Outterson, *Patent Buy-Outs for Global Disease Innovations for Low- and Middle-Income Countries*, 32 Am. J. L. & Med. 159, 171–3 (2006). A somewhat analogous proposal has also been made by James Love, *Measures to Enhance Access to Medical Technologies, and New Methods of Stimulating Medical R&D*, 40 (3) U.C. Davis L. Rev. 679, 713 (2007), available at <http://www.keionline.org/ misc-docs/DavisVol40No3_Love.pdf> (accessed 24 October 2013). See also Amy Kapczynski et al., *Addressing Global Health Inequities: An Open Licensing Approach for University Innovations*, 20 Berkeley Tech L. J. 1031 (2005), available at <http://digitalcommons.law.yale.edu/cgi/viewcontent.cgi?article=4297&context= fss_papers> (accessed 24 October 2013).

63. Press Release, Drugs for Neglected Diseases Initiative (DNDi), *DNDi Partners with Pharma, Biotech, Academia, Public Health Institutes and NGOs to Deliver Lifesaving Drugs*, DNDi (June 23, 2008), <http://www.dndi.org/cms/public_html/insidearticleListing.asp?CategoryId=166&SubCategoryId=167&ArticleId=490&TemplateId=1> (accessed 24 October 2013); see also Ahmed Abdel Latif et al., Overcoming the Impasse on Intellectual Property and Climate Change at the UNFCCC: A Way Forward (ICTSD, Pol'y Brief No. 11, Nov. 2011), available at <http://ictsd.org/i/publications/120254/?view=document> (accessed 24 October 2013).

64. Heleen de Coninck et al., *International Technology-Oriented Agreements to Address Climate Change*, 36 Energy Pol'y 335–6 (2008); IEA, Energy Technology Perspectives 2008 (2008), available at <http://www.iea.org/publications/freepublications/publication/etp2008.pdf> (accessed 24 October 2013).

65. de Coninck et al., *supra* note 64.

66. See Newell, *supra* note 58.

67. See Newell, *supra* note 58.

68. European Comm'n, European Strategic Energy Technology Plan (Nov. 2007), available at <http://eur-lex.europa.eu/LexUriServ/LexUriServ.do?uri=CELEX:-52007DC0723:EN:HTML> (accessed 24 October 2013): See also Latif et al., *supra* note 63.

69. Ministry of Econ., Trade & Indus. (METI), Cool Earth: Innovative Energy Technology Program (March 2008), available at <http://www.meti.go.jp/english/newtopics/data/pdf/031320CoolEarth.pdf> (accessed 24 October 2013).

70. U.S. Dep't of Energy, U.S. Climate Change Technology Program, Strategic Plan (Sept. 2006), available at <http://www.climatetechnology.gov/stratplan/final/CCTP-StratPlan-Sep-2006.pdf> (accessed 24 October 2013).

71. IEA, Towards a Sustainable Energy Future (2008), available at <http://ccs101.ca/assets/Documents/g8_towards_sustainable_future.pdf .

72. See Newell, *supra* note 58.

73. See Newell, *supra* note 58.

74. Org. for Econ. Co-operation & Dev. (OECD), OECD Science, Technology and Industry Scoreboard 2007 (2007), available at <www.oecd.org/sti/oecdsciencetech-nologyandindustryscoreboard2011innovationandgrowthinknowledgeeconomies.htm> (accessed 24 October 2013).

75. A copy of the proposal can be found at <http://www.cptech.org/workingdrafts/rndtreaty4.pdf> (accessed 24 October 2013). See Love and Hubbard, *supra* note 59, for a related background discussion.

76. See Newell, *supra* note 58.

77. IEA, *Publications*, <http://www.iea.org/publications> (accessed 24 October 2013).

78. Frederick M. Abbott, *Protecting First World Assets in the Third World*, 22 Vand. J. Transnat'l L. 689 (1989), available at <http://ssrn.com/abstract=1918346> (accessed 24 October 2013); Jerome H. Reichman, *From Free Riders to Fair Followers: Global Competition under the TRIPS Agreement*, 29 N.Y.U. J. Int'l L. & Pol. 11–93 (1996–97); Jerome H. Reichman, *Intellectual Property Rights in the Twenty-First Century: Will the Developing Countries Lead or Follow?* (this volume, Chapter 4).

79. Keith E. Maskus and Jerome H. Reichman, *The Globalization of Private Knowledge Goods and the Privatization of Global Public Goods*, in International Public Goods and Transfer of Technology under a Globalized Intellectual Property Regime (Keith E. Maskus and Jerome H. Reichman, eds.,) (Cambridge University Press, 2005), 3–45.

80. Agreement on Trade-Related Aspects of Intellectual Property Rights arts. 41–9, 15 April 1994, 108 Stat. 4809, 1869 U.N.T.S. 299 [hereinafter TRIPS Agreement]. See Jerome H. Reichman, *Enforcing the Enforcement Provisions of the TRIPS Agreement*, 37 Va. J. Int'l L. 335 (1997), available at <http://scholarship.law.duke.edu/cgi/viewcontent.cgi?article=1406&context=faculty_scholarship> (accessed 24 October 2013).

81. See, e.g., Reichman, Green Tulips, *supra* note 33. See also Joshua D. Sarnoff, *The Patent System and Climate Change*, 16 U. Va. J. L. 8 Tech 301, 336–52 (2011).

82. Paris Convention for the Protection of Industrial Property art. 4*bis*, 20 March 1883, *as amended on* 28 September 1979, 21 U.S.T. 1583; TRIPS Agreement, *supra* note 78, art 2.1.

83. TRIPS Agreement, *supra* note 80, art. 31; see Jerome H. Reichman, *Compulsory Licensing of Patented Pharmaceutical Inventions: Evaluating the Options*, 37 J. L. Med. & Ethics 247 (2009), available at <http://scholarship.law.duke.edu/cgi/viewcontent.cgi?article=2747&context=faculty_scholarship> (accessed 24 October 2013). Abbott & Reichman, *supra* note 60.

84. TRIPS Agreement, *supra* note 81, art. 31.l.

85. See *Gene Patents and Public Health* pt. 2, sec. 2 (Geertrui van Overwalle, eds, 2007).

86. See Abbott & Reichman, *supra* note 60, at 973–7 (with regard to pooled procurement strategies in the pharmaceutical sector).

87. Abbott & Reichman, *supra* note 86.

88. Abbott & Reichman, *supra* note 86.

89. For the unsettled state of this thesis, see Abbott and Reichman, *supra* note 60, at 957–78.

90. See IEA (2007), supra note 4; *China to Top USA in Greenhouse Emissions*, USA Today, 24 April 2007, <http://www.usatoday.com/weather/climate/globalwarming/2007-04-24-china-emissions_N.htm> (accessed 24 October 2013); *A Large Black Cloud: Rapid Growth Is Exacting a Heavy Environmental Price*, The Economist, 15 March 2008, at 17, 21, available at <http://www.economist.com/node/10795813> (accessed 24 October 2013).

91. See David Barboza, *China Unveils Sweeping Plan for Economy*, N.Y. Times, 9 November 2008, <http://www.nytimes.com/2008/11/10/world/asia/10china.html> (accessed 24 October 2013).

92. See David G. Streets, *Black Smoke in China and Its Climate Effects*, 4(2) Asian Econ. Papers 1 (2005); Fei Teng and Alun Gu, *Climate Change: National and Local Policy Opportunities in China* (Fondazione Eni Enrico Mattei, Working Paper No. 74.2007, 2007), available at <http://ssrn.com/abstract=999926> (accessed 24 October 2013).

93. See *China to Top USA in Greenhouse Emissions*, *supra* note 90; *A Large Black Cloud*, *supra* note 90; Elizabeth C. Economy, *The Great Leap Backward?*, Foreign Aff., Sept./Oct. 2007, at 38, 47 (citing 400,000 to 750,000 deaths per year);

V. Ramanathan and G. Carmichael, *Global and Regional Climate Changes due to Black Carbon*, 1 Nature Geoscience 221, 226 (2008) (finding that black carbon makes a significantly greater contribution to global warming than earlier estimates, and observing that reductions in black carbon could yield major public health benefits, especially in China, India, and other developing countries). Note that black carbon is not yet included in the Kyoto Protocol, Annex A, list of regulated GHGs, but could be added in a future international accord. See Kyoto Protocol to United Nations Framework Convention on Climate Change, Annex A, 11 December 1997, 2303 U.N.T.S. 148.

94. The World Bank & State Envtl. Prot. Admin., People's Rep. of China, Costs of Pollution in China, at xvii (2007) (citing a cost of 5.78 per cent of GDP).

95. See Jonathan B. Wiener, *Climate Change Policy and Policy Change in China*, 55 UCLA L. Rev. 1805, 1818–21 (2008).

96. See Shulin Gu and Bengt Åke-Lundvall, *China's Innovation System and the Move Toward Harmonious Growth and Endogenous Innovation*, 8 Innovation: Mgmt., Pol'y & Prac. 1 (2006).

97. See further Latif et al., *supra* note 63. Of course, the U.S. and China have had disputes over IPRs in China. See David R. Weisman, *US Toughens Its Position on China Trade*, N.Y. Times, Apr. 10, 2007, <http://www.nytimes.com/2007/04/10/business/worldbusiness/10trade.html> (accessed 24 October 2013). Chinese leaders say they seek a stronger system of IPRs. See *China Needs to Perfect its Intellectual Property System*, Xinhua News Serv., Oct. 29, 2008, <http://news.xinhuanet.com/english/2008-10/29/content_10276636.htm> (accessed 24 October 2013) ("Zhang Qin, deputy director of State Intellectual Property Office . . . [said] the country's intellectual property system still lagged behind developed countries and needs improvement. The country also encourages the enterprise to upgrade their innovation level."). Meanwhile, in a sign of further movement toward a full market economy, China has been authorizing property rights in land. See Edward Wong, *China May Let Peasants Sell Rights to Farmland*, N.Y. Times, 11 October 2008, at A1, available at <http://www.nytimes.com/2008/10/11/world/asia/11china.html> (accessed 24 October 2013).

98. In the June 2012 *Doing Business* rankings posted by the World Bank—China, India, and Brazil ranked 91st, 132nd and 130th (out of 185 countries) in overall ease of doing business. See World Bank Group, *Economy Rankings*, Doing Business Project (June 2012), <http://www.doingbusiness.org/rankings> (accessed 24 October 2013).

99. For surveys of IPRs in China, see William P. Alford, To Steal a Book Is an Elegant Offense: Intellectual Property Law in Chinese Civilization (Stanford University Press, 1995); Peter Feng, Intellectual Property in China (Sweet and Maxwell, 2nd ed., 2003).

13

Legal and Economic Perspectives on International Technology Transfer in Environmentally Sound Technologies

Keith E. Maskus and Ruth L. Okediji

1. INTRODUCTION

The task of stabilizing the accumulation of greenhouse gases (GHGs) in the atmosphere rests in large part on the development and transfer of technologies (Barrett, 2009). In this chapter we consider policy approaches that may help achieve an effective framework for encouraging and supporting innovation and international technology transfer (ITT) of environmentally sound technologies (ESTs).[1]

Transferring and adapting effective technologies to developing countries (DCs) on a sustainable basis is critical for addressing the adverse effects of climate change. As noted in Article 4.5 of the United Nations Framework Convention on Climate Change (UNFCCC), developed countries are required to promote and help finance ITT and access to ESTs and know-how to enable DCs to implement provisions of the Convention.[2] One potential means of supporting such ITT is to rely on the global intellectual property (IP) system, which, in principle, is designed to encourage innovation and facilitate trade in technology. However, many DCs are deeply skeptical of the efficacy of this system, seeing it as an impediment to achieving their technology needs. This tension between innovation and diffusion of ESTs has made IP reforms a difficult and contentious issue in ongoing climate-change negotiations.

Fundamental questions arise in the UNFCCC process about the classic justifications for private intellectual property rights (IPRs) in ESTs, which bear characteristics of public goods. Arguments for IPRs are that they facilitate investments in research and development (R&D), reduce licensing costs, add to the knowledge base, and enhance follow-on inventive activity. If one takes this view, it follows that DCs should enhance and enforce their legal regimes, because private firms will not license technologies without adequate compensation and credible protection from misappropriation. Regarding climate change, however, these positive aspects are highly uncertain. First, patents incentivize private R&D only when there is strong demand for new technological solutions, which, in the absence of policies to support high prices for GHG emissions, is unlikely. Second, to the extent that IPRs limit access to new ESTs, they will reduce local mitigation and adaptation investments. Third, limited availability of suitable technologies, offered on reasonable terms, could lower the willingness of DCs to participate in negotiating a climate treaty. Finally, the market demands for ESTs that are specially tailored to the needs of poor DCs are likely to be too weak for IPRs alone to incentivize the necessary R&D.

Thus, in regards to ESTs, incentives are needed for all product phases, from R&D to commercialization, and from ITT to local adoption. A complex mixture of IPRs and policy initiatives will be necessary; the challenge is to identify the relevant variables at each stage. The difficulty of this task is compounded by the fact that the countries most vulnerable to climate change generally have weak policy institutions and legal systems. Thus, relying on property rights as the primary access mechanism for developing countries is inadequate.

Two opposing views have dominated the global policy debate. The first view argues that IPRs, per se, are sufficient to achieve optimal innovation and ITT to manage climate change. It denies the role of limitations and exceptions to proprietary rights, focusing instead on the importance of enforcing transparent legal provisions. The second view favors the importance of dissemination, arguing for strong limits on exclusive rights, including the liberal use of compulsory licenses (CLs) and other government interventions in the technology market. This approach finds systemic failures in the global IP system's ability to support ITT of key public goods to developing countries.

In this chapter, we explore a third approach, which proposes specific government measures, combined with IPRs, to provide a sound set of incentives to invent and diffuse ESTs. We do not advocate generalized IPR reforms because they would entail large political costs without clear evidence of enhanced access for DCs. However, there is value in targeted revisions to support access to new technical knowledge, to improve domestic adaptive innovation in DCs, and to facilitate a more balanced global system. This more nuanced approach to the role of IPRs is complemented by additional policy options regarding the innovation and diffusion of public goods more generally.

In section 2 we review the role of patents in developing and transferring ESTs. In section 3 we discuss the complex interactions among IPRs, ESTs, and policymaking, and note weaknesses in the system preventing efficient dissemination. In section 4 we describe and analyze a variety of new approaches intended to support innovation and access in this area, including potential adaptation incentives. Finally, in section 5, we offer some proposals for IPR reforms specifically targeted at improving access to ESTs in the IP system.

2. IPRs AND TECHNOLOGY TRANSFER IN ESTs

Dealing with climate change is a massive economic and political challenge that will require considerable action beyond the IP arena. For example, the International Energy Agency (IEA, 2008) estimates that to meet global goals, needed investments in clean-technology innovation will be around $1.1 trillion per year (in real terms) through 2050, or around 1.1 per cent of global GDP. Part of this cost arises from the great heterogeneity of technology needs in particular sectors and countries (Maskus, 2010). Such investments are more likely to be attained if a sustainably high price on carbon emissions is established to encourage conservation and to spur investments in alternative energy sources. Public subsidies encouraging the development of new technologies and the deployment of these technologies into DCs are also important.

2.1 Evidence on patents, innovation, and ITT in clean technologies

The limited evidence available suggests that there are four factors driving the bulk of investment in ESTs: anticipated market demand, relative prices of alternative energy sources, costs of investment, and public research subsidies. Existing studies take patent applications as a measure of innovative output and statistically relate them to indicators of environmental policy. For example, Brunnermeier and Cohen (2003) found a positive correlation between the number of environment-related U.S. patents granted and abatement expenditures across U.S. manufacturing industries. There was also evidence that more internationally competitive U.S. industries invest more in environmental R&D. Popp (2006) found a strong effect of tighter air-quality regulation on domestic patenting of pollution-abatement equipment in the United States, but not in Germany or Japan. Johnstone et al. (2009) gathered evidence from 25 countries between 1978 and 2003 and noted that environmental policies can effectively spur innovation (as measured by patent applications). Policies increasing the cost of fossil fuels support innovation in alternative technologies that are close substitutes for carbon-based technologies. However, inducing patentable innovation in broader alternative energy technologies requires subsidies and other support.

The number of patents registered in green technologies is increasing rapidly. The World Intellectual Property Organization (WIPO) reports that solar-energy-related patent applications filed under the Patent Cooperation Treaty (PCT) tripled between 2004 and 2008, rising to 1,411 (Castonguay, 2009). Another study reviewed patent applications between 1998 and 2008 in seven environmental technologies: waste, solar, ocean, fuel cell, biomass, geothermal, and wind power (Copenhagen Economics, 2009). It identified 215,000 total worldwide applications, 22,000 of which were in a sample of developing economies, including the major emerging economies.

Taken together, these studies found a marked expansion of patent applications in DCs, with a growth of over 500 per cent between 2004 and 2008. Virtually all of this growth was in a small group of emerging economies, including Argentina, Brazil, Russia, Ukraine, India, China, and the Philippines. Fewer than ten applications per year were submitted in the group of DCs. More than one-third of the applications in DCs were registered by inventors from those countries, primarily China. China is a significant source of new environmental technologies and its entities hold major shares of global patents in solar energy and fuel cells. China's enterprises also invest large R&D sums in clean coal technologies (Jessup, 2008).

The most comprehensive analysis was performed by the United Nations Environment Programme (UNEP), European Patent Office (EPO), and the International Centre for Trade and Sustainable Development (ICTSD).[3] These organizations reviewed the universe of recent applications and described the existence and ownership of patents in major clean-energy technologies (CETs), a subset of ESTs. They discovered that patenting rates of CETs have gone up by 20 per cent per year since 1997, faster than the rate of traditional energy technologies. Patenting CETs is still dominated by industrialized nations, but several emerging economies, including Mexico in hydro/marine activities and India in solar-photovoltaic inventions, are important sources of technology.

It is also important to note that although the number of patent applications in ESTs has risen rapidly, ownership of patents within any particular technology field tends to be diffused across countries and firms. One study argues that this dispersed ownership of patents implies little risk of monopoly pricing or anticompetitive behavior in their use, even in emerging and developing economies (Copenhagen Economics, 2009). It argues further that patents cannot be an impediment to ITT to the poorest countries, since virtually no patents exist there.

Barton (2007) qualitatively reviewed patenting in solar-photovoltaics, biofuels, and wind technologies, and reached similar conclusions about the effect of IPRs on the transfer of ESTs. In these areas, many of the fundamental technologies have long been off-patent, while existing patents usually protect moderate improvements and specific features. These incremental changes generally compete with numerous substitute technologies both within and across invention classes, and generally arise in sectors with relatively free entry. Thus, licensing is available from numerous sources and the resulting competition would likely restrain pricing power in reasonably competitive DC markets. Both Barton (2007) and Copenhagen Economics claim that the real barriers to ITT arise from impediments to trade, impediments to investment, and from limited adaptation capabilities in DCs. This notion is consistent with the observation of many analysts that the effectiveness of transferring ESTs is critically dependent on the general investment climates of recipient nations (Maskus, 2010; Maskus, 2012).

This generally optimistic situation could drastically change as additional investments are made in ESTs in the future. If, for example, the global community agreed on an international cap-and-trade system elevating fossil-fuel prices, new and critical technologies eligible for patent protection may emerge. In many sectors, access to these new ESTs would likely not be unduly restricted, since the high carbon price would induce numerous competing projects across multiple technologies. However, a specific, yet important, concern is that particular patented enzymes or new micro-organisms will be the basis for second-generation biofuels and synthetic fuels (Barton, 2007; Saez, 2009). This possibility is similar to the current situation in biotechnology, where many observers claim that patent thickets and transaction costs reduce R&D and sustain market power, impairing access to knowledge (Newell et al., 2008). More generally, patents for some ESTs could increase access problems in technologies that address specific local ecological needs (e.g. in agriculture) or market conditions. In sum, constraints on ITT from the exercise of patent rights in ESTs are quite feasible going forward, even if there is limited evidence of its past occurrence.

At least two other potential concerns with regard to limiting ITT should be highlighted. First, an extensive investigation of patent ownership and market adoption rates of six energy technologies—wind, solar photovoltaic, concentrated solar power, biofuels, cleaner coal, and carbon capture and storage—over the last 30 years found that innovation and international adoption are lengthy processes, often taking 20 or 30 years (Lee et al., 2009). Because this slow diffusion rate cannot meet global needs for rapid ITT and deployment, the authors argue for targeted supports to speed up adaptation and diffusion as new technologies come on line.

Moreover, governments in a small number of countries finance much of the basic research performed at universities and public research laboratories in the heterogeneous realm of ESTs (Barton, 2007). These countries also have programs to encourage innovation and commercialization to promote the global competitiveness of domestic firms. For example, the Environmental Technologies Action Plan (ETAP) of the European Commission provides fiscal support to firms creating ESTs.[4] Similarly, the United States makes large investments in solar power, wind power, hydrogen cells, and biofuels (Hargreaves, 2009). Many other developed economies offer similar research subsidies, while China invests significant amounts in the development of biotechnology, solar power, and fuel cells (Climate Group, 2009).

Thus, the second concern about possibly limiting ITT is that because the bulk of scientific research in basic technologies will be funded by government grants, their deployment will take on protectionist elements. For example, key features of U.S. innovation policy permit patenting of new technologies developed under public support, and the rules favor commercialization approaches that discriminate in favor of domestic firms (Barton, 2007). It is likely that other nations will pursue similar favoritism in their innovation systems, raising the possibility of fragmentation in access to ESTs developed from public research supports.

2.2 Structural issues involving IPRs and technology diffusion

The primary economic justification for IPRs is that they facilitate private solutions to information-based market failures (Maskus, 2000). Exclusive property rights are given to qualified authors and inventors in return for the public disclosure of their creative work and results of their scientific inquiry. A patent claiming an invention that satisfies criteria of novelty, non-obviousness, and utility gives the inventor an exclusive right to prevent others from making, using, or selling the invention for 20 years. Copyrights provide longer exclusive protection against unauthorized copying of expressions of ideas, including software and original databases. Trade secrets also offer exclusivity so long as the firm takes reasonable precautions to keep its information confidential. These three main categories of intellectual property offer well-defined property rights that provide legal security to preclude misappropriation and to encourage public disclosure of new concepts.

Mature patent systems also are designed to foster dynamic competition through improvements of inventions and through downstream innovation. This process is made possible through provisions regarding the scope and duration of protection; exclusions to facilitate research by third parties; measures that permit government use; and mechanisms to challenge the validity of a patent. There are also limitations on the scope of copyright, including a range of permissible uses without the authorization of the owner, and other limitations and exceptions consistent with the Berne Convention (Okediji, 2006), which arguably remain intact notwithstanding the TRIPS Agreement. Properly deployed, these intentional "gaps" in the IP system support the goals of diffusing knowledge, facilitating access, and fostering further innovation.

The globally harmonized regime of IPRs is rationalized on similar grounds, specifically that such harmonization will encourage innovation and beneficial

ITT (Lamy, 2004; Yu, 2009).[5] Advocates claim that strong IPRs will encourage robust flows of cross-border technology transactions and facilitate the absorption of new inventions into foreign markets.[6] Indeed, ITT flows can contribute to economic development by strengthening domestic capacity to absorb new knowledge and generate new goods and services with which to trade in global markets (Yang and Maskus, 2009). Members of the World Trade Organization adopted the TRIPS Agreement in 1995, in part, to pursue these outcomes. The TRIPS Agreement, however, achieves partial harmonization at best and recognizes limitations and exceptions (L&Es) to exclusive IP rights. It does not address a number of issues currently under debate, such as the role of L&Es in improving access to new technologies, including ESTs, which remains highly controversial.

Indeed, it is difficult to determine empirically whether the TRIPS Agreement achieves an appropriate and workable balance between the needs for coordinated innovation incentives and access to new products and technologies. Available evidence does not clearly find that encouraging foreign firms to enter DC markets generates positive productivity and competition spillovers (Maskus, 2004). Rather, some studies have found negative externalities because multinational enterprises (MNEs) may displace rival local firms. There are incentives for MNEs to prevent information spillovers to horizontal competitors. In contrast, there is evidence that global firms often transfer new technologies to local input suppliers, generating important backward spillovers (Javorcik, 2004). This is potentially an important factor for DCs, especially if domestic and international regulations require compliance with minimum environmental standards.

It should also be noted that technology transfer comes at a cost to local recipients. For example, a study by the World Bank (2001) found that implementing TRIPS would have required ten middle-income and developing nations markedly to increase patent-based royalty payments to firms in high-income countries. Other costs arise, such as transactions costs related to negotiating terms and conditions of access, opportunity costs for diverting skilled labor from other productive activities, and the costs of adapting technology to efficient local uses. While transaction costs may be reduced by more legal certainty regarding the scope of IPRs, adaptation costs can be substantial and subject to additional fees, particularly if local use would impinge on other exclusive rights. Thus, stronger patent protection can considerably raise the costs of imitation on the part of local competing firms in DCs. Conversely, well-designed and effectively deployed limitations on patent rights can establish more balanced competition between international firms and domestic licensees and imitators.

This analysis suggests that while more harmonized IPRs could induce greater inward flows of ESTs, there is a corresponding risk that licensing costs would raise the expense of mitigating GHGs. Some of these problems can be avoided by supporting adaptation of new technologies to local conditions and domestic production capacities. Such adaptation could even generate positive externalities to the extent that it contributes to the supply of skilled labor and supports employment while reducing emissions.

Thus, there is an argument for public intervention to support investments in modifying ESTs for local conditions. One means of doing so is to establish an IP system in which contracting regulations and L&Es are sufficiently well defined to allow modifications and follow-on innovation to occur with relatively minimal transaction costs. With regard to IPRs, the ease with which downstream innovators and local firms can adapt technologies will depend on the transparency and efficacy of the patent system, which can play an important role in reducing information asymmetries (Arora et al., 2001). These positive impacts could be supported further by various forms of open-source collaboration based on full disclosure of know-how associated with patented technologies.

In any event, it is evident that while many DCs need to improve their institutional environment for IPRs, they would benefit from sustaining robust criteria for issuing patents, whether through rigorous novelty standards, a high inventive step requirement, or well-crafted exclusions. Further, it makes sense to establish transparent limits on claims, to facilitate challenges to validity, competition enforcement, and compulsory licensing under appropriate circumstances. Doing so could achieve gains in terms of local knowledge diffusion. That strategy is indeed consistent with central goals of the global IP system, which include efficient international dissemination of new technical knowledge. Of course, robust patentability standards mean that local inventions may not qualify for protection. However, DCs can establish a system of utility models to encourage domestic innovation while limiting the development and dissemination costs associated with broad patent claims.

3. NEW GLOBAL APPROACHES TO INNOVATION AND ACCESS

To summarize the prior analysis, the patent system does not appear to be a primary determinant of R&D for most ESTs and government programs largely subsidize basic and applied climate-change research. Further, while IPRs can be an important support for building markets in technology, there are difficult structural problems in making this support effective for ITT to DCs. Moreover, even if patents do not currently limit access to the use of many ESTs, it does not imply that the current system is the most effective mechanism for encouraging effective innovation and diffusion of clean technologies.

These factors suggest that an IPR-centered system of investment incentives is inadequate for inducing and disseminating new technologies quickly enough to reduce GHG emissions sufficiently to mitigate climate change. Indeed, in real terms, the levels of R&D spending by members of the International Energy Agency (IEA) on critical alternative energy sources and mitigation technologies fell in the 1990s (Barrett, 2009). More recently these expenditures have increased, but much of that rise is due to public investments.

Thus, in the following subsections we describe alternative innovation and access models, based more on public financing and access sharing, which may be needed to complement increasing government and private investments in ESTs. In so doing, we reiterate that at least two fundamental conditions need to be met in order to provide general incentives for technological development and dissemination. The first would be a sustained and significant increase in global costs of emitting GHGs or using fossil-fuels, whether through coordinated taxes or cap-and-trade systems, in order to provide a significant boost to profitable R&D in ESTs. The second would be macroeconomic and innovation policies in DCs that improve investment climates and reduce costs of transferring and adapting new technologies. Assuming these outcomes are feasible in the medium term, the proposals listed below could offer significant complementary benefits.

3.1 Grants and prizes

One idea is to open up competition for public research grants. Granting agencies in the United States, EU, Canada and other national governments could be encouraged to set aside some of their funds devoted to environmental research and make them available for specific projects in poor nations. These grants would best be awarded competitively to research teams involving national and international collaborations among universities, public research institutions, and NGOs. The granting terms could encourage linkages with private enterprises for effective testing of new technologies under local environmental and market conditions and conducting randomized field tests and other preliminary implementation processes. Note that participants would likely register exclusive rights on their inventions in major markets, the allocation of which is best left to the collaborative partners, subject to appropriate competition regulation. However, the basic knowledge generated by such publicly financed R&D should be placed in the public domain, with the applied proprietary results made available for widespread licensing in DCs on advantageous terms.

The politics of permitting national agencies to open targeted grant competitions this way are likely to limit such possibilities and may not ensure sustainable funding. Thus, a second suggestion is to establish a Global Emissions Reduction Fund (GERF) to incentivize investments in technical solutions to specific mitigation needs in the developing world.[7] Donors could include public agencies, foundations, and private enterprises, all having some stake in the distribution of funds. One use of a GERF would be similar to the Global Fund to fight AIDS, Tuberculosis, and Malaria: to purchase ESTs embodied in goods and services that can be implemented effectively in particular locations. Given sufficient funds, the facility could also negotiate concessional prices and licensing terms.

To induce innovation, a mix of direct grants, prizes, and geographically limited patent buyouts could be envisaged. Specific innovation prizes are promising for incentivizing particular solutions in developing markets (Erren, 2007; Bays and Jansen, 2009). Prize programs can take two general approaches. The more common is for a donor to describe the technical problem and offer a pre-specified monetary reward for the first technology that solves it effectively, thereby focusing investment efforts on well-defined solutions. This strategy can also be effective for ESTs with wider, cross-border applications, though here it is difficult to judge how much money to set aside *ex ante* and the first invention may not be the most efficient one or ensure applicability to needs of specific locations.

Thus, we also suggest provision of funds to a second prize mechanism, which would pre-specify target regions and particular needs (e.g., adoption of drought-resistant crops in sub-Saharan Africa) without choosing the form of technology. A critical feature would be the funding formula that defines the prize. Rather than a fixed dollar amount, a reward could capture some proportion of the social (economic and broader spillover) value the invention seems likely to create in the specific market.[8] For this purpose, the inventing team would need to demonstrate applicability and utility in the targeted location through field research describing experimental data, market surveys of economic needs, and the technical feasibility of adoption prospects. For approved inventions, a prize would be released, set at some percentage of the value of identified national or regional market needs. To maximize diffusion prospects, the recipient would forego patent or other IP protection in the target location (and preferably in other poor countries). The prize agency would make the invention available to all who wish to use or sell it locally, including to the original inventor.

Designers of either prize model would have to consider the possible ramifications of patents on follow-on inventions. It is possible that a prize-winning invention, with its technical details entering the public domain, could give rise to subsequent innovations for which the inventor (or a third party) would seek patent protection in developing countries. It is inefficient to use public funds to incentivize an early invention if it becomes supplanted by a subsequent and privately owned technology. Thus, we argue for provisions disallowing patents in poor countries in cases of clear sequential innovation, though the follow-on inventor could earn licensing royalties in a liability-rule regime (Antonelli, 2007).

It is not straightforward to determine how much funding might be necessary or where to locate a facility like a GERF. Because addressing climate change is a global public good, nearly all governments should be expected to contribute in some form. So too should private interests that take advantage of the subsidies proffered or benefit from proprietary rights in rich-country markets. Both consumers and producers of fossil fuels could be induced to contribute through a carbon tax or cap-and-trade system, with some revenues devoted to this purpose. We argue further that even the least-developed countries should be expected to make some contributions as a form of co-payment for participation.

3.2 Patent extension

Another possibility is to provide more incentives for innovation through explicitly differentiating the terms of protection for particularly effective ESTs. Thus, the duration of patents could be extended for technologies with demonstrated utility in reducing GHG emissions, especially perhaps in DCs. However, we would not anticipate *ex ante* patent-term extensions to stimulate much innovation in this area. Firms already benefit from market lead-times, making longer patents less relevant as an inducement. Moreover, specific ESTs have fairly rapid life cycles, while "inventing around" patents is often fairly straightforward (Barooah, 2008). In consequence, patents generally are of low value prior to their regular expiry dates. If the extension were to be awarded *ex post* (i.e. after an invention reveals itself to be particularly effective), the implied uncertainty would limit any additional R&D incentive. It could be argued that some innovation gains could be achieved from extending market rents through longer patents if those revenues were devoted to R&D in new ESTs. However, this is surely a costly means of incentivizing such investments.

In addition, many important ESTs, such as solar-photovoltaic cells, hydrogen batteries, and hybrid engines, are characterized by cumulative invention, whereby current projects build on prior knowledge (IETC/UNEP, 2003). In such cases, patent extensions on longer-living technologies can raise costs of subsequent innovation (Encaoua et al., 2006). It should be noted that there is little indication to date that failures to license have diminished subsequent invention in general (Gallini, 2002).

Patent-term extensions presumably should be provided only for modifications or adaptations of existing inventions to create new useful technological solutions to relevant climate-change problems. It is important to encourage adaptive investments because they can meet smaller market needs and spur rapid technological changes (Maskus, 2001). However, patents are generally viewed as heavy protection for small improvements, suggesting that shorter terms and narrower claims, like those in design patents or utility models, make more sense (UNCTAD, 2007). If a short period of extended protection on legitimate adaptations of an existing patent were permitted, rather than on the basic invention itself, it could achieve the same goal. If, on the other hand, the extension were provided to the original patented invention, it would be important for policymakers to garner a commitment by the patentee to offer widespread licensing in developing countries on reasonable terms.

Finally, there is the question of where such patent extensions would occur and under what terms. Inventors would likely benefit most if the extensions were in the largest markets, such as the United States, EU, Japan, and China. Assuming there is a demand for the invention or its adaptation in those locations, a meaningful fee should be imposed on applications for extensions. If the adaptation were really more suitable for conditions in DCs, it would lapse into the public domain upon original expiry, unless patentable novelty could be demonstrated to authorities in those jurisdictions.

Overall, we doubt there is much welfare gain available from patent extensions for ESTs. Such a policy would not offer much invention stimulus, while providing a thick wedge of protection. If extensions were to be offered to specific technologies, clear criteria would need to be established for certifying eligibility. Given the disparity of economic and environmental interests across countries, it would be hard to achieve an international agreement on those criteria. However, as a means of encouraging ITT, developed economies could offer patent extensions—even midway through the patent term—in return for a commitment to open licensing, especially in DCs.

3.3 Wild-card patents

Another suggestion is that firms be permitted to extend patents on an invention of their choice within their patent portfolios in return for commercializing a second environmental technology for which there is a limited market. This policy has been proposed in the United States to encourage pharmaceutical companies to develop new antibiotics to overcome drug resistance (Spellberg et al., 2007). In principle, this approach could be useful for incentivizing R&D into the mitigation and adaptation needs of smaller countries in specific technologies (Torrance, 2007; Weilbaecher, 2009). Since wild-card extensions would only be offered in return for successful development and commercialization of small-market technologies, profits would only be made on extended patents in return for verifiable and beneficial outcomes.[9] Original firms presumably would apply to extend protection on one of their most valuable technologies in order to maximize revenues. In that context, the proposal establishes a potentially effective *ex ante* incentive to invest in secondary technologies.

Still, the policy would be effective only to the extent that anticipated revenues from the wild-card designation exceed the net costs of secondary technology development. Because the useful lifetimes of original ESTs are frequently less than standard patent terms, the approach may not offer much stimulus to small-market technology development. It could also slow down investments by other firms in substitutes for both the original and secondary technologies, depending on the scope of that protection (Gallini, 2002). The most significant objection is simply that there are costs associated with slower entry of the original invention into the public domain.

Note further that with ESTs the objective is to encourage development of technologies for specific environmental needs that generally exist outside the original patent jurisdiction. Thus, if the United States or EU were to extend wild-card protection on widely used, basic ESTs, in order to promote private development and transfer of specific technologies for DCs, the effect would be a tax on users in the former regions to pay for environmental benefits in the latter. Beyond the political difficulty of such an arrangement, it is not likely to be an efficient tax. There is also likely to be significant international free-riding on the costs of patent extensions, which would limit the R&D incentive. Overall, there is promise in this idea, but it is not likely to become a priority compared to more direct subsidies for R&D and technology transfer.

3.4 Voluntary patent networks

An approach of considerable promise would be to facilitate the emergence of voluntary patent pools or networks into which patent holders—including firms, universities, and research institutions—would deposit their relevant IP (Cahoy and Glenna, 2009). Users could then acquire the licenses needed for specific mitigation and adaptation technologies from members of the network in return for royalties paid at *ex ante* agreed rates. These rates could be differentiated in favor of uses in DCs. These patent cooperatives offer a single location for the dissemination of technologies, which can markedly reduce the costs of licensing to multiple markets (Lerner and Tirole, 2004; Picker, 2006). They are especially helpful in circumstances where there are multiple patents on complementary inputs and where private technology brokers would not bundle these rights, except at a high cost.

History suggests that private patent pools among competing firms within a country offer mixed benefits and costs (Nelson, 2007). Each firm sometimes innovates and sometimes needs access to other patents and thus has an interest in participating and cross-licensing. However, exclusive pools may be anticompetitive under certain circumstances, while some firms may choose not to license blocking patents. Thus, countries should exercise vigilance on the part of competition authorities. The situation would be different for global patent pools, however, where licensees in DCs are less likely to be future licensors in the medium term. Structured properly, patent networks would amount to open licensing in return for an agreed payment, effectively a liability rule regime (Flynn et al., 2009). Such an arrangement has been established by UNITAID in the area of antiretroviral drugs (Weilbaecher, 2009).

The primary difficulty with voluntary licensing pools is that inventors may refuse to place their patents in the pool, particularly for inventions with high global commercial value. Firms also may not participate if their IPRs are capable of blocking implementation of ESTs that embody their technologies as components. Thus, the ability of licensing pools to promote ITT depends on how much they reduce transactions costs, the size of potential markets, and the nature of relevant technologies.[10] Here an argument arises for public subsidization of license fees to build a secure market where the technologies in question bear external environmental benefits. This is especially true where the license provides access to know-how, which can provide spillover dynamic gains in recipient countries by reducing the costs of future adaptive technologies (Popp, 2009).

One means of facilitating patent pools would be to establish a system in which patent application and renewal fees in the major developed markets would be reduced in return for participation in those pools for ESTs with demonstrable environmental benefits. While this approach has rarely been attempted, the strategic use of patent fees to facilitate global access to technologies that address significant public goods is appropriate and could be achieved via an agreement among the legislative and patent authorities in major economies.

Finally, even if voluntary pools failed to attract significant participation by private firms, universities and public research institutes could be encouraged to place their technologies into public databases in return for licensing fees differentiated by development levels and needs in recipient nations. Doing so would require grant-funding authorities to recognize the public-good nature of the basic technologies they support (Adelman and Engel, 2008; Barton and Maskus, 2006). This offers additional justification for targeted pooling of grant funds and opening competition for grants to partner institutions in the developing world.

4. ACCESS OPTIONS UNDER THE GLOBAL IP SYSTEM

The prior section considered policy approaches that may be implemented largely without reference to global norms of IP protection as set out in the TRIPS Agreement. It is equally important to clarify how the legal provisions of that agreement may be used to enhance access to ESTs, which we do in the next subsection.[11] Following that we outline potential revisions to TRIPS itself that may be beneficial in this context.

4.1 Access options within TRIPS

As extensively discussed in the literature, the provisions of TRIPS offer flexibility to DCs in establishing IP protection standards and associated L&Es to private rights (Maskus and Reichman, 2005; Reichman, 2010; Deere, 2009). For example, Article 30 is a general statement that governments may provide "limited exceptions" to exclusive patent rights so long as they do so in a way that does not "unreasonably prejudice" the legitimate interests of rights holders and does not "unreasonably conflict" with normal exploitation of the patent. They must also take account of the interests of third parties. Subject to this basic proscription, the scope of which remains under debate, a number of key L&Es may be envisioned. We briefly review those possibilities that are particularly relevant for access to ESTs and adaptation to local needs.

Patent standards. As noted earlier, it makes sense for DCs to sustain robust criteria for patentability. Patents should be provided only to genuine inventive advances, with minor inventions receiving lesser protection or relying on trade secrecy. Developing countries may choose fairly stiff non-obviousness and inventiveness standards, which India has done with respect to pharmaceuticals in its recent patent law. The utility standard in particular may help keep the results of basic science in the public domain. Next, while rigorous eligibility standards can prevent excessive patenting, DCs may deploy pre-grant or post-grant opposition procedures. This element is particularly useful in poor countries that cannot afford their own examination offices and, therefore, rely largely on simple registration procedures or the results of novelty examinations abroad.

While applying rigorous standards to invention patents is sensible, it is also important not to extinguish small-scale inventive and adaptive efforts, particularly by local entrepreneurs. In this regard, a robust utility model or petty patents system can be effective. These devices offer shorter-term and narrow protection for adaptive inventions, with limited requirements for demonstrated novelty. Statistical evidence suggests that utility models have contributed to productivity growth in Brazil, Korea, and Japan (Maskus, 2000). They could be of particular value in meeting local mitigation needs.

Research exemption. The procedures above can help sustain information in the public domain while rewarding small-scale innovation. They may be inadequate for supporting local science and encouraging competition, however. In that regard, a broad research exemption for experimental users (including both firms and research organizations) of patented ESTs in order to develop new inventions and invent around, or significantly improve, existing ones can be beneficial. Establishing or sustaining a limited research exemption in agricultural varieties may be of particular importance as developing economies deal with GHGs by deploying drought-resistant crops or plants for biofuels.

Compulsory licensing. A compulsory license (CL) allows a non-patent holder to produce or import the patented product or process without the permission of the patent owner, though the latter is generally due compensation. Article 31 creates room for countries to issue CLs for technology on a case-by-case basis.[12] Paragraph 5 of the Doha Declaration on TRIPS and Public Health further clarifies that members have "the right to grant compulsory licenses and the freedom to determine the grounds upon which such licenses are granted."[13] While Article 31 has so far only been used explicitly to authorize CLs for essential medicines, it could in principle extend to patented technology in ESTs.

Article 31 sets out procedural conditions that safeguard the rights of patent owners. For example, Article 31(b) requires the proposed licensees to have sought a voluntary license from the patent holder "on reasonable commercial terms and conditions" prior to applying for the CL. While it may be burdensome to seek a voluntary license first, the requirement does not greatly diminish the scope for DCs to authorize CLs for ESTs. This is because the restriction can be waived in the case of "a national emergency or other circumstances of extreme urgency" or "public non-commercial use." Each country may decide what constitutes a national emergency since this term is not defined in TRIPS. Some have argued that the anticipated consequences of climate change could create a situation of extreme urgency that may waive the obligation of Article 31(b) (Adam, 2009).

Next, Article 31(f) limits the issuance of a CL "predominantly for the supply of the domestic market of the member authorizing such use," except in cases where it is granted to remedy an anticompetitive practice. Thus, countries cannot authorize CLs to produce for export markets unless the requirements of Article 31(f) are waived. This provision has had important consequences in public health (Abbott and Reichman, 2007). As in that case, WTO Members with no manufacturing capabilities cannot authorize a CL for a domestic manufacturer to make ESTs domestically available nor can they turn to other members for imports. Nevertheless, in 2005 the WTO adopted an amendment to Article 31(f) that would allow a permanent waiver of the domestic market requirement for pharmaceuticals. A similar waiver for ESTs could be possible in the future and may be an option.

According to Article 31(k), meeting the various restrictions is not required in cases where CLs are issued to remedy anticompetitive practices in licensing IPRs. All that is required is that an administrative or judicial process has determined the existence of an anticompetitive practice, possibly including refusals to deal or license ESTs. It is sensible for DCs to enact appropriate regulations and policies supporting IPRs that could provide a basis to utilize the opportunities provided by his provision.

Elements of all these provisions exist in the patent laws of major developed economies, so they are not radical departures from accepted practice. For example, compulsory licensing provisions exist to ensure that patented technologies are used effectively. These may include provisions to remedy anticompetitive behavior, licensing to permit exercise of dependent patents, conditions for government-use licenses, and other situations. Still, it must be recognized that the effective exercise of complex patent standards, compulsory licenses, and accompanying judicial procedures requires significant administrative and judicial expertise. In that regard, they may be of limited utility in the poorest countries, though there is scope for considering their use on the basis of regional cooperation. Thus, a complementary commitment to building expertise and capacity in this regard is needed to effectuate the approach.

Exclusions. Article 27 of TRIPS allows for the exclusion of patent rights to inventions whose commercial use must be prevented to "protect human, animal or plant life or health or to avoid serious prejudice to the environment." It is possible that some environmental technologies could fall under this exemption. Indeed, ESTs are rarely environmentally neutral and if an invention improves one aspect of the environment it may worsen another aspect. For example, some authors estimate that it would take over seventy-five years for the carbon emissions saved from using biofuels to compensate for those emitted through forest conversion to produce it (Danielson et al., 2009). For another, technologies that limit over-catching in fisheries may also have adverse effects on other ecological dimensions of the coastal zone. This problem has received administrative attention in Europe. In the *Plant Genetic Systems* case, the EPO Technical Board of Appeals expressed concern that, while the genetically engineered plant cells at issue would effectively combat weeds, there were several countervailing environmental concerns.[14]

A per se exemption for technology on environmental grounds would be politically difficult and seemingly inconsistent with the terms of the TRIPS Agreement. It is also uncertain that limiting patentability would improve either access to ESTs or the environment itself. Nevertheless, Article 27 may permit patent offices to balance, in the context of national mitigation or adaptation strategies, the anticipated impact of the technology on environmental goals when assessing patentability.

4.2 Access-oriented modifications to TRIPS

It may also be feasible to increase access to ESTs in DCs by modifying or further clarifying certain provisions in the Agreement (Abbott and Reichman, 2007). First, the WTO waiver of Article 31(f) granting compulsory import licenses of essential medicines could, in principle, be extended to ESTs (Littleton, 2008). Doing so may be impractical due to difficulties in defining ESTs. Nevertheless, the Doha Development Round, if the current impasse is overcome, offers an opportunity to define conditions of the waiver specifically tailored for ESTs.

Second, it would be useful to have an authoritative interpretation of the scope of the unauthorized use exception under Article 30. The unprecedented declaration by the Max Planck Institute offers a useful starting point to review how such limitations may be defined and yet meet the basic three criteria of Article 30 (Max Planck Institute, 2009). Perhaps most promising, given its potential efficiency, would be liability rules designed around a modified Article 30. These rules might well meet the interests and expectations of both patent holders and local inventors. Another idea would be to permit temporary licenses in which a patent holder could provide users in DCs access to an EST for a limited period with the expectation of receiving payment once the technology is adapted to local requirements (Littleton, 2008).

Third, to encourage participation by technology suppliers, it is important to guard against the possibility that technologies targeted for specific nations and acquired under a CL mechanism are not diverted to third markets. If a CL scheme places the enforcement responsibility solely on patent holders, developed countries would probably find it harder to join such a global licensing scheme.

Finally, any modification of the TRIPS Agreement to facilitate EST transfer should create a balanced solution that incorporates the concerns of both developed and developing countries. The global legal framework for innovation and its benefits can only be realized if both the affirmative rights to IP protection and the access needs of developing countries are respected and enforced. In this regard, more serious attention should be paid to finding means of effectively implementing the obligations of developed countries with regard to facilitating ITT to the least-developed countries as provided under TRIPS Article 66(2).

5. CONCLUDING REMARKS

To date, international climate-change negotiations under the aegis of the UNFCCC have achieved some successes with respect to technology transfer, most notably the establishment of a funding mechanism that remains largely unfulfilled. These talks have made little progress, however, in determining means by which such funding may be effectively deployed or patent regimes may be used or modified to enhance global access. It is vital that such deliberations move forward, in light of the enormous scale of the climate-change problem and the major needs of DCs to acquire and adapt ESTs to heterogeneous local conditions.

In this chapter we reviewed the primary possibilities available in both dimensions. Outside the realm of IPRs, our suggestions range from allocating funding to prize mechanisms and targeted interventions of demonstrated effectiveness, to greater use of voluntary patent pools and research networks, often based on concessional licensing terms for use in poor countries. Even those licenses may need subsidization in light of the public-goods importance of ESTs. Within the patent arena we reaffirm the importance of taking advantage of flexibilities offered by the TRIPS Agreement in terms of IP standards, limitations, and exceptions. We also note the potential for adjustments to existing mechanisms in the TRIPS Agreement to make ITT more effective.

While these approaches are important, and indeed some combination of them likely is necessary, we reiterate the basic need for a macroeconomic environment in both developed and developing countries that greatly incentivizes innovation in ESTs and encourages their transfer to locations of greatest need. For these purposes, sustainably higher charges for emitting GHGs must be established, while DCs are well advised to invest in improvements in local business climates and infrastructure. In summary, building administrative and managerial capacity is essential if the gains from policy reforms are to be realized.

NOTES

1. This chapter draws on the analysis in Maskus and Okediji (2010).
2. The UNFCCC entered into force on 21 March 1994, 31 I.L.M. 849 (1992).
3. See UNEP, EPO, and ICTSD, 2010.
4. <http://ec.europa.eu> (last accessed October 5, 2009).
5. The preamble to the TRIPS Agreement recognizes such gains, as does Article 7, which lists, as one objective, "the promotion of technological innovation . . . and the transfer and dissemination of technology."
6. The empirical evidence underlying such claims is mixed, as noted in Park (2008).

7. A proposal was adopted at the December 2009 UNFCC meeting in Copenhagen to establish the "Copenhagen Green Climate Fund" to set aside funds for technology transfer and mitigation assistance in DCs. The accord called for developed countries to "provide new and additional resources" approaching $30 billion in the 2010–12 period. See <www.sourcewatch.org/index.php?title=Copenhagen_Green_Climate_Fund> (last accessed 12 September 2013). As of this writing, however, the institutional arrangements and financing levels remain unclear.

8. See, e.g., Masters and Delbecq (2008) who set out a proposal for proportional "prize rewards" dividing available funds among multiple winners in proportion to measured achievement.

9. Torrance (2007) notes the importance of a strict certification requirement as part of the wild-card extension.

10. Lee (2006) lists a number of factors affecting the viability of patent pools.

11. To conserve space, what follows is only an outline. Details may be found in Maskus and Okediji, 2010.

12. Some observers consider the general exceptions provision in Article 30 to constitute justification for CLs in almost any legitimate public purpose (Correa, 1999).

13. WTO Ministerial Declaration of 14 November 2001, WT/MIN(01)/DEC/1, 41 I.L.M. 746 (2002) [hereinafter Doha Declaration].

14. See *Plant Genetic Systems N.V. v. Greenpeace Ltd.*, [1995] E.P.O.R. 357: IX(c) (Technical Bd. App.).

REFERENCES

Abbott, F. M. and Reichman, J. H., (2007). "The Doha Round's Public Health Legacy: Strategies for the Production and Diffusion of Patented Medicines under the Amended TRIPS Provisions," *Journal of International Economic Law* 10 (4): 921–87.

Adam, A., (2009). "Technology Transfer to Combat Climate Change: Opportunities and Obligations under TRIPS and Kyoto," *Journal of High Technology Law* 9 (1): 1–20.

Adelman, D. E. and Engel, K. H., (2008). "Reorienting State Climate Change Policies to Induce Technological Change," *Arizona Law Review* 50 (3): 835–78.

Antonelli, C., (2007). "Technological Knowledge as an Essential Facility," *Journal of Evolutionary Economics* 17 (4): 451–71.

Arora, A., Fosfuri, A. and Gambardella, A., (2001). *Markets for Technology: The Economics of Innovation and Corporate Strategy.* (Cambridge, MA: MIT Press).

Barooah, S. P., (2008). "UNFCCC Requiring a New Patent Regime?" Available online at: <http://spicyipindia.blogspot.com> (last accessed 10 November 2009).

Barrett, S., (2009). "The Coming Global Climate—Technology Revolution," *Journal of Economic Perspectives* 23 (2): 53–75.

Barton, J. H., (2007). "Intellectual Property and Access to Clean Energy Technologies in Developing Countries," ICTSD Programme on Trade & Environmental, Issue Paper No. 2. Available online at: <http://ictsd.org> (last accessed 4 November 2009).

Barton, J. H. and Maskus, K. E., (2006). "Economic Perspectives on a Multilateral Agreement on Open Access to Basic Science and Technology," in Simon J. Evenett and Bernard M. Hoekman, eds., *Economic Development and Multilateral Trade Cooperation*. (Washington, DC: Palgrave/MacMillan and World Bank).

Bays, J. and Jansen, P., (2009). "Prizes: A Winning Strategy for Innovation." Available online at: <http://whatmatters.mckinseydigital.com> (last accessed 10 November 2009).

Brunnermeier, S. B. and Cohen, M. A., (2003). "Determinants of Environmental Innovation in U.S. Manufacturing Industries," *Journal of Environmental Economics & Management* 45 (2): 278–93.

Cahoy, D. R. and Glenna, L., (2009). "Private Ordering and Public Energy Innovation Policy," *Florida State University Law Review* 36 (3): 415–58.

Castonguay, S., (2009). "Photovoltaic Technology—Sunny Side Up," *WIPO Magazine* 3: 2–4.

Climate Group, (2009). "China's Clean Revolution II: Opportunities for a Low Carbon Future," Available online at: <http://www.theclimategroup.org> (last accessed 5 November 2009).

Cohen, W. M., Nelson, R. R. and Walsh, J. P., (2000). "Protecting Their Intellectual Assets: Appropriability Conditions and Why U.S. Manufacturing Firms Patent (or Not)," National Bureau of Economic Research, Working Paper No. 7552. Available online at: <http://www.nber.org> (last accessed 4 November 2009).

Copenhagen Economics/The IPR Company, (2009). "Are IPRs a Barrier to the Transfer of Climate Change Technology?" Report commissioned by DG Trade, European Commission. Available online at: <http://trade.ec.europa.eu> (last accessed 5 November 2009).

Correa, Carlos M., (1999). "Intellectual Property Rights and the Use of Compulsory Licenses: Options for Developing Countries," T.R.A.D.E Working Paper no. 5, Geneva: South Centre.

Danielsen, F. et al., (2009). "Biofuel Plantations on Forested Lands: Double Jeopardy for Biodiversity and Climate," *Conservation Biology* 23 (2): 348–58.

Deere, Carolyn, (2009). *The Implementation Game: The TRIPS Agreement and the Global Politics of Intellectual Property Reform in Developing Countries*. (Oxford: Oxford University Press).

Encaoua, D. et al., (2006). "Patent Systems for Encouraging Innovation: Lessons from Economic Analysis," *Research Policy* 35 (9): 1423–40.

Erren, T. C., (2007). "Prizes to Solve Problems in and beyond Medicine, Big and Small: It Can Work," *Medical Hypotheses* 68 (4): 732–4.

Flynn, S., Hollis, A. and Palmedo, M., (2009). "An Economic Justification for Open Access to Essential Medicine Patents in Developing Countries," University of Calgary Department of Economics, Working Paper No. 2009-01. Available online at: <https://econ.ucalgary.ca> (last accessed 10 November 2009).

Gallini, N. T., (2002). "The Economics of Patents: Lessons from Recent U.S. Patent Reform," *Journal of Economic Perspectives* 16 (2): 131–54.

Hargreaves, S., (2009). "Obama Budget Boosts Green Spending," *CNN Money*, 26 February 2009. Available online at: <http://money.cnn.com> (last accessed 5 November 2009).

IEA, (2008). "Energy Technology Perspectives 2008 Executive Summary," International Energy Agency. Available online at: <http://www.iea.org> (last accessed 12 September 2013).

IETC/UNEP (2003). Available at <http://www.unep.or.jp/ietc/techtran/focus/sustdev_est_background.pdf> (accessed 10 October 2013).

Javorcik, B. S., (2004). "Does Foreign Direct Investment Increase the Productivity of Domestic Firms? In Search of Spillovers through Backward Linkages," *American Economic Review* 94 (3) 605–27.

Jessup, S., (2008). "Climate Change: China Innovating in the Clean Coal Technology Market," *WIPO Magazine*, 5: 14.

Johnstone, N., Hascic, I. and Popp, D., (2009). "Renewable Energy Policies and Technological Innovation: Evidence Based on Patent Counts," National Bureau of Economic Research, Working Paper No. 13760. Available online at: <http://www.nber.org> (last accessed 4 November 2009).

Klevorick, A. K., Levin, R. C., Nelson, R. R. and Winter, S. G., (1987). "Appropriating the Returns from Industrial Research and Development," *1987 Brookings Papers on Economic Activity*: 783–820.

Lamy, P., (2004). "The TRIPs Agreement 10 Years On," Speech to the International Conference on the 10th Anniversary of the WTO TRIPs Agreement, 23 June 2004.

Lee, A., (2006). "Examining the Viability of Patent Pools for the Growing Nanotechnology Patent Thicket," *Nanotechnology Law & Business* 3 (3): 317–27.

Lee, B., Iliev, I. and Preston, F., (2009). "Who Owns our Low-Carbon Future? Intellectual Property and Energy Technologies," Chatham House Report.

Lerner, J. and Tirole, J., (2004). "Efficient Patent Pools," *American Economic Review* 94 (3): 691–711.

Littleton, M., (2008). "The TRIPS Agreement and Transfer of Climate Change-Related Technologies to Developing Countries," UN Department of Economic & Social Affairs, Working Paper No. 71. Available online at: <http://www.un.org> (last accessed 8 November 2009).

Maskus, K., (2000). *Intellectual Property Rights in the Global Economy* (Washington DC: Institute for International Economics).

Maskus, K. E., (2001). "Intellectual Property Challenges for Developing Countries: An Economic Perspective," *University of Illinois Law Review* 2001 (1): 457–73.

Maskus, K. E., (2004). "Encouraging International Technology Transfer," UNCTAD-ICTSD Project on IPRs & Sustainable Development: Issue Paper No. 7. Available online at: <http://www.iprsonline.org> (last accessed 4 November 2009).

Maskus, K. E., (2010). "Differentiated Intellectual Property Regimes for Environmental and Climate Technologies," OECD Environmental Working Papers No. 7.

Maskus, K. E. and Okediji, R. L. (2010). "Intellectual Property Rights and International Technology Transfer to Address Climate Change: Risks, Opportunities and Policy Options." ICTSD Project on IPRs & Sustainable Development: Issue Paper No. 32.

Maskus, K. E. and Reichman, J. H., (2005). "The Globalization of Private Knowledge Goods and the Privatization of Global Public Goods," *Journal of International Economic Law* 7(2): 279–320.

Masters, W. A. and Delbecq, B., (2008). "Accelerating Innovation with Prize Rewards: History and Typology of Technology Prizes and a New Contest Design for Innovation in African Agriculture," IFPRI, Discussion Paper No. 00835. Available online at: <http://www.ifpri.org> (last accessed 12 September 2013).

Max Planck Institute, (2009). "Declaration on the Three-Step Test," Max Planck Institute for Intellectual Property, Competition & Tax Law. Available online at: <http://www.ip.mpg.de> (last accessed 4 November 2009).

Nelson, P. B., (2007). "Patent Pools: An Economic Assessment of Current Law and Policy," *Rutgers Law Journal* 38 (2): 539–72.

Newell, R. G., Rai, A. K., Reichman, J. and Wiener, J. B., (2008). "Intellectual Property and Alternatives: Strategies for Green Innovation," Energy, Environment and Development Programme Paper No. 08/03. Chatham House. Available online at: <http://www.chathamhouse.org.uk> (last accessed 12 September 2013).

Park, W. G., (2008). "Intellectual Property Rights and International Innovation," in K. E. Maskus, ed., *Frontiers of Economics and Globalization*, ii: Intellectual Property, Growth and Trade. (Amsterdam: Elsevier North Holland).

Picker, R. C., (2006). "Mistrust-Based Digital Rights Management," *Journal on Telecommunications & High Technology Law* 5 (1): 47–71.

Popp, D., (2006). "International Innovation and Diffusion of Air Pollution Control Technologies: The Effects of NO_X and SO_2 Regulation in the U.S., Japan, and Germany," *Journal of Environmental Economics & Management* 51 (1): 46–71.

Popp, D., (2009). "A Perspective Paper on Technology Transfers as a Response to Climate Change," Copenhagen Consensus Centre.

Reichman, Jerome H., (2010). "Intellectual Property in the Twenty-First Century: Will the Developing Countries Lead or Follow?" *Houston Law Review* 46 (4): 1115–85.

Saez, C., (2009). "Enzymes a Potential Planet-Saver, But Heavy Patenting Necessary, Industry Says." Intellectual Property Watch. Available online at: <http://www.ip-watch.org> (last accessed 5 November 2009).

Spellberg, B. et al., (2007). "Societal Costs Versus Savings from Wild-Card Patent Extension Legislation to Spur Critically Needed Antibiotic Development," *Infection* 35 (3): 167–74.

Torrance, A. W., (2007). "Patents to the Rescue—Disasters and Patent Law," *DePaul Journal of Health Care Law* 10 (3): 309–58.

Travis, H., (2008). "Opting out of the Internet in the United States and the European Union: Copyright, Safe Harbors, and International Law," *Notre Dame Law Review* 84 (1): 331–407.

UNCTAD, (2007). "The Least Developed Countries Report 2007: Knowledge, Technological Learning and Innovation for Development 124," UN document: Geneva and New York.

UNEP, EPO, and ICTSD, (2010). "Patents and Clean Energy: Bridging the Gap between Evidence and Policy: Final Report." Available online at: <http://ictsd.org/downloads/2010/09/study-patents-and-clean-energy_159101.pdf> (last accessed 12 September 2013).

Weilbaecher, A., (2009). "Diseases Endemic in Developing Countries: How to Incentivize Innovation," *Annals of Health Law* 18 (2): 281–305.

World Bank, (2001). *Global Economic Prospects 2002: Making Trade Work for the World's Poor.* (Washington, DC: World Bank).

Yang, Lei and Keith E. Maskus, (2009). "Intellectual Property Rights, Technology Transfer and Exports in Developing Countries," CES-ifo Working Paper No. 2464, *Journal of Development Economics* 90 (2): 232–6.

Yu, Peter K., (2009). "The Objectives and Principles of the TRIPS Agreement," *Houston Law Review* 46 (4): 979–1019.

Part IV

Challenges for Governance and Policymaking

14

Multilateral Agreements and Policy Opportunities

Carlos M. Correa

INTRODUCTION

This chapter analyzes the opportunities for local production and technological learning allowed by the use of some of the "flexibilities" contained in the TRIPS Agreement. The chapter is structured as follows. First, it presents the concept of TRIPS "flexibilities" and the main areas where they apply. This section will briefly examine the interpretive value of the Doha Declaration on TRIPS and Public Health which confirmed some of those flexibilities. Second, the chapter will explore the extent to which some of the flexibilities in the area of patent and test data protection may create a favorable policy space to promote domestic production in developing countries. Finally, the chapter provides recommendations for developing countries in terms of both domestic and international policies.

TRIPS FLEXIBILITIES GENERALLY

The term "flexibilities" has become a common way of designating various legal doctrines and mechanisms that help to mitigate the effects deriving from the exclusive rights conferred by IPRs. The degree to which such flexibilities are incorporated into national laws determine the room available to adopt measures to protect legitimate competition and consumers' welfare. As examined below, some of these measures may be specifically used, within certain limits, to allow for the domestic production of IPR-protected products.

The "flexibilities" allowed by the TRIPS Agreement have been extensively explored in academic analyses[1] and authoritative reports.[2] There is broad consensus that the TRIPS Agreement does not establish a set of uniform rules and that, despite some detailed provisions and the incorporation of the obligations under pre-existing IPR conventions, it does not cover all aspects of IPRs. Moreover, there are ambiguities in the text that allow for different modalities of implementation whereas in some cases, notably in the area of enforcement, the treaty provisions indicate the objectives to be met rather than the specific ways in which they may be achieved.

The TRIPS flexibilities may be useful for different objectives, ranging from local production to the importation of protected products at the lowest possible price. Examples of possible objectives for the application of such flexibilities are given in Table 14.1.

The existence of a number of flexibilities in the TRIPS Agreement has been confirmed by the WTO Ministerial Conference, the highest WTO body, through the Declaration on the TRIPS Agreement and Public Health, adopted in Doha in November 2001.[3] The Declaration is the first WTO instrument to specifically use the concept of "flexibility" with regard to the TRIPS Agreement. Although the Doha Declaration focused on IPRs related to public health, it is relevant to IPRs in any field of technology.[4]

Paragraph 5 of the Doha Declaration specifies some of the flexibilities available to facilitate access to pharmaceutical products. The wording of the *chapeau* of this paragraph makes it clear that it only enumerates some of the possible flexibilities. Sub-paragraphs (a) and (b) are particularly relevant to the implementation of measures intended to expand domestic production with the use of protected technologies.

Sub-paragraph (a) of paragraph 5 of the Doha Declaration confirms the relevance of article 7 of the TRIPS Agreement for the interpretation of its provisions.[5] This article provides that the protection and enforcement of intellectual property rights "should contribute to the promotion of technological

Table 14.1 TRIPS flexibilities: For what purposes?

Purpose	Flexibilities	Relevant TRIPS provisions
Prevent the appropriation of subject matter existing in nature	Definition of invention	Article 27.1
Avoid patents on minor developments, undue limitations to legitimate competition	Determination of level of patentability requirements	Article 27.1
Access to products at lower prices	Parallel imports; compulsory licenses	Article 6, article 31
Remedy anti-competitive practices	Compulsory licenses	Article 31 (k)
Permit the local exploitation of patented inventions	Compulsory licenses	Article 31
Allow follow-on innovation	Research exception	Article 30
Speed up competition after patent expiry	"Bolar exception"	Article 30

innovation and to the transfer and dissemination of technology," thereby suggesting that the TRIPS Agreement must be interpreted in a manner that favors access by third parties to technology necessary to further innovation and domestic production. The Agreement should not be regarded as a charter of absolute rights to control the exploitation of protected technologies, but rather as an instrument that requires the use of such technologies "to the mutual advantage of producers and users of technological knowledge and in a manner conducive to social and economic welfare" (article 7).

The confirmation of the members' leeway to determine the grounds for the granting of compulsory licenses in sub-paragraph (b) opens the possibility of providing for such licenses in cases of lack of industrial exploitation of a patent, as further discussed below.

PRESERVING THE FREEDOM TO OPERATE

Patenting in developing countries is—with the exception of China—overwhelmingly of foreign origin.[6] Given the control that foreigners may exert through the patent system over technologies necessary to undertake local production, a key policy issue is what concepts and criteria are applied to determine the patentability of inventions. Although the TRIPS Agreement specifies the standards to be used (novelty, inventive step or non-obviousness, industrial applicability or utility), governments enjoy considerable room to determine several important aspects of this as well as of other important components of their patent policy (see Table 14.2).

Defining the concept of invention raises several issues of interest for a policy aiming at promoting local production. One of such issues is whether "invention" should be broadly understood, as in many developed countries, so as to encompass claims on genes and other substances found in nature, even if

Table 14.2 Flexibilities regarding patentability criteria and claims' coverage

Flexibility	Possible use	Relevant TRIPS provisions
Definition of invention	Determining the admissibility or not of patents on natural substances, including genes	Article 27.1
Patentability criteria	Establish the level of the inventive step requirement; avoid "evergreening" patents	Article 27.1
Disclosure	Information sufficient to execute the invention	Article 29
Scope of claims	Protection limited to actually obtained embodiments of an invention	None
Doctrine of equivalents	Literal infringement or infringement by equivalence	None

merely isolated or purified. It may be argued that countries rich in genetic resources have a lot to gain if patents of that kind were allowed, as they may encourage investment in developing and commercializing new products. However, most of those countries lack the technological capacity and, above all, the capital required to initiate and sustain viable activities in this field. The window of opportunity to file patents on natural substances may be exploited more effectively by foreign companies. Local patenting, in the absence of a robust domestic industry and a supportive scientific and technological infrastructure, may be small or null. In addition, allowing patents for natural substances such as genes may generate high social costs, for instance, if the realization of diagnostic tests is subject to the control of the patent owner.[7]

Deciding where to set the bar of inventiveness is one of the critical aspects in patent policy. Patents may be conferred on the basis of a more or less strict scrutiny of the level of inventive step. A low requirement leads to the proliferation of patents—sometimes called "low quality" patents[8]—that may be used to keep competitors out of the market, especially if they are unable or unwilling to bear the costs of challenging the validity of wrongly granted patents.

Despite its importance for some public policies, such as public health, competition and industrial development, governments commonly pay little attention to the determination of the optimum level of inventive step to be applied. Rather than a deliberate state policy, as noted by Drahos, "[I]t is the daily patent office routines of a country that determine the build-up of patents in an economy."[9] Patent offices tend to establish the criteria for patentability on the basis of their own choices, often with the assumption that the more patents granted the better. Some patent offices, such as those from the U.S., Japan, Australia and the European Patent Office (EPO) have significantly influenced, through technical assistance (provided directly or through WIPO) the way in which developing-country patent offices operate. Broad interpretations of the patentability standards and of the scope of claims have led many of such offices to ordinarily grant patents on minor developments, as illustrated by the proliferation of "evergreening" patents in the pharmaceutical sector.[10] In fact, developing-country patent offices "have been integrated into a system of international patent administration in which the grant of low-quality patents by major patent offices is a daily occurrence."[11] Another illustration is provided by the acceptance by some patent offices,[12] under the influence of the EPO, of patents on the "second indication" of known pharmaceuticals, even where the respective national laws exclude the patentability of methods of medical treatment and other subject matter without industrial applicability.

It has been argued that the application of lax patentability standards in developing countries could have beneficial effects, as it would allow small and medium companies to apply for and obtain patents that would not be viable if stricter standards were applied. This is a questionable argument, though. First, there is no justification to detract knowledge from the public domain to favor some local companies over others, when all may utilize the same set of technologies in a competitive environment. Second, marginal changes to the state of the art are generally low-risk and require small investment. The argument of recovering high costs in R&D does not apply in these cases. Third, other titles, such as utility models, or new schemes based on liability rules,[13] could be more appropriate than patents to promote minor innovations in a manner that optimizes social benefits. Fourth, foreign applicants are generally much better equipped than local companies to take advantage from lax patentability standards. The World Bank has been right in recommending developing countries apply more flexible IPR standards than do their developed counterparts, and particularly, that they "could set high standards for the inventive step, thereby preventing routine discoveries from being patented. Regarding patent scope, it is sensible to exercise strict claims and discourage multiple claims in patent applications."[14]

Patent laws generally establish the extent to which an invention needs to be disclosed in order to obtain a valid patent. The general standard is that disclosure should be "sufficiently clear and complete for the invention to be carried out by a person skilled in the art" (article 29, TRIPS Agreement). Some laws, such as in the U.S., also require the applicant to indicate the *best mode* for carrying out the invention known to the inventor at the filing date or, where priority is claimed, at the priority date of the application.

The general rule about disclosure, however, is differently applied by patent offices. Many follow a very flexible approach and allow, for instance, the so-called "Markush claims" which cover a large number of possible embodiments of an invention, even if never empirically obtained and tested for the claimed application of the invention. In the chemical field such claims permit the protection of a chemical structure with multiple functionally equivalent chemical entities allowed in one or more parts of the compound, thereby sometimes covering millions of possible compounds. After a patent containing Markush claims has been granted, it is common for the patent owner to select a number of the embodiments and obtain, in some jurisdictions, a new patent on the selection for an additional period.

Another relevant issue is the level of detail that patent specifications should include in order to adequately disclose the invention. Although the concept of "person skilled in the art" is generally considered as a notion of universal applicability, the information contained in the specifications may need to be more comprehensive in applications filed in countries with a low local scientific and technological capacity than in those with a pool of people that may understand the technical complexities.

It is important to note that the TRIPS Agreement does not prevent a member country from adopting a strict concept of "a person skilled in the art" for assessing the patentability (for instance, a person with a university degree or significant experience in a technological field) while resorting to a less qualified "person skilled in the art" to consider the extent of disclosure of an invention. In fact, the disclosure requirement could be set in developing countries in accordance with the average knowledge of a skilled person in such countries.[15]

The scope of claims may have important implications for establishing the "freedom to operate" with regard to production and follow-on innovation. Broad claims may be rarely justified, such as in the cases of "pioneer" inventions. They distort competition and discourage production and innovation, particularly when systematically allowed for merely incremental innovations.[16]

One modality of broad claims is that based on *functional* terms, that is, claims that describe what an invention does, not what the invention structurally is. Functional claims cover all possible ways of obtaining a given result. One example is U.S. patent 4.627.192 granted over sunflower seeds that produce certain levels of oleic acid. It discloses a sunflower seed having an oleic acid content of 80 per cent and a low linoleic acid content. Any sunflower variety producing these levels would be covered under the patent, and not only that identified by the "inventor."[17]

An example of a legislation that applies a strict approach to patent scope is provided by Pakistan's Patents Ordinance, as revised in 2002. Section 13(3) requires that "[E]ach application shall relate to one invention only." As a result, separate applications need to be filed for intermediates and the final product, and eventually for processes of manufacture. Moreover, the new subsections 15(2A) and (8) require the structural definition of chemical products and separate applications for an active ingredient and their derivatives and salts. Hence, patent applications generally claiming the "pharmaceutically acceptable salts, prodrugs, etc." without disclosing its physical, chemical, pharmacological, and pharmaceutical properties would not be acceptable.

The post-war Japanese patent policy provides an interesting example of a system deliberately designed to increase the room for local companies to produce and innovate around foreign patented technologies. In accordance with Section 1 of the Japanese patent law the purpose of the patent system was "to encourage inventions by promoting their protection and utilization *so as to contribute to the development of industry*" (emphasis added). One of the key elements of that policy was to allow patents with narrowly defined claims. The system was effective in enhancing the negotiating capacity of domestic companies to obtain technology transfer from, or to establish other agreements with, foreign patent owners. The alleged pro-industrial bias of the Japanese patent law raised considerable criticism in U.S. circles. The U.S. General Accounting Office (GAO) undertook a survey of U.S. firms with experience in patenting in Japan, which identified a number of practices that favored the dissemination of technology amongst domestic companies and the development of their own patent packages.[18] Such practices included:

- laying open patent applications for public examination during the examination process, combined with long delays prior to the actual commencement of (deferred) examination (on average, approximately three years);
- allowing for pre-grant opposition;
- allowing compulsory cross-licensing in the event of an improvement patent;
- patent flooding, that is, surrounding a patent with a number of patents on improvements in order to force the owner of the first patent to enter into negotiations with or grant a license to the owner of the subsequent patents. For instance, "a U.S. firm reported to GAO that a Japanese competitor had surrounded its patents for a 'breakthrough synthetic fiber' with 150 patents on incremental improvements to the U.S. company's invention, and that the Japanese firm subsequently tried to pressure the U.S. firm into cross-licensing its 'core' technology."[19]

In accordance with GAO's 1993 report, the Japanese patent law was biased in favor of industrial development, and against the individual inventor: "patent experts contend that the Japanese patent system seeks to promote technology development by disseminating technology, rather than rewarding inventors with exclusive rights."[20]

The worst combination for a patent policy aiming at promoting both industrial development and innovation is a low inventive-step standard coupled with broad patent claims. Such combination is "not in the interest of developing nations (nor, in the judgment of many, of the developed nations either)."[21]

Finally, the methods used for interpretation of patent claims and, particularly, when an infringement may be established or not, may greatly affect the space left for local production and innovation. One of the main methods applied for claim interpretation is the "doctrine of equivalents." This doctrine has greatly attracted the interest of scholars and professionals in developed countries, but its applicability and implications have been scarcely explored in developing countries. Commonly, this doctrine is not spelled out in the statutes, but results from case law. Thus, this important body of policy is determined by judges rather than by the agencies responsible for industrial and technological development. An expansive doctrine of equivalents may have negative effects on innovation,[22] as it may allow the patent owner to block follow-on innovations based on the original invention.

The basic issue addressed by the doctrine of equivalents[23] is whether non-literal infringement may be prevented by the patent owner. The way in which issues such as how an "equivalent" is defined and at what date its existence is judged are key to determine how much space competitors have to work around a patented invention. Thus, if a monohydrate variant of a pharmaceutical product is deemed equivalent to a patented trihidrate variant, the production and sale of a competitive product, not strictly claimed in the patent, may be banned by the patent owner.

Countries have a number of options to deal with the doctrine of equivalents, ranging from requiring literal infringement to considering that infringement exists when a substantially similar means is used to perform a substantially similar function, independently of the inventive step exhibited by the variant used. Judging the equivalence at the date of infringement (as is currently done, for instance, under U.S. and Japanese law) rather than at the date of the patent application, expands the control of the patent owner on innovations around its patent.

EXCEPTIONS TO PATENTABILITY

There are a few cases in which the TRIPS Agreement allows WTO members not to grant patents based on the type or certain characteristics of the subject matter (see Table 14.3).

According to article 27.2 of the TRIPS Agreement, members "may exclude from patentability inventions, the prevention within their territory of the commercial exploitation of which is necessary to protect *ordre public* or morality, including to protect human, animal or plant life or health or to avoid serious prejudice to the environment, provided that such exclusion is not made merely because the exploitation is prohibited by their law."

Non-patentability may only be established under article 27.2 if the commercial exploitation of the invention is prevented in the respective country and such prevention is necessary to protect the interests referred to above.

Table 14.3 Flexibilities about patentable subject matter

Flexibility	Possible use	Relevant TRIPS provisions
Non patentability of inventions contrary to *ordre public* or morality in deciding public health	Harmful or morally unacceptable products	Article 27.2
Non patentability of diagnostic, therapeutic, and surgical methods	Allows, e.g., the exclusion of patents on second uses of known products	Article 27.3 (a)
Plants and animals	Permits the exclusion, e.g., of genetically modified plants or animals	Article 27.3 (b)

This exclusion would not allow the determination, for instance, of the non-patentability of an HIV/AIDS vaccine, even if that were necessary to protect public health, since the ban to circulate the invention in the territory of the country where the patent was filed is a condition for the TRIPS-consistency of the exclusion.

Of immediate relevance to public health policy is Article 27.3 (a) of the Agreement, which permits members to exclude from patentability "diagnostic, therapeutic and surgical methods for the treatment of humans or animals." Most countries in the world do not grant patents over such methods due to ethical or public health reasons, or simply because they do not meet the industrial applicability requirement imposed by most patent laws.

The exclusion of therapeutic methods may constitute one of the grounds for denying patents covering "second indications" of pharmaceutical products, as patents regarding such indications are essentially equivalent to patents on methods to treat a disease. This may be particularly important in countries with manufacturing capacity in pharmaceuticals, where second indication patents may be used to block the introduction of generics. In fact, Argentina, Brazil,[24] and India do not grant patents on second indications. They have rejected the rather elusive argument that second-indication patents may benefit local producers as they may be able to find new applications for existing drugs without incurring the costs of developing them. Marketing a known product for a new indication requires new clinical studies that demonstrate the efficacy and safety of the product. The cost of such studies is too high for most domestic pharmaceutical companies and poses a high barrier for the hypothetical use of second indication patents as a window of opportunity to expand their business.

RESEARCH AND "EARLY WORKING" EXCEPTIONS

Can experimentation, including for commercial purposes, be legitimately conducted by third parties on patented inventions? Or is the patent owner entitled to block it? Can the producer of generic pharmaceutical or agrochemical products undertake tests to carry out the procedures for marketing approval before the expiry of the relevant patent? The reply to these questions depends on national laws. The TRIPS Agreement, in article 30, permits members to provide for limited exceptions to the exclusive rights conferred by a patent, subject to a three-step test.[25]

The patent holder's legitimate interests do not include the faculty to control further experimentation or research on a patented invention.[26] It is vital for society to ensure sustained scientific and technological progress based on past innovations. The patent owner cannot be given the power to prevent new

Table 14.4 Flexibilities regarding research and product approvals

Flexibility	Possible use	Relevant TRIPS provisions
Experimentation or research on patented invention	To challenge the validity of a patent; request a voluntary or compulsory license; invent around a patented product or process; improve a patented invention	Article 30
Early working ("Bolar") exception	Approval of pharmaceutical products before the expiry of relevant patents	Article 30

generations of innovators to rely on an invention that, in turn, was derived from the pool of knowledge available to the inventor. Innovators ought to have the possibility of using their predecessors' work to develop their own creative and inventive capacities: "[T]he ability to experiment free from the threat of patent infringement or from the tax of patent licenses is critical to scientists and to competitors seeking to develop non-infringing or blocking improvements. A broad experimental use exception is therefore essential to furthering scientific knowledge and technological development to benefit humanity."[27]

Allowing for the experimentation on patented inventions may be important to initiate or expand industrial activities in various situations (see Table 14.4).

A research or experimentation exception would seem to be clearly validated under the first and second steps of article 30 ("limited exceptions" that "do not unreasonably conflict with a normal exploitation of the patent") of the TRIPS Agreement. If patent protection is conceived as a "means to induce inventors to disclose their invention to the public in order to facilitate the dissemination and advancement of technical knowledge, it appears illegitimate to prevent experimental use during the term of the patent."[28]

Such an exception may foster "inventing around" patented inventions and follow-on innovations. It may also facilitate challenges to the validity of wrongly granted patents or the request of a compulsory license. Such an exception may also legitimize the undertaking of the tests necessary to obtain the marketing approval of a pharmaceutical product when an "early working" exception (discussed below) is not formally provided for.

In order to ensure a sufficient freedom to experiment or carry out research on a patented invention, the exception should desirably meet the following requirements:[29]

- the exception may be invoked by any party, including commercial entities, and not only when experimentation or research is done privately or in an academic environment;[30]
- the exception should cover acts done with or without gainful intent;
- the exception should cover any acts done for experimental purposes, including production, importation and use of samples of the patented

product, or implementation of the patented process for testing and research;

- the exception should be applicable to acts conducted for scientific or technological purposes; it should not be limited to academic activities.

The formulation of the research or experimentation exception, if intended to promote follow-on innovation and industrial development, should clearly distance itself from the very narrow interpretation given by the U.S. courts.[31]

A well-crafted experimentation or research exception serves both the interests of public policies in reducing prices of drugs via generic competition, and industrial policies aimed at expanding local production. A comparative review of current legislation,[32] however, reveals that policymakers in developing countries have not paid significant attention to the problems associated with experimentation or research on patented inventions and many countries, including some with significant scientific and technological potential have not fully utilized the room left by the TRIPS Agreement to provide for such exception.[33]

Some countries have also incorporated the so-called "early working" or "Bolar exception," which allows a generic pharmaceutical company to conduct the acts necessary to carry out tests and obtain marketing approval of a generic product before the expiry of the patent, for commercialization thereof after its expiry.[34] As mentioned, a Bolar-type exception results from the application of an experimental exception.

The TRIPS consistency of the "Bolar exception" was confirmed by the WTO Dispute Settlement Body in "Canada—Patent Protection of Pharmaceutical Products."[35] It may be important to encourage the development of a domestic pharmaceutical industry, as it allows an early entry into the market with generic versions of off-patent products. In order to maximize such effect, the exception should be framed in a manner that:

- Does not require an extension of the patent term in exchange for the availability of the exception. Although such extension has been provided for under the U.S. law and the law of a few other countries (e.g., Australia), it is not a condition for the TRIPS-consistency of the exception and would unnecessarily delay the market entry of generic products.
- Allows for acts required to obtain marketing approval domestically and abroad, thus allowing the generic companies to export and exploit economies of scale.[36]

DATA EXCLUSIVITY

The protection of undisclosed test data necessary for the marketing approval of pharmaceutical and agrochemical products was first introduced in an international instrument by the TRIPS Agreement in article 39.3. This has been one of the most controversial provisions in the implementation of the Agreement. Under a literal interpretation of the TRIPS obligation, in accordance with the Vienna Convention on the Law of the Treaties, such data must be protected under unfair competition rules (article 10bis of the Paris Convention for the Protection of Industrial Property), which does not require the grant of exclusive rights.

The application of unfair competition rules has a clear pro-competitive and pro-development effect, as it allows domestic companies to enter the market as long as patent protection does not exist, without the need of unnecessarily duplicating trials to obtain test data that are already available (see Table 14.5).

However, the U.S., the European Union, and other developed countries have adopted *sui generis* regimes that provide for a term of exclusivity for the use of test data by the originator company, even in the absence of patent protection. Many developing countries have been coerced to accept a similar solution, through unilateral pressures or in the context of their accession to the WTO[37] or the negotiation of FTAs. Notably, the U.S. FTAs drastically depart from the TRIPS standard with regard to data protection. They generally oblige parties to grant exclusive rights for at least five years for pharmaceuticals and ten years for agrochemicals counted from the date of approval of the product in their territory, irrespective of whether the data are undisclosed or not. Such exclusivity would also apply irrespective of whether the national health authority requires or not the submission of the data, that is, even in cases where the authority relies on the approval made in a foreign country. "Data exclusivity" covers chemical entities that are not "new," as they may have been previously approved in other countries or in the same country (in the case of new indications).

An extreme version of data exclusivity was incorporated into the CAFTA-Dominican Republic FTA, where a waiting period of five years was provided for. According to article 15.10.1 (b), a party may require that the person providing the information in another territory seek approval in the party within five years after obtaining marketing approval in the other territory. Thus, in accordance with one interpretation, the originator of the test data would enjoy a full ten-year period of exclusivity during which no other party

Table 14.5 Protection of test data

Flexibility	Possible use	Relevant TRIPS provisions
Protection of test data against unfair competition	Approval of generic products may rely on existing test data or prior approval of the originator's product in the country or abroad	Article 39.3

would be able to use, without his consent, directly or indirectly, the relevant test data.[38]

In recognizing the negative effects of data exclusivity on access to medicines in developing countries, a bipartisan agreement reached in June 2007 between the Republican and Democratic parties at the U.S. Congress made concrete suggestions to mitigate the data exclusivity requirements in the FTAs, albeit only limited to those agreements signed by the U.S. government with Peru and Panama. It introduced the concept of "concurrent" protection, that is, the term of data exclusivity protection may be counted from the date of marketing approval in the United States and not in the Party where protection is sought. In addition, data exclusivity is mandated for a period that "shall normally mean five years from the data on which the Party granted approval to the person that produced the data for approval to market its product, taking account of the nature of the data and the person's efforts and expenditures in producing them." This means that the period of exclusivity could be less than five years, that a country may require disclosure of information about the cost of producing the data and establish the period of exclusivity on a case-by-case basis.

The EU has concluded or currently pursues trade negotiations with a number of countries including the Andean Community, MERCOSUR, CARIFORUM (Caribbean), and ACP countries.[39] The EU CARIFORUM Economic Partnership Agreement (EPA) includes a number of TRIPS-plus provisions with regard to copyright, databases, trademarks, industrial designs, and geographical indications, as well as with regard to enforcement, but does not contain additional substantive standards on health-related issues.[40] This approach would be limited, nevertheless, in accordance with the EU Commissioner, to those countries considered sufficiently "poor" by the EU to receive such special treatment. More advanced developing countries are subject to demands of TRIPS-plus standards, particularly with regard to test data.[41]

COMPULSORY LICENSES

Compulsory licenses, including non-commercial government use, are important TRIPS flexibilities that may be used, inter alia, to allow or encourage local production of protected products. Such licenses may be used both for local production as well as for importation of patented products. When these are inputs for the production of other products, importation under such licenses may be a requisite to permit local production on viable economic conditions.

Prior to the TRIPS Agreement, it was well accepted that under the Paris Convention for the Protection of Industrial Property (the Paris Convention), countries could issue compulsory licenses to address situations of "lack of working" of a patent.[42] The paradigm that underpinned this Convention included the transfer of technology and the development of industrial capacities through compulsory licenses. The lack of working was qualified as an "abuse."[43]

Compulsory licenses have been extensively used in Canada since the 1960s in order to promote the development of a local pharmaceutical industry.[44] The policy was widely successful. When Canada was forced to change it, as a result of U.S. pressures and the adoption of the North American Free Trade Agreement, a vibrant domestic pharmaceutical industry had already been established.[45] The U.S. has also made a broad use of compulsory licenses. Although they were granted to remedy anti-competitive practices (particularly in the context of companies' mergers that might have led to a monopolistic market position) or for government use, their impact on local production was probably significant.[46]

During the Uruguay Round of negotiations, developed countries made intense efforts to secure that the TRIPS Agreement would not allow the granting of compulsory licenses in cases of lack of local exploitation of a patent. This position obviously aimed at preserving the room for transnational enterprises to decide where to set up production facilities and where to exploit their IPRs merely through importation. Such efforts concluded with an ambiguous compromise contained in article 27.1 of the Agreement.[47] While the U.S. and some commentators have read this article as the death sentence of any working obligations for patent owners, a proper interpretation of the provision does not support this view.[48]

The obligation to work a patent—understood as the local manufacture of the patented product or the industrial use of the patented process—was first established in the United Kingdom and incorporated into many national laws during the nineteenth and twentieth centuries. During the twentieth century, however, most industrialized countries relaxed or eliminated such an obligation in order to facilitate the trans-border activities of transnational corporations in increasingly globalized markets.

Although the WTO bodies have not confirmed—or denied—the possibility of granting compulsory licenses in cases of lack of local exploitation of a patent, the Doha Declaration (paragraph 5) confirmed the right of WTO members to determine the *grounds* for the granting of a compulsory license. In January 2001, the U.S. brought a complaint against Brazil arguing that the Brazilian law's authorization to grant compulsory licenses when patents were not worked was TRIPS-inconsistent.[49] However, the U.S. withdrew the complaint before a panel was established. It is unclear whether U.S. feared loosing the case and setting a negative precedent for the interests of the U.S. companies or whether the agreement reached with the Brazilian authorities gave the U.S. enough comfort to withdraw the complaint.[50] The issue has never been raised again before the WTO, despite the fact that several national laws contain provisions allowing for compulsory licenses in cases of lack of working.

In some cases, "working" is defined by national laws as encompassing local production or importation of the patent product.[51] This obviously dilutes the working obligation. In some cases, however, national laws include provisions that seem to allow the granting of compulsory licenses in the absence of domestic production.[52] These provisions are, in some cases, subject to additional conditions, such as the supply of the domestic market through imports. Examples are provided by Section 48(3) of the UK Patents Act 1977, Chapter 37 (as amended by the Copyright, Designs and Patents Act 1988) and Section 70(2) of the Patents Act 1992 (of 27 February 1992) of Ireland.

Although the FTAs and bilateral IPRs agreements signed by the U.S. with some countries (e.g. Jordan and Sri Lanka) limited the grounds for the granting of compulsory licenses, in the FTAs signed after the Doha Declaration the U.S. seems to have restrained itself from requesting a limitation of that kind, openly inconsistent with the Declaration.

As mentioned above, and although limited to LDCs, paragraph 7 of the Doha Declaration requires the transfer of manufacturing technology in pharmaceuticals. Moreover, the WTO Decision of 30 August 2003 sets out a mechanism to facilitate exports of pharmaceutical products to countries with insufficient manufacturing capacity in the field.[53] In adopting the WTO decision and the amendment to the TRIPS Agreement, and in order to overcome U.S. opposition, the chairman read a statement indicating, inter alia, that "Members recognize that the system that will be established by the Decision should be used in good faith to protect public health and, without prejudice to paragraph 6 of the Decision, not be an instrument to pursue industrial or commercial policy objectives."

However, the statement may only serve as an auxiliary means of interpretation. It cannot add obligations or restrictions to those set out in the decision/amendment.

A member country can legitimately apply the decision in order to expand exports from its domestic industry while contributing to the solution of health problems in other developing countries. A chair's statement cannot create obligations to which members have not consented to, nor provide an authentic interpretation of, WTO rules. Such statements share the legal status of the minutes of an international agreement and can only be considered as "circumstances of conclusion" in accordance with article 32 of the Vienna Convention on the law of the Treaties.[54]

Another option for undertaking local production is the use of "refusal to deal" as a ground for the granting of compulsory licenses.[55] Given the freedom that WTO members have to determine such grounds, "refusal to deal" may therefore be deemed an *autonomous* ground.[56] Compulsory licenses for "refusal to deal" are specifically provided for in some cases in national laws, such as under Section 24(1) of the German Patent Law (Text of 16 December 1980, as last amended by the Laws of 16 July and 6 August 1996) and Section 70 (2) of the aforementioned patent law of Ireland. However, even in the absence of such provisions, those licenses may be based on the application of competition laws. The "essential facilities" doctrine[57] has been applied in some jurisdictions to deal with situations where access to a technology is essential to undertake production. For instance, the Italian Competition Authority (ICA) decided to grant a compulsory license for an alleged abuse of a dominant position through the refusal by Merck to grant Dobfar (a chemical pharmaceutical manufacturer) a license to produce an active ingredient (ceimipenem/cilastatina-IC) needed for the production of an antibiotic (carbapenems). The ICA considered that Merck's refusal to license its product amounted to an abuse of dominant position "since it prevented Dobfar from producing the IC and enabled Merck to maintain its dominance over the relevant pharmaceutical markets, cutting out potential competitors. Namely, the IC was deemed to be an essential resource for the production of generics by Merck's potential competitors, whereas Dobfar was considered an indispensable supplier for such competitors and in turn, Merck was seen as an indispensable supplier for Dobfar."[58]

Despite the importance of compulsory licenses as a means for opening the door to local production, it must be borne in mind that such a license does not entail per se access to the know-how required for actual production, which is not normally contained in the patent specifications. Hence, the recipient of the license should possess the required technological capacity or obtain external support to effectively execute the invention at a reasonable cost.

CONCLUSIONS

The multilateral rules on IPRs set out by the TRIPS Agreement limit the WTO members' room to use foreign protected technologies for local production. However, governments retain certain policy space under the Agreement to promote local production, although it is much narrower than in the pre-TRIPS era.

The so-called "flexibilities" in the TRIPS Agreement may be used for a multiplicity of purposes. In some cases, the intended policy objectives may be achieved through the importation of the required products. This may be the case, for instance, when an emergency occurs and immediate supplies are necessary. In other cases, the flexibilities of the Agreement may be used to facilitate domestic production and thereby foster technological learning and advance in the development process.

As examined in this chapter, there are various flexibilities that well-informed governments may exploit if they desire to expand the "freedom to operate" in relation to local production. First and foremost, they may adopt exceptions to the patentability, as allowed by the TRIPS Agreement, and define such critical aspects as the concept of "invention" and the bar with which the requirement of inventive step is to be assessed. These constitute core flexibilities regarding patent protection. If strict patentability criteria are applied to refuse low inventive patents, there would be no need to confer at a later stage a compulsory license to allow for domestic production (or other purposes). Developing countries are more exposed to pressures by foreign governments and companies when a compulsory license is issued—what is seen as a "political" decision affecting acquired "property rights"—than in cases where a patent is refused for "technical" arguments relating to the lack of inventive step.

There are a variety of measures that countries may apply to mitigate the monopolistic effects of granted patents. Some of them may be instrumental, directly or indirectly, to policies that encourage domestic production. For example, the experimentation exception may facilitate "inventing around," the acquisition of voluntary or compulsory licenses, or legal challenges against invalid patents. The "Bolar exception" and protection of test data under unfair competition law (without exclusivity) may widen the room for the operation of the local pharmaceutical industry. Compulsory licenses for failure to work a patent or for "refusal to deal" may open the necessary space for local production in various industries.

The extended use by developing countries of the TRIPS flexibilities will serve the purposes of the individual countries and contribute to set precedents that other countries may benefit from. However, such countries should avoid accepting—in the WTO accession process or in entering into trade agreements—requirements that erode such flexibilities. Understandably, the offers of WTO or bilateral preferential access to large markets with quantifiable benefits are in some cases too attractive to be turned down, and governments are ready to make concessions in the area of IPRs, where costs and benefits are more difficult to quantify. But market access may bring ephemeral gains in the face of growing competition from other countries equally entitled to preferential treatment, while the limitations imposed on local production and innovation by TRIPS-plus standards may have enduring effects on the development prospects of the countries that, for whatever reason, accept them.

In sum, there is room for developing countries to use TRIPS flexibilities to open space for local production. They face, however, the multiple challenges of preserving such space in bilateral and multilateral negotiations, effectively implementing the permitted flexibilities in national laws, and applying them when IPRs may emerge as a stumbling block against domestic production or other legitimate states' objectives.

NOTES

1. See, e.g. J.H. Reichman, "From Free Riders to Fair Followers: Global Competition Under the TRIPS Agreement," *N.Y.U. J. Int'l L. & Pol.* 29 (1997): 11; S. Musungu and C. Oh, *The Use of Flexibilities in TRIPS by Developing Countries: Can They Promote Access to Medicines?* Geneva: South Centre and WHO, 2006; C. Correa, *Trade Related Aspects of Intellectual Property Rights (Commentaries on the GATT/ WTO Agreements, vi)*. Oxford: Oxford University Press, 2007.

2. See the "Report of the Commission on Intellectual Property Rights" (CIPR) established by the government of United Kingdom, 2002 <www.iprcommission. org> (last visited 25 October 2007), and the "Report of the WHO Commission on Intellectual Property Rights, Innovation and Public Health" (CIPIH), 2006, available at <www.who.int> (last visited 25 October 2007).

3. WT/MIN(01)/DEC/W/2, 14 November 2001, hereinafter "the Doha Declaration."

4. A declaration is not, under WTO law an "authoritative interpretation" in terms of Article IX.2 of the Marrakesh Agreement Establishing the WTO. However, in practice it may have equivalent effects. Members have provided in paragraph 5 of the Doha Declaration an agreed interpretation of certain aspects of the TRIPS Agreement that future panels and the Appellate Body cannot ignore.

5. It is worth noting that before the adoption of the Doha Declaration, in "Canada – Patent Protection of Pharmaceutical Products," a WTO panel argued, in connection with TRIPS Article 30, that "the goals and the limitations stated in Articles 7 and 8" as well as those of "other provisions of the TRIPS Agreement which indicate its object and purposes…must obviously be borne in mind" (WT/ DS114/R, 17 March 2000, para. 7.26).

6. Patenting countries' profiles are available at <www.wipo.int/ipstats/en/statistics/ country_profile/> (last accessed 20 September 2013).

7. As illustrated by the affordability problems created by Myriad Genetic's patents over *BRCA1* and *BRCA2* breast cancer genes. See "BC sidesteps patent claim, transfers BRCA gene testing to Ontario," *CMAJ*, 21 January 2003; 168 (2), available at <www.cmaj.ca/content/168/2/211.1.full.pdf> (last accessed 20 September 2013). The US Supreme Court declared, in *Association for Molecular Pathology et al. v. Myriad Genetics Inc. et al.* (13 June 2013) the invalidity of patents covering merely isolated DNA, but left open the possibility of patenting cDNA, that is, a biotechnologist's copy of DNA. See, e.g., http://www.newrepublic. com/article/113476/supreme-court-genetics-ruling-reveals-judges-ignorance (last accessed 20 September 2013).

8. For the US case, see generally A. Jaffe and J. Lerner, *Innovation and Its Discontents: How Our Broken Patent System Is Endangering Innovation and Progress, and What to Do about It*. Princeton: Princeton University Press, 2004.

9. P. Drahos, "'Trust Me': Patent Offices in Developing Countries," Centre for Governance of Knowledge and Development available at <http://papers.ssrn. com/sol3/papers.cfm?abstract_id=1028676> (last accessed 19 September 2013).

10. In *AstraZeneca Canada Inc. v. Canada (Minister of Health)* (2006 SCC 49), for instance, the Supreme Court of Canada referred to "commercial strategy of the innovative drug companies to evergreen their products by adding bells and

whistles to a pioneering product even after the original patent for that pioneering product has expired even if the generic manufacturer (and thus the public) does not thereby derive any benefit from the subsequently listed patents."

11. P. Drahos, "'Trust Me': Patent Offices in Developing Countries."

12. This is the case, for instance, of China and Vietnam. See on the latter N. Dzung, "Vietnam Patent Law: Substantive Law Provisions and Existing Uncertainties," *Chicago-Kent Journal of Intellectual Property Law* 6 (2007): 138–56.

13. See J. Reichman, "Of Green Tulips and Legal Kudzu: Repackaging Rights in Subpatentable Innovation," *Vanderbilt Law Review* 53 (2000): 1743–98.

14. World Bank, *Global Economic Prospects and the Developing Countries 2002.* Washington, DC: World Bank, 2002, p. 43.

15. See, e.g. UNCTAD, *The TRIPS Agreement and Developing Countries.* Geneva and New York, United Nations, 1996, p. 33.

16. See, e.g., R. Mazzoleni and R. Nelson, "The Benefits and Costs of Strong Patent Protection: A Contribution to the Current Debate," *Research Policy* 27 (1998): 273–84.

17. This was the "Pervenets" variety only.

18. United States General Accounting Office, "Intellectual Property Rights: U.S. Companies' Patent Experiences in Japan," (GAO/GGD-93-126), Washington, DC: GAO, 1993, quoted in R. Girouard, "U.S. Trade Policy and the Japanese Patent System," BRIE Working Paper 89, 1996, available at <http://brie.berkeley.edu/publications/WP%2089.pdf> (last accessed 3 October 2013).

19. Girouard, *U.S. Trade Policy and the Japanese Patent System.*

20. GAO Report, quoted in Girouard, *U.S. Trade Policy and the Japanese Patent System*, p. 17.

21. J. Barton, "Integrating IPR Policies in Development Strategies," background paper for Bellagio meeting, 30 October–2 November 2002, available at <www.ictsd.org> (iprsonline) (last accessed 20 December 2007).

22. See, e.g., R. Merges, *Patent Law and Policy: Cases and Materials.* Boston: Contemporary Legal Educational Series, 1992, p. 705.

23. T. Adam, "Patent Scope and Doctrine of Equivalence: Critical Aspects," in Chamas, C., Nogueira, M., and Scholze, S., eds, *Intellectual Property for the Academy.* Fundacao Oswaldo Cruz, Ministerio da Ciencia e Tecnologia, Fundacao Konrad Adenauer, Brazil, 2000.

24. Divergences arose in Brazil between the Instituto Nacional de Propriedade Industrial, which favored second indication patents, and ANVISA (the national health authority) which aimed at excluding such patents. See, e.g., M. Basso, "Intervention of Health Authorities in Patent Examination: The Brazilian Practice of the Prior Consent ," *International Journal of Intellectual Property Management,* 1 (1) (2006).

25. See, e.g. C. Correa, *Trade Related Aspects of Intellectual Property Rights (Commentaries on the GATT/WTO Agreements, vi).* Oxford: Oxford University Press, 2007.

26. See e.g. H. Holzapfel and J. Sarnoff, "A Cross-Atlantic Dialog on Experimental Use and Research Tools," American University, WCL Research Paper No. 2008–13, available at <papers.ssrn.com/abstract=1005269> (last accessed 18 September 2013).

27. Brief of *Amici Curiae* Consumer Project on Technology, Electronic Frontier Foundation and Public Knowledge in Support of Petitioner, *Merck Kgaa v. Integra Lifesciences I, Ltd.* and The Burnham Institute, on writ of certiorari to the United States Court of appeals for the Federal Circuit, 22 February 2005, available at <http://www.wcl.american.edu/ipclinic/documents/Integrav.Merck-Oct2005.pdf> (last accessed 19 September 2013).

28. M. Senftleben, *Copyright Limitations and the Three-Step Test: An Analysis of the Three-Step Test in International and EC Copyright Law.* The Hague: Kluwer Law International, 2004, p. 229.

29. For an analysis of comparative law on the subject see C. Correa, "International Dimension of the Research Exception," SIPPI Project, AAAS, Washington D.C., 2005, available at <http://sippi.aaas.org/intlexemptionpaper.shtml> (last accessed 16 September 2013).

30. See, however, the Mexican and Argentine laws according to which the exception applies to a third party who performs research "privately or in an academic environment" (article 22(1) and 36(a) respectively).

31. See *Madey v. Duke University*, 307 F.3d 1351 (Fed. Cir. 2002).

32. See C. Correa, 2005, "International Dimension of the Research Exception."

33. Correa, 2005, "International Dimension of the Research Exception."

34. For instance, the Thai Patent Act B.E 2522 (1979), as amended by B.E 2535 (1992), provides that the patentee's exclusive rights shall not apply to "any act in respect of applications for drug registration, the applicant intending to produce, sell or import the patented pharmaceutical when the patent expires" (article 36.5).

35. See Report of the WTO Panel, "Canada—Patent Protection of Pharmaceutical Products," WT/DS114/R (2000).

36. See, for instance, Section 55(2)(2) of the Patent Act of Canada, which has become a model for other national laws.

37. See F. Abbott and C. Correa, "Intellectual Property Issues in WTO Accession Negotiations," QUNO, Geneva, 2007, available at <http://www.quno.org/geneva/pdf/economic/Issues/WTO-IP-English.pdf> (last accessed 3 October 2013).

38. However, the five-year term may be interpreted as allowing a party to establish the obligation to seek approval in its territory within a shorter term (e.g. one year) in order to secure data protection. See C. Correa, "Implementación de la protección de datos de prueba de productos farmacéuticos y agroquímicos en DR-CAFTA-Ley Modelo," ICTSD, Geneva, available at <www.ictsd.org> (last accessed 3 October 2013).

39. That is, the countries from Africa, the Caribbean and the Pacific signatories of the Lomé Convention (1975), succeeded by the Cotonou Agreement (2000).

40. However, the proposed standards on enforcement (e.g. expanded border measures) may affect trade in medicines and active ingredients.

41. A European Parliament resolution of 12 July 2007 on the TRIPS Agreement and access to medicines called on the European Council "to meet its commitments to the Doha Declaration and to restrict the Commission's mandate so as to prevent it from negotiating pharmaceutical-related TRIPS-plus provisions affecting public health and access to medicines, such as data exclusivity, patent extensions and limitation of grounds of compulsory licences, within the framework of the EPA

negotiations with the ACP countries and other future bilateral and regional agreements with developing countries."

42. See, e.g., M. Halewood, "Regulating Patent Holders: Local Working Requirements and Compulsory Licences at International Law," *Osgoode Hall L.J.* 35 (1997): 243.

43. See article 5A of the Paris Convention.

44. See, e.g., J. Reichman and C. Hasenzahl, "Non-Voluntary Licensing of Patented Inventions: Historical Perspective, Legal Framework under TRIPS and an Overview of the Practice in Canada and the United States of America," Issues Paper No. 5, UNCTAD and ICTSD, Geneva, 2002.

45. At the end of 2006, generic medicines accounted in Canada for 44 per cent of all prescriptions and 18 per cent of the $17 billion market. It invested 15 per cent of sales in R&D. See <www.canadiangenerics.ca/en/issues/economic_benefits.shtml> (last visited 24 November 2007).

46. See e.g., J. Reichman and C. Hasenzahl, "Non-Voluntary Licensing of Patented Inventions."

47. Article 27.1: "[P]atent rights shall be enjoyable without discrimination . . . whether the products are imported or locally produced."

48. See e.g., C. Correa, "Can the TRIPS Agreement Foster Technology Transfer to Developing Countries?" in Keith E. Maskus and Jerome H. Reichman, eds, *International Public Goods and Transfer of Technology under a Globalized Intellectual Property Regime.* Cambridge: Cambridge University Press, 2005; B. Mercurio and M. Tyagi, "Treaty Interpretation in WTO Dispute Settlement: The Outstanding Question of the Legality of Local Working Requirements," *Minnesota Journal Of Int'l Law,* 19 (2010): 275–326.

49. See "Brazil—Measures Affecting Patent Protection," Request for the Establishment of a Panel by the United States, 9 January 2001, WT/DS199/3.

50. Without prejudice to their respective positions, the United States and Brazil agreed to enter into bilateral discussions before Brazil makes use of Article 68 against a U.S. patent holder. "Brazil—Measures Affecting Patent Protection," Notification of Mutually Agreed Solution, WT/DS199/4, G/L/454, IP/D/23/Add.1, 19 July 2001.

51. See, e.g., Decision 486 of the Andean Community (article 60).

52. It should be borne in mind that the grant of compulsory licenses due to failure to work is subject to the terms provided for by article 5A of the Paris Convention (three years from grant of the patent, four from the application date). Such terms do not apply to compulsory licenses granted on other grounds.

53. The text of the decision was incorporated into a new article (31bis) of the TRIPS Agreement, still pending of ratification in accordance with WTO rules.

54. H. Ruse-Khan, "The Role of the Chairman's Statements in the WTO," *Journal of World Trade* 41 (3) (2007): 524.

55. See generally C. Correa, "Intellectual Property and Competition Law: Exploring Some Issues of Relevance to Developing Countries," Geneva, ICTSD, 2007; available at <http://ictsd.org/i/publications/11376/> (last accessed 19 September 2013).

56. This is not prevented by the fact that article 31(b) of the TRIPS Agreement only refers to the refusal of a voluntary license as a pre-condition for granting compulsory licenses, except in the cases where this requirement is waived.

57. See C. Correa, "Intellectual Property and Competition Law."
58. R. Coco and P. Nebbia, "Compulsory Licensing and Interim Measures in Merck: A Case for Italy or for Antitrust Law?" *Journal of Intellectual Property Law & Practice* 2 (7) (2007): 452. See also, for other cases, C. Correa, "Intellectual Property and Competition Law."

15

Preferential Trade Agreements and Intellectual Property Rights

Pedro Roffe and Christoph Spennemann*

Adopting different modalities and denominations, new preferential trade agreements (PTAs), with the view of intensifying and deepening the World Trade Organization's (WTO) commitments, have proliferated in recent years. According to WTO, the surge in this kind of agreement has continued unabated since the early 1990s. As of 31 July 2010, some 474 Regional Trade Agreements (RTAs) have been notified and at that same date, 283 agreements were in force.[1] While the main aim of PTAs is to expand trade liberalization in goods and services, and to improve market access conditions, most agreements signed contemporarily or after the establishment of WTO also include a number of trade-related rules on investment, intellectual property (IP) and government procurement. With respect to IP, these new trade agreements elaborate further on the TRIPS minimum standards of protection and enforcement, representing a strong manifestation of an upward move towards expansion and strengthening of intellectual property rights (IPRs).[2]

The political economy of why governments enter into PTAs responds to a number of sovereign considerations that are beyond the scope of analysis of this chapter.[3] In our understanding, developing countries tend to be *demandeurs* of PTAs mainly to gain better access for their goods and services to more affluent markets, but developed-country partners are those that push for the incorporation of strong IP rules in the belief that this is the way of reaffirming their technological competitive advantages.[4]

Our analysis focuses on recent trends in PTAs tracing the evolution that has taken place since the conclusion of the North American Free Trade Agreement (NAFTA)[5]—the first major agreement signed by the USA with Canada and Mexico—and their broad implications for the international system. Overall, we seek to show the extent and breadth of the novelties introduced by PTAs and how they affect the balance between private rights and public interests, the possible consequences for access to medicines, genetic resources and knowledge, and of the challenges posed to countries in the implementation of these new obligations.

OVERVIEW OF RECENT PTAs

Until lately and unlike the US agreements, the IP chapters in the European PTAs did not follow a single model. By and large there was an emphasis on reinforcing the existing international IP architecture by committing parties to adhere to multilateral IP-related agreements.[6] For example, in the 2003 Chile-European Association Agreement,[7] the parties agreed to accede to a number of WIPO-administered treaties[8] and to make "every effort" to ratify other conventions.[9] The adherence to these agreements is reinforced by the overarching obligation of ensuring adequate and effective protection to IPRs in accordance with the highest international standards, including effective means of enforcing such rights.[10]

A major shift took place in 2008 with the signature of the European Partnership Agreement (EPA) with the countries of the CARIFORUM.[11] The Agreement and the model being used in ongoing negotiations with a diversity of countries[12] show that the EU is now following a similar approach to that of the USA in the specificity and breadth of their commitments. This concerns, in particular, the series of EU negotiations of EPAs with six regional groupings of the African, Caribbean and Pacific (ACP) states,[13] the recently signed Trade and Association Agreements with Colombia and Peru,[14] the Central American countries,[15] the Free Trade Agreement (FTA) with the Republic of Korea,[16] and the ongoing negotiations with India.[17] All of these agreements put greater emphasis on IP provisions particularly with respect to enforcement.

Prior to CARIFORUM, the most significant IP-related provisions in the EU agreements—beyond the obligation to accede, ratify or adhere to a number of WIPO administered treaties—included specific arrangements on the reciprocal protection of geographical indications (GIs) related to wines and spirits, and the protection of traditional expressions. In more recent agreements, the EPAs provide further strengthening of the provisions of GIs in a clear and determined way of aligning parties[18] to the position sustained by the EU in multilateral discussions and deliberations regarding the international registry for wines and spirits and the expansion of the protection afforded to wines and spirits to all other products.[19]

The European Free Trade Agreement (EFTA) model has followed closely the EU approach,[20] but incorporates the specific protection of data provided to national authorities on the safety and efficacy of pharmaceutical and agrochemical products. While all EFTA trade agreements contain references to treaties that parties should adhere to—as in the case of the EU—they follow various schemes to achieve the same objective.[21]

With respect to agreements to which the USA is a party they have traditionally been more ambitious with a comprehensive coverage on disciplines. Prior to the completion of the TRIPS Agreement, the USA already concluded a bilateral agreement with Canada,[22] in which IP features prominently.[23] Then, in NAFTA, the IP provisions became an important component of the treaty, surpassing the minimum standards of the TRIPS Agreement. Following NAFTA, the agreement with the Hashemite Kingdom of Jordan[24] anticipated the policy, which the USA later adopted in the Trade Promotion Authority of 2002. The latter set general principles and objectives that guide the negotiations to the achievement of a number of objectives, including the accelerated and full implementation of the TRIPS obligations and to "reflect a standard of protection similar to that found in US law"[25] in the provisions of any trade agreement. The subsequent agreements have followed this expansive and strong IP agenda.

As in the case of TRIPS, the breadth and scope of the agreements sponsored by the USA relate to all major IP disciplines. The IP chapters are an integral part of the PTAs that include, in a single undertaking, a number of trade disciplines and general chapters dealing with settlement of disputes and the administration of the Agreement. While the structure and specific contents of these agreements may vary slightly in terminology, they generally follow a common comprehensive pattern with a robust emphasis on enforcement issues.

An important development in the evolution of US policies—examined in more detail in subsequent sections—constitute the changes introduced in May 2007, after the expiration of the Trade Promotion Authority of 2002, as a result of a bipartisan understanding on the ratification of outstanding trade agreements.[26] Amendments were thus introduced to the agreements signed with Colombia, Panama and Peru with respect to provisions dealing with pharmaceutical products, reflecting concerns voiced on the impact of those agreements on public health policies.[27] The changes relate to topics such as extensions of the patent term, data exclusivity, the patent-regulatory linkage and the appropriate treatment of the Doha Declaration on TRIPS and Health.[28]

Some peculiarities of US law: the "certification" process

TRIPS recognizes a certain degree of autonomy in the application of the Agreement in the sense that members are free to determine the appropriate method of implementation, "within their own legal system and practice."[29] In the case of agreements signed with the USA, because of the peculiarities of its legislative process, this freedom of implementation appears to have been severely constricted. The implementation bills passed by Congress condition the entry into force of the agreements, in the USA, upon the satisfaction expressed by the Executive branch that the other party has taken the necessary measures to implement effectively the provisions of the agreement.[30] This aspect, known in some quarters as the "certification" act, commits the other party to adopt the necessary-IP-implementation legislation that meets the expectations of the USA. In practical terms, this means that once the formal negotiations have been concluded and the agreement signed by the parties, a new negotiating process begins with respect to the implementing legislation, which in most cases demands a major redesign—in the case of developing countries—of their legal and institutional base.[31] This important aspect of the implementation process has been hard-pressed and highlighted by some industry lobbies as one major feature that needs to be strengthened further.[32]

Another important quality of the domestic US legal system is that in the case of PTA the agreements are not expressly self-executing,[33] which means that, unless passed into domestic law, nothing in the trade agreements shall be construed to amend or modify any law of the United States, or to limit any authority conferred under any law of the USA.[34]

These peculiarities of the US legal system put partner countries under the obligation to take measures to adjust their internal IP regimes to the new standards set in the trade agreement and to the perceived expectations of the stronger party, which questions the relevance of the principle of freedom of implementation sanctioned by TRIPS. USTR, in this context, has advised Congress that it may accordingly adopt subsequent legislation inconsistent with the terms of free trade agreements, taking account of their lack of self-executing character in domestic law.[35] This practice of "certification" has rendered US trade agreements legally asymmetric in terms of their actual implementation, namely in the pursuit of the ultimate objective of reflecting in the legislation of the other party standards of "protection similar to that found in US law." In recent studies carried out for the Inter-American Development Bank on the implementation of free trade agreements in four countries in Latin America, officials interviewed claimed that the so called "certification" process has been one of the most strenuous and demanding part of the negotiations.[36]

CONTROVERSIAL ISSUES

As noted, while developing countries have often been actively involved in securing PTAs with major trading blocks, they have been rather diffident with respect to the IP demands of their trading partners.[37] Difficulties in this area relate to the fact that the new IP obligations go beyond the TRIPS minimum standards ("TRIPS-plus") or include obligations not even contemplated in TRIPS ("TRIPS-extra").[38] Such obligations constitute a major challenge for developing countries for at least three main reasons. First, as pointed out, the freedom of implementation recognized in TRIPS is seriously hampered in these agreements, aggravated by the fact that the assumed new obligations limit the ability to make use of the flexibilities provided under TRIPS. Second, their implementation arguably adds another layer of complexities and costs to the administration and enforcement of IP obligations, in addition to the many challenges that most developing countries face already in implementing the minimum standards of the TRIPS Agreement. Third, TRIPS-plus and TRIPS-extra commitments may compromise or affect positions that countries might pursue or sustain with like-minded countries in multilateral negotiations. In other words, the bilateral track—legitimatized by the TRIPS Agreement[39]— might be detrimental to the pursuit of more balanced outcomes that could be achieved through the multilateral system.

Advocates of stronger IP obligations argue that the latter are mere elaborations of the TRIPS minimum standards. A case in point would be, for example, the provisions dealing with the protection of undisclosed information and, in general, on the enforcement of IPRs.[40]

On the whole, few would dispute that the IP provisions have been one of the most contentious aspects of the negotiations of new trade agreements. The general critique is that these provisions tend to affect the general balance achieved in TRIPS by overemphasizing protection aspects while reducing policy spaces otherwise available to safeguard broader public interests. The rest of the paper elaborates further on this general observation with respect to developing countries' public policy objectives in areas such as access to medicines, genetic resources, access to knowledge and enforcement issues in general.

THE ACCESS TO MEDICINES ISSUE

The relationship between IPRs, public health and access to medicines in general has been one of the most controversial multilateral trade-related topics of recent years. Precisely in this area the TRIPS Agreement introduced fundamental changes to the international IP architecture; prior to TRIPS, countries, for example, were free to grant or not process or product patents in this technological field.[41] The Doha Declaration on the TRIPS Agreement and Public Health of 2001[42] was an important step in easing tensions in this area. It reiterated, among others, the right of WTO members "to use, to the full, the provisions in the TRIPS Agreement, which provide flexibility" for the purpose of "WTO members' right to protect public health and in particular, to promote access to medicines for all."[43] With the adoption of the Doha Declaration, the WTO General Council Decision for the implementation of Paragraph 6 of that Declaration and the subsequent amendment of the TRIPS Agreement, the focus of the debate has shifted away from the multilateral level to the regional and bilateral front and the impact of public-health-related TRIPS-plus provisions in PTAs.[44]

The TRIPS-plus nature of provisions found in new trade agreements has been characterized as having a major undermining effect on the use of internationally agreed flexibilities[45] and making accessibility to medicines a major hardship for developing countries.[46] Concerns raised by the expansive character of exclusive rights on pharmaceutical products are not limited to access issues, but extend to the building of technological capacities in developing countries. Overly broad exclusive rights may threaten the ability of local innovators to engage in R&D through reverse engineering and the creation of functional generic equivalents and improvements.[47] Extended exclusive rights might discourage potential generic investors from investing in existing local production plants, thus denying important opportunities for technology transfer to local producers of pharmaceuticals.[48] Thus, PTA provisions, where implemented without due regard to their potential impact on innovation, may seriously hamper developing countries' efforts of technological catching-up.[49] As noted, some of these concerns were reflected in the changes introduced in recent trade agreements signed by the USA to echo more accurately the need to conform trade agreements to the spirit and letter of the Doha Declaration on TRIPS and Public Health.[50]

The twenty years plus

Under the TRIPS Agreement (Article 33), the minimum term of patent protection is twenty years from the filing date. In the case of regulated products such as medicines, the period during which the patentee may actually take advantage of its exclusive rights may be affected by administrative delays in the granting of the patent and in the marketing approval process of the medicine. This is the apparent rationale behind provisions in all US agreements requiring an extension of the patent term in such circumstances.[51] Such extensions respond to demands of the R&D-based industry. However, from a public-health policy standpoint, they further delay, beyond the original patent term, the entry of competing medicines into the market.

While patent extensions of this type had been an obligation incorporated in trade agreements since NAFTA,[52] this approach has been modified in more recent US agreements following the 2007 bipartisan understanding in the US

Congress, reported above. In the revised version of more recent agreements,[53] the obligation in earlier agreements to compensate for delays in the patent granting or marketing approval process is made optional in the case of pharmaceutical products. In the event of patents not related to pharmaceutical products, the patent extensions remain mandatory. In the case of pharmaceutical products, parties, in order to resort to the option of not extending the patent term, need to make best efforts to process patent and marketing approval applications expeditiously with a view to avoiding unreasonable delays.[54] Peru, for example, has taken advantage of this option in its domestic law.[55]

This shift in US policies is an interesting development that confirms the line of reasoning that non-discrimination, as recognized in TRIPS,[56] does not exclude differentiation among sectors, as noted in the WTO case on "Canada—Patent Protection of Pharmaceutical Products."[57]

The new EU free trade and association agreements follow no uniform approach with respect to the restoration of the patent term for delays in regulatory approval procedures. While the Republic of Korea Free Trade Agreement includes mandatory patent term extension of up to five years,[58] the EU–Colombia/Peru Trade Agreement—in line with recent US trends as discussed above—makes such extension optional,[59] and the EU–Central America Association Agreement contains no such provision.

Patents on new uses

Developing countries' subscribers of free trade agreements may face further challenges to domestic innovation and access to medicines as a result of requirements to patent new uses of known products (sometimes referred to as "ever-greening" of existing patents).[60] The TRIPS Agreement contains no obligation to make patents available for new (or second) uses of known patented products.[61] By contrast, certain agreements such as those between the USA, respectively, with Australia, Bahrain, Morocco and Oman make mandatory the protection of any new uses or new methods of using a known product, including new uses and new methods for the treatment of particular medical conditions.[62] This is not the case of the free trade agreements involving Latin American countries.

It should be noted, however, that this type of provision does not expressly state whether new uses should cover only the new process or even the known product as such. To the extent that a government intends to promote generic competition, it would appear to be free to follow the US domestic system, which limits the patentability of new uses to process patents ("method-of-use" claims).[63] New uses could arguably provide innovators with incentives to engage in incremental innovation, but the original patentee would seem to have the greatest opportunities to develop new uses of the patented product, due to his often dominant and exclusive position.

Compulsory licenses and exhaustion of rights

The TRIPS Agreement leaves national jurisdictions free to determine the substantive grounds for the issuance of a compulsory license and for the appropriate regime for the exhaustion of IPRs.[64] While most of the US agreements do not interfere with these flexibilities, some PTAs do introduce limitations.

The agreements with Australia, Jordan, Singapore and Vietnam limit the grounds for the use of compulsory licenses to cases of anti-trust remedies, public non-commercial use and national emergencies or other circumstances of extreme urgency.[65] This excludes the granting of compulsory licenses on other essential grounds, such as the promotion of innovation and research in case of one patent blocking the exploitation of another one ("dependent patents," TRIPS Article 31 (l)), or in case of the unavailability of an essential research tool for the development of new products. Concern has been expressed on the impact of such limitations not only on the mere granting of compulsory licenses but on the potential of constraining states' abilities to draw effective benefits from a domestic research exception or "otherwise restrict the scope of patents in research tools, even to benefit the enterprise of innovation."[66]

Exhaustion of exclusive rights means, in practical terms, the authorization of parallel imports of IP protected products. This was one of the most difficult issues that arose during the negotiation of the TRIPS Agreement.[67] The compromise at that time was that each WTO member would be entitled to adopt its own exhaustion regime. This understanding was framed in Article 6, precluding anything in TRIPS from being used to address the exhaustion of rights in a dispute settlement, subject to the provisions on national and MFN treatment. This was reaffirmed in the Doha Declaration on TRIPS and Public Health, which stated that each WTO member is free to establish its own system of exhaustion.

A number of US free trade agreements—i.e. those with Australia, Morocco and Singapore—expressly acknowledge the patent holder's right to prevent parallel imports through the use of contracts or other means.[68] This approach, apparently affecting the freedom of countries to import goods, which IPRs have been exhausted, was criticized in 2005 in a House of Representatives report as contrary to US national interests.[69]

Trade agreements signed with Latin American countries and recent PTAs subscribed by the USA with Bahrain and Morocco do not include limitations on the use of compulsory licenses or intrude on questions of parallel imports. These agreements incorporate also side letters with special reference to the "WTO health solution." The free trade agreement with Chile, for its part, expressly refers to the Doha Declaration on TRIPS and Public Health in a Preamble to the IP Chapter, a practice that was not followed in subsequent negotiations.

With respect to European-sponsored agreements there has been a consistent policy to include references to the Doha Declaration, the Decision of the WTO General Council of 30 August 2003 as well as the need to take the necessary steps to accept the Protocol amending the TRIPS Agreement of 6 December 2005.[70]

Protection of clinical test data

The TRIPS Agreement (Article 39.3) obliges members to protect undisclosed test or other data, involving considerable effort for the originator, against "unfair commercial use." Whether this implies the protection of test data through exclusive rights is a controversial issue.[71]

The US agreements have introduced a new regime of test data exclusivity, providing that once a firm has submitted original data on a pharmaceutical product, regulatory authorities shall not permit competing producers to rely on that data for a period of five years from the date of marketing approval (ten years in the case of agricultural chemical products).[72] This type of provision effectively requires generic producers to come up with their own test data, which very often is not economically feasible and rather questionable on ethical grounds.[73] The PTAs, thus, provide the data originator with a further period of exclusivity, including in cases of non-patented pharmaceutical or agrochemical products, thus creating a new form of exclusive rights not mandatory under TRIPS.[74]

In the case of US agreements negotiated, more recently, with Colombia, Panama and Peru, pursuant to the bipartisan agreement reached by Congress in 2007, some flexibility was introduced to soften the strictures of past agreements. In the case of Peru, the PTA stipulates that the protection of undisclosed test or other data should not exceed "a reasonable period of time." The relevant provision clarifies that for this purpose, such a timeframe shall normally mean five years, taking into account the nature of the data and the degree of effort and expenditure required to produce it. The provision further clarifies that parties shall be allowed to implement abbreviated approval procedures for such products on the basis of bioequivalence or bioavailability studies, subject to the requirement to implement the data exclusivity obligation.[75] Contrary to, for example, the CAFTA–DR or the Bahrain FTAs, the new PTAs leave room, in theory, for a more balanced domestic implementation of the norms including, for example, a protection for less than five years when the originator of such data has not involved considerable efforts and expenditures.[76]

In another important departure, the revised Peru-PTA provides that the reasonable period of exclusive use shall begin with the date of the first marketing approval in any one of the PTA signatories (i.e., in general, in the USA)—a so-called "concurrent period"—on condition that Peru grants the approval of the compound within six months of an application.[77] This new mechanism provides an incentive for rapid marketing approval in the country where the drug is approved subsequently, in exchange for a shorter period of effective protection in that country. This important change responds to criticisms targeted to earlier agreements that allowed for a priority period of five years since obtaining the first approval abroad, within which the innovator could claim exclusivity in the other country. Such a priority right could generate, as in the case of CAFTA–DR, Bahrain and others, a de facto extension of the period of protection up to ten years in the countries of subsequent approvals.[78]

A much more liberal approach to the concurrent period has been adopted by Chile in the implementation of the FTA with the USA. Chile's domestic law provides that data exclusivity will not be granted in Chile if the data originator has not applied for regulatory approval in Chile within twelve months from receiving approval for the same substance abroad.[79]

Departing from the earlier US agreements, the amended texts of the Colombia, Panama and Peru PTAs also call on the parties, in the main text and not in side letters, to reaffirm their commitments to the Doha Declaration, particularly emphasizing that the provisions on data exclusivity should be subordinated to the right of a party to take measures to protect public health. The revised texts further oblige the parties to respect existing waivers granted by WTO members regarding provisions of the TRIPS Agreement.[80]

The EFTA countries, in their agreements, have not followed a uniform approach to the protection of undisclosed pharmaceutical test data. While the EFTA–Chile agreement obligates parties to provide a data exclusivity regime for at least five years,[81] the EFTA–Egypt accord broadly refers to Article 39, TRIPS Agreement, without further specification.[82]

Yet, another option is provided under the agreements between EFTA and the Republic of Korea and Colombia, respectively, where protection of undisclosed information may be granted either through exclusivity or through a regime of compensatory liability.[83] This option seems to be based on suggestions made by scholars[84] and deserves further consideration in the implementation of data exclusivity regimes. The above-mentioned EFTA–Colombia agreement also provides for the compensatory liability option, but with an important qualification: this option applies only to agricultural chemical products involving vertebrate animals.[85] In the case of test data related to pharmaceuticals, the trade agreement insists on protection through a regime of exclusivity, "which in the case of pharmaceutical products means normally five years."[86] In a way comparable to the more recent US PTAs, the

EFTA–Colombia agreement refers to parties' rights to "take measures to protect public health" in accordance with the implementation of the Doha Declaration, any related waiver of any TRIPS obligation, and any related amendment to the TRIPS Agreement.[87]

In the case of the EU trade agreements, significant developments have taken place over the past two years, albeit without showing a uniform approach: the agreements with the Republic of Korea[88] and Colombia/Peru[89] have introduced exclusive rights in pharmaceutical test data, lasting for five years from the first grant of domestic marketing approval. There is no comparable provision in the EU–Central America Association Agreement probably due to already existing data exclusivity obligations under the US–DR/CAFTA FTA.[90] India has, for the time being, rejected the inclusion of pharmaceutical test data exclusivity provisions in the trade negotiations with the EU.

The linkage issue

While the above observations may relate also to non-patented pharmaceutical and agrochemical products, most of the trade agreements with the USA contain an additional provision that can have an important impact in the area of patented pharmaceutical and agrochemical products. These provisions subject the decision by regulatory authorities to grant marketing approval to third parties to the acquiescence of the patent holder, thereby "linking" the separate realms of drug regulation and patent law.[91] Such a requirement effectively transforms the regulatory agencies into patent enforcement authorities—a facet that is not even a feature in US law.[92] Besides the difficulties created for regulatory authorities to determine the validity of patents, and besides the fact that according to the preamble of TRIPS, IPRs are private rights—and private parties bear the primary responsibility of enforcing them—this linkage has been interpreted as potentially precluding, among others, the recourse to compulsory licenses to increase the availability of low-priced pharmaceutical products.[93] As a matter of principle, regulatory approval is independent of patent law, and the third party authorized to produce a patented product under compulsory license would arguably depend—in the case of linkage—on the patentee's consent or acquiescence for the actual marketing of the product.[94]

In view of criticisms raised with respect to past agreements, the new US PTAs with Peru, Colombia and Panama make such linkage optional and in particular do not require that sanitary authorities withhold approval until they can certify that no patent would be violated if the generic product were marketed.[95] Peru has taken advantage of this option in its implementing legislation.[96] Instead, the revised PTAs require parties to provide procedures and remedies (judicial or administrative proceedings, including injunctions or equivalent effective provisional measures) for adjudicating expeditiously any patent infringement or validity dispute that arises with respect to a product for which marketing approval is sought.[97] The new texts also require parties to provide—as in the case of the US Hatch-Waxman Act[98]—effective rewards for a successful challenge to the validity or applicability of the patent.[99] In other words, the revised PTAs seek to balance the rights of patent holders with opportunities for generic producers to challenge patented products that might prevent competing products from entering the market. They shift the primary responsibility for patent enforcement back to the patent owner. The potential of adequately and actually using the flexibilities included in these newer agreements will much depend on the abilities and margin of implementation left to local authorities.[100]

BEYOND MEDICINES

As pointed out, with respect to the broad implications of PTAs, access to medicines has been the central focus of attention. However, a number of scholars, civil society groups and private actors have identified several other aspects as being contentious for expanding the WTO minimum standards by upsetting the structural balance reached in TRIPS between private rights and public-interest considerations. Among these other issues, we discuss in this chapter the treatment of genetic resources, protection of life forms and related questions and the circumvention of technological measures in the digital environment and their potential impact on access and dissemination of knowledge. To complete this broad picture of the significance of PTAs, it is extremely important to also consider the ramifications of the enforcement measures and dispute settlement aspects provided for by these agreements that add extra "teeth" to what TRIPS achieved in this area. Without these important additions, the consequences for access to medicines, genetic resources and knowledge and the general implementation challenges posed by these new obligations would not be the same.

PROTECTION OF LIFE FORMS AND RELATED QUESTIONS

PTAs go beyond TRIPS in a number of instances by imposing, for example, the obligation to grant patent protection to plants and animals.[101] Also, in some cases they tend to suggest—in the view of the authors, prematurely—modalities of treatment of genetic resources and traditional knowledge still under conceptualization and deliberations in competent international forums. The latter places weaker countries in apparent contradiction with positions sustained side by side with other like-minded countries in these same international forums reflecting a manifest internal lack of coherence on these matters.

PTAs in a number of ways preclude parties from taking advantage of the general principles and exclusions acknowledged in TRIPS. For example, the UPOV Convention is listed in almost all agreements as one of the international treaties that parties should subscribe or endeavor to adhere to as the modality of protection for plant varieties. The TRIPS Agreement does oblige countries to prescribe protection for plant varieties but offers various options including an effective *sui generis* system of protection.[102]

UPOV provides a framework for the protection of plant varieties.[103] However, there are two main versions of the Convention: UPOV 1978 and UPOV 1991. In both versions, the breeders' right may be subject to two exceptions: the "breeders' exemption" and the "farmers' privilege." The rights of breeders—both to use protected varieties as an initial source of variation for the creation of new varieties and to market these varieties without authorization from the original breeder (the "breeder exemption")—are covered in both versions of the Convention under different modalities. The trade agreements obligate countries to opt for the 1991 version of UPOV, which is seen as less flexible and more stringent than its previous incarnations.[104] UPOV's plant breeders' rights regimes have been questioned, in general, on grounds that they better respond to conditions prevailing in industrialized countries and thereby risk undermining the food security of communities in less advanced countries.[105]

Countries party to PTAs undertake further commitments to "make efforts" to introduce legislation concerning the patenting of plants that is not mandatory under TRIPS (Article 27.3(b)).[106] Contrary to this best-effort clause, in the case of the FTA between the USA and Morocco, the parties assume the obligation to grant patents to inventions on animals and plants.[107] An intermediary approach is followed in the USA–Bahrain Agreement that makes mandatory the patenting of "plant inventions," but not of animals.[108]

In addition, according to a number of trade agreements, any party that provides patent protection for plants and animals as of, or after, the date of its entry into force needs to maintain such protection.[109] This means a practical derogation from the TRIPS flexibility to determine the appropriate method of implementation by "locking-in" countries to maintain such protection without alteration. This is no doubt a clear signal of the pervasive nature of these agreements that as a matter of principle would not allow parties to amend their national legislation if conditions and circumstances changed.[110]

Contrary to the US trend, the European trade agreements appear not to interfere on the topic of life forms and thus do not alter the TRIPS status quo. They do, however, generally contain an obligation for parties to comply with UPOV 1991.[111] The 2011 EU–Central America Association Agreement does not make reference to UPOV but reiterates the TRIPS principle that parties "shall provide for the protection of plant varieties either by patents or by an effective *sui generis* system or by any combination thereof." It adds the understanding of the parties "that no contradiction exists between the protection of plant varieties and the capacity of a party to protect and conserve its genetic resources." Finally, it provides for, apparently, a more generous right to provide for exceptions—compared to UPOV 1991[112]—"to exclusive rights granted to plant breeders to allow farmers to save, use and exchange protected farm-saved seed or propagating material."[113]

A related question might arise as to whether parties to these agreements may incorporate substantial requirements at the domestic level on the disclosure in patent applications of origin of genetic resources and associated traditional knowledge (TK). The TRIPS Agreement is silent in this respect, with the exception of the general provision regarding applicants' obligation to disclose the invention in a manner sufficiently clear and complete for the invention to be carried out by a person skilled in the art.[114] As a matter of principle, TRIPS does not limit members to place further conditions to the disclosure of inventions. As such, the disclosure of origin at the domestic level is, in principle, TRIPS-compliant.[115] Those opposed to the mandatory disclosure of origin have argued in the Council for TRIPS that such a requirement would add a further obligation to applicants and would not be TRIPS-compliant.[116]

Some have argued that in the case of a number of PTAs—for example, the trade agreements by the USA, respectively, with CAFTA–DR, Peru and Colombia—"governments will no longer be able to reject a patent application because a firm fails to indicate the origin of a plant or show proof of consent for its use from a local community."[117] This assertion finds its basis in two provisions that namely state that parties shall provide that a "disclosure of a claimed invention shall be considered to be sufficiently clear and complete if it provides information that allows the invention to be carried out by a person skilled in the art" and that a claimed invention is sufficiently supported by its disclosure if the latter reasonably conveys that the "applicant was in possession of the claimed invention as of the filing date."[118]

The extent to which these provisions would inhibit the possibility of introducing disclosure requirements at the domestic level remains a matter of interpretation. But if this were their effect, as argued by some,[119] there would be some political ramifications for countries' signatories of PTAs that are at the same time proponents for amending TRIPS to accommodate a disclosure of origin requirement to combat bio-piracy and the misappropriation of TK and thus make TRIPS fully consistent with the Convention on

Biological Diversity (CBD).[120] Such a stance at the multilateral front would arguably lose credibility if parties were inhibited of implementing disclosure requirements at the domestic level because of their PTA obligations.

Side letters have been included in agreements negotiated by the USA with Colombia[121] and Peru,[122] respectively, recognizing "the potential contribution of traditional knowledge and biodiversity to cultural, economic, and social development." The side letters reaffirm the importance of obtaining prior informed consent and the equitable sharing of benefits as provided in the CBD—even if the USA is not a party to the latter Convention.

The side letters on biodiversity were at a point in time highlighted by the Andean negotiators as constituting a major success in the negotiations with the USA because, for the first time, a formal recognition of the importance of preserving biodiversity and respecting TK was documented. This apparent success responded to many criticisms made by civil society groups that if concessions were to be made on IP in general, positive commitments would need to be made on biodiversity and TK.[123] In the case of Peru this was particularly important, because the country has been an active advocate of the reform of TRIPS by incorporating a new provision into the Agreement (i.e. a proposed Article 29*bis*). However, a critical point in the side letters appears to reaffirm the position taken by the USA, namely that a contract-based approach should be favored for the protection of TK and genetic resources,[124] contrary to the position taken multilaterally by a number of developing countries calling for an international legal instrument in this area.

Compared to the USA, European countries appear to take a different approach on these matters. This may be seen in the context of the current efforts to secure developing countries' support for increased protection of geographical indications at the multilateral level, accompanied by corresponding concessions in the area of biodiversity.[125] Further, with the desire of promoting consistency between TRIPS and the CBD, the agreement between the EU and CARIFORUM acknowledges that the patent provisions of the EPA and the CBD shall be implemented in a mutually supportive way and that parties may require the identification, by the applicant, of the sources of the biological material used by the applicant and described as part of the invention.[126] The same Agreement also commits parties to regularly exchange views and information on relevant multilateral discussions such as in WIPO, on the issues dealt with in the framework of the Intergovernmental Committee on Genetic Resources, Traditional Knowledge and Folklore.[127]

The EU–Republic of Korea Free Trade Agreement encourages the sharing of benefits arising from the use of knowledge owned by traditional communities (Article 10.40); while the Colombia/Peru Trade Agreement goes a step further by acknowledging the usefulness of disclosure requirements in patent applications and containing an obligation of parties to render such requirement effective, in accordance with domestic laws (Article 201(7), (8)). No similar provision on disclosure is found in the EU–Central American Association Agreement but a general statement is made which relates that nothing should "prevent the Parties from adopting or maintaining measures to promote the conservation of biological diversity, the sustainable utilization of its components and the fair and equitable participation in the benefits arising from the utilization of genetic resources, in conformity with what is established in" the CBD.[128]

THE CIRCUMVENTION OF TECHNOLOGICAL MEASURES

As argued in this chapter, the PTAs have deepened the process of upward harmonization initiated by TRIPS that in the case of copyright enforcement has a number of manifestations. This applies to both the US and, albeit to a more limited degree, also to the copyright provisions under the EU trade agreements (i.e. Central America; Colombia/Peru; Republic of Korea). One manifestation relates to the noticeable expansion of the duration of copyright and related rights by twenty years in addition to the fifty years, as generally established under TRIPS.[129]

The provisions on effective technological protection measures (TPMs) in US agreements go beyond the WIPO "Internet treaties" of 1996 (the WIPO Copyright Treaty, WCT; and the WIPO Performances and Phonograms Treaty, WPPT), which state that parties "shall provide adequate legal protection and effective legal remedies" against the circumvention of TPMs,[130] leaving it to each party to decide the way in which it will implement the provisions and whether it will apply civil and/or criminal sanctions to infringers. The WIPO Internet treaties are not incorporated in the TRIPS system and by themselves they are already an indication of a determination in subsequent trade agreements to go beyond the requirements of the latter.

The free trade arrangements, in general, contain detailed rules aimed at providing adequate legal protection and effective legal remedies to fight against the circumvention of effective TPMs used by authors, performers and producers of phonograms to protect their works, performances and phonograms protected by copyright and related rights.[131] In a common provision that can be found, with minor variations, in all agreements signed with the USA there is the obligation to provide for a detailed system of protection from circumvention that practically exports the US domestic law into the domestic legislation of its partners. In addition, PTAs provide for the requirement to make available adequate and effective legal remedies to protect rights management information.[132]

The terminology found in the US trade agreements draws from the US Digital Millennium Copyright Act (DMCA),[133] which was "nominally intended to bring US law into compliance with the 1996 WIPO Treaties on copyright and the Internet. In fact, it went well beyond what those treaties required,"[134] *inter alia* by undue restrictions of fair and other legitimate uses of digital content; unnecessary obstacles to competition within the content industry; and inappropriate obstacles to competition in the market for TPMs.[135]

DMCA and US trade agreements' provisions make it a civil and criminal offence to tamper with embedded anti-piracy measures that control access to works and phonograms. They also provide for civil liability, and, when done willfully and for prohibited commercial purposes, criminal liability for the manufacture and offering to the public of devices, products or components that serve the purpose of circumventing TPMs that control access and the exclusive rights in a work or phonogram.[136]

The incidence of these anti-circumvention provisions in PTAs has been criticized precisely for limiting access to technology and making these DMCA-like provisions a de facto model for global implementation of the WCT, leading to increased difficulty in access to content material and adding further layers of impediments to developing countries in utilizing information technology, among others by raising costs.[137] It remains to be seen whether the Trans-Pacific Partnership (TPP) Agreement,[138] which is currently being negotiated among Australia, Brunei Darussalam, Canada, Chile, Japan, Malaysia, Mexico, New Zealand, Peru, Singapore, the United States and Vietnam[139] would go beyond existing provisions in free trade agreements already negotiated between these countries and the USA.

In order to overcome some of the difficulties posed by PTAs to the legitimate use of traditional copyright exceptions and fair-use norms, a number of proposals have been advanced in the literature, such as the development of "smart DRM" (digital rights management) technologies with the inbuilt capacity to recognize and accommodate traditional copyright exceptions, and the negotiation of an international agreement restricting the use of DRMs in cases where digital objects carry a high proportion of public interest-relevant information.[140] Other proposals focus on remedial action to be taken by domestic courts when dealing with anti-circumvention provisions.[141]

The trade agreements under consideration do provide for limited exceptions that need to be activated by the countries concerned. For example, the USA–Peru Agreement—as it is the case of most PTAs—recognizes exceptions in cases of "noninfringing reverse engineering activities with regard to a lawfully obtained copy of a computer program concerned," for the sole purpose of achieving program-to-program interoperability.[142] Further, the US agreements, following the model of the DMCA, also provide for exceptions for "noninfringing uses of a work, performance, or phonogram, in a particular class of works, performances, or phonograms, provided that any exception or limitation adopted . . . shall be based on the existence of substantial evidence, as found in a legislative or administrative proceeding."[143] This model requires a particular institutional infrastructure not common in developing countries. In the case of the DMCA the process to establish such exceptions is conducted by the Librarian of the Library of Congress that periodically reviews existing exceptions.[144]

Finally, the EU trade agreements also provide for measures targeting the circumvention of TPMs but appear to give parties greater freedom to provide for exceptions, in accordance with domestic laws and international treaties, such as the WCT and WPPT.[145]

DISPUTE SETTLEMENT AND ENFORCEMENT ISSUES

As observed in this chapter, important ingredients of PTAs are the robust provisions on dispute settlement and more specifically on enforcement of IPRs. In fact, trade agreements subsequent to TRIPS incorporate general dispute settlement chapters, applicable to all disciplines, and detailed provisions—beyond those related to anti-circumvention measures—on IP enforcement. An important difference, in this respect, in the approach followed by the USA and EU relates to the scope of application of the dispute settlement mechanism. The US agreements allow the parties to bring not only cases that address inconsistencies with the obligations of the parties, but also cases described in the WTO system as non-violation and situation complaints.[146] In the TRIPS context, the latter are subject, for the time being, to a de facto moratorium in the sense that they are not fully operational.[147] In the US agreements, by contrast, non-violation complaints are in force and thus not subject to the existing WTO moratorium. In a clear manifestation of their intrusion in multilateral processes, these PTAs make operational these types of situations in their specific context.

Affected parties bringing non-violation cases might eventually argue, in the case of IP, that certain public policies restricting market access of protected products deprive rights holders of certain expectations arising from the substantive rules in PTAs. For example, recourse to price controls, particularly in the area of pharmaceutical products, could be considered as impairing marketing expectations on the part of foreign patent holders. Also, the use by governments of flexibilities, such as the grant of a compulsory license or the narrow design of patentability criteria, might trigger the recourse to non-violation complaints. This could be extended, in theory, to public policy choices pursued through internal taxes, packaging and labeling requirements, consumer protection rules and environmental standards that might be perceived as causing nullification or impairment.[148]

US trade agreements have traditionally laid more emphasis on detailed IP enforcement provisions than those of the EU. However, recent developments in the EU suggest a dramatic change and an even more ambitious and drastic approach to enforcement issues.[149] These trends, in general, reflect the new enforcement agenda[150] led at the international level by these same countries with a clear manifestation in the concluded negotiations of an Anti-Counterfeiting Trade Agreement (ACTA).[151] In many respects the latter mirrors the major provisions already present in most PTAs.

In general, the enforcement provisions of PTAs follow the same structure as the TRIPS Agreement. Accordingly, they contain provisions dealing with general obligations; civil and administrative procedures; provisional measures; border measures; and criminal procedures. For the USA, probably the most important achievement in this area has been to make mandatory many of the discretionary remedies included under TRIPS.[152] An important novelty of the PTAs, as far as TRIPS and the WIPO Internet treaties are concerned, is that they provide for "Limitations on Liability of Internet Service Providers."[153]

Inspired by TRIPS, PTAs provide that there is no need to create a special enforcement system for IPRs, distinct from the one that exists for law enforcement in general. There is neither an obligation to assign special resources for the enforcement of IPRs, different from that for the law in general, but this shall not excuse a party from non-compliance with the provisions on enforcement of the PTA.[154]

Trade agreements signed with the USA provide for the important legal copyright presumption that all works bearing a name in a usual manner should be considered protected (copyrighted), except for subject matter that evidently has fallen into the public domain.[155] In other words, the burden of proving that a work is not protected—as a defense to infringement claims— falls on the general public that uses original works and not on the author.[156]

The same trade agreements further provide that damages should be paid by the infringer to compensate for the injuries suffered by the right holder,[157] without qualifying the nature of the infringement. The equivalent provision in the TRIPS Agreement limits damages to a contravention of the rights by an infringer who is "knowingly, or with reasonable grounds to know, engaged in infringing activity."[158] Therefore, innocent infringement according to TRIPS may be excluded; however, it is not apparent whether that possibility is open in the PTAs.

As far as border measures are concerned, free trade agreements once again go beyond TRIPS, particularly in one aspect. TRIPS provides for border measures, including *ex officio* actions—under some conditions[159]—only for the importation of counterfeit trademarks or pirated goods. The application of border measures to goods being exported and to goods in transit[160] is optional. PTAs are in a TRIPS-plus mode by providing for *ex officio* measures for goods being imported, as well as for those destined for export or moving in transit.[161] An important aspect in the US trade agreements is that they provide for a clear authority to exercise legal action, *ex officio*, without the need for a formal complaint to initiate border measures with respect to imported, exported, or in-transit merchandise.[162]

Border measures also appear to be an important feature of newer agreements signed with the EU as exemplified by the original proposals made in the negotiations initiated by the EU with Andean countries and India.[163] The Economic Partnership Agreements (EPA) signed with CARIFORUM appears to go even beyond the agreements sponsored by the USA. The latter stick to the minimum standard of TRIPS in the sense that border measures apply to counterfeit trademark or pirated copyright goods. In the case of EU–CARIFORUM, border measures apply in general to "goods infringing an intellectual property right," a concept that embraces a wide range of IPRs including designs and geographical indications. CARIFORUM states agree also "to collaborate to expand the scope of this definition to cover goods infringing all intellectual property rights."[164] However, the EU has followed no uniform approach on this matter. Regardless of the original proposals by the EU, the Trade Agreement with Colombia/Peru[165] is less restrictive than the CARIFORUM standard limiting border measures to goods infringing copyright or trademarks, in line with the minimum standard of the TRIPS Agreement (i.e. Article 51). By contrast, the Free Trade Agreement with the Republic of Korea includes the most expansive standard by subjecting, *inter alia*, patent-infringing products to border measures.[166]

Additionally, PTAs, particularly those signed by the USA, expand the provisions in TRIPS on criminal measures. According to TRIPS, criminal measures apply, for example, to cases of willful trademark counterfeiting or copyright piracy on a commercial scale. The agreements in question make no reference to the quantitative "commercial scale" requirement in TRIPS and replace it with the notion of a "commercial advantage or financial gain" element, which focuses more on the purpose of the infringement, even if it is not made at a commercial scale.[167] Other examples of provisions that go beyond TRIPS deal with criminal procedures, specifically the detailed rules on seizure, forfeiture and destruction of infringing goods and elements used in the infringements.[168]

As noted, PTAs—both in the case of the USA and EU—include specific rules on liability of and limitation of the liability of Internet services providers (ISPs) for infringing content that is transmitted or stored in their networks when they perform certain functions, such as hosting, caching or linking. The rules include the requirement to provide (a) legal incentives for service providers to cooperate with copyright owners in deterring the unauthorized storage and transmission of copyrighted materials; and (b) limitations in domestic law regarding the scope of remedies available against service providers for copyright infringements that they do not control, initiate or direct, and that take place through systems or networks controlled or operated by them or on their behalf.[169]

CONCLUSIONS

This chapter shows how PTAs have deepened the process of harmonization initiated by TRIPS and have expanded protection and enforcement measures to new frontiers altering in many respects the balance achieved on the multilateral front between private rights holders and consumers in general. The potential impact of these agreements in hampering access to essential products—such as medicines or educational material—and in narrowing down the public domain of essential information needed for the development of technological skills, creative works, and by further restraining competition should be a source of concern. To restore the necessary balance between producers, consumers and the public interest, policymakers need to become aware of and make use of the flexibilities that remain in place and implement their new IP commitments in the context of a broader framework of policies that promote creativity, innovation and a pro-competitive environment.

Despite its importance for technological innovation and cultural progress, the public domain has been seriously affected by an expansion of private rights, both under the TRIPS Agreement and even more so under the new generation of PTAs. It has been observed that a fundamental tension is emerging "between the public purposes of intellectual property and the tendency toward the commodification (and attendant rationing) of an increasing number of forms of basic information."[170] This tendency has been supported by the belief in many countries that stronger exclusive rights will necessarily yield higher levels of creativity and innovation, despite the lack of concrete empirical evidence in this regard. Taken together, these trends have upset the balance between private rights and the free dissemination of knowledge. It has been correctly pointed out in the case of advanced countries—and this is a relevant lesson for those implementing IP reform—that there is an optimal level of protection, beyond which ever-expansive exclusive rights will prove counterproductive to society at large.[171]

One needs to continue bearing in mind that historically IP systems have been constructed around the need for public policy interventions securing exclusive rights to reward innovators and creators for their contributions to society. Society prospers, culturally and economically, through innovation and the creation of new ideas.[172] Implicit in this conception is that the exclusive rights granted to authors and innovators should be premised on the encouragement of future authors and innovators to use those contributions to further technological and cultural progress.[173] Thus, the dissemination of knowledge has been at the heart of the IP system, a goal that was well captured in the TRIPS Agreement as part of its objectives and principles.[174]

Accordingly, the IP system is premised on the dissemination of knowledge and improved forms of transfer of technology. Access and dissemination of knowledge is thus the quid pro quo for the exclusive rights accorded to authors and innovators in general. However, one could question whether the bargain between society at large—benefiting from the knowledge produced and disseminated by IP—and the right holders—extracting rents from their time-limited monopoly—is indeed being promoted by new initiatives such as the ones analyzed in this chapter.

Society is highly dependent on the dissemination of knowledge goods. For example, the activities of researchers, follow-on entrepreneurs, software developers, libraries, educational institutions, publishers and media rely heavily on a robust public domain[175] and on the delimitation of the boundaries of exclusive property rights through the establishment of exceptions to and limitations of those rights. For example, limiting the use of exceptions and limitations, restricting possibilities for reverse engineering, and the extensive use of digital TPMs combined with criminal sanctions for their circumvention, although useful to protect works, may also have unintended consequences in terms of erecting fundamental roadblocks for the national and global provision of public goods, including scientific research, education, health care, biodiversity and environmental protection.[176] The agreements analyzed in this chapter do provide for exceptions to the use of these measures but their actual use in the case of countries with weak human and institutional infrastructures is not so obvious—as briefly mentioned below.

Taking account of the need for follow-on inventors and creators to access protected information or works at some point, the IP system has been built on the assumption that once the exclusive temporal rights of authors and inventors expire, they fall into the public domain. In addition, the IP system is constructed on the notion that certain things are not protected because the burden on society would be too heavy and general access to the respective subject matter should be provided at all times. Expanding the boundaries of protection—as the case of PTAs shows—for instance through constraints on reverse engineering, neglects this basic assumption.[177]

Leaving aside the systemic issues discussed here, a question arises regarding what conclusions one could reach on the involvement of developing countries in trade agreements with strong chapters on IPRs. There is no doubt, in the view of the authors, that PTAs represent agreements freely entered into, where developing countries seek a number of aggressive trade and political objectives.[178] However, this is not the case with respect to the IP obligations where the latters' stand has been merely self-defensive. One of the difficulties—as pointed out in this chapter—relates to the complex negotiation process and the renegotiation of commitments. As reported, the negotiations do not end with the subscription of the agreement but become more burdensome in the so-called "certification" act as it is in the case of US trade agreements. This objectionable certification process nullifies the TRIPS principle of freedom of implementation and questions the legitimacy and consensual character of these agreements.

Countries negotiating PTAs need to be aware of these complexities and the consequences of reaching agreements that will be the subject of stringent monitoring processes by private parties and by the USTR through its 301 Annual reviews. An interesting exercise would be to examine how many countries party to PTAs are subject to the different characterizations made by the USTR on performing countries in the area of IPRs. For instance, how many PTAs partners are on the priority watch list? It is obvious that by adhering to new IP obligations countries become more exposed to the private and public scrutiny of their implementation measures in line with these new commitments. In the case of Latin American countries party to PTAs, they have often being listed by USTR in their unilateral categorization as non-performing countries.[179] The fear of being portrayed as a non-performing IP country may have a deterring effect on assertive national reforms and on the adoption of innovative forms of implementation of PTAs.

The other important consideration that countries need to bear in mind in negotiating PTAs is that the obligations made in the area of IP, thanks to the most-favored nation principle of TRIPS (Article 4), are extensive in scope. These new commitments would have to be translated into national legislation and thus applied without discrimination to all countries. In this respect, negotiating PTAs parallel to or subsequently with different trading partners means, in the area of IP, the potential addition of new commitments that would apply *erga omnes*.

The serious challenge for developing countries is the fact that when importing foreign systems of IPRs, including sophisticated pieces of legislation such as, for example the DMCA, they do so without ensuring the necessary checks and balances[180] that exist in the "exporting" countries. As described in this chapter, PTAs do include exceptions to the stringent provisions related to the circumvention of TPMs reproducing a successful model conducted by the sophisticated resources of the US Library of Congress.

Less advanced countries, due to lack of resources and capabilities, have major institutional shortcomings for assuming an adequate implementation of PTAs. Their weak judiciary and administrative system and an almost non-existent critical academic and skilled professional bar make this implementation dilemma difficult to surmount.[181] As a result, there is a lack of critical capacity and boldness to implement, for example, legitimate exceptions—as in the case of anti-circumvention measures—and more generally limited experience on the implementation of competition instruments. There are cases where countries have understood that PTAs represent major challenges, among them a challenge of modernization that demands major investments in various fields. But, to face those challenges, IP alone would not be the answer. IP reform should be part of a major design anchored in wide-ranging sustainable development objectives, where protection and enforcement goes par to par with access to knowledge, transfer and dissemination of technology, the promotion of innovation and competition policies, and, overall, the recognition of the important role the public domain plays for innovation and creativity.

NOTES

* Pedro Roffe is Senior Associate at the International Centre for Trade and Sustainable Development (ICTSD), Project on Intellectual Property and Sustainable Development. Christoph Spennemann is Legal Expert at the United Nations Conference on Trade and Development (UNCTAD), Intellectual Property Unit, Investment Capacity-Building Branch, Division on Investment and Enterprise. This chapter builds on work carried out by the authors in recent years in their respective capacities in ICTSD and UNCTAD. It draws, but differs substantially in its coverage, contents and focus, from "Intellectual Property Rights in Free Trade Agreements: Moving beyond TRIPS Minimum Standards," by the same authors and Johanna von Braun in Carlos M. Correa, ed., *Research Handbook on the Protection of Intellectual Property Law under WTO Rules: Intellectual Property in the WTO*, vol. I. Edward Elgar Publishing, 2010. Finally, the views expressed in this chapter are the authors' personal views and may not be attributed to ICTSD or UNCTAD.

1. "Of these, 351 RTAs were notified under Article XXIV of the GATT 1947 or GATT 1994; thirty-one under the Enabling Clause; and ninety-two under Article V of the GATS." WTO information, available at <http://www.wto.org/english/tratop_e/region_e/region_e.htm> (28 April 2011). See also Horn, Mavroidis and Sapir (2010) reporting that between 1995 and 2009, more than 250 agreements were notified to the trading body.

2. Some scholars have made valuable distinctions between WTO-plus obligations compared to those that could be characterized as WTO-extra. The former would consist of new commitments building on those already agreed at the multilateral level. WTO-extra would be those commitments dealing with issues going beyond the current WTO mandate. See Horn, Mavroidis and Sapir (2010). The distinction is important from a system-wide approach (i.e. application of the MFN principle to TRIPS-plus obligations, as opposed to any TRIPS-extra commitments). But, for purposes of the impact of those agreements, the consequences for the parties would be the same: assuming more obligations than those contemplated in WTO and more precisely, in our case, going beyond the TRIPS Agreement.

3. For details, see Roffe, Vivas, and von Braun (2008).

4. See Bhagwati (1991); Stewart (1999); Ryan (1998); Sell (2003); Drahos and Braithwaite (2002); von Braun (2008); Roffe (2004).

5. Available at <https://www.nafta-sec-alena.org/Default.aspx> (20 September 2013).

6. Santa Cruz (2007).

7. Text available at <http://www.sice.oas.org/Trade/chieu_e/chieu1_e.asp#Title6p4> (23 September 2013) and in general in OAS-SICE which has a complete database of all trade agreements figuring countries of the Americas: <http://www.sice.oas.org/> (3 May 2011).

8. For example: the World Intellectual Property Organization (WIPO) Copyright Treaty, WCT, 1996; the WIPO Performances and Phonograms Treaty, WPPT, 1996; the Patent Cooperation Treaty of 19 June 1970, Washington Act amended in 1979 and modified in 1984.

9. For example: the Protocol to the Madrid Agreement Concerning the International Registration of Marks; the Madrid Agreement concerning the International Registration of Marks, Stockholm Act 1967, as amended in 1979; and the Vienna Agreement establishing an International Classification of Figurative Elements of Marks, 1973, amended in 1985.

10. Roffe and Santa Cruz (2006).

11. See Economic Partnership Agreement between the CARIFORUM states, of the one part, and the European Community and its member states, of the other part, L 289/I/4 EN Official Journal of the European Union, 30 October 2008. See also OAS-SICE.

12. See Seuba (2008).

13. Santa Cruz (2007).

14. See <http://trade.ec.europa.eu/doclib/docs/2011/march/tradoc_147704.pdf> (3 May 2011). The Trade Agreement was signed in April 2011, see also ICTSD *Bridges Weekly Trade News Digest*, 15, (4): 20 April 2011 <http://ictsd.org/i/news/bridgesweekly/104884/> (3 May 2011).

15. See <http://trade.ec.europa.eu/doclib/press/index.cfm?id=689> (3 May 2011). The Association Agreement was signed in May 2010.

16. See <http://ec.europa.eu/trade/creating-opportunities/bilateral-relations/countries/korea/> (3 May 2011). The Free Trade Agreement was signed in October 2010, approved by the European Parliament in February 2011 and is scheduled to enter into force on 1 July 2011. See <http://www.ip-watch.org/weblog/2011/02/20/stronger-ip-rights-granted-in-eu-korea-fta-precedent-for-future-ftas/?utm_source=post&utm_medium=email&utm_campaign=alerts> (3 May 2011).

17. See <http://ec.europa.eu/trade/creating-opportunities/bilateral-relations/countries/india/> (3 May 2011). Negotiations are expected to conclude in the course of 2011, see <http://www.business-standard.com/india/news/india-eu-stepefforts-to-reach-fta-this-year/132472/> on (3 May 2011).

18. See, for example, Article 145 A.2/3, 145 B.3(b) of the EU–CARIFORUM EPA.

19. On the latest status of the negotiations at the World Trade Organization "Multilateral System of Notification and Registration of Geographical Indications for Wines and Spirits," Report by the Chairman, Ambassador Darlington Mwape (Zambia) to the Trade Negotiations Committee, TN/IP/21, 21 April 2011.

20. Roffe and Santa Cruz (2006).

21. For example, in the agreement between EFTA and Tunisia it is stipulated that the latter "will do its outmost to accede to the international conventions concerning IPRs to which EFTA States are Parties" (Abdel Latif (2009)). On the other hand, the trade agreement between EFTA and the states of the Southern African Customs Union (SACU) provides no particular obligation in respect to IPRs, but remains limited to a few general principles, such as national treatment and MFN. But, it states: "With the objective of progressively harmonizing their legal framework on intellectual property rights, the EFTA States and the SACU States

affirm their commitment to review this Chapter not later than five years after the entry into force of this Agreement." (Article 26.5).

22. The Canada–USA Free Trade Agreement entered into force on 1 January 1989.

23. The USA had in that instance a particular concern regarding the liberal Canadian policies of allowing compulsory licensing in support of its pharmaceutical domestic generic industry. See Reichman and Hasenzahl (2003).

24. The agreement was signed on 24 October 2000; <http://www.ustr.gov/trade-agree ments/free-trade-agreements/jordan-fta> (3 May 2011).

25. See, among others, Section 2102 of the Trade Promotion Authority, Trade Act of 2002.

26. Congressional leaders reached a compromise with the Administration on issues related to IP, labor standards and the environment with respect to three of the PTAs pending for ratification by Congress (Colombia, Republic of Korea, Panama; see http://www.ustr.gov/trade-agreements/free-trade-agreements). The Peru Trade Promotion Agreement, by contrast, entered into force in February 2009. See <http://www.ustr.gov/trade-agreements/free-trade-agreements/peru-tpa and OAS-SICE> and <http://www.sice.oas.org/Trade/PER_USA/PER_USA_s/Index_ s.asp> (1 May 2011).

27. See for example GAO (2007).

28. Roffe and Vivas-Eugui (2007).

29. See Article 1.1, TRIPS Agreement and UNCTAD-ICTSD (2005: 25–7).

30. For instance, Dominican Republic–Central American–United States Free Trade Agreement Implementation Act, Pub.L. 109–53, 109th Cong., 1st sess. (2005), Section 101. See also the text of H.R. 3688 [110th]: United States-Peru Trade Promotion Agreement Implementation Act, Section 102, available at <http:// www.govtrack.us/congress/billtext.xpd?bill=h110-3688> (21 April 2011).

31. In the recent case of the PTA between the USA and Peru, this process meant the enactment of several legislative acts that had to be revised a few weeks before President G.W. Bush put his signature to the Agreement, just days before he concluded his mandate. See Roca (2009).

32. In its report of February 2006, the Industry Trade Advisory Committee on Intellectual Property Rights (ITAC-15), stated with respect to Peru: "ITAC 15 urges the US not only to monitor very closely the implementation by Peru (and other FTA partners) of their FTA obligations but also to ensure that Peru and other FTA partners have in place, before the entry into force of the FTAs, national legislation that faithfully reflects their FTAs obligations.... IFAC-15 commends the US for working with FTA partners to secure fully-compliant national legislation before each agreement enters into force. ITAC-15 considers it essential that, if need be, entry into force be postponed until full compliance is achieved."

33. See Abbott (2006).

34. See Section 102 of the Congressional Implementation Bill of the CAFTA–DR Agreement on the Relationship of the Agreement to United States and State Law of the Dominican Republic–Central American–United States Free Trade Agreement Implementation Act (2005).

35. USTR has also advised Congress that decisions of dispute settlement panels under the FTAs do not affect US Federal law unless those decisions are expressly given effect by Congress. Abbott (2006: 5).

36. See Roffe and Genovesi (2010).
37. Roffe (2004: 9) and Roffe and Genovesi.
38. Horn, Mavroidis and Sapir (2010).
39. This legitimatization, based on Article 1.1, TRIPS, has limitations. See, Kur and Grosse Ruse-Khan (2011).
40. For an overview of the push for TRIPS-plus, see Deere (2009: 114–18).
41. See Bodenhausen (1968).
42. Declaration on the TRIPS Agreement and Public Health, WTO document WT/MIN(01)/DEC/2 of 20 November 2001; see related work by Abbott (2005).
43. See paragraph 4 *in fine* of the Declaration on the TRIPS Agreement and Public Health, available at <http://www.wto.org/english/thewto_e/minist_e/min01_e/mindecl_trips_e.htm> (1 May 2011).
44. Roffe and Spennemann (2006); Abbott and Reichman (2007).
45. "In the 2002 Trade Promotion Authority Act, Congress directed the Administrative branch to adhere to the Doha Declaration as a 'principal negotiating objective' in U.S. trade negotiations. Regrettably, recent . . . FTAs appear to undermine this commitment with provisions that strip away flexibilities to which countries are entitled under TRIPS. The FTAs provisions also appear to upset an important balance between innovation and access by elevating intellectual property at the expense of public health. The end result is that they threaten to restrict access to life-saving medicines and create conditions where poor countries could wait even longer than the Unites States for affordable generic medicines." Public letter dated 12 March 2007 addressed to the USA Trade Representative, signed by 12 members of the US Congress.
46. Nobel Prize laureate Joseph Stiglitz (2004) observed with respect to the agreement with Morocco that "The new agreement, many Moroccans fear, will make generic drugs needed in the fight against AIDS even less accessible in their country than they are in the United States."
47. Jaszi (2009: 8).
48. In February 2009, a joint venture between the Indian producer Cipla and the domestic Ugandan producer Quality Chemicals began producing anti-retroviral drugs at a modern production site near Kampala. One of the factors attracting the Indian investor was reportedly the implementation by Uganda of the LDC transition period on pharmaceutical product patents accorded by the WTO Council for TRIPS. See Rocks (2008) and UNCTAD-ICTSD (2010: 7). In a recent decision by the Indian pharmaceutical producer Cadila Pharmaceuticals to establish a manufacturing plant for active pharmaceutical ingredients (APIs) in Rwanda (see <http://www.in-pharmatechnologist.com/Industry-Drivers/Cadila-JV-to-set-up-plant-in-Rwanda> (1 May 2011)), the fact that Rwanda as an LDC is authorized to delay the introduction of pharmaceutical product patents until at least 2016 has been considered by Cadila as one element in their investment decision. Personal communication from Cadila management staff to one of the authors, April 2011.
49. UNCTAD (2011).
50. Details of these amendments are discussed, respectively, in the analysis of the PTAs provisions dealing with pharmaceutical products, below.
51. For example, Article 15.9.7, USA–Morocco.

52. Roffe (2004).
53. See, for example, Article 16.9.6(b) of the USA–Peru PTA; and Article 15.9.6(b) of the USA–Panama Promotion Trade Agreement.
54. See Article 16.9.6(a) of the USA–Peru PTA.
55. See Peru, Decreto Legislativo 1075, Articles 32 of 28 June 2008.
56. Article 27.1, TRIPS: "patent protection shall be available and patents rights enjoyable without discrimination . . . as to the field of technology."
57. WTO document WT/DS114/R of 17 March 2000. In this case, the panel held that WTO members can adopt different rules for particular product areas, provided that the differences are adopted for bona fide purposes. See UNCTAD-ICTSD (2005: 370–1) and Roffe and Spennemann (2010).
58. See Article 10.35(2).
59. See Article 223(4).
60. For instance, Sildenafil (Viagra) was first patented by Pfizer to treat heart disease. After finding out that it also served to treat impotence, Pfizer filed a second patent for this new use of the same drug. This second patent has been invalidated in some countries because of lack of novelty or because it was found obvious. See Jeffrey A. Andrews, "Pfizer's Viagra Patent and the Promise of Patent Protection in China," 28 *Loy. L.A. Int'l & Comp. L. Rev.* 1 (2006): 13. See <http://www.lockeliddell.com/files/News/ab9ebdd4-621f-4432-a383-1cae37df9ea1/Presentation/NewsAttachment/c5a9d67e-bdd9-4c7e-97e9-1d6efb6314dc/Andrews_Pfizers%20Viagra%20Patent.pdf> (3 May 2011).
61. UNCTAD (2011: 49ff; 74ff).
62. See, e.g., Article 15.9.2 of the PTA USA–Morocco: (Article 15.8.1(b) of the PTA USA–Oman: <http://www.ustr.gov/trade-agreements/free-trade-agreements/oman-fta> (1 May 2011).
63. Thomas (2005: 37–8).
64. See Articles 31 and 6, TRIPS.
65. See, e.g., Article 4. 20 of the USA–Jordan FTA.
66. Jaszi (2009: ch. 1).
67. Gervais (1998: 61) and Dreyffus et al. (1997).
68. See e.g. Chapter 15, Article 15.9.4 of the USA–Morocco FTA, and Chapter 17, Article 17.9.4 of the USA–Australia FTA.
69. United States House of Representatives (2005).
70. For example, Article 147 B, CARIFORUM; Article 10.34 EU–Republic of Korea; Article 197(2) EU–Colombia/Peru, together with other general principles of importance to ensuring balance between the interests of owners and users of IP rights.
71. On the one hand, it has been argued that Article 39.3 of the TRIPS Agreement merely obligates members to protect test data against misappropriation, through non-exclusive means. See Correa (2006: 84). See also Reichman (2006: 142). Others have interpreted Article 39.3, TRIPS Agreement as implying an obligation for members to protect test data through exclusive right, see International Federation of Pharmaceutical Manufacturers Associations (IFPMA) (2004: 40); Gorlin (2000). For an overview of the different positions and supporting arguments, see UNCTAD (2011: 161ff).

72. See, e.g., Chapter 15, Article 15.10.1(a) of CAFTA, or Article 14.9.1 (a), Bahrain–USA.
73. See World Medical Association Declaration of Helsinki: <http://www.wma.net/en/30publications/10policies/b3/> (23 September 2013).
74. Abbott (2004: 7). Abbott observes that such exclusivity renders illegal the actual marketing of generic drugs produced under a compulsory or public non-commercial use license (2004: 8). This is so because the exclusive nature of the test data prevents reliance by the drug regulatory authority on these data, which will render it practically impossible for the compulsory licensee to be granted approval. In addition, the actual grant of approval will often be illegal because of provisions that link marketing approvals to the patent status of pharmaceutical substances.
75. See Article 16.10.2 (b), Peru–USA PTA and the implementing legislation (Decreto Legislativo 1072, Article 5).
76. See Article 16.10.2 (b), Peru–USA PTA.
77. Peru PTA, Article 16.10.2(c).
78. See Article 15.10.1(b) of the US–CAFTA PTA, and its interpretation by Correa (2006: 89) and Abbott (2004: 7).
79. Decree 153 (2005) of the Health Ministry, Mechanisms for the Protection of Undisclosed Data; see discussion by Roffe (2006). It should be noted that the text of the PTA with Chile is not identical to other PTAs (Roffe 2004). The USA and the EFTA countries have challenged the treatment of this and other matters in the Chilean law. In the case of the USA it has prompted the USTR to place Chile in the Priority Watch List of its 2006 annual report. See Roffe (2007) and Roffe and Genovesi (2010).
80. In the case of the PTA with Peru, see Article 16.13.
81. Annex XII, Article 4.2 of the EFTA–Chile PTA.
82. Annex V, Article 3(e) of the EFTA–Egypt PTA.
83. See Annex XIII (Article 3) to the EFTA–Korea FTA, <http://www.efta.int/free-trade/free-trade-agreements/korea/fta.aspx> (1 May 2011).
84. See Reichman and Lewis (2005), Reichman (2009) and Weissman (2006).
85. Article 6.11.3(b), EFTA–Colombia.
86. Article 6.11.2, EFTA–Colombia. Footnote 15 to this provision states that "normally" means that the protection shall extend to five years, unless there is an exceptional case, where the public health interests would need to take precedence over the rights provided for in this paragraph.
87. Article 6.11.4, EFTA–Colombia.
88. Article 10.36. A broad reference to the Doha Declaration and its principles under Article 10.34 could be used to offset potential negative implications of data exclusivity on access to affordable medicines.
89. Article 231(2). Under Article 231(4a), the agreement provides for the possibility to invoke exceptions to data exclusivity, *inter alia* in case of public interest.
90. In an "EU Declaration on data protection of certain regulated products" at the very end of the Association Agreement Title VI on IP, the EU expresses satisfaction with Central American implementation of data exclusivity obligations arising from the USA–DR/CAFTA FTA. It should be noted that this consideration would have also applied to the trade agreements with Colombia and Peru that both had similar obligations in their FTAs with the USA.

91. See, e.g., Article 17.10.2 (c), Chile–USA.
92. See Abbott (2006).
93. Abbott (2004: 8).
94. See UNCTAD-ICTSD (2005: 537).
95. See Article 16.10.2(d) and 16.10.4 of the United States–Peru PTA.
96. See Article 4, *Decreto Legislativo* 1074 of 28 June 2008.
97. For example, Article 16.10.3, USA–Peru.
98. See Drug Price Competition and Patent Term Restoration Act of 1984, Pub. L. No. 98-417, 1984 Stat. 1538.
99. According to the revised version of the agreement with Peru, a party may comply with this clause by providing a period of marketing exclusivity for the first applicant to successfully challenge the validity or applicability of the patent (footnote 18 in chapter 16 of that agreement).
100. See our earlier discussion on the peculiarities of the US legislative process.
101. Article 27.3(b) of the TRIPS Agreement authorizes members to exclude plants and animals from patentability, subject to some qualifications.
102. Article 27.3.b.
103. The Convention was first signed in 1961 and revised in 1972, 1978 and 1991. It entered into force in 1968. It established the International Union for the Protection of New Varieties of Plants, based in Geneva and associated with WIPO.
104. For details, see UNCTAD-ICTSD (2003: 53–4).
105. See UNCTAD-ICTSD (2003: 105). See also Oxfam (2007: 12–13). Then and Tippe (2009) and G. Dutfield. For a more positive assessment of the impact of UPOV, see UPOV (2005).
106. See, e.g., Chile–USA, Article 17.9.2.
107. Morocco–USA, Article 15.9.2.
108. Bahrain–USA, Article 14.8.2.
109. See, e.g., the USA–CAFTA/DR PTA, Article 15.9.2. See also the USA–Peru PTA, Article 16.9.2.
110. This apparently would not be the case with the USA that according to its respective implementation bills makes these PTAs subordinate to US law. See discussion *supra* on this matter.
111. Article 10.39, EU–Republic of Korea; Article 232, EU–Colombia/Peru.
112. Article 15(2) of UPOV 1991 provides "Notwithstanding Article 14, each Contracting Party may, within reasonable limits *and subject to the safeguarding of the legitimate interests of the breeder*, restrict the breeder's right in relation to any variety in order to permit farmers to use *for propagating purposes, on their own holdings*, the product of the harvest which they have obtained by planting, on their own holdings, the protected variety or a variety covered by Article 14(5)(a)(i) or Article 14(5)(a)(ii)." (emphasis added).
113. See Article 259, EU–Central America Association Agreement, available at <http://trade.ec.europa.eu/doclib/docs/2011/march/tradoc_147664.pdf> (29 April 2011).
114. Article 29.1, TRIPS.
115. For example, the Swiss government has amended its patent law precisely to include such a requirement. See Article 49 a II of the Swiss Patent Act as entered

into force on 1 July 2008 (French language version available at <http://www.admin.ch/ch/f/rs/232_14/> (18 September 2013)).

116. See, for example, US communications in IP/C/W/209 and IP/C/W/162; and Australia's communication in IP/C/W/310. See also World Trade Organization (2011) for the latest developments on this issue.

117. Oxfam (2007: 14).

118. See Articles 16.9.9 and 16.9.10, USA–Peru. Similar provisions are found in USA–Morocco, see Articles 15.21.10 and 15.21.11.

119. Oxfam (2007: 14).

120. See *Bridges Weekly* (2008) and latest report by WTO Director-General on the status of negotiations on the relationship between TRIPS and CBD, see reference at note 122, *supra*.

121. See USTR at <http://www.ustr.gov/sites/default/files/uploads/agreements/fta/colombia/asset_upload_file953_10182.pdf> (3 October 2013).

122. See <http://www.ustr.gov/sites/default/files/uploads/agreements/fta/peru/asset_upload_file719_9535.pdf> (3 May 2011).

123. See *Bridges Monthly* (2006: 17–19).

124. In this sense, critics have questioned the merits of this kind of side agreement (von Braun 2008). See also Ruiz (2006), reflecting different views on this matter.

125. See proposal TN/C/W/52 at the WTO Council for TRIPS by the EU and 110 other WTO members.

126. EC–CARIFORUM, Article 150.4.

127. See Article 150 EC–CARIFORUM.

128. Articule 229.4, EU–Central America.

129. See, e.g., USA–Bahrain, Article 14.4.4, and EU–Colombia/Peru, Article 218(1).

130. WCT, Article 11; WPPT, Article 18.

131. "Effective technological measure means any technology, device, or component that, in the normal course of its operation, controls access to a work, performance, phonogram, or any other protected material, or that protects any copyright or any rights related to copyright, and cannot, in the usual case, be circumvented accidentally." Article 17.7.5 (f), PTA USA–Chile.

132. According to Article 16.7.5 (c) of the US PTA with Peru—almost identical in all respective provisions of PTAs—rights management information means: "(i) information that identifies a work, performance, or phonogram; the author of the work, the performer of the performance, or the producer of the phonogram; or the owner of any right in the work, performance, or phonogram; (ii) information about the terms and conditions of the use of the work, performance, or phonogram; or (iii) any numbers or codes that represent such information, when any of these items is attached to a copy of the work, performance, or phonogram or appears in connection with the communication or making available of a work, performance, or phonogram, to the public."

133. USC. Title 17 § 1201.

134. Lemley et al. (2000: 89).

135. See Samuelson and Scotchmer (2002: 1637).

136. "The DMCA was a bit of law intended to back up the protection of [this] code designed to protect copyrighted material. It was, we could say, *legal code* intended

to buttress *software code* which itself was intended to support the *legal code of copyright.*" Lessig (2004).

137. Okediji (2004: 24).

138. See information on TPP available at <http://www.ustr.gov/tpp> (1 May 2011).

139. For information on the TPP, see official USTR site http://www.ustr.gov/tpp (24 Sept. 2013), for a brief and preliminary assessment of the US negotiating text, see The South Centre (2011: 8).

140. Jaszi (2009).

141. Depending on the domestic design of anti-circumvention regimes, courts should, according to this suggestion, enable information users to notify copyright owners of their intent to make public good uses of technologically protected copyrighted works, triggering the rights owners' responsibility to take down the TPMs or otherwise make lawful uses possible (Reichman, Dinwoodie and Samuelson (2007)).

142. Article 16.7.4 (e) (i), USA–Peru.

143. Article 16.7.4 (f), USA–Peru.

144. See recent directive in Library of Congress, Copyright Office, Exemption to Prohibition on Circumvention of Copyright Protection Systems for Access Control Technologies, 75 Fed. Reg. 43825, 43839 (27 July 2010) (to be codified at 37 CFR 201.40).

145. Article 221 Colombia/Peru; Article 10.12 Republic of Korea; and Article 5.1 Central America.

146. See in general UNCTAD-ICTSD (2005: 680). See in particular Article 21.2.1 of the USA–Peru PTA. For a more detailed discussion of non-violation complaints under the Chile–USA PTA, see Roffe (2004: 47–8).

147. See, UNCTAD-ICTSD (2005: 673–6), with an overview of various interpretations. The latest moratorium on non-violation complaints was made at the ninth WTO Ministerial Conference in December 2013.

148. See UNCTAD-ICTSD (2005: 681).

149. Seuba (2008).

150. See ICTSD, Correa (2009).

151. See Sell (2008), Abdel Latif (2010). For the ACTA text see USTR, <http://www.ustr.gov/webfm_send/2379> (30 April 2011).

152. Note for example the IFAC-3 Chile Report (2003: 17) stating that the agreement makes some "significant advances" towards deterring further infringements, and clarifies and builds upon existing TRIPS standards. Cited in Roffe (2004).

153. e.g. Articles 10.62-10.66 EU–Republic of Korea.

154. See Article 17.11.2 (b) PTA with Chile and Article 16.11.4, PTA with Peru.

155. See, for example, the USA–Peru PTA, Article 16.11.5. An identical provision may be found in USA–CAFTA/DR, Article 15.11.5.

156. Chile–USA, Article 17.11.6(b).

157. In a similar provision in Chile–USA, parties, however, are free to provide that the presumption will only be valid on two conditions: that the work appears on its face to be original and that it bears a publication date not more than seventy years prior to the date of the alleged infringement. The seventy years from publication

term is the equivalent to the term of protection granted to legal persons. See, USA–Chile, Article 17.11.8(a).
158. Article 45.1, TRIPS.
159. See Article 58, TRIPS.
160. Footnote 13, TRIPS.
161. See Article 16.11.23, USA–Peru. See also Article 249(1) EU–Colombia/Peru.
162. See, for example, USA–Peru, Article 16.11.11.
163. Seuba (2008).
164. See footnote 3 to Article 163(1) CARIFORUM.
165. Article 249(1), EU–Colombia.
166. Footnote 27 to Article 10.67(1). The Republic of Korea has two years from the entry into force of the PTA to implement the obligation related to patents and registered designs, see Article 10.67(4).
167. See, for example, USA–Peru, Article 16.11.26.
168. See, for example, USA–Peru, Article 16.11.17.
169. See, for example, Article 17.11.29, USA–Australia FTA, Article 16.9.22, USA–Singapore FTA and Article 15.11.27, CAFTA. See in the case of the EU, Articles 250–254, EU–Colombia.
170. Jaszi (2009).
171. See, for example, Thumm 2006.
172. This concept is well expressed in the Constitution of the United States: "The Congress shall have the power to promote the Progress of Science and useful Arts, by securing for limited Times to Authors and Inventors the exclusive Right to their respective Writings and Discoveries." US Constitution, Article 1, Section 8, Clause 8.
173. Jaszi (2009).
174. Article 7, TRIPS.
175. See, for example, Boyle (2008).
176. Maskus and Reichman (2004: 7).
177. Roffe and Santa Cruz (2007).
178. Roffe (2004).
179. See for example, USTR (2010) and analysis in Roffe and Genovesi (2010).
180. See Abbott (2006).
181. On the difficulties of implementation, see Deere (2009).

REFERENCES

I. Publications

Abbott, Frederick M. (2004), "The Doha Declaration on the TRIPS Agreement and Public Health and the Contradictory Trend in Bilateral and Regional Free Trade Agreements," QUNO Occasional Paper 14, QUNO, Geneva, available at: <http://www.quno.org/geneva/pdf/economic/Occassional/TRIPS-Public-Health-FTAs.pdf> (19 September 2013).

Abbott, Frederick M. (2005), "The WTO Medicines Decision: The Political Economy of World Pharmaceutical Trade and the Protection of Public Health," *The American Journal of International Law*, 99: 317–58.

Abbott, Frederick M. (2006), "Intellectual Property Provisions of Bilateral and Regional Trade Agreements of the United States in Light of U.S. Federal Law," UNCTAD-ICTSD Issue Paper No. 12, Geneva, available at: <http://www.iprsonline.org/resources/docs/Abbott%20-%20US%20bilateral%20and%20regional%20trade%20agreements%20-%20Blue%2012.pdf> (19 September 2013).

Abbott, Frederick M. and Reichman, Jerome H. (2007), "The Doha Round's Public Health Legacy: Strategies for the Production and Diffusion of Patented Medicines under the Amended TRIPS Provisions," *Journal of International Economic Law*, 10: 921 et seq.

Abdel Latif, Ahmed (2009), "A Perspective on Reform in Arab Countries," in Ricardo Melendez and Pedro Roffe, (eds) ICTSD (2009), *Intellectual Property and Sustainable Development: Development Agendas in a Changing World*. Cheltenham, UK: Edward Elgar.

Andrews, Jeffrey A. (2006), "Pfizer's Viagra Patent and the Promise of Patent Protection in China," *Loyola Los Angeles International and Comparative Law Review* 28 (1): 13

Bhagwati, Jagdish (1991), *The World Trading System at Risk*. Princeton: Princeton University Press.

Bodenhausen, G. H. C. (1968), "Guide to the Application of the Paris Convention for the Protection of Industrial Property," 71, BIRPI, Geneva.

Boyle, James (2008), *The Public Domain: Enclosing the Commons of the Mind*. New Haven and London: Yale University Press.

Bridges Monthly (2006), "IP Standards in the US–Peru FTA: Health and Environment" *Bridges Monthly*, January–February 2006, ICTSD, Geneva.

Bridges Monthly (2007), "Thailand Continues the Battle for Cheaper Drugs," in *Bridges Monthly*, February–March 2007, ICTSD, Geneva.

Commission on Intellectual Property Rights (2002), "Integrating Intellectual Property Rights and Development Policy, Report London," <http://www.iprcommission.org/> (19 September 2013).

Correa, Carlos (2006), "Protecting Test Data for Pharmaceutical and Agrochemical Products under Free Trade Agreements," in P. Roffe, D. Vivas-Eugui and G. Tansey, eds, *Negotiating Health: Intellectual Property and Access to Essential Medicines*. London: Earthscan.

Correa, Carlos (2007), *Trade Related Aspects of Intellectual Property Rights: A Commentary on the TRIPS Agreement*. Oxford: Oxford University Press.

Correa, Carlos (2009), "The Push for Stronger Enforcement Rules: Implications for Developing Countries" in *The Global Debate on the Enforcement of Intellectual Property Rights and Developing Countries*, ICTSD, Issue Paper 22, <http://www.iprsonline.org/New%202009/fink-correa_feb2009.pdf> (19 September 2013).

Deere, Carolyn (2009), *The Implementation Game: The TRIPS Agreement and the Global Politics of Intellectual Property Reform in Developing Countries*. Oxford: Oxford University Press.

Drahos, Peter and Braithwaite, John (2002), *Information Feudalism: Who Owns the Knowledge Economy?* New York: New Press.

Dreyffus, Rochelle C. and Lowenfeld, Andreas F. (1997), "Two Achievements of the Uruguay Round: Putting TRIPS and Dispute Settlement Together," *Virginia Journal of International Law*, 37.

Dutfield, Graham (2011), "The Role of the International Union for the Protection of New Varieties of Plants (UPOV)," Intellectual Property Issue Paper No. 9, Quaker United Nations Office.

Horn, Henrik, Mavroidis, Petros, and Sapir, Andre (2010), "Beyond the WTO? An Anatomy of EU and US Preferential Trade Agreements," *The World Economy* 33 (11): 1565–88.

IFAC 3 (2003), "The U.S.–Chile Free Trade Agreement (FTA)—The Intellectual Property Provisions," Report of the Industry Functional Advisory Committee on Intellectual Property Rights for Trade Policy Matters (IFAC-3), see: http://www. ustr.gov/assets/Trade_Agreements/Bilateral/Chile_FTA/Reports/asset_upload_ file799_4936.pdf (3 October 2013).

International Federation of Pharmaceutical Manufacturers and Associations (IFPMA) (2004), "The Pharmaceutical Innovation Platform—Sustaining Better Health for Patients Worldwide," Geneva.

Jaszi, Peter (2009), "Rights in Basic Information: A general perspective," in Ricardo Melendez and Pedro Roffe, eds, *Intellectual Property and Sustainable Development: Development Agendas in a Changing World*. Cheltenham, UK: Edward Elgar.

Kur, Annette and Grosse Ruse-Khan, Henning (2011), "Enough is Enough: The Notion of Binding Ceilings in International Intellectual Property Protection," in Kur and Levin, eds, *Intellectual Property Rights in a Fair World Trade System*. Cheltenham, UK: Edward Elgar, pp. 359–407.

Lessig, Lawrence (2004), *Free Culture: How Big Media Uses Technology and the Law to Lock Down Culture and Control Creativity*. New York: The Penguin Press, available at <http://www.free-culture.cc/freecontent/> (19 September 2013).

Maskus, Keith E. and Reichman, Jerome H. (2004), "The Globalization of Private Knowledge Goods and the Privatization of Global Public Goods," *Journal of International Economic Law*, 7: 279–320.

Maskus, Keith E. and Reichman, Jerome H., eds. (2005), *International Public Goods and Transfer of Technology: Under a Globalized Intellectual Property Regime*. Cambridge: Cambridge University Press.

Okediji, Ruth (2004), "The International Copyright System: Limitations, Exceptions and Public Interest Considerations for Developing Countries," UNCTAD-ICTSD Issue Paper No. 15, Geneva.

Oxfam International (2007), "Signing Away the Future: How trade and investment agreements between rich and poor countries undermine development," Briefing Paper 101, http://www.oxfam.org/sites/www.oxfam.org/files/Signing%20Away% 20the%20Future.pdf (23 September 2013).

Reichman, Jerome H. (2006), "Compulsory Licensing of Patented Inventions: Comparing United States Law and Practice with Options under the TRIPS Agreement," Paper presented to the American Association of Law Schools Mid-Year Workshop on Intellectual Property (Vancouver, Canada, 14 June).

Reichman, Jerome H., (2006), "The International Legal Status of Undisclosed Clinical Trial Data: From Private to Public Goods?" in Roffe, Tansey, and Vivas-Eugui, eds,

Negotiating Health: Intellectual Property and Access to Medicines. London: Earthscan.

Reichman, Jerome H. (2009), "Rethinking the Role of Clinical Trial Data in International Intellectual Property Laws: The Case for a Public Goods Approach," *Marquette Intellectual Property Law Review*, 13 (1): 1ff.

Reichman, Jerome H., Dinwoodie, Graeme B., and Samuelson, Pamela (2007), "A Reverse Notice and Takedown Regime to Enable Public Good Uses of Technically Protected Copyrighted Works," Social Science Research Network (SSRN) at <http://papers.ssrn.com/sol3/papers.cfm?abstract_id=1007817> (19 September 2013).

Reichman, Jerome H. and Hasenzahl, Catherine H. (2003), "Nonvoluntary Licensing of Patented Inventions: Historical Perspective, Legal Framework under TRIPS and an Overview of the Practice in Canada and the United States of America," UNCTAD-ICTSD Issue Paper No. 5, Geneva; available at <http://www.iprsonline.org/resources/docs/Reichman%20-%20Non-voluntary%20Licensing%20-%20Blue%205.pdf> (19 September 2013).

Reichman, Jerome H. and Lewis, Tracy (2005), "Using Liability Rules to Stimulate Local Innovation in Developing Countries: Application to Traditional Knowledge," in Keith Maskus and Jerome Reichman, eds., *International Public Goods and Transfer of Technology: Under a Globalized Intellectual Property Regime*. Cambridge: Cambridge University Press.

Roca, Santiago (2009), "Demócratas, salud pública y propiedad intelectual en el APC Perú–EE.UU," *Puentes* 10.

Rocks, David (2008), "Cheap AIDS Drugs Bring Uganda Hope," *Business Week*, 14 July 2008, available at <http://www.businessweek.com/globalbiz/content/jul2008/gb20080714_399079.htm> (19 September 2013).

Roffe, Pedro (2004), "Bilateral Agreements and a TRIPS-plus World: The Chile–USA Free Trade Agreement," TRIPS Issues Paper No. 4, Quaker International Affairs Programme, Ottawa.

Roffe, Pedro (2006), "Intellectual Property Provisions in Bilateral and Regional Trade Agreements: the Challenges of Implementation,", Issue Paper No. 12, CIEL, Geneva.

Roffe, Pedro (2007), "Chile and the Priority Watch List: Some Considerations," *Bridges Monthly*, 11/2: 18, ICTSD, Geneva, available at <www.ictsd.org/monthly/> (3 October 2013).

Roffe, Pedro and Genovesi, Luis Mariano (2009), "Propuesta De Estrategia y Plan De Accioín: Implementacioín Del Acuerdo De Promocioín Comercial Con Los EEUU. En el Aírea De Propiedad Intelectual," BID. Washington DC, Informe Final, Febrero 2009.

Roffe, Pedro and Genovesi, Luis Mariano (2010), "Implementacioín y Administracioín de los Capiítulos de Propiedad Intelectual en los Acuerdos de Libre Comercio con los Estados Unidos: La Experiencia de Cuatro Paiíses de Ameírica Latina", Banco Interamericano de Desarrollo, Vicepresidencia de Sectores y Conocimiento Sector de Integracioín y Comercio, Octubre 2010.

Roffe, Pedro and Santa Cruz, Maximiliano (2006), "Los derechos de propiedad intelectual en los acuerdos de libre comercio celebrados por países de America Latina con países desarrollados," Serie Comercio Internacional, Numero 70, CEPAL, Chile.

Roffe, Pedro and Spennemann, Christoph (2006), "The impact of FTAs on public health policies and TRIPS flexibilities," *International Journal Intellectual Property Management*, 1 (1/2): 75–93.

Roffe, Pedro and Spennemann, Christoph (2010), "Canada—Patent Protection of Pharmaceutical Products" in Carlos M. Correa, ed., *Research Handbook on the Interpretation and Enforcement of Intellectual Property under WTO Rules*. Cheltenham, UK: Edward Elgar.

Roffe, Pedro and Vivas-Eugui, David (2007), "A Shift in Intellectual Property Policy in US FTAs?" in *Bridges Monthly*, 11 (5): 15–16.

Roffe, Pedro, von Braun, Johanna, and Vivas-Eugui, David (2007), "A New Generation of Regional and Bilateral Trade Agreements: Lessons from the US–CAFTA/DR," in Blouin, Chantal, Heymann, Jody, and Drager, Nick (eds.) *Trade and Health, Seeking Common Ground: Integrating Health Objectives and International Trade Policies*. Montreal: McGill, Queen's University Press.

Ruiz, Manuel (2006), "The Not-So-Bad US–Peru Side Letter on Biodiversity," *Bridges Monthly* 10: 17–19, ICTSD, Geneva.

Ryan, Michael. P. (1998) *Knowledge Diplomacy: Global Competition and the Politics of Intellectual Property*. Washington, DC: Brookings Institution Press.

Samuelson, Pamela and Scotchmer, Suzanne (2002), "The Law and Economics of Reverse Engineering," *Yale Law Journal* 111: 1575.

Santa Cruz, Maximiliano (2007), "Intellectual Property provisions in European Union Trade Agreements: implications for developing countries," ICTSD Issue Paper No. 20, ICTSD, Geneva.

Sell, Susan (2003), *Private Power, Public Law: The Globalization of Intellectual Property Rights*. Cambridge: Cambridge University Press.

Sell, Susan (2008), "The Global IP Upward Ratchet, Anti-Counterfeiting and Piracy Enforcement Efforts: The State of Play," available at <http://digitalcommons.wcl.american.edu/research/15/> (23 September 2013).

Stiglitz, Joseph (2004), "New Trade Pacts Betray the Poorest Partners," *New York Times*, 10 July.

The South Centre (2011), "IP Negotiations Monitor," Issue No. 4, March 2011.

Then, Christoph and Tippe, Ruth (2009), "The Future of Seeds and Food: Under the Growing Threat of Patents and Market Concentration," Déclaration de Berne, Greenpeace et al., April.

Thomas, John R. (2005), *Pharmaceutical Patent Law*. Washington, DC: BNA Books.

Thumm, Nikolaus (2006), "Reasonable Patent Protection with a Statutory Research Exemption," *IPR Helpdesk Bulletin*, No. 29, September–October 2006, available at <http://www.ipr-helpdesk.org> (3 October 2013).

UNCTAD (2011), *Using Intellectual Property Rights to Stimulate Pharmaceutical Production in Developing Countries: A Reference Guide*. New York and Geneva: United Nations. Available at <http://www.unctad.org/en/docs/diaepcb2009d19_en.pdf> (19 September 2013).

UNCTAD-ICTSD (2003), "Intellectual Property Rights: Implications for Development," Policy Discussion Paper, Geneva.

UNCTAD-ICTSD (2005), *Resource Book on TRIPS and Development*. Cambridge: Cambridge University Press.

UNCTAD-ICTSD (2010), "Development Dimensions of Intellectual Property in Uganda: Transfer of Technology, Access to Medicines and Textbooks," available at: <http://www.unctad.org/en/docs/diaepcb200913_en.pdf> (19 September 2013).

United States Government Accountability Office (GAO) (2007), "Intellectual Property: US Trade Policy Guidance on WTO Declaration on Access to Medicines May Need Clarification," GAO-07-1198, September, available at <http://www.gao.gov/new.items/d071198.pdf> (19 September 2013).

United States House of Representatives (2005), "Trade Agreements and Access to Medications under the Bush Administration, Committee on Government Reform," Minority Staff Special Investigations Division, prepared for Rep. Henry A. Waxman, June, Washington, DC.

UPOV (2005), "Report on the Impact of Plant Variety Protection," UPOV Publication No. 353, available at <http://www.upov.int/export/sites/upov/en/publications/pdf/353_upov_report.pdf> (29 April 11).

USTR (2010), "2010 Special 301 Report Watch List," available at <http://www.ustr.gov/webfm_send/1906> (30 April 11).

von Braun, Johanna (2008), "Do Public Policy Objectives Have a Space in the Negotiation of Bilateral Free Trade Agreements? A Study of Multi-Level Diplomacy and the Making of Intellectual Property Law," draft thesis document, unpublished, available at request with author.

Watal, Jayashree (2001), *Intellectual Property Rights in the WTO and Developing Countries*. Oxford: Oxford University Press.

Weissman, Robert (2006), "Data Protection: Options for Implementation," in Roffe, Tansey, Vivas-Eugui, eds, *Negotiating Health: Intellectual Property and Access to Medicines*. London: Earthscan.

World Trade Organization (2011), "Report by the Director-General to the General Council-Trade Negotiations Committee, Issues Related to the Extension of the Protection of Geographical Indications Provided for in Article 23 of the TRIPS Agreement to Products other than Wines and Spirits and those Related to the Relationship Between the TRIPS Agreement and the Convention on Biological Diversity," WT/GC/W/633, TN/C/W/61, 21 April.

II. Websites of main relevance

<http://www.ustr.gov/>.
<http://www.sice.oas.org/>.
<http://ec.europa.eu/trade/creating-opportunities/bilateral-relations/>.
<http://www.efta.int/free-trade.aspx>.
<http://www.wto.org/>.

16

Industrial Policy and IPR: A Knowledge Governance Approach

Leonardo Burlamaqui and Mario Cimoli

INTRODUCTION

This chapter discusses the role of IPR within the broader set of industrial policies aimed at catching up in technological production capabilities. In particular, we shall argue, the transformation of productive structures occurs together with the accumulation of knowledge and technological capabilities. Active and strong industrial policies are necessary conditions for this achievement, and only as a follow-up to these policies may IPR have some positive effect on innovation in some sectors, but not necessarily. We shall also highlight the fact that IPR regimes have remained lax in all preceding waves of industrialization, so as to allow for learning processes through imitation, reverse engineering and copying.

The chapter is organized as follows: the first section outlines the debate on industrial development and IPR. Next, we describe the common ingredients of industrial policies that succeeded in promoting accumulation of technological capabilities in advanced countries. The following section provides a general picture of the intricate context for knowledge transfer and learning in catching up economies under the TRIPS regime. The last part sketches a criterion for knowledge governance and the basis of the timing and main features of industrial policies and IPR regimes. Finally, some concluding remarks are presented.

TECHNOLOGICAL SPECIALIZATION AND IPR

Industrial development is a long-term process of accumulation of technological capabilities and diversification of knowledge. As noted in Chapter 2, catching up and transformation of productive structures entails "the development of pools of indigenous competence in various scientific and technological fields, fostering the emergence and growth of new corporate actors, and affecting directly and indirectly the allocation of resources." It results in a rupture with familiar practices from the past and an intensification of manufacturing activities (nowadays also advanced services) able to systematically learn how to generate and carry out new ways of producing new products under conditions of dynamic increasing returns (Cimoli, Dosi and Stiglitz, 2009). In short, industrial development encompasses the transformation of a country's productive structure.

Rather than being automatic or spontaneous, industrialization is shaped by policies and institutions helping to facilitate learning processes on different levels within a complex network. Firms, research institutions, governments and other organizations all take part in these processes. Although economic history does not account for any evidence of industrial development taking place without an effective underlying public policy, during the 1990s an uncritical confidence in the capacity of market forces to deliver the best outcomes prevailed internationally. It inspired major economic reforms in Latin America and other regions, leading to an important shift regarding the role of the state. The "market-friendly approach" was the ideological pillar of this process supported by international organizations, where industrial policy came to be shunned (World Bank, 1991).

It was argued that by increasing the flows of trade and technology between countries at different stages of economic development, it would naturally bring about convergence across them. Accordingly, the recipe for structural adjustment programs comprised trade liberalization, privatization of large domestic firms and deregulation of labor and financial markets (Stallings and Peres, 2000). In this view, industrial and technological policies were regarded as barriers to the well functioning of markets, hence, as sources of inefficiency, and they were kept inactive in many countries.

Strengthening intellectual property regimes emerges as a component of this free-trade fundamentalist discourse. Under the assumption that stronger IPR would lead to increased knowledge transfer, trade and foreign direct investments from the developed world towards emerging and developing countries, in the 1986–94 WTO–Uruguay Round, countries agreed on standardizing and deepening their IPR national systems (World Bank, 1991; OECD, 1997). The Trade-Related Aspects of Intellectual Property Rights (TRIPS) agreement went into force in 1995 spreading the belief that there would be a sequential order between IPR reinforcement and industrial development, where "getting IPR right"—meaning TRIPS compliance—would necessarily come first.

Graph 16.1 portrays a sort of "knowledge curve" showing the comparative technological intensity of production structures of countries and their corresponding patenting activity (Cimoli, Coriat and Primi, 2009). We order countries

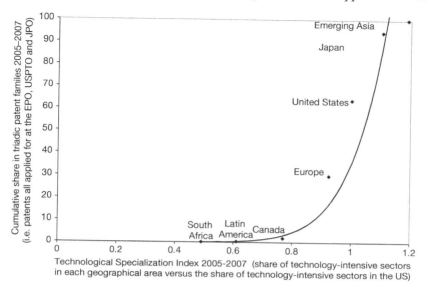

Graph 16.1 The knowledge curve: production structure specialization and patenting[12]

Source: Authors' elaboration based on OECD Patent Database, 2009; OECD Factbook, 2010; and UNIDO Database, 2010.

Note: Emerging Asia includes India, The Republic of South Korea and Singapore. Latin American countries include Argentina, Brazil, Chile and Mexico. European countries include Finland, France, Ireland, Israel, Norway, Sweden and the UK. The value for each group of countries is calculated as the simple average of the value for each member country.

along the horizontal axis pursuant to their technological specialization with respect to the United States. At the same time, for each country (or group of countries) we plot the cumulative share of patents per capita applied for at the three major world-patenting offices (the European, the Japanese and the North American one, altogether named as "triadic patents") on the vertical axis.

First, we observe a clear differentiation between industrialized countries and industrializing ones. The group led by Emerging Asia, including Japan, the United States, Europe, and Canada, show similar technological specialization, at least in terms of share of high-tech industries in total manufacturing. Regarding the share of technology-intensive sectors in total value-added manufacturing, within the same group of countries and geographical regions, the share of those sectors is near 50 per cent on average. In industrializing countries, however, it does not go beyond 30 per cent, the rest of production being concentrated in labor and natural-resource-intensive sectors. Second, in the vertical axis, the graph shows an asymmetry in patent applications. The countries which obtain higher levels of accumulation of capabilities, such as Emerging Asia, Japan, the United States and the European countries, also account for the highest shares in triadic patent family per capita. Alternately, South Africa and countries in Latin America, where natural resources or labor-intensive activities have generally had a dominant position in exports and in total value-added manufacturing, the role of patenting activity has been residual.

Emerging Asian economies have experienced an extraordinary growth in export shares of medium- and high-tech manufacturing: the percentage has tripled, rising from 18.7 per cent (average, during 1970–79) to 56.3 per cent in 2000–07. It corresponds to the most significant growth in terms of patenting applications over time: from 1970–79 to 2000–07, the annual average of patent applications per capita grew around 13,700 per cent (Table 16.1). The transformation of the productive structure and the development of technological capabilities constitute a preliminary step toward IPR reinforcement and an increase in the number of patent applications. It can be noted that the United States, which during 2000–07 is the leader in patenting per capita, is followed by Japan, Canada and Europe, which have also reached considerable levels of applications as their exports' share of medium- and high-tech manufacturing increases.

Table 16.1 confirms, and history also demonstrates, that the free-trade prescription differs largely from what happened during past industrialization experiences. Ranging from the United States to Japan to recent catching up in Emerging Asia, the accumulation of technological capabilities has taken place under lax IPR, by means of imitation, reverse engineering and copying (Chang, 2007; Reinert, 2009; Cimoli, Dosi and Stiglitz, 2009; Mowery, 2010; Odagiri et al., 2010). IPR have only become relevant as economies reach a higher degree of industrialization and, particularly, specialization in technology-intensive sectors (i.e. medium- and high-tech manufacturing).

Two different views towards accumulation of technological capabilities and IPR are illustrated in Graph 16.2. The orthodox perspective can be stylized by the solid (lower) curve, which implies that IPR reinforcement must lead to increased innovation and, therefore, to a higher accumulation of capabilities. It claims that without well-founded IPR regimes (especially patents) there would be no economic incentive for innovative activities. Patents would work as a reward, ensuring that the rent generated by the innovative firm does not vanish as others start copying the novel product. Under the guarantee (IPR) that the economic benefits will be higher than the costs of innovative processes, firms engage in innovative activities, for the purpose of developing their productive and technological capabilities as well (World Bank, 1991; OECD, 1997).

By contrast, the evolutionary approach suggests that the relationship between IPR and the process of accumulation of technological capabilities is not deterministic or linear (David, 1993; Heller and Eisenberg, 1998; Mazzoleni and Nelson, 1998; Dosi et al., 2006; Cimoli, Dosi and Stigltiz, 2009; and

Table 16.1 Importance of technology-intensive sectors (exports shares and shares in total manufactures) and IPR.[13]

Countries	Export shares of medium and high-tech manufactures in total exports (%, annual averages)				Shares of medium and high-tech manufactures in total manufacturing value added (%, annual averages)				Number of Utility Patent Applications per capita in the USPTO (annual averages, per 10.000 inhabitants)			
	1970–1979	1980–1989	1990–1999	2000–2007	1970–1979	1980–1989	1990–1999	2000–2007	1970–1979	1980–1989	1990–1999	2000–2007
South Africa	9.9	14.1	20.4	24.6	28.7	30.8	28.2	23.9	62	63	48	51
Latin America	11.3	16.1	27.5	31.4	19.7	26.3	32.3	31.0	10	8	11	18
Canada	32.4	39.6	48.0	43.0	31.4	34.4	40.8	39.1	902	948	1.523	2.580
Europe	34.7	39.2	47.3	50.9	34.8	39.2	42.8	45.0	779	867	1.064	1.703
United States	53.6	58.0	64.9	67.3	45.1	48.5	49.7	49.5	3.045	2.797	4.211	6.751
Japan	66.1	79.3	83.4	83.4	43.0	47.8	49.8	53.2	788	1.717	3.168	5.163
Emerging Asia	18.7	30.4	48.4	56.3	35.3	44.5	53.2	57.3	1	3	34	138

Source: Authors' elaboration based on U.S. Patent and Trademark Office, 2011; and UNIDO Database, 2010. The value for each group of countries is calculated as the simple average of the value for each member country.

Note: According to USPTO's glossary, "utility" patent refers to inventions or discoveries of any new, useful, and non-obvious process, machine, article of manufacture, or composition of matter, or any new and useful improvement thereof <http://www.uspto.gov/main/glossary/index.html#u> (last accessed 24 September 2013).

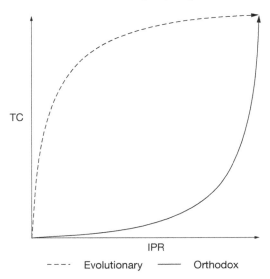

TC

IPR

- - - - Evolutionary   ——— Orthodox

Graph 16.2 Accumulation of technological capabilities and IPR: Evolutionary vs. Orthodox perspective

Note: TC-Technological Capabilities; IPR-Patenting Activity.

Chapter 2 of this book). It is intrinsically related to the productive structure, in which each sector has its own technological and innovative dynamics. Achieving a specialization pattern in technology-intensive goods, and higher innovative performance, is the result of a specific productive structure aimed to favor the accumulation of technological capabilities. It is only when their capabilities are already developed that (frontier) firms, sectors and countries invoke IPR protection as a means to preserve national dominance in specific fields, and not the other way around (Cimoli, Coriat and Primi, 2009). This perspective is described by the broken line in the Graph 16.2.

The analysis of two divergent experiences concerning the accumulation of technological capabilities and IPR—Emerging Asia and Latin America—supports our point: productive structures and the stage of industrial development *do* matter and influence the role of IPR in each country (Graph 16.3). Asia describes a virtuous process of knowledge governance, where industrial policies were enacted to benefit Asian economies, reinforce their technological capabilities and increase the share of medium- and high-tech manufacturing in their manufacturing industries. The levels of IPR protection and patenting activity were only enhanced after that.

Latin America provides an example in which enhancing IPR protection and patenting activity did not by itself lead to the accumulation of technological capabilities. Instead, the region presents a truncated development trajectory, stopping the industrialization in earlier stages. Economic structure

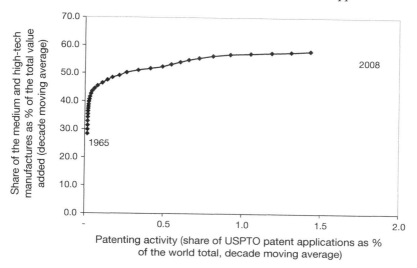

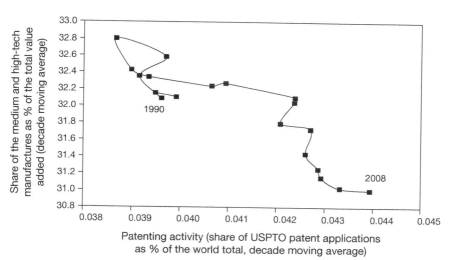

Graph 16.3 A virtuous and vicious development of the production structure and IPR

Source: Authors' elaboration based on U.S. Patent and Trademark Office 2011 and UNIDO 2010 database.

Note: Emerging Asia includes India, The Republic of South Korea and Singapore. Latin American countries include Argentina, Brazil, Chile and Mexico. The value for each group of countries is calculated as the simple average of the value for each member country.

and specialization pattern remained intensive in natural resources and raw labor. In this case, the poor accumulation of capabilities seems to be related to the lack of a favorable learning environment that enables structural change. While the Latin American pattern reflects major consequences of a history of policy shocks, recurrent crises and the characteristics of the institutional setting, these conditions were exasperated by rapid trade liberalization, appreciation of domestic currencies, large inflows of foreign capital and absence of sustained industrial policies (Cimoli and Porcile, 2011).

Inquiring *how* countries have succeeded in catching up, as is the case with several Asian economies, leads us back to the drivers of their historical processes of industrialization. Evidence shows that they all experienced relatively high degrees of state intervention (including industrial and technology policies) in order to foster structural change and to induce transformations of productive structures, but typically no IPR-enforcing ones.

"FIRST THINGS FIRST": INDUSTRIAL POLICY AND ACCUMULATION OF CAPABILITIES

Countries that succeed in getting closer to the technological frontier differ in terms of prevailing instruments and institutional arrangements but they all share some "philosophy of intervention" and the recognition, even if sometimes implicit, that the rationale for industrial policies is the need to induce the accumulation of technological capabilities. Thus, promoting learning both in the technologies already in use and in the "strategic" and "uncertain" new technologies has been at the core of state policies towards industrial development. The following are all domains where an appropriate mix of policies help countries—as historical experiences have shown—to "delock" from the past and foster novel developmental trajectories (Cimoli, Dosi and Stiglitz, 2009). Broadly speaking, there are four common elements that have sustained effective industrial policies and supported structural change in the medium term and economic development in the long run, and which relate directly or indirectly.

First, as a general rule, *emulation of production and technological activities* are the premises for the accumulation of technological capabilities and a corresponding process of industrialization. Making an effort to match or surpass others in any achievement or quality standard has been the rationale of economic policy for the past 500 years. Countries that became rich have done so through an emulation strategy,[1] i.e. developing capacities in the areas where technological progress was concentrated at that time, as is currently the case of the information and communication technologies, biotechnologies, nanotechnologies and new materials (Reinert, 2007, 2009).

In fact, countries have historically protected their industries that were using the "key" prevailing technology at that time; and they all favored the transfer of knowledge and capabilities by supporting direct interchange between "experts in art." This has been the case for the UK, which protected its manufacturing industry until reaching the frontier; the United States, which has been protecting their industry since its foundation; and more recently the Republic of South Korea, China and India. However, protectionism needs not to be "fixed" or constant: once a certain domestic industrial capacity is reached, sustaining competitiveness, especially in smaller countries, demands access to larger markets.

Second, institutional building: linking learning activities with the political economy shaping the environment where they take place, with particular emphasis on the economy's degree of openness, macroeconomic governance and competition policies. Institutions can be seen as the social construct that governs externalities, interaction among agents and complementarities between learning patterns in different activities. Under this premise, policies and other activities of "institutional engineering" simultaneously affect: (i) the technological capabilities of firms and the rate at which they actually learn; (ii) the economic signals that they face (including profitability signals and perceived opportunity costs); (iii) the ways they interact with each other and with non-market institutions (research universities, public research centers, medical institutes, space and military agencies, primary education, polytechnics, U.S.-style "land-grant colleges," state-owned holdings, public merchant banks, public "venture capitalists," public utilities, regulatory agencies, agencies governing research and production subsidies, trade controlling entities, agencies granting and controlling IPR, anti-trust or competition authorities, institutions governing bankruptcy procedures, etc).

Market incentives are often not enough, and market signals can sometimes discourage the accumulation of technological capabilities. Thus, institutions play the crucial role of creating the conditions for inducing the development of the capabilities of actors, both in the case of the emergence of new technological paradigms, and also in cases of catching up whereby no reasonable incentive structure might be sufficient to motivate private actors to surmount big technological lags.

Third, managing rents in ways that create an incentive and provide credible compulsions for learning and accumulation of technological capabilities (cf. Blankenburg and Kahn, 2009). Institutions and policies shape the incentives for learning, for which they need to have credibility and be able to impose costs and sanctions on industries and firms that fail to achieve a satisfactory rate of learning.

Fiscal policies play a key role in this regard as they may be capable of transferring rents, for example, from those sectors that benefit from the cyclical advantages in terms of trade and/or those which exploit natural resources.

However, providing a learning rent for too short a period is just as ineffective as providing it for too long. If the state does not have the credibility to withdraw a subsidy when there is underperformance, then not only will there be a short-term cost, but there will also be a permanent cost because infant industries will not be able to mature. These conditions are particularly demanding because the satisfactory period of rent allocation for learning will vary from sector to sector, and across countries depending on the initial capacities of capitalists, managers and workers.

The institutional conditions for "developmental compulsion" (via rent management strategies) can vary significantly given different internal political configurations of power. However, interestingly, "developmental rents" never included monopolistic profits stemming from IPR.

Fourth, the recognition of complementarities between learning in technologies and the development of productive capacity. Technological learning entails the generation and acquisition of novel technological knowledge. Productive capacity embodies this new knowledge.

Considerable evidence on micro-behavior highlights the mechanisms that stimulate and limit endogenous learning in developing countries, such as the use of equipment, the development of engineering skills and the adaptation of existing machines and final products to specific environmental and local conditions. Significant factors favoring this process include: the quality of human capital, the skills and technical competences of engineers and designers in the mechanical artifacts, and increasingly, the existence of managers capable of efficiently running complex organizations.

The generation of technological and production capabilities demands time and it is largely based on progressive learning in organizations. In the case of catching-up economies, the process of industrialization is also closely associated with access to global knowledge—through trade, foreign direct investment, technology licensing, copying and reverse engineering, foreign education and training, and accessing foreign technical information. These processes of adoption and adaptation of technologies, in turn, are influenced by the specific abrogative capabilities (cf. Cohen and Levinthal, 1990) already accumulated in each economy.

What past industrialization episodes tell us about the role of IPR in these processes is that *tight intellectual property regimes have not been helpful.* On the contrary, lax IPR conditions have been a constant feature. Countries have also caught up through a lot of imitation, reverse engineering and straightforward copying; this includes one-time episodes from the nineteenth century, such as the United States and Germany, and the cases of late-industrializing countries in the second half of the twentieth century like Japan, South Korea, China, India and so on (Mowery, 2010; Odagiri et al., 2010; Reinert, 2009; Cimoli, Dosi and Stiglitz, 2009).

As noted in Chapter 2, it is recognized that British patent law ("Statute of Monopolies"), for example, came into being in 1623, but it did not really take up the status of a "patent law" until its reform in 1852,[2] that is, after the Industrial Revolution. Other patent regulations emerged in France (1791), the United States (1793) and Austria (1794), but most industrialized countries established their patent laws during the first half of the nineteenth century: Russia (1812), Belgium and the Netherlands (1817), Spain (1820), Sweden (1834), Portugal (1837) and Japan (1885).[3] Yet, all those early IPR regimes were flexible and quite weak in comparison to the standards of our time: many patent systems lacked disclosure requirements, incurred very high costs in filing and processing patent applications and afforded inadequate protection to the patentees, also being lax in checking the originality of the invention (Chang, 2007), and often included strong biases in favor of domestic partners.

The principles mentioned above are the baseline for industrialization and development, and set up the conditions for a virtuous governance of knowledge. They can also be understood in terms of National Systems of Innovation (NSI) (Freeman, 1987; Nelson, 2003; Lundvall, 1992; Metcalfe, 1995; and Edquist, 1997, among others). As a variety of complementary actors, often including business firms, public training and research institutions, technical societies, trade unions, etc., are involved in all the processes of generating scientific and technological knowledge as well as technological imitation and adaptation, the virtuous interaction between them plays a key role in fostering development and diffusion of new technology processes. In such a context, the TRIPS Agreement and its adoption in national IPR regimes can be seen as an important change that distorts the NIS configuration and performance (Foray, 1993; David, 1992; Aboites and Cimoli, 2002).

As discussed at greater length in Chapter 2, the TRIPS agreement expanded patenting subject matter and raised minimum common standards of IPR protection, resulting in the standardization of national regimes. By doing so, it neglected the striking heterogeneity lying behind production structures. Moreover, after TRIPS, many countries have negotiated trade agreements with TRIPS "extra" and "plus" provisions, generally in response to foreign pressures, motivated by the primary interest in market access rather than in creating domestic capabilities. The result appears to be the increased exclusion of domestic actors from markets for knowledge and the reinforcement of the pattern of specialization in low-intensive technology sectors.

TRIPS AND BILATERAL AGREEMENTS: ANY ROOM LEFT FOR INDUSTRIALIZATION?

During the 1980s, two major facts led to radical changes in intellectual property regulation and consolidation of regimes of supranational scope.

First, both the new institutional framework and the delimitation of increased IPR standards in the United States influenced IPR reconfiguration internationally. The main modifications carried out in the United States were: (a) the expansion of the patentable frontier (Hunt, 2001); (b) the predominance of a legal stance oriented to strengthen the protection of intellectual property;[4] and (c) the transition from a model of open science to one that is more proprietary and oriented to commercialization (Dasgupta and David, 1994).[5]

Second was the incorporation of IPR in the international trade domain, culminating in the adoption of TRIPS and further bilateral agreements with stronger IPR provisions (TRIPS "extra" and "plus").[6] The determination of minimum common standards of IPR protection, minimum patent terms of twenty years from filing, expansion of patent subject matter and authorization for the importation of patented products being considered "sufficient exploitation" of a patent, are some of the novelties TRIPS introduced in national regimes (ECLAC, 2010b).

However, IPR homogenization even if it tends to reduce the spaces for policy maneuver, did not end the "implementation game" by local legal entities, as accounted by Deere (2009). Within the new international framework, there remains room for countries to push for some strategic intellectual property management. TRIPS provides some flexibilities, although scant, that may be further exploited and adapted consistently with local needs (Correa, 2000, and Chapter 14 in this volume). Let us briefly address some of them.[7]

In fact, TRIPS includes some special and differential treatment provisions and flexibilities that might be used to pursue industrial development objectives, such as the compulsory license provision (Art. 31), parallel imports or "exceptions to rights conferred" (Art. 30), among others. Table 16.2 sketches these possibilities outlining a taxonomy, as follows:

Table 16.2 SDT, flexibilities, and self-determination provisions: A taxonomy of TRIPS' (effective) degrees of freedom for policies

Provision	Article of reference	(Effective) Policy Spaces
Special and Differential Treatment (SDT)		
Transitional Periods	TRIPS, art. 65, par. 2–5 Developing countries are entitled to delay for a given period the date of application of (given) provisions of the agreement.	The Doha Declaration on TRIPS Agreement and Public Health extended the window for LDC's even beyond the original TRIPS allowance.
	TRIPS, art. 66.1 Least developing countries (LDCs) are entitled to delay for a period of 10 years the application of TRIPS provisions, other than	

	articles 3, 4 and 5. Upon motivated request by a LDC, the Council for TRIPS may accord extensions of this period.	
Technical and Financial Cooperation	TRIPS, art. 67 On request and on mutually agreed terms and conditions, developed countries shall provide technical and financial cooperation to developing and LDCs.	Non-legally binding provision
Technology Transfer	TRIPS, art. 66.2 Developed countries should provide incentives to enterprises and institutions in their territory to promote and encourage technology transfer to LDCs. **Doha Declaration, art.7** Reaffirms the commitment of developed countries to provide incentives to promote and encourage technology transfer.	Non-legally binding provision
Flexibilities		
Compulsory Licensing (CL)	TRIPS, art. 31 Governments are allowed to authorize a party other than the holder of a patent on an invention to use that invention without the consent of the patent holder, on the condition that efforts have been made to obtain the authorization from the right holder on reasonable commercial terms within a reasonable period of time. In case of national emergency, other circumstances of extreme urgency and public non-commercial use the requirement of prior efforts does not apply.	Only countries with a certain production and technological capacity may make use of this provision. If the country is credible (in terms of industrial capacities, market structure and public policy) this instrument can be used as a negotiation threat. Strong political will and commitment is necessary. TRIPS does not stipulate the grounds upon which a compulsory license should be granted. Thus member countries can make provisions for CL on any ground. TRIPS only mandates certain procedural prerequisites such as voluntary negotiation prior to the grant of a license etc. In the case of national emergencies, or if the CL is being granted to remedy an anticompetitive practice, then these prerequisites need not be met. If the country in

(Continued)

Table 16.2 Continued

Provision	Article of reference	(Effective) Policy Spaces
		question lacks the necessary manufacturing and technological capacities, the Doha declaration and its 2003 implementation provide for a CL that would enable export from countries that have such manufacturing capabilities.
Exhaustion (national, regional and international exhaustion) (Parallel Imports)	TRIPS, art. 6 For the purposes of dispute settlement under this Agreement, subject to the provisions of art. 3 and 4, nothing in this Agreement shall be used to address the issue of the exhaustion of IPRs. This article addresses the exhaustion of IPRs that is crucial in international trade because it addresses the point at which the IPR ceases. This provision implicitly addresses the issue of parallel imports (i.e. products placed on the market in one country and subsequently imported into a second country without the permission of the owner of the intellectual property right in the second country).	The only obligations under the TRIPS Agreement that can be used by one country to challenge another country's position on parallel imports are those relating to national treatment (Article 3) and most-favored-nation treatment (Article 4). The exhaustion regime of IPRs depends on national laws.
Exceptions to rights conferred	TRIPS, art. 30 Members may provide limited exceptions to exclusive rights conferred by a patent, provided that such exceptions do not unreasonably conflict with a normal exploitation of the patent and do not unreasonably prejudice the legitimate interests of the patent owner, taking account of the legitimate interests of third parties.	National law can introduce exceptions according to art. 30.
Bolar Exception	The Bolar exception was first introduced in the U.S. Drug Price Competition and Patent Term Restoration Act in 1984 following the court ruling Roche vs. Bolar	According to a WTO dispute settlement in April 2000 Canadian law conforms to TRIPS in allowing manufacturers to exploit this exception. (WTO case

Pharmaceuticals. The U.S. law enables testing to establish bioequivalency of generic drugs before patent expiration. This mechanisms allows generic producers to place their products on the market when the original patent expires

"Canada: Patent Protection for Pharmaceutical Products"). This exception has been explicitly adopted by Canada, Australia, Israel, Argentina and Thailand. In the EU it has been used case by case to solve disputes. In the Canadian case, the WTO upheld the "Bolar" provision but struck down the "stockpiling" provision, stating that this contravened article 30.

Source: Cimoli, Coriat and Primi (2009).

Special and Differential Treatment provisions (SDT) confer specific rights to developing and least developed countries (LDC) in the framework of TRIPS, recognizing their status as "developing economies." However, SDT do not eliminate the one-size-fits-all nature of the agreement: they simply grant a time lag for implementing the homogeneous minimum standards established by TRIPS itself. SDT do not confer the right to implement an intellectual property regime in accordance with the stage of development of the economy, but recognize the right to benefit from transitional periods for the implementation of the agreement (transitional periods, arts. 65 and 66).

Additionally, according to Article 31, governments may issue a compulsory license and authorize a party other than the patent holder of an invention to make use of it even without the consent of the patent holder. This would be the case when the party has unsuccessfully tried to obtain such a license on "reasonable commercial terms within a reasonable period of time." The conditions under which it is possible to issue a compulsory license restrict the potential use of this flexibility, being difficult to fulfill and subject to subjective interpretation of "reasonable." However, the quite restrictive requirement does not apply in the cases of national emergencies, extreme urgency and public non-commercial use, though the right holder shall be notified as soon as possible.

Parallel imports, in turn, address the different exhaustion regimes of patent protection (national, regional or international), covering situations when products are purchased in one market and subsequently sold in a second market without the authorization of the right holder. Thus, prior to a patent's expiration, countries can take advantage of products manufactured under license in other countries or for other markets and benefit from international price differentials.

With regards to the "exceptions to rights conferred," Article 30 establishes that member countries "may provide limited exceptions to the exclusive rights

conferred by a patent, provided that such exceptions do not unreasonably conflict with a normal exploitation of the patent and do not unreasonably
prejudice the legitimate interests of the patent owner, taking into account of
the legitimate interests of third parties." This provision recognizes the possibility to grant limited exceptions to the rights conferred by a patent, including
the "Bolar" exception, also known as "early working." It gives permission to
generic producers to import, manufacture and carry out experiments on
patented products before the patent expires. In other words, it allows firms
to carry out experimental R&D to produce generic products without violating
the patent.

However, legal feasibility and awareness of the existence of these flexibilities
in the implementation of TRIPS are not sufficient for countries to take
advantage of them. The lack of ability to exploit them is also associated with
the lack of accumulation of technological capabilities. If IPR are enforced
where productive and technological capabilities are weak and industrial policies are absent, countries have no bargaining power, and little capacity to
recur to TRIPS flexibilities. At the same time, if these policy spaces remain
unexplored and no active industrial policies are effectively implemented,
the adoption of stronger IPR regimes will make the process of creation of
capabilities even more difficult.

For example SDT provisions concerning technical and financial cooperation and technology transfer, which open a window of opportunity for
developing and least developed countries, contain minimal effectiveness because they are not legally binding and their implementation is dependent on
each country's decision to execute them. Parallel imports are also scantly used
by developing countries, in part due to the lack of qualified technical personnel
and institutional apparatus needed to carry out this practice. The use of the
Bolar exception, too, requires certain thresholds of accumulated technological
capabilities and public and private incentives to engage in research efforts,
without which a demand for this flexibility is not generated. Moreover, a
sufficient degree of institutional organization and ability in IPR management
is also required, together with the integration of (anti-) IPR policies into
national development strategies (CIPR, 2002; ECLAC, 2010a).

The process of reconfiguration of IPR regulation was consistent with a
period of liberalization and market-friendly reforms. In the context of inter-
ruption of industrialization and destruction of existent capabilities, the adoption of international agreements standardizing and strengthening IPR systems
in fact forged a more complex and restrictive environment for knowledge
transfer, imitation, copying and thus for domestic learning and innovation.

All this notwithstanding, recent trade negotiations resulted in the incorporation of IPR standards which are even higher than those agreed under
TRIPS, and a reduction of the room for policymaking for the implementation
of some TRIPS flexibilities. It has happened in all bilateral agreements—either

Free Trade Agreements (FTAs) or Bilateral Investment Treaties (BITs)—signed between the United States and developing economies after TRIPS ratification (Fink and Reichenmiller, 2005; and Chapter 15 in this volume).

This occurs through the application of the "most favored nation clause," which stipulates that any concession or enhanced standard brought into a bilateral treaty should be automatically extended to the nationals (holders of IPR) of other member states of the WTO that are not party to these agreements (Moncayo, 2006). A few examples of FTAs and BITs recently signed by the United States lately, which incorporate such higher IPR standards, are the following: Bahrain (FTA signed in 2004), Jordan (2000), DR–CAFTA (Dominican Republic–Central America Free Trade Agreement, 2004), Australia (2004), Chile (2003), Morocco (2004), Singapore (2003), Peru, Colombia and Panama (2006).

Some of the common elements of these agreements engender IP-strengthening objectives (Moncayo, 2006): (i) the extension of patent terms as a way to "compensate" for any delays in the granting of a patent (usually five extra years); (ii) the provision of a grace period before patent application, aiming to avoid publicizing a discovery before patent filing so as to erode its novelty (in the United States it covers 12 months preceding the application); (iii) expanding the frontiers of patenting subject matter and strengthening the rights of patent holders;[8] (iv) the reduction of the grounds on which a patent can be revoked by the States; and (v) in some cases, the prohibition of parallel imports and limitation of the scope of compulsory license. All these new regulations reduce the possibility of maneuvering around TRIPS implementation.

In addition, stronger IPR have been accompanied by an increased effort from the developed countries to ensure compliance with the new standards. The United States, for example, engaged in a worldwide campaign against IPR violations. This occurs under the provisions of Section 301 of the 1974 Trade Act, further amended in 1984 and 1988, which allows the United States "to impose trade sanctions against foreign countries that maintain acts, policies and practices that violate, or deny US rights or benefits under trade agreements, or are unjustifiable, unreasonable or discriminatory and burden or restrict US commerce," including IPR violations. For this purpose, the Special 301 Report (also known as "the watch list")—an annual review of the global state of IPR protection and enforcement conducted by the Office of the United States Trade Representative (USTR)—was established (Coriat, 2000).

This more restricted IPR environment has not facilitated knowledge flows towards countries aiming at catching up. On the contrary, the lack of active and sustained industrial policies in combination with strict IPR norms concurred to magnify the obstacles for the accumulation of technological capabilities. Other things being equal, a greater exclusion from the "markets for knowledge" and the "reinforcement of the pattern of specialization in low technology intensive sectors" has been the outcome stemming from the new institutional setting (Cimoli, Coriat and Primi, 2009).

A "TIME CONSISTENT" KNOWLEDGE APPROACH

To repeat, the transformation of production and technological capabilities by catching-up countries encompasses processes of accumulation and of knowledge in turn shaped by a set of complementary public policies inspired by what we shall call a *knowledge governance approach*.

Broadly speaking, such a knowledge-centered perspective to industrial development and IPR contains few main elements. In general, it calls for active and selective industrial policies, as means to promote and support the general argumentation of capabilities. More specifically, these policies historically happened to involve, to different degrees and according to specific local conditions, the following elements consistent with the ingredients we have previously identified in industrialization processes: (i) state ownership; (ii) selective credit allocation; (iii) favorable tax treatment to selective industries; (iv) restrictions on foreign investment; (v) local context requirements; (vi) special IPR regimes; (vii) government procurement; and (viii) promotion of large domestic firms (Cimoli, Dosi and Stiglitz, 2009).[9]

It should also comprise a variety of institutions to be created, strengthened and linked—governing, for example, scientific and technological research, education, and competition. For this purpose, obtaining better calibration of IPR regimes is required as well, to make them conducive to knowledge transfer and learning processes, particularly in those sectors or technologies where they proved to be an obstacle.

The necessity of ensuring conditions that make learning processes through imitation possible is a central knowledge governance task. As it has already been remarked, imitation, copying and reverse engineering are crucial, especially if adopted in the early stages of catching up: improved calibration of IPR regimes could bring major effects at this point. Since the importance of IPR is sector- and technology-specific, it is precisely in the cases where IPR act as effective appropriation mechanisms that they should be managed to allow domestic learning processes.

Figure 16.1 illustrates the distinct outcomes delivered by varying combinations of industrial policies and IPR regimes. A virtuous knowledge governance corresponds to the quadrant number I, where all past and recent successful industrialization episodes are located. They have been achieved by means of active industrial policies along with lax IPR regimes, as is the case for Asia and industrialized countries like the United States, England, Germany, etc.

Most countries, as is the case in Latin America, could fit in the other spaces. For example, in the opposite direction (quadrant number III), where industrial policy is kept inactive, adopted passively or with pure horizontal incentives in combination with tighter intellectual property regimes, the processes of accumulation of knowledge and technological capabilities do not occur in a

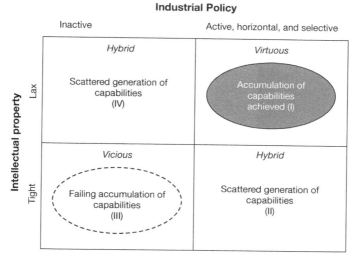

Figure 16.1 The "intensity" and "time consistency" of knowledge governance

sustained manner. This has been typically the case for Central America after TRIPS enforcement, where some neglect of industrial policies associated with increased IPR standards has helped to perpetrate a truncated industrialization process and reinforce the specialization pattern in goods with low technology intensity ("vicious"). In turn, a dispersed generation of technological capabilities and localized in few specific economic fields ("scattered") might occur in those situations where either a mix of too tight intellectual property regimes could limit the scope of active, horizontal and selective industrial policies (quadrant II), or passive industrial policy together with lax IPR regimes take place (quadrant IV). Both correspond to a hybrid scheme of governance.

Can improved competition (and anti-trust) policies be a tool for helping to counterbalance the effects of strong IPR? That might be the case in sectors and technologies where IPR performs as a barrier to knowledge access that is essential for competitors. In this sense, either resorting to an "essential facility" doctrine[10] or getting inspiration on U.S. courts longstanding tradition of applying a "patent misuse" doctrine (as mentioned in Chapter 12 of this volume), it would require improvement of competition-policy institutions and better connection with IPR domains. Finally, competition policy could also be useful in addressing practices of strategic patenting—the proliferating business strategy of applying for patents that firms have no intention of using or exploiting, with the exclusive aim of preventing others from taking profit from the innovation (Varian, Farrel and Shapiro, 2004)[11]—which again may also hinder the diffusion of knowledge and innovation. However, it generally holds that "competitive compensation" may, in general, be partial at best.

CONCLUDING REMARKS

The increasingly binding environment for knowledge transfer entails the urgency of rethinking intellectual property in relation to development strategies, and reframing both into a knowledge governance approach. Emphasis should be given to both industrial policies for generating technological and production capabilities, and strategic (largely *anti-*) IPR management to uphold the industrial development effort. These would form the basic ingredients of a "virtuous" path for development.

Past and recent experiences of industrialization followed this "virtuous" pathway. In terms of time sequencing, first came active industrial policies which helped the achievement of production and innovation capabilities and the diffusion of knowledge through the different sectors. Only later on did industrializing countries adopt reinforced IPR regimes.

The current scenario has increasingly shifted into a more constraining one for today's catching-up economies, thus also constraining industrial development strategies. Under the influence of the trade liberalization recommendations, many developing countries implemented economic reforms encompassing obliteration of industrial policies and strengthened IPR regimes. The adoption of the TRIPS agreement resulted in expanded patenting subject matter, raised minimum common standards of IPR protection and standardized national regimes. And, it neglected the striking heterogeneity lying behind production structures. Moreover, many countries have negotiated trade agreements with TRIPS "extra" and "plus" provisions, in part reflecting their primary interest in market access rather than in creating capabilities. Some of the implications have been more *exclusion* from markets for knowledge. In other words, the "market-friendly" measures turned to be a "vicious" path.

Even if there were also intermediary (or "hybrid") situations in which countries obtained a limited and scarce generation of capabilities and diffusion of knowledge, as a rule, trade liberalization reforms and the TRIPS recommendations did not deliver industrialization to the developing world. Rather, industrial development demands a better calibration of industrial policies and IPR management, both in terms of "intensity" and "time consistency."

NOTES

1. The strategy of trying to do what leading economies are doing also takes place at the micro level, where learning "how" to do it becomes of major relevance. As for products, it first involves achieving the corresponding manufacturing abilities which allows for efficacy in the process of reproduction of the characteristics and properties of that same product. After that, the aim becomes profitability and efficiency, measured in terms of costs or time per unit produced.

2. See MacLeod, 1988 and H.-J. Chang, 2007.
3. For a historical review on the emergence of patent law, see Penrose, 1951.
4. See the studies by Adelman, 1987; Merges, 1992; Mazzoleni and Nelson, 1998; Jaffe, 2000; Hall and Ziedonis, 2001; Cohen and Lemely, 2001; Gallini, 2002; Bessen and Hunt, 2004; Hall, 2003; Graham and Mowery, 2003.
5. For a discussion on the possible effects of the adoption of the Bayh-Dole paradigm in developing countries, see Chapter 6 in this volume.
6. A treaty or agreement with TRIPS-plus provisions means that: (i) State's governments are obliged to implement an enhanced standard of IPR protection that exceeds the level of protection required by TRIPS, or (ii) it is removed as an option, possibility or flexibility allowed by the TRIPS Agreement, namely the possibility, for example, that national legislature establishes the proper interaction of TRIPS standards with other multilateral conventions (such as the Convention on Biodiversity) or regulate and define concepts that are not defined in the TRIPS Agreement. However, the Free Trade Agreements (FTAs) also have clauses that can be considered "TRIPS-extra" when they include a new area, category or institution concerning IPR, which is not contemplated or required by TRIPS (Moncayo, 2006).
7. For a more detailed analysis see Chapter 14 in this volume. See also Fink and Reichenmiler, 2005; Abbott, 2006; and Moncayo, 2006, among others.
8. For example, allowing the patenting of business methods and software, as well as limiting the exclusions so as to facilitate the patenting of new or second indications.
9. Beyond these traditional mechanisms, and in response to the increasingly binding WTO environment, innovation in the design of industrial policy instruments is also desirable. Tax incentives, non-refundable grants, subsidized credits, and subventions, which are not forbidden under WTO rules when intended to promote firms' R&D and innovation are some of the fields to explore in the future.
10. "Any input which is deemed necessary for all industry participants to operate in a given industry and which is not easily duplicated might be seen as an *essential facility*" (Motta, 2004: 66), therefore engendering the obligation to make the facility available to competitors.
11. See also Landes and Posner, 2003.
12. This is an updated version of a graph elaborated by Cimoli, Coriat, and Primi (2009).
13. We take patent applications at the United States Patent Office (USPTO) considering its strategic importance in terms of the market it serves and because it is where the majority of technology-related transactions take place. Additionally, the data series available cover a wider period of time that other patent databases.

REFERENCES

Abbott, F.M. (2006), "Intellectual Property Provisions of Bilateral and Regional Trade Agreements of the United States in the Light of U.S. Federal Law," UNCTAD-ICTSD, issue paper 12 <http://ictsd.org/i/publications/11732/> (last accessed 16 September 2013).

Aboites, J. and Cimoli, M. (2002), "Intellectual Property Rights and National Innovation Systems: Some Lessons from the Mexican Experience," *Revue d' Economie Industrielle*, 99: 215–33.

Adelman, M.J. (1987), "The New World of Patents Created by the Court of Appeals for the Federal Circuit," *Journal of Law Reform*, 20: 979–1007.

Bessen, J. and Hunt, R.M. (2004), "An Empirical Look at Software Patents," WP, 03/17R, Federal Reserve Bank of Philadelphia, available at <http://papers.ssrn.com/sol3/papers.cfm?abstract_id=461701> (last accessed 24 September 2013).

Blankenburg, S. and Khan, M. (2009), "The Political Economy of Industrial Policy in Asia and Latin America," in M. Cimoli, G. Dosi, and J.E. Stiglitz, eds, *Industrial Policy and Development: The Political Economy of Capabilities Accumulation*. Oxford: Oxford University Press.

Cimoli, M., Coriat, B., and Primi, A. (2009), "Intellectual Property and Industrial Policy: A Critical Assessment," in M. Cimoli, G. Dosi, and J. Stiglitz, eds, *Industrial Policy and Development*. Oxford: Oxford University Press.

Cimoli, M., Dosi, G., and Stiglitz, J.E. (2009), "The Political Economy of Capabilities Accumulation: The Past and Future of Policies for Industrial Development" (Preface), in M. Cimoli, G. Dosi, and J. Stiglitz, eds, *The Political Economy of Capabilities Accumulation: The Past and Future of Policies for Industrial Development*. Oxford: Oxford University Press.

Cimoli, M. and Porcile, G. (2011), "Learning, Technological Capabilities and Structural Dynamics," in J.A. Ocampo and J. Ros, eds, *The Oxford Handbook of Latin American Economies*. Oxford: Oxford University Press.

Chang, H.-J. (2007), *Kicking Away the Ladder: Development Strategy in Historical Perspective*. London: Anthem Press.

Cohen, J.E. and Lemely, M.A. (2001), "Patent Scope and Innovation in the Software Industry," *Columbia Law Review*, 89 (1): 1–57.

Cohen, W. and Levinthal, D. (1990), "Absorptive Capacity: A New Perspective on Learning and Innovation," *Administrative Science Quarterly*, 35: 128–52.

Coriat B. (2000), "Entre Politique de la Concurrence et Politique Commerciale: quelle place pour la politique industrielle de l'Union Européenne" in Lorenzi and Cohen, eds, *Les politiques Industrielles Européennes*. Paris: Cahiers du Conseil d'Analyse Economique, 1[ier] Ministre, La Documentation Française.

Correa, C. (2000), *Intellectual Property Rights, the WTO and Developing Countries: The TRIPS Agreement and Policy Options*. London: Zed Books.

Dasgupta, P. and David, P.A. (1994), "Toward a New Economics of Science," *Research Policy* 23 (5): 487–521.

David, P.A. (1992), "Knowledge, Property and the System Dynamics of Technological Change," World Bank Annual Conference on Development Economics, Washington, DC.

David, P.A. (1993), "Intellectual Property Institutions and the Panda's Thumb: Patents, Copyrights and Trade Secrets in Economic Theory and History," in M. B. Wallerstein, M.E. Mogee, and R.A. Schoen, eds, *Global Dimensions of Intellectual Property Rights in Science and Technology*. Washington, DC: National Academy Press.

Deere, C. (2009), *The Implementation Game*. Oxford: Oxford University Press.

Dosi, G., Marengo, L., and Pasquali, C. (2006), "How Much Should Society Fuel the Greed of Innovators? On the Relations between Appropriability, Opportunities and the Rates of Innovation," available at <http://www.academia.edu/1433221/How_much_should_society_fuel_the_greed_of_innovators_On_the_relations_between_appropriability_opportunities_and_rates_of_innovation> (accessed 17 October 2013).

Dosi, G., Pavitt, K., and Soete, L. (1990), *The Economics of Technical Change and International Trade*. London and New York: Harvester Wheatsheaf Press/New York University Press.

ECLAC (2008), "Structural Change and Productivity Growth, 20 Years Later: Old Problems, New Opportunities Santiago," LC/G.2367(SES.32/3), May 2008.

ECLAC (2010a), "Time for Equality: Closing Gaps, Opening Trails," Santiago, LC/G.2432(SES.33/3), May 2010.

ECLAC-SEGIB (2010b), *Innovar para crecer: desafíos y oportunidades para el desarrollo sostenible e inclusivo en Iberoamerica*. Santiago de Chile: UN.

Edquist, C (1997), *Systems of Innovation: Technologies, Institutions and Organizations*. London: Pinter.

Fink, C. and Reichenmiller, P. (2005), "Tightening TRIPS: The Intellectual Property Provisions of Recent US Free Trade Agreements," World Bank Trade Note, No. 20, February 2005.

Foray, D. (1993), "Feasibility of a Single Regime of Intellectual Property Rights," in H. Humbert, ed., *The Impact of Globalization of Europe's Firms and Industries*. London and New York: Pinter.

Freeman, C. (1987), *Technology Policy and Economic Performance: Lessons from Japan*. London: Pinter.

Gallini, N. (2002), "The Economics of Patents: Lessons from the Recent US Patent Reform," *Journal of Economic Perspectives*, 16: 131–54.

Graham, S. and Mowery, D.C. (2003), "Intellectual Property Protection in the US Software Industry," in W.M. Cohen and S. Merrill, eds., *Patents in the Knowledge Based Economy*. Washington, DC: National Academic Press.

Hall, B.H. (2003), "Business Methods Patents, Innovation and Policy," Economics Department, University of California Berkeley, Working Paper E03–331.

Hall, B.H. and Ziedonis, R.H. (2001), "The Patent Paradox Revisited: An Empirical Study of Patenting in the US Semiconductor Industry, 1979–1995," *RAND Journal of Economics*, 32: 101–28.

Heller, M.A. and Eisenberg, R.S. (1998), "Can Patents Deter Innovation? The Anti-Commons in Biomedical Research," *Science*, 280: 698–701.

Hunt, R.M. (2001), "You Can Patent That? Are Patents on Computer Programs and Business Methods Good for the New Economy?" *Business Review*, Q1, 2001, Federal Reserve Bank of Philadelphia.

Jaffe B.J. (2000), "The US Patent System in Transition: Policy Innovation and the Innovation Process," *Research Policy*, 29: 531–57.

Landes, D. (1969), *The Unbound Prometheus*. Cambridge: Cambridge University Press.

Landes, W. and Posner, R. (2003), *The Economic Structure of Intellectual Property Law*. Cambridge, MA: Belknap Press.

Lundvall, B.-A. (1992), *National Systems of Innovation: Towards a Theory of Innovation and Interactive Learning*. London: Pinter.

MacLeod, C. (1988), *Inventing the Industrial Revolution: The English Patent System 1660–1800*. Cambridge: Cambridge University Press.

Maskus, Keith E. (2004), "Integrating Intellectual Property Rights and Development Policy: Report of the Commission on Intellectual Property Rights," *Journal of International Economics*, 62 (1): 237–9.

Mazzoleni, R. and Nelson, R. (1998), "The Benefits and Costs of Strong Patent Protection: A Contribution to the Current Debate," *Research Policy*, 27: 273–84.

Merges, R.P. (1992), *Patent Law and Policy*. Charlottesville, VA: Michie Company.

Metcalfe, J.S. (1995), "Technology Systems and Technology Policy in an Evolutionary Frame-Work," *Cambridge Journal of Economics*, 19: 25–46.

Moncayo, A. (2006), "Bilateralismo y multilateralismo en materia de patentes de invención: una interacción compleja," in *Sistemas de Propiedad Intelectual y Gestión Tecnológica en Economías Abiertas: Una Visión Estratégica para América Latina y el Caribe*. Estudio OMPI-CEPAL.

Motta, M. (2004), *Competition Policy: Theory and Practice*. Cambridge: Cambridge University Press.

Mowery, D.C. (2010), "IPR and US Economic Catch-Up" in Odagiri et al., eds, *Intellectual Property Rights, Development, and Catch Up*. Oxford: Oxford University Press.

Nelson, R.R. (2003) "The Market Economy and the Scientific Commons," LEM Working Paper Series, 2003/24.

Odagiri, H., Goto, A., Sunami, A., Nelson, R.R. (eds.) (2010), *Intellectual Property Rights, Development, and Catch Up: An International Comparative Study*. Oxford: Oxford University Press.

OECD (1997), "Patents and Innovation in the International Context," January 1997, available at <http://www.oecd.org/dataoecd/35/13/2101372.pdf> (last accessed 24 September 2013).

Penrose, E.T. (1951), *The Economics of the International Patent System*. Baltimore, MA: Johns Hopkins University Press.

Peres, W. and Primi, A. (2009), "Theory and Practice of Industrial Policy: Evidence from the Latin American Experience," Santiago, Chile: ECLAC-UN.

Peres, W. and Stallings, B. (2000), *Growth, Employment and Equity*. Washington, DC: Brookings Institute Press.

Reinert, E.S. (2007), *How Rich Countries Got Rich . . . and Why Poor Countries Stay Poor*. London: Constable.

Reinert, E.S. (2009), "Emulation v. Comparative Advantage: Competing and Complementary Principles in the History of Economic Policy," in M. Cimoli, G. Dosi, and J.E. Stiglitz, eds, *The Political Economy of Capabilities Accumulation: The Past and Future of Policies for Industrial Development*. Oxford: Oxford University Press.

Stallings, B. and Wilson, P. (2000), *Crecimiento, empleo y equidad: el impacto de las reformas económicas en América Latina y el Caribe*. Santiago: Fondo de Cultura Económica: CEPAL.

Varian, H., Farrel, J., and Shapiro, C. (2004), *The Economics of Information Technology*. Cambridge: Cambridge University Press.

World Bank (1991), *World Development Report 1991: The Challenge of Development*. New York: Oxford University Press and The World Bank.

Part V

Conclusion

17

The Role of Intellectual Property Rights in Developing Countries: Some Conclusions

Mario Cimoli, Giovanni Dosi, Keith E. Maskus, Ruth L. Okediji, Jerome H. Reichman, and Joseph E. Stiglitz

It is not a surprise that, as the global economy has increasingly become based on knowledge and innovation, the question of intellectual property rights has become central in the global economics debate.

It is usually suggested that because the advanced industrial countries have a comparative advantage in innovation and knowledge production (a by-product of their relatively more effective and advanced "national systems of innovation"), a tough IPR regime is in their interests. It would also ensure a flow of funds—mostly in the form of patent and copyright royalties—from the developing to developed countries, to replace the lost revenue from previous exports of traditional manufacturing products that are now mostly imported from developing countries.

But such an interpretation is incomplete, if not wrong, for several reasons. First, a "tough" IPR regime may not even be in the interests of the advanced countries; as explained in Chapter 1, all innovations build on previous innovations, and by making the fruits of existing innovations less accessible, the progress of science and technology may be inhibited. Indeed, with modern innovations requiring a myriad of ideas and access to a myriad of patents, holdups and patent thickets have become a significant problem, and the patent system is increasingly seen as an impediment to scientific progress.

Second, even the advanced industrial countries have an interest in the rapid growth of *all* other countries: growth in emerging markets and developing countries can be complementary to that of the advanced countries. Indeed, in recent years, emerging markets and developing countries have been the engine of global economic growth. A *better* IPR regime—which fosters more innovation and more access to knowledge—would facilitate growth in developing countries, reducing the knowledge gap, which remains a critical distinction between developed and developing countries.

Third, everyone has an interest in the promotion of global public goods—in doing something, for instance, about global warming. For example, concerns about having to pay large rents to developed countries that control access to emission-reducing technologies is one important impediment to reaching a global climate accord. At the same time, without some incentives to undertake risky innovation, there may be fewer emission-reducing technologies available.[1]

Finally, we have a humanitarian interest in avoiding unnecessary suffering (either for lack of food or healthcare or the like. This means at the very least there should be access to life-saving medicines and better seeds and agricultural technologies. The IPR system has to be designed to facilitate both innovation and access, without imposing unnecessary impediments, as the current system does.

It is not just a matter of "strong" vs. "weak" rights, but the appropriate design of the IPR regime. The current IPR regime may serve a few industries well (such as pharmaceuticals), but the extent to which it serves the interests of other industries or society as a whole is open to question. The authors of the papers in this volume differ in how each might design the "optimal" IPR regime—some putting more emphasis on the role of IPRs in providing incentives, others on the role of IPRs in inhibiting the free flow of knowledge. Several papers argue for a much more circumscribed IPR regime—indeed, some contributions to this book seem to ask whether we need IPRs at all— while others do not object too much to a "tough" regime although most would agree that there is considerable room for improvement in dominant IPR regimes.[2] Those who are most critical of IPRs find it hard to see any compelling evidence that IPRs have been a key driver of the capitalist search for innovation. Rather, they see *IPRs as an obstacle to further innovation,* as Boldrin and Levine (2008b) suggest was the case with Watt's stream engine patents. There is indeed a long list of cases in which similar obstacles have been reported, from patents on automobiles to those on the OncoMouse (see Chapters 1 and 2). These scholars believe that even without IPRs, there is sufficient ability for innovators to appropriate returns on investment—for example through secrecy, first mover advantages, and *tacit knowledge—* for innovation to be adequately incentivized. On that premise, IPRs might become an *obstacle to innovation even in "frontier" countries,* or at the very least give rise to unnecessary patent rents. As is often the case, rent-seeking can have adverse effects on both economic efficiency and distribution.[3]

Even if some IPRs remain desirable in some form, the current system is not designed to maximize welfare-enhancing innovations, even in developed countries. It may, for instance, result in excessive *"protection" of intellectual property,* as a result, for instance, of the enclosure of the knowledge commons. This critique applies to patents and, even more so, to copyrights and certain other forms of IPR protection: the notion that a copyright royalty paid on, say, a book up to 70 years after the death of the author would be an incentive to the creativity of its writer is quite debatable, particularly where such term extensions are granted retroactively.

Still, while the various contributors to this volume might differ in what they would see as an ideal IPR regime, we think they all would agree on four propositions: (1) an IPR regime that is well-suited for advanced industrial countries may not be so well-suited for developing countries; the trade-offs between the benefits from improved incentives and the benefits of greater access to knowledge may differ markedly; (2) IPRs are only one component of a country's innovation system, and at least in many countries there has been excessive emphasis on IPRs relative to other ways of supporting, funding, and incentivizing innovation; (3) there are ways to reform IPR regimes, and more broadly the innovation system, in both advanced countries and developing countries that would enhance innovation together with societal welfare. Moreover (4), the adverse consequences for welfare and growth generated by the current IPR regime (including the TRIPS Agreement) are worse for the developing than for the developed countries; the existing regime poses formidable impediments to closing the knowledge gap, which is so essential to developmental success.

The policy prescriptions in this book reflect the variety of views summarized above. They address two different sets of questions.

The first set asks whether one should seek to change the current international IPR regime (basically TRIPS and "TRIPS-plus" standards), and if so, in which directions. The following is a short list of some proposed reforms to IPRs in general.

SOME MODEST PROPOSALS FOR REFORM

1. Push forward the boundaries of Open Science

Private appropriation of basic scientific discoveries in general, and those publicly financed in particular, is bad for science and in the long-term also for industry: it tends to slow down the drive along Vannevar Bush's (1945) *Endless Frontier* of Open Science. As So et al. argue in this volume, one should guarantee at the very least that the fruits of government-funded research be made available on the basis of non-exclusive licensing, that government should retain use rights, and that end products stemming from publicly funded research should be made affordable to the public at large.

We are arguing, in other words, for a rethinking of the ways in which the Bayh-Dole Act put the United States (followed by other countries and piece-meal in the European Union, even if not by a single piece of legislation like in the United States[4]) on the path of allowing universities to appropriate for themselves the fruits of government-funded research. As universities try to glean for themselves as much of the rents from the innovative activity that occurs on their campuses as they can, it has the adverse effect of moving universities away from what they have traditionally been—open and collaborative.

Relatedly we think efforts should be made to

(i) Prevent the patenting of research platforms and research tools;
(ii) Prevent the patenting or copyrighting of algorithms and other research methods.

Some of the authors also argue for measures to:[5]

(iii) Ensure access to life-saving medicines for poor people (in both devel-oped and developing countries) that are produced as a result of government-funded research.
(iv) Ensure access to knowledge that pertains to global warming and other essential public goods.

2. Reinstate the once "universally accepted principle that plant and animal genetic resources are a heritage of mankind and consequently should be available without restrictions"

This principle from the "International Undertaking on Plant Genetic Resources," (1983), (see Chapter 10 in this volume) has been a controversial aspect of on-going international negotiations on the legal framework that should govern access, use and transfer of genetic materials and goods derived therefrom. As Halewood shows, over the last three decades one has seen the proliferation of exclusive forms of control of plants, seeds and living organisms. At the very least—Halewood argues and we fully agree—it is urgent to fully implement the international "quasi-commons" prescribed by the International Treaty on Plant Genetic Resources for Food and Agriculture (ITPGRFA) (2001), notwithstanding its acknowledgement of national sover-eignties and IPRs. Similarly, the Convention on Biological Diversity attempts to balance the rights of those countries having an abundance of genetic resources (biodiversity), with the need for incentives to preserve that biodiver-sity (for those countries largely in the South), and with incentives for corpor-ate interests, some in developing countries and many in developed ones exploiting these genetic resources.

3. A major change in the boundaries between public research and for-profit activities in medical research and pharmaceuticals?

One of the sectors in which IPRs in the form of patents *do* matter is pharmaceuticals. But this is also where the current IPR regime reveals how deeply flawed, expensive and possibly counterproductive it is. In a nutshell, the current system works as follows. The first stage of research on new molecules addressing particular pathologies and on the mappings between genes and pathologies themselves is overwhelmingly undertaken in public institutions, including universities, and financed by public entities, such as the National Institutes of Health (NIH) in the United States. Promising molecules and promising genetic targets are then picked up by private firms, generally with the acquisition of a universally held patent with the intermediation of a (rent-seeking) biotech, which in turn transfers it to "big pharma" companies.

The drugs that make it to clinical trials are then tested, typically by the pharmaceutical companies, on humans in hospitals which are partly (in the United States) or almost entirely (in Continental Europe) public, under condition of conflict of interest,[6] since the drug companies want the data to support the approval of the drug. Finally, if the drug obtains the approval of the FDA or equivalent agencies in Europe and Japan, it is put on the market. A large fraction of the sales is to a public buyer—more than 50 per cent in the United States and a much higher share in Europe, at a price incorporating a mark-up on research and testing costs. At the end of the day, the public pays for the drug both through backing the original research, and then again by buying the drug itself on behalf of the patients. And all this without controlling the directions of research, that is the selection of the would-be drugs which are taken through clinical trials (and thus, indirectly, of the pathologies which are addressed).[7] In the United States and most other countries, the drug companies have even resisted creating a formulary, which would pay for drugs on the basis of efficacy and cost effectiveness.

The system, while very costly, does not appear even to be efficient in terms of innovative output: the New Chemical Entities (that is, discretely novel drugs as opposed to marginal variations over existing ones) approved by the FDA are of the order of a couple of dozen per year at best; drug firms undertake marketing expenditures that are more than three times their research spending (Angell, 2004). The drug companies have been especially neglectful of the diseases that most afflict the developing countries, and especially the poor in those countries.[8]

There are many alternatives to this system, including moving to a prize system; and/or to have the public (i.e. public agencies such as the NIH) not only perform the research but also fund the clinical trials,[9] and then license on a non-exclusive basis the production of the drugs to pharmaceutical companies, which at that point would have to price at (near) marginal costs. Not only would such a system be socially more efficient and reliable (without the inherent conflicts of interest in the current arrangements), but it would actually save the taxpayer money. At present, given that a very large percentage of the costs of medicine are paid for by the public, the consequences of inefficiencies and monopoly pricing are inevitably borne by taxpayers.

SOME POLICY OPTIONS CONCERNING "CATCHING-UP" IN DEVELOPING COUNTRIES

The second set of questions posed in this book is about how developing countries can best cope with the imperfections of the current IPR regime while, for instance, preserving their chances of catching up in the knowledge economy and protecting the health of their citizens. We also ask how the world as a whole can safeguard the openness of scientific discoveries, encourage the preservation of and access to biological diversity, and ensure the full humanitarian use of technological advances.

The advocates of the current regime claim that it will benefit developing countries, and not just provide more rents for the firms of the developed countries. By contrast, we hope to convince readers of this book that the historically unprecedented international harmonization of IPRs, "upward" toward a tighter regime under the TRIPS Agreement and subsequent bilateral or regional Free Trade Agreements, is harmful for the development process in general and for developing countries in particular. It not only fails to enhance the process of accumulating technological capabilities by domestic firms—which is at the core of the development process (more in Cimoli, Dosi and Stiglitz, 2009)—it also hinders learning by putting serious limits on access to knowledge (and thus presents impediments to closing the knowledge gap) so essential if firms in developing countries are to catch up with the more technically advanced countries.[10] It also harms developing countries because of the increased rents that they have to pay, especially for pharmaceuticals, which not only reduces funds available for a broad range of developmental objectives, but also undermines public health.

It would be different if these stronger IPRs, say, for medicines, had led to more innovation focused on the diseases and health problems prevalent in developing countries. But it has not. While the evidence of adverse effects from tighter IPRs, especially in pharmaceuticals, is clear, the purported developmental benefits—that some firms with high IPR content in their products will be deterred from locating in countries with weak IPR protection—is ambiguous at best.[11]

Hence, from a normative point of view, reforms of the TRIPS-based international regime in the direction of *looser* IPR protection—towards what is sometimes called a TRIPS-minus regime—should be welcomed in developing countries. Unfortunately, the United States, with its bilateral Free Trade Agreements, and Europe, with its so-called Economic Partnership Agreements, have been pushing the world towards a TRIPS-plus regime.[12]

We should emphasize (as many of the chapters in this book do), that it is wrong to view IPR regimes through a simplistic lens that sees them as just tougher or looser. Rather, there are a myriad of provisions that affect the developmental impact of IPRs. We agree with the General Assembly of the World Intellectual Property Organization (WIPO) that we need a *developmentally oriented intellectual property regime,* and that TRIPS is *not* such a regime as it stands.

However, even if the TRIPS Agreement is not reformed, there is much that developing countries can do *within* the current regime to promote innovation and societal well-being, as discussed in several chapters in this volume (in particular those by Allarakhia; Reichman; Maskus and Okediji; Correa; and also Maskus and Reichman (2005).

They include:

(i) The development of open source commons, such as those illustrated by Chapter 11 in this volume on biotechnological and pharmaceutical knowledge in India and Brazil, and a legal framework to support the commons.

(ii) A more extensive use of utility models (petty patents) that protect small-scale innovations essentially by domestic producers in developing countries.[13]

(iii) A greater use of prizes and grants (both in developed and developing countries) for rewarding innovators as an alternative to patents. (Even better, would be a global framework for prizes, as suggested by the World Health Organization for diseases affecting the developing countries.)[14]

(iv) There are many choices in the design of an IPR regime even within TRIPS: more restrictive granting of patents, e.g. avoiding minor variations that attempt to "evergreen" patent products, easier forms of opposition to the granting of patents;[15] and use of a "liability" rule, whereby injunctive relief for violating a patent would be severely limited, and those who used existing inventions in follow-on innovation would have to pay appropriate compensation for the use of someone else's intellectual property.[16]

(v) A fuller exploitation of the "flexibilities" allowed by TRIPS, such as those allowing in some circumstances compulsory licensing and other exceptions to the full IPR protection.[17]

(vi) Excluding from patent eligibility all claims on human life or life processes and reaffirming that patents on environmentally sound technologies are subject to the full range of limitations and exceptions set out in TRIPS, at a minimum.[18]

(vii) Resisting provisions in bilateral or multilateral preferential trade agreements involving "super-TRIPS" clauses that basically eliminate the "flexibilities" allowed by TRIPS or require the parties not to trade in goods originating from third countries making use of such "flexibilities."[19]

We believe that these measures could be beneficial to the development process as a whole. However, as discussed in Cimoli, Dosi and Stiglitz (2009), one should not forget that IPR-related measures—and even the broader reforms in national innovation systems—are just a part of a much larger picture of broadly defined industrial policies which, if well designed, can nurture the birth and growth of technologically competent and increasingly innovative firms in catch-up countries.

Intellectual property rights are not, as we have emphasized, an end in themselves. They are a means to forging more prosperous economies, with rising standards of living. Developing countries should subject all proposals for IPR regimes to a simple standard: the extent to which such a regime promotes the prosperity and well-being of their citizens.

NOTES

1. Maskus & Okediji (this volume).
2. There is a long line of papers that are critical of the current IPR regime. See Boldrin and Levine (2008b), Odagiri et al. (2010), Jaffe (2000).
3. Chapter 1, as well as several of the other chapters, have detailed the precise mechanisms through which patents impede innovation—including adverse effects on openness and the flow of information.
4. See Siepmann (2004).
5. Chapters 5 and 7 in this volume argue that scientific research has to be properly supported in *ethical terms*. (See also the concluding remarks in Mazzucato and Dosi, 2006). There are public policies which are *good in their own right*, from the safeguard of justice to the pursuit of knowledge, to the right of access to health care.
6. The testing system's reliability is not only compromised by these conflicts of interest, but costs are increased, since testing is often intertwined with marketing. Doctors who participate in the testing of a successful drug are more likely to prescribe that drug, and perhaps even to convince others of its benefits.
7. Reichman (2009b).
8. Not a surprise, as several chapters point out in so far as profits drive innovation (which is not even often the case), and the poor do not have the money to spend on drugs that the rich do.
9. Jayadev, A. and Stiglitz, J.E. (2009, 2010); Reichman (2009b).

10. Our findings are thus consistent with (though go beyond) those of the World Commission on the Social Dimensions of Globalization (2004).

11. For some discussion of this see Chapter 2 in this volume. See also, Keith E. Maskus (2012).

12. E.g. with data exclusivity. See Charlton and Stiglitz, 2005 and Stiglitz, 2006. As this book goes to press, there is concern, for instance, that the Trans Pacific Partnership agreement, now under negotiation, will provide still further impediments in the access to generic medicines, rolling back improvements that were incorporated into, e.g., the Peru–U.S. bilateral trade agreement.

13. Utility models, as discussed also in several chapters of this book, are minor variations on incumbent product and processes, most often undertaken by local producers in catching-up countries, but too "minor" to fulfil the criteria of a nonobviousness (inventive step) enshrined in contemporary patent regimes. In fact they were widely used by now developed countries, such as Germany and Japan, in their industrialization phase (see Chapter 2 in this volume and Odagiri et al., 2010). Our proposal is indeed that their use should be confined to developing countries only and in that to domestic producers who undertake often minor "creative imitations." On the contrary, allowing the use of utility models by "frontier" companies and countries would just strengthen their monopolistic positions and increase entry barriers into innovative activities. We note that this is an area where the IPR regime for developing and developed countries should probably differ, which would require amending the national treatment rules of the Paris Convention and TRIPS. Strong arguments have been put forward that for developed countries, utility models actually impede the pace of innovation, encouraging research, e.g. on small innovations rather than larger, more transformative ones.

14. See also Love (2005) and Stiglitz, (2004, 2006).

15. See Henry and Stiglitz (2010).

16. See Chapter 1 and Reichman, Lewis (2005), and generally UNCTAD (2011).

17. Reichman, Chapter 4 in this volume.

18. In fact, some of the co-editors would go further by imposing restrictions that go beyond those explicitly stated in TRIPS: a sort of "TRIPS minus" somewhat along the lines suggested by, e.g., the ILO World Commission on the Social Dimension of Globalization (ILO, 2004). The Rio Convention also imposed "flexibilities" in the form of compulsory licensing for technologies related to climate change.

19. See Chapter 15 in this volume.

REFERENCES

Angell, M. (2004), *The Truth about the Drug Companies: How They Deceive Us and What to Do about It*. New York: Random House.

Boldrin, M. and Levine, D.K. (2008a), "Perfectly Competitive Innovation," *Journal of Monetary Economics*, 55 (3): 435–53.

Boldrin, M. and Levine, D.K. (2008b), *Against Intellectual Monopoly*. New York: Cambridge University Press.

Bush, V. (1945), *Science, The Endless Frontier*. A Report to the President, United States Government Printing Office, Washington.

Charlton, A. and Stiglitz, J.E. (2005), *Fair Trade for All*. New York: Oxford University Press.

Cimoli M., Dosi, G., and Stiglitz J.E. (eds.) (2009), *Industrial Policy and Development: The Political Economy of Capabilities Accumulation*. New York: Oxford University Press.

Gana, Ruth L. (1996), "Prospects for Developing Countries under the TRIPS Agreement," *Vand. J. Transnat'l. L.*, 29: 735.

Henry, C. and Stiglitz, J.E. (2010), "Intellectual Property, Dissemination of Innovation and Sustainable Development," *Global Policy*, 1: 237–51.

Hertel, G., Krishnan, M., and Slaughter, S. (2003), "Motivation in Open Source Projects: An Internet-Based Survey of Contributors to the Linux Kernel," *Research Policy*, 32 (7): 1159–77.

ILO (International Labor Office) (2004), *A Fair Globalization: Creating Opportunities for All*. Geneva.

Jayadev, A. and Stiglitz, J.E. (2009), "Two Ideas to Increase Innovation and Reduce Pharmaceutical Costs and Prices," *Health Affairs*, 28 (1): 165–8.

Jayadev, A. and Stiglitz, J.E. (2010), "Medicine for Tomorrow: Some Alternative Proposals to Promote Socially Beneficial Research and Development in Pharmaceuticals," *Journal of Generic Medicines*, 7 (3): 217–26.

Jaffe, A. (2000), "The US Patent System in Transition: Policy Innovation and the Innovation Process," *Research Policy*, 29: 531–57.

Love, J. (2005), "Remuneration Guidelines for Non-Voluntary Use of a Patent on Medical Technologies," working paper of the World Health Organization and United Nations Development Programme, Health Economics and Drugs TCM Series No. 18, available at <http://www.undp.org/content/dam/aplaws/publication/en/publications/poverty-reduction/poverty-website/renumeration-guidelines-for-non-voluntary-use-of-a-patent-on-medical-techologies-/RenumerationGuidelines.pdf> (accessed 24 September 2013).

Maskus, Keith E. (2012), *Private Rights and Public Problems: The Global Economics of Intellectual Property in the 21ˢᵗ Century*. Washington, DC: Peterson Institute for International Economics.

Maskus, Keith E. and Reichman, Jerome H. (eds.) (2005), "The Globalization of Private Knowledge Goods and the Privatization of Global Public Goods," in *International Public Goods and Transfer of Technology Under a Globalized Intellectual Property Regime*. Cambridge: Cambridge University Press.

Mazzucato, M. and Dosi, G. (eds.) (2006), *Knowledge Accumulation and Industry Evolution*. Cambridge: Cambridge University Press.

Odagiri, H., Goto, A., Sunami, A., and Nelson, R.R. (eds.) (2010), *Intellectual Property Rights, Development, and Catch Up: An International Comparative Study*. Oxford and New York: Oxford University Press.

Okediji, Ruth, and Bagley, M.A. (eds.) (2013), *Patent Law in Global Perspective*. New York: Oxford University Press.

Okediji, Ruth, (2013), "Public Welfare and the International Patent System," in Ruth L. Okediji and Margo A. Bagley, eds, *Patent Law in Global Perspective*. New York: Oxford University Press.

Okediji, Ruth, (2013), "The Role of WIPO in Access to Medicines" in Rochelle Dreyfuss and Cesar Rodriguez-Garavito, eds, *Balancing Wealth and Health: Global Administrative Law and the Battle over Intellectual Property and Access to Medicines in Latin America*. Oxford: Oxford University Press.

Reichman, Jerome H. (2010), "Lessons to be Learned in Europe from the International Discourse on Patents and Public Health," in Christine Godt, ed., *Differential Pricing of Pharmaceuticals Inside Europe*. Baden-Baden, Germany: Nomos Publishers.

Reichman, Jerome H. (2009a), "Compulsory Licensing of Patented Pharmaceutical Inventions: Evaluating the Options," *Journal of Law, Medicine, and Ethics*, 37 (2): 247–63.

Reichman, Jerome H. (2009b), "Rethinking the Role of Clinical Trial Data in International Intellectual Property Law: The Case for a Public Goods Approach," *Marquette Intellectual Propertly Law Review*, 13: 1–68.

Reichman, J. and Lewis, T. (2005), "Using Liability Rules to Stimulate Local Innovation in Developing Countries: Application to Traditional Knowledge," in K. Maskus and J. Reichman, eds, *International Public Goods and Transfer of Technology under a Globalized Intellectual Property Regime*. Cambridge: Cambridge University Press.

Siepmann, Thomas J. (2004), "The Global Exportation of the U.S. Bayh-Dole Act," *University of Dayton Law Review*, 30 (2): 209–44.

Stiglitz, J. (2004), "Towards a Pro-Development and Balanced Intellectual Property Regime," keynote address presented at the Ministerial Conference on Intellectual Property for Least Developed Countries, World Intellectual Property Organization (WIPO), Seoul, 25 October 2004, available at <http://www2.gsb.columbia.edu/faculty/jstiglitz/download/2004_TOWARDS_A_PRO_DEVELOPMENT.htm> (accessed 5 November 2012).

Stiglitz, J. (2006), *Making Globalization Work*. New York: W.W. Norton.

UNCTAD (United Nations Conference on Trade and Development) (2011), *Using Intellectual Property Rights to Stimulate Pharmaceutical Production in Developing Countries*. United Nations Press.

World Commission on the Social Dimension of Globalization (2004), "A Fair Globalization—Creating Opportunities for All," available at <http://www.ilo.org/fairglobalization/report/lang–en/index.htm> (accessed 24 September 2013).

Index

abuses (of power/dominant position) 3, 9,
        132–3, 170, 363, 379, 430, 432
access:
  access-oriented modifications to
        TRIPS 409
  global 406–9
  to knowledge 1–3, 7–8, 10–12, 32, 74,
        128–9, 132, 135, 138–9, 143–4, 163,
        180, 187, 224, 335, 347, 349, 396, 405,
        443, 461, 503–8
  within TRIPS 406–9
  see also access to medicines
access to medicines 8, 17, 139, 167, 230, 429,
        136, 440, 443–50, 465, 504, 506
  compulsory licenses/exhaustion of
        rights 446–7
  linkage 449–50
  patents on new uses 445–6
  protection of clinical test data 447–9
  twenty years plus, the 444–5
accumulation:
  of (technological) capabilities 27, 34, 36,
        57–8, 67–8, 81, 104, 168, 477, 479–87,
        492–5
  evolutionary perspective 480, 482
  of knowledge 58, 164, 332, 477, 494
  orthodox perspective 480, 482
  of patent portfolios 65, 364
Africa 136, 138, 172, 237, 289–93, 401,
        436, 440
agriculture:
  appropriability in 242–63
  chemical product use 245–8
  crop transfers 244–5
  cultivation practices, improvements
        in 244–5
  diffusion of innovations 270–5
  failure of convergence in 266–70
  innovation in 242–63
  international legal support in 298–307
  mechanization of 244–8, 259, 266
  productivity growth in 242–63
  transformation of 243–50
  see also crop genetic resources; plant
        varieties
AIDS 28, 44, 79, 161, 214, 219, 230–1, 233–7,
        401, 425, 465
algorithms, patenting of 74, 506
Allarakhia, M. 262, 331–2, 336–7, 347, 509

Allen, D.E. 248–9
allocation of resources 9, 27, 44, 68, 96, 196,
        286, 347, 400, 478, 486, 494
  of (R&D) funds 12, 196
  and prizes 400, 410
alternatives to patents/intellectual
        property 59, 356–91, 507
  international context 372–83
  prizes 28–32, 44, 125–6, 140, 160, 235, 247,
        357, 371–3, 388, 400–2, 410–11,
        507, 509
  technology pools 126, 359, 371
"American preference" 73, 75–6
antitrust 123, 146, 169–70
Apple 16, 38, 42
appropriability 5, 8–9, 14, 18, 22–6, 59–66,
        81–2, 242–63, 295, 326, 329
  in agriculture 242–63
  regimes 60–2, 64, 81, 243
  role of 24–5
  see also innovation; inventions;
        knowledge; patents
appropriation 7–8, 21, 23, 25–7, 65, 72, 76,
        153, 253, 326–8, 342, 348, 350, 418,
        494, 505
  misappropriation, see misappropriation
  see also patents; returns
approval 23, 44, 49, 62, 225, 235, 401, 467, 507
  marketing 30, 425–9, 444–5, 447–50
Arrow, K. 10
ARV drugs 230, 232–4, 236–7
automobile patents 17–18, 63, 362, 504

Barro, R. 271–2, 276
Barton, J. 12, 369, 395–6, 405
Bayh-Dole Act 16–17, 23, 42, 75–6, 83, 91, 93,
        124–5, 150, 160, 171, 188, 201–15, 226,
        325, 328, 366, 497, 506
  instituting safeguards 207–10
  overstating claims 202–4
  sources of concern 204–7
  see also publicly funded research
BD, see Bayh-Dole Act
Bessen, J. 23, 156, 384
"big pharma" 24, 225, 231, 507
  see also pharmaceutical industry, the
bilateral agreements and TRIPS 487–93
  see also TRIPS
BiOS, see CAMBRIA